Students'

English – Tibetan Colloquial Dictionary

(Text incorporating corrections listed in the Errata)

by

C.A. Bell

C.M.G., C.I.E.

D.K. Printworld (P) Ltd.

Publishers of Indian Traditions

Cataloging in Publication Data — DK
[Courtesy: D.K. Agencies (P) Ltd. <docinfo@dkagencies.com>]

Bell, Charles Alfred, *Sir*, 1870-1945.
Students' English-Tibetan colloquial dictionary.

ISBN 13: 9788124601594 (Hb)
ISBN 13: 9788124601600 (Pb)
1. English language — dictionaries — Tibetan.
I. Title.

First published in India 1905
Second edition published in 1920
D.K. Printworld's Edition 2000
Second Impression 2011
ISBN 13: 978-81-246-0159-4 (Hb) ISBN 10: 81-246-0159-3
ISBN 13: 978-81-246-0160-0 (Pb) ISBN 10: 81-246-0160-7

Published and printed by:
D.K. Printworld (P) Ltd.
Regd. office : *'Vedaśrī'*, F-395, Sudarshan Park
Ramesh Nagar Metro Station
New Delhi – 110 015
Phones : (011) 2545 3975; 2546 6019; *Fax* : (011) 2546 5926
E-mail: indology@dkprintworld.com
Web: www.dkprintworld.com

PREFACE TO SECOND EDITION.

1. In the first edition this dictionary was published as the second part of a "Manual of Colloquial Tibetan," the first part consisting of a Grammar of Colloquial Tibetan. In this second edition both parts have not only been revised, but have also been considerably enlarged. The map accompanying this edition—the latest from the Indian Survey Department—is bulkier than the Royal Geographical Society's map of 1904, with which the first edition was furnished. It has therefore been found best to bring out the Grammar and Dictionary as separate books. The map accompanies the Grammar.

2. The Tibetan words are romanized, as in the first edition, for the convenience of those, who lack either the time or the inclination to master the Tibetan character. But the first Chapter of the Grammar, that on "The alphabet and its pronunciation," is reprinted at the commencement of this dictionary, in order that the student, who learns the Tibetan letters, may understand the structure and the pronunciation of the words more clearly than can be expressed by any system of romanization.

3. Some two thousand fresh words have been added in this edition, which now contains between eleven and twelve thousand words. As Political Officer in Sikkim,—a post to which I have recently been recalled, though I retired from the service of Government ten months ago,—I am in charge of the diplomatic relations of the British Government not only with Sikkim, but with Tibet and Bhutan also. Many therefore of these new words, as well as the revision of a few in the earlier edition, have been gained in conversation with my Tibetan friends of all classes, High Priests, Cabinet Ministers, civil and military officers, shopkeepers, mule-drivers, shepherds, peasants, etc., etc., during my fifteen years' service in Tibet and on the borderland. Among all

these my thanks are especially due to Rai Sahib Kusho Pahlese of the noble family of Pahla in Lhasa. And Mr. David Macdonald, British Trade Agent at Yatung, Tibet, has again rendered valuable assistance.

4. My acknowledgments are also due to the Government of Bengal, who have defrayed the cost of this edition also, in retnrn for its copyright.

5. This book has been adopted as one of the text-books in the High Proficiency examination in the Tibetan language, held under the auspices of the Government of India.

6. In conclusion I must express my pleasure at finding that a second edition was called for owing to the first edition being sold out,—a rare occurrence among books on Tibet,—for it may be hoped that some have found it useful.

GANGTOK, SIKKIM :
January, 1920.

C. A. BELL.

PREFACE TO FIRST EDITION OF "MANUAL OF COLLOQUIAL TIBETAN."

1. The object of this little work is to provide a practical handbook for those who wish to acquire a speedy knowledge of Colloquial Tibetan. It, therefore, does not deal with the written language, which differs widely from the colloquial, and is useless for conversational purposes.

2. Notwithstanding the political and commercial importance of Tibet it is remarkable that so few Europeans are able to converse with the people in their own tongue. The language is undoubtedly a hard one to acquire on account of the complexity of the grammar, the intricacy of the spelling, the fine shades of pronunciation, the different terminology, known as the honorific, employed in addressing the higher classes, the variety of dialects, and the distinction, already noted, between the literary and spoken language. To minimise these difficulties and to make the approach to the colloquial as easy as possible, is the aim of this handbook. It seeks to do so by giving a minimum of grammatical notes, fully explained by examples, a clear statement of the rules of pronunciation, a simple system of phonetic spelling in the Roman character, a set of conversational exercises and a sufficiently full vocabulary of both common and honorific words to meet the ordinary requirements of conversation with all classes.

3. Tibet is essentially a country of dialects. A well-known proverb says—

།ལུང་པ་རེ་རེ་སྐད་ལུགས་རེ།
།བླ་མ་རེ་རེ་ཆོས་ལུགས་རེ།།

"Every district its own dialect;
Every lama his own doctrine."

Under these circumstances it was necessary to select the dialect most widely spoken, and that of Lhasa has been chosen accordingly. It is not only the dialect of the Central Province, but may be said to be also the *lingua franca* of the whole of Tibet. It is more generally spoken than any other, and is recognized as the most correct form of speech by all.

4. The Vocabulary contains somewhat less than ten thousand Tibetan words, the number of separate English words being some seven thousand or about twice as many as those contained in any colloquial Tibetan vocabulary up to date. The remaining three thousand words are made up of about two thousand honorific words and one thousand extra Tibetan words. Where two or more Tibetan words are given for one English equivalent, all are in common colloquial use and the one placed first is the commonest. It is hoped that the honorific words given may be found useful. Existing vocabularies give but few. A knowledge of honorific words is essential for talking to or of Tibetans of good position. It is hoped also that the exercises in Tibetan handwriting given in Part I, Chapter XVII, may assist any student, who so desires, to learn how to write Tibetan letters and other documents in a clear and correct style.

5. It is recommended that the grammar be used as follows: The rules of each Chapter should be perused and their accompanying examples learnt by heart. The *Words* at the end of the Chapter should then be committed to memory as far as possible, and the exercise (for reading and copying) should be read aloud to the teacher to ensure correct pronunciation, and every word should be understood. After this the other Exercise (for translation) should be translated *vivâ voce* and then written down, care being taken, when writing, to verify the spelling, as very few Tibetan teachers can spell correctly. On the following day the Tibetan half of the reading exercise should be covered up, and the English half re-translated into Tibetan, first *vivâ voce* and then in writing. If the above plan is followed the student will gain the soundest possible knowledge of the language. But if the student has not time for the above thorough system, he should omit the writing of both exercises and limit himself to the *vivâ voce*.

6. As regards teachers it is best to obtain at first one who speaks English. If the teacher can speak the Lhasa language also, so much the better, but very few of the English-speaking Tibetans in the Darjeeling district or in Sikkim are really proficient in the latter. As soon as he can converse a little, the student should change to a Lhasa man that speaks Tibetan only, so as to be certain of always speaking in Tibetan. When the teacher knows English or Hindustani there is always a tendency for the conversation to drop into the latter languages. The Lhasa teacher should of course be as well educated a man as is procurable. The student should also, when he is able to understand and converse a little, call in Tibetans of the Lhasa province to talk to him, one at a time, changing them every two or three weeks. Tibetans are generally ready to talk; they have not the formal constraint of manner which characterizes so many of the Indian races. The more he calls in thus, the better will he be able to understand and reply to any chance Tibetan he meets.

7. A word as to the system of romanization. In this, which is believed to be as phonetic as possible, I had reluctantly to differ from the various systems of my predecessors, as none of them seemed to me to reproduce the sounds in the dialect of Lhasa, though some reproduced those in the Sikkimese and other dialects. The system followed in this book is nearly the same as that recommended to Government for official reports, etc., by Captain O'Connor, C.I.E., Trade Agent at Gyangtse, and the author, but distinguishes the different sounds with greater accuracy than was considered necessary in the Government system.

8. The Tibetan words and syllables in brackets are those used in the simple form of book-language. Where the pronunciation of the literary and spoken form of a word is the same, the literary form alone is given, since the sole object of entering the spoken form is to show the exact pronunciation of the word.

9. In conclusion, I must acknowledge my obligations to the Government of Bengal for their patronage, to the Grammars of the Rev. Graham Sandberg, the Rev. H. A. Jäschke and the Rev.

Father A. Desgodins, and especially to Mr. Henderson's Tibetan Manual, which marks a great advance in the Tibetan colloquial over any of its predecessors. And most of all are my thanks due to Mr. David Macdonald, who has revised this book throughout, and to whose unrivalled knowledge of both colloquial and literary Tibetan are largely due whatever merits the work may possess.

CHUMBI, TIBET: *March*, 1905. C. A. BELL.

ABBREVIATIONS.

Adj. = adjective.
Adv. = adverb.
Art. = article.
Ch. = Chinese.
Conj. = conjunction.
C.T. = Central Tibet, *i.e.* the provinces of U and Tsang.
Def. = definite.
Do. = ditto.
E.G. = for instance.
F. = female, feminine.
Hin. = Hindi.
Hon. = honorific.
H. hon. = high honorific.
Imp. = imperative.
Inf. = inferior.
Interj. = interjection.
Interr. = interrogative.
Lit. = literally.
M. = male, masculine.
Mon. = Mongolian.
Neg. = negative.
Opp. = opposed.
Post. = postposition.
Pron. = pronoun.
Rel. = relative.
S. = substantive.
Sik. = Sikkimese.
Sup. = superior.
Ts. = Tsang province.
V.I. = verb intransitive.
V.T. = verb transitive.
W. = with.

Attention Please !

To facilitate our readers, all the corrections listed in the errata of the second edition have been carried out in the main text.

D.K. Printworld (P) Ltd.

NOTE.—Where the colloquial and the literary forms differ appreciably, the latter are given in brackets in the Tibetan character. In the romanized Tibetan he colloquial forms alone are given.

THE ALPHABET AND ITS PRONUNCIATION.

1. The Tibetan Alphabet was originally taken from the Sanskrit Devanagari in the 7th century A.D., but many of the letters, especially in Central Tibet, now represent sounds different from their prototypes. Both the Sanskrit and the Tibetan pronunciations have changed considerably during this period.

2. The Tibetan letters are as follow :—

Consonants and their romanized equivalents.

	Surds.	Aspirates.	Sonants.	Nasals.
Gutturals	ཀ་ *ka*	ཁ་ *kha*	ག་ *ḱa*	ང་ *nga*
Palatals	ཅ་ *cha*	ཆ་ *chha*	ཇ་ *cȟa*	ཉ་ *nya*
Dentals	ཏ་ *ta*	ཐ་ *tha*	ད་ *t́a*	ན་ *na*
Labials	པ་ *pa*	ཕ་ *pha*	བ་ *ṕa*	མ་ *ma*
Sibilants	ཙ་ *tsa*	ཚ་ *tsha*	ཛ་ *tśa*	
Semi-vowels	ཝ་ *wa*	ཞ་ *sȟa*	ཟ་ *śa*	འ་ (not romanized)
	ཡ་ *ya*	ར་ *ra*	ལ་ *la*	
	ཤ་ *sha*	ས་ *sa*	ཧ་ *ha*	ཨ་ *a*

3. In this Chapter I endeavour to give as nearly as possible the sound represented by each Tibetan letter. The romanization throughout is intended only as a rough guide to the pronunciation for those who are unable to give the time for studying the exact pronunciation. The consonants when used as initials, *i.e.*, when immediately preceding the vowel of a syllable, are pronounced as below.

ཀ་ The *k* in the Hindustani word *kam*. To be pronounced with the tongue between the teeth and without breathing.

ཁ་ an aspirated *k*, e.g., *block-head*, pronounced in one breath. The same as the aspirated *k* in Hindustani words, *e.g.*, *khana*.

ག་ also a *k* but pronounced through the throat and in a lower tone than ཀ་

ང་ like the *ng* in *coming*. Say *coming in*, eliminating the first four letters *comi*.

ཅ་ *ch* in *chin*. To be pronounced with the tongue between the teeth and without breathing.

ཆ་ *ch* aspirated, e.g., *touch-hands* pronounced in one breath, *i.e.*, like the aspirated *ch* in Hindustani.

ཇ་ is also a *ch* pronounced through the throat and in a lower tone than ཅ་

ཉ་ as the initial sound in *nuisance*.

ཏ་ a Dental *t* to be pronounced with the tongue between the teeth and without breathing. This ཏ་ and ན་ differ from the English *t* and *n*, in that the English letters require the tongue to be placed against the roof of the mouth and so have a heavier sound.

ཐ་ aspirated *t*, e.g., *thora* in Hindustani; or—subject to the difference noted under ཏ་—*pat hard* pronounced in one breath. Not to be confused with the English *th* sound, in words like *the.*

ད་ is like ཏ་ but pronounced through the throat and in a lower tone than ཏ་

ན་ is like English *n*, e.g., in *nest* subject to the difference noted under ཏ་

པ་ like English *p* as in *pear,* to be pronounced with the tongue between the teeth and without breathing.

ཕ་ aspirated *p*, e.g., *stop here* pronounced as one word. Not to be confused with *ph* sound occurring in English words like *phantasy*, etc.

བ་ is also a *p* but pronounced through the throat and in a lower tone than པ་ If it forms the second syllable of a word whose first syllable ends with a vowel or with ང་འ་ར་ or ལ་ it is pronounced as *w*.

མ་ as English *m*, e.g., in *man*.

ཙ་ *ts* is pronounced like *weights* eliminating the letters *weigh*.

To be pronounced with the tongue between the teeth ,and without breathing.

ཚ་ as *ts* aspirated, *e g.*, in *pats hard* pronounced as one word.

ཛ་ is also a *ts*, but pronounced through the throat and in a lower tone than ཙ་

ཝ་ like *w* in English, *e.g.*, in *wing*.

ཞ་ Something like *sh* in English, but pronounced in a lower tone and more through the throat.

ཟ་ Something like *s* in English, but pronounced in a lower tone and more through the throat.

འ་ has no pronunciation of its own. When it precedes ག་ཇ་ད་བ་ or ཛ་; these letters are pronounced respectively like *g* in *gun*, *j* in *jam*, *d* in *den*, *b* in *bend*, and *ds* in *pads*. See also para. 23

ཡ་ like *y* in English, *e.g.*, in *yacht*.

ར་ is short like *r* in English, *e.g.*, in *rat*. It is never rolled.

ལ་ like *l* in English, *e.g.*, in *linger*.

ཤ་ like *sh* in English, but pronounced sharply and through the teeth.

ས་ like *s* in English, but pronounced sharply and through the teeth.

ཧ་ like *h* aspirated in English, *e.g.*, in *hand*.

ཨ་ When a vowel is initial, either ཨ་ or འ་ is used as its base. The difference in pronunciation of these two is that the throat is opened for ཨ་ and kept closed for འ་ The result is that ཨ་ carries the ordinary vowel sound, whatever the vowel may be; while འ་ in the case of ུ or ོ gives a slight, but very slight sound of *w*; e.g., འུར་ *noise*=something between *ur* and *wur* though more like *ur*.

4. The five vowels are called དབྱངས་ལྔ་ *Yang-nga*: ཨ་ (a) ཨི་ (i) ཨུ་ (u) ཨེ་ (e) ཨོ། (o)

The four vowel-signs are ི *i* ུ *u* ེ *e* ོ *o*.

Every consonant implies a following *a*, unless another vowel is attached. This *a* is sounded like the English *u* in *rub*.

ི named གི་གུ་ *ki-ku*, like *i* in *in* or *tin*, e.g., མི་ man=*mi*.

ུ named ཞབས་ཀྱུ་ *sKap-kyu*, like *oo* in *root* when initial or final. Like *u* in *pull*, when medial, *e.g.*, གྲུ་ boat=*tru*; ནུབ་ west=*nup*.

named འགྲེང་བུ་ *Deng-bu*, like *e* in *men*. But when final also often like *i* in *tin*, e.g., ལེན་པ་ to take=*lem-pa*; ལྡེ་མིག་ *key=di-mi*.

named ན་རོ་ *na-ro*, like *o* in hole; e.g., ལོག་པ་ to come back=*loḱ-pa*.

5. The Tibetan letters with the four vowel-signs are as follow:—

ཀི་ *ki.*	ཁུ་ *khu.*	གེ་ *ḱe.*	ངོམས། *ngom.*
ཅི་ *chi.*	ཆུ་ *chhu.*	ཇེ་ *cḱe.*	ཉོན། *nyön.*
ཏི་ *ti.*	ཐུ་ *thu.*	དེ་ *t́e.*	ནོར། *nor.*
པི་ *pi.*	ཕུ་ *phu.*	བེ་ *ṕe.*	མོས། *mö.*
ཙི་ *tsi.*	ཚུ་ *tshu.*	ཛེ་ *tśe.*	ཝོལ། *wöl.*
ཞི་ *sḱi.*	ཟུ་ *śu.*	འེ་ *e.*	ཡོད། *yö.*
རི་ *ri.*	ལུ་ *lu.*	ཤེ་ *she.*	སོང་། *song.*
	ཧེ་ *he.*	ཨོཾ། *Om.*	

(The *o* is named "*le-kor*," and represents the letter མ་).

The above set of examples is that ordinarily used in Tibetan schools and monasteries.

6. **Final Consonants.**—The preceding paragraph shows the ordinary pronunciation of the vowels which is, however, further affected by some of the final consonants. Of final con-

sonants there are only ten; that is to say, though any consonant may begin a syllable only one of these ten consonants may end it. These ten final consonants are as follow :—

ག་ང་ད་ན་བ་མ་འ་ར་ལ་ས་ Let us briefly consider the pronunciation of each as a final, and its effect upon the pronunciation of the preceding vowel.

ག་ is pronounced so slightly as hardly to be heard and shortens the preceding vowel. When followed, however, by another consonant in a second syllable of the same word it is clearly pronounced, and does not affect the pronunciation of the preceding vowel, thus མིག་ eye =*mi*, but འཕོག་པ་ to hit=*phok̄-pa*.

ང་ is pronounced more sharply than when an initial. It does not affect the pronunciation of the preceding vowel, *e.g.*, མིང་ name=*ming*, but sounded sharply. The sound of final ག་ and ང་ can be obtained from the teacher with but little practice.

ད་ } These all modify the sounds of the preceding vowels *a*, *u*
ལ་ } and *o*; i.e., *a* into *e* (in French *les*); *u* into *ü* (in French *sur*); *o* into *ö* (*e.g.*, *hören* in German or *eu* in French
ས་ } *peu*). These modified sounds will, therefore, be romanized into *e*, *ö*, *ü*, respectively.

The final consonant itself is not pronounced; *e.g.*, ལུད་ manure=*lü*, བལ་ wool=*p̄ē*, བྲོས་པ་ to flee=*t́rö-pa*.

ད་ makes the preceding vowel short; ལ་ and ས་

make it long, thus ལུད་ manure=*lü* (short *u*); but ལུས་ body=*lü* (long *u*).

ན་ modifies vowels as ད་ལ་ and ས་ modify them, but is itself pronounced, *e.g.*, ལན་ answer=*len*. When followed by པ་ཕ་བ་ or མ་ in the same word it is pronounced as *m*, e.g., རིན་པོ་ཆེ་ precious=*rim-po-chhe*.

བ་ }
མ་ }
ར་ } Do not affect the pronunciation of the vowel, and are themselves pronounced the same as when initial, *e.g.*, ཚབ་ delegate=*tshaṕ*, ཟམ་པ་ bridge=*śam-pa*, ཟུར་ corner = *śur*. But ར་ like ག་ is sometimes pronounced so lightly as hardly to be heard.

འ་ is not itself pronounced but lengthens the sound of the vowel preceding it. No vowel except the indirect *a* precedes it, *e.g.*, ནམ་མཁའ་ sky = *nam-khā*.

7. **Affix.**—The letter ས་ also occurs as a second final consonant or affix after either of the four letters ག་ང་བ་མ་ It is not pronounced, but in the case of ག་ preceded by *a*, it has the effect of lengthening the *a*, e.g., ལགས་སོ་ yes = *lā-si*. It is sometimes written in an incomplete form below the final consonant thus ལགྶ་སོ་

8. **Sanskrit Letters.**—The following six letters taken from the Sanskrit are occasionally used in the Colloquial language, namely :—

ཊ་	ཋ་	ཌ་	ཎ་	ཥ་	ཀྵ་
tra	*thra*	*dra*	*na*	*kha*	*khya.*

ཊ་ is known as *ta-lo-tra,* which means "*ta* reversed is *tra*";

ཎ་ as *na-lo-na,* "*na* reversed is *na*"; and so on.

9. **Examples.**

[The student is recommended to cover the romanized Tibetan letters with a piece of paper and thus to test his knowledge of the alphabet and its pronunciation.]

ཀོ་བ་ leather = *ko-wa.*	ས་ earth = *sa.*
སྒར་ encampment = *gar.*	ཟ་བ་ to eat = *śa-wa.*
ཤིང་ tree = *shing.*	དད་པ་ faith = *t́e-pa.*
ཆུ་ water = *chhu.*	དང་ and = *t́ang.*
ཨ་མ་ mother = *a-ma.*	ལས་ཀ་ work = *le-ka.*
འོད་ light, *s.* = *ö.*	ལུག་ sheep = *lŭ.*
ཕན་ profit = *phen.*	ལག་པ་ hand = *laḱ-pa.*
ཞོན་པ་ to ride = *sḱöm-pa.*	ཇོ་བོ་ lord = *cḱo-wo.*

10. **Diphthongs.**—There are no real diphthongs, but under this head may be classed the combination *ai, oi, ui,* occurring when the one syllable of a word ends in *a, o,* or *u,*

and the next begins with *i*; e.g., རོ་ and འི་ of the corpse = *ro-i,* pronounced almost like *rö,* but with a slight sound of *i*; similarly ཁ and འི་ of the mouth = *kha-i* and almost = *khē*; བུ་ and འི་ of the son = *ṕu-i* and almost = *ṕü.* In fact the འི་ modifies the preceding vowels in practically the same way as ས་ would do.

The other combinations of vowels are *ao, io, uo, eo, oo, au, iu, eu*; e.g., ཟའོ། ཤིའོ། དུའོ། ཚེའོ། ཏོའོ། གའུ། ཁྲིའུ། ལེའུ། They are not often used in the colloquial and are not really diphthongs, as each vowel is clearly though rapidly pronounced.

Note that འ་ and not ཨ་ is always used as the base of the second vowel; that is, the letter over which the second vowel must be written; *e.g.,* ཁ and འི་ and not ཁ་ and ཨི་

11. **Compound Consonants.**—These are of two kinds, namely Subjoined and Superadded. These subjoined consonants are:—

ཝ་ཡ་ར་ལ་ and ཧ་ They are known respectively as ཝ་ཟུར་ *wa-śur,* "*wa* on the edge"; ཡ་བཏགས་ *ya-ta,* "*ya* subjoined"; ར་བཏགས་ *ra-ta,* "*ra* subjoined"; ལ་བཏགས་ *la-ta,* "*la* subjoined"; and ཧ་བཏགས་ *ha-ta,* "*ha* subjoined."

12. Wasurs.—*Wasur* may be joined to sixteen consonants, *viz.* —

ཀྭ་ ཁྭ་ གྭ་ ཅྭ་ ཉྭ་ ཏྭ་ དྭ་ ཙྭ་ ཚྭ་ ཞྭ་ ཟྭ་ རྭ་ ལྭ་ ཤྭ་ སྭ་ ཧྭ་

The effect on the pronunciation is to lengthen the sound of the vowel in the same way as final འ་ but not quite so much, *e.g.*, ཚྭ་ salt = *tshā.*

13. Of *yatas* there are seven, which are joined to the following letters, thus—

ཀྱ་ *kya*, ཁྱ་ *khya*, གྱ་ *ḱya*, པྱ་ *cha*, ཕྱ་ *chha*, བྱ་ *cḱa*, མྱ་ *nya*.

Note the pronunciation of the last four.

Thus གྱོང་པོ་ hard = *ḱyong-po.*

ཕྱིན་པ་ to go = *chhim-pa.*

བྱ་ bird = *cḱa.*

14. *Rata* is joined to thirteen consonants, namely :—

ཀྲ་ *tra*, ཁྲ་ *thra*, གྲ་ *t́ra.*

ཏྲ་ *tra*, དྲ་ *t́ra.*

པྲ་ pronounced *tra.* or *pa*, ཕྲ་ *thra*, བྲ་ pronounced *t́ra*, *ṕa* or *ra.*

Note that gutturals and labials take the sound of dentals. *Rata* is also joined to ནྲ་ *na*, མྲ་ *ma*, ཤྲ་ *sha*, སྲ་ *sa* or

NOTE.—Several English grammars also give ཧྲ་ *thra*, but this is neither given in Tibetan primers nor used in the colloquial language.

tra or *hra,* ཧྲ་ *hra,* e.g., ཁྲག་ blood = *thra,* གྲུ་ boat = *t́ru,* དྲིལ་བུ་ bell = *t́ri-ṕu,* བྲིས་པ་ (འབྲི་བ་) to write = *t́ri-pa,* སྲས་ son = *se,* སྲབ་ bridle = *traṕ.*

Note that where any of the first nine *ratas* are followed by the vowels ི or ེ the *r* is pronounced less strongly than when followed by the other vowels. And in no case is the *r* pronounced as strongly as in English.

15. *Hata* in the colloquial language is not used except with ལ་, *e.g.,* ལྷ་ a god = *hla,* the *h* being pronounced before the *l.* It is also joined to ག་ད་བ་ཛ་ and ཪ་ and is then written གྷ་དྷ་བྷ་ཛྷ་ and ཪྷ་ respectively, but these last five cases only occur in transcribing Sanskrit words, and are of little use for colloquial purposes.

16. *La-ta* is joined to six consonants, thus—

ཀླ་གླ་བླ་ཟླ་རླ་སླ་ These are all sounded as *la* in a high tone, except ཟླ་ which is pronounced *da,* e.g., གླུ་ song = *lu* ; ཟླ་བ་ month = *da-wa.*

17. **Examples.**

བྲག་ rock = *t́ra.*

སྨྱུ་གུ་ reed-pen = *nyu-gu.*

སླེ་ཀོག་ basket = *le-ko.*

ངའི་སྲབ་ my bridle = *nge-traṕ.*

ཁྱོད་ཀྱི་སྲོག་ your life = *khyö-kyi so.*

ཁོའི་གླུ་ his song = *khö lu.*

ཞབས་བྲོ་ dance = *sḱaṕ-ro.*

བྲང་ཁོག་ chest (of body) = *ṕang-kho.*

སྲང་འགག་ lane = *hrang-ga.*

18. **Superscribed Consonants.**—There are three of these, namely, ར་ལ་ and ས་ They are placed on the tops of other letters.

ར་ is placed on the top of twelve consonants, thus·

རྐ་	རྒ་	རྔ་	རྗ་	རྙ་	རྟ་	རྡ་	རྣ་	རྦ་	རྨ་	རྩ་	རྫ་
ka	*ga*	*nga*	*ja*	*nya*	*ta*	*da*	*na*	*ba*	*ma*	*tsa*	*dza.*

Note that the ར་ is written as ˇ ; except with ཉ་ when the full ར་ is written. Note also that རྒ་ is pronounced as *ga*, རྗ་ as *ja*, རྡ་ as *da*, རྦ་ as *ba* and རྫ་ as *dza*. The others differ from the ordinary ཀ་ང་ etc., in that they are pronounced in higher tone.

19. **Examples.**

རྐང་པ་ foot = *kang-pa,* རྒད་པོ་ old man = *ge-po,* རྒྱན་ ornament = *gyen,* རྡོ་ stone = *do,* རྣོ་པོ་ sharp = *no-po,* རྩ་བ་ root = *tsa-wa,* ལུག་རྫི་ shepherd = *luḱ-dzi.* The ར་ itself is not pronounced except sometimes when occurring in the second syllables of words; *e.g.*, རྡོ་རྗེ་ sacred thunder-bolt = *dor-je*. When ར་ surmounts a consonant as above, it is named ར་མགོ་ *rang-go,* i.e., ra-head, and the consonant is said to be "tied on" or "subjoined" as the *ya-tas, ratas,* etc., above. Thus རྐ་ is named *ra-ka-ta,* i.e., *ra* with *ka* subjoined, རྒ་ is named *ra-ga-ta,* and so on.

20. ལ་ similarly named ལ་མགོ་ *lang-go,* i.e., la-head, is superadded to ten consonants as follow:—

ལྐ་ ལྒ་ ལྔ་ ལྕ་ ལྗ་ ལྟ་ ལྡ་ ལྤ་ ལྦ་ ལྷ་

ལྷ་ is pronounced *hla.* The rest are pronounced in the same way as the corresponding consonants with superadded ར། ལྕ་ and ལྤ་ are pronounced in a high tone as *cha* and *pa* respectively.

21. ས་ similarly named ས་མགོ་ *sang-go,* i.e., sa-head, is superadded to eleven consonants as follow:—

སྐ་ སྒ་ སྔ་ སྙ་ སྟ་ སྡ་ སྣ་ སྤ་ སྦ་ སྨ་ སྩ་

These are pronounced in the same way as the corresponding consonants with superadded ར་ or ལ་ The consonants surmounted by ལ་ or ས་ are similarly said to be "tied on," e.g., ལྔ་ is named *la-nga-ta,* and སྡ་ is named *sa-da-ta.*

22. **Examples.**

ལྔ་ five = *nga.*

སྔ་དྲོ་ morning = *nga-t́ro.*

ལྕགས་ iron = *cha.*

ལྡིང་བ་ to soar (in the air) = *ding-wa.*

སྡིག་པ་ sin = *diḱ-pa.*

སྨན་ medicine = *men.*

23. **Prefixed Letters.**—The five letters ག་ད་བ་མ་འ་ are found in many words before the initial consonant. These prefixes are not themselves pronounced, but affect the pronunciation in the same way as superadded ར་ལ་ or ས་

ག་ occurs before ཅ་ཉ་ཏ་ད་ན་ཙ་ཞ་ཟ་ཡ་ཤ་ས་

ད་ before ཀ་ག་ང་པ་བ་མ་

བ་ before ཀ་ག་ཅ་ཇ་ཉ་ཏ་ད་ན་ཙ་ཛ་ཞ་ཟ་ཟླ་ཤ་ས་

མ་ before ཁ་ག་ང་ཆ་ཇ་ཉ་ཐ་ད་ན་ཚ་ཛ་

འ་ before ཁ་ག་ཆ་ཇ་ཐ་ད་ཕ་བ་ཚ་ཛ་

Examples.

གཅིག་ one = *chi.*

གསར་པ་ new = *sa-pa.*

གདན་ bolster = *den.*

དངུལ་ silver = *ngü.*

བཏང་བ་ to send = *tang-wa*. བདུན་ seven = *dün*.

མཁས་པོ་ skilful = *khe-po*. འཛོམ་པ་ to assemble = *dzom-pa.*

24. Confusion might arise in the case of one of the prefixed letters making a word with one of the final consonants, the vowel being the inherent *a*, e.g., དག་ as to whether it represents *tă* or *gā*. The confusion is obviated as follows. If it is the initial ད་, the word is written དག་ *ťă*. If it is the prefix, འ་ is added thus, དགའ་ = *gā*.

25. When བ་ as initial consonant follows ད་ as prefix, the combination is either sounded as *w* or not sounded at all. If accompanied by a *yata* or a vowel sign, it is not sounded at all; *e.g.*, དབུགས་ breath = *u*, དབྱངས་ tune, melody = *yang*; དབྱུག་པ་ to throw = *yuǩ-pa*. If accompanied by *rata*, it follows the ordinary rule of *ratas* (para. 14) and prefixed ད་ (para. 23) and is pronounced *dr*. In other cases it is pronounced as *w*, e.g., དབང་ power, authority = *wang*.

26. Sentences for Pronunciation.

Bring some hot water. ཆུ་ཚ་པོ་འཁྱེར་ཤོག་ *chhu tsha-po khe sho.*

This water is not hot. ཆུ་འདི་ཚ་པོ་མི་འདུག་ *chhu di tsha-po min-du.*

It is cold. གྲང་མོ་རེད་ *ťrang-mo re.*

You can go now. ད་འགྲོ་ཆོག་གི་རེད་ *ťa dro chhoǩ-ǩi-re.*

27. **Irregular Sounds.**—In the following cases the pronunciation is modified for the sake of euphony.

(*a*) *m* and *n* sounds.—When one syllable is followed by another beginning with a prefixed letter the sound of *m* or *n* is often introduced. This occurs especially when the first syllable ends in ག་ *e.g.*

ཕྱག་ལྡེ་ key, *hon.* = *chhan di.*

ཕྱག་འབྲུ་ grain, *hon.* = *chhan-dru.*

མི་འདུག་ is not = *min-du.*

ན་བཟའ་ clothes, *hon.* = *nam-śa.*

(*b*) *Reduplicated Sounds.*—When the following final consonants, or affixes, namely, ག་གས་ང་ངས་ར་ and ལ་, are followed by པ་ or བ་, the sound of the final consonant is reduplicated, *e.g.*, བཀག་ (འགོགས་) པ་གནང་བ་ to hinder, *hon.* = *kak̄-k̄a nang-wa*; གསུངས་པ་རེད་ he said, *hon.* = *sung-nga-re.* ཉར་བ་ གནང་བ་ to take care of, *hon.* = *ngar-ra nang-wa*; ཚིལ་བུ་ fat = *tshil-lu*; དཔོན་པོས་གནང་བ་རེད། the official has given, *pöm-pö nang-nga-re.*

(*c*) བ་ following a vowel or ལ་. When བ་ follows a vowel its sound is sometimes omitted altogether, *e.g.*, ལྦ་བ་ goitre = *ba-a.*

ཀ་བ་ pillar = *ka-a.*

བ་ after ལ་ is often pronounced as *r*, e.g.,—

རྒྱལ་བ་གནང་བ་ to conquer, hon. = *gye-ra nang-wa.*

(*d*) Other changed sounds

བཞིས་ཐུར་ spoon = *sǩip-thu.*

རྒྱ་ར་ (རྒྱ་བྲ་) sweet buck-wheat = *gyap-ra.*

(*e*) There are also other irregular sounds, but it seems unnecessary to enumerate them all here. They will be picked up more easily in the course of conversation.

28. **The Tones.**—In Tibetan the tone, that is to say the pitch of the voice, varies, each word in this language having a tone in which it should be pronounced. It is very important for the student to render these tones with substantial accuracy; otherwise the pronunciation becomes uncertain and many of his words will assume meanings which he does not intend for them.

29. For practical purposes we must discriminate between three tones, *viz.* the high, the medium, and the low. The initial letter and the prefix govern the tone.

High Tone.—Use this in a word beginning with a prefix except when the initial letter is ཁ་ག་ཆ་ཇ་ཐ་ད་ཕ་བ་ཚ་ or ཛ་ Use it also with any of the following initials, *viz.* ཀ་ཅ་ཏ་པ་ ཙ་ཤ་ས་ཧ་

Medium Tone.—Use this in a word beginning with ཁ་ཆ་ཐ་ཕ་ཚ་ as initals whether with or without prefixes.

Low Tone.—Use this in a word beginning with any of the following letters as initials ག་ང་ཇ་ཉ་ད་ན་བ་མ་ཛ་ཝ་ཞ་ཟ་ཡ་ ར་ལ་འ་ also in words in which a prefix precedes the initials ག་ཇ་ད་བ་ or ཛ་ Such initials are in this case, as previously noted in paragraph 23, pronounced as *g, j, d, b* and *dz,* respectively. For effect of ག་ང་ད་བ་ལ་ས་ in lengthening or shortening the preceding vowel see above paras. 6 and 7.

Examples.

ཀོ་བ་ leather = *ko-wa,* high tone.

སྤོས་ incense = *pö,* high tone and lengthened.

ཕག་ brick = *pă,* high tone and shortened.

ཆམ་པ་ cold (in the head) = *chham-pa,* medium tone.

ཐབས་ opportunity = *thaṕ,* medium tone.

ཐག་པ་ rope = *thaḱ-pa,* medium tone and shortened.

ལ་ to (postposition) *la,* low tone.

ལགས་ yes (a polite affirmative) = *lā,* low tone and lengthened.

བོད་ Tibet = *ṕö,* low tone and shortened.

Note the d[illegible] in above examples between སྤོས་ and བོད་ and between ལ་ and ལགས་

30. **Punctuation.**—It will have been noticed from the examples that at the end of each syllable a dot is placed at the top right-hand corner. This dot is named ཚེག *tshe.* A comma, semi-colon or colon is indicated by a vertical line (།) called *she,* a full-stop by a double line (༎) called *nyi-she,* and the end of a chapter by four lines (༎ ༎) called *sk̄i-she.* In hand-writing a mark (‘) is usually placed between each syllable instead of the *tshe,* but is sometimes incorporated with the last letter of the syllable.

31. **Spelling.**—The Tibetan method of spelling words should be acquired, as the teacher, in common with all Tibetans, will use it.

32. Pronounce the first consonant or compound consonant, add the vowel and pronounce the two together.

Thus, ཀོ་; *ka-na-ro, ko.* སྐི་; *sa-ka-ta, ka, ka k̄i-k̄u, ki.*

It is as if to say *sa* with *ka-ta* makes *ka, ka* with *k̄i-k̄u* makes *ki.*

33. If there is a final consonant, pronounce the whole word with it, then the consonant itself, and then the whole word again. Thus, ཀོང་; *ka-na-ro, ko, kong-nga-kong.* Again ཀྱོང་; *ka ya-ta, kya, kya-na-ro, kyo, kyong-nga, kyong.*

34. If the vowel is the inherent *a,* pronounce the first consonant, then the whole word, then the final consonant, and then the whole word again, *e.g.* ཁང་; *k̄a, k̄ang-nga, k̄ang.* སྒང་; *sa-ga-ta, ga, gang-nga, gang.* ལྟོགས; *la-ta-ta, ta, ta-na-ro, to, tok-k̄a-sa, tok.*

35. When a prefixed letter begins the syllable, *e.g.* ག་ད་ etc., it is pronounced as *ḱa-wo, ťa-wo*; *e.g.* གཉེན; *ḱa-wo-nya-deng-bu, nye, nyen-na, nyen.* དགབ; *ťa-wo-ga, gaṕ-ṕa gaṕ.* This *wo* is pronounced very shortly.

36. A syllable containing only a consonant and the inherent *a*, e.g., མ་, is called *ma-kyang, i e.* "only *ma*," to distinguish it from the consonant accompanied by one of the other vowels. Thus, to enquire whether a syllable is སོ་ or ས་, you may say, "Is it *sa-na-ro* or *sa-kyang*?"

36. **Examples.**

ལུང་ handle. *la sḰaṕ-kyu, lu, lung-nga, lung.*

རས་ cotton. *ra, re-sa, re.*

བཏང་བ་ to send. *ṕa-wo-ta-tang-nga, tang; wa: tang-wa.*

འཁྱུད་པ་ to embrace. *a-wo-kha-ya-ta khya, khya shaṕ-kyu, khyu, khyü-ťa, khyü; pa: khyü-pa.*

དགྲ་ enemy. *tá-wo-ga-ra-ta, dra.*

ལྷ་ spirit. *la-ha-ta, hla.*

བསོད་ནམས་ good fortune. *ṕa-wo-sa-na-ro, so, sö-ťa, sö; na, nam-ma-sa, nam: sö-nam.*

ཞྭ་མོ་ hat. *sḰa-wa-sur, sḰa; ma na-ro, mo: sḰa-mo.*

དཔེ་ཆ་ book. *Tá-wo-pa-deng-bu, pe; chha: pe-chha.*

གློག་ lightning. *ḱa-la-ta, la, la-na-ro, lo, lo-ḱa, lo.*

རྒྱུག་པ་ to run. *ra-ga-ta, ga, ga ya-ta gya, gya sḱaṕ-kyu, gyu, gyuḱ-ḱa, gyuḱ; pa: gyuḱ-pa.*

རིགས་བརྒྱུད་ lineage. *ra-ḱi-ḱu, ri, ri-ḱa-sa, riḱ; ṕa-wo-ra-ga-ta, ga, ga ya-ta, gya, gya-sḱaṕ-kyu, gyu, gyü-ťa, gyü: riḱ-gyü.*

37. **Sentences.**

Where are you going to? ཁྱོད་ག་པ་འགྲོ་གི་ཡིན་པ་ *khyö ḱa-pa dro-ḱi yim-pa?*

I am going to Darjiling, Sir. ལགས་ང་རྡོ་རྗེ་གླིང་ལ་འགྲོ་གི་ཡིན་ *lā nga Dor-je-ling lă dro-ḱi yin.*

What have you got in the bundle? རྡོག་ཐྲེད་ནང་ལ་ག་རེ་ཡོད་པ་ *doḱ-thre nang-la ḱa-re yö-pa?*

Different kinds of things, Sir. ལགས་ཆ་ལག་སྣ་ཚོགས་ཡོད་ *lā cha-lă na-tsho yö.*

Have you a tea-pot among them? དེའི་ནང་ལ་ཁོ་ཏིང་ཡོད་པས་ *ťe-ï nang-la kho ting yö-pē?*

Yes, Sir, I have. ལགས་ཡོད་ *lā-yö.*

What is its price? གོང་ག་ཚོད་ཡིན་པ་ *ḱong ḱa-tshö yim-pa?*

Twenty rupees. ལགས་སྒོར་མོ་ཉི་ཤུ་ཐམ་པ་ཡིན་ *lā gor-mo nyi-shu tham-pa yin.*

Will you let me have it for fifteen rupees? སྒོར་མོ་བཅོ་ལྔ་ལ་གཏོང་གི་ཡིན་པས་ *gor-mo che-nga la tong-ḱi yim-pē?*

No, Sir. ལགས་མིན་ *la-men.*

Well, good-day! འོ་ན་ག་ལེ་རྒྱུག་ *o-na ḱa-le gyu.*

Good-day, Sir! ད་འོ་ན་ག་ལེ་འཆིབ་རྒྱུ་གནང་ *ťa o-na ḱa-le chhiṕ-gyu-nang.*

ENGLISH-TIBETAN COLLOQUIAL DICTIONARY.

NOTE.

1. To understand fully the pronunciation of the Tibetan words, and the transliteration into the Roman character, reference should be made to the preliminary chapter on the "The Alphabet and its Pronunciation." It is not possible to represent all the Tibetan sounds by Roman letters with exactitude; hence the importance of mastering that chapter before using this dictionary.

2. Where the colloquial and the literary forms differ appreciably, the latter are given in brackets in the Tibetan character. In the romanized Tibetan the colloquial forms alone are given.

3. Where two or more Tibetan words are entered against the same English word, the first is the one most commonly used.

A

A, An, *art.*	ཅིག་	*chi.*
Do. (in the sense of full or complete)	གང་	*kang.*
Aback	རྒྱབ་ལོགས་ལ་	*gyap-lo-la.*
Abaft	གཤུག་ལ་	*sKu-la.*
Abandon, to	བཞག་པ་ (འཇོག་པ།) སྤང་བ་	*sKak-pa; pang-wa.*
Do. *hon.*	གཞོག་ག་ (འཇོག་པ་) གནང་བ་	*sKok-Ka nang-wa.*
	སྤོང་ང་ (བ་) གནང་བ་	*pong-nga nang-wa.*

Abate, to (in price)	བཅག་པ་ (གཅོག་པ་)	*chaḱ-pa.*
Do. *hon.*	གཅོག་ག་ (པ་) གནང་བ་	*choḱ-ḱa nang-wa.*
Abbess	ཨ་ནི་དབུ་མཛད་	*a-ni um-dze.*
Abbot	མཁན་པོ་	*khem-po.*
Abbreviate, to	སྡུད་པ། རྡུམ་རྡུམ་བྱེད་པ་	*dü-pa; dum dum cḱe-pa.*
Abdomen	གྲོ་ཁོག་ (གྲོད་ཁོག་)	*t́ro-kho.*
Do. *hon.*	གསོལ་གྲོད་	*sö-t́rö.*
Abide, to	བསྡད་པ་ (སྡོད་པ་)	*de-pa.*
Do. *hon.*	བཞུགས་པ་	*sḱu-pa*
Ability	དབང་	*wang.*
Abject	སྡུག་པོ་	*duḱ-po.*
Able, *adj.*	མཁས་པོ་	*khe-po.*
Able, to be	ཐུབ་པ་	*thuṕ-pa.*
Do. *hon.*	ཐུབ་པ་གནང་བ་	*thuṕ-pa nang-wa.*
Able, to be (in the sense of knowing how)	ཤེས་པ་	*she-pa.*
Do. *hon.*	མཁྱེན་པ་	*khyem-pa.*
Able-bodied	སྟོབས་ཆེན་པོ་	*toṕ chhem-po.*
Ablution	ཁྲུས་	*thrü.*
Do. *hon.*	སྐུ་ཁྲུས་	*ku-thrü.*

Abode	ཁང་པ། ནང་	*khang-pa; nang.*
Do. *hon.*	གཟིམ་ཁང་	*śim-khang.*
Do. *h. hon*	གཟིམ་ཤག་	*śim-sho*
Abolish, to	མེད་པར་བཟོ་བ་	*me-pa śo-wa.*
Do. *hon.*	མེད་པར་བཟོ་བ་གནང་བ་	*me-pa śo-wa nang-wa.*
Abominable	སྐྱུག་བྲོ་པོ་	*kyuḱ-t́ro-po.*
Abortion	བུ་གུ་ཤོར་བ་	*pu-gu shor-wa.*
About (approximately)	ཙ་ (ཙམ་)	*tsa.*
About (concerning)	དོན་ལ། སྐོར་ལ་	*t́ön-la; kor-la.*
Above (on top of)	སྟེང་ལ། སྒང་ལ་	*teng-la; gang-la.*
Above (higher up a hill)	ཡར་ལ་	*ya-la.*
Abridge, to	སྡུད་པ་	*dü-pa.*
Do. *hon.*	སྡུད་པ་གནང་བ་	*dü-pa nang-wa.*
Abruptly	ལམ་སང་	*lam-sang.*
Abscess	ཤུ་བ་	*shu-wa.*
Do. *hon.*	སྐུ་ཤུ་	*ku-shu.*
Abscond, to	བྲོས་པ་ (འབྲོས་པ་)	*t́rö-pa.*
Do. *hon.*	བྲོས་ (འབྲོས་) ཕེབ་པ་	*t́rö-phe-pa.*
Absence	མེད་དུས་	*me-t́ü.*
Absent, to be	མེད་པ་	*me-pa.*

Absolutely (used negatively)	ཐད་དེ། ཁྱོན་ནས་	*be te ; khyön-ne.*
Absolve, to	སེལ་བ་	*sel-wa.*
Do. *hon.*	སེལ་ལ་ (བ་) གནང་བ་	*sel-la nang-wa.*
Abstain from, to (certain kinds of food, &c.)	སྤང་བ་	*pang-wa.*
	བཅད་པ་ (གཅོད་པ་)	*che-pa.*
Do. *hon.*	སྤོང་ང་ (བ་) གནང་བ་	*pong-nga nang-wa.*
	བཅད་ (གཅོད་) པ་གནང་བ་	*che-pa nang-wa.*
Absurd, to be	དོན་དག་མེད་པ་	*t̔ön-t̔a me-pa.*
Abundant	འབེལ་པོ། ཛག་དོ་	*be-po ; dzak-t̔o.*
Abuse, *s.*	སྨད་ར་	*me-ra.*
Abuse, to	སྨད་ར་བཏང་ (གཏོང་) བ་	*me-ra tang-wa.*
Do. *hon.*	སྨད་ར་གཏོང་ང་ (བ་) གནང་བ་	*me-ra tong-nga nang-wa.*
Do. *inf.* to *sup.*	སྨད་ར་ཞུ་བ་	*me-ra sku-wa.*
Abyss	གཡང་གཟར་པོ་	*yang-śar-po.*
Accede, to	ཁས་ལེན་པ་	*khe-lem-pa.*
Do. *hon.*	ཞལ་བཞེས་གནང་བ།	*ske-ske nang-wa ;*
	ཞལ་གྱིས་བཞེས་པ་	*ske-kyi ske-pa.*
Accept, to	ལེན་པ་	*lem-pa.*
Do. *hon.*	བཞེས་པ་	*ske-pa.*
Access, to have	འགྲོ་ཚོག་པ། ཕྱིན་ཚོག་པ་	*dro-chhok-pa ; chhin-chhok-pa.*

Access, *hon.*	ཕེབ་ཆོག་པ་	*phe-chhok-pa.*
Accident	བར་ཆད་	*par-chhe.*
Accommodation	ཤོང་ས་	*shong-sa.*
Accompany, to	མཉམ་དུ་ཡོང་བ་	*nyam-tu yong-wa.*
Do. *hon.*	མཉམ་དུ་ཕེབ་པ་	*nyam-tu phe-pa.*
Do. *h. hon.*	ལྷན་རྒྱས་འཆིབ་རྒྱུ་གནང་བ་	*hlen-gye chhip-gyu nang-wa.*
Accomplice	རོགས་	*ro.*
Accomplished, to be (completed)	འཚར་བ་	*tshar-wa.*
Do. *hon.*	གྲུབ་པ་	*trup-pa.*
According to	ནང་བཞིན་	*nang-skin.*
Account	རྩིས་	*tsi.*
Account Book	རྩིས་ཐོ་	*tsi-tho.*
Do. *hon.*	ཕྱག་ཐོ་	*chha-tho.*
Account of, on	རྐྱེན་གྱིས་	*kyen-kyi.*
Accounts, to do	རྩིས་རྒྱབ་པ་	*tsi-gyap-pa.*
Do. *hon.*	ལྗགས་རྩིས་གནང་བ་	*ja-tsi nang-wa.*
	ལྗགས་རྩིས་སྐྱོན་པ་	*ja-tsi kyöm-pa.*
Accountant	རྩིས་པ་	*tsi-pa.*
Do. Chief	རྩིས་དཔོན་	*tsi-pön.*

Accountant, Office of an	རྩིས་ཁང་	*tsi-khang.*
Accumulate, to (money)	བསག་པ་ (གསོག་པ་)	*sak̄-pa.*
Do. *hon.*	བསག་ག་(གསོག་ཀ་)གནང་བ་	*sak̄-k̄a nang-wa.*
Accurate	ཁྲིག་ཁྲིག། ཏེན་ཏེན་	*thrik̄-thrik̄ ; ten-ten.*
Accusation	སྙད་	*nye.*
Accuse, to	སྙད་བཙུགས་ (འཛུགས་) པ་	*nye-tsuk̄-pa.*
Do. *hon.*	སྙད་བཙུགས་ཀ་ (འཛུགས་པ་) གནང་བ་	*nye-tsuk̄-k̄a nang-wa.*
	སྙད་སྐོ་བ་གནང་བ་	*nye-k̄o-wa nang-wa.*
Accustomed, to be	གོམས་པ་	*k̄om-pa.*
Do. to become	གོམས་སོང་བ་	*k̄om-song-wa.*
Ache, *s.*	གཟུག་	*suk̄.*
Do. *hon.*	སྙུང་གཞི་	*nyung-sk̄i.*
Ache, to	ན་བ་	*na-wa.*
Do. *hon.*	སྙུང་བ་	*nyung-wa.*
Achieve, to	བྱེད་པ་	*ck̄e-pa.*
Do. *hon.*	གནང་བ་	*nang-wa.*
Acid	སྐྱུར་པོ་	*kyur-po.*
Aconite	བཙན་དུག་	*tsen-ťu.*
Acquaintance (friend)	ངོ་ཤེས་པའི་མི་	*ngo-shem-pe-mi.*

Acquainted, to be	ངོ་ཤེས་པ་	*ngo-shem-pa.*
Do. *hon.*	ཐུགས་ངོ་མཁྱེན་པ་	*thu-ngo-khyem-pa.*
Do. *inf.* to *sup.*	ཞལ་ཚོ (ཚོར་) བ་	*sKe-tsho-wa.*
Acquainted, to get	ངོ་ཤེས་བཏང་ (གཏོང་) བ་	*ngo she tang-wa.*
Do. *hon.*	ངོ་ཤེས་གཏོང་ང་ (བ་) གནང་བ་	*ngo-she tong-nga nang-wa.*
Acquire, to	འབྱོར་བ། ཐོབ་པ་	*jor-wa ; thop-pa.*
Do. *hon.*	ཕྱག་འབྱོར་བྱུང་བ་	*chhan-jor cKung-wa.*
Acquirement (skill)	ཡོན་ཏན་	*yön-ten.*
Acquit, to	གློས་པ། བཏང་བ་	*lö-pa ; tang-wa.*
Acquitted, to be (in a case)	བཏང་བཞག་པ་	*tang-sKaK-pa.*
Do. *hon.*	བཏང་བཞག་ག་ (པ་) གནང་བ་	*tang-sKaK-Ka nang-wa.*
Across	ཕར་	*pha.*
Act, to	བྱེད་པ་	*cKe-pa.*
Do. *hon.*	གནང་བ་	*nang-wa.*
Action (law suit)	ཁ་མཆུ་	*kham-chhu.*
Do. (deed)	ལས་ཀ་	*le-ka.*
Do. *hon.*	ཕྱག་ལས་	*chha-le.*
Active	ཧུར་པོ་	*hur-po.*
Actor	ཨ་ཆེ་ལྷ་མོ་	*a-chhe-hla-mo.*
Actress	ཨ་ཆེ་ལྷ་མོ་	*a-chhe-hla-mo.*

Actual	ངོ་ཐོག་	*ngo-tho.*
Acute (knife)	རྣོ་པོ་	*no-po.*
Adage	གཏམ་དཔེ་	*tam-pe.*
Adams-apple	ཨོག་ལྡོམ་	*ok-dom.*
Add, to	སྣོན་འབེལ་སྤྲད་པ་	*nöm-be tre-pa.*
Do. *hon.*	སྣོན་འབེལ་གནང་བ་	*nöm-be nang-wa.*
Do. (figures)	སྡོམ་པ་	*dom-pa.*
Additional	སྣོན་གས་	*nön-ke.*
Adequate, to be	འགྲིག་པ་	*drik-pa.*
Adhere, to, *v.i.*	འབྱར་བ་	*jar-wa.*
Adieu (to a person departing)	ག་ལེ་ཕེབས་	*ka-le phe.*
Do. (to a person remaining)	ག་ལེ་བཞུགས་	*ka-le sku.*
Adjourn, to	བཞག་པ་ (འཇོག་པ་)	*skak-pa.*
Adjourn, to, *hon.*	གཞོག་ག་ (འཇོག་པ་) གནང་བ་	*skok-ka nang-wa.*
Adjust, to	སྒྲིག་པ་	*drik-pa.*
Do. *hon.*	སྒྲིག་ག་ (པ་) གནང་བ་	*drik-ka nang-wa.*
Admiration	མོས་པ་	*mö-pa.*
Admire, to	མོས་པ་བྱེད་པ་	*mö-pa che-pa.*

Admire, to (things)	སེམས་ཤོར་བ་	*sem-shor-wa.*
Do. *hon.*	ཐུགས་སེམས་ཤོར་བ་	*thu-sem shor-wa.*
Admittance, to grant	མཇལ་ཁ་གནང་བ་	*je-kha nang-ua.*
Admonish, to	བསླབ་བྱ་བྱེད་པ་	*lap-cha che-pa.*
Do. *hon.*	བསླབ་བྱ་གནང་བ་	*lap-cha nang-wa.*
Admonition	བསླབ་བྱ་	*lap-cha.*
Adopted child	གསོས་ཕྲུག་	*sö-thruk.*
Adore, to	མོས་གུས་བྱེད་པ་	*mö-kü che-pa.*
Adorn, to	རྒྱན་ཆ་བཏགས་ (འདོགས་) པ་	*gyen-chha tak-pa.*
Adornment	རྒྱན་ཆ་	*gyen-chha.*
Do. *hon.*	སྐུ་རྒྱན་	*ku-gyen.*
Adrift, to be	ཆུའི་སྒང་ལ་ལྡིང་བ་	*chhü-gang-la ding-wa.*
Adroit	རྩལ་ཆེན་པོ་	*tse-chhem-po.*
Adult	ལོ་དར་མ། གཞོན་པ་	*lo-tar-ma; shöm-pa.*
Adulterate, to	འདྲེས་བཏང་ (གཏོང་) བ་	*dre-tang-wa.*
Do. *hon.*	འདྲེས་གཏོང་ང་ (བ་) གནང་བ་	*dre-tong-nga nang-wa.*
Adulterer	ཆལ་པོ་	*chhe po.*
Adulteress	ཆལ་མོ་	*chhe-mo.*
Advance (of money)	སྔ་ཁྲི་	*ngam-chhi.*
Advantage	ཕན། ཕན་ཐོགས་	*phen; phen-tho.*

Advantage, *hon.*	ཐུགས་ཕན་	*thu-phen*
Do. to be of	ཕན་ཐོགས་པ་	*phen-thoǩ-pa.*
Do. *hon.*	ཐུགས་ཕན་གསོ་བ་	*thu-phen so-wa.*
Adversary	དགྲ་	*dra.*
Advice	གྲོས་	*ťrö.*
Advice, to ask	གྲོས་དྲི་ (འདྲི་) བ་	*ťrö-ťri-wa.*
Do. *hon.*	བཀའ་འདྲི་ཞུ་བ་	*kan-dri sǩu-wa.*
Do. *h. hon.*	བཀའ་སྨོན་ (སྨོལ) ཞུ་བ་	*ka-mön sǩu-wa.*
Advice, to give	གྲོས་བྱེད་པ་	*ťrö-cǩe-pa.*
Do. *hon.*	བཀའ་གྲོས་གནང་བ་	*ka-ťrö nang-wa.*
Aeroplane	གནམ་གྲུ་	*nam-ťru.*
Afar, *adv.*	ཐག་རིང་པོ་	*tha-ring-po.*
Affair (business)	ལས་ཀ། དོན་དག་	*le-ka ; ťön-ťa.*
Do. *hon.*	ཕྱག་ལས། སྐུ་དོན་	*chha-le ; ku-ťön.*
Affection	བྱམས་པོ་	*cǩam-po.*
Affectionate, to be	བྱམས་པོ་བྱེད་པ་	*cǩam-po cǩe-pa.*
Do. *hon.*	བྱམས་པོ་གནང་བ་	*cǩam po nang-wa.*
Affirm, to	ལབ་པ་	*lap̌-pa.*
Do. *hon.*	གསུང་བ་	*sung wa.*
Affix, *s.* (grammatical)	རྗེས་འཇུག་	*ǰen-ǰu.*

Affix, to	སྦྲེལ་བ་	*drel-wa.*
Do. *hon.*	སྦྲེལ་ལ་ (བ་) གནང་བ་	*drel-la nang-wa.*
Afflicted, to be	དཀའ་ལས་བྱུང་བ་	*ka-le cḱung-wa.*
Affliction	དཀའ་ལས་	*ka-le.*
Afford, to	སྟེར་བ་	*ter-wa.*
Do. *hon.*	གནང་བ་	*nang-wa.*
Afloat, to be	ཆུའི་སྒང་ལ་གཡང་ (གཡིང་) བ་	*chhü-gang-la yang-wa.*
Afoot (on foot)	རྐང་ཐང་ལ་	*kang-thang-la.*
Do. *hon.*	ཞབས་ཐང་ལ་	*sḱaṕ-thang-la.*
Afraid, to be	ཞེད་པ་	*sḱe-pa.*
Do. *hon.*	ཞེད་པ་གནང་བ་	*sḱe-pa nang-wa.*
Affray, to commit an	ལག་འཛིང་བྱས་པ་	*laḱ-dzing cḱe-pa.*
After	གཞུག་ལ། རྗེས་ལ་	*sḱu-la ; je-la.*
Afternoon	དགོངས་དག་	*gong-t́a.*
Afterwards	གཞུག་ལ། རྗེས་ལ་	*sḱu-la ; je-la.*
Again	ཡང་སྐྱར་	*yang-kyar.*
Against, over	ཁ་ཐུག་ལ་	*kha-thu-la.*
Age (of a human being) .	ལོ་	*lo.*
Do. *hon.*	དགོང་ལོ་ (དགུང་ལོ་)	*gong-lo.*
Age (of an animal)	ན་	*na.*

Aged, *m.*	རྒ་ཕུ་ (རྒད་པོ་)	*ga-p̄u.*
Do. *f.*	རྒ་སྨུ་ (རྒད་མོ་)	*ga-mu.*
Do. *hon.*	སྐུ་ནས་བགྲེས་པོ་	*ku-ne dre-po.*
Agent	ལས་ཚབ་	*le-tshap̄.*
Do. *hon.*	སྐུ་ཚབ་	*ku-tshap̄.*
Aggravated, to be (angry)	ཚིག་པ་ཟ་བ་	*tshik̄-pa śa-wa.*
Do. *hon.*	དགོངས་པ་ཚུང་པ་	*gong-pa tshung-pa.*
Agile	ཧུར་པོ་	*hur po.*
Agitate, to (shake)	དཀྲུག་པ་	*truk̄-pa.*
Do. *hon.*	དཀྲུག་ག་ (པ་) གནང་བ་	*truk̄-k̄a nang-wa.*
Agitated, to be	སེམས་འཚབས་པ་	*sem tshap̄-pa.*
Do. *hon.*	ཐུགས་སེམས་འཚབས་པ་ གནང་བ་	*thu-sem tshap̄-pa nang-wa.*
Agony	སྡུག་བསྔལ་	*du-nge.*
Do. *hon.*	ཐུགས་འཁྲལ་	*thu-thre.*
Agree, to	འགྲིག་པ། འཆམ་པ་	*drik̄-pa ; chham-pa.*
Agreeable	མཐུན་པོ་	*thüm-po.*
Agreeable (in taste)	ཞིམ་པོ་	*sk̄im-po.*
Do. *hon.*	སྤྲོ་པོ་	*tro-po.*
Agreement (bond)	གམ་རྒྱ་ (གན་རྒྱ་)	*k̄am-gya.*

Agriculture	སོ་ནམས་	*so-nam.*
Agriculturist	སོ་ནམས་བྱེད་མཁན	*so-nam cKe-khen.*
Ague	ཚད་ནད་	*tshe-ne.*
Ague, to have	འདར་རྒྱབ་པ་	*dar-gyap-pa*
Ahead (in front)	སྔན་ལ་ (སྔོན་ལ་)	*ngen-la.*
Aid	རོགས་	*ro.*
Do. *hon.*	མགོ་འདྲེན་	*gön-dren.*
Aid, to	རོགས་བྱེད་པ་	*ro-cKe-pa.*
Do. *hon.*	མགོ་འདྲེན་གནང་བ་	*gön-dren nang-wa.*
Ail, to	ན་བ་	*na-wa.*
Do. *hon.*	སྙུང་བ་	*nyung-wa.*
Ailment	ན་ཚ་	*na-tsha.*
Do. *hon.*	སྙུང་བ་	*nyung-wa.*
Air (atmospheric wind)	ལྷགས་པ། རླུང་	*hlak-pa ; lung.*
Air (mien)	མདངས། གདོང་	*dang ; dong.*
Alarm, to	ཞེད་སྐྲག་སླང་བ་	*sKe-tra lang-wa.*
Do. *hon.*	ཞེད་སྐྲག་སློང་ང་ (བ་) གནང་བ་	*sKe-tra long-nga nang-wa.*
Alas	ཨ་ཁ་ཁ་ (ཀྱི་མ་)	*a-kha-kha.*
Alert	གཅང་པོ་	*chang-po.*
Do. *hon.*	ཐུགས་གཅང་པོ་	*thu-chang-po.*

Alien	ཕྱོགས་མི་	*chho-mi.*
Alight, to (*e.g.*, from horse)	བབ་པ་ (འབབ་པ་)	*ṕaṕ-pa.*
Alight, to be (of fire)	འབར་བ་	*bar-wa.*
Alike	གཅིག་པ་	*chiḱ-pa.*
Alive, to be	གསོན་པོ་ཡོད་པ་	*söm-po yö-pa.*
All	ཚང་མ། ཐམས་ཅད། སྐང་ཁ། རུ་	*tshang-ma; tham che; gang-ḱha; ru.*
All day	ཉིན་གང་	*nyin-ḱang.*
All right (very well)	ལགས་སོ། ལགས་ལགས་སི་	*la-so; la-la-si.*
Allot, to	བགོད་པ་	*gö-pa.*
Do. *hon.*	བགོད་པ་གནང་བ་	*gö-pa nang-wa.*
Alliance (relation)	བརྒྱུད་ཚ་	*gyü-tsa.*
Do. *hon.*	སྐུ་བརྒྱུད་	*ku-gyü.*
Allied, to be	ཁ་མཐུན་པ་	*ḱha-thüm-pa.*
Do. *hon.*	ཞལ་མཐུན་གནང་བ་	*sḱe-thün-nang-wa.*
Allotment (share allotted)	སྐེ་ལ་ (སྐལ་བ་)	*ke-la.*
Do. *hon.*	སྐུ་སྐལ་	*ku-ke.*
Allow, to	བཅུག་པ་ (འཇུག་པ་)	*chuḱ-pa.*
Do. *hon.*	བཅུག་ག་ (འཇུག་པ་) གནང་བ་	*chuḱ-ḱa nang-wa.*
Allowed, to be	ཆོག་པ་	*chhoḱ-pa.*

Alloy	ལྷད་	*hle.*
Allure, to	སླུ་བ་	*lu-wa.*
All-wise	ཐམས་ཅད་མཁྱེན་པ་	*tham-che khyem-pa.*
Almanack	ཟླ་ཐོ། ལེ་ཐོ་ (ལོ་ཐོ་)	*da-tho; le-tho.*
Do. *hon.*	གཟིགས་ཐོ་	*śiǩ-tho.*
Almighty	སྐུ་དབང་ཆེན་པོ་	*ku-wang chhem-po.*
Almond	རྒྱ་དཀར་སྟར་ཀ་	*gya-kar tar-ka.*
Almost	ཧ་ལམ་	*ha-lam.*
Alms	སྦྱིན་པ་	*jim-pa.*
Alms, to ask	སློང་བ་	*long-wa.*
Alms, to give	སྦྱིན་པ་བཏང་ (གཏོང་) བ་	*jim-pa tang-wa.*
Alone	གཅིག་པོ་	*chiǩ-po.*
Do. *hon.*	སྐུ་རྐྱང་	*ku kyang.*
Along with	དང་མཉམ་དུ་	*ťang-nyam-ťu.*
Aloud	སྐད་ཆེན་པོ་བརྒྱབ་ནས་	*ke-chhem-po gyap̆-ne.*
Do. *hon.*	གསུང་སྐད་ཆེན་པོ་སྐྱོན་ནས་	*sung-ke chhem-po kyön-ne.*
Alphabet	ཀ་ཁ་	*ka-kha.*
Already	ད་གི་ནས་	*ťa-ki-ne.*
Also	ཡང་	*yang.*
Altar	མཆོད་བཤམས་	*chhö-sham.*

Alter, to, *v.t.*	རྗེ་བ། སྒྱུར་བ་	*je-wa; gyur-wa.*
Do. *hon.*	རྗེ་བ་གནང་བ། སྒྱུར་ར་ (བ་) གནང་བ་	*je-wa nang-wa; gyur-ra nang-wa.*
Alter, to (fit of clothes, etc.)	བཟོ་བཅོས་རྒྱབ་པ་	*śop-chö gyap-pa.*
Do. *hon.*	བཟོ་བཅོས་སྐྱོན་པ་	*śop-chö kyöm-pa.*
Alternately	རེ་མེད་ (མོས་) བྱས་ནས་	*re-me cKe-ne.*
Although	ཀྱང་། རུང་། ན། ཡང་།	*kyang; rung; na; yang.*
Altogether (in total)	ཐམས་ཅད་བསྡོམས་ནས་	*tham-che dom-ne.*
Do. (quite)	ཐད་	*be.*
Alum	སྐྱུར་མོ་ཚ་	*kyu-mu-tsha.*
Always	རྣམ་རྒྱུན། དུས་རྒྱུན་	*nam-gyün; tü gyün.*
Am	ཡོད་	*yö.*
Amass, to	སྡུད་པ་	*dü-pa.*
Do. *hon.*	སྡུད་པ་གནང་བ་	*dü-pa nang-wa.*
Amaze, to	ཡ་མཚན་བྱེད་པ་	*yam-tshen cKe-pa.*
Do. *hon.*	ཡ་མཚན་གནང་བ་	*yam-tshen nang-wa.*
Amazement	ཡ་མཚན་	*yam-tshen.*
Amazing	ཡ་མཚན་པོ་	*yam-tshem-po.*
Ambassador	སྐུ་ཚབ་	*ku-tshap.*

Amber	སྤོས་ཤེལ་	*pö-she.*
Ambition	མཐོ་འདོད་	*thon-dö.*
Ambitious	མཐོ་འདོད་ཆེན་པོ་	*thon-dö chhem-po.*
Amble (of a horse)	འགྲོས་	*drö.*
Amble, to (horse)	འགྲོས་རྒྱབ་པ་	*drö-gyap-pa.*
Do. *hon.*	ཆིབས་འགྲོས་རྒྱབ་པ་	*chhim-drö gyap-pa.*
Ambling pony	འགྲོས་མ་	*drö-ma.*
Amend, to	བཟོ་སྐྱོར་བྱེད་པ་	*śo-kyor cKe-pa.*
Do. *hon.*	བཟོ་སྐྱོར་གནང་བ་	*śo-kyor nang-wa.*
Amendment (correction)	ཞུ་དག་	*sKu-t́a.*
Amicable	མཐུན་པོ་	*thüm-po.*
Amicable relationship (state of)	མཐུན་ལམ་	*thün-lam.*
Amidst	དཀྱིལ་ལ་	*kyi-la.*
Ammunition	རྫས་རྡེ་	*dzen-de.*
Among	དཀྱིལ་ལ་	*kyi-la.*
Among ourselves (yourselves, themselves)	ནང་ཚག་	*nang-tsa.*
Amount, total	ཁྱོན་བསྡོམས་	*khyön-dom.*
Ample	མང་པོ་	*mang-po.*

Amusement	རྩེད་མོ་	*tse-mo.*
Do. *hon.*	སྐུ་རྩེད་	*ku-tse.*
Amusement, to have	ཐུགས་སྤྲོ་བཏང་ (གཏོང་) བ་	*thu-tro tang-wa.*
Do. *hon.*	ཐུགས་སྤྲོ་གཏོང་ང་(བ་)གནང་བ་	*thu-tro tong-nga nang-wa.*
Analogy	དཔེ་	*pe.*
Ancestry	རིགས་བརྒྱུད། མི་བརྒྱུད་	*ri-gyü ; mi-gyü.*
Do. *hon.*	སྐུ་བརྒྱུད་	*ku-gyü.*
Ancestry of Lama	གདུང་བརྒྱུད་	*dung-gyü.*
Anchor	གཏིང་རྡོ་	*ťing-do.*
Ancient (of former time)	སྔོན་གྱི་	*ngön-ḱyi.*
Do. (old)	རྙིང་པ་	*nying-pa.*
Anciently	སྔོན་ལ། སྔོན་དུས་	*ngön-la ; ngön-ťü.*
And	ཡང་། དང་	*yang ; ťang.*
Anecdote	སྒྲུམ་ (སྒྲུངས་)	*drum.*
Anecdote, to relate	སྒྲུམ་ (སྒྲུངས་) བཤད་པ་	*drum she-pa.*
Do. *hon.*	སྒྲུམ་ (སྒྲུངས་) གསུང་བ་	*drum sung-wa.*
Angel	ཕོ་ཉ་	*pho-nya.*
Anger	ཚིག་པ། ཁོང་ཁྲོ་	*tshiḱ-pa ; khong-thro.*
Angle (corner)	ཟུར་	*śur.*
Angry, to be	ཚིག་པ་ཟ་བ། ཁོང་ཁྲོ་ཟ་བ་	*tshiḱ-pa śa-wa ; khong thro śa-wa.*

Angry, to be *hon*	དགོངས་པ་ཚུང་བ་ རྣམ་མཁྱེན་འགལ་བ་	*gong-pa tshung-pa ; nam-khyen gel-wa.*
Angry and suspicious, to be	བལྟ་ཕྱོགས་བྱེད་པ་	*ta-chhok che-pa.*
Do. *hon.*	གཟིགས་ཕྱོགས་གནང་བ་	*śi-chhok nang-wa.*
Angular	ཟུར་མང་པོ་ཡོད་པ་	*śur-mang-po yö-pa.*
Animal	སེམས་ཅན་	*sem-chen.*
Animal (wild)	རི་དྭགས་	*ri-ťa.*
Animal (beast of prey)	གཅན་གཟན་	*chen-śen.*
Ankle	རྐང་པའི་ཚིགས་ཏོག་	*kang-pe tshik-do.*
Do. *hon.*	ཞབས་ཀྱི་ཚིགས་ཏོག་	*shap-kyi tshik-do.*
Annals	ལོ་རྒྱུས་	*lo-gyü.*
Annals (of kings)	རྒྱལ་རབས་	*gye-rap.*
Annihilate, to	ཐམས་ཅད་མེད་པར་བཟོ་བ་	*tham-che me-pa śo-wa.*
Announce, to	ལན་ (ལོན་) སྤྲོད་པ། ལན་ (ལོན་) སྐྱེལ་བ་	*len-tre-pa ; len-kyel-wa.*
Do. *inf.* to *sup.*	ལྗགས་ལན་ཕུལ་ (འབུལ་) བ་	*ja-len phü-wa.*
Annoy, to	ཁོང་ཁྲོ་སློང་བ	*khong-thro lang-wa.*
Do. *hon.*	དགོངས་པ་དཀྲུག་པ་	*gong-pa truk-pa.*
Annoyed, to be	འཚེར་བ་	*tsher-wa.*
Do. *hon.*	ཐུགས་འཚེར་གནང་བ་	*thu-tsher nang-wa.*

Annually	ལོ་རེ་རེ་	*lo-re-re.*
Anoint, to	བྱུགས་པ་ (འབྱུག་པ།) སྐུ་བ་	*cḱuḱ-pa ; ku-wa.*
Do. *hon.*	བྱུགས་ག་ (འབྱུག་པ་) གནང་བ། བསྐུས་པ་ (སྐུ་བ་) གནང་བ་	*cḱuḱ-ḱa nang-wa ; kü-pa nang-wa.*
Another	གཞན་པ། ཡན་པ་	*sḱem-pa ; yem-pa.*
Answer, *s.*	ལན་	*len.*
Do. *hon.*	བཀའ་ལན་	*ka-len.*
Answer, to	ལན་རྒྱབ་པ་	*len-gyaṕ-pa.*
Do. *hon.*	ལྗགས་ལན་སྐྱོན་པ་	*ja-len kyöm-pa.*
Answer, to (in anger)	ཁ་ལན་ལོག་པ་	*kha-len loḱ-pa.*
Answer letter, to	ཡིག་ལན་ལོག་པ། ཡིག་ལན་བཏང་ (གཏོང་) བ་	*yiḱ-len loḱ-pa ; yiḱ-len tang-wa.*
Do. *hon.*	ཕྱག་བྲིས་བཀའ་ལན་གནང་བ་	*chha-ri ka-len nang-wa.*
Ant	གྲོག་མ་	*t́ro-ma.*
Antagonist	དགྲ་	*dra.*
Antelope	གཙོད་	*tsö.*
Antique	རྙིང་པ་	*nying-pa.*
Anus	ཀུབ་	*kuṕ.*
Do. *hon.*	ཞབས་ཕོངས་	*sḱam-phong.*
Anvil	འོག་ཙ་	*oḱ-tsa.*

Anxiety	སེམས་འཁྲལ་	*sem-thre.*
Do. *hon.*	ཐུགས་འཁྲལ་	*thu-thre.*
Anxious, to be	སེམས་འཁྲལ་བྱེད་པ་	*sem-thre cḱe-pa.*
Do. *hon.*	ཐུགས་འཁྲལ་གནང་བ་	*thuḱ-thre nang-wa.*
Any	གང་ཡང་	*ḱang yang.*
Anybody (with negative)	སུ་གང་། སུ་ཡང་	*su-ḱang; su-yang.*
Anyhow (in any case)	ག་རེ་ཡིན་ན་ཡང་	*ḱa-re yin-ne yang.*
Apartment	ཁང་མིག་	*khang-miḱ.*
Do. *hon.*	གཟིམ་ཆུང་	*śim-chung.*
Ape	སྤེའུ་ (སྤྲེའུ་)	*pe-u.*
Aperture	སྒི་ཁུང་	*gi-khung.*
Apologize, to	ཐུགས་དགོངས་དག་ཞུ་བ་	*thu-gong-t́a sḱu-wa.*
Apology	ཐུགས་དགོངས་དག་	*thu-gong-t́a.*
Apoplexy	གཟའ་རྒྱབ་པ་	*sa gyaṕ-pa.*
Apothecary's shop	སྨན་ཁང་	*men-khang.*
Apparatus	ལག་ཆ་	*laḱ-chha.*
Apparel	ཆུ་པ་	*chhu-pa.*
Apparel, *hon.*	ན་བཟའ་	*nam-śa.*
Appeal, to	ཞུ་བ་	*sḱu-wa.*
Appear to be, to	ཡིན་འགྲོ་	*yin-dro.*

Appear, to (to be seen)	མཐོང་བ་	*thong-wa.*
Appear, to cause to (ghost, etc.)	སྤྱན་འདྲེན་ཞུ་བ་	*chen-dren sḱu wa.*
Appearance	དབྱིབས། བཟོ་ལྟ་	*y'ṕ ; sóp-ta.*
Appetite	དང་ག་	*t́ang-ḱa.*
Do. *hon.*	གསོལ་དང་	*sö-t́ang.*
Applaud, to	སྟོད་ར་བཏང་ (གཏོང་) བ་	*tö-ra tang-wa.*
Do. *hon.*	སྟོད་ར་གཏོང་ང་ (བ་) གནང་བ་	*tö-ra tong-nga nang-wa.*
Do. *inf.* to *sup.*	སྟོད་ར་ཞུ་བ་	*tö-ra sḱu-wa.*
Applause	སྟོད་ར་	*tö-ra.*
Apple	ཀུ་ཤུ་	*ku-shu.*
Application (inferior to superior)	སྙན་ཞུ་	*nye-sḱu.*
Application, written (by inferior to superior)	ཞུ་ཡིག་	*sḱu-yi.*
Apply, to (by inferior to superior)	སྙན་ཞུ་ཕུལ་ (འབུལ་) བ་	*nye-sḱu-phü-wa.*
Apply in writing, to (by inferior to superior)	ཞུ་ཡིག་ཕུལ་བ་	*sḱu-yi phü-wa.*
Appoint, to (an officer)	སྐོ་བ་	*ko-wa.*
Do. *hon.*	བསྐོས་བཞག་གནང་བ་	*kö-sḱa nang-wa.*
Appoint, to (a menial servant)	བཞག་པ་ (འཇོག་པ་)	*sḱak-pa.*

Appoint, to (a menial servant) *hon.*	གཞོག་ག་ (འཇོག་པ་) གནང་བ་	*sḰok-Ḱa nang-wa.*
Approach, to (an object)	འགྲམ་ལ་འགྲོ་བ། འགྲམ་ལ་ཡོང་བ་	*dram-la dro-wa ; drum-la yong-wa.*
Do. *hon.*	འགྲམ་ལ་ཕེབ་པ་	*dram-la phe-pa.*
Approve, to (sanction)	བཀའ་གནང་བ་	*ka-nang-wa.*
Appurtenance	ཅ་ལག་ (ཆ་ལག་)	*cha-la.*
Do. *hon.*	སྐུ་ཅས་ (སྐུ་ཆས་)	*ku-che.*
Apricot	ཁམ་བུ་	*kham-ṕu.*
Do. (a quick-growing, with good fruit)	ལོ་གསུམ་ཁམ་བུ་	*lo-sum kham-ṕu.*
Do. (dried, from Balti)	མངའ་རིས་ཁམ་བུ་	*nga-ri kham-ṕu.*
Apron	པང་གདན་	*pang-den.*
Do. *hon.*	སྐུ་པང་	*ku-pang.*
Aqueduct	ཡོ་པོ་ (ཡུར་པོ་)	*yo-po.*
Arbitrate, to	བར་མི་བྱེད་པ་	*ṕar-mi cḰe-pa.*
Do. *hon.*	བར་མི་གནང་བ་	*ṕar-mi nang-wa.*
Archer	མདའ་པ་	*da-pa.*
Do. *hon.*	ཕྱག་མདའ་གནང་མཁན་	*chhan-da nang-khen.*
Arduous	དཀའ་ལས་ཁག་པོ་	*ka-le khaḱ-po.*
Do. *hon.*	སྐུ་མཉེལ་པོ་	*ku-nye-po.*

Are	ཡོད། འདུག། རེད་	*yö ; du ; re.*
Area	རྒྱ་	*gya.*
Argue, to	རྩེ་རྒྱབ་པ་	*t e-gyap-pa.*
Do. *hon.*	ཞལ་རྩེ་སྐྱོན་པ་	*sKe-tse kyöm-pa.*
Argument	རྩོད་པ་	*tsö-pa.*
Arid	སྐམ་པོ་	*kam po.*
Arise, to	ལང་བ་	*lang-wa.*
Do. *hon.*	བཞང་བ་ (བཞེང་བ་)	*sKang-wa.*
Do. *h. hon.*	སྐུ་བཞང་ (བཞེང་) གནང་བ་	*ku-sKang nang-wa.*
Arithmetic	རྩིས་	*tsi.*
Do. *hon.*	ཕྱགས་རྩིས་	*ja-tsi.*
Arm	ལག་པ་	*lak-pa.*
Do. *hon.*	ཕྱག་	*chha.*
Arm, upper	ལག་པའི་ཉ་	*lak-pe-nya.*
Do. *hon.*	ཕྱག་གི་ཉ་	*chha-ki-nya.*
Armful	པང་ག་ (པ་) གང་	*pang-ka-kang.*
Armlet	སྒྲོག་གདུང་	*dro-dung.*
Do. *hon.*	ཕྱག་གདུང་	*chha-dung.*
Armour	ཁྲབ་	*thrap.*
Arm-pit	མཆན་ཁུང་	*chhen-khung.*

Arms (weapon)	མཚོན་ཆ་	*tshön-chha.*
Army	དམག་དཔུང་	*mak̄-pung.*
Do. (first militia, consisting of Tibetan laymen)	འདོན་དམག་	*dön-ma.*
Do. (second militia consisting of Tibetan monks)	སེར་དམག་	*ser-ma.*
Do. (last militia, consisting of all males between 18 and 60)	བཅོ་བརྒྱད་དྲུག་ཅུ་	*chop̄-gye truk̄-chu.*
Around	འཁོར་ལ་	*khor-la.*
Arouse, to (from sleep)	གཉིད་སད་པ་	*nyi-se-pa.*
Do. *hon.*	གཉིད་སད་པ་གནང་བ་	*nyi-se-pa nang-wa.*
Arrange, to	སྒྲིག་པ་	*drik̄-pa.*
Do. *hon.*	སྒྲིག་ག་ (པ་) གནང་བ་	*drik̄-ka nang-wa.*
Arrest, to	ཟིན་པ་	*ṡim-pa.*
Do. *hon.*	ཟིན་པ་གནང་བ་	*sim-pa nang-wa.*
Arrive, to	སླེབ་པ་	*lep̄-pa.*
Do. *hon.*	ཕེབ་པ་	*phe-pa.*
Do. *h. hon.*	འཆིབ་རྒྱུ་གནང་བ་	*chhip̄-gyu nang wa.*
Arrogant	ཉམས་ཆེན་པོ། ཛ་ཁོག་ཆེན་པོ་	*nyam-chhem-po; dza-kho chhem-po.*

Arrow	མདའ་	*da.*
Do. *hon.*	ཕྱག་མདའ་	*chhan-da.*
Art, *s.*	ཡོན་ཏན་	*yön-ten.*
Artery	རྩ་	*tsa.*
Artful	གཙང་པོ་	*chang-po.*
Do. *hon.*	ཐུགས་གཙང་པོ་	*thu-chang-po.*
Article	སྤྱད་ལག ། དངོས་རིགས་	*cha-la ; ngö ri.*
Artist (painter)	ལྷ་རི་ (འབྲི་) པ་	*hla-ri-pa.*
As (like)	ནང་བཞིན། འདྲ་པོ་	*nang-shin ; dra-po.*
As far as	བར་དུ། ཐུག་	*par-tu ; thu.*
Ascend, to	འཛེག་པ་ (འཛེག་པ་)	*dzak-pa.*
Do. *hon.*	འཛེག་ག (འཛེག་པ་) གནང་བ་	*dzak-ka nang-wa.*
Ascent (uphill)	གྱེན་	*kyen.*
Ascertain, to	ཧ་གོ་བ་བྱེད་པ་	*ha-ko-wa che-pa.*
Do. *hon.*	མཁྱེན་པ་གནང་བ་	*khyem-pa nang-wa.*
Ascetic	སྒོམ་ཆེན་	*gom-chhen.*
Ashamed	ངོ་ཚ་པོ་	*ngo-tsha-po.*
Ashamed, to feel	ངོ་ཚ་བ་	*ngo-tsha-wa.*
Do. *hon.*	ཐུགས་ངོ་ཚ་བ་	*thu-ngo-tsha-wa.*
Ashes	གོག་ཐལ་	*ko-the.*

Aside	ཟུར་དུ་	*śur-ťu.*
Ask, to	དྲི་བ་ (འདྲི་བ་)	*ťri-wa.*
Ask, to (inferior asking superior)	ཞུ་བ་	*sḱu-wa.*
Asleep, to fall	གཉིད་ཁུག་པ་	*nyi-khuḱ-pa.*
Do. *hon.*	མཉན་ (མཉལ་) གཟིམ་པ་	*nye-śim-pa.*
Ass	བུང་གུ་ (བོང་བུ་)	*ṕung-ḱu.*
Do. (wild)	རྐྱང་	*kyang.*
Assail, to	རུབ་རྒྱབ་པ་	*ruṕ-gyaṕ-pa.*
Assassin	མི་གསོད་མཁན་	*mi-sö-khen.*
Assassinate, to	བསད་པ་ (གསོད་པ་)	*se-pa.*
Assault, to	རྡུང་བ་	*dung-wa.*
Do. *hon.*	ཕྱག་འཇུག་ (འཇུས་) གནང་བ་	*chhan-juḱ nang-wa.*
Assemble, to	འཚོགས་པ་	*tshoḱ-pa.*
Do. *hon.*	ཚོགས་འདུ་འཚོགས་ཀ་ (པ་) གནང་བ་	*tshon-du-tshoḱ-ḱa nang-wa.*
Assembly-hall	ཚོམས་ཆེན་	*tshom-chhen.*
Do. for monks	འདུ་ཁང་	*du-khang.*
Assiduous	བརྩོན་འགྲུས་ཆེན་པོ་	*tsön-drü chhem-po.*
Do. to be	སྙིང་རུས་བྱེད་པ་	*nying-rü cḱe-pa*

Assiduous, to be *hon.*	ཐུགས་རུས་གནང་བ་	*thu-rü nang-wa.*
Assist, to	རོགས་བྱེད་པ་	*ro-cKe-pa.*
Do. *hon.*	མགོན་འདྲེན་གནང་བ་	*gön-dren nang-wa.*
Assistance	རོགས་	*ro.*
Do. *hon.*	མགོན་འདྲེན་	*gön-dren.*
Assistant	རོགས་བྱེད་མཁན་	*ro-cKe-khen.*
Do. *hon.*	མགོན་འདྲེན་གནང་མཁན་	*gön-dren nang-khen.*
Associate	དགའ་པོ་ཉེ་པོ་	*ga-po nye-po.*
Do. *hon.*	ཐུགས་ཉེ་ཆག་པོ་	*thuK-nye chhaK-po.*
Associate with, to	དགའ་པོ་ཉེ་པོ་ཡོད་པ་	*ga-po nye-po yö-pa.*
Aster	སྐལ་བཟང་མེ་ཏོག་	*ke-śang me-to.*
Astonish, to	ཡ་མཚན་བྱེད་པ་	*yam-tshen cKe-pa.*
Do. *hon.*	ཡ་མཚན་གནང་བ་	*yam-tshen nang-wa.*
Astonished	ཡ་མཚན་པ་	*yam-tshem-pa.*
Astonishing	ཡ་མཚན་པོ་	*yam-tshem po.*
Astonishment	ཡ་མཚན་	*yam-tshen.*
Astride, to put	སྐྱོན་པ་	*kyöm-pa.*
Astrologer	རྩིས་པ་	*tsi-pa.*
Astrology	སྐར་རྩིས་	*kar-tsi.*
Astronomer	རྩིས་པ་	*tsi-pa.*

Astronomy	སྐར་རྩིས་	*kar-tsi.*
Asunder	སོ་སོ་	*so-so.*
At	ལ་	*la.*
At all (negatively)	ཙ་ནས་	*tsa-ne.*
Athletic	རྩལ་ཆེན་པོ་	*tse-chhem-po.*
Atlas	ས་ཁྲ་	*saṕ-thra.*
At once	ལམ་སང་	*lam-sang.*
Attach, to	རྒྱབ་པ་	*gyaṕ-pa.*
Do. *hon.*	སྐྱོན་པ་	*kyöm-pa.*
Attach, to (by sticking together)	སྦྱར་བ་	*jar-wa.*
Do. *hon.*	སྦྱར་ར་ (བ་) གནང་བ་	*j̣ar-ra nang-wa.*
Attached, to be (long for)	དྲན་པ་	*t́rem-pa.*
Do. *hon.*	དྲན་པ་གནང་བ་	*t́rem-pa nang-wa.*
Attached, to be (love)	སེམས་ཆགས་པ་	*sem chhaḱ-pa.*
Do. *hon.*	ཐུགས་སེམས་ཆགས་པ་	*thu-sem chhaḱ-pa.*
Attack, to	རུབ་རྒྱབ་པ་	*ruṕ-gyaṕ-pa.*
Attain, to	འབྱོར་བ། ཐོབ་པ་	*jor-wa ; thoṕ-pa.*
Do. *hon.*	འབྱོར་ར་ (བ་) གནང་བ། ཕྱག་སོན་ཕྱུང་བ་	*jor-ra nang-wa ; chhaḱ-sön ćhung-wa.*

Attempt	བརྩོན་འགྲུས་	*tsön-drü.*
Attempt, to	བརྩོན་འགྲུས་བྱེད་པ་	*tsön-drü cḱe pa.*
Do. *hon.*	བརྩོན་འགྲུས་གནང་བ་	*tsön-drü nang-wa.*
Attend, to (servant on master)	ཞབས་ཕྱི་ཞུ་བ་	*sḱap-chhi sḱu-wa.*
Attend, to (before a superior)	སྐུ་མདུན་ལ་བཅར་བ་	*kun-dün-la char-wa.*
	སྐུ་བཅར་ཞུ་བ་	*ku-char sḱu-wa.*
Attend, to (before Lama)	སྐུ་མདུན་ལ་མཇལ་བ་	*kun-dün-la je-wa.*
Attend, to (heed)	ཉན་པ། ཨམ་ཅོག་ཉན་པ་	*nyem-pa ; am-cho nyem pa.*
Do. *hon.*	གསན་པ། སྙན་ལ་གསན་པ་	*sem pa ; nyen-la-sem-pa.*
Attendant	གཡོག་པོ་	*yoḱ-po.*
Do. *hon.*	ཞབས་ཕྱི་	*sḱap-chhi.*
Attendant, female	གཡོག་མོ་	*yo mo.*
Do. *hon.*	ཞལ་ཏ་མ་	*sḱe-ta-ma.*
Attentive, to be	ཧུར་ཐག་བྱེད་པ་	*hur-tha cḱe-pa.*
Do. *hon.*	ཧུར་ཐག་གནང་བ་	*hur-tha nang-wa.*
Aunt (paternal)	ཨ་ནི་ (ཨ་ནེ་)	*a ni.*
Do. (maternal)	སྲུ་མོ་	*su-mo.*
Auspices (omens)	རྟེན་འབྲེལ་	*tem-dre.*
Authentic	དངོས་ནས། ངོ་ཐོག་	*ngö-ne ; ngo-tho*
Author	རྩོམ་མཁན་	*tsom-khen.*

Author, *hon.*	རྩོམ་པ་གནང་མཁན་	*tsom-pa nang-khen.*
Authority	དབང་	*wang.*
Authorize	དབང་སྤྲད་པ་	*wang-tre-pa.*
Do. *hon.*	དབང་གནང་བ་	*wang-nang-wa.*
Autumn	སྟོན་ཀ་	*tön-ka.*
Auxiliary troops	རྒྱབ་སྣོན་	*gyam-nön.*
Avalanche	གངས་རུད་	*ḱang-rü.*
Avarice	ཧམ་པ་	*ham-pa.*
Avaricious	ཧམ་པ་ཆེན་པོ་	*ham-pa chhem-po.*
Avenge, to	དགྲ་ལན་ལོག་པ་	*dra-len loḱ-pa.*
Do. *hon.*	དགྲ་ལན་ལོག་ག་(པ་) གནང་བ་	*dra-len loḱ-ḱa nang-wa.*
Avoid, to (a person)	དབྱོལ་བ། ཟུར་ནས་འགྲོ་བ་	*yö-wa; śur-ne dro-wa.*
Do. *hon.*	གཟུར་ནས་ཕེབ་པ་	*śur-ne phe-pa.*
Awake, to	གཉིད་སད་པ་	*nyi-se-pa.*
Do. *hon.*	མཉན་ (མནལ་) སད་པ་	*nyen-se-pa.*
Await, to	སྒུག་པ་	*guḱ-pa.*
Do. *hon.*	སྒུག་པ་གནང་བ་	*guḱ-pa nang-wa.*
Away	ཕར་	*pha.*
Awkward	སྡུག་རུས་	*duḱ-rü.*
Axe	སྟ་རི་ (སྟ་རེ་)	*ta-ri.*

Ay (yes)	ལགས་སོ། ལགས་ལགས་སི། ལ་ཧྲོང་	*la-so; la-la-si; la-ong.*
Azure	སྔོན་པོ་	*ngöm-po.*

B

Baby (of few months)	མ་འབྱར་	*man-ja.*
Baby (older)	ཕྲུ་གུ་ཆུང་ཆུང་	*pu-gu chhung-chhung.*
Do. *hon.*	ཨ་ལྲྭ་	*a-wa.*
Bachelor	ཕོ་ཧྲང་ང་	*pho-hrang-nga.*
Back (of body)	རྒྱབ་	*gyap̌.*
Do. *hon.*	སྐུ་རྒྱབ་	*ku-gyap̌.*
Back (behind in place)	རྒྱབ་ལ་	*gyap̌-la.*
Backbite	ཁ་བཏང་ (གཏོང་) བ་	*kha-tang-wa.*
Do. *hon.*	ཞལ་གཏོང་ང་ (བ) གནང་བ་	*sȟe-tong-nga nang-wa.*
Backbone	སྒལ་ཚིགས་	*ge-tshi.*
Do. *hon.*	སྐུ་སྟོད་ཚིགས་	*ku-tö tshi.*
Backside	ཀུབ་	*kup̌.*
Do. *hon.*	ཞབས་ཕོངས་	*sȟam-phong.*
Backwards	རྒྱབ་ལོགས་ལ་	*gyap̌-lo-la.*
Bad (wicked)	ངན་པ། སྐྱུག་བྲོ་པོ་	*ngem-pa ; kyuǩ ťro-po.*
Do. (decomposed, *e.g.*, of meat)	རུལ་པ་	*rü-pa.*
Do. (of things offensive in smell, &c.)	སྐྱུག་བྲོ་པོ། སྡུག་རུལ་	*kyuǩ-ťro-po ; duǩ-rü.*

Bad, to be (of things generally)	ཡག་པོ་མེད་པ་	*yak-po me-pa.*
Bag (large)	སྒྲེ་མོ་	*gye-mo.*
Do. (small)	ཕད་ཀོག་	*phe-ḱo.*
Do. (made of leather)	ཀྱལ་པ་	*kye-pa.*
Badge	རྟགས་	*ta.*
Baggage	དོས་པོ་	*t́ö-po.*
Bail	ཁས་ཁྱགས་	*khe-khya.*
Do. *hon.*	ཞལ་ཁྱགས་	*sḱe-khya*
Bail, to	ཁས་ཁྱགས་བྱེད་པ་	*khe-khya cḱe-pa.*
Do. *hon.*	ཞལ་ཁྱགས་གནང་བ་	*sḱe-khya nang-wa.*
Bake, to	བག་ལེབ་སྲེག་པ་	*ṕa-le traḱ-pa.*
Bakshish	གསོལ་རས་	*sö-re.*
Balance (what is wanting)	ལྷག་མ་	*hla-ma.*
Do. (for small weights)	རྒྱ་འཐུར་	*gya-thu.*
Do. (for larger weights)	ཉ་ག་	*nya-ḱa.*
Do. (for very large weights)	རྒྱ་མ་	*gya-ma.*
Balanced evenly, to be	ཡང་ལྗི་མེད་པ་	*yang ji me-pa.*
Bald	ཟངས་ཁོགས་	*śang-kho.*
Do. *hon.*	དབུ་རིལ་	*u-ri.*

Bale	དོས་པོ་	*tö-po.*
Do. (of wool)	བལ་དོས་	*p̓e-t̓ö.*
Ball	རྡིའུ་ (རྡེའུ་)	*di-u.*
Ball-cartridge	མདེ་རིལ་	*dik̓-ri.*
Ball (of gun)	རྡིག་རིལ་	*dik̓-ri.*
Balloon	རླུང་གྲུ་	*lung-t̓ru.*
Bamboo	སྨྱུག་མ་	*nyung-ma.*
Banana	སྐྱེ་སྡོང་ *Sik.*	*k̓ye-dong.*
Band (gang of men)	ཚོགས་	*tsho.*
Band (hoop)	ཤན་	*shen.*
Do. (of iron)	ལྕགས་ཤན་	*cha-shen.*
Do. (of silver)	དངུལ་ཤན་	*ngü-shen.*
Do. (of brass)	རག་ཤན་	*ra-shen.*
Do. (of gold)	གསེར་ཤན་	*se-shen.*
Bandit	ཇག་པ་	*cK̓ak̓-pa.*
Bandy-legged	རྐང་ཀྱོག་	*kang-k̓yȯ.*
Do. *hon.*	ཞབས་ཀྱོག་	*sK̓ap̓-kyo.*
Banish, to	རྒྱང་ཕུད་ (འབུད་) བཏང་ (གཏོང་) བ་	*gyam-phü tang-wa.*

Banish, to, *hon.*	རྒྱང་ཕུད་ (འཕུད་) གཏོང་ང་ (བ་) གནང་བ་	*gyam-phü tong-nga nang-wa.*
Bank (of river, &c.)	འགྲམ་	*d̓ram.*
Banker	ཕུན་བདག་	*p̓ün-da.*
Banner	དར་འཕྱར་	*t̓ar-chhar.*
Do. (of victory)	རྒྱལ་མཚན་	*gyen-tshen.*
Banquet	མགྲོན་པོ་ (མགྲོན་)	*dröm-po.*
Do. *hon.*	ཐུགས་སྤྲོ་	*thuk̓-tro.*
Do. to give a	མགྲོན་པོ་ (མགྲོན་) བཏང་ (གཏོང་) བ་	*dröm-po tang-wa.*
Do. *hon.*	ཐུགས་སྤྲོ་གཏོང་ང་(བ་)གནང་བ་	*thuk̓-tro tong-nga nang-wa.*
Baptism	ཁྲུས་གསོལ་	*thrü-sö.*
Baptize, to	ཁྲུས་གསོལ་གནང་བ་	*thrü-sö nang-wa.*
Bar	དུམ་བུ་	*t̓um-p̓u.*
Barbarian	མཐའ་འཁོབ་པ་	*tha-khop̓-pa.*
Barber	སྐྲ་བཞར་ར་ (བ་)	*tra-sk̓ar-ra.*
Do. *hon.*	དབུ་སྐྲ་བཞར་མཁན་	*u-tra sk̓ar-k̓k̓en.*
Bare (naked)	དམར་ཧྲང་ང་	*ma-hrang-nga.*
Barefooted	རྐང་རྗེན་མ་	*k̓ang-je-ma.*
Do. *hon.*	ཞབས་རྗེན་མ་	*shap̓-je-ma.*

Bargain, *s.*	ཚོང་	*tshong.*
Do. to	ཚོང་རྒྱབ་པ་	*tshong gyaṕ-pa*
Do. *hon.*	རྒྱ་ཚོང་གནང་བ་	*gya-tshong nang-wa.*
Bark	པགས་པ་	*paḱ-pa.*
Bark, to (of dogs)	འཆང་བ་	*chhang-wa.*
Barley	ནས་	*ne.*
Do. *hon.*	ཕྱག་འབྲུ་	*chhan-dru.*
Barley-flour	རྩམ་པ་	*tsam-pa.*
Do. *hon.*	གསོལ་ཞིབ་	*sö-sḱiṕ.*
Barn	འབྲུ་ཁང་	*dru-khang.*
Barrel (of gun)	ལྕགས་ཧྲང་	*ċha-hrang.*
Barren (of women)	རབས་ཆད་	*raṕ-chhe.*
Do. (of cow)	བཞོས་སྐམ་	*sḱö-kam.*
Barrier (fence)	ར་བ་	*ra-wa.*
Barter	རྗེ་བ་	*je-wa.*
Bashful, to be	ངོ་ཚ་བ་	*ngo-tsha-wa.*
Do. *hon.*	ཞལ་རས་ཚ་བ་	*sḱe-re tsha-wa.*
Basin (for washing hands)	ཏུང་བན་	*ťung-ṕen.*
Do. (wooden)	གཞོང་པ་	*sḱong-pa.*
Do. (round copper basin)	ཀ་ཏོ་ར་	*ka-to-ra.*

Basket	སླེ་ཀོག། སླེ་པོ་	*le-ko̤; le-po.*
Bat	ཕྭམ་པོ་ (ཕྭ་ཝོང་)	*gam-po.*
Bath	ཆུ་གཞོང་	*chhu-sKong.*
Do. *hon.*	ཆབ་གཞོང་	*chhap̤-sKong.*
Bathe, to	འཁྲུད་པ་	*thrü-pa.*
Do. *hon.*	འཁྲུད་པ་གནང་བ་	*thrü-pa nang-wa.*
Battle	དམག་	*ma.*
Bay-coloured (horse)	སྐྱང་པོ་	*kyang-po.*
Do. (light)	སྐྱང་དཀར་	*kyang-ka.*
Do. (dark)	སྐྱང་ནག་	*kyang-na.*
Bazaar	ཁྲོམ	*throm.*
Be, to	རེད་པ། ཡིན་པ། ཡོད་པ། འདུག་པ་	*re-pa; yim-pa; yö-pa; duk-pa.*
Bead	འཕྲང་ང་ (འཕྲེང་བ་)	*thrang-nga.*
Do. *hon.*	ཕྱག་འཕྲེང་	*chhan-threng.*
Beak	མཆོ་ལྟོ་ (མཆུ་ལྟོ་)	*chho-to.*
Beam, large	གདུང་མ་	*dung-ma.*
Do. small	ལྕམ་ཤིང་	*cham-shing.*
Bean	སྲན་མ་	*tre-ma.*
Bear, to (bring forth).	སྐྱེད་པ་	*kye-pa.*

Bear, to (bring forth) *hon.*	འཁྲུང་བ་	*thrung wa.*
Bear, to (carry)	འཁྱེར་བ་	*khyer-wa.*
Bear, *s.*	དོམ་	*tom.*
Beard	ཨོག་ཞོལ་	*oḱ-sḱö.*
Do. (with whiskers)	རྒྱ་	*gya.*
Beard, a person having a	རྒྱའུ་ (རྒྱ་བོ་)	*gya-u.*
Beast	དུད་འགྲོ། སེམས་ཅན་	*ťün-dro ; sem-chen.*
Beast (of prey)	གཅན་ཟན་	*chen-śen.*
Beat, to	རྡུང་བ་	*dung-wa.*
Do. *hon.*	ཕྱག་འཇུག་གནང་བ་	*chhan-ju nang-wa.*
Beaten, to be (in a contest)	འཕམ་པ་	*pham-pa.*
Beautiful	མཛེས་པོ་	*dze-po.*
Do. *hon.*	ཐུགས་ཚར་པོ་	*thu tshar-po.*
Beaver	ཆུ་སྲམ་	*chhu-tram.*
Because	རྐྱེན་གྱིས། དོན་ལ་	*kyen-ḱyi ; ťön-la.*
Beckon, to	གཡས་དབྱུག་རྒྱབ་པ་	*ye-yu gyap̃-pa.*
Do. *hon.*	གཡས་དབྱུག་སྐྱོན་པ་	*ye-yu kyöm-pa.*
Become, to	བྱུང་བ་ (འབྱུང་བ་)	*cḱung-wa.*
Becoming	འོས་པོ་	*ö-po.*

Bed	ཉལ་ཁྲི་	*nye-thri.*
Do. *hon.*	གཟིམ་ཁྲི་	*sim-thri.*
Bedaub, to	བྱུགས་པ་ (འབྱུག་པ།) སྐུ་བ་	*cḱuḱ-pa ; ku-wa.*
Do. *hon.*	བྱུགས་ག་ (འབྱུག་པ་) གནང་བ། སྐུ་བ་གནང་བ་	*cḱuḱ-ḱa nang-wa ; ku-wa nang-wa.*
Bedding	ཉལ་གཟན་	*nye-śen.*
Do. *hon.*	གཟིམ་གཟན་	*śim-śen.*
Bedroom	ཉལ་ས་	*nye-sa.*
Do. *hon.*	གཟིམ་ཁང་	*śim-khang.*
Bee	སྦྲང་མ་	*drang-ma.*
Bee-hive	སྦྲང་ཚང་	*drang-tshang.*
Beef	གླང་ཤ་	*lang-sha.*
Beer	ཆང་	*chhang.*
Do. *hon.*	མཆོད་ཆང་	*chhö-chhang.*
Do. (spirit)	ཨ་རག་	*a-ra.*
Do. *hon.*	བཞེས་རག་	*sḱe-ra.*
Beer-shop	ཆང་ཁང་	*chhang-khang.*
Beer-seller	ཆང་མ། འཕྲུང་མ་	*chhang-ma ; thrung-ma.*
Bees-wax	སྦྲ་ཚིལ་	*traḱ t́shi.*
Beetle	སྦྲང་བུ་	*drang-ṕu.*

Befitting, *adj.*	འོས་པོ་	*ö-po.*
Befool, to	མགོ་སྐོར་བ་	*go-kor-wa.*
Do. *hon.*	དབུ་སྐོར་ར་ (བ་) གནང་བ་	*u-kor-ra nang-wa.*
Before (*adv.* & *prep.* of place)	མདུན་ལ་	*dün-la.*
Do. *hon.*	སྐུ་མདུན་ལ་	*kun-dün-la.*
Before (*adv.* & *prep.* of time)	སྔན་ལ་ (སྔོན་ལ)	*ngen-la.*
Do. (with verb)	མ་...གོང་ལ་	*ma...kong-la.*
Beg, to (request)	ཞུ་བ་	*sku-wa.*
Do. *hon.*	ཞུ་བ་གནང་བ་	*sku-wa nang-wa.*
Do. to (alms)	སློང་བ་	*long-wa.*
Do. *hon.*	བསོད་སྙོམས་ཞུ་བ་གནང་བ་	*sö-nyom sku-wa nang-wa.*
Beget, to	སྐྱེད་པ་	*kye-pa.*
Do. *hon.*	འཁྲུང་བ་	*thrung-wa.*
Beggar	སྤྲང་གོ་ (སྤྲང་པོ་)	*pang-ko.*
Begin, to	མགོ་བཙུགས་ (འཛུགས་) པ་	*go-tsuk-pa.*
Do. *hon.*	དབུ་བཙུགས་ཀ་ (འཛུགས་པ་) གནང་བ་	*u-tsuk-ka nang-wa.*
Beginning	མགོ་	*go.*
Do. in the	སྔོན་དང་པོ་	*ngön-tang-po.*
Beguile, to	མགོ་སྐོར་བ་	*go-kor-wa.*

Beguile, to, *hon.*	དབུ་སྐོར་ར་ (བ་) གནང་བ་	*u-kor-ra nang-wa.*
Behalf of, on	དོན་ལ་	*ťön-la.*
Behaviour	བྱེད་སྟངས་ (སྤྱོད་པ་)	*cḱe-tang.*
Behead, to (common person)	སྐེ་བཅད་ (གཅོད་) པ་	*ke-che-pa.*
Do. (superior person)	མགུལ་བཅད་ (གཅོད་) པ་	*gül-che-pa.*
Behind (*adv.* & *prep.*)	རྒྱབ་ལ། གཞུག་ལ་	*gyaṕ-la ; sḱu-la.*
Behind hand, to be	ཕྱི་པོ་བྱེད་པ་	*chhi-po cḱe-pa.*
Do. *hon.*	ཕྱི་པོ་གནང་བ་	*chhi-po nang-wa.*
Behold, to	མཐོང་བ་	*thong-wa.*
Do. *hon.*	གཟིགས་པ་	*śi-pa.*
Belch, to	འགག་དྲི་རྒྱབ་པ་	*gaḱ-ťri gyaṕ-pa.*
Do. *hon.*	འགག་དྲི་སྐྱོན་པ་	*gaḱ-ťri kyöm-pa.*
Belief (religion)	དད་པ་	*ťe-pa.*
Believe, to	ཡིད་ཆེས་པ་	*yi-chhe-pa.*
Do. *hon.*	ཐུགས་ཡིད་ཆེས་པ་	*thu-yi chhe-pa.*
Do. (in religious sense)	དད་པ་བྱེད་པ་	*ťe-pa cḱe-pa.*
Do. *hon.*	དད་པ་གནང་བ་	*ťe-pa nang-wa.*
Bell	དྲིལ་བུ་	*ťri-ṕu.*
Do. *hon.*	ཕྱག་དྲིལ་	*chha-ťri.*
Bell-metal	ལི་	*li.*

Bellows	སྦུད་པ་	*bü-pa.*
Do. iron tube of	ཤན་མཆུ་ (སྦུད་མཆུ་)	*shen-chhu.*
Belly	གྲོ་ཁོག་ (གྲོད་ཁོག །) ཁོག་པ་	*t́ro-kho; khoḱ-pa.*
Do. *hon.*	གསོལ་གྲོད་	*sö-t́rö.*
Belong, to (to me)	ཡིན་པ་	*yim-pa.*
Do. (to you or to third person)	རེད་པ་	*re-pa.*
Beloved	གཅེས་པོ་	*che-po.*
Below (lower down)	མ་	*ma.*
Do. *prep.*	འོག་ལ། གཤམ་ལ་	*o-la; sham-la.*
Belt	སྐེ་རགས་	*ke-ra.*
Do. *hon.*	སྐུ་རགས་	*ku-ra.*
Bench	ཀུབ་ཀྱག ཁྲིའུ་ཤིང་	*kuṕ-kya; thri-u-shing.*
Do. *hon.*	ཞབས་ཀྱག་	*sḱaṕ-kya.*
Bend, to, *v.t.*	བཀུག་པ་ (འགུག་པ་)	*kuḱ-pa.*
Do. *hon.*	བཀུག་ག་ (འགུག་པ་) གནང་བ་	*kuḱ-ḱa nang-wa.*
Bend, to (stoop)	གུག་གུག་བྱེད་པ་	*ḱu-ḱu cḱe-pa.*
Do. *hon.*	གུག་གུག་གནང་བ་	*ḱu-ḱu nang-wa.*
Beneath	འོག་ལ་	*o-la.*
Benediction	བྱིན་རླབས་	*cḱin-laṕ.*
Benefaction	མགོ་འདྲེན་	*gön-dren.*

Benefactor	མགོ་འདྲེན་གནང་མཁན་	*gön-dren nang-khen.*
Do. *hon.*	དབུ་འདྲེན་གནང་མཁན་	*u-dren nang-khen.*
Benefit, to	ཕན་ཐོགས་པ་	*phen-thoḱ-pa.*
Benefit of, for the	ཕན་པའི་དོན་ལ་	*phen-pe-tön-la.*
Benevolence	དྲིན་	*t́rin.*
Do. *hon.*	བཀའ་དྲིན་	*ka-t́rin.*
Benevolent	དྲིན་ཆེན་པོ་	*t́rin-chhem-po.*
Do. *hon.*	བཀའ་དྲིན་ཆེན་པོ་	*ka-t́rin chhem-po.*
Benevolent, to be	དྲིན་བྱེད་པ་	*t́rin-cḱe-pa.*
Do. *hon.*	བཀའ་དྲིན་གནང་བ་	*ka-t́rin nang-wa.*
Bent, to be	གུག་གུག་བྱས་ནས་བསྡད་ (སྡོད་) པ་	*ḱu-ḱu cḱe-ne de-pa.*
Beseech, to	ཞུ་བ་ཕུལ་ (འབུལ་) བ་	*sḱu-wa phü-wa.*
Beside	རྩ་ལ་	*tsa-la.*
Besides, *prep.*	མ་གཏོགས། མིན་པ་	*ma-to; mem-pa.*
Besmear, to	བྱུགས་པ་ (འབྱུག་པ་)	*cḱuḱ-pa.*
Do. *hon.*	བྱུགས་ག་ (འབྱུག་པ་) གནང་བ་	*cḱuḱ-ka nang-wa.*
Besprinkle with water, to	ཆུ་ཆག་རྒྱབ་པ་	*chhu-chha gyap-pa.*
Best	ཡག་ཤོས། ཡག་ཐག་ཆོད་	*yaḱ-shö; yaḱ-thaḱ-chhö.*
Bestow, to	སྟེར་བ་	*ter-wa.*

Bestow, to, *hon.*	གནང་བ་	*nang-wa.*
Bet	རྒྱན་	*gyen.*
Do. *hon.*	སྐུ་རྒྱན་	*ku-gyen.*
Bet, to	རྒྱན་བཞག་ (འཛོག་) པ་	*gyen-sḰaḱ-pa.*
Do. *hon.*	སྐུ་རྒྱན་གཞོག་ག་ (འཛོག་པ་) གནང་བ་	*ku-gyen sḰoḱ-ḱa nang-wa.*
Betel-nut	གོ་ཡུ་	*ḱo-yu.*
Betray, to	དགྲའི་དབང་ལ་བཏང་ (གཏོང་) བ་	*dra-i wang-la tang-wa.*
Better	ཡག་ག་	*yaḱ-ḱa.*
Better, to get the (in a fight, &c.)	རྒྱལ་བ་	*gye-wa.*
Between	བར་ལ་	*ṕa-la.*
Beware, to	དོགས་ཟོན་བྱེད་པ་	*t́oḱ-śön cḰe-pa.*
Do. *hon.*	ཐུགས་ཟོན་གནང་བ་	*thuḱ-śön nang-wa.*
Bewildered, to be	མགོ་འཁོར་བ་	*go-khor-wa.*
Do. *hon.*	དབུ་འཁོར་ར་ (བ་) གནང་བ་	*u-khor-ra nang-wa.*
Beyond	ཕར་ཕྱོགས་ལ་	*pha-chho-la.*
Bhutan	འབྲུག་ཡུལ་	*druḱ-yü.*
Bhutanese	འབྲུག་པ་	*druḱ-pa.*
Bible	གསུང་རབ་	*sung-raṕ.*

Bicycle	ཁང་སྒ་རི་	*kang-ga-ri.*
Bid, to	བཀའ་གནང་བ་	*ka-nang-wa.*
Bier	ཤིང་ཁྲི་	*ching-thri.*
Big	ཆེན་པོ་	*chhem-po.*
Bile	མཁྲིས་པ་	*thri-pa.*
Bill (amount)	རྩིས་ཐོ་	*tsi-tho.*
Do. *hon.*	ཕྱག་ཐོ་	*chha-tho.*
Bill (of bird)	མཆོ་ལྟོ་ (མཆུ་ལྟོ་)	*chho-to.*
Billow	ཕ་རླབས་	*ba-lap̓.*
Bind, to	བསྡམས་པ་ (སྡོམ་པ་)	*dam-pa.*
Biography	རྣམ་ཐར་	*nam-tha.*
Do. *hon.*	གསུང་ཐར་	*sung-tha.*
Birch tree	སྟག་པ་ཤིང་	*tak̓-pa-shing.*
Bird	བྱ་	*cḱa.*
Bird-cage	རླུང་ཙེ་	*lung-tse.*
Bird's-nest	བྱ་ཚང་	*cḱa-tshang.*
Birthday	སྐྱེ་ཚེས་	*kye-tshe.*
Do. *hon.*	འཁྲུང་ཚེས་	*thrung-tshe.*
Birth, high	སྐྱེ་ས་མཐོ་པོ་	*kye-sa tho-po.*
Birth, low	སྐྱེ་ས་དམའ་པོ་	*kye-sa ma-po.*

Birth-place	སྐྱེ་ས། སྐྱེ་སའི་ལུང་པ་	*kye-sa; kye-se lung-pa.*
Do. *hon.*	འཁྲུངས་ས་	*thrung-sa.*
Bishop	མཁན་པོ་	*khem-po.*
Bit (of a bridle)	སྲབ་ལྕགས་	*trap-cha.*
Bit (piece)	དུམ་བུ་	*t́um-ṕu.*
Bitch	ཁྱི་མོ་	*khyi-mo.*
Bite, to	སྨུག་པ། སོ་རྒྱབ་པ་	*muk-pa; so-gyap-pa.*
Bitter	ཁག་ཐིག་	*khak-thi.*
Black	ནག་པོ་	*nak-po.*
Blacksmith	མགར་ར་ (བ་)	*gar-ra.*
Bladder	གླང་ཕུག་	*gang-phu.*
Blade (of grass)	ལྗང་པ་	*jang-pa.*
Blade (of sword)	དངོ་	*ngo.*
Blame, to	སྐྱོན་བདོན་པ་	*kyön töm-pa.*
Do. *hon.*	སྐྱོན་བདོན་པ་གནང་བ་	*kyön töm-pa nang-wa.*
Blank	སྟོང་པ་	*tong-pa.*
Blanket	ཉལ་གཟན་	*nye-śen.*
Do. *hon.*	གཟིམ་གཟན་	*śim-śen.*
Blaspheme, to	སྨད་ར་བཏང་ (གཏོང་) བ་	*me-ra tang-wa.*
Do. *hon.*	སྨད་ར་གཏོང་ང་(བ་) གནང་བ་	*me-ra tong-nga nang-wa.*

Blaze, *s.*	མེ་	*me.*
Blaze, to (of fire)	འབར་བ་	*bar-wa.*
Bleat, to	ལུག་སྐད་རྒྱབ་པ་	*luk̑-ke gyap̑-pa.*
Bleed, to, *v.i.*	ཁྲག་འཐོན་པ་	*thra-thöm-pa.*
Do. (of doctor), *v.t.*	ཁྲག་རྒྱབ་པ་	*thra-gyap̑-pa.*
Blemish, *s.*	སྐྱོན་	*kyön.*
Blend, to	འདྲེ་བ་	*dre-wa.*
Do. *hon.*	འདྲེ་བ་གནང་བ་	*dre-wa nang-wa*
Bless, to	བྱིན་རླབས་གནང་བ་	*ck̑in-lap̑ nang-wa.*
Do. to (dead person)	བསྔོ་བ་རྒྱབ་པ་	*ngo-wa gyap̑-pa.*
Blessing (by placing book on head)	བྱིན་རླབས་	*ck̑in-lap̑.*
Do. (by laying hand on head)	ཕྱག་དབང་	*chha-wang.*
Blind	ལོང་ང་ (ལོང་བ་)	*long-nga.*
Do. *hon.*	སྤྱན་ལོང་ང་ (བ་)	*chen-long-nga.*
Blind of one eye	མིག་ཞར་ར་ (བ་)	*mik̑-sk̑ar-ra.*
Do. *hon.*	སྤྱན་ཞར་ར་ (བ་)	*chen-sk̑ar-ra.*
Blink, to	མིག་བཙུམ་རྒྱབ་པ་	*mik̑-tsum gyap̑-pa.*
Do. *hon.*	སྤྱན་བཙུམ་སྐྱོན་པ་	*chen-tsum kyöm-pa.*
Blister, *s.*	ཆུ་གང་	*chhu-k̑ang.*

Blistered, to be	ཆུ་གང་འཐོན་པ་	*chhu-kang thöm-pa.*
Blithe	སྐྱིད་པོ་	*kyi-po.*
Block, to	བཀག་པ་ (འགེགས་པ་)	*kak-pa.*
Blockhead	ཀླུགས་པ། གླེན་པ་	*kuk-pa; lem-pa.*
Blood	ཁྲག་	*thra.*
Do. *hon.*	སྐུ་ཁྲག་	*ku-thra.*
Blossom	མེ་ཏོག་	*me-to.*
Blot, *s.*	ནག་ཐིག་	*nak-thi.*
Blow (with fist)	ཛོག་རམ་ (ཛོག་རིལ་)	*dzo-ram.*
Do. (with open palm)	ཐལ་ལྕག་	*the-cha.*
Blow, to, *v.t.*	ཕུ་རྒྱབ་པ་	*phu-gyap-pa.*
Do. *hon.*	ལྗགས་ཕུ་གནང་བ་	*ja-phu nang-wa.*
Do. (of wind), *v.i.*	རྒྱབ་པ་	*gyap-pa.*
Blue	སྔོན་པོ་	*ngöm-po.*
Blue, dark	སྔོ་ནག་	*ngo-nak.*
Blue Book	དེབ་སྔོན་པོ་	*tep ngöm-po.*
Blue, light	སྔོ་སྐྱ་	*ngo-kya.*
Blunder, to	ཁ་ནོར་བ་	*kha-nor-wa.*
Do. *hon.*	ཞལ་ནོར་ར་ (བ་) གནང་བ་	*ske-nor ra nang-wa.*
Blunt, to be	རྣོ་པོ་མེད་པ་	*no-po me-pa.*

Blush, to	ངོ་ཚ་བ་	*ngo-tsha-wa.*
Do. *hon.*	ཞལ་རས་ཚ་བ་གནང་བ། ཐུགས་ངོ་ཚ་བ་གནང་བ་	*sḱe-re tsha-wa nang-wa; thu-ngo tsha-wa nang-wa.*
Boar	ཕག་པ་	*phaḱ-pa.*
Do. (wild)	རི་ཕག་	*ri-pha.*
Board	སྤང་ལེབ་	*pang-le.*
Boast, to	རང་སྟོད་བྱེད་པ་	*rang-tö cḱe-pa.*
Boat (of wood)	གྲུ་	*t́ru.*
Boatman (of wooden boat)	གྲུ་པ་	*t́ru-pa.*
Do. *hon.*	གྲུ་དཔོན་	*t́ru-pön.*
Boat (of hide)	ཀོ་བ་	*ko-wa.*
Do. *hon.*	ཕེབ་ཀོ་	*phe-ko.*
Boatman (of hide boat)	མཉན་པ་	*nyem-pa.*
Do. *hon.*	མཉན་དཔོན་	*nyem-pön.*
Body	གཟུགས་པོ། ལུས་	*śuḱ-po; lü.*
Do. *hon.*	སྐུ་གཟུགས། སྐུ་ལུས་	*ku-śuḱ; ku-lü.*
Body (corpse of human being)	རོ་	*ro.*
Do. *hon.*	སྐུ་ཕུང་	*ku-phung.*
Body (dead body of animal)	ཤི་རོ་	*shi-ro.*
Boil	གཉན་ཕུར་	*nyen-ṕur.*

Boil (watery)	ཆུ་བུར་	*chhu-pur.*
Do. to, *v.i.*	འཁོལ་བ་	*khöl-wa.*
Do. *v.t.*	བསྐོལ་བ་ (སྐོལ་བ་)	*kö-wa.*
Boiler (cauldron)	དཀྱིལ་ཁྲོ་	*kyị-thro.*
Boiling, *adj.*	ཁོལ་མ་	*khöl-ma.*
Bold	བློ་ཁོག་ཆེན་པོ་	*lo-kho chhem-po.*
Do. *hon.*	ཐུགས་ཁོག་ཆེན་པོ་	*thu-kho chhem-po.*
Bolt	སྒོ་ལྕགས་	*gön-cha.*
Do. *hon.*	གཟིམ་ལྕགས། ཕྱག་ལྕགས་	*śim-cha; chha-cha.*
Bolt, to (of horse), *v.i.*	ངར་ནས་ཕྱིན་པ་	*ngar-ne chhim-pa.*
Bolt, to (door, &c.)	སྒོ་ལྕགས་རྒྱབ་པ་	*gön-cha gyap-pa.*
Do. *hon.*	གཟིམ་ལྕགས་སྐྱོན་པ་	*śim-cha kyöm-pa.*
Bolting, *adj.* (of horse)	འདྲོག་པ་	*drok-pa.*
Bond (for large amount)	གམ་རྒྱ་ (གན་རྒྱ་)	*kam-gya.*
Do. *hon.*	ཕྱག་གན་	*chha-gen.*
Do. (for small amount)	འཛིན་	*dzin.*
Do. *hon.*	ཕྱག་འཛིན་	*chhan-dzin.*
	བཀའ་འཛིན་	*kan-dzin.*
Bone	རུས་ཁོག་	*rü-kho.*
Do. *hon.*	སྐུ་རུས་	*ku-rü.*

Book	དཔེ་ཆ་	*pe-chha.*
Do. *hon.*	ཕྱག་དཔེ་	*chha-pe.*
Book-language	ཆོས་ཚིག་	*chhö-tshi.*
Book, printed	པར་མ་	*par-ma.*
Do. written	བྲིས་མ་	*ťri-ma.*
Boon	དྲིན་	*ťrin.*
Do. *hon.*	བཀའ་དྲིན་	*ka-ťrin.*
Boot	ལྷམ། ལྷམ་ཁོག་	*hlam ; hlam-kho.*
Do. *hon.*	ཞབས་ཆགས་	*sǩaṕ-chha.*
Boot (of European style)	འཇུ་ཏ་	*ju-ta.*
Bootmaker	ངོ་བཟོ་	*ngoṕ-śo.*
Do. *hon.*	དབུ་མཛད་	*um-dze.*
Borax	ཚ་ལི་	*tsha-li.*
Border	ཟུར་	*sur.*
Do. (of land)	ས་མཚམས་	*san-tsham.*
Bore a hole, to	ཨི་ཁུང་ཕིད་ (འབིག་) པ་	*i-khung pi-pa.*
Born, to be	སྐྱེ་བ་	*kye-wa.*
Do. *hon.*	འཁྲུངས་བ་	*thrung-wa.*
Borrow, to	གཡར་བ་	*yar-wa.*
Do. to (ask a loan)	སྐྱི་བ་	*kyi-wa.*

Borrow, to, *hon.*	གཡར་པོ་ཞུ་བ་གནང་བ་	*yar-po sKu-wa nang-wa.*
Bosom	བང་ཁོག་ (བྲང་ཁོག་)	*pang-kho.*
Do. *hon.*	སྐུ་བང་ (སྐུ་བྲང་)	*ku-pang.*
Both, *pron.*	གཉིས་ཀ་	*nyi-ka.*
Bothersome	ཅ་སྨྱུན་པོ་	*cha-sim-po.*
Do. *hon.*	ཐུགས་ཅ་སྨྱུན་པོ་	*thu-cha sim-po.*
Bottle	ཤེལ་དམ་	*she-tam.*
Bottom	གཏིང་	*ting.*
Do. (anus)	ཀུབ་	*kup.*
Do. *hon.*	ཞབས་ཕོངས་	*sKam-phong*
Bough	ཡལ་ག་	*ye-ka.*
Bound, to (jump)	མཆོངས་པ། མཆོངས་རྒྱག་རྒྱབ་པ་	*chhong-pa; chhong-gya gyap-pa.*
Do. *hon.*	མཆོངས་རྒྱག་སྐྱོན་པ་	*chhong-gya kyöm-pa.*
Boundary	ས་མཚམས་	*san-tsham.*
Bountiful	ལག་པ་ཤོག་པོ་	*lak-pa shok-po.*
Do. *hon.*	ཕྱག་ཤོག་པོ་	*chha-shok-po.*
Bow (for shooting)	གཞུ་	*sKu.*
Do. *hon*	ཕྱག་གཞུ་	*chha-sKu.*
Bow, to (taking hat)	ཕྱག་འབུལ་ཞུ་པ	*chham-bü sKu-wa.*

Bow-legged	རྐང་ཀྱོག་	*kang-kyo.*
Bowel	རྒྱུ་མ་	*gyu-ma.*
Bowl (for drinking tea, &c.)	ཕོར་པ་	*phor-pa.*
Do. *hon.*	མཆོད་ཞལ་	*chhö-she.*
Bowl (of tobacco pipe)	གང་མགོ་	*kang-go.*
Box (chest)	སྒམ་	*gam.*
Do. *hon.*	ཕྱག་སྒམ་	*chha-gam.*
Boy	བུ་གུ་	*pu-gu.*
Do. *hon.*	ཨ་ལྦུ་	*a-wa.*
Bracelet	སྒྲོག་གདུང་	*dro-dung.*
Do. *hon.*	ཕྱག་གདུང་	*chha-dung.*
Brahma	ཚངས་པ་	*tshang-pa.*
Brahman (caste)	བྲམ་ཟེ་	*tram-se.*
Brain	ཀླད་པ་	*le-pa.*
Bramble	ཚེར་མ་	*tsher-ma.*
Bran	ཕུང་མ་	*phung-ma.*
Branch	ཡལ་ག་	*ye-ka.*
Brandish, to	དབྱུག་དབྱུག་བྱེད་པ་	*yu-yu che-pa.*
Do. *hon.*	དབྱུག་དབྱུག་གནང་བ་	*yu-yu nang-wa.*
Brandy	ཨ་རག་	*a-ra.*

Brandy, *hon.*	བཞེས་རག་	*sḱe-ra.*
Brass	རག་	*ra.*
Brave, *adj.*	སྙིང་ཆེན་པོ་	*nying-chhem-po.*
Do. *hon.*	ཐུགས་སྙིང་ཆེན་པོ་	*thu-nying-chhem-po.*
Brawl	རྒྱབ་འདྲེ། འཁྲུག་པ་	*gyam-dre ; thruḱ-pa.*
Bray	བོང་སྐད་རྒྱབ་པ་	*ṕong-ke-gyaṕ-pa.*
Bread	བག་ལེབ་	*ṕa-le.*
Do. *hon.*	བཞེས་བག་	*sḱe-ṕa.*
Breadth	ཞང་ (ཞེང་)	*sḱang.*
Break, to, *v.t.*	བཅག་པ་ (གཅོག་པ་)	*chaḱ-pa.*
Do. *hon.*	གཅོག་ག་ (གཅོག་པ་) གནང་བ་	*choḱ-ḱa nang-wa.*
Break, to, *v.i.*	འཆག་པ་	*chhaḱ-pa.*
Breakfast (at 10 or 11 A.M.)	ཚ་གདིང་མའི་ཁ་ལག་	*tsha-ting-me kha-la.*
Do. *hon.*	ཚ་གདིང་མའི་ཞལ་ལག་	*tsha-ting-me sḱe-la.*
Breakfast (at 7 to 9 A.M.)	ཞོགས་གེའི་ཁ་ལག་	*sḱo-ḱe kha-la.*
Do. *hon.*	ཞོགས་གེའི་ཞལ་ལག་	*sḱo-ḱe sḱe-la.*
Breast	བང་ཁོག་ (བྲང་ཁོག་)	*ṕang-kho.*
Do. *hon.*	སྐུ་བང་ (སྐུ་བྲང་)	*ku-ṕang.*
Breath	དབུགས་	*u.*

Breath, *hon.*	ལྗགས་དབུགས་	*ja-u.*
Breathe, to	དབུགས་བཏང་ (གཏོང་) བ་	*u-tang-wa.*
Do. *hon.*	ལྗགས་དབུགས་གཏོང་ང་ (བ་) གནང་བ་	*ja-u tong-nga nang-wa.*
Breathless, to be	དབུགས་བསག་ (གསོག་) པ་	*u sak-pa.*
Do. *hon.*	ལྗགས་དབུགས་བསག་ག་ (གསོག་པ་) གནང་བ་	*ja-u sak-ka nang-wa.*
Breed (of men)	བརྒྱུད་	*gyü.*
Do. *hon.*	སྐུ་བརྒྱུད་	*ku-gyü.*
Do. (of animals)	བརྒྱུད་དག་	*gyü-ta.*
Breeze	ལྷགས་པ། རླུང་	*hlak-pa; lung.*
Bribe	རྩིག་ཐོ་	*tsik-tho.*
Do. *hon.*	སྐྱབས་འཇུག་	*kyam-ju.*
Bribe, to give	རྩིག་ཐོ་རྒྱབ་པ་	*tsik-tho gyap-pa.*
Do. (*inf.* to *sup.*)	སྐྱབས་འཇུག་ཞུ་བ་	*kyam-ju sku-wa.*
Bribe, to take	རྒྱུ་ཟ་བ་	*gyu-sa-wa.*
Do. *hon.*	རྒྱུ་བཞེས་པ་	*gyu-ske-pa.*
Brick	ས་པག་	*sa-pa.*
Brick of tea	ཇ་བག་	*cka-pa.*
Do. *hon.*	གསོལ་ཇ་བག་	*so-cka pak-ka.*

Bride	མནའ་མ་	*na-ma.*
Bridegroom	མག་པ་	*maḱ-pa.*
Bridesmaid	བག་རོགས་	*ṕa-ro.*
Bridge	ཟམ་པ་	*śam-pa.*
Do. *hon.*	ཕེབས་ཟམ་	*phe-śam.*
Bridge, iron	ལྕགས་ཟམ་	*cha-śam.*
Do. *hon.*	ལྕགས་ཀྱི་ཕེབ་ཟམ་	*cha-kyi phe-śam.*
Bridle	སྲབ་	*traṕ.*
Do. *hon.*	ཆིབས་སྲབ་	*chhiṕ-traṕ.*
Brief	ཐུང་ཐུང་	*thung-thung.*
Brier	ཚེར་མ་	*tsher-ma.*
Brigand	ཇག་པ་	*cḱaḱ-pa.*
Bright (clear)	གསལ་པོ་	*se-po.*
Do. (dazzling)	འོད་ཆེན་པོ་	*ö-chhem-po.*
Brightness	འོད་	*ö.*
Brilliant	འོད་ཆེན་པོ་	*ö-chhem-po.*
Brim, to fill to the	དག་དག་ཀླུག་པ་	*ťaḱ-ťaḱ luḱ-pa.*
Do. *hon.*	དག་དག་ཀླུག་ག་ (པ་) གནང་བ་	*ťaḱ-ťaḱ luḱ-ka nang-wa.*
Brimstone	མུ་ཟི་	*mu-śi.*
Bring, to (by carrying)	འཁྱེར་ཡོང་བ་	*khyer-yong-wa.*

Bring, to, *hon.*	བསྣམས་ (སྣོམ་) ཕེབ་པ་	*nam-phe-pa.*
Bring, to (by leading along, *e.g.*, horse)	འཁྲིད་ཡོང་བ་	*thri-yong-wa.*
Do. *hon.*	འཁྲིད་ཕེབ་པ་	*thri-phe-pa.*
Brink	འགྲམ་	*dram.*
Brisk	ཧུར་པོ་	*hur-po.*
Bristle	ཕག་ཟྲེ་	*phak-se.*
British	དབྱིན་ཇི་	*in-ji.*
Do. Government	དབྱིན་གཞུང་	*in-sKung.*
Broadcloth	འགོ་སྣམ་	*go-nam.*
Broad	ཞང་ (ཞེང་) ཆེན་པོ་	*sKang-chhem-po.*
Broad (of land)	རྒྱ་ཆེན་པོ་	*gya-chhem-po.*
Broil	རྒྱབ་འདྲེ་	*gyam-dre*
Broken, to be	ཆག་པ་	*chhak-pa.*
Bronchitis	གློ་ཡུའི་ནད་	*lo-yü-ne.*
Bronze	ཁྲོ་	*thro.*
Brooch	སྐེ་འཕྲུག་	*ke thru.*
Do. *hon.*	མགུལ་འཕྲུག་	*gü-thru.*
Brood, to (of fowls)	སྒོ་ང་བསྙལ་བ་	*go-nga nyal-wa.*
Brook, *s.*	རྒྱུག་ཆུ་	*gyuk-chhu.*

Broom	ཕྱག་མ་	*chha-ma.*
Broth	ཁུ་བ་	*khu-a.*
Do. *hon.*	སྐྲུང་ཁུ་ (སྐྲུམ་ཁུ་)	*trung-khu.*
Broth (made from meat)	ཤ་ཁུ་	*sha-khu.*
Do. *hon.*	སྐྲུང་ཁུ་ (སྐྲུམ་ཁུ་)	*trung-khu.*
Brother	སྤུན་ཀྱག་	*pün-kya.*
Do. *hon.*	སྐུ་མཆེད་	*kum-chhe.*
Brother, mother's	ཨ་ཞང་	*a-sKang.*
Do. *hon.*	ཞང་ཞང་ལགས་	*sKang-sKang-la.*
Brother, elder	ཇོ་ཇོ་	*cKo-cKo.*
Do. *hon.*	ཇོ་ལགས་	*cKo-la.*
Brother, younger	སྤུན་ཆུང་ང་ (བ་)	*pün-chhung-nga.*
Do. *hon.*	སྐུ་མཆེད་ཆུང་ང་ (བ་)	*kum-chhe chhung-nga*
Brother-in-law (wife's brother)	སྐྱེ་དམན་གྱི་སྤུན་ཀྱག་	*kyi-men Kyi pün-kya.*
Do. *hon*	སྐུ་ཟླའི་སྐུ་མཆེད་	*kum-de kum-chhe.*
Do. (sister's husband)	སྤུན་ཀྱག་གི་ཁྱོ་ག་	*pün-Kya Ki khyo-ga.*
Do. *hon.*	སྐུ་མཆེད་ཀྱི་སྐུ་ཟླ་	*kum-chhe kyi kum-da.*
Brown	སྨུག་པོ་	*muK-po.*
Bruised, to be	སྤྲག་པ་	*traK-pa.*

Bruised, *hon.*	སྤྲག་ཀ་ (པ་) གནང་བ་	*traḱ-ḱa nang-wa.*
Bruised, to be	ཁི་ཤུས་ལོག་པ་	*ki-shü loḱ-pa.*
Brush	ཕག་ཟེ་	*pha-śe.*
Brute	ཏྲོལ་སོང་	*cḱö-song.*
Bubble	ལྦུ་བ་	*bu-wa.*
Buck	ཤྭ་ (ཤྭ་བ་)	*sha-a.*
Bucket	ཆུ་བཟོམ་	*chhu-śom.*
Do. *hon.*	ཆབ་བཟོམ་	*chhaṕ-śom.*
Buck wheat, bitter	བྲའུ་ (བྲ་བོ་)	*ťra-u.*
Do. sweet	རྒྱ་བྲ་	*gyaṕ-ra.*
Bud, *s.*	ཐེའུ་	*theu.*
Bud, to	སྐྱེ་བ་	*kye-wa.*
Buddha	སངས་རྒྱས་	*sang-gye.*
Buddhist	ནང་པ་	*nang-pa.*
Buffalo	མ་ཧེ་	*ma-he.*
Buffoonery	སྤྲེ་རྩེད་	*tre-tse.*
Bug	འདྲེ་ཤིག་	*dre-shi.*
Bugle	དམག་དུང་	*maḱ ťung.*
Build, to	བཟོ་བ་	*śo-wa.*
Do. *hon.*	བཟོ་བ་གནང་བ་	*śo-wa nang-wa.*

Building	ཁང་པ་	*khang-pa.*
Do. *hon.*	གཟིམ་ཁང་	*śim-khang.*
Do. *h. hon.*	གཟིམ་ཤག་	*śim-sha.*
Bulk	ཆེ་ཆུང་	*chhe-chhung.*
Bulky	སྦོམ་པོ་	*bom-po.*
Bull	གླང་། གླང་གོག་	*lang ; lang-ko.*
Bullet	རྡིག་རིལ་ (མདེའུ་)	*dik-ri.*
Bullock	གླང་། གླང་གོག་	*lang ; lang-ko.*
Bunch	ཚག་པ་	*chhak-pa.*
Bundle of clothes	གོས་སྒྲིལ་	*kö-dril.*
Do. of papers	ཤུག་གུའི་ (ཤོག་བུའི་) ཚག་པ་	*shuk-ku-i chhak-pa.*
Do. of sticks	ཤིང་འཁུར་	*shing-khur.*
Burden (of animal)	ཁལ། ཏོས་པོ་	*khe ; tö-po.*
Do. (of human being)	རྡོག་ཐྲེད་། རྒྱབ་འཁུར་	*dok-thre ; gyap-khur.*
Buriat	སྤྲོ་རས་ཐུ་	*po-re-thu.*
Burn, to, *v.i.*	འཚིག་པ་	*tshik-pa.*
Do. *v.t.*	སྲེག་པ་	*trak-pa.*
Burnt-offering	སྦྱིན་སྲེག་	*jin-se.*
Burrhel (sheep)	གནའ་བ་	*na-wa.*
Burst, to, *v.i*	གས་པ་ (འགས་པ་)	*ke-pa.*

Burst, to, *v.t.*	བཅག་པ་ (གཅོག་པ་)	*chak-pa.*
Do. *hon.*	གཅོག་ག་ (གཅོག་པ་) གནང་བ་	*chok-ka nang-wa.*
Bury, to	ས་ལ་སྦེད་པ་	*sa-la be-pa.*
Do. *hon.*	ས་སྦེད་གནང་བ་	*sa-be nang-wa.*
Burying-place	དུར་ཁྲོད་	*ťu-thrö.*
Bush	ཤིང་སྡོང་ཆུང་ཆུང་	*shing-dong chhung-chhung.*
Business	ལས་ཀ། དོན་དག་	*le-ka.; ťön-ťa.*
Do. *hon.*	ཕྱག་ལས། སྐུ་དོན་	*chha-le ; ku-ťön.*
Busy, I am	ང་ཅོག་གི་མི་འདུག! ང་དལ་ཀྱི་མི་འདུག་	*nga cho-ki min-duk ; nga ťe-kyi min-du.*
Busy, he is, *hon.*	ཁོང་ཐུགས་ཅོག་ག་ གནང་གི་མི་འདུག་	*khong thu-chok-ka nang-gi min-du.*
Do. *h. hon.*	སྐུ་གཉོགས་ཐུགས་ཅོག་ག་ (པ་) གནང་གི་མི་འདུག་	*ku-sko thu-cho-ka nang-gi min-du.*
But	ཡིན་ཀྱང་། ཡིན་ན་ཡང་	*yin-kyang ; yin-na-yang.*
Butcher	ཤན་པ། ཡར་པོ་	*shem-pa ; ya-po.*
Butler	གཟིམ་དཔོན་	*śim-pön.*
Butt (of gun)	སྒྲུམ་ཤིང་། ཉ་གཞུག་	*gum-shing ; nya-sku.*
Butter	མར་	*mar.*
Do. *hon.*	གསོལ་མར་	*sö-ma.*

Butterfly	ཕྱེ་འདྲེན་མ་	*chhem-drem-ma.*
Butter-milk	དར་ར་ (བ་)	*t́ar-ra.*
Do. *hon.*	བཞེས་དར་	*sḱe-t́ar.*
Buttock	ཀུབ་	*kuṕ.*
Do. *hon.*	ཞབས་ཕོངས་	*sḱam-phong.*
Button	ཐུབ་ཆི་	*thuṕ-chhi.*
Do. *hon.*	མགུལ་ཐུབ་	*gü-thuṕ.*
Button-hole	ཐོབ་ལུང་	*thoṕ-lung.*
Do. *hon.*	མགུལ་ལུང་	*yü-lung.*
Button (of rank)	དོག་	*to.*
Do. *hon.*	དབུ་དོག་	*u-to.*
Buy, to	ཉོ་བ་	*nyo-wa.*
Do. *hon.*	གཟིགས་པ་	*śi-pa.*
Do. *h. hon.*	ལྗགས་གཟིགས་གནང་བ་	*ja-śi nang-wa.*
Buzz, to	སྦྲང་སྐད་རྒྱབ་པ་	*drang-ke gyaṕ-pa.*
By (*post*)	གིས། ཀྱིས། གྱིས།	*ki; kyi; ḱyi.*
By reason of	རྐྱེན་གྱིས་	*kyen-ḱyi.*

C

Cabbage	པེ་ཚལ་ *ch.*	*pe-tshe.*
Cage	ལྕགས་ཁྲ་	*cha-thra.*
Cairn	རྡོ་སྤུང་	*do-pung.*
Cake	ཏེན་ཤིན་ *ch.*	*ten-shin.*
Do. (of tea)	པག་ཀ་	*ṕa-ḱa.*
Calamity	བཀྲ་མི་ཤིས་	*ťra-mi-shi.*
Calculate, to	རྩིས་རྒྱབ་པ་	*tsi gyaṕ-pa.*
Do. *hon.*	ཕྱགས་རྩིས་སྐྱོན་པ་	*ja-tsi kyöm-pa.*
Calculation	རྩིས་	*tsi.*
Do. *hon.*	ཕྱགས་རྩིས	*ja-tsi.*
Caldron	དཀྱིལ་ཁྲོ་	*kyi-thro.*
Calendar	ཟླ་ཐོ་	*da-tho.*
Do. *hon.*	གཟིགས་ཐོ་	*śi tho.*
Calf (of the cow)	བེ་བེ་ (བེའུ་)	*ṕe-ṕe.*
Do. (of the leg)	རྐང་པའི་ཉ་	*ḱang-pe nya.*
Do. *hon.*	ཞབས་ཀྱི་ཉ་	*sħaṕ ḱyi-nya.*
Call, to	སྐད་བཏང་ (གཏོང་) བ་	*ḱe-tang-wa.*
Do. *hon.*	གསུང་གནང་བ། སྐད་གཏོང་ང་ (བ་) གནང་བ་	*sung-nang-wa; ḱe-tong-nga nang-wa.*

Call! (a person)	སྐད་གཏོང་ཤོག	*ke-tong-sho.*
Do. *hon.*	ཕེབས་ཞུས་ཤོག	*pḱe-sḱü-sho.*
Do. *h. hon.*	འཆིབ་རྒྱུ་གནང་ཞུས་ཤོག	*chhiṕ-gyu-nang sḱü-sho.*
Call, to (on a person)	བཙར་བ	*char-wa.*
Call, to (on superior)	སྐུ་མདུན་ལ་བཙར་བ	*kun-dün-la char-wa.*
Call up, to (a ghost, etc.)	སྤྱན་འདྲེན་ཞུ་བ	*chen-dren sḱu-wa.*
Calm (condition of country)	ཧླིངས་ཆག་པོ། འཇམ་ཐིང་ཐིང	*hling-chaḱ-po; jam-thing-thing.*
Cambric	དར་རས	*ťar-re.*
Camel (male or female)	ཨ་མོང་ (རྔ་མོང་)	*a-mong.*
Camel hair	ཨ་མོང་སྤུ་ (རྔ་མོང་སྤུ)	*a-mong-pu.*
Camp	སྒར	*gar.*
Camping ground	སྒར་ས	*ga-sa.*
Camphor	ག་བུར	*ḱa-ṕur.*
Canal	ཡོ་པོ་ (ཡུར་པོ་)	*yo-po.*
Cancel, to (blot out)	སུབ་པ	*suṕ-pa.*
Do. *hon.*	སུབ་པ་གནང་བ	*suṕ-pa nang-wa*
Cancel, to (set aside)	མེད་པར་བཟོ་བ	*me-pa śo-wa.*
Do. *hon.*	མེད་པར་བཟོ་བ་གནང་བ	*me-pa śo-wa nang-wa.*
Cancel, to (writing)	བྲིས་སུབ་བཏང་ (གཏོང་) བ	*ťri-suṕ tang-wa.*
Do. *hon.*	བྲིས་སུབ་གནང་བ	*ťri-suṕ nang-wa.*

Candid	དྲང་པོ་	*ťrang-po.*
Do. *hon.*	ཐུགས་རྒྱུ་དྲང་པོ་	*thu-gyu ťrang-po.*
Candle (of Chinese make)	ལཱ་	*la.*
Candle (of English make)	རྒྱ་གར་ལཱ་	*gya-ǩar-la.*
Cane	སྦ་	*pa.*
Cannibal	མིའི་ཤ་ཟ་མཁན་	*mi-i sha-śa-khen.*
Cannon	མེ་སྒྱོགས་	*me-gyo.*
Cannon-ball	མེ་སྒྱོགས་ཀྱི་མདེའུ་	*me-gyoǩ-ǩi di-u.*
Canter, to	འཛོག་རྒྱབ་པ་	*dzo-gyap̌-pa.*
Cap	ཞྭ་མོ་	*sǩa-mo.*
Do. *hon.*	དབུ་ཞྭ་	*u-sǩa.*
Capable	ནུས་པོ་	*nü-po.*
Capable, to be	ཐུབ་པ་	*thup̌-pa.*
Do. *hon.*	ཐུབ་པ་གནང་བ་	*thup̌-pa nang-wa.*
Capital, *s.* (as opposed to interest)	ངོ་བོ་ (དངོས་པོ་)	*ngo-po.*
Capital (letters)	དབུ་ཅན་	*u-chen.*
Capital, *s.* (chief city)	རྒྱལ་ཁབ། རྒྱལ་ས་	*gye-khap̌, gye-sa.*
Capital, *adj.* (excellent)	ཡག་ཐག་ཆོད། ཨང་གི་དང་པོ་	*yaǩ-thaǩ-chhö ; ang-gi ťang-po.*

Capitulate, to	མགོ་དགུར་བ་	*go-gur-wa.*
Do. *hon.*	དབུ་དགུར་ར་ (བ་) གནང་བ་	*u-gur-ra nang-wa.*
Capsize, to	མགོ་གཞུག་ལོག་པ་	*go-sku lok-pa.*
Captain (officer in command of 100 men)	བརྒྱ་དཔོན་	*gya-pön.*
Captive	བཙོན་པ་	*tsöm-pa.*
Capture, to	ཟིན་པ་ (འཛིན་པ་)	*śim-pa.*
Do. *hon.*	ཟིན་པ་ (འཛིན་པ་) གནང་བ་	*śim-pa nang-wa.*
Carcass	རོ་	*ro.*
Do. (of animal killed for meat)	ཤི་རོ་	*shi-ro.*
Card	ཡི་གེ་	*yi-ge.*
Cards, playing	ཤོན་	*shön.*
Do. *hon.*	ཕྱག་ཤོན་	*chha-shön.*
Cardamums	སུག་སྨེལ་	*su-me.*
Care (anxiety)	སེམས་འཁྲལ་	*sem-thre.*
Do. *hon.*	ཐུགས་འཁྲལ་	*thu-thre.*
Care, to take (be careful)	བརྟན་བརྟན་བྱེད་པ་	*ten-ten cḱe-pa.*
Care of, to take (keep carefully)	ཉར་བ། ཅག་ག་བྱེད་པ་	*nyar-wa ; chaḱ ḱa cḱe-pa.*

Care of, to take *hon.*	ཉར་ར་ (བ་) གནང་བ་	*nyar-ra nang-wa.*
Do. *h. hon.*	ཐུགས་ཅག་གནང་བ་	*thu-cha nang-wa.*
Career (manner of life)	བྱེད་སྟངས་	*cḱe-tang.*
Do. *hon.*	གནང་སྟངས་	*nang-tang.*
Carefully	ཅག་ག་བྱས་ནས་	*cha-ḱa cḱe-ne.*
Do. *hon.*	ཐུགས་ཅག་གནང་ནས་	*thu-cha nang-ne.*
Caress, to	བྱམས་པོ་བྱེད་པ་	*cḱam-po cḱe-pa.*
Do. *hon.*	བྱམས་པོ་གནང་བ་	*cḱam-po nang-wa.*
Carpenter	ཤིང་བཟོ་བ་	*shing-śo wa.*
Do. *hon.*	དབུ་མཛད་ལགས་	*um-dze-la.*
Carpet	ས་གདན་	*sa-den.*
Carriage	ཤིང་རྟ་འཁོར་ལོ་	*shing-ta ḱhor-lo.*
Carrier	དོས་པོ་འཁྱེར་མཁན་	*ṫö-po ḱhyer-khen.*
Carrot	གུང་ལ་ཕུག་	*ḱung-la-phuḱ.*
Carry, to	འཁྱེར་བ། འཁུར་བ་	*ḱhyer-wa ; ḱhur-wa.*
Do. *hon.*	སྣོམ་པ་	*nom-pa.*
Cart, bullock	གླང་སྒ་རི་	*lang-ga-ri.*
Cartridge	རྡིག་རིལ་	*diḱ-ri.*
Carve to (on wood, iron, etc.)	སྤྱོས་རྒྱབ་པ་	*trö-gyap̄-pa.*
Do. *hon.*	སྤྱོས་སྐྱོན་པ་	*trö-kyöm-pa.*

Cascade	བབ་ཆུ་ (འབབ་ཆུ་)	*ṕaṕ-chhu.*
Do. (over rocks)	བྲག་ཆུ་	*t́raḱ-chhu.*
Case (law suit)	ཁ་མཆུ་	*kham-chhu.*
Do. (box)	སྒམ་	*gam.*
Do. *hon.*	ཕྱག་སྒམ་	*chha-gam.*
Do. (covering)	ཤུབས་	*shuṕ.*
Cash	དངུལ་	*ngü.*
Do. *hon.*	ཕྱག་དངུལ་	*chha-ngü.*
Cashier	ཕྱག་མཛོད་	*chhan-dzö.*
Cashmere	ཁ་ཆེའི་ལུང་པ་	*kha-chhe lung-pa.*
Cask	ཆུ་རུམ་མ། ཆུ་བཟོམ་	*chhu-rum-ma; chhu-śom.*
Cast away, to	དབྱུག་པ་	*yuḱ-pa.*
Do. *hon.*	དབྱུག་ག་ (པ་) གནང་བ་	*yuḱ ḱa nang-wa.*
Caste	རུས་	*rü.*
Do. *hon.*	སྐུ་རུས་	*ku-rü.*
Castle	རྫོང་	*dzong.*
Castrate, to	ཤ་བཅད་ (གཅོད་) པ་	*sha-che-pa.*
Cat	ཞི་མི་	*sḱi-mi.*
Cataract	ཧ་རི་ལོང་ང་	*ha-ri-long-nga.*
Catarrh	ཆམ་པ་	*chham-pa.*

Catarrh, *hon.*	མཁྲུལ་ཆམ་	*gün-chham.*
Catch, to	ཟིན་པ་ (འཛིན་པ་)	*śim-pa.*
Do. *hon.*	ཟིན་པ་ (འཛིན་པ་) གནང་བ་	*śim-pa nang-wa.*
Catechu	དོས་ཇ་	*tö-ja.*
Caterpillar	སའབུ་	*sa-bu.*
Cattle	བ་གླང་	*pa-lang.*
Cattle-disease	ཕྱུགས་ནད་	*chhu ne.*
Cauliflower	ཀོ་པི་མེ་ཏོག་	*ko-pi me-tok.*
Cause (reason)	རྐྱེན། རྒྱུ་རྐྱེན་	*kyen ; gyu-kyen.*
Cautious, to be	ཧེན་ལྡན་བྱེད་པ་	*ten-den cke-pa.*
Do. *hon.*	ཧེན་ལྡན་གནང་བ་	*ten-den nang-wa.*
Cavalry	རྟ་དམག་	*ta-ma.*
Cave of earth	ས་ཕུག་	*sa-phu.*
Cave of rock	བྲག་ཕུག་	*t́rak-phu.*
Cavity	ཨི་ཁུང་	*i-khung.*
Cease, to	འཆད་པ་	*chhe-pa.*
Ceaseless	རྒྱུན་མི་ཆད་པ་	*gyün-mi-chhe-pa.*
Ceiling	ཐོག་ཁ་	*tho-kha.*
Celebrated	སྙན་གྲགས་ཆེན་པོ་	*nyen-t́ra chhem-po.*
Do. *hon.*	མཚན་སྙན་གྲགས་ཆེན་པོ་	*tshen nyen-t́ra chhem-po.*

Cell (of hermit)	རི་ཁྲོད་	*ri-thrö.*
Do. (of monks)	གྲྭ་ཤག་	*ťra-sha.*
Cemetery	དུར་ཁྲོད་	*ťu-thrö.*
Censer	སྤོས་ཕོར་	*pö-phor.*
Censure, to	གཤེ་གཤེ་བཏང་ (གཏོང་) བ་	*she-she tang-wa.*
Do. *hon.*	བཀའ་བསྐྱོན་གནང་བ་	*kap-kyön nang-wa.*
Centipede	རྐང་བརྒྱ་ལག་བརྒྱ་	*kang-gya lak-gya.*
Centre	དཀྱིལ་	*kyi.*
Centurion	བརྒྱ་དཔོན་	*gya-pön.*
Ceremony	ལུགས་སྲོལ་	*luk-sö.*
Ceremony (religious)	ཆོ་ག། སྐུ་རིམ་	*chho-ga ; ku-rim.*
Certain	ངེས་པ་	*nge-pa.*
Do. *hon.*	ཐུགས་ངེས་པ་	*thu-nge-pa.*
Certainly	ཏེན་ལྡན། ངོ་ཐོག་	*ten-den ; ngo-tho.*
Certainty	བརྟན་པོ། ངེས་པ། ཏེན་ལྡན་	*tem-po ; nge-pa ; ten-den.*
Certificate	བཀའ་ཤོག་	*ka-sho.*
Chaff (of grain)	ཕུང་མ་	*phung-ma.*
Chain, iron	ལྕགས་ཐག་	*chak-tha.*
Do. brass	རག་ཐག་	*rak-tha.*
Chair	རྐུབ་ཀྱག །་ ཁྲིའུ་ཤིང་	*kup-kya ; thri-u-shing.*

Chair, *hon.*	ཞབས་ཀྱག་	*sḱap-kya.*
Do. (high chair used as throne)	བཞུགས་ཁྲི་	*sḱuk-ṭhri.*
Chairman	འཁྲིད་པ་	*thri-pa.*
Chalk	ས་དཀར། དཀར་རྩི་	*sa-kar ; kar-tsi.*
Chamber	ཁང་མིག་	*khang-mi.*
Do. *hon.*	གཟིམ་ཆུང་	*śim-chhung.*
Chamber, sleeping	ཉལ་ས་	*nye-sa.*
Do. *hon.*	གཟིམ་ཁང་	*śim-khang.*
Chamberlain	གཟིམ་དཔོན་ཆེན་པོ་	*śim-pön chhem-po.*
Chance (accident)	བར་ཆད་	*ṕar-chhe.*
Do. (luck)	བསོ་བདེ་ (བསོད་བདེ་)	*so-de.*
Do. *hon.*	སྐུ་བསོད་	*ku-sö.*
Change, to, *v.t.*	སྒྱུར་བ་	*gyur-wa.*
Do. *hon.*	སྒྱུར་ར་ (བ་) གནང་བ་	*gyur-ra nang-wa.*
Change, to, *v.i.*	འགྱུར་བ་	*gyur-wa.*
Change, to, (exchange)	རྗེ་པོ་རྒྱབ་པ་	*je-po gyaṕ-pa.*
Do. *hon.*	རྗེ་པོ་སྐྱོན་པ་	*je-po kyöm-pa.*
Channel (for irrigation)	ཡོ་པོ་ (ཡུར་པོ་)	*yo-po.*
Chap, to (of skin)	གས་པ་	*ḱe-pa.*

Chapel	ཆོས་ཁང་	*chhö-khang.*
Chapter	ལེའུ་	*li-u.*
Character	བྱེད་སྟངས་	*cḱe-tang.*
Do. *hon.*	གནང་སྟངས་	*nang-tang.*
Charcoal	སོལ་ལ་ (སོལ་བ་)	*sö-la.*
Charge, to (price)	གོང་ལབ་པ་	*ḱong laṕ-pa.*
Charge of, to give into	རྩིས་སྤྲོད་པ་	*tsi tre-pa.*
Charge of, to take	རྩིས་ལེན་པ་	*tsi lem-pa.*
Charitable	དགེ་སེམས་ཆེན་པོ་	*ge sem chhem-po.*
Charity (alms)	སྦྱིན་པ། བསོད་སྙོམས་	*jim-pa ; sö-nyom.*
Charity of mind	སྙིང་རྗེ། དགེ་སེམས་	*nying-je ; ge-sem.*
Charm (amulet)	རྟེན་	*ten.*
Do. (worn on person)	སྲུང་ང་ (སྲུང་བ་)	*trung-nga.*
Do. *hon.*	མགུལ་སྲུང་	*gü-sung.*
Charm-box	གའུ་	*ḱa-u.*
Do. *hon.*	མགུལ་གའུ་	*gü-ḱa-u.*
Chase, to	གཤུག་རེད་ཕྱིན་པ་	*sḱuḱ-t́e chhim-pa.*
Do. *hon.*	གཤུག་རེད་ཕེབ་པ་	*sḱuḱ-t́e phe-pa.*
Chasm	སེར་ཀ་	*ser-ka.*
Chat, to	ཁ་ལས་ང་ཤད་ (ཤོད་) པ་	*khaṕ-le she-pa.*

Chat, to *hon.*	ཞལ་ལས་གསུང་བ་	*sḱe-le sung-wa.*
Cheap	ཁེ་པོ་	*khe-po.*
Cheat, to	མགོ་སྐོར་བཏང་ (གཏོང་) བ། མགོ་སྐོར་བ་	*go-kor tang-wa.* *go kor-wa.*
Do. *hon.*	མགོ་སྐོར་གཏོང་ང་ (བ་) གནང་བ་	*go-kor tong-nga nang-wa.*
Do. *inf.* to *sup.*	དབུ་སྐོར་ཞུ་བ་	*u-kor sḱu-wa.*
Check, to (stop)	བཀག་པ་ (འགེགས་པ)	*kaḱ-pa.*
Do. *hon.*	བཀག་ག་ (བཀག་པ་) གནང་བ་	*kaḱ-ḱa nang-wa.*
Cheek	འདན་ཁོག། འགྲམ་པ་	*den-kho ; dram-pa.*
Do. *hon.*	ཞལ་འགྲམ་	*sḱen-dram.*
Cheeky	གྱོང་པོ་	*ḱyong-po.*
Cheerful, to be	སེམས་དགའ་བ་	*sem-ga-wa.*
Do. *hon.*	ཐུགས་མཉེས་པ་	*thu-nye-pa.*
Cheese	ཆུར་ར་	*chhu-ra.*
Do. *hon.*	བཞེས་ཆུར་	*sḱiṕ-chhur.*
Do. (mixed with butter)	ཐུད་	*thü.*
Do. *hon.*	བཞེས་ཐུད་	*sḱiṕ-thü.*
Do. (another kind)	ཆུར་ཞིབ་	*chhur-sḱiṕ.*

Chemist	སྨན་ཚོང་པ་	*men tshong-pa.*
Chess	མིག་དམག་ (མིག་མངས་)	*mi-ma.*
Do. *hon.*	སྤྱན་དམག་ (སྤྱན་མངས་)	*chen-ma.*
Chest	སྒམ་	*gam.*
Do. *hon.*	ཕྱག་སྒམ་	*chha-gam.*
Do. (of body)	བྲང་ཁོག་	*p̓ang-k̇ho.*
Do. *hon.*	སྐུ་བྲང་	*ku-p̓ang.*
Chestnut (horse), *m.*	སྐྱང་པོ་	*kyang-po.*
Do. *f.*	སྐྱང་མོ་	*kyang-mo.*
Chicken	བྱ་ཕྲུག་	*cḣap̓-thru.*
Chide, to	གཤེ་གཤེ་བཏང་ (གཏོང་) བ་	*she-she tang-wa.*
Do. *hon.*	བཀའ་བཀྱོན་གནང་བ་	*kap̓-kyön nang-wa.*
Chief (among officials, etc.)	གཙོ་བོ་	*tso-o.*
Chief Minister	བློན་ཆེན་	*lön-chhen.*
Chiefly	ཕལ་ཆེར་	*phe-chher.*
Chilblains, to suffer from	འཁྱགས་འབོས་འཐེབ་པ་	*khyak̇-bö thep̓-pa.*
Child	བུ་གུ་	*pu-gu.*
Do. *m. hon.*	སྲས་	*se.*
Do. *f. hon.*	སྲས་མོ་	*tre-mo* or *se-mo.*
Children	བུ་བུ་མོ་	*p̓u p̓u-mo.*

Children, *hon.*	ཨ་བྲ་སྲས་སྲོས་	*a-wa se-sö.*
Chilli	སིལ་པན་	*si-pen.*
Do. *hon.*	སྐྲུམ་སྨན་	*trum-men.*
Chilly	གྲང་མོ། བསིལ་པོ་	*t́rang-mo; si-po.*
Do. *hon.*	སྐུ་བསིལ་པོ་	*ku-si-po.*
Chimney	དུ་ཁུང་ (དུད་ཁུང་)	*t́u-khung.*
Chin	མས་ལེ་	*me-le.*
Do. *hon.*	ཞལ་མལ་ (ཞལ་མས་)	*sḱe-mel.*
China (country)	རྒྱ་ནག་	*gya-na.*
China, *adj.* (porcelain)	དཀར་ཡོལ་	*ka-yö.*
Do. *hon.*	ཞལ་དཀར་	*sḱe-ka.*
Chinaman	རྒྱ་མི་	*gya-mi.*
Chinese, *adj.* and *s.*	རྒྱ་མི་	*gya-mi.*
Chinese Emperor	རྒྱ་ནག་གོང་མ། གོང་མ་ཆེན་པོ་	*gya-na kong-ma; kong-ma chhem-po.*
Chinese language	རྒྱ་སྐད་	*gya-ke.*
Chink (in wall, etc.)	སེར་ཀ་	*se-ka.*
Chisel	ཟོང་	*śong.*
Choke, to	གློ་སུབ་རྒྱབ་པ་	*lo-suṕ gyaṕ-pa.*
Do. *hon.*	གློ་སུབ་སྐྱོན་པ་	*lo-suṕ kyöm-pa.*

Choked, to be	འགགས་པ་	*gaḱ-pa.*
Cholera	སྐྱུག་བཤལ་	*kyuḱ-she.*
Choose, to (appoint)	སྐོ་བ་	*ko-wa.*
Do. *hon.*	སྐོ་བ་གནང་བ་	*ko-wa nang-wa.*
Choose, to (select)	འདམས་པ་	*dam-pa.*
Do. *hon.*	འདམས་པ་གནང་བ་	*dam-pa nang-wa.*
Chop (mutton chop)	ལུག་ཤའི་རྩིབ་མ་	*luḱ-she tsi-ma.*
Do. *hon.*	གསོལ་སྐྲུམ་ལུག་ཤའི་རྩིབ་མ་	*sö-trum luḱ-she tsi-ma.*
Do. to (meat)	བཙབ་པ་	*tsaṕ-pa.*
Do. *hon.*	བཙབ་པ་གནང་བ་	*tsaṕ-pa nang-wa.*
Do. to (wood, metal, etc.)	བཅད་པ་ (གཅོད་པ་)	*che-pa.*
Do. *hon.*	བཅད་ (གཅོད་) པ་གནང་བ་	*che-pa nang-wa.*
Chopper	ཚེས་དོ་	*tshe-t́o.*
Chopsticks	ཁོ་ཙེ་ *ch.*	*khö-t́se.*
Do. *hon.*	བཞེས་ཙེ་	*sḱe-tse.*
Christ	མ་ཤི་ཀ་	*ma-shi-ka.*
Chronicle	ལོ་རྒྱུས་	*lo-gyü.*
Chum (in a monastery)	ཆོས་གྲོགས་	*chhö-t́ro.*
Church	ཆོས་ཁང་	*chhö-khang.*
Churn, *s.*	ལྡོང་མོ་	*dong-mo.*

Churn for milk	ཞོ་ལྡོང་	*sḰo-dong.*
Do. for tea	ཇ་ལྡོང་	*cḰan-dong.*
Do. *hon.*	གསོལ་ལྡོང་	*sön-dong.*
Do. to (tea)	སྲུས་པ་ (སྲུབ་པ་)	*sü-pa.*
Do. *hon.*	སྲུས་ (སྲུབ་) པ་གནང་བ་	*sü-pa nang-wa.*
Churn, to (milk)	ཞོ་དཀྲོག་པ་	*sḰo-troḰ-pa.*
Cicatrice	རྨ་ཤུལ་	*ma-shü.*
Cinder (hot)	མེ་མདག་	*men-da.*
Cipher (zero)	ཀླད་ཀོར་	*le-kor.*
Circle	སྒོ་སྒོར་ (སྒོར་སྒོར་)	*go-kor.*
Circular	ཀོར་ཀོར་	*kor-kor.*
Circumference	སྒོར་ཐིག་	*gor thiḰ.*
Circumstance	རྐྱེན་	*kyen.*
Citadel	རྫོང་	*dzong.*
City	གྲོང་ཁྱེར་	*t́rong-khyer.*
Civil, (honorific, of conversation)	ཞེ་ས་	*sḰe-sa.*
Claim	ཐོབ་སྐལ་	*thoṕ-ke.*
Clairvoyance	མངོན་ཤེས་	*ngön she.*
Do. *hon.*	མངོན་མཁྱེན་	*ngön-khyen.*
Clamour	ཨུར་སྒྲ་	*u-dra.*

Clap, the hands, to	ལག་པ་རྡབ་པ་	*lak̄-pa dap̄-pa.*
Do. *hon.*	ཕྱག་རྡབ་པ	*chha-dap̄-pa.*
Clarified butter	མར་ཁུ་	*mar-khu.*
Clarify, to (butter)	མར་བསྐུ་བ	*mar sk̄u-wa.*
Clarionet	རྒྱ་གླིང་	*gya-ling.*
Clasp, to	འཁྱུད་པ་	*khyü-pa.*
Do. *hon.*	འཁྱུད་པ་གནང་བ་	*khyü-pa nang-wa.*
Class (kind)	རིམ་པ་	*rim-pa.*
Do. (in school)	གྲལ་	*t́re.*
Do. *hon.*	བསྐུགས་གྲལ་	*sk̄u-t́re.*
Claw	སྡེར་མོ་	*der-mo.*
Clay	འདག་པ་	*dak̄-pa.*
Clean	གཙང་མ་	*tsang-ma.*
Do. to	འཁྲུ་བ་	*thru-wa.*
Do. *hon.*	འཁྲུད་པ་གནང་བ་	*thrü-pa nang-wa.*
Clean, to (by wiping)	འཕྱིད་པ་	*chhi-pa.*
Do. *hon.*	འཇག་ཕྱིད་གནང་བ་	*ja-chhi nang-wa.*
Clean, to (by rubbing and wiping)	འཕྱིད་དར་གཏོང་བ་	*chhi-t́ar tong-wa.*
Do. *hon.*	འཇག་འཕྱིད་གནང་བ་	*ja-chhi nang-wa.*
Clean, to (by sweeping)	གེ་རྒྱབ་པ་	*k̄e-gyap̄-pa.*

Clean, to (by sweeping) *hon.*	ཁེ་སྐྱོན་པ་	*ǩe-kyöm-pa.*
Cleansed (purified)	དག་པོ་	*ťaǩ-po.*
Clear (of glass)	གསལ་པོ་	*se-po.*
Do. (of air)	དྭངས་པོ་	*ťang-po.*
Cleave, to (wood etc.)	གཤགས་པ་ (གཤོག་པ་)	*shaǩ-pa.*
Do. *hon.*	གཤགས་ག་ (གཤོག་པ་) གནང་བ་	*shaǩ-ǩa nang-wa.*
Cleft	སེར་ཀ་	*se-ka.*
Clergy	གྲྭ་པ་	*ťra-pa.*
Do. *hon.*	དགེ་འདུན་	*gen-dün.*
Clerk	དྲུང་ཡིག་	*ťrung-yi.*
Do. *hon.*	དྲུང་ཡིག་ལགས་	*ťrung-yi-la.*
Clever	རིག་པ་ཆེན་པོ་	*riǩ-pa chhem-po.*
Do. *hon.*	ཐུགས་རིག་ཆེན་པོ་	*thu-riǩ chhem-po.*
Climate	བསིལ་དྲོས་	*si-ťrö.*
Climb, to	འཛེག་པ་ (འཛོག་པ་)	*dzaǩ-pa.*
Do. *hon.*	འཛེག་ག་ (འཛོག་པ་) གནང་བ་	*dzaǩ-ǩa nang-wa.*
Cling, to	འཛུས་པ་	*jü-pa.*
Do. *hon.*	འཛུས་པ་གནང་བ་	*jü-pa nang-wa.*
Cloak	ཆུ་པ་	*chhu-pa.*

Cloak, *hon.*	ན་བཟའ་	*nam-śa.*
Clock	ཆུ་ཚོད་འཁོར་ལོ་	*chhu-ťshö khor-lo.*
Cloisonné	གུ་གུ་ཤ་	*ǩu-ǩu-sha.*
Close to, *adv.* and *post.*	ཙཱ་ (ཙར།) ཐག་ཉེ་པོ་	*tsa ; tha-nye-po.*
Do. to	བཀག་པ་ (འགེགས་པ་)	*kaǩ-pa.*
Do. *hon.*	བཀག་ག་ (འགེགས་པ་) གནང་བ་	*kaǩ-ǩa nang-wa.*
Close up, *v.i.* (of flowers, etc.)	ཁ་ཟུམ་པ་	*kha-śum-pa.*
Close fisted	ལག་པ་དམ་པོ་	*laǩ-pa ťam-po.*
Do. *hon.*	ཕྱག་དམ་པོ་	*chha-ťam-po.*
Cloth, cotton	རས་	*re.*
Do. *hon.*	སྐུ་རས་	*ku-re.*
Cloth, woollen (of European or Indian make)	འགོ་སྣམ་	*go-nam.*
Do. (of Tibetan make)	སྣམ་བུ་	*nam-ṕu.*
Do. *hon.*	ཕྱག་སྣམ་	*chha-nam.*
Clothe, to	གོན་པ་	*ǩöm-pa.*
Do. *hon.*	བཞེས་པ་	*sǩe-pa.*
Clothes	དུག་ལོག་	*ťu-lo.*
Do. *hon.*	ན་བཟའ་	*nam-śa.*

Clothes, to put on	དུག་ལོག་གོན་པ་	*ťu-lo ǩöm-pa.*
Do. *hon.*	ན་བཟའ་བཞེས་པ་	*nam-śa sǩe-pa.*
Do. to take off	དུག་ལོག་ཕྱིས་ (འབུད་) པ་	*ťu-lo pi-pa.*
Do. *hon.*	ན་བཟའ་བསིལ་བ་	*nam-śa si-wa.*
Cloud (in sky)	སྤྲིན་པ་	*trim-pa.*
Do. (fog)	རྨུགས་པ་	*muǩ-pa.*
Cloudy, to become	འཐིབ་པ་	*thiṕ-pa.*
Clove	ལི་ཤི་	*li-shi.*
Clown	དབུ་འཁོར་ཞུ་མཁན་	*wu-khor sǩu-khen.*
Clumsy	སྡུག་རུལ་	*duǩ-ru.*
Coagulate, to (of blood, etc.)	འཁྱག་པ་	*khyaǩ-pa.*
Coal	རྡོ་སོལ་	*do-sö.*
Coarse	རྩུབ་པོ་	*tsuṕ-po.*
Coast	ཆུ་འགྲམ་	*chhu-dram.*
Coat	ཆུ་པ་	*chhu-pa.*
Do. *hon.*	ན་བཟའ་	*nam-śa.*
Do. of mail	ཁྲབ་	*thraṕ.*
Coax, to (for good object)	བསླབ་བྱ་རྒྱབ་པ་	*laṕ cǩa gyaṕ-pa.*
Do. *hon.*	བཀའ་སློབ་གནང་བ་	*ka-loṕ nang-wa.*
Coax, to (for bad object)	སླུ་བ་	*lu-wa.*

Coax, to (for bad object) *hon.*	སླུ་བ་གནང་བ་	*lu-wa nang-wa*
Cobbler	དོང་བཟོ་	*ngop-so.*
Comforter. *hon.*	སེམས་གསོ་གཏོང་ང་ (ན) གནང་མཁན་	*sem-so tong-nga nang-khen.*
Do. *hon.* (*inf.* to *sup.*)	ཐུགས་གསོ་ཕུལ་མཁན་	*thuk so phü-khen.*
Confidential	གསང་བ་	*sang-wa.*
Cobweb	སྡོམ་ཐག་	*dom-tha.*
Cock	བྱ་ཕོ་	*cKa-pho.*
Code of law	ཁྲིམས་ཡིག་	*thrim-yi.*
Coffer	སྒམ་	*gam.*
Do. *hon.*	ཕྱག་སྒམ་	*chha-gam.*
Coffin	རོ་སྒམ་	*ro-gam.*
Do. *hon.*	སྤུར་སྒམ་	*pur-gam.*
Cohere, to, *v.i.* (stick together)	འབྱར་བ་	*jar-wa.*
Coil, to (of snake)	སྒོ་འཁོར་བྱེད་པ་	*go-khor cKe pa.*
Coin (silver, value four annas)	ཊཾ་ཀ་	*tang-ka.*
Do. (silver, value two and half annas)	ཞོ་གང་	*sKo-kang.*
Do. (silver, value two annas)	ཕྱེད་གས་	*chhi-ke.*

Coin (silver, value one anna and one pice)	སྐར་མ་ལྔ་	*ka-ma-nga.*
Do. (silver, value three pice)	ཁ་གང་	*kha-ḱang.*
Do. (silver, value four pies)	ཁ་ཕྱེད་	*khaṕ-chhe.*
Do. (Chinese pice)	ཏོང་ཙེ་	*ťong-tse.*
Cold, *adj.* (of body, meat, etc.)	གྲང་མོ། བསིལ་པོ་	*ťrang-mo ; si-po.*
Do. *hon.*	སྐུ་བསིལ་པོ་	*ku si-po.*
Do. (to feel)	འཁྱགས་པ་	*khyaḱ-pa.*
Do. *hon.*	སྐུ་བསིལ་བ་	*ku-si-wa.*
Cold, *s.*	འཁྱགས་པ་	*khyaḱ-pa.*
Do. (catarrh)	ཆམ་པ་	*chham-pa.*
Do. *hon.*	མགུལ་ཆམ་	*gü-chham.*
Do. to have (in the head)	ཆམ་པ་ན་བ་	*chham-pa na-wa.*
Do. *hon.*	མགུལ་ཆམ་སྙུང་བ་	*gü-chham nyung-wa.*
Colic	རྒྱུ་གཟེར་	*gyu-śer.*
Collar	གོང་ང་ (གོང་བ་)	*ḱong-nga.*
Do. (after Chinese fashion)	ལིང་ཙེ་	*ling-tse.*

Collar (after Chinese fashion) *hon.*	མགུལ་གླིང་	*gü-ling.*
Colleague	རོགས་བྱེད་མཁན་	*ro-cḱe-khen.*
Collect, to	སྡུད་པ་	*dü-pa.*
Do. *hon.*	སྡུད་པ་གནང་བ་	*dü-pa nang-wa.*
Collect, to (wood, etc.)	སྒྲུག་པ་	*druḱ-pa.*
Do. *hon.*	སྒྲུག་ག་ (པ་) གནང་བ་	*druḱ-ḱa nang wa.*
College (of monks)	གྲྭ་ཚང་	*t́ra-tshang.*
Colloquial (language)	ཕལ་སྐད་	*phe-ke.*
Colonel (officer in command of 500 men to 1,000 men)	མདའ་དཔོན་	*de-pön.*
Colour (dye)	ཚོས་	*tshö.*
Do. natural	མདོག་	*do.*
Do. to lose	ཚོས་ཡལ་བ་	*tshö-ye-wa.*
Colt	རྟི་གི་ (རྟེའུ་)	*ti-ḱi.*
Do. of an ass	ཨུ་རྟཱི་	*u-ti.*
Column	ཀ་ (ཀ་བ་)	*ka.*
Comb	སྐྲ་གཤད་	*tra-she.*
Do. *hon.*	དབུ་བཤད་	*u-she.*
Do. to	སྐྲ་གཤད་པ་	*tra-she-pa.*
Do. *hon.*	དབུ་གཤད་སྐྱོན་པ་	*u-she kyöm-pa*

Combat	རྒྱབ་འདྲེ་	*gyam-dre.*
Come, *imp.*	ཤོག་	*sho.*
Do. to	ཡོང་བ་	*yong-wa.*
Do. *hon.*	ཕེབ་པ་	*phe-pa.*
Do. *h. hon.*	འཆིབ་རྒྱུ་གནང་བ་	*chhiṕ-gyu nang-wa.*
Come back, to	ལོག་ཡོང་བ་	*lo-yong-wa.*
Do. *hon.*	ལོག་ཕེབ་པ་	*lo-phe-pa.*
Do. *h. hon.*	འཆིབ་རྒྱུ་གནང་བ་	*chhiṕ-gyu nang-wa.*
Come, to (before *sup.*)	མཇལ་བ་	*je-wa.*
Do. *hon.*	མཇལ་ར་ (བ་) གནང་བ་	*je-ra nang-wa.*
Come out, to	འཐོན་པ་	*thöm-pa.*
Do. *hon.*	ཕྱི་ལོགས་ལ་ཕེབ་པ་	*chhi-lo la pheṕ-pa.*
Come together (of persons)	འཛོམ་པ། འཚོགས་པ་	*dzom-pa ; tshoḱ-pa.*
Do. *hon.*	ལྷན་རྒྱས་ཚོགས་པ་གནང་བ་	*lhen-gye tshoḱ-pa nang-wa.*
Comet	དུ་བ་མཇུག་རིང་	*ťu-wa juḱ-ring.*
Comfortable	སྐྱིད་པོ་	*ḱyi-po.*
Do. *hon.*	སྤྲོ་པོ་	*tro-po.*
Comic	བགད་མོ་བྲོ་པོ་	*ge-mo ťro-po.*
Do. *hon.*	ཞལ་མོ་བྲོ་པོ་	*sḱe-mo ťro-po.*
Command, commandment	བཀའ་	*ka.*

Command, to (give order)	བཀའ་གནང་བ་	*ka-nang-wa.*
Do. to (be in command of)	འགོ་བྱེད་བྱེད་པ་	*go-cḱe cḱe-pa.*
Do. *hon.*	འགོ་བྱེད་གནང་བ་	*go-cḱe nang-wa.*
Commander	དམག་དཔོན་	*maḱ-pön.*
Commander-in-Chief	སྤྱི་མདའ་	*chin-da.*
Commence, to	མགོ་བཙུགས་ (འཛུགས་) པ་	*go-tsuḱ-pa.*
Do. *hon.*	དབུ་བཙུགས་ (འཛུགས་) པ་	*u-tsuḱ-pa.*
Commencement	ཐོག་མ་	*tho-ma.*
Commend, to	བསྟོད་ར་བཏང་ (གཏོང་) བ་	*t́ö-ra tang-wa.*
Do. *hon.*	བསྟོད་ར་གཏོང་ང་ (བ་) གནང་བ་	*tö-ra tong-nga nang-wa.*
Commendation	བསྟོད་ར་	*tö-ra.*
Commerce	ཚོང་	*tshong.*
Do. *hon.*	རྒྱ་ཚོང་	*gya-tshong.*
Commissary (delegate)	ཚབ་	*tshaṕ.*
Do. *hon.*	སྐུ་ཚབ་	*ku-tshaṕ.*
Commit, to	བྱེད་པ་	*cḱe-pa.*
Do. *hon.*	གནང་བ་	*nang-wa.*
Do. to (to one's care)	བཅོལ་བ་ (འཆོལ་བ་)	*chöl-wa.*
Do. *hon.*	བཅོལ་ར་ (བ་) གནང་བ་	*chö-ra nang-wa.*

Common, *adj.* (vulgar)	དཀྱུས་མ་	*kyü-ma.*
Do. (plentiful)	འབེལ་པོ་	*be-po.*
Do. (of language *opp.* to *hon.*)	ཞེ་ས་མེད་པ་	*sKe-sa me-pa.*
Do. in (jointly)	མཉམ་འབྲེལ་	*nyam-dre.*
Do. *hon.*	ཕྱག་འབྲེལ་	*chha-dre.*
Companion	རོགས་	*ro.*
Do. (in work)	ལས་རོགས་	*le-ro.*
Do. *hon.*	ཕྱག་འབྲེལ་	*chha-dre.*
Company (of persons)	མི་ཚོགས་	*mi-tsho.*
Compare, to	སྡུར་བ་	*dur-wa.*
Do. *hon.*	སྡུར་ར་ (བ་) གནང་བ་	*dur ra nang-wa.*
Comparison	དཔེ་	*pe.*
Compasses (a pair of)	སྐོར་ཐིག་	*kor-thi.*
Compassion	སྙིང་རྗེ་	*nying-je.*
Do. *hon.*	ཐུགས་རྗེ་	*thu-je.*
Compel, to	ཨུ་ཚུགས་བྱེད་པ་	*u-tshu cKe-pa.*
Do. *hon.*	ཨུ་ཚུགས་གནང་བ་	*u-tshu nang-wa.*
Compelled, to be	དགོས་པ་	*gö-pa.*
Compensate, to	འགྲོ་སོང་སྟེར་བ་	*dro-song ter-wa.*
Compensation	འགྲོ་སོང་	*dro-song.*

Compete, to	སྡུར་བ་	*dur-wa.*
Do. *hon.*	སྡུར་ར་ (བ་) གནང་བ་	*dur-ra nang-wa.*
Competent	འོས་པོ་	*ö-po.*
Competitor	སྡུར་མཁན་	*dur-khen.*
Do. *hon.*	སྡུར་ར་ (བ་) གནང་མཁན་	*dur-ra nang-khen.*
Compile, to	སྒྲིག་པ་	*driḱ-pa.*
Complain, to (in writing)	སྙན་ཞུ་ཕུལ་ (འབུལ་) བ་	*nye-sḱu phü wa.*
Do. to (verbally)	ཞུ་ཐུག་བྱེད་པ་	*sḱu-thu cḱe-pa.*
Do. *hon.*	ཞུ་ཐུག་གནང་བ་	*sḱu-thu nang-wa.*
Complaint (petition)	སྙན་ཞུ་	*nye-sḱu.*
Complete, to	ཚར་བ་	*tshar-wa.*
Do. *hon.*	འགྲུབ་པ་	*druṕ-pa.*
Completely	བད་དེ་	*be-ṫe.*
Complicated	མགོ་རྙོག་ཚ་པོ་	*go-nyo tsha-po.*
Compliment	ཕྱག་འབུལ་	*chham-bü.*
Compliment, to (a superior)	ཕྱག་འབུལ་ཞུ་བ་	*chham-bü sḱu-wa.*
Do. to (equals)	འདྲིས་མི་བཏང་ (གཏོང་) བ་	*dri-me tang-wa.*
Compose, to (writing, &c.)	རྩོམ་པ་	*tsom-pa.*
Do. *hon.*	རྩོམ་པ་གནང་བ་	*tsom-pa nang-wa.*
Do. *h. hon.*	བཀའ་རྩོམ་གནང་བ་	*ka-tsom nang-wa.*

Comprehend, to (understand)	ཧ་གོ་བ་	*ha-ko-wa.*
Do. *hon.*	མཁྱེན་པ་	*khyem-pa.*
Compress, to	བཙིར་བ་	*tsir-wa.*
Do. *hon.*	བཙིར་ར་ (བ་) གནང་བ་	*tsir-ra nang-wa.*
Comprise, to	སྡུད་པ་	*dü-pa.*
Compromise, to (by mutual concession)	ནང་འགྲིག་བྱེད་པ། བར་འདུམ་བྱེད་པ་	*nang-drik che-pa, par-dum che-pa.*
Do *hon.*	བཀའ་བསྡུམ་གནང་བ་	*nan-dum nang-wa.*
Computation	རྩིས་	*tsi.*
Do. *hon.*	ཕྱག་རྩིས་	*ja-tsi.*
Compute, to	རྩིས་རྒྱབ་པ་	*tsi-gyap-pa.*
Do. *hon.*	ཕྱག་རྩིས་གནང་བ་	*ja-tsi nang-wa.*
Comrade	རོགས་	*ro.*
Do. *hon.*	ཕྱག་འབྲེལ་	*chha-dre.*
Concave	ཀོང་ཀོང་	*kong-kong.*
Conceal, to	སྦེད་པ་	*be-pa.*
Do. *hon.*	སྦེད་པ་གནང་བ་	*be-pa nang-wa.*
Concede, to	སྟེར་བ་	*ter-wa.*
Do. *hon.*	གནང་བ་	*nang-wa.*
Conceited	ལྟ་བ་མཐོ་པོ་	*ta-wa tho-po.*

Conceive, to (a child)	བུ་གུ་འཁོར་བ། བུ་ཚ་འཆག་པ་	*pu-gu khor-wa, pu-tsha chhak-pa.*
Do. *hon.*	ཨ་ལྷ་འཁོར་བ་	*a-wa khor-wa.*
Concerning	དོན་ལ། སྐོར་ལ་	*ťön-la; kor-la.*
Conch-shell	དུང་	*ťung.*
Do. bracelet	དུང་སྐོར་	*ťung-ko.*
Do. *hon.*	ཕྱག་དུང་	*chha-ťung.*
Conclude, to	འཚར་བ་	*tshar-wa.*
Do. *hon.*	འགྲུབ་པ་	*drup-pa.*
Concur, to	མཐུན་པ་	*thüm-pa.*
Do. *hon.*	མཐུན་པ་གནང་བ་	*thüm-pa nang-wa.*
Condemn, to (as judge)	ཁྲིམས་བཏང་ (གཏོང་) བ་	*thrim-tang-wa.*
Condemn, to, *hon.*	ཁྲིམས་གཏོང་ང་ (བ་) གནང་བ་	*thrim tong-nga nang-wa.*
Do. *h. hon.*	བཀའ་ཁྲིམས་གནང་བ་	*ka-thrim nang-wa.*
Condiment	ཤ་སྨན་	*sha-men.*
Condition (state)	གནས་ཚུལ་	*ne-tshü.*
Condole, to	སེམས་གསོ་བཏང་ (གཏོང་) བ་	*sem-so tang-wa.*
Conduct, *s.*	བྱེད་སྟངས	*cḱe-tang.*
Do. *hon.*	གནང་སྟངས་	*nang-tang.*
Do. to (towards)	འཁྲིད་ཡོང་བ་	*thri-yong-wa.*
Do. *hon.*	འཁྲིད་ཕེབ་པ་	*thri-phe-pa.*

Conduct to (away)	འཁྲིད་འགྲོ་བ་	*thri-dro-wa.*
Do. *hon.*	འཁྲིད་ཕེབ་པ་	*thri-phe-pa.*
Conduit (drain)	ཡོ་པོ་ (ཡུར་པོ་)	*yo-po.*
Cone of clay (with figures of gods)	ཚ་ཚ་	*tsha-tsha.*
Confer, to (converse)	གྲོས་བྱེད་པ་	*t́rö-cḱe-pa.*
Do. *hon.*	བཀའ་གྲོས་གནང་བ་	*ka-t́rö nang-wa.*
Confer, to (give)	སྟེར་བ་	*ter-wa*
Do. *hon.*	གནང་བ་	*nang-wa.*
Conference	གྲོས་	*t́rö.*
Do. *hon.*	བཀའ་གྲོས་	*ka-t́rö.*
Confess, to	བཤགས་པ་	*shaḱ-pa.*
Do. *hon.*	མཐོལ་བཤགས་ཕུལ་ (འབུལ་) བ་	*thö-sha phü-wa.*
Do. *h. hon.*	མཐོལ་བཤགས་འབུལ་ལ་ (བ་) གནང་བ་	*thö-sha bül-la nang-wa.*
Confide, to	བློ་གཏད་བྱེད་པ་	*lo-te cḱe-pa.*
Do. *hon.*	བློ་གཏད་གནང་བ་	*lo-te nang-wa.*
Confidence	བློ་གཏད་	*lo-te.*
Confine, to	བཙུག་པ་ (འཛུག་པ་)	*chuḱ-pa.*
Do. *hon.*	བཙུག་ག་ (འཛུག་པ་) གནང་བ་	*chuḱ-ka nang-wa.*

Confirm, to (statement etc.)	གཏན་ལྡན་བྱེད་པ་	*ten-den cḱe-pa.*
Do. *hon.*	གཏན་ལྡན་གནང་བ་	*ten-den nang-wa.*
Confiscate, to	གཞུང་བཞེས་བཏང་ (གཏོང་) བ་	*shung-sḱe tang-wa.*
Do. *hon.*	གཞུང་བཞེས་གནང་བ་	*sḱung-sḱe nang-wa.*
Confiscation	གཞུང་བཞེས་	*sḱung-sḱe.*
Conflict	རྒྱབ་འདྲེ་	*gyam-dre.*
Confounded, to be	མགོ་འཁོར་བ། མགོ་འཐོམས་པ་	*go-ḱhor-wa ; go-thom-pa.*
Do. *hon.*	དབུ་འཁོར་བ། དབུ་འཐོམས་པ་	*u-khor-wa ; u-thom-pa.*
Confront, to	རབ་འཕྲོད་བཏང་ (གཏོང་) བ་	*rap̒-thrö tang-wa.*
Do. *hon.*	རབ་འཕྲོད་གཏོང་ང་ (བ་) གནང་བ་	*rap̒-thrö tong-nga nang-wa.*
Confused, to be	མགོ་འཁོར་བ་	*go-khor-wa.*
Do. *hon.*	དབུ་འཁོར་བ་	*u-khor-wa.*
Confusing (intricate)	མགོ་ཉོག་ཚ་པོ། མགོ་ཉོག་ཆེན་པོ་	*go-nyo tsha-po ; go-nyo chem-po.*
Do. *hon.*	དབུ་ཉོག་ཚ་པོ་	*u-nyo tsha-po.*
Confusion (of speech)	ཁ་རྗོད་	*khan-jö.*
Confusion	མགོ་དཀྲོག་	*go-tro.*
Congeal, to	འཁྱགས་པ་	*khyaḱ-pa.*
Congregate, to	འཛོམས་པ་	*dzom-pa.*
Do. *hon.*	ལྷན་རྒྱས་ཚོགས་པ་	*hlen-gye tshoḱ-pa.*

Congregation	ཚོགས་	*tsho.*
Conjure, to (do conjuring tricks)	མིག་འཕྲུལ་རྩེད་པ་	*mik-thrü tse-pa.*
Do. *hon.*	མིག་འཕྲུལ་རྩེད་པ་གནང་བ་	*mik-thrü tse-pa nang-wa.*
Conjure, to (implore)	ནན་ཏན་ཞུ་བ་	*nen-ten sKu-wa.*
Do. *hon.*	ནན་ཏན་ཞུ་བ་གནང་བ་	*nen-ten sKu-wa nang-wa.*
Conjure up, to (ghost, etc.)	སྤྱར་འདྲེན་ཞུ་བ་	*chen-dren sKu-wa.*
Do. *hon.*	སྤྱན་འདྲེན་ཞུ་བ་གནང་བ་	*chen-dren sKu-wa nang-wa.*
Conjuring tricks	མིག་འཕྲུལ་	*mik-thrü.*
Do. *hon.*	སྤྱན་འཕྲུལ་	*chen-thrü.*
Conjurer	མིག་འཕྲུལ་རྩེད་མཁན་	*mik-thrü tse-khen.*
Do. *hon.*	མིག་འཕྲུལ་གནང་མཁན་	*mik thrü nang-khen.*
Connect, to (join together)	འཐུད་པ་	*thü-pa.*
Do. *hon.*	འཐུད་པ་གནང་བ་	*thü-pa nang-wa.*
Conquer, to	རྒྱལ་བ་	*gye-wa.*
Do. *hon.*	རྒྱལ་ར་ (བ་) གནང་བ་	*gye-ra nang-wa.*
Conquered, to be	འཕམ་པ་	*pham-pa.*
Do. *hon.*	ཐུགས་འཕམ་པ་གནང་བ་	*thu pham-pa nang-wa.*
Conscience, to have a	བཟང་ངན་ཤེས་པ་	*sang-ngen she-pa.*
Do. *hon.*	བཟང་ངན་མཁྱེན་པ་	*śang-ngen khyem-pa.*
Conscious, to be	དྲན་པ་	*trem-pa.*

Conscious, to be *hon.*	ཐུགས་དྲན་གསོ་བ་	*thu-t́ren so-wa.*
Consecrate, to	རབ་གནས་བྱེད་པ་	*raṕ-ne cḱe-pa.*
Do. *hon.*	རབ་གནས་གནང་བ་	*raṕ ne nang wa.*
Consecration	རབ་གནས་	*raṕ-ne.*
Consent, to	ཉན་པ་	*nyem-pa.*
Do. *hon.*	གསན་པ་	*sem pa.*
Consequence of, in	རྐྱེན་གྱིས་	*kyen-ḱyi.*
Consequently	དེའི་རྐྱེན་བྱས་ནས་	*t́ei-kyen cḱe-ne.*
Consider, to	བསམ་བློ་བཏང་ (གཏོང་) བ་	*sam lo tang-wa.*
Do. *hon.*	ཐུགས་བསམ་བཞེས་པ་	*thu-sam sḱe-pa.*
Considerable number of, a	མང་ཉུང་སྙོམ་པོ་གཅིག་	*mang-nyung nyom-po-chi.*
Console, to	སེམས་གསོ་བཏང་ (གཏོང་) བ་	*sem-so tang-wa.*
Do. *inf.* to *sup.*	སེམས་གསོ་ཞུ་བ་	*sem so sḱu-wa.*
Consonant, *s.*	གསལ་བྱེད་	*se-cḱe.*
Conspicuous	མངོན་གསལ་ཆེན་པོ་	*ngön-se chhem-po.*
Constable	སྐོར་ཅག་པ་	*ko-chaḱ-pa.*
Constant	བརྟན་པོ་	*tem-po.*
Constantly	རྟག་པ་རེ་བཞིན་	*taḱ-pa re-sḱi.*
Constellation	གཟའ་སྐར་	*za-ka.*
Constipation	རྩ་འགག་པ་	*tsa-gak pa.*

Construct, to	བཟོ་བ་	*śo-wa.*
Do. *hon.*	བཟོ་བ་གནང་བ་	*śo-wa nang-wa.*
Consult, to	གྲོས་དྲི་ (འདྲི་) བ་	*t́rö-t́ri-wa.*
Do. *hon.*	བཀའ་གྲོས་གནང་བ་	*ka t́rö nang-wa.*
Consumed, to be	རྫོགས་པ་	*dzoḱ-pa.*
Do. *hon.*	རྫོགས་ག་ (པ་) གནང་བ་	*dzoḱ-ḱa nang-wa.*
Consumption (pulmonary)	གཅོང་ནད་	*chong-ne.*
Contamination	གྲིབ་	*t́riṕ.*
Do. *hon.*	སྐུ་གྲིབ་	*ku-t́riṕ.*
Contemplate, to (consider)	བསམ་བློ་བཏང་ (གཏོང་) བ་	*sam-lo tang-wa.*
Do. *hon.*	ཐུགས་བསམ་བཞེས་པ་	*thu-sam sḱe-pa.*
Do. to (meditate on religious things)	སྒོམ་རྒྱབ་པ་	*gom-gyaṕ-pa.*
Do. *hon.*	སྒོམ་སྐྱོན་པ་	*gom kyöm-pa.*
Contemporary	ལོ་ཟླ་	*lon-da.*
Do. *hon.*	དགོང་ཟླ་ (དགུང་ཟླ་)	*gong-da.*
Contend, to (in war)	དམག་རྒྱབ་པ་	*ma-gyaṕ-pa.*
Do. *hon.*	དམག་སྐྱོན་པ་	*ma-kyöm pa.*
Contented, to be	འདོད་པ་གང་བ་	*dö-pa ḱang-wa.*
Do. *hon.*	ཐུགས་འདོད་གང་བ་	*thung-dö ḱang-wa*

Continent, *s.*	གླིང་	*ling.*
Continually	ནམ་རྒྱུན། དུས་རྒྱུན་	*nam-gyün.; tü-gyün.*
Contract, a large written	གན་རྒྱ་	*ḱam-gya.*
Do. a small written	འཛིན་	*dzin.*
Do. *hon.*	བཀའ་འཛིན། ཕྱག་འཛིན་	*kan-dzin; chha-dzin.*
Do. to let out on	ཕོགས་མ་ལ་བཏང་ (གཏོང་) བ་	*ṕoḱ-ma-la tang-wa.*
Do. *hon.*	ཕོགས་གཏོང་གནང་བ་	*ṕoḱ-tong nang-wa.*
Contractor	ཕོགས་འཛིན་པ་	*ṕoḱ-dzin-pa.*
Contradict, to	རྒྱབ་འགལ་བྱེད་པ་	*gyam-ge cḱe-pa.*
Do. *hon.*	ཐུགས་འགལ་གནང་བ་	*thuk-ge nang-wa.*
Contradictory	རྒྱབ་འགལ་	*gyam-ge.*
Contrite, to be	འགྱོད་པ་སྐྱེད་པ་	*gyö-pa kye-pa.*
Do. *hon.*	ཐུགས་འགྱོད་གནང་བ་	*thung-gyö nang-wa.*
Contrition	འགྱོད་པ་	*gyö-pa.*
Do. *kon.*	ཐུགས་འགྱོད་	*thung-gyö.*
Control	དབང་	*wang.*
Do. *hon.*	སྐུ་དབང་	*ku-wang.*
Control, to	དབང་བྱེད་པ་	*wang-cḱe-pa.*
Do. *hon.*	སྐུ་དབང་གནང་བ་	*ku-wang nang-wa.*
Controversy	རྩོད་པ་	*tsö-pa.*

Convent	ཨ་ནིའི་དགོན་པ་	*a-ni-i göm-pa.*
Conversation	སྐད་ཆ་	*ke-chha.*
Do. *hon.*	གསུང་གྲོས་	*sung-ťrö.*
Converse, to	སྐད་ཆ་བྱེད་པ་	*ke-chha cȟe-pa.*
Do. *hon.*	གསུང་གྲོས་གནང་བ་	*sung-ťrö nang-wa.*
Do. *inf.* to *sup.*	གསུང་གྲོས་ཞུ་བ་	*sung-ťrö sȟu-wa.*
Convex	འབུར་འབུར་	*bur-bur.*
Convey, to	སྐྱེལ་བ་	*kye-wa.*
Do. *hon.*	སྐྱེལ་ར་ (ཟ་) གནང་བ་	*kye-ra nang-wa.*
Convulsions (of baby, etc.)	རྒྱལ་གཟེར་རྒྱབ་པ་	*ge-śer gyap̌-pa.*
Cook	མ་ཆེན་	*ma-chhen.*
Do. to	བཙོས་པ་ (འཚོད་པ་)	*tsö-pa.*
Cookroom	ཐབ་ཚང་	*thap̌-tshang.*
Do. *hon.*	གསོལ་ཐབ་	*sö-thap̌.*
Cool	གྲང་མོ། བསིལ་པོ་	*ťrang-mo ; si-po.*
Do. *hon.*	སྐུ་བསིལ་པོ་	*ku-si-po.*
Cooly (labourer)	ཨར་པོ་བ་	*ar-po.*
Cooly (carrier of load)	དོས་པོ་འཁྱེར་མཁན། མི་ཧྲང་	*ťö-pokhyer-khen ; mi-hrang.*
Copious	མང་པོ། འཕེལ་པོ་	*mang-po ; be-po.*
Copper	ཟངས་	*śang.*

Coppersmith	ཟངས་བཟོ་བ་	*śang-śo-wa.*
Do. *hon.*	དབུ་མཛད་	*um-dze.*
Copulate, to	རྒྱོ་བ་	*gyo-wa.*
Copy	དཔེ་	*pe.*
Do. to	དཔེ་ཤུ་བ་	*pe-shu-wa.*
Do. *hon.*	དཔེ་ཤུ་བ་གནང་བ་	*pe-shu-wa nang-wa.*
Copy, true	ངོ་ཤུས་	*ngo-shü.*
Coral	བྱི་རུ་	*cḱi-ru.*
Do. *hon.*	མགུལ་བྱི་	*gü-cḱi.*
Cord	ཐག་པ་	*thȧḱ-pa.*
Cork (lid)	ཁ་གཅོད་	*khaṕ-chö.*
Do. *hon.*	ཞལ་གཅོད་	*śhe-chö.*
Corn (grain)	འབྲུ་	*dru.*
Do. *hon.*	ཕྱག་འབྲུ་	*chhan-dru.*
Do. parched	ཡོས་	*yö.*
Do. *hon.*	བཞེས་ཡོས་	*śke-yö.*
Corner	ཟུར་	*śur.*
Corporal (in command of 10 men)	བཅུ་དཔོན་	*chu-pön.*
Corpse	རོ་	*ro.*
Do. *hon.*	སྐུ་ཕུང་ (སྐུ་སྤུར་)	*ku-phung.*

Corpulent	རྒྱགས་པ་	*gyaǩ-pa.*
Do. *hon.*	སྐུ་ཤ་འབྱོར་པོ་	*ku-sha jo-po.*
Correct (of words spoken)	སྒྲ་དག་པོ་	*dra-ťaǩ-po.*
Do. (of a thing done)	རྟེན་ལྡན་	*ten-den.*
Do. to (any writing)	ཞུ་དག་བྱེད་པ་	*sǩu-ťa cǩe-pa.*
Do. *hon.*	ཞུ་དག་གནང་བ་	*sǩu--ťa nang-wa.*
Correction	ཞུ་དག་	*sǩu-ťa.*
Correctly (of words spoken)	སྒྲ་དག་པོ་བྱས་ནས་	*dra-ťaǩ-po cǩe-ne.*
Do. (of a thing done)	རྟེན་ལྡན་བྱས་ནས་	*ten-den cǩe-ne.*
Corrupt, to	མེད་པར་བཟོ་བ་	*me-pa śo-wa.*
Do. *hon.*	མེད་པར་བཟོ་བ་གནང་བ་	*me-pa śo-wa nang-wa.*
Cost	གོང་	*ǩong.*
Do. *hon.*	ཕྱགས་གོང་	*ja-ǩong.*
Costly	གོང་ཆེན་པོ་	*ǩong-chhem-po.*
Do. *hon.*	ཕྱགས་གོང་ཆེན་པོ་	*ja-ǩong chhem-po.*
Costume	ཆས་	*chhe.*
Cotton	རས་	*re.*
Cotton-cloth	རས་གོས། རས་ཆ་	*re-ǩö ; re-chha.*
Cotton-thread	རས་སྐུད་	*re-ǩü.*
Do. *hon.*	ཕྱག་སྐུད་	*chha-ǩü.*

Cotton-yarn	སྲིང་	*sing.*
Cotton-wool	སྲིང་བལ་	*trim-ṕe.*
Couch	ཀུབ་ཀྱག། ཁྲིའུ་ཤིང་	*kuṕ-kya; thri-u-shing.*
Do. *hon.*	ཞབས་ཀྱག་	*sḱaṕ-kya.*
Cough, to	གློ་རྒྱབ་པ་	*lo-gyaṕ-pa.*
Do. *hon.*	མགུལ་གློ་སྐྱོན་པ་	*gü-lo kyöm-pa.*
Counsel	གྲོས་	*ťrö.*
Do. *hon.*	བཀའ་གྲོས་	*ka-ťrö.*
Do. to ask	གྲོས་དྲི་ (འདྲི་) བ་	*trö-ťri-wa.*
Do. *hon.*	བཀའ་གྲོས་གནང་བ་	*ka-ťrö nang-wa.*
Council, Head	བཀའ་གཤགས་ལྷན་རྒྱས་	*ka-sha hlen-gye.*
Count, to	གྲངས་ཀ་རྒྱབ་པ་	*ťrang-ka gyaṕ-pa.*
Do. *hon.*	ཕྱགས་གྲངས་སྐྱོན་པ་	*ja-ťrang kyöm-pa.*
Countenance	གདོང་	*dong.*
Do. *hon*	ཞལ་རས་	*sḱe-re.*
Counterfeit, *adj.* (of coin)	མ་ཕིན་	*ma-pin.*
Do. (of other things)	རྫུས་མ་	*dzü-ma.*
Do. to (of coin)	མ་ཕིན་བཏང་ (གཏོང་) བ་	*ma-pin tang-wa.*
Do. (of other things)	རྫུས་མ་བཏང་ (གཏོང་) བ་	*dzü-ma tang-wc.*
Counting	གྲངས་ཀ་	*ťrang-ka.*

Counting, *hon.*	ལྗགས་གྲངས་	*ja-ťrang.*
Country	ལུང་པ་	*lung-pa.*
Do. (native land)	སྐྱེ་ས་	*kye-sa.*
Do. *hon.*	འཁྲུང་ས་	*thrung-sa.*
Country (as opposed to town)	གྲོང་སེབ་	*ťrong-se.*
Country-house	གཞི་ཀ་	*sǩi-ka.*
Couple, *s.* (a pair)	ཆ་	*chha.*
Do. (two)	གཉིས། དོ་	*nyi ; ťo.*
Do. a married	ནང་ཚང་གཉིས་	*nang-tshang-nyi.*
Courageous	སྙིང་ཆེན་པོ། བློ་ཁོག་ཆེན་པོ་	*nying-chhem po ; lo-kho chhem-po.*
Do. *hon.*	ཐུགས་སྙིང་ཆེན་པོ། ཐུགས་ཁོག་ཆེན་པོ་	*thu-nying chhem-po ; thu-kho chhem-po.*
Courier	ཕང་ཆེན་	*ṕang-chhen.*
Do mounted	ཨ་དྲུང་རྟ་བཞོན་	*a-trung tap-sǩön*
Court (of justice)	ཁྲིམས་ཁང་	*thrim-khang.*
Court-yard	སྒོ་ར་	*go-ra.*
Cousin	སྤུན་ཀྱག་	*pün kya.*
Covenant	ཁ་ཏེན། ཁ་ཆད་	*kha-ten ; kha-chhe.*
Do. *hon.*	ཞལ་ཏེན། ཞལ་ཆད་	*sǩe-ten ; sǩe-chhe.*
Cover, *s.* (lid)	ཁ་གཅོད་	*khaṕ-chö.*

Cover, to	བཀབ་པ་ (འགེབས་པ་)	*kaṕ-pa.*
Covering	ཁེབས་	*kheṕ.*
Covet, to	ཧམ་པ་བྱེད་པ་	*ham-pa cḱe-pa.*
Do. *hon.*	ཧམ་པ་གནང་བ་	*ham-pa nang-wa.*
Covetous	ཧམ་པ་ཆེན་པོ་	*ham-pa chhem-po.*
Covetousness	ཧམ་པ་	*ham-pa.*
Cow	བ་	*ṕa.*
Do. (of yak)	འབྲི་	*dri.*
Coward	སེམས་ཆུང་ཆུང་	*sem-chhung-chhung.*
Do. *hon.*	ཐུགས་སེམས་ཆུང་ཆུང་	*thu-sem chhung-chhung.*
Cowherd	འབྲོག་པ་	*droḱ-pa.*
Cowshed	བ་ར་	*ṕa-ra.*
Cowry	འགྲོན་བུ་	*dröm-ṕu.*
Crab	སྡིག་སྲིན་	*diḱ-sing.*
Crack, to, *v.i.*	གས་པ་ (འགས་པ་)	*ḱe-pa.*
Do. *hon.*	གས་ (འགས་) པ་གནང་བ་	*ḱe-pa nang-wa.*
Do. a	སེར་ཀ་	*se-ka.*
Crafty	གཡོ་ཆེན་པོ་	*yo-chhem-po.*
Cramp	རྩ་ཁུམ་པ་	*tsa-khum-pa.*

Crane (bird)	བྱ་ཁྲུང་ཁྲུང་	*cḱa-thrung-thrung.*
Crawl, to	ཁ་བུབ་གོག་པ་	*kha-ṕu ḱok-pa.*
Crazy	སྨྱོན་པ་	*nyöm-pa.*
Cream	སྤྲི་མ་	*tri-ma.*
Do. *hon.*	བཞེས་སྤྲི་	*sḱe-tri.*
Create, to	བཀོད་པ་	*kö-pa.*
Do. *hon.*	བཀོད་པ་གནང་བ་	*kö-pa nang-wa.*
Credible	འོས་པ་	*ö-pa.*
Credit, to	ཡིད་ཆེས་པ་	*yi-chhe-pa.*
Do. *hon.*	ཐུགས་ཡིད་ཆེས་པ་གནང་བ་	*thu-yi chhe pa nang-wa.*
Creditor	བུན་བདག་	*ṕün-da.*
Creed	དད་པ་	*t́e-pa.*
Creek (in a lake)	མཚོ་ལག་	*tsho-la.*
Do. (in a river)	ཆུ་ལག་	*chhu-la.*
Creep, to	ཁ་བུབ་གོག་པ་	*ḱa-ṕu ḱok-pa.*
Crevice	སེར་ཀ་	*se-ka.*
Crime, to commit	ཁྲིམས་འགལ་བ་	*thrim gel-wa.*
Do. *hon.*	བཀའ་ཁྲིམས་འགལ་ར་ (བ་) གནང་བ་	*ka-thrim ge-ra nang-wa.*
Criminal, *adj.*	འཛབ་ཆེན་	*dzaṕ-chhen.*

Crimson	དམར་པོ་	*mar-po.*
Crippled	རྐང་ཀྱོག་	*kang-kyo.*
Do. *hon.*	ཞབས་ཀྱོག་	*sḱaṕ-kyo.*
Crocodile	ཆུ་སྲིན་	*chhu-sin.*
Crooked (with one bend)	གུག་གུག་	*ḱu-ḱu.*
Do. (with several bends)	ཀྱོག་ཀྱོག་	*kyo-kyo.*
Crop (of corn, etc.)	སྟོན་ཐོག་	*tön-tho.*
Cross, to	རྒལ་བ་	*gel-wa.*
Do. *hon.*	བརྒལ་ནས་ཕེབ་པ་	*ge-ne phe-pa.*
Do. *h. hon.*	བརྒལ་ནས་འཆིབ་རྒྱུ་གནང་བ་	*ge-ne chhiṕ-gyu nang-wa.*
Cross, to be	ཚིག་པ་ཟ་བ་	*tshiḱ-pa śa-wa.*
Do. *hon.*	དགོངས་པ་ཚུང་པ་	*gong-pa tshung-wa.*
Cross of wood (on which criminals are bound)	རྒྱངས་ཤིང་	*gyang-shing.*
Cross-legged	སྐྱིལ་ཀྲུམ་ (སྐྱིལ་ཀྲུང་)	*kyi-trum.*
Crow, *s.*	ཁྭ་ཏ་	*kha-ta.*
Do. to (of cock) .	བྱ་སྐད་རྒྱབ་པ་	*cḱa-ke gyaṕ-pa.*
Crowd, *s.*	ཚོགས་	*tshoḱ.*
Crown of the head	སྤྱི་གཙུག་	*chi-tsu.*
Do. *hon.*	དབུ་གཙུག་	*u-tsu.*

Crucify, to	རྒྱངས་ཤིང་ལ་བརྐྱང་ (རྐྱོང་) བ་	*gyang-shing-la. kyang-wa.*
Do. *hon.*	རྒྱངས་ཤིང་ལ་རྐྱོང་ང་ (བ་) གནང་བ་	*gyang shing la kyong-nga nang-wa.*
Cruel, to be	སྙིང་རྗེ་མེད་པ་	*nying-je me-pa.*
Crupper	རྨེད་	*me.*
Crush, to	རྫི་བ་	*dzi-wa.*
Do. *hon.*	རྫི་བ་གནང་བ་	*dzi-wa nang-wa.*
Cry, to (weep)	ངུ་བ་	*ngu-wa.*
Do. *hon.*	ཤུམ་པ་	*shum-pa.*
Crystal	ཤེལ་	*she.*
Cubit	ཁྲུ་	*thru.*
Do. *hon.*	ཕྱག་ཁྲུ་	*chha-thru.*
Cub of fox	ཝ་ཕྲུག་	*wa-thru.*
Do. of bear	དོམ་ཕྲུག་	*t́om-thru.*
Do. of leopard	གཟིག་ཕྲུག་	*śiḱ-thru.*
Do. of tiger	སྟག་ཕྲུག་	*ta-thru.*
Cuckoo	ཁུ་ཡུག་	*khu-yu.*
Culprit	འཛབ་ཆེན་	*dzaṕ-chhen.*
Cultivate, to	ཞིང་ལས་བྱེད་པ་	*sḱing-le cḱe-pa.*
Cultivation	སོ་ནམས་	*so-nam.*

Cultivator	སོ་ནམས་བྱེད་མཁན་	so-nam cḱe-khen.
Cunning	གཅང་པོ་	chang-po.
Do. *hon.*	ཐུགས་གཅང་པོ་	thu-chang-po.
Cup (earthen-ware)	དཀར་ཡོལ་	ka-yö.
Do. *hon.*	ཞལ་དཀར་	sḱe-ka.
Do. (wooden)	ཕོར་པ་	phor-pa.
Do. *hon.*	མཆོད་ཞལ་	chhö-sḱe.
Curds	ཞོ་	sḱo.
Do. *hon.*	གསོལ་ཞོ་	sö-sḱo.
Cure, to	དྲག་པ་བཟོ་བ་	ṫrak-pa ṡo-wa.
Do. *hon.*	དྲག་པ་བཟོ་བ་གནང་བ་	ṫrak-pa ṡo-wa nang-wa.
Do. (patient, of good position)	སྐུ་དྭངས་ང་ (བ་) བཟོ་བ་ གནང་བ་	ku-ṫang-nga ṡo-wa nang wa.
Cured, to be	དྲག་པ་	ṫrak-pa.
Do. *hon.*	སྐུ་དྭངས་པ་	ku-ṫang-pa.
Curious	ཁྱད་མཚར་པོ་	khye-tshar-po.
Curly (of hair)	སུ་ལུ་	su-lu.
Current	ཆུ་རྒྱུན་	chhu-gyün.
Curse, to	དམོད་མོ་རྒྱབ་པ་	mö-mo gyaṕ-pa.
Do. *hon.*	དམོད་མོ་སྐྱོན་པ་	mö-mo kyöm-pa.

Curtail, to	ཉུང་རུ་ (དུ་) བཏང་ (གཏོང་) བ་	*nyung-ru tang-wa.*
Do. *hon.*	ཉུང་རུ་ (དུ་) གཏོང་ང་ (བ་) གནང་བ་	*nyung-ru tong-nga nang-wa.*
Curtain	ཡོལ་ལ་ (ཡོལ་བ་)	*yö-la.*
Do. *hon.*	གཟིམ་ཡོལ་	*śim-yö.*
Curve, to	ཀུག་ཀུག་བྱེད་པ་	*ḱuk-ḱu cḱe-pa.*
Do. *hon.*	ཀུག་ཀུག་གནང་བ་	*ḱuk-ḱu nang-wa.*
Curved	ཀུག་ཀུག་	*ḱuk-ḱu.*
Cushion	གདན་	*den.*
Do. *hon.*	བཞུགས་གདན་	*sḱu-den.*
Cushion (small, placed on chair)	ཁ་གདན་	*kha-den.*
Do. (large, placed on ground)	འབོལ་གདན་	*bö-den.*
Custody (care)	རྩིས་	*tsi.*
Custom (manner)	ལུགས་སྲོལ་	*luḱ-sö.*
Customs (duty)	ཤོ་ཁྲལ་	*sho-thre.*
Cut, *s.* (blow with whip, etc.)	ལྕག་	*cha.*
Do. (wound)	རྨ་	*ma.*
Cut, to	བཅད་པ་ (གཅོད་པ་)	*che-pa*
Do. *hon.*	བཅད་ (གཅོད་) པ་གནང་བ་	*che-pa nang-wa.*
Cut, to (by chopping)	བཙབ་པ་	*tsaṕ-pa.*

Cut, to *hon.* (by chopping)	བཙབ་པ་གནང་བ་	*tsaṕ-pa nang wa.*
Cutch	སྤོད་ཛ་	*tö-cḱa.*
Cycle (of 12 years)	ལོ་འཁོར་	*lo-khor.*
Do. (of 60 years)	རབ་བྱུང་	*rab-cḱung.*
Cyclone	རླུང་ཚུབ་	*lung-tshuṕ.*
Cylinder	འཁོར་ལོ་	*khor-lo.*
Do. (praying)	མ་ཎི་	*ma-ni.*
Cymbal	རོལ་མོ་	*rö-mo.*
Cypress	ཤུག་པ་	*shuḱ-pa.*

D

Dacoit	ཇག་པ་	*cḱak-pa.*
Dagger	ཨམ་གྲི། མགར་ཟྲོར་	*am-t́ri ; ga-śo.*
Do. *hon.*	ཕྱག་ཤན་	*chha-shen.*
Daily	ཉི་མ་རྟག་པ་རེ་བཞིན་	*nyi-ma taḱ-pa ri-sḱi.*
Dainty	ཡག་པོ་	*yaḱ-po.*
Dairy-farm	འབྲོག་ས་	*droḱ sa.*
Dalai Lama	སྐྱབས་མགོན་རིན་པོ་ཆེ། རྒྱལ་བ་རིན་པོ་ཆེ་	*kyam-gön rim-po-chhe.; gya-wa rim-po chhe.*
Dale	ལུངས་	*lung.*
Dam, *s.* (for water)	ཆུ་རགས་	*chhu-ra.*
Damage	སྐྱོན་	*kyön.*
Do. to	སྐྱོན་བྱེད་པ་	*kyön-cḱe-pa.*
Damp	རློན་པ་	*löm-pa.*
Damsel	བུ་མོ་	*ṕu-mo.*
Do. *hon.*	སྲས་མོ་	*se-mo* or *tre-mo.*
Dance, ordinary	ཞབས་བྲོ་	*sḱaṕ-ro.*
Do. with dramatic entertainment	འཁྲབ་པ་	*thraṕ-pa.*
Do. religious, performed by monks	འཆམ་	*chham.*

Dance, to	ཞབས་བྲོ་རྒྱབ་པ་	*sḱaṕ-ro gyaṕ-pa.*
Do. *hon.*	ཞབས་བཞེས་གནང་བ་	*sḱaṕ-sḱe nang-wa.*
Dandy (sedan-chair)	འཁྱོགས་དཔྱང་	*gyo-chang.*
Do. *hon.*	ཕེབ་དཔྱང་	*phe-chang.*
Danger	ཉེན་	*nyen.*
Dangerous	ཉེན་ཀ་ཆེན་པོ་	*nyen-ka chhem-po.*
Dare, to	ནུས་པ་	*nü-pa.*
Do. *hon.*	ནུས་པ་གནང་བ་	*nü-pa nang-wa.*
Daring	སྙིང་ཆེན་པོ་	*nying-chhem-po.*
Do. *hon.*	ཐུགས་སྙིང་ཆེན་པོ་	*thu nying chhem-po.*
Dark	ནག་པོ་	*naḱ-po.*
Do. to become (from clouds)	འཐིབས་པ་	*thiṕ-pa.*
Darkness (of night)	མུན་ནག་	*min-na.*
Darling (favourite)	སྙིང་སྡུག་	*nying-du.*
Darn, to	གྲོག་ (སྒྲོག་) དུག་རྒྱབ་པ་	*t́ro-t́uḱ gyaṕ-pa.*
Do. *hon.*	གྲོག་ (སྒྲོག་) དུག་སྐྱོན་པ་	*t́ro-t́uḱ kyöm-pa.*
Dart	མདའ་	*da.*
Do. *hon.*	ཕྱག་མདའ་	*chhan-da.*
Date	ཚེས་པ་	*tshe-pa.*
Daub, to	སྐུ་བ་	*ku-wa.*

Daub, to *hon.*	སྐུ་བ་གནང་བ་	*ku-wa nang-wa.*
Daughter	བུ་མོ་	*ṕu-mo.*
Do. *hon.*	སྲས་མོ་	*se-mo.*
Daughter-in-law	མནའ་མ་	*na-ma.*
Dawn, *s.*	ནམ་ལངས་	*nam-lang.*
Do. to	ཤར་མདའ་བཏང་ (གཏོང་) བ་	*shan-da tang-wa.*
Day (as opposed to night)	ཉི་མ་	*nyi-ma.*
Do. (of twenty-four hours)	ཞག་པོ་	*sꝁak-po.*
Do. *hon.*	བཞུགས་ཞག	*sꝁu-sꝁa.*
Do. (all the day long)	ཉིན་གང་	*nyin-ꝁang.*
Day, each	ཉི་མ་རེ་རེ་	*nyi-ma re-re.*
Do. every	ཉི་མ་རྟག་པ་རེ་བཞིན་	*nyi-ma tak-pa ri-ꝁi.*
Day-break	ནམ་ལངས་	*nam-lang.*
Day after to-morrow	ནངས་	*nang.*
Day before yesterday	ཁའི་ཉི་མ་	*khe-nyi-ma.*
Do. last of a month	གནམ་གང་	*nam-ꝁang.*
Dazzling	འོད་ཆེམ་ཆེམ་	*ö-chhem-chhem.*
Dead man (corpse)	རོ་	*ro.*
Do. *hon.*	སྐུ་ཕུང་	*ku-phung.*
Dead, *adj.* (deceased)	ཤི་མཁན་	*shi-khen.*

Dead, *adj.* (deceased) *hon.*	གྲོངས་མཁན་	*ťrong-khen.*
Do. *h. hon.*	དམ་པ་	*ťam-pa.*
Dead, is	ཤི་སོང་	*shi-song.*
Do. *hon.*	གྲོངས་སོང་	*ťrong-song.*
Do. *h. hon.*	གཤགས་སོང་ (གཤེགས་སོང་)	*sha-song.*
Deaf	འོན་པ་	*öm-pa.*
Deal, a great (large quantity)	ཛག་ཏོ་	*dzaǩ-ťo.*
Dealer	ཚོང་པ་	*tshong-pa.*
Do. *hon.*	ཚོང་དཔོན་ལགས་	*tshong-pön-la.*
Dear (expensive)	གོང་ཆེན་པོ། གུས་པོ་	*ǩong-chhem-po ; ǩü-po.*
Do. *hon.*	ལྗགས་གོང་ཆེན་པོ་	*ja-ǩong chhem-po.*
Dear (beloved)	གཅེས་པོ་	*che-po.*
Debar, to	བཀག་པ་ (འགེགས་པ་)	*ǩaǩ-pa.*
Do. *hon.*	བཀག་ག་ (འགེགས་པ་) གནང་བ་	*ǩaǩ-ǩa nang-wa.*
Debate, to	རྩོད་པ་རྒྱབ་པ་	*tsö-pa gyap̌-pa.*
Do. *hon.*	ཐུགས་རྩོད་སྐྱོན་པ་	*thuǩ-tsö kyöm-pa.*
Debt	བུ་ལོན་	*p̌u-lön.*
Do. *hon.*	ཕྱག་བུན་	*chha-p̌ün.*
Debtor	བུ་ལོན་ལེན་མཁན་	*p̌u-lön len-khen.*

Debtor, *hon.*	ཕྱག་བུན་བཞེས་མཁན་	*chha-p̓un sḱe-khen.*
Decapitate, to	སྐེ་བཅད་ (གཅོད་) པ་	*ke-che-pa.*
Do. (person of high position)	མགུལ་བཅད་ (གཅོད་) པ་	*gü-che-pa.*
Decay, to	རུལ་བ་	*rül-wa.*
Deceased, the	ཤི་མཁན་	*shi-khen.*
Do. *hon.*	གྲོངས་མཁན་	*ťrong-khen.*
Do. *h. hon.*	དམ་པ་	*ťam-pa.*
Deceit	མགོ་སྐོར་	*go-kor.*
Do. *hon.*	དབུ་སྐོར་	*u-kor.*
Deceitful	གཡོ་ཅན། བློ་སྐྱོགས་སྐྱོགས་	*yo-chen ; lo kyoḱ-kyoḱ.*
Do. *hon.*	ཐུགས་གཡོ་ཅན། ཐུགས་སྐྱོགས་སྐྱོགས་	*thu yo-chen ; thu kyoḱ-kyoḱ.*
Deceive, to	མགོ་སྐོར་བཏང་ (གཏོང་) བ་	*go-kor tang-wa.*
Do. *hon.*	མགོ་སྐོར་གཏོང་ང་ (བ་) གནང་བ་	*go-kor tong-nga. nang-wa.*
Do. *inf.* to *sup.*	དབུ་སྐོར་ཞུ་བ་	*u-kor sḱu-wa*
Deceiver	མགོ་སྐོར་གཏོང་མཁན་	*go-kor tong-khen.*
Decent (becoming)	འོས་པོ་	*ö-po.*
Deception	གཡོ་སྒྱུ་	*yo-gyu.*
Decide, to (judge)	ཐག་བཅད་ (གཅོད་) པ་	*tha-che-pa.*

Decide, to (judge) *hon.*	ཐག་གཅོད་པ་གནང་བ་	*tha-chö-pa nang-wa.*
Do. *h. hon.*	ཐུགས་ཐག་གཅོད་པ་གནང་བ་	*thu-tha chö-pa nang-wa.*
Decidedly	ཐག་ཆོད་	*thak-chhö.*
Declare, to	བཤད་པ་ (འཆད་པ་)	*she-pa.*
Do. *hon.*	གསུང་བ་	*sung-wa.*
Declivity	ཐུར་	*thur.*
Decorate, to	རྒྱན་ཆ་བཏགས་ (འདོགས་) པ་	*gyen-chha tak-pa.*
Do. *hon.*	སྐུ་རྒྱན་བཏགས་ཀ་ (འདོགས་པ་) གནང་བ་	*ku-gyen tak-ka nang-wa.*
Decoration	རྒྱན་ཆ་	*gyen-chha.*
Do. *hon.*	སྐུ་རྒྱན་	*ku-gyen.*
Decrease, to (in numbers)	ཉུང་རུ་ (དུ་) ཕྱིན་པ་	*nyung-ru chhim-pa.*
Do. to (in size)	ཆུང་རུ་ (དུ་) ཕྱིན་པ་	*chhung-ru chhim-pa.*
Do. *hon.*	ཆུང་རུ་ (དུ་) ཕེབ་པ་	*chhung-ru-phe-pa.*
Decree (of court of justice)	བཀའ་ཁྲིམས་	*ka-thrim.*
Do. (of secular authority)	བཀའ་ཤོག་	*ka-sho.*
Do. (religious)	ཆོས་ཁྲིམས་	*chhö-thrim.*
Decrepit	འཁོགས་པ་	*khok-pa.*
Dedicate, to	རབ་གནས་བྱེད་པ་	*ram-ne che-pa.*
Do. *hon.*	རབ་གནས་གནང་བ་	*ram-ne nang-wa.*

Dedication	རབ་གནས་	*ram-ne.*
Deduct, to	འཐེན་པ་	*them-pa.*
Do. *hon.*	འཐེན་པ་གནང་བ་	*them-pa nang-wa.*
Deed	ལས་ཀ་	*le-ka.*
Do. *hon.*	ཕྱག་ལས་	*chha-le.*
Deep	གཏིང་རིང་པོ་	*ting-ring-po.*
Deer	ཤ་ (ཤ་བ་)	*sha.*
Do. male	ཤ་ཕོ་	*sha-pho.*
Do. female	ཤ་མོ་	*sha-mo.*
Do. young	ཤ་ཕྲུག་	*sha-thru.*
Deface, to	སུབ་པ་	*suṕ-pa.*
Do. *hon.*	སུབ་པ་གནང་བ་	*suṕ-pa nang-wa.*
Defamation	སྨད་ར་	*me-ra.*
Defame, to	སྨད་ར་བཏང་ (གཏོང་) བ་	*me-ra tang-wa.*
Do. *hon.*	སྨད་ར་གཏོང་ང་ (བ་) གནང་བ་	*me-ra tong-nga nang-wa.*
Defeat, to	རྒྱལ་བ་	*gye-wa.*
Do. *hon.*	རྒྱལ་ར་ (བ་) གནང་བ	*gye-ra nang-wa.*
Defeated, to be	འཕམ་པ་	*pham-pa.*
Do. *hon.*	འཕམ་པ་གནང་བ་	*pham-pa nang-wa.*
Defect	སྐྱོན་	*kyön.*

Defective	སྐྱོན་ཆེན་པོ་	*kyön-chhem-po.*
Defend, to	བསྐྱབས་པ་ (སྐྱོབ་པ།) སྐྱོང་བ་	*kyaṕ-pa; kyong-wa.*
Do. *hon.*	སྐྱབས་འཇུག་གནང་བ་	*kyam-juḱ nang-wa.*
Defendant	ཞུ་གདུག་བྱེད་པའི་ཁ་ཐེག་	*sḱu-tuḱ cḱe-pe khaṕ-the.*
Defer, to	པ་རུ་བཞག་ (འཛོག་) པ་	*pa-ru sḱak-pa.*
Do. *hon.*	པ་རུ་གཞོག་ག་གནང་བ་	*pa-ru sḱoḱ-ḱa nang-wa.*
Deficient	ཆད་པ་	*chhe pa.*
Defile, to	བཙོག་པ་བཟོ་བ་	*tsoḱ-pa śo-wa.*
Do. *hon.*	བཙོག་པ་བཟོ་བ་གནང་བ་	*tsoḱ-pa śo-wa nang-wa.*
Defilement	གྲིབ་	*t́riṕ.*
Define, to	དོན་དག་བཤད་ (འཆད་) པ་	*t́ön-t́a she-pa.*
Do. *hon.*	སྐུ་དོན་གསུང་བ་	*ku-t́ön sung-wa.*
Definite (certain)	ངེས་པ། ཏེན་ཏེན་	*nge-pa; ten-ten.*
Do. *hon.*	ཐུགས་ངེས་པ་	*thu-nge-pa.*
Definitely	ཏེན་ཏེན་བྱས་ནས་	*ten-ten cḱe-ne.*
Deformed, to be	དབང་པོ་མ་ཚང་བ་	*wang-po ma-tshang-wa.*
Defraud, to	མགོ་སྐོར་བཏང་ (གཏོང་) བ་	*go-kor tang-wa.*
Do. *hon.*	མགོ་སྐོར་གཏོང་ང་ (བ་) གནང་བ་	*go-kor tong-nga nang-wa.*
Degenerate, to	ཉམས་པ་	*nyam-pa.*

Degenerate, to *hon.*	ཐུགས་ཉམས་པ་	*thu-nyam-pa.*
Degrade, to	གོ་གནས་བབ་པ་	*k̓o-ne p̓ap-pa.*
Degree (series)	རིམ་པ་	*rim-pa.*
Do. (rank)	གོ་གནས་། གོ་ས་	*k̓o-ne ; k̓o-sa.*
Degrees, by	རིམ་བཞིན་	*rim-sK̓in.*
Dejected, to be	མི་...དགའ་བ་	*mi...ga-wa.*
Do. *hon.*	མཉེས་པོ་མི་...གནང་བ་	*nye-po mi... nang-wa.*
Do. *h. hon.*	ཐུགས་དགྱེས་པོ་མི་...གནང་བ་	*thu-gye-po mi ...nang-wa.*
Deity	ལྷ་	*hla.*
Delay	འགོར་པོ་	*gor-po.*
Delay, without	འགོར་པོ་མ་བྱེད་པར་	*gor-po ma-cK̓e-par.*
Do. *hon.*	ཐུགས་འགོར་མེད་པ་	*thung-gor me-pa.*
Delay, to	འགོར་པོ་བྱེད་པ་	*gor-po cK̓e-pa.*
Do. *hon.*	ཐུགས་འགོར་གནང་བ་	*thung-gor nang-wa.*
Delegate	ཚབ་	*tshap̓.*
Do. *hon.*	སྐུ་ཚབ་	*ku-tshap̓.*
Delegate, to	ངོ་ཚབ་བཏང་ (གཏོང་) བ་	*ngo-tshap̓ tang-wa.*
Do. *hon.*	སྐུ་ཚབ་གཏོང་ང་ (བ་) གནང་བ་	*ku-tshap̓ tong-nga nang-wa.*
Deliberate, to	གྲོས་བྱེད་པ་	*t̓rö-cK̓e-pa.*
Do. *hon.*	བཀའ་གྲོས་གནང་བ་	*ka-t̓rö nang-wa.*

Delicate (weak), to be	ཐང་པོ་མེད་པ་	*thang-po me-pa.*
Delicious	ཞིམ་ཐག་ཆོད་	*sḱim-thaḱ-chhö.*
Do. *hon.*	སྦྲོ་ཐག་ཆོད་	*trö-thaḱ-chhö.*
Delight	དགའ་ཚོར་	*ga-tshor.*
Do. *hon.*	མཉེས་ཚོར་	*nye-tshor.*
Delight in, to take	དགའ་བ་	*ga-wa.*
Do. *hon.*	མཉེས་པོ་གནང་བ་	*nye-po nang-wa.*
Do. *h. hon.*	ཐུགས་དགྱེས་པོ་གནང་བ་	*thu-gye-po nang-wa.*
Deliver, to (rescue)	བསྐྱབས་པ་ (སྐྱོབ་པ།) སྐྱོང་བ་	*kyap̄-pa; kyong-wa.*
Do. *hon.*	སྐྱབས་འཇུག་གནང་བ་	*kyam-juḱ nang wa.*
Deliver, to (give)	སྤྲད་པ་	*tre-pa.*
Do. *hon.*	གནང་བ་	*nang-wa.*
Deliverance	ཐར་པ་	*thar pa.*
Delude, to	མགོ་སྐོར་བཏང་ (གཏོང་) བ་	*go-kor tang-wa.*
Do. *hon.*	མགོ་སྐོར་གཏོང་ང་(བ་)གནང་བ་	*go-kor tong-nga nang-wa.*
Do. *inf.* to *sup.*	དབུ་སྐོར་ཞུ་བ་	*u-kor sḱu-wa.*
Deluge (flood)	ཆུ་རུད་	*chhu-rü.*
Demand, to	དགོ་ (དགོས་) ཟེར་བ་	*go-śer-wa.*
Do. *hon.*	དགོ་ (དགོས) གསུང་བ་	*go-sung-wa.*

Demeanour	བྱེད་སྟངས་	*cke-tang.*
Do. *hon.*	གསུང་སྟངས་	*nang-tang.*
Demented	སྨྱོན་པ་	*nyöm-pa.*
Demi-god	ལྷ་མ་ཡིན་	*lha-ma-yin.*
Demolish, to	བཤིག་པ་ (འཇིག་པ་)	*shik-pa.*
Do. *hon.*	བཤིག་ག་ (འཇིག་པ་) གནང་བ་	*shik-ka nang-wa.*
Demon	གདོང་འདྲེ། བདུད་	*dong-dre; dü.*
Den	ཚང་	*tshang.*
Denomination	ཆོས་ལུགས་	*chhö-lu.*
Dense	འཐུག་པོ་	*thuk-po.*
Deny, to	ཁྱབ་འགལ་བྱེད་པ་	*gyam-ge cke-pa.*
Do. *hon.*	ཁྱབ་འགལ་གནང་བ་	*gyam-ge nang-wa.*
Depart, to	འཐོན་པ། ཕྱིན་པ་	*thöm-pa; chhim-pa.*
Do. *hon.*	ཕེབ་པ་	*phe-pa.*
Do. *h. hon.*	འཆིབ་རྒྱུ་གནང་བ་	*chhip-gyu nang-wa.*
Departed (deceased)	ཤི་མཁན་	*shi-khen.*
Do. *hon.*	གྲོངས་མཁན་	*trong-khen.*
Do. *h. hon.*	དམ་པ་	*tam-pa.*
Depend upon, to	བློས་ (བློ་) བཀལ་བ་	*lö-kel-wa.*

Depend upon, to *hon.*	ཐུགས་བློ་བཀལ་ར་ (བ་) གནང་བ་	*thu-lo ḱe-ra nang-wa.*
Deportment	བྱེད་སྟངས་	*cḱe-tang.*
Do. *hon.*	གནང་སྟངས་	*nang-tang.*
Deposit, to	བཞག་པ་ (འཇོག་པ་)	*sḱaḱ-pa.*
Do. *hon.*	གཞོག་ག་ (འཇོག་པ་) གནང་བ་	*sḱoḱ-ḱa nang-wa.*
Depositary	མཛོད་	*dzö.*
Depraved, *adj.*	སྡུག་རྩུལ་	*duḱ-rü.*
Deprive, to	འཕྲོག་པ་	*throḱ-pa.*
Do. *hon.*	འཕྲོག་ག་ (པ་) གནང་བ་	*throḱ-ḱa nang wa.*
Depth	གཏིང་རིང་ཐུང་	*ting-ring-thung.*
Depute, to (send)	ཚབ་བཏང་ (གཏོང་) བ་	*tshaṕ-tang-wa.*
Do. *hon.*	སྐུ་ཚབ་གཏོང་ང་ (བ་) གནང་བ་	*ku-tshaṕ tong-nga nang-wa.*
Deputy	ཚབ་	*tshaṕ.*
Do. *hon.*	སྐུ་ཚབ་	*ku-tśhaṕ.*
Derangement	སྐྱོན་	*kyön.*
Descend, to	བབ་ (འབབ་) ཡོང་བ་ (or འགྲོ་བ་)	*ṕaṕ-yong-wa* (or *dro-wa*).
Do. *hon.*	བབ་ (འབབ་) ཕེབ་པ་	*ṕaṕ-phe-pa.*

Descend, to *h. hon.*	བབ་ (འབབ་) འཆིབ་རྒྱུ་ གནང་བ་	*p̓ap-chhip̓-gyu nang-wa.*
Descendants	རིགས་བརྒྱུད། མི་བརྒྱུད་	*ri-gyü ; mi-gyü.*
Do. *hon.* (of laymen)	སྐུ་བརྒྱུད་	*ku-gyü.*
Do. *hon.* (of lamas)	གདུང་བརྒྱུད་	*dung-gyü.*
Descent	ཐུར་	*thur.*
Describe, to	བཤད་པ་ (འཆད་པ་)	*she-pa.*
Do. *hon.*	གསུང་བ་	*sung-wa.*
Desert, *s.*	བྱེ་ཐང་	*cKe-thang.*
Do. to	སྤང་བ་	*pang-wa.*
Do. *hon.*	སྤོང་ང་ (བ) གནང་བ་	*pong-nga nang-wa.*
Deserve, to	འོས་པ་	*ö-pa.*
Design (sketch)	རི་མོ་	*ri-mo.*
Do. (pattern)	དཔེ་	*pe.*
Do. to (sketch, &c.)	རི་མོ་བྲིས་པ་ (འབྲི་བ་)	*ri-mo t́ri-pa.*
Do. *hon.*	རི་མོ་བྲིས་པ་ (འབྲི་བ་) གནང་བ་	*ri-mo t́ri-pa nang-wa.*
Design, to (copy)	དཔེ་བྲིས་པ་ (འབྲི་བ་)	*pe t́ri-pa.*
Do. *hon.*	དཔེ་བྲིས་པ་ (འབྲི་བ་) གནང་བ་	*pe t́ri-pa nang-wa.*
Desire, *s.*	འདོད་པ་	*dö-pa.*
Do. *hon.*	ཐུགས་འདོད་	*thung-dö.*

Desire, to	འདོད་པ་བྱེད་པ་	*dö-pa cKe-pa.*
Do. *hon.*	ཐུགས་འདོད་གནང་བ་	*thung-dö nang-wa.*
Desist, to	སྤང་བ་	*pang-wa.*
Do. *hon.*	སྤོང་ང་ (བ) གནང་བ་	*pong-nga nang-wa.*
Despair, to	ཡིད་མུག་པོ་བྱེད་པ་	*yi-muk-po cKe-pa.*
Despatch, to	བཏང་བ་ (གཏོང་བ་)	*tang-wa.*
Do. *hon.*	གཏོང་ང་ (བ་) གནང་བ་	*tong-nga nang-wa.*
Desperate, to be (hopeless)	བློ་ (ཁོ་) ཐག་བཅད་ (གཅོད་) པ་	*lo-tha che-pa.*
Despise, to	དམའ་འབེབས་བྱེད་པ་	*ma-bep̂ cKe-pa.*
Do. *hon.*	དམའ་འབེབས་གནང་བ་	*ma-bep̂ nang-wa*
Do. *inf.* to *sup.*	དམའ་འབེབས་ཞུ་བ་	*ma-bep̂ sKu-wa.*
Despondent, to be	སེམས་སྐྱོ་བ་	*sem-kyo-wa.*
Do. *hon.*	ཐུགས་སེམས་སྐྱོ་བ་གནང་བ་	*thu-sem kyo-wa nang-wa.*
Destiny (fate)	བསོ་བདེ་ (བསོད་བདེ་)	*so-de.*
Do. *hon.*	སྐུ་བསོད་	*ku-sö.*
Destitute	གང་ཡང་མེད་པ་	*Kang-yang me-pa.*
Destroy, to	མེད་པ་ (པར་) བཟོ་བ་	*me-pa śo-wa.*
Do. *hon.*	མེད་པ་ (པར་) བཟོ་བ་གནང་བ་	*me-pa śo-wa nang-wa.*
Detail, in	ཞིབ་པ་	*sKip̂-pa.*

Detailed account	ཐོ་	*tho.*
Do. *hon.*	ཕྱག་ཐོ་	*chha-tho.*
Detain, to	བཀག་པ་ (འགེགས་པ་)	*kaḱ-pa.*
Do. *hon.*	བཀག་ག་ (པ་) གནང་བ་	*kaḱ-ka nang-wa.*
Determine, to	ཐག་བཅད་ (གཅོད་) པ་	*tha-che-pa.*
Do. *hon.*	ཐག་གཅོད་པ་གནང་བ་	*tha-chö pa nang-wa.*
Do. *h. hon.*	ཐུགས་ཐག་གཅོད་པ་གནང་བ་	*thu-tha chö-pa nang-wa.*
Detest, to	དགྲ་བྱེད་པ་	*dra-cḱe-pa.*
Do. *hon.*	དགྲ་གནང་བ་	*dra nang-wa.*
Device	ཇུས་	*chü.*
Do. *hon.*	སྐུ་ཇུས་	*ku-cḱü.*
Devil	གདོང་འདྲེ། བདུད་	*dong-dre ; dü.*
Devotee (hermit)	མཚམས་པ། སྒོམ་ཆེན་	*tsham-pa ; gom-chhen.*
Devotion (faith)	དད་པ་	*t́e-pa.*
Devour, to	ཧ་ཕེ་ཧོ་ཕེ་ (ཧབ་ཧོབ་) ཟ་བ་	*ha-phe ho-phe śa-wa.*
Do. *hon.*	ཧ་ཕེ་ཧོ་ཕེ་ (ཧབ་ཧོབ་) བཞེས་པ་	*ha-phe ho-phe sḱe-pa.*
Devout	ཆོས་སེམས་ཆེན་པོ་	*chhö-sem chhem-po.*
Dew	ཟིལ་པ་	*śi-pa.*
Dexterous	གཅང་པོ་	*chang-po.*
Do. *hon.*	ཐུགས་གཅང་པོ་	*thu-chang-po.*

Diadem	ཅོད་པན་	*chö-pen.*
Dialect	སྐད་ལུགས་	*ke-lu.*
Diamond	རྡོ་རྗེ་ཕ་ལམ་	*do-je pha-lam.*
Diarrhœa	བཤལ་ནད་	*she-ne.*
Do. to have	འགྲིམ་པ། བཤལ་བ་	*drim-pa ; she-wa.*
Do. *hon.*	འགྲིམ་པ་གནང་བ། བཤལ་ར་ (བ་) གནང་བ་	*drim-pa nang-wa ; she-ra nang wa.*
Dice, to play at	ཤོ་རྒྱབ་པ་	*sho-gyaṕ-pa.*
Do. *hon.*	ཕྱག་ཤོ་སྐྱོན་པ་	*chha-sho kyöm-pa.*
Dictionary	ཚིག་མཛོད་	*tshiḱ-dzö.*
Die, Dice, *s.*	ཤོ་	*sho.*
Do. *hon.*	ཕྱག་ཤོ་	*chha-sho.*
Die, to	ཤི་བ་	*shi-wa.*
Do. *hon.*	གྲོངས་པ་ (འགྲོང་བ་)	*t́rong-pa.*
Do. *h. hon.*	གཤགས་པ་ (གཤེགས་པ་)	*shaḱ-pa.*
Die, to (of great Lama)	སྐུ་ཞིང་ལ་ཕེབ་པ་	*ku-sḱing-la phe-pa.*
Diet	ཁ་ལག། ལྟོ་ཆས་	*kha-la ; toṕ-chhe.*
Do. *hon.*	ཞལ་ལག་	*sḱe-la.*
Differ, to	ཁྱད་ཡོད་པ་	*khye yö-pa.*
Do. *hon.*	ཐུགས་ཁྱད་ཡོད་པ་	*thu-khye yö-pa.*

Difference	ཁྱད། ཧེ་བག་	khye ; he-ᵽa.
Do. *hon.*	ཐུགས་ཁྱད་	thu-khye.
Different	མི་གཅིག་པ་	mi-chiꝁ-pa.
Difficult	དཀའ་ལས་ཁག་པོ་	ka-le khaꝁ-po.
Do. *hon.*	སྐུ་མཉེལ་པོ་	ku-nye-po.
Dig, to	རྐོ་བ་	ko-wa.
Do. *hon.*	རྐོ་བ་གནང་བ་	ko-wa nang-wa.
Digest, to	འཇུ་བ་	ju-wa.
Do. *hon.*	འཇུ་བ་གནང་བ་	ju-wa nang-wa.
Dignity	གོ་ས། གོ་གནས་	ꝁo-sa ; ꝁo-ne.
Dilate, to	ཁ་ཕྱེ་བ་	kha-chhe wa.
Dilatory	ཉ་སི་དགུ་སི་	nya-si gu-si.
Diligence	སྙིང་རུས་	nying-rü.
Do. *hon.*	ཐུགས་རུས་	thuꝁ-rü.
Diligence, to use	སྙིང་རུས་བྱེད་པ་	nying-rü cħe-pa.
Do. *hon.*	ཐུགས་རུས་གནང་བ་	thuꝁ-rü nang-wa.
Diligent	སྙིང་རུས་ཆེན་པོ་	nying-rü chhem-po.
Do. *hon.*	ཐུགས་རུས་ཆེན་པོ་	thuꝁ-rü chhem-po.
Diligently	སྙིང་རུས་བྱས་ནས་	nying-rü cħe-ne.
Do. *hon.*	ཐུགས་རུས་གནང་ནས་	thuꝁ-rü nang-ne.

Dim	སྲབ་སྲིབ་	*hrap-hrip.*
Dimension	ཆེ་ཆུང་	*chhe-chhung.*
Diminish, to (in number)	ཉུང་རུ་ (དུ་) འགྲོ་བ་	*nyung-ru dro-wa.*
Do. to (in size)	ཆུང་རུ་ (དུ་) འགྲོ་བ་	*chhung-ru dro-wa.*
Do. *hon.*	ཆུང་རུ་ (དུ་) ཕེབ་པ་	*chhung-ru phe-pa.*
Dinner (in evening)	དགོང་མོའི་ཁ་ལག་	*gong-mö kha-la.*
Do. *hon.*	དགོང་མོའི་ཞལ་ལག་	*gong-mö sKe-la.*
Dip, to (into water, &c.)	བཙུག་པ་ (འཛུག་པ་)	*chuk-pa.*
Do. *hon.*	བཙུག་ག་ (པ་) གནང་བ་	*chuk-ka nang-wa.*
Diploma	བཀའ་ཤོག་	*ka-sho.*
Direction	ཕྱོགས་	*chho.*
Directly	ལམ་སང་	*lam sang.*
Dirt	བཙོག་པ་	*tsok-pa.*
Do. *hon.*	སྐུ་བཙོག་	*ku-tso.*
Dirt (mud)	རྫབ་	*dzap.*
Dirty	བཙོག་པ་	*tsok-pa.*
Do. to make	བཙོག་པ་བྱེད་པ་	*tsok-pa cKe-pa.*
Do. *hon.*	སྐུ་བཙོག་གནང་བ་	*ku-tso nang-wa.*
Dirty, to become	བཙོག་པ་ཤོར་བ་	*tsok-pa shor-wa.*
Do. *hon.*	སྐུ་བཙོག་ཤོར་བ་	*ku-tso shor-wa.*

Disadvantageous, to be	ཕན་ཐོགས་མེད་པ་	*phen-tho me-pa.*
Do. *hon.*	ཐུགས་ཕན་མི་གསོ་བ་	*thu-phen mi so-wa.*
Disagree, to	མི་མཐུན་པ་	*mi thüm-pa.*
Do. *hon.*	མཐུན་པ་མི་གནང་བ་	*thüm-pa mi nang-wa.*
Disappear, to	ཡལ་བ་	*ye-wa.*
Disbelieve, to	ཡིད་མི་ཆེས་པ་	*yi mi chhe-pa.*
Do. *hon.*	ཐུགས་ཡིད་མི་ཆེས་པ་གནང་བ་	*thu-yi mi chhe-pa nang-wa.*
Disc	འཁོར་ལོ་	*khor-lo.*
Discharge, to (dismiss)	དགོངས་པ་སྟེར་བ་	*gong-pa ter-wa.*
Do. *hon.*	དགོངས་པ་གནང་བ་	*gong-pa nang-wa.*
Discharge, to (fire off)	རྒྱབ་པ་	*gyap-pa.*
Do. *hon.*	སྐྱོན་པ་	*kyöm-pa.*
Discharge to (free)	བཏང་བ་ (གཏོང་བ་)	*tang-wa.*
Do. *hon.*	གཏོང་ང་ (བ་) གནང་བ་	*tong-nga nang-wa.*
Disciple	ཉེ་གནས་	*nye-ne.*
Discipline	སྒྲིག་ལམ་	*drik-lam.*
Discontented, to be	འདོད་པ་མི་ཁང་བ་ (འཁངས་པ་)	*dö-pa mi khang-wa.*
Do. *hon.*	ཐུགས་འདོད་མི་ཁང་བ་ (འཁངས་པ་)	*thung-dö mi khang-wa.*

Discourse	སྐད་ཆ་	*ke-chha.*
Do. *hon.*	གསུང་གྲོས་	*sung-t́rö.*
Discourse, to	སྐད་ཆ་བྱེད་པ་	*ke-chha cḱe-pa.*
Do. *hon.*	གསུང་གྲོས་གནང་བ་	*sung-t́rö nang-wa.*
Discover, to (see)	མཐོང་བ་	*thong-wa.*
Do. *hon.*	གཟིགས་པ་	*śi-pa.*
Discreet (in speech)	ཁ་བཙན་པོ་	*kha tsem-po.*
Do. *hon.*	ཞལ་བཙན་པོ་	*sḱe tsem-po.*
Discuss, to	རྩོད་པ་རྒྱབ་པ་	*tsö-pa gyaṕ-pa.*
Do. *hon.*	རྩོད་པ་སྐྱོན་པ་	*tsö-pa kyöm-pa.*
Disease	ན་ཚ་	*na-tsha.*
Do. *hon.*	སྙུང་གཞི་	*nyung-sḱi.*
Disgrace	ཞབས་འདྲེན་	*sḱam-dren.*
Disgraced, to be	ཞབས་འདྲེན་ཞུ་བ་	*sḱam-dren sḱu-wa.*
Do. *hon.*	ཞབས་འདྲེན་ཞུ་བ་གནང་བ་	*sḱam-dren sḱu-wa nang-wa.*
Disguised, to be	ཆ་ལུགས་མི་གཅིག་པ་སྤྲད་པ་	*chha-lu mi-chiḱ-pa tre-pa.*
Do. *hon.*	ཆ་ལུགས་མི་གཅིག་པ་བཞེས་པ་	*chha-lu mi-chiḱ-pa sḱe-pa.*
Disgusting	སྐྱུག་བྲོ་པོ་	*kyuḱ-t́ro-po.*
Dish	སྡེར་མ་	*der-ma.*
Do. *hon.*	གསོལ་སྡེར་	*sö-der.*

Disheartened	སེམས་སྐྱོ་པོ་	*sem-kyo-po.*
Disk	འཁོར་ལོ་	*khor-lo.*
Dislike, to	མི་དགའ་བ་	*mi-ga-wa.*
Do. *hon.*	མི་མཉེས་པ་	*mi-nye-pa.*
Dislocate, to (joint)	ཚིགས་སྤྲོག་པ་	*tshik̄-throk̄-pa.*
Dismantle, to	བཤིག་པ་ (འཇིག་པ་)	*shik̄-pa.*
Do. *hon.*	བཤིག་ག་ (པ་) གནང་བ་	*shik̄-ka nang-wa.*
Dismiss, to (*e.g.*, servant)	དགོངས་འཕོག་བཏང་ (གཏོང་) བ།	*gong-pho tang-wa;*
	གནས་དབྱུང་བཏང་ (གཏོང་) བ་	*ne-yung tang-wa.*
Do. *hon.*	གནས་དབྱུང་གཏོང་ང་ (བ་) གནང་བ།	*ne-yung tong-nya nang-wa ,*
	དགོངས་འཕོག་གནང་བ་	*gong-pho nang-wa.*
Dismount, to	བབ་པ་ (འབབ་པ་)	*p̄ap̄-pa.*
Do. *hon.*	ཆིབས་གཞོལ་གནང་བ་	*chhip̄-sk̄ö nang-wa.*
Disobey, to	ཁ་ལ་མི་ཉན་པ་	*kha-la mi-nyem pa*
Do. *hon.*	ཞལ་ལ་མི་གསན་པ་	*sk̄e-la mi-sem-pa.*
Disorder	མགོ་དཀྲུག་	*go-tro.*
Dispatch, to	བཏང་བ་ (གཏོང་བ་)	*tang-wa.*
Do. *hon.*	གཏོང་ང་ (བ་) གནང་བ་	*tong-nya nang-wa.*

Dispensary	སྨན་ཁང་	*men-khang.*
Disperse, to, *v.i.*	གྲོལ་བ། གྱེས་པ་	*ťröl-wa ; ƙye-pa.*
Do. *hon.*	ལྷན་རྒྱས་གྲོལ་ར་(བ་) གནང་བ་	*lhen-gye trö-ra nang-wa.*
Disposition (temper)	སེམས་	*sem.*
Do. *hon.*	ཐུགས་སེམས་	*thu-sem.*
Disputation	རྩོད་པ་	*tsö-pa.*
Dispute	ཡབ་གཞི། རྩོད་པ་	*lap̌-shi ; tsö-pa.*
Do. to	རྩོད་པ་རྒྱབ་བ་	*tsö-pa gyap̌-pa.*
Do. *hon.*	རྩོད་པ་སྐྱོན་པ་	*tso-pa ƙyöm-pa.*
Disrobe, to	ཕྱིས་པ་ (འབུད་པ་)	*pi-pa.*
Do. *hon.*	ཕྱིས་ (འབུད་) པ་གནང་བ་	*pi-pa nang-wa.*
Dissatisfied, to be	འདོད་པ་མི་ཁང་བ་(འཁེངས་པ)	*dö-pa mi-khang-wa.*
Do. *hon.*	ཐུགས་འདོད་མི་ཁང་བ་ (འཁེངས་པ་)	*thung-dö mi-khang-wa.*
Dissension	སྡེ་དཀྲུག་	*de-tru.*
Dissimilar	མི་གཅིག་པ་	*mi-chiƙ-pa.*
Dissimilarity	ཁྱད་པར་	*khye-par.*
Do. *hon.*	ཐུགས་ཁྱད་	*thu-khye.*
Dissolve, to	བཞུ་བ་	*sƙu-wa.*
Do. *hon.*	བཞུ་བ་གནང་བ་	*sƙu-wa nang-wa.*

Dissuade, to	སེམས་སྒྱུར་བ་	*sem-gyur-wa.*
Do. *hon.*	ཐུགས་སེམས་སྒྱུར་ར་ (བ་) གནང་བ་	*thu-sem gyur-ra nang-wa.*
Distance	ཐག་རིང་ཐུང་	*tha-ring-thung.*
Do. *hon.*	ཕེབ་ཐག་རིང་ཐུང་	*phep̃-tha-ring-thung.*
Distant	ཐག་རིང་པོ་	*tha-ring-po.*
Do. *hon.*	ཕེབ་ཐག་རིང་པོ་	*phep̃-tha-ring-po.*
Distinct (clear)	གསལ་པོ་	*se-po.*
Distinction, to make a	དབྱེན་ (དབྱེ་བ་) ཕྱེ་བ་	*yen chhe-wa.*
Distinction (difference)	ཁྱད་	*khye.*
Do. *hon.*	ཐུགས་ཁྱད་	*thu-khye.*
Distinctly (intelligibly)	སྒྲ་དག་པོ་	*dra-ťak-po.*
Distinguish, to	དབྱེན་ (དབྱེ་བ་) ཕྱེ་བ་	*yen-chhe-wa.*
Do. *hon.*	དབྱེན་ (དབྱེ་བ་) ཕྱེ་བ་གནང་བ་	*yen-chhe-wa nang-wa.*
Distinguished (well-known)	སྐད་གྲགས་ཆེན་པོ་	*ke-ťra chhem-po.*
Do. *hon.*	མཚན་སྙན་གྲགས་ཆེན་པོ་	*tshen-nyen-ťra chhem-po.*
Distress	སྡུག་བསྔལ་	*du-nge.*
Distressed, to be	སེམས་སྡུག་པ་	*sem-duk-pa.*
Do. *hon.*	ཐུགས་སེམས་སྡུག་ག་ (པ་) གནང་བ་	*thu-sem duk-ǩa nang-wa.*

Distribute, to	བགོད་པ། བགོ་བཤའ་རྒྱབ་པ་	*gö-pa ; goṕ-sha gyaṕ-pa.*
Do. *hon.*	བགོད་པ་གནང་བ། བགོ་བཤའ་སྐྱོན་པ་	*gö-pa nang-wa ; goṕ-sha kyöm-pa.*
District (tract of country)	ལུང་པ། ཡུལ་	*lung-pa ; yü.*
Do, (jurisdiction of a dzong pön)	རྫོང་ཁག་	*dzong-kha.*
Distrust, to	བློས་མི་ཁེད་པ་	*lö mi khe-pa.*
Do. *hon.*	ཐུགས་བློས་མི་ཁེད་པ་	*thuḱ-lö mi khe-pa.*
Disturbance	རྒྱབ་འདྲེ་	*gyam-dre.*
Do. *hon.*	གསུང་འཁྲུག་	*sung-thru.*
Ditch	ཆུ་དོང་	*chhu-t́ong.*
Dive, to	ཆུའི་གཏིང་ལ་འཛུལ་འགྲོ་བ་	*chhu-i-ting-la dzü-dro-wa.*
Divers (various)	སོ་སོ་	*so-so.*
Divest, to (of clothes)	ཕིས་པ་ (འབུད་པ་)	*pi-pa.*
Do. *hon.*	ཕིས་ (འབུད་) པ་གནང་བ་	*pi-pa nang-wa.*
Divide, to	བགོད་པ། བགོ་བཤའ་རྒྱབ་པ་	*gö-pa ; goṕ-sha gyaṕ-pa.*
Do. *hon.*	བགོད་པ་གནང་བ་	*gö-pa nang-wa.*
Divorce, to	ཁ་བྲལ་ (འབྲལ་) བ་	*kha-t́rel-wa.*
Do. *hon.*	ཁ་བྲལ་ར་ (འབྲལ་བ་) གནང་བ་	*kha-t́re-ra nang-wa.*
Divorce money (paid to divorce)	དབྱུག་འཇལ་	*yuḱ-je.*
Dizzy, to be	མགོ་ཡུ་འཁོར་བ་	*go-yu khor-wa.*

Dizzy, to be *hon.*	དབུ་ཡུ་འཁོར་བ་	*u-yu khor-wa.*
Do, to	བྱེད་པ་	*cḱe-pa.*
Do. *hon.*	གནང་བ་	*nang-wa.*
Do, that will (that is enough)	ད་འགྲིག་ག་	*t́a-driḱ-ḱa.*
Doctor	ཨམ་ཆི་ (ཨེམ་ཆི་)	*am-chhi.*
Do. *hon.*	ཨམ་ (ཨེམ་) ཆི་ལགས་	*am-chhi-la.*
Doctrine	ཆོས་ལུགས་	*chhö-lu.*
Document	འཛིན་	*dzin.*
Do. *hon.*	ཕྱག་འཛིན་	*chha-dzin.*
Dog	ཁྱི་	*khyi.*
Do. *hon.*	གཟིམ་ཁྱི་	*śim-khyi.*
Dog (for hunting)	ཤ་ཁྱི་	*sha-khyi.*
Dominion	རྒྱལ་ཁག་	*gye-kha.*
Dominoes, to play at	སྦག་རྒྱབ་པ་	*ba gyaṕ-pa.*
Do. *hon.*	ཕྱག་སྦག་སྐྱོན་པ་	*chha-ba kyöm-pa.*
Donkey	བུང་གུ་ (བོང་བུ་)	*ṕung-gu.*
Door	སྒོ་	*go.*
Do. *hon.*	གཟིམ་སྒོ་	*śim-go.*
Door (large outside)	རྒྱལ་སྒོ་	*gye-go.*
Door-frame	སྒོའི་རི་བཞི་	*gö-riṕ-sḱi.*

Door-keeper	སྒོ་རག་པ་ (སྒོ་སྲུང་བ་)	*go-ra-pa.*
Dose (of medicine)	སྨན་ཐུན་	*men-thün.*
Dot	ཚག་ (ཚེག)	*tsha.*
Double	གཉིས་ལྡབ་	*nyi-daṕ.*
Doubt	ཐེ་ཚོམ་	*the-tshom.*
Do. to	ཐེ་ཚོམ་ཟ་བ་	*the-tshom śa-wa.*
Do. *hon.*	ཐེ་ཚོམ་གནང་བ་	*the-tshom nang-wa.*
Doubtful	གཉིས་བཟོ་	*nye-śo.*
Dough	སྤགས་	*pa.*
Dove	ཏུད་ཏུད་ཀུ་ཀུ་	*ťu-ťu ku-ku.*
Down	མར་	*ma.*
Down hill	ཐུར་	*thur.*
Down there	མ་གི་	*ma-gi.*
Downwards	མར་	*ma.*
Doze, to	གཉིད་ཙོག་རྒྱབ་པ་	*nyi-tso gyaṕ-pa.*
Do. *hon.*	མཆན་ (མནལ་) ཙོག་སྐྱོན་པ་	*nye-tso kyöm-pa.*
Drag, to	འཐེན་པ་	*them-pa.*
Do. *hon.*	འཐེན་པ་གནང་བ་	*them-pa nang-wa.*
Dragon	འབྲུག་	*druḱ.*
Drain (on ground)	ཡོ་པོ་ (ཡུར་པོ་)	*yo-po.*

Drain (on roof of house)	འོག་ཆུ་	*o-chhu.*
Draw, to (pull)	འཐེན་པ་	*them-pa.*
Do. *hon.*	འཐེན་པ་གནང་བ་	*them-pa nang-wa.*
Draw lots, to	མོ་རྒྱབ་པ་	*mo-gyaṕ-pa.*
Do. *hon.*	ཕྱག་མོ་སྐྱོན་པ་	*chha-mo kyöm-pa.*
Draw up, to (documents &c.)	རྩོམ་པ་	*tsom-pa.*
Do. *hon.*	རྩོམ་པ་གནང་བ་	*tsom-pa nang-wa.*
Do. *h. hon.*	བཀའ་རྩོམ་གནང་བ	*ka-tsom nang-wa.*
Draw out, to (in length)	རིང་དུ་བཏང་ (གཏོང་) བ་	*ring-ťu tang-wa.*
Do. *hon.*	རིང་དུ་གཏོང་ང་ (བ་) གནང་བ་	*ring-ťu tong-nga nang-wa.*
Draw pictures, to	རི་མོ་བྲིས་པ་ (འབྲི་བ་)	*ri-mo ťri-pa.*
Do. *hon.*	རི་མོ་བྲིས་པ་ (འབྲི་བ་) གནང་བ་	*ri-mo ťri-pa nang-wa.*
Drawers (in table, &c.)	ཤུར་སྒམ་ (ཤུབས་སྒམ་)	*shur-gam.*
Drawers, chest of	སྒམ་	*gam.*
Do. *hon.*	ཕྱག་སྒམ་	*chha-gam.*
Drawers (garment)	གོ་ཐུང་ (གོས་ཐུང།) དོར་མ་	*ḱo-thung ; ťo-ma.*
Do. *hon.*	ཞབས་ཁྲིན། ཞབས་དོར་	*sh́aṕ-khyen ; sh́aṕ-ťo.*
Dread, to	ཞེད་པ་	*sh́e-pa.*
Do. *hon.*	ཞེད་པ་གནང་བ་	*sh́e-pa nang-wa.*

Dreadful	ཞེད་སྐྲག་ཚ་པོ་	*sḱe-tra tsha-po.*
Dream	གཉིད་ལམ་	*nyi-lam.*
Do. *hon.*	མཉན་ལམ་ (མནལ་ལམ་)	*nye-lam.*
Dream, to	གཉིད་ལམ་བཏང་ (གཏོང་) བ་	*nyi-lam tang-wa.*
Do. *hon.*	མཉན་ (མནལ་) ལམ་གཏོང་ང་ (བ་) གནང་བ་	*nye-lam tong-nga nang-wa.*
Dress	དུག་ལོག་	*ťu-lo.*
Do. *hon.*	ན་བཟའ་	*nam-śa.*
Dress, to (clothe)	གྱོན་པ་	*ḱyöm-pa.*
Do. *hon.*	བཞེས་པ་	*sḱe-pa.*
Dress ostentatiously, to	དང་འདོད་བྱེད་པ་	*ťang-dö cḱe-pa.*
Do. *hon.*	ཐུགས་དང་འདོད་གནང་བ་	*thu ťang-dö nang-wa.*
Dried	སྐམ་པོ་	*kam-po.*
Drill, to (soldiers)	དམག་སྦྱོང་བྱེད་པ་	*ma-jong cḱe-pa.*
Do. *hon.*	དམག་སྦྱོང་གནང་བ་	*ma-jong nang-wa.*
Drink, to	འཐུང་བ་	*thung-wa.*
Do. *hon.*	བཞེས་པ་	*sḱe-pa.*
Drinking-water	འཐུང་ཡ་གི་ཆུ་	*thung-ya-ḱi chhu.*
Do. *hon.*	བཞེས་ཡ་གི་ཆབ་	*sḱe-ya-ḱi chhaṕ.*
Drip, to (of water)	ཐིགས་པ་རྒྱབ་པ་	*thiḱ-pa gyaṕ-pa.*

Drive, to (pursue)	དེད་པ་	*ťe-pa.*
Do. *hon.*	དེད་པ་གནང་བ་	*ťe-pa nang-wa.*
Drop	ཐིགས་པ་	*thiḱ-pa.*
Drop, to, *v.t.*	བཏང་བ་ (གཏོང་བ་)	*tang-wa.*
Do. *hon.*	གཏོང་ང་ (བ་) གནང་བ་	*tong-nga nang-wa.*
Drop, to *v.i.*	གཟག་པ་	*śaḱ-pa.*
Dropsy, to have	གཟུགས་པོ་ལ་ཆུ་བསགས་ (གསོག་) པ་	*śuḱ-po-la chhu-saḱ-pa.*
Do. *hon.*	སྐུ་གཟུགས་ལ་ཆབ་བསགས་ (གསོག་) པ་	*ku-śuḱ-la chhaṕ saḱ-pa.*
Dross (alloy)	ལྷད་	*hle.*
Drowned, to be	ཆུ་ལ་ཤོར་བ་	*chhu-la shor-wa.*
Do. *hon.*	ཆབ་ལ་ཤོར་ར་ (བ་) གནང་བ་	*chhaṕ-la shor-ra nang-wa.*
Drug	སྨན་	*men.*
Do. *hon.*	གསོལ་སྨན་	*sö-men.*
Drum	རྔ་	*nga.*
Do. *hon.*	ཕྱག་རྔ་	*chha-nga.*
Drum-skin	རྔ་ལྤགས་	*nga-pa.*
Drum-stick	རྔ་ཡོག་ (རྔ་དབྱུགས་)	*nga-yo.*
Drunk	ར་བཟི་	*raṕ-śi.*

Drunk, to be	ར་བཟི་བ་	*ra-śi-wa.*
Do. *hon.*	སྐུ་ར་ཐྲད་པ་	*ku-ra be-pa.*
Drunken fit, to quarrel in a	ར་བཟི་བྱེད་པ། ཀྱོང་ཁོང་བྱེད་པ་	*rap̆-śi cḱe-pa; kyong-khong cḱe-pa.*
Do. *hon.*	ར་བཟི་གནང་བ། ཀྱོང་ཁོང་གནང་བ་	*rap̆-śi nang-wa; kyong-khong nang-wa.*
Dry	སྐམ་པོ་	*kam-po.*
Dry to	བསྐམ་པ་ (སྐེམ་པ་)	*kam-pa.*
Duck	ཡ་ཚེ་ ch.	*ya-tse.*
Dull (stupid)	ལྐུགས་པ། གླེན་པ་	*kuḱ-pa; lem pa.*
Dumb	ཁ་ལྐུགས་པ་	*kha-kuḱ-pa.*
Do. *hon.*	ཞལ་ལྐུགས་པ་	*sḱe-kuḱ-pa.*
Dung (of sheep, goats, mice, etc.)	རིལ་མ་	*ri-ma.*
Do. of horse	རྟའི་སྦྲངས་	*te-bang.*
Do. of cattle	ལྕུ་བ་ (ལྕི་བ་)	*chu-a.*
Do. of human beings.	སྐྱག་པ་	*kyaḱ-pa.*
Dupe, to	མགོ་སྐོར་བཏང་ (གཏོང་) བ་	*go-kor tang-wa.*
Do. *hon.*	མགོ་སྐོར་གཏོང་ང་ (བ་) གནང་བ་	*go-kor tong-nga nang-wa.*
Durable	ཀྲོག་ཆེན་པོ་	*tro-chhem-po.*

During	དུས་ལ་	*t́ü-la.*
Dusk	ས་རིབ་ (སྲོད་ཏུབ་)	*sa-riṕ.*
Dust	ཐལ་ལ (ཐལ་བ་)	*thel-la.*
Dust-storm	ཐལ་རླུང་	*the-lung.*
Duty (tax)	ཞོ་ཁྲལ་	*sho-thre.*
Dwarf	མི་ཆུང་དེ་ལེབ་	*mi-chhung te-le.*
Do. *hon.*	སྐུ་གཟུགས་ཆུང་ཆུང་	*ku-śuḱ chhung-chhung.*
Dwell, to	བསྡད་པ་ (སྡོད་པ་)	*de-pa.*
Do. *hon.*	བཞུགས་པ་	*sḱu-pa.*
Do. *h. hon.*	བཞུགས་གདན་འཛག་པ་	*sḱu-den jaḱ-pa.*
Dweller	སྡོད་མཁན་	*dö-khen.*
Do. *hon.*	བཞུགས་མཁན་	*sḱu-khen.*
Do. *h. hon.*	བཞུགས་གདན་འཛག་མཁན་	*sḱu-den ja-khen.*
Dwelling, *s.*	ཁང་པ། ནང་། སྡོད་ས་	*khang-pa ; nang ; dö-sa.*
Do. *hon.*	གཟིམ་ཁང་། བཞུགས་ས་	*śim-khang ; sḱuḱ-sa.*
Do. *h. hon.*	གཟིམ་ཤག། བཞུགས་གདན་འཛག་ས་	*śim-sha ; sḱu-den ja-sa.*
Dwindle, to (in size)	ཆུང་རུ་ (དུ་) འགྲོ་བ་	*chhung-ru dro-wa.*
Do. *hon.*	ཆུང་རུ་ (དུ་) ཕེབ་པ་	*chhung-ru phe-pa.*
Dwindle, to (in numbers)	ཉུང་རུ་ (དུ་) འགྲོ་བ་	*nyung-ru dro-wa.*

Dye	ཚོས་	*tshö.*
Do. red lac	རྒྱ་ཚོས་	*gya-tshö.*
Dye, to	ཚོས་རྒྱབ་པ་	*tshö-gyaṕ-pa.*
Do. *hon.*	ཚོས་སྐྱོན་པ་	*tshö-kyöm-pa.*
Dynasty	རྒྱལ་བརྒྱུད་	*gye-gyü.*
Dysentery	འབྲུ་ནད་	*thru-ne.*
Dyspepsia	ལྟོ་མ་འཇུ་བའི་ནད་	*to ma-ju-we ne.*

E

Each	རེ་རེ་	*re-re.*
Eager	སྙིང་འདོད་པོ། སྙིང་བྲོ་པོ་	*nying-dö-po ; nying-ťro-po.*
Eager to do	བྱེད་སྙིང་འདོད་པོ་	*cḱe nying dö-po.*
Eager to go	འགྲོ་སྙིང་འདོད་པོ་	*dro-nying dö-po.*
Eagle	གོ་བོ་	*ḱo-wo.*
Ear	ཨམ་མཆོག་ (རྣ་མཆོག་)	*am-chho.*
Do. *hon.*	སྙན་མཆོག་	*nyen-chho.*
Ear-hole	ཨམ་མཆོག་ (རྣ་མཆོག་) གི་ཨི་ཁུང་	*am-chho-ḱi i-khung.*
Do. *hon.*	སྙན་མཆོག་གི་ཨི་ཁུང་	*nyen-chho-ḱi i-khung.*
Ear of corn	སྙེ་མ་	*nye-ma.*
Early (in morning)	སྔ་པོ་	*nga-po.*
Earnest, *adj.*	སྙིང་རུས་ཆེན་པོ་	*nying-rü chhem-po.*
Do. *hon.*	ཐུགས་རུས་ཆེན་པོ་	*thu-rü chhem-po.*
Earnestly	སྙིང་རུས་བྱས་ནས་	*nying-rü cḱe-ne.*
Earring (man's)	སོ་བྱིས་ (སོ་གོང་)	*so-cḱi.*
Do. *hon.*	སྙན་བྱིས་	*nyen-cḱi.*
Earring (woman's)	ཨས་སྐོར་	*e-kor.*
Do. *hon.*	སྙན་སྐོར་	*nyen-kor.*

Earring (of turquoises)	གཟི་གཡུ་	*sí-yu.*
Do. *hon.*	སྙན་གཡུ་	*nye-yu.*
Earth	ས་	*sa.*
Earthen vessel	ཁོག་མ་	*kho-ma.*
Do. *hon.*	བཞེས་ཁོག་	*sḱe-kho.*
Earthenware	ཛ་སྣོད་	*dza-nö.*
Earthquake	ས་གཡོམ་ (ས་གཡོས།) ས་འགུལ་	*sa-yom ; sa-gü.*
Earth-work	ས་ལས་	*sap-le.*
Easily	ལས་སླ་པོ་	*le-la-po.*
East	ཤར་	*shar.*
Easy	ལས་སླ་པོ་	*le-la-po.*
Eat, to	ཟ་བ་	*śa-wa.*
Do. *hon.*	བཞེས་པ་	*sḱe-pa.*
Eating-house	ཟ་ཁང་	*śa-khang.*
Echo	བ་ཆ་ (བྲག་ཆ་)	*ṕa-chha.*
Do. to	བ་ཆ་ (བྲག་ཆ་) འཁོར་བ་	*ṕa-chha khor-wa.*
Eclipse of the moon	ཟླ་འཛིན་	*dan-dzin.*
Do. of the sun	ཉིན་འཛིན་	*nyin-dzin.*
Edict	བཀའ་རྒྱ་	*ka-gya.*

Edge (of knife, etc.)	ངོ་	*ngo.*
Do. (of land, water, etc.)	ཙར། འགྲམ་	*tsa ; dram.*
Do. (of table, etc.)	ཟུར་	*śur.*
Edged	རྣོ་པོ་	*no-po.*
Edible, to be	ཟ་ཉན་པ་	*śa-nyem-pa.*
Do. *hon.*	མཆོད་ཉན་པ་	*chhö-nyem-pa.*
Editor	རྩོམ་པ་རྒྱབ་མཁན་	*tsom-pa gyaṕ-khen.*
Educate, to	ཡི་གེ་བསླབས་ (སློབ་) པ། སྦྱོང་དར་སྤྲད་པ་	*yi-ge laṕ-pa ; jong-ṫar tre-pa.*
Do. *hon.*	ཕྱག་བྲིས་བསླབས་ (སློབ་) པ་གནང་བ་	*chha-ri laṕ-pa nang-wa.*
Efface, to	སུབ་པ་	*suṕ-pa.*
Do. *hon.*	སུབ་པ་གནང་བ་	*suṕ-pa nang-wa.*
Effect, to (perform)	བྱེད་པ་	*cḱe-pa.*
Do. *hon.*	གནང་བ་	*nang-wa.*
Effects (goods)	ཅ་ལག་ (ཆ་ལག་)	*cha-la.*
Do. *hon.*	སྐུ་ཅས་ (སྐུ་ཆས་)	*ku-che.*
Effort	བརྩོན་འགྲུས་	*tsön-drü.*
Effort, to make an	བརྩོན་འགྲུས་བྱེད་པ་	*tsön-drü cḱe-pa.*
Do. *hon.*	ཐུགས་བརྩོན་གནང་བ་	*thuḱ-tsön nang-wa.*

Egg	སྒོ་ང་	*go-nga.*
Do. *hon.*	བཞེས་སྒོང་	*sḱe-gong.*
Egg, white of an	དཀར་སྤྲིན་	*kar-trin.*
Eggs, to lay	སྒོ་ང་བཏང་ (གཏོང་) བ་	*go-nga tang-wa.*
Eight	བརྒྱད་	*gye.*
Eighteen	བཅོ་བརྒྱད་	*choṕ-gye.*
Eighteenth	བཅོ་བརྒྱད་པ་	*choṕ-gye-pa.*
Eighth	བརྒྱད་པ་	*gye-pa.*
Eightieth	བརྒྱད་བཅུ་པ་	*gye-chu-pa.*
Eighty	བརྒྱད་བཅུ་	*gye-chu.*
Either, *conj.*	ཡང་མིན་ན། ཡང་ན་	*yang-men-na ; yang-na.*
Eject to	བཏོན་པ་ (འདོན་པ་)	*töm-pa.*
Do. *hon.*	བཏོན་ (འདོན་) པ་གནང་བ་	*töm-pa nang-wa.*
Elbow	གྲུ་མོ་	*t́re-mo.*
Elder, *adj.*	རྒན་པ་	*gem-pa.*
Elder brother	ཇོ་ཇོ་	*cḱo-cḱo.*
Do. *hon.*	ཇོ་ལགས་	*cḱo-la.*
Eldest	རྒན་ཤོས་	*gen-shö.*
Do. *hon.*	བགྲེས་ཤོས་	*dre-shö.*
Elect, to (appoint)	སྐོ་བ་	*ko-wa.*

Elect, to (appoint) *hon.*	སྐོ་བ་གནང་བ་	*ko-wa-nang-wa.*
Electric light	གློག་ཤུ་	*loḱ-sḱu.*
Elegant	འདྲ་ཆགས་པོ་	*dra-chhaḱ-po.*
Element (fire, earth, etc.)	འབྱུང་བ་	*jung-wa.*
Elephant	གླང་པོ་ཆེ། གླང་ཆེན་	*lang-po-chhe; lang-chhen.*
Elevation	མཐོ་དམན་	*tho-men.*
Eleven	བཅུ་གཅིག་	*chuḱ-chi.*
Eleventh	བཅུ་གཅིག་པ་	*chuḱ-chi-pa.*
Else	དེ་མིན་ན་	*t́e-min-na.*
Elsewhere	གཞན་པ་	*sḱem-pa.*
Embarrassed, to be	མགོ་འཐོམས་པ་	*go-thom-pa.*
Do. *hon.*	དབུ་འཐོམས་པ་	*u-thom-pa.*
Ember	མེ་མདག་	*men da.*
Emblem	རྟགས་	*ta.*
Embrace, to	འཁྱུད་པ་	*khyü-pa.*
Do. *hon.*	འཁྱུད་པ་གནང་བ་	*khyü-pa nang wa.*
Embroidery	ཀྱིང་ཁབ་ (ཀྱིང་ཁེབས་)	*kying-khaṕ.*
Do. gold	ཟར་བབས་	*śar-ṕaṕ.*
Do. best quality	རྒྱ་གསེར་	*gya-ser.*
Emerald	མ་རྐད་	*ma-ge.*

Emetic	སྐྱུག་སྨན་	*kyuk-men.*
Eminence, *s.*	སྒང་། རྩེ་	*gang ; tse.*
Eminent, *adj.*	སྐད་གྲགས་ཆེན་པོ་	*ke-ťra chhem-po.*
Do. *hon.*	སྙན་གྲགས་ཆེན་པོ་	*nyen-ťra Chhem-po.*
Emperor	རྒྱལ་པོ་	*gye-po.*
Do. of China	རྒྱ་ནག་གོང་མ་	*gya-na ǩong-ma.*
Emperor's administration	རྒྱལ་སྲིད་	*gye-si.*
Empire	རྒྱལ་ཁམས་	*gyeng-kham.*
Employ, to	སྐོ་བ་	*ko-wa.*
Do. *hon.*	སྐོ་བ་གནང་བ་	*ko-wa nang-wa.*
Employ, to (servant)	བཞག་པ་ (འཇོག་པ་)	*sǩak-pa.*
Do. *hon.*	གཞོག་ག་ (པ་) གནང་བ་	*sǩok-ǩa nang-wa.*
Employment	ལས་ཀ་	*le-ka.*
Do. *hon.*	ཕྱག་ལས་	*chha-le.*
Empty, *adj.*	སྟོང་པ་	*tong-pa.*
Do. to	སྟོང་པ་བཟོ་བ་	*tong-pa śo-wa.*
Do. *hon.*	སྟོང་པ་བཟོ་བ་གནང་བ་	*tong-pa śo-wa nang-wa.*
Enabled, to be	ཐུབ་པ་	*thuṕ-pa.*
Do. *hon.*	ཐུབ་པ་གནང་བ་	*thuṕ-pa nang-wa.*
Enamelware	ཀུ་ཀུ་ཤ་	*ǩu-ǩu-sha.*

Encamp, to	སྒར་རྒྱབ་པ་	*gar-gyap̄-pa.*
Do. *hon.*	སྒར་སྐྱོན་པ་	*gar-kyöm-pa.*
Encampment	སྒར་	*gar.*
Encircle, to	སྐོར་བ་	*kor-wa.*
Do. *hon.*	སྐོར་ར་ (བ་) གནང་བ་	*kor-ra nang-wa.*
Enclosure (fence)	ར་བ་	*ra-wa.*
Encounter, to (meet)	ཐུག་པ་	*thuk̄-pa.*
Do. *inf.* meeting *sup.*	མཇལ་བ་	*jel-wa.*
Encourage, to	བློ་ཁོག་ཆེ་རུ་བཏང་ (གཏོང་) བ་	*lo-kho chhe-ru tang-wa.*
Do. *hon.*	བློ་ཁོག་ཆེ་རུ་གཏོང་ང་ (བ་) གནང་བ་	*lo-kho chhe-ru tong-nga nang-wa.*
End	མཐའ་	*tha.*
Do. to be at an (consumed)	རྫོགས་པ་	*dzok̄-pa.*
Do. to be at an (accomplished)	འཚར་བ་	*tshar-wa.*
Endeavour, to	བརྩོན་འགྲུས་བྱེད་པ་	*tsön-drü ck̄e-pa.*
Do. *hon.*	ཐུགས་བརྩོན་གནང་བ་	*thu-tsön nang-wa.*
Endless	རྫོགས་རྒྱུ་མེད་པ་	*dzo-gyu me-pa.*
Endure, to, *v.t.*	བཟོད་པ་སྒོམ་པ་	*śö-pa gom-pa.*
Do. *hon.*	བཟོད་པ་སྒོམ་པ་གནང་བ་	*śö-pa gom-pa nang-wa.*
Enemy.	དགྲ་	*dra.*

Energetic	བརྩོན་པོ། སྙིང་རུས་ཆེན་པོ་	*tsöm-po ; nying-rü chhem-po.*
Do. *hon.*	ཐུགས་རུས་ཆེན་པོ་	*thuḱ-rü chhem-po.*
Engage on hire, to	གླ་པ་	*la-pa.*
Do. *hon.*	གླ་གནང་བ་	*la nang-wa.*
Enhance, to	འཕར་བ་	*phar-wa.*
Enjoin, to	བཀའ་གནང་བ་	*ka-nang-wa.*
Enough, to be	འགྲིག་པ་	*driḱ-pa.*
Enjoy, to	སྐྱིད་པོ་བྱེད་པ་	*kyi-po cḰe-pa.*
Do. *hon.*	སྤྲོ་པོ་གནང་བ་	*tro-po nang-wa.*
Enlarge, to	ཆེ་རུ་བཏང་ (གཏོང་) བ་	*chhe-ru tang-wa.*
Do. *hon.*	ཆེ་རུ་གཏོང་ང་ (བ་) གནང་བ་	*chhe-ru tong-nga-nang-wa.*
Enmity	གཏིང་ནད་	*ting-ne.*
Enormous	ཆེ་ཐག་ཆོད་	*chhe-thaḱ-chhö.*
Enquire, to (ask)	དྲི་བ་ (འདྲི་བ་)	*t́ri-wa.*
Do. *hon.*	བཀའ་འདྲི་གནང་བ་	*kan-dri nang-wa.*
Enquire, to (investigate)	ཞིབ་དཔྱོད་བྱེད་པ་	*sḰiṕ-chö cḰe-pa.*
Do. *hon.*	ཞིབ་དཔྱོད་གནང་བ་	*sḰiṕ-chö nang-wa.*
Do. *h. hon.*	བཀའ་ཞིབ་གནང་བ་	*ka-sḰiṕ nang-wa.*
Ensnare, to	རྙི་བཙུགས་ (འཛུགས་) པ་	*nyi-tsuḱ-pa.*

Ensnare, to *hon.*	ཉི་བཙུགས་ཀ་ (འཛུགས་པ་) གནང་བ་	*nyi-tsuk-ka nang-wa.*
Enter, to	འཛུལ་བ་	*dzü-wa.*
Do. *hon.*	ཕེབ་པ་	*phe-pa.*
Do. *h. hon.*	འཆིབ་རྒྱུ་གནང་བ་	*chhip-gyu nang-wa.*
Entertainment (feast)	མགྲོན་པོ་	*dröm-po.*
Do. *hon.*	ཐུགས་སྤྲོ་	*thu-tro.*
Entice, to	སླུ་བ་	*lu-wa.*
Do. *hon.*	སླུ་བ་གནང་བ་	*lu-wa nang-wa.*
Entire	ཚང་མ། ཐམས་ཅད། སྒང་ཁ་	*tshang-ma ; tham che ; gang-kha.*
Entirely	བད་དེ་	*be-te.*
Entomb, to	ས་སྦེད་བཏང་ (གཏོང་) བ་	*sa-be tang-wa.*
Do. *hon.*	ས་སྦེད་གཏོང་ང་ (བ་) གནང་བ་	*sa-be tong-nga nang-wa.*
Entrails	རྒྱུ་མ་	*gyu-ma.*
Do. *hon.*	སྐུ་རྒྱུ་	*ku gyu.*
Entreat, to	ཞུ་བ་	*sku-wa.*
Entrust, to	བཅོལ་ (འཆོལ་) གཞག་ (འཇོག་) པ་	*chö-skok-pa.*
Do. *hon.*	བཅོལ་ (འཆོལ་) གཞག་ཀ་ (འཇོག་པ་) གནང་བ་	*chö-skok-ka nang-wa.*

Envelope (Tibetan)	རྒྱ་མ་	*gya-ma.*
Do. (English)	ཡིག་ཤུབས་	*yiḱ-shuṕ.*
Envious	ཕྲ་དོག་ཚ་པོ་	*thra-ťo tsha-po.*
Envoy	ཕོ་ཉ་	*pho-nya.*
Envy, *s*	ཕྲ་དོག་	*thra-ťo.*
Envy, to	ཕྲ་དོག་བྱེད་པ་	*thra-ťo cḱe-pa.*
Do. *hon.*	ཕྲ་དོག་གནང་བ་	*thra-ťo nang-wa.*
Epilepsy	གཟའ་ནད་	*śa-ne.*
Epistle	ཡི་གེ་	*yi-ge.*
Do. *hon.*	ཕྱག་བྲིས་	*chha-ri.*
Equal	གཅིག་པ། འདྲ་འདྲ་	*chiḱ-pa ; dran-dra.*
Equitable	འདྲ་དྲང་	*dra-ťrang.*
Erase, to	སུབ་པ་	*suṕ-pa.*
Do. *hon.*	སུབ་པ་གནང་བ་	*suṕ-pa nang-wa.*
Erect	ཀྱེ་རེ་	*kye-re.*
Do. to stand	ཀྱེ་རེ་ལང་བསྡད་ (སྡོད་) པ་	*kye-re lang-de-pa.*
Do. *hon.*	ཀྱེ་རེ་བཞང་(བཞེང་)བཞུགས་པ་	*kye-re sḱang-sḱu-pa.*
Erect, to (build)	རྩིག་པ་	*tsiḱ-pa.*
Do. *hon.*	རྩིག་ག་ (པ་) གནང་བ་	*tsiḱ-ka nang-wa.*
Err, to	ནོར་བ་	*nor-wa.*

Err, to *hon.*	ནོར་ར་ (བ་) གནང་བ་	*nor-ra nang-wa.*
Error	ནོར་	*nor.*
Eruption (on skin)	བྲ་ཚ་ (བྲ་པ་)	*ba-tsha.*
Escape, to	ཤོར་བ་	*shor-wa.*
Escort, *s.*	སྐུ་སྲུང་།	*ku-sung.*
	དཔུང་རོགས་	*pung-ro.*
Do. to	དཔུང་རོགས་འཁྲིད་པ་	*pung-ro thri-pa.*
Do. *hon.*	དཔུང་རོགས་འཁྲིད་པ་གནང་བ་	*pung-ro thri-pa nang-wa.*
Do. to (of person in superior position)	སྐུ་སྲུང་འཁྲིད་པ་གནང་བ་	*ku-sung thri-pa nang-wa.*
Especially	ཁྱད་པར་དུ་	*khye par-t̔u.*
Eternal	རྫོགས་རྒྱུ་མེད་པ།	*dzo-gyu-me-pa ; tha-me-pa.*
	མཐའ་མེད་པ་	
Europe	ཕྱི་གླིང་	*chhi-ling.*
European, *adj.*	ཕྱི་གླིང་གི་	*chhi ling-k̔i.*
Do. (a man)	ཕྱི་གླིང་གི་མི་	*chhi-ling-k̔i-mi.*
Evaporate, to	ཡལ་བ་	*ye-wa.*
Even, *adj.* (level)	སྙོམས་པོ་	*nyom-po.*
Even, *adv.*	ཡང་	*yang.*
Evening	དགོང་མོ་	*gong-mo.*
Do. this	དོ་དགོང་	*t̔o-gong.*

Evenly balanced, to be	ཡང་ལྗི་མེད་པ་	*yang-ji me-pa.*
Events, at all	གང་ཡིན་ཀྱང་། ག་རེ་ཡིན་རུང་	*ḱang-yin-kyang ; ḱa-re yin-rung.*
Ever (always)	ནམ་རྒྱུན། དུས་རྒྱུན། དག་པ་རེ་བཞིན་	*nam-gyün ; tü-gyün ; taḱ-pa re-sḱi.*
Everlasting	རྫོགས་རྒྱུ་....མེད་པ། མཐའ་མེད་པ་	*dzo-gyu me-pa ; tha-me-pa.*
Every	རེ་རེ་	*re-re.*
Everybody	མི་སྐང་ཁ་	*mi gang-kha.*
Every day	ཞག་མ་རེ་རེ་	*sḱa-ma re-re.*
Every kind	སྣ་ཚོགས་	*na-tsho.*
Everywhere	ག་ས་ག་ལ་	*ḱa sa ḱa-la.*
Evidence	རྒྱུ་མཚན་	*gyum-tshen.*
Evident	ངེས་པ། དངོས་ནས་	*nge-par ; ngön-ne.*
Evil	ངན་པ་	*ngen-pa.*
Evil spirit	འདྲེ་	*dre.*
Exact	ཁྲིག་ཁྲིག་	*thriḱ-thri.*
Exactly	རང་	*rang.*
Exactly so	ད་ག་རེད་	*ťa-ḱa-re.*
Do. *hon.*	ད་ག་རང་རེད་	*ťa-ḱa rang-re.*
Do. *h. hon.*	བཀའ་གནང་རང་རེད་	*ka-nang rang-re.*

Exaggerate, to	སྐད་ཆ་སྒྲོ་འདོགས་པ་	*ke-chha dro-doḱ-pa.*
Exalt, to	མཐོ་ས་སྐྱེལ་བ་	*tho-sa kyel-wa.*
Do *hon.*	མཐོ་ས་སྐྱེལ་ར་ (བ་) གནང་བ་	*tho-sa kye-ra nang-wa.*
Examination (of student)	རྒྱུགས་	*gyuḱ.*
Do. (investigation)	ཞིབ་དཔྱོད་	*sḱiṕ-chö.*
Do. *hon.*	བཀའ་ཞིབ་	*ka-sḱiṕ.*
Examine, to (student)	རྒྱུགས་ལེན་པ་	*gyuḱ-lem-pa.*
Do. *hon.*	རྒྱུགས་བཞེས་པ་	*gyuḱ-sḱe pa.*
Examine, to (investigate)	ཞིབ་དཔྱོད་བྱེད་པ་	*sḱiṕ-chö cḱe-pa.*
Do. *hon.*	ཞིབ་དཔྱོད་གནང་བ་	*sḱiṕ-chö nang-wa.*
Do. *h. hon.*	བཀའ་ཞིབ་གནང་བ་	*ka sḱiṕ nang-wa.*
Examined, to be (student)	རྒྱུགས་ཕུལ་ (འབུལ་) བ་	*gyuḱ-phül-wa.*
Example	དཔེ་	*pe.*
Example, for	དཔེ་ན་ཡིན་ན། དཔེ་ན་ (དཔེར་ན་)	*pe-na yin-na; pe-na.*
Excavation	དོང་	*ťong.*
Excavate, to	རྐོ་བ་	*ko-wa.*
Do. *hon.*	རྐོ་བ་གནང་བ་	*ko-wa nang-wa.*
Exceed, to	ལྷག་པ་	*hlaḱ-pa.*
Exceedingly	ཐག་ཆོད་	*thaḱ-chhö.*

Exceedingly many	མང་ཐག་ཆོད་	*mang-thak-chhö.*
Excellency, His	རིན་པོ་ཆེ་	*rim-po-chhe.*
Excellent	ཡག་ཐག་ཆོད་	*yak-thak-chhö.*
Except	མ་གཏོགས། མེན་པ་ (མིན་པ་)	*ma-to ; mem-pa.*
Exchange	རྗེ་པོ་རྒྱབ་པ་	*je-po gyap-pa.*
Do. *hon.*	རྗེ་པོ་སྐྱོན་པ་	*je-po kyöm-pa.*
Excessive	མང་ཐག་ཆོད། ཛག་ཏོ་	*mang-thak-chhö ; dzak-to.*
Excessive appetite	གྲོད་ཁོག་ཆེན་པོ་	*trö-kho chhem-po.*
Exclaim, to	སྐད་བཏང་ (གཏོང་) བ་	*ke-tang-wa.*
Do. *hon.*	སྐད་གཏོང་ང་ (བ་) གནང་བ་	*ke tong-nga nang-wa.*
Excluding (except)	མ་གཏོགས། མེན་པ་ (མིན་པ་)	*ma-to ; mem-pa.*
Excrement (human)	སྐྱག་པ་	*kyak-pa.*
Excuse, *s.*	ཁ་འདྲི་	*khan-dri.*
Do. *hon.*	ཞལ་འདྲི་	*sken-dri.*
Excuses, to make	ཁ་འདྲི་བཤད་པ་	*khan-dri she-pa.*
Do. *hon.*	ཞལ་འདྲི་གནང་བ་	*sken-dri nang-wa.*
Do. *inf.* to *sup.*	ཁ་འདྲི་ཞུ་བ་	*khan dri sku-wa.*
Exercise, literary	ཡིག་རྒྱུགས་	*yik-gyu.*
Exert one's self, to	སྙིང་རུས་བྱེད་པ་	*nying-rü che-pa.*
Do. *hon.*	ཐུགས་རུས་གནང་བ་	*thuk-rü nang-wa.*

Exhausted, to be (tired)	ཐང་ཆད་པ་	*thang-chhe-pa.*
Do. *hon.*	སྐུ་ཐང་ཆད་པ་གནང་བ་	*ku thang chhe-pa nang-wa.*
Exhaustion	ངལ་	*ngel.*
Do. *hon.*	སྐུ་ངལ་	*ku-ngel.*
Exhibit, to	བསྟན་པ་ (སྟོན་པ་)	*tem-pa.*
Exist, to	ཡོད་པ་	*yö-pa.*
Exhort, to	བསླབ་བྱ་བྱེད་པ་	*laṕ-cḰa cḰe-pa.*
Do. *hon.*	བསླབ་བྱ་གནང་བ་	*laṕ-cḰa nang wa.*
Do. *h. hon.*	བཀའ་སློབ་གནང་བ་	*ḱa-loṕ nang-wa.*
Exhortation	བསླབ་བྱ་	*laṕ-cḰa.*
Do. *hon.*	བཀའ་སློབ་	*ka loṕ.*
Exorcise, to	དམ་ལ་བཏགས་ (འདོགས་) པ་	*ťam-la taḱ-pa.*
Do. *hon.*	དམ་འདོགས་གནང་བ་	*ťam-doḱ nang-wa.*
Expanse	ཁ་ཞེང་	*kha-sḰeng.*
Expect, to (wait for)	སྒུག་བསྡད་ (སྡོད་) པ་	*gu-de pa.*
Do. *hon.*	སྒུག་བཞུགས་པ	*gu sḰu-pa.*
Expect, to (hope for)	རེ་བ་བྱེད་པ་	*re-wa cḰe pa.*
Do. *hon.*	ཐུགས་རེ་གནང་བ་	*thu-re nang-wa.*
Expectation	རེ་བ་	*re-wa.*
Do. *hon.*	ཐུགས་རེ་	*thu-re.*

Expedite, to	བྲེལ་བ་བྱེད་པ་	*ťre-wa cḱe-pa.*
Do. *hon.*	ཐུགས་བྲེལ་གནང་བ་	*thuḱ-ťre nang-wa.*
Expel, to	བཏོན་པ་ (འདོན་པ་)	*töm-pa.*
Do. *hon.*	འདོན་པ་གནང་བ་	*döm-pa nang-wa.*
Expense	འགྲོ་སོང་	*dro-song.*
Do. *hon.*	ཐུགས་འགྲོན་ (ཐུགས་འགྲོ་)	*thung-drön.*
Expensive	གོང་ཆེན་པོ། གུས་པོ་	*ḱong-chhem-po ; ḱü-po.*
Do. *hon.*	ལྗགས་གོང་ཆེན་པོ་	*ja-ḱong chhem-po.*
Experienced (skilled)	མཁས་པོ་	*khe-po.*
Explain, to	ངོ་སྤྲོད་སྤྲད་པ། དོན་དག་བཤད་པ་	*ngo-trö tre-pa ; ťon-ťa she-pa.*
Do. *hon.*	ངོ་སྤྲོད་གནང་བ། སྐུ་དོན་གསུང་བ་	*ngo-trö nang-wa ; ku-ťön sung-wa.*
Explain, to (by sign)	ལག་བརྡ་བྱེད་པ་	*laḱ-da cḱe-pa.*
Do. *hon.*	ཕྱག་བརྡ་གནང་བ་	*chha-da nang-wa.*
Explanation (apology)	སེབ་བཀྲོལ་	*seṕ-trö.*
Exports	འཐོན་ཁུངས་	*thön-khung.*
Extensive	རྒྱ་ཆེན་པོ་	*gya-chhem-po.*
External	ཕྱིའི་	*chhi-i.*
Extinct, to become	ཆད་པ་	*chhe-pa.*

Extinguish, to	བསད་པ་ (གསོད་པ་)	*se-pa.*
Do. *hon.*	གསོད་པ་གནང་བ་	*sö-pa nang-wa.*
Extort, to	དབང་ཡོད་བྱས་ནས་ལེན་པ་	*wang-yö cKe-ne lem-pa.*
Extra	འཕྲིབ་པ་	*thep-pa.*
Extract, to	བཏོན་པ་ (འདོན་པ་)	*töm pa.*
Do. *hon.*	འདོན་པ་གནང་བ་	*döm-pa nang-wa.*
Extraction (descent)	རྒྱུད་	*gyü.*
Extraordinary	ཡ་མཚན་པོ། ཁྱད་མཚར་པོ།	*yam-tshen po ; khye-tsha-po.*
Extremity	མཐའ་	*tha.*
Exult, to (rejoice)	དགའ་བ་	*ga-wa.*
Do. *hon.*	མཉེས་པོ་གནང་བ་	*nye-po nang-wa.*
Do. *h. hon.*	ཐུགས་དགྱེས་པོ་གནང་བ་	*thu-gye-po nang-wa.*
Exultation	དགའ་ཚོར་	*ga-tshor.*
Eye	མིག་	*mik.*
Do. *hon.*	སྤྱན་	*chen.*
Eye-ball	མིག་རིལ་	*mik-ri.*
Do. *hon.*	སྤྱན་རིལ་	*chen-ri.*
Eye-brow	མིག་ཟྲི་ (མིག་ཛྲི་)	*mik-śi.*
Do. *hon.*	སྤྱན་ཟྲི་ (སྤྱན་ཛྲི་)	*chen-śi.*
Eye-glass	མིག་ཤེར་ (མིག་ཤེལ་)	*mik-sher.*

Eye-glass, *hon.*	སྤྱན་ཤེར་ (སྤྱན་ཤེལ་)	*chen-sher.*
Eye-lash	མིག་སྤུ་	*miḱ-pu.*
Do. *hon.*	སྤྱན་སྤུ་	*chem-pu.*
Eye-lid	མིག་ལྤགས་	*miḱ-pa.*
Do. *hon.*	སྤྱན་ལྤགས་	*chem-pa.*
Eye-lid, lower	མིག་ལྤགས་སྨད་	*miḱ-pa me.*
Do. *hon.*	སྤྱན་ལྤགས་སྨད་	*chem-pa me.*
Eye-lid, upper	མིག་ལྤགས་ཡས་	*miḱ pa-ye.*
Do. *hon.*	སྤྱན་ལྤགས་ཡས་	*chem-pa ye.*
Eye-shade (of hair)	མིག་ར་	*miḱ-ra.*
Do. *hon.*	སྤྱན་ར་	*chen-ra.*

F

Fable	སྒྲུམ་ (སྒྲུང་)	*drum.*
Do. *hon.*	ཞལ་སྒྲུམ་ (ཞལ་སྒྲུང་)	*sḱe-drum.*
Fabrication (lie)	ཧམ་པ། སྐྱག་རྫུན་	*ham-pa ; ḱyaḱ-dzün.*
Do. *hon.*	ཞལ་རྫུན་	*sḱe-dzün.*
Face	གདོང་	*dong.*
Do. *hon.*	ཞལ་རས་	*sḱe-re.*
Facsimile	འདྲ་ཤུས་	*dra-shü.*
Fact	དོན་སྙིང་	*ťön-nying.*
Factory	བཟོ་ཁང་	*śo-khang.*
Fade, to (wither)	རྙིད་པ་	*nyi-pa.*
Do. to (of colour)	གཞུད་པ་	*sḱü pa.*
Fail, to (miss)	མི་…ཐུབ་པ་	*mi...thup̒-pa.*
Do. *hon.*	མི་…ཐུབ་པ་གནང་བ་	*mi...thup̒-pa nang-wa.*
Fail, without (in any event)	ཡིན་གཅིག་མིན་གཅིག། ཏེན་ལྡན་	*yin-chi min-chi ; ten-den.*
Faint-hearted	སེམས་ཆུང་ཆུང་། སྙིང་ཆུང་ཆུང་	*sem chhung-chhung ; nying-chhung-chhung.*
Do. *hon.*	ཐུགས་སེམས་ཆུང་ཆུང་	*thu-sem chhung-chhung.*

Faint, to	དྲན་མེད་བརྒྱལ་བ་	*t́ren me gye-wa.*
Do. *hon.*	དྲན་མེད་བརྒྱལ་ར་ (བ་) གནང་བ་	*t́ren me gye-ra nang-wa.*
Fair	མཛེས་པོ་	*dze-po.*
Do. *hon.*	ཐུགས་ཚར་པོ་	*thu tshar-po.*
Fair (just)	ཁྲིམས་དྲང་པོ་	*thrim-t́rang-po.*
Do. *hon.*	བཀའ་ཁྲིམས་དྲང་པོ་	*ka-thrim t́rang-po*
Fairy	ལྷ་མོ་	*hla-mo.*
Faith	དད་པ་	*t́e-pa.*
Faithful	དམ་ཚིག་ཡག་པོ་	*t́am-tshi yaḱ-po.*
Fakir	གྲུབ་ཐོབ་	*t́rup-tho.*
Falcon	ཁྲ་	*thra.*
Fall, to (on ground which one is already touching)	འགྱེལ་བ་	*gye-wa.*
Do. *hon.*	འགྱེལ་ར་ (བ་) གནང་བ་	*gye-ra nang-wa.*
Fall, to (from a height)	གཟགས་པ་ (འཛོག་པ་)	*śaḱ-pa.*
Do. *hon.*	གཟགས་ག་ (འཛོག་པ་) གནང་བ་	*śaḱ-ḱa nang-wa.*
Fall, to (descend)	བབ་ (འབབ་) ཡོང་བ་ (or འགྲོ་བ་)	*ṕap-yong-wa* (or *dro-wa*).

Fall, to (descend) *hon.*	བབ་ (འབབ་) ཕེབ་པ་	*pap-phe-pa.*
Do. *h. hon.*	བབ་ (འབབ་) འཆིབ་རྒྱུ་ གནང་བ་	*pap-chhip-gyu nang-wa.*
Fall head-over-heels, to	མགོ་གཞུག་ལོག་པ་	*go-sku lok-pa.*
Do. to (in drops)	འཐིག་པ་རྒྱབ་པ་	*thik-pa gyap-pa.*
Do. to (of flood, etc.)	ཆག་པ་	*chhak-pa.*
Fallow	ས་སྟོང་	*sa-tong.*
False	ཧམ་བ། སྐྱག་རྫུན།	*ham-pa ; kyak-dzün.*
Falsehood	ཧམ་པ། སྐྱག་རྫུན་	*ham-pa ; kyak-dzün.*
Do. *hon.*	ཞལ་རྫུན་	*ske-dzün.*
Falter, to (waver)	ཐེ་ཚོམ་ཟ་བ་	*the-tshom sa-wa.*
Do. hon.	ཐེ་ཚོམ་གནང་བ་	*the-tshom nang-wa.*
Fame	སྐད་གྲགས་	*ke-tra.*
Do. *hon.*	སྙན་གྲགས་	*nyen-tra.*
Familiar	གློ་དཀར། ཉེ་པོ་	*lo-ka ; nye-po.*
Family	མི་ཚང་	*mi-tshang.*
Family (lineage)	རིགས་བརྒྱུད་	*ri-gyü.*
Do. *hon.*	སྐུ་བརྒྱུད་	*ku-gyü.*
Family, member of	ནང་མི་	*nang-mi.*
Family priest	མཆོད་གནས་	*chhö-ne.*

Famine	མུ་གེ་	*mu-ḱe.*
Famous (celebrated)	སྙན་གྲགས་ཆེན་པོ་	*ke-t́ra chhem-po.*
Do. *hon.*	སྙན་གྲགས་ཆེན་པོ་	*nyen-t́ra chhem-po.*
Fan	རླུང་ཡབ་	*lung-yaṕ.*
Fancy (opinion)	བསམ་པ་	*sam-pa.*
Do. *hon.*	ཐུགས་སེམས་	*thu-sem.*
Fancy (wish)	འདོད་པ་	*dö-pa.*
Do. *hon.*	ཐུགས་འདོད་	*thung-dö.*
Fancy, to (like)	དགའ་བ་	*ga-wa.*
Do. *hon.*	ཐུགས་མཉེས་པ་	*thu-nye-pa.*
Do *h. hon.*	ཐུགས་དགྱེས་པ་	*thu-gye-pa.*
Fancy to, (suppose)	བསམ་པ་	*sam-pa.*
Do. *hon.*	དགོངས་པ་	*gong-pa.*
Fang (of tiger, etc.)	མཆེ་བ་	*chhe-wa.*
Far	ཐག་རིང་པོ་	*tha-ring-po.*
Do. how	ཐག་རིང་ཐུང་ག་ཚོད་	*tha-ring-thung ḱa-tshö.*
Fare (food)	ཁ་ལག ། ཏོ་	*kha-la ; to.*
Do *hon.*	ཞལ་ལག་	*sḱe-la.*
Farewell! (to person going away)	འོ་ན་རྒྱུག་ཨ་	*o-na gyu-a.*
Do. *hon.*	ག་ལེ་ཕེབས་	*ḱa-le phe*

Farewell! (to person going away) *h. hon.*	ག་ལེ་འཆིབ་རྒྱུ་གནང་	*ka-le chhip-gyu-nang.*
Farewell! (to person remaining)	འོ་ན་སྡོད་ཨ་	*o-na dö-a.*
Do. *hon.*	ག་ལེ་བཞུགས་	*ka-le sku.*
Do. *h. hon.*	ག་ལེ་བཞུགས་གདན་འཇག་	*ka-le sku-den-ja.*
Farm	ཕ་གཞིས་	*pha-ski.*
Farmer	སོ་ནམས་བྱེད་མཁན་	*so-nam cke-khen.*
Farming, *s.* (agriculture)	སོ་ནམས་	*so-nam.*
Farrier	རྨིག་ལྕགས་རྒྱབ་མཁན་	*mik-cha gyang-khen.*
Farther	ཕ་ཙ་ (ཕར་ཙམ་)	*pha-tsa.*
Fascinate, to	བློ་ལ་ཕྱིན་པ་	*lo-la chhim-pa.*
Do. *hon.*	ཐུགས་ལ་ཕེབ་པ་	*thu-la phe-pa.*
Fashion (custom)	ལུགས་སྲོལ་	*luk-sö.*
Do. (form)	བཟོ་ལྟ་	*sop-ta.*
Do. *hon.*	སྐུ་བཟོ་	*ku-so.*
Fast (faithful)	དམ་ཚིག་ཡག་པོ་	*tam-tshi yak-po.*
Do. (firm)	བརྟན་པོ་	*tem-po.*
Do. (quick)	མགྱོགས་པོ་	*gyok-po.*
Do. *hon.*	རྩོལ་པོ་	*tsö-po.*
Fast, to	སྨྱུང་གནས་སྲུང་བ་	*nyung-ne sung-wa.*

Fast, to, ***hon.***	སྨྱུང་གནས་སྲུང་ང་ (བ་) གནང་བ་	*nyung-ne sung-nga nang-wa.*
Fasten, to (with rope, etc.)	བསྡམས་པ་ (སྡོམ་པ་)	*dam-pa.*
Do. *hon.*	བསྡམས་ (སྡོམ་) པ་གནང་བ་	*dam-pa nang-wa.*
Fasten, to (with glue, etc.)	སྦྱར་བ་	*jar-wa.*
Do. *hon.*	སྦྱར་ར་ (བ་) གནང་བ་	*jar-ra nang-wa.*
Fasten on, to (affix)	སྦྲེལ་བ་	*drel-wa.*
Do. *hon.*	སྦྲེལ་ལ་ (བ་) གནང་བ་	*drel-la nang-wa.*
Fasting, *s.*	སྨྱུང་གནས་	*nyung-ne.*
Fat, *adj.*	ཤ་རྒྱགས་པ་	*sha-gyak-pa.*
Do. *hon.*	སྐུ་ཤ་འབྱོར་པོ་	*ku-sha jor-po.*
Fat, *s.* **(suet, lard)**	ཚིལ་ལུ་ (ཚིལ་བུ་)	*tshi-lu.*
Do. *hon.*	བཞེས་ཚིལ་	*sḱe-tshi.*
Fate	བསོ་བདེ་ (བསོད་བདེ་)	*so-de.*
Do. *hon.*	སྐུ་བསོད་	*ku-sö.*
Father	ཨ་ཕ་	*a-pha.*
Do. *hon.*	ཡབ་	*yaṕ.*
Fatherland	ལུང་པ་	*lung-pa.*
Do. *hon.*	འཁྲུངས་ས་	*thrung-sa.*
Father-in-law	པ་ལགས། གྱོས་པོ་	*pa-la ; ḱyö-po.*

Fatigue	ངལ་	*ngel.*
Do. *hon.*	སྐུ་ངལ་	*ku-ngel.*
Fatigued, to be	ཐང་ཆད་པ་	*thang-chhe-pa.*
Do. *hon.*	སྐུ་ཐང་མཉེལ་བ་	*ku-thang nye-wa.*
Fatiguing	དཀའ་ལས་ཁག་པོ་	*ka-le khaḱ-po.*
Do. *hon.*	སྐུ་མཉེལ་པོ་	*ku-nye-po.*
Fault	སྐྱོན་	*kyön.*
Favonr	དྲིན་	*t́rin.*
Do. *hon.*	བཀའ་དྲིན་	*ka-t́rin.*
Favourite (official, etc.)	མིག་གསལ་	*miḱ-se.*
Do. *hon.*	སྤྱན་གསལ་	*chen-se.*
Fawn	ཤ་ཕྲུག་	*sha-thru.*
Fear	ཞེད་སྐྲག་	*sḱe-tra.*
Fear, to	ཞེད་པ་	*sḱe-pa.*
Do. to *hon.*	ཞེད་པ་གནང་བ་	*sḱe-pa nang-wa.*
Fearful	ཞེད་སྐྲག་ཚ་པོ་	*sḱe-tra tsha-po.*
Fearless, to be	ཞེད་རྒྱུ་ཙ་ནས་མེད་པ་	*sḱe-gyu tsa-ne me-pa.*
Feast	མགྲོན་པོ་	*dröm-po.*
Do. *hon.*	ཐུགས་སྒྲོ་	*thuḱ-tro.*
Feather (small)	སྤུ་	*pu.*

Feather (large)	སྒྲོ་	*dro.*
Features	བཟོ་བལྟ་	*sop-ta.*
Fee	རྔན་པ། གླ་	*ngem-pa ; la.*
Feeble (infirm)	ཀྱ་རེ་ཀྱོ་རེ། ཉ་རེ་ (ར) ཉོ་རེ་	*kya-re kyo-re ; nya-re nyo-re.*
Do. *hon.*	སྐུ་ཀྱོར་ཀྱོར་	*ku-kyor-kyor.*
Feed, to, *v.t.*	ལྟོ་སྟེར་བ་	*to ter-wa.*
Do. *hon.*	ལྟོ་གསོལ་རས་གནང་བ་	*to sö-re nang-wa.*
Do. *inf.* to *sup.*	ཞལ་ལག་ཕུལ་ (འབུལ་) བ་	*sKe la phü-wa.*
Feed, to, *v.i.*	ཁ་ལག་ཟ་བ། ལྟོ་ཟ་བ་	*kha-la śa-wa ; to śa-wa*
Do. *hon.*	ཞལ་ལག་བཞེས་པ་	*sKe-la sKe-pa.*
Feel, to, (touch)	ཐུག་པ་	*thuK-pa.*
Do. *hon.*	ཐུག་ག་ (པ་) གནང་བ་	*thuK-Ka nang-wa.*
Feel cold, to	འཁྱགས་པ་	*khyaK-pa.*
Do. *hon.*	སྐུ་བསིལ་ར་ (བ་) གནང་བ་	*ku-si-ra nang-wa*
Feign, to	གྱོད་བཤད་པ་	*Kyö-she-pa*
Do. *hon.*	གྱོད་གསུང་བ་	*Kyö-sung-wa.*
Feign illness, to	ན་ཚུ་ (རྫུ) བཏབ་ (འདེབས་) པ་	*na-tshu tap̄-pa.*
Do. *hon.*	སྙུང་ཚུ་ (རྫུ) བཏབ་ (འདེབས་) པ་	*nyung-tshu tap̄-pa.*
Feign stupidity, to.	ལྐུགས་ཚུལ་བཏབ་ (འདེབས་) པ་	*kuK-tshü tap̄-pa.*

Feign stupidity, to, *hon.*	ལྐུགས་ཚུལ་གསུང་བ་	*kuḱ-tshü sung-wa.*
Fellow-labourer	ལས་རོགས་	*le-ro.*
Do. *hon.*	ཕྱག་སྦྲེལ་	*chha-drel.*
Fellow-traveller	ལམ་རོགས་	*lam-ro.*
Do. *hon.*	ཕེབ་རོགས་	*pheṕ-ro.*
Felon	བཙོན་པ་	*tsöm-pa.*
Felt	ཕྱིང་པ་	*chhing-pa.*
Female	མོ་	*mo.*
Fence	ར་བ་	*ra-wa.*
Ferment, to (wine)	བསྙེལ་བ་ (སྙོལ་བ་)	*nyel-wa.*
Fern	སྐྱེ་མ་	*kye-ma.*
Ferocious (of human beings)	ངན་པ་	*ngem-pa.*
Do. (of animals)	ཚུབ་པོ་	*tshuṕ-po.*
Ferry	གྲུ་ཁ་	*t́ru-kha.*
Ferry-boat	གྲུ་	*t́ru.*
Do. *hon.*	ཕེབ་གྲུ་	*pheṕ t́ru.*
Ferry-man	གྲུ་པ་	*t́ru-pa.*
Do. *hon.*	གྲུ་དཔོན་	*t́ru-pön.*
Fertile	ལུད་ཆུ་འཛོམ་པོ་	*lü-chhu dzom-po.*
Fervent	སྙིང་རུས་ཆེན་པོ་	*nying-rü chhem-po.*

Fervent, *hon.*	ཐུགས་དྲུས་ཆེན་པོ་	*thu-rü chhem-po*
Festival	དུས་ཆེན་	*t́ü-chhen.*
Fetch, to (by carrying)	འཁྱེར་བ་	*ḱhyer-wa.*
Do. *hon.*	སྣོམས་པ་	*nom-pa.*
Fetch, to (by leading)	འཁྲིད་པ་	*thri-pa.*
Do. *hon.*	འཁྲིད་པ་གནང་བ་	*t́hri-pa nang-wa.*
Fetlock, fore (of horse)	ལག་གུག་	*laḱ-ku.*
Do. hind	རྐང་གུག་	*kang-ḱu.*
Fetters (for hands)	ལག་ལྕགས་	*laḱ-cha.*
Do. (for feet)	རྐང་ལྕགས་	*kang-cha.*
Fever	ཚད་པ་	*tshe-pa.*
Do. *hon.*	སྐུ་ཚད་	*ku-tshe.*
Fever, to have	ཚད་པ་ན་བ་	*tshe-pa na-wa.*
Do. *hon.*	སྐུ་ཚད་སྙུང་བ་	*ḱu-tshe nyung-wa.*
Few	ཏོག་ཙ་ (ཏོག་ཙོད་)	*toḱ-tsa.*
Do., only a	ཁ་ཤས་ཅིག་	*ḱha-she-chi.*
Fibre	རྒྱུས་པ་	*gyü-pa.*
Fickle, to be	བརྟན་པོ་...མེད་པ་	*tem-po ...... me-pa.*
Fiddle	པི་ཝང་	*pi-wang.*
Field	ཞིང་ཁ་	*sḱing-kha.*

Fiend	བདུད་	*dü.*
Fierce (of human beings)	ངན་པ་	*ngem-pa.*
Do. (of animals)	རྩུབ་པོ་	*tshup-po.*
Fifteen	བཅོ་ལྔ་	*chö-nga.*
Fifteenth	བཅོ་ལྔ་པ་	*chö-nga-pa.*
Fifth	ལྔ་པ་	*nga-pa.*
Fiftieth	ལྔ་བཅུ་པ་	*ngap-chu-pa.*
Fifty	ལྔ་བཅུ་	*ngap-chu.*
Fight	རྒྱབ་འདྲེ་	*gyam-dre.*
Do. to (with words or blows)	རྒྱབ་འདྲེ་རྒྱབ་པ་	*gyam-dre gyap-pa.*
Do. *hon.*	གསུང་འཁྲུག་སྐྱོན་པ་	*sung-thru kyöm-pa.*
Fight, to (make war)	དམག་རྒྱབ་པ་	*ma-gyap-pa.*
Do. *hon.*	དམག་སྐྱོན་པ་	*ma-kyöm-pa.*
Fight, to (with blows)	འཛིང་བ་	*dzing-wa.*
Do. *hon.*	འཛིང་རེས་གནང་བ་	*dzing-re nang-wa.*
Figurative	སྙན་ངག་	*nye-nga.*
Figure (painting)	རི་མོ་	*ri-mo.*
Do. (number)	ཨང་ཀི་	*ang-ki.*
Do. (shape)	བཟོ་བལྟ་	*śop-ta.*
Do. *hon.*	སྐུ་བཟོ་	*ku-śo.*

File	ལྕགས་སག་	*chak̄-sa.*
Fill, to	གང་གླུག་པ་	*k̄ang-luk̄-pa.*
Do. *hon.*	གང་གླུག་ག་ (ཀ་) གནང་བ་	*k̄ang-luk̄-k̄a nang-wa.*
Do. *inf.* to *sup.*	གང་ཞུ་བ་	*k̄ang-sk̄u-wa.*
Filter (for tea)	ཇ་ཚགས་	*ck̄a-tsha.*
Filthy	བཙོག་པ་	*tsok̄-pa.*
Do. *hon.*	སྐུ་བཙོག་	*ku-tso.*
Filthy, to be	བཙོག་པ་ཡོད་པ་	*tsok̄-pa yö-pa.*
Do. to become	བཙོག་པ་ཤོར་བ་	*tsok̄-pa shor-wa.*
Do. *hon*	སྐུ་བཙོག་ཤོར་བ་	*ku-tso shor-wa.*
Fin	ཤོག་པ་	*shok̄-pa.*
Final	གཞུག་ཤོས་	*sk̄uk̄-shö.*
Find, to	རྙེད་པ་	*nye-pa.*
Do. *hon.*	རྙེད་པ་གནང་བ་	*nye-pa nang-wa.*
Fine (beautiful)	མཛེས་པོ་	*dze-po.*
Do. (minute)	ཞིབ་པོ་	*sk̄ip̄-po.*
Do. (thin, of round objects)	ཕྲ་པོ་	*thra-po.*
Do. (thin, of flat objects)	སྲབ་པོ་	*trap̄-po.*
Fine, *s.*	དངོས་པོའི་ཉེས་པ་	*ngö pö nye-pa.*

Fine, *hon.*	དངོས་པོའི་བཀའ་ཉེས་	*ngö-pö ka-nye.*
Fine, to	དངོས་པོའི་ཉེས་པ་བཏང་ (གཏོང་) བ་	*ngö-pö nye-pa tang-wa.*
Do. *hon.*	དངོས་པོའི་བཀའ་ཉེས་གནང་བ་	*ngö-pö ka-nye nang wa.*
Fine (for murder, paid as compensation to the relatives of the deceased)	སྟོང་	*tong.*
Do. (for theft)	བཀུས་འཇལ་ (ཀུ་འཇལ་)	*kün-jel.*
Finger	མཛུག་གུ་	*dzu-ku.*
Do. *hon.*	ཕྱག་མཛུག་	*chhan-dzu.*
Finger (fore-finger)	མཛུག་གུ་	*dzu-ku*
Do. (middle finger)	དཀྱིལ་མཛུག་	*kyi-dzu.*
Do. (third finger)	སྲིན་མཛུག་	*trin-dzu.*
Do. (little finger)	མཛུག་ཆུང་། ཨི་ཆུང་ང་	*dzuk-chhung; i-chhung-nga.*
Finger-nail	སེན་མོ་	*sen-mo.*
Do. *hon.*	ཕྱག་སེན་	*chha-sen.*
Finish, to (complete)	འཚར་བ་	*tshar wa*
Do. *hon.*	འགྲུབ་པ་	*drup-pa.*
Fir-tree (Abies Webbiana)	གདུང་ཤིང་	*dung-shing.*

Fire	མེ་	*me.*
Do. *hon.*	སྐུགས་མེ་	*sḰu-me.*
Fire, to catch	མེ་ཤོར་བ་	*me-shor-wa.*
Fire, to, *v.t.*	མེ་སྦར་བ་	*me-bar-wa.*
Fire a gun, to	མེ་མདའ་རྒྱབ་པ་	*men-da gyaṕ-pa.*
Do. to *hon.*	ཕྱག་མདའ་སྐྱོན་པ་	*chhan-da-kyöm-pa.*
Fire-place	ཐབ་	*thaṕ.*
Fire-works	ཤོག་པག་	*sho-pa.*
Firm (not shaky)	བརྟན་པོ་	*tem-po.*
Do. (tight)	དམ་པོ་	*t́am-po.*
Firmament	གནམ། ནམ་མཁའ་	*nam ; nam-kha.*
First	དང་པོ་	*t́ang-po.*
Firstborn	རྒན་པ་	*gem-pa.*
First class (excellent)	ཨང་གི་དང་པོ་	*ang-Ḱi t́ang-po.*
First-rate	ཨང་གི་དང་པོ་	*ang-Ḱi t́ang-po.*
Firstly	དང་པོ་ (དང་པོར་)	*t́ang-po.*
Fish	ཉ་	*nya.*
Do. to	ཉ་ཟིན་པ་	*nya śim-pa.*
Do. *hon.*	ཉ་ཟིན་པ་གནང་བ་	*nya śim-pa nang-wa.*
Fish-bone	ཉ་རུས་	*nya-rü.*

Fisherman	ཉ་རྡུང་ང་། ཉ་ཟྲིན་མཁན་	*nyap dung-nga; nya-sim-khen.*
Fish-hook	ལྕགས་ཀྱུ། ཉ་ཀྱུག་	*cha-kyu; nya-ku.*
Fishing-net	ཉ་དོལ་	*nya-töl.*
Fish's fin	ཉའི་ཤོག་པ་	*nya-i shok-pa.*
Fissure	སེར་ཀ་	*ser-ka.*
Fist	ཛོག་མགོ་	*dzong-go.*
Fisted, close-	ལག་པ་དམ་པོ་	*lak-pa tam-po.*
Do. *hon.*	ཕྱག་དམ་པོ་	*chha-tam-po.*
Fit, to (of clothes, &c.)	འགྲིག་པ་	*drik-pa.*
Do. *hon.*	འགྲིག་ག་ (པ་) གནང་བ་	*drik-ka nang-wa.*
Fitful, to be	བརྟན་པོ་མེད་པ་	*tem-po....me-pa.*
Fitting (proper)	འོས་པོ་	*ö-po.*
Do. to be	འགྲིག་པ་	*drik-pa.*
Five	ལྔ་	*nga.*
Fix, to (place)	བཞག་པ་ (འཛོག་པ་)	*skak-pa.*
Do. *hon.*	གཞོག་ག་ (པ་) གནང་བ་	*skok-ka nang-wa.*
Fix a time, to	དུས་ཚོད་བྱེད་པ་	*tü-tshö che-pa.*
Do. *hon.*	དུས་ཚོད་གནང་བ་	*tü tshö nang-wa.*
Flag, large	དར་ཆེན་	*tar-chhen.*
Do. small	དར་ལྕོག་	*tar-cho.*

Flagstaff	དར་ཤིང་	*ťar-shing.*
Flame	མེ་ལྕེ་	*me-che.*
Flannel, thin	ཐེར་མ་	*ther-ma.*
Do. thick	སྤུ་རུག་	*pu-ru.*
Flat	ལེབ་ལེབ་	*leṕ-leṕ.*
Flatten, to	ལེབ་ལེབ་བཟོ་བ་	*leṕ-leṕ śo-wa.*
Do. *hon.*	ལེབ་ལེབ་བཟོ་བ་གནང་བ་	*leṕ-leṕ śo-wa nang-wa.*
Flatter, to	དཔལ་ལས་བཤད་པ་	*pe-le she-pa.*
Do. *inf.* to *sup*	དཔལ་ལས་ཞུ་བ་	*pe-le sǩu-wa.*
Flaunt, to (boast)	རང་སྟོད་བྱེད་པ་	*rang-tö cǩe-pa.*
Flavour	བྲོ་བ་	*ťro-wa.*
Do. *hon.*	ལྗགས་བྲོ་	*ja-ťro.*
Flaw	སྐྱོན་	*kyön.*
Flay, to	ཤུ་བ་	*shu-wa.*
Do. *hon.*	ཤུ་བ་གནང་བ་	*shu-wa nang-wa.*
Flea	འཇོ་འོ་ (འཇུ་བ་)	*jo.*
Flee, to	བྲོས་ཕྱིན་པ་	*ṕö chhim-pa.*
Do. *hon.*	བྲོས་ཕེབ་པ་	*ṕö-pheṕ-pa.*
Do. *h. hon.*	བྲོས་འཆིབ་རྒྱུ་གནང་བ་	*ṕö chhiṕ-gyu nang-wa.*

Fleet (quick)	མགྱོགས་པོ་	*gyok-po.*
Do. *hon.*	རྩོལ་པོ་	*tsö-po.*
Flesh	ཤ་	*sha.*
Do. *hon.*	སྐུ་ཤ་	*ku-sha.*
Flesh, for eating, *hon.*	གསོལ་སྒྲུང་ (གསོལ་སྒྲུམ་)	*sö-trung.*
Fleshy (fat)	ཤ་རྒྱགས་པ་	*sha-gyak-pa.*
Do. *hon.*	སྐུ་ཤ་འབྱོར་པོ་	*ku-sha jor-po.*
Flexible	མཉེན་པོ་	*nyem-po.*
Fling, to	དབྱུག་པ་	*yuk-pa.*
Do. *hon.*	དབྱུག་ག་ (པ་) གནང་བ་	*yuk-ka nang-wa.*
Flint	མེ་རྡོ་	*me do.*
Flip, to	ཨེ་ཀོག་གཞུ་བ་	*e-ko sku-wa.*
Float, to	ལྡིང་བ་	*ding-wa.*
Flock, *s.*	ཁྱུ་	*khyu.*
Flog, to	གཞུ་བ་	*sku-wa.*
Flood	ཆུ་རུད་	*chhu rü.*
Do. to	ཆུ་ཡིས་གནོན་པ་	*chhu-yi nem-pa*
Floor, boarded	སྤང་ལེབ་	*pang-lep.*
Do. of earth	ས་	*sa.*
Do. plastered	ཞལ་ (ཞལ་ལ་	*ska-la.*

Flour, barley	ཙམ་པ་	*tsam-pa.*
Do. *hon.*	གསོལ་ཞིབ་	*sö-sḱip̣.*
Flour, wheat	གྲོ་ཞིབ་	*ṫro-sḱip̣.*
Do. rice	འབྲས་ཙམ་	*dre-tsam.*
Flourishing	གཡང་ཆེན་པ་	*yang-chhem-po.*
Flout, to (scoff)	ཀྱག་ཀྱག་བྱས་ནས་ལབ་པ་	*kya-kya cḱe-ne lap̣-pa.*
Do. *hon.*	ཀྱག་ཀྱག་གནང་ནས་གསུང་བ་	*kya-kya nang-ne sung-wa.*
Flout, to (insult)	སྨད་ར་བཏང་ (གཏོང་) བ་	*me-ra tang-wa.*
Do. *hon.*	སྨད་ར་གཏོང་ང་ (བ་) གནང་བ་	*me-ra tong-nga nang-wa.*
Flow, to	རྒྱུག་པ་	*gyuḱ-pa.*
Flow out, to	འཐོན་པ་	*thöm-pa.*
Flower	མེ་ཏོག་	*me-to.*
Do. garden.	མེ་ཏོག་ལྡུམ་ར་	*me-to dum-ra.*
Fluently	ཆུ་རྒྱུག་རྒྱུག	*chhu-gyuḱ-gyu.*
Fluid (food)	ཁུ་བ་	*khu-wa.*
Flute (small)	གླིང་བུ་	*ling-ṗu.*
Flute (large, held across the body)	ཕྲེད་གླིང་	*thre-ling.*
Do. *hon.*	ཞལ་གླིང་	*sḱe-ling.*
Fly, *s.*	སྦྲང་མ་	*drang-ma.*
Do. to (of bird)	འཕིར་བ་ (འཕུར་བ་)	*phir-wa.*

Foal, *s.*	ཏི་གི་ (ཏེའུ་)	*ti-ḱi.*
Do. of an ass	ཨུ་ཏིའི་ (ཨུ་ཏི་)	*u-ti-i.*
Foam	ལྦུ་བ་	*bu-wa.*
Fodder (grass and grain)	རྩ་ཆག་	*tsa-chha.*
Foe	དགྲ་	*dra.*
Fog	སྨུགས་པ་	*muḱ-pa.*
Fold, to	ལྟབ་རྩིས་ (རྩིགས་) རྒྱབ་པ་	*taṕ-tsi gyaṕ-pa.*
Do. *hon.*	ལྟབ་རྩིས་ (རྩིགས་) སྐྱོན་པ་	*taṕ-tsi kyöm-pa.*
Foliage	ལོ་མ་	*lo-ma.*
Folk	མི་	*mi.*
Follow, to	གཞུག་ལ་ཕྱིན་པ་	*sḱu-la chhim-pa.*
Do. *hon.*	གཞུག་ལ་ཕེབ་པ་	*sḱu-la phe-pa.*
Do. *h. hon.*	གཞུག་ལ་འཆིབ་རྒྱུ་གནང་བ་	*sḱu-la chhiṕ-gyu nang-wa.*
Fond of, to be (of persons and things)	ཞེན་ཆགས་བྱེད་པ་	*sḱen-chha cḱe-pa.*
Do. *hon.*	ཞེན་ཆགས་གནང་བ་	*sḱen-chha nang-wa.*
Fondle, to	བྱམས་པོ་བྱེད་པ་	*cḱam po cḱe-pa.*
Do. *hon.*	བྱམས་པོ་གནང་བ་	*cḱam-po nang-wa.*
Fondness	བྱམས་པོ་	*cḱam-po.*
Food	ཁ་ལག། ལྟོ་	*kha-la; to.*
Do. *hon.*	ཞལ་ལག	*sḱe-la.*

Fool	གླེན་པ། ལྐུགས་པ་	*lem-pa ; kuk̓-pa.*
Foolhardy (rash)	ཁ་མེད་མིག་མེད་	*kha-me mik̓-me.*
Foolish (weak in intellect)	ལྐུགས་པ། གླེན་པ་	*kuk̓-pa ; lem-pa.*
Do. (senseless, of things)	དོན་མེད་	*tön-me.*
Foot	རྐང་པ་	*kang-pa.*
Do. *hon.*	ཞབས་	*sh̓ap̓.*
Foot, to go on	རྐང་ཐང་ལ་འགྲོ་བ་	*kang-thang-la dro-wa.*
Do. *hon.*	ཞབས་ཐང་ལ་ཕེབ་པ་	*sh̓ap̓-thang-la phep̓-pa.*
Do. *h. hon.*	ཞབས་ཐང་ལ་འཆིབ་རྒྱུ་ གནང་བ་	*sh̓ap̓-thang-la chhip̓-gyu nang-wa.*
Foot and mouth disease	ཁ་ཚ་	*kha-tsha.*
Foot-bridge	ཟམ་པ་ཆུང་ཆུང་	*śam-pa chhung-chhung.*
Do. *hon.*	ཕེབ་ཟམ་ཆུང་ཆུང་	*phep̓-śam. chhung-chhung.*
Foot-path	རྐང་ཐང་ལ་འགྲོ་ས་	*kang-thang-la dro-sa.*
Do. *hon.*	ཞབས་ཐང་ལ་ཕེབ་ས་	*sh̓ap̓-thang-la phep̓-sa.*
Foot-path (alongside of cliff)	འཕྲང་	*thrang.*
Foot-print	རྐང་རྗེས་	*kang-je.*
Do. *hon.*	ཞབས་རྗེས་	*sh̓ap̓-je.*
Foot-race	མི་རྒྱུག	*mi-gyu.*
Foot-soldier	དམག་མི་	*ma-mi.*

Footstool	རྐང་སྟེགས་	*kang-teḱ.*
Do. *hon.*	ཞབས་སྟེགས་	*sḱap-teḱ.*
For (because)	ག་རེ་རེད་ཟེར་ན་	*ḱa-re re śe-na.*
For instance	དཔེ་ན་ (དཔེར་ན་)	*pe-na.*
For the sake of	དོན་ལ་	*ťön-la.*
Forage (grass)	རྩྭ་	*tsa.*
Forbear, to	ཁོག་པ་བྱེད་པ་	*khoḱ-pa cḱe-pa.*
Do. *hon.*	ཐུགས་ཁོག་གནང་བ་	*thu-kho nang-wa.*
Forbear, to (of monks)	བཟོད་པ་སྒོམ་པ་	*śö-pa gom-pa.*
Do. *hon.*	བཟོད་པ་བཞེས་པ་	*śö-pa sḱe-pa.*
Forbid, to	བཀག་པ་ (འགོགས་པ་)	*kaḱ-pa.*
Do. *hon.*	བཀག་ག་ (འགོགས་པ་) གནང་བ་	*kaḱ ḱa nang-wa.*
Forbidding (repulsive)	སྐྱུག་བྲོ་བོ་	*kyuḱ-ťro-po.*
Force (strength)	ཤེད་	*she.*
Do. *hon.*	སྐུ་ཤེད་	*ku-she.*
Force (authority)	དབང་	*wang.*
Do. *hon.*	སྐུ་དབང་	*ku-wang.*
Force, to (compel)	ཨུ་ཚུགས་བྱེད་པ་	*u-tshu cḱe-pa.*
Do. *hon.*	ཨུ་ཚུགས་གནང་བ་	*u-tshu nang-wa.*

Forcible	ཤུགས་ཆེན་པོ་	*shuk-chhem-po.*
Ford, *s.*	རབ་	*rap.*
Forearm	ལག་ངར་	*la-ngar.*
Do. *hon.*	ཕྱག་ངར་	*chha-ngar.*
Forecast	ལུང་བསྟན་	*lung-ten.*
Do. *hon.*	བཀའ་ལུང་	*ka-lung.*
Forego, to (renounce)	སྤང་བ་	*pang-wa.*
Do. *hon.*	སྤོང་ང་ (བ་) གནང་བ་	*pong-nga nang-wa.*
Foregoing	སྔོན་གྱི་	*ngön-kyi.*
Forehead	དཔལ་ཁོག་ (ཐོད་པ་)	*pe-kho.*
Do. *hon.*	དབུ་དཔལ་	*u-pe.*
Foreign	ཕྱི་གླིང་	*chhi-ling.*
Foreigner	ཕྱི་གླིང་ང་ (བ་)	*chhi-ling-nga.*
Foreign country	ཕི་ (ཕྱི་) གླིང་ལུང་པ་	*phi-ling lung-pa.*
Foreign Secretary	ཕྱི་རྒྱའི་བློན་ཆེན་	*chhi-gye lön-chhen.*
Foreknowledge	མངོན་ཤེས་	*ngön-she.*
Do. *hon.*	མངོན་མཁྱེན་	*ngön-khyen.*
Forenoon (8 a.m. to 10 a.m.)	ཚ་ཏིང་	*tsha-ting.*
Forerunner	སྔན་ (སྔོན་) བགྲོད་པ་	*ngen-drö-pa.*
Foretell, to	མངོན་ཤེས་ཤེས་པ་	*ngön-she she-pa.*

Foretell, to, *hon.*	མངོན་མཁྱེན་མཁྱེན་པ་	*ngön-khyen khyem-pa.*
Foretell, to (in a trance)	ལུང་བསྟན་ (སྟོན་) པ་	*lung-tem-pa.*
Do. *hon.*	ལུང་བསྟན་ (སྟོན་) པ་གནང་བ་	*lung-tem pa nang-wa.*
Forest	ཤིང་ནགས། ནགས་གསེབ་	*shing-na ; naḱ-seṕ.*
Forever	ནམ་རྒྱུན། དུས་རྒྱུན་	*nam-gyün ; ťü-gyün.*
Forge, *s.*	བཟོ་ཐབ་	*śo-thaṕ.*
Forget, to.	བརྗེད་པ། བརྗེད་ནས་མེད་པ་	*je-pa ; je-ne-me-pa.*
Do. *hon.*	བསྙེལ་བ། ཐུགས་བསྙེལ་ཤོར་བ་	*nyel-wa ; thu-nye shor-wa.*
Forgive, to	དགོངས་པ་བཏང་ (གཏོང་) པ། སྙིང་རྗེ་ལྟ་བ་	*gong-pa tang-pa ; nying-je ta-wa.*
Do. *hon.*	དགོངས་པ་གཏོང་ང་ (བ་) གནང་བ། སྙིང་རྗེ་གཟིགས་པ་	*gong-pa tong-nga nang-wa nying-je śiḱ-pa.*
Fork	ཤ་འཛིན་	*shan-dzin.*
Form, *s.* (shape)	བཟོ་བལྟ་	*śoṕ-ta.*
Do. *hon.*	སྐུ་བཟོ་	*ku-śo.*
Form, to (make)	བཟོ་བ་	*śo-wa.*
Do. *hon.*	བཟོ་བ་གནང་བ་	*śo-wa nang-wa.*
Formally	ལུགས་སྲོལ་ནང་བཞིན་	*luḱ-sö nang shin.*
Former	སྔོན་གྱི། དང་པོ་	*ngön-ḱyi ; ťang-po.*

Formerly (a short time ago)	སྔན་ལ་ (སྔོན་ལ་)	*ngen-la.*
Do. (a long time ago)	སྔར་	*ngar.*
Formidable	ཞེད་སྐྲག་ཚ་པོ་	*ske-tra tsha-po.*
Forsake, to	དབྱུག་བཞག་ (འཇོག་) པ་	*yuk-skak-pa.*
Do. *hon.*	དབྱུག་ག་ (པ་) གནང་བ་	*yuk-ka nang-wa.*
Fort	རྫོང་	*dzong.*
Forthwith	ལམ་སང་། ལམ་ཀྱང་	*lam-sang ; lam-kyang.*
Fortieth	བཞི་བཅུ་པ་	*skip-chu-pa.*
Fortification	འཛིང་ར་	*dzing-ra.*
Fortnight	བདུན་ཕྲག་གཉིས། བདུན་གཉིས་	*dün-thra nyi ; dün-nyi.*
Fortress	རྫོང་	*dzong.*
Fortunate	བསོ་ (བསོད་) བདེ་ཆེན་པོ། བསོད་ནམས་ཆེན་པོ་	*so-de chhem-po ; sö-nam-chhem-po.*
Do. *hon.*	སྐུ་བསོད་ཆེན་པོ་	*ku-sö chhem-po.*
Fortune, good	བསོ་བདེ་ (བསོད་བདེ་།) བསོད་ནམས་	*so-de ; sö-nam.*
Do. *hon.*	སྐུ་བསོད་	*ku-sö.*
Fortune, bad	བསོ་ (བསོད་) བདེ་སྐམ་པོ། བསོད་ནམས་ཆུང་ཆུང་	*so-de kam-po ; sö-nam chhung-chhung.*

Fortune, bad, *hon.*	སྐུ་བསོད་ཆུང་ཆུང་	*ku-sö chhung-chhung.*
Forty	བཞི་བཅུ་	*ship-chu.*
Foster, to	གསོ་བ་	*so-wa.*
Do. *hon.*	གསོ་བ་གནང་བ་	*so-wa nang-wa.*
Foul	བཙོག་པ་	*tsok-pa.*
Do. *hon.*	སྐུ་བཙོག་	*ku-tsho.*
Foul, to be	བཙོག་པ་ཡོད་པ་	*tsok-pa yö-pa.*
Do. to become	བཙོག་པ་ཤོར་བ་	*tsok-pa shor-wa.*
Do. *hon.*	སྐུ་བཙོག་ཤོར་བ་	*ku-tso shor-wa.*
Found, to (institute)	བཙུགས་པ་ (འཛུག་པ་)	*tsuk-pa.*
Do. *hon.*	བཙུགས་ག་ (འཛུག་པ་) གནང་བ་	*tsuk-ka nang-wa.*
Foundation of wall	རྩིག་རྟེན་	*tsik-ten.*
Fountain	ཆུ་མིག	*chhu-mi.*
Four	བཞི་	*shi.*
Fourth	བཞི་པ་	*shi-pa.*
Fourteen	བཅུ་བཞི་	*chup-shi.*
Fourteenth	བཅུ་བཞི་པ་	*chup-shi-pa.*
Fowl	བྱ་	*cha.*
Do. domestic	བྱ་དེ་	*cha-te.*

Fox	ཝ་མོ་	*wa-mo.*
Fractured, to be (of bones)	རུས་ཁོག་ཆག་པ་	*rü-kho chhak-pa.*
Fragment	ཆག་དུམ་	*chhak-tum.*
Fragrance	དྲི་མ་	*tri-ma.*
Frail (infirm)	ཀྱ་རེ་ཀྱོ་རེ། ཉ་རེ་ (ར་) ཉོ་རེ་	*kya-re kyo-re; nya-re nyo-re.*
Do. *hon.*	སྐུ་ཀྱོར་ཀྱོར་	*ku-kyor-kyor.*
Frame, *s.*	ཁྲི་	*thri.*
Do. to (construct)	བཟོ་བ་	*so-wa.*
Do. *hon.*	བཟོ་བ་གནང་བ་	*so-wa nang-wa.*
Frank	དྲང་པོ་	*trang-po.*
Do. *hon.*	ཐུགས་རྒྱུ་དྲང་པོ་	*thu-gyu trang-po.*
Frankincense	སྤོས་	*pö.*
Frankly	མ་...གསང་བ་	*ma...sang-wa.*
Fraud, to commit	མགོ་སྐོར་བ་	*go-kor-wa.*
Do. *hon.*	མགོ་སྐོར་ར་ (བ་) གནང་བ་	*go-kor-ra nang-wa.*
Do. *inf.* on *sup.*	དབུ་སྐོར་ཞུ་བ་	*u-kor sku-wa.*
Free, to, *v.t.*	ཐར་ར་ (བར་) བྱེད་པ། བཏང་ (གཏོང་) བ་	*thar-ra che-pa; tang-wa.*
Do. *hon*	ཐར་ར་ (བར་) གནང་བ། གཏོང་ང་ (བ་) གནང་བ་	*thar-ra nang-wa; tong-nga nang-wa.*

Free, to become	ཐར་བ་	*thar-wa.*
Free, to (by ransom)	བླུ་བ་	*lu-wa.*
Do. *hon.*	བླུ་བ་གནང་བ་	*lu-wa nang-wa.*
Freedom	ཐར་པ་	*thar-pa.*
Freeze, to	ཁྱགས་པ་ཆགས་པ་	*khyaḱ-pa chhaḱ-pa.*
Frequently	ཚར་མང་པོ་	*tshar mang-po.*
Fresco	རི་མོ་	*ri-mo.*
Fresh	གསར་པ་	*sa-pa.*
Fret, to	སེམས་འཕྲུལ་བྱེད་པ། སེམས་འཚབས་པ་	*sem thre ḱe-pa ; sem-tshaṕ-pa.*
Do. *hon.*	ཐུགས་འཕྲུལ་གནང་བ། ཐུགས་སེམས་འཚབས་པ་གནང་བ་	*thuḱ-thre nang-wa ; thu-sem tshaṕ-pa nang-wa.*
Friction (disagreement)	འཁྲུག་གཞི་	*thruḱ-śi.*
Friday	གཟའ་སྤ་སངས་	*śa-pa-sang.*
Friend, *m.*	གྲོགས་པོ་	*t́roḱ-po.*
Friend, *f.*	གྲོགས་མོ་	*t́ro-mo.*
Friendly relationship (between governments, etc.)	མཐུན་ལམ་	*thün-lam.*
Friends, to make	གྲོགས་པོ་རྒྱབ་པ་	*t́roḱ-po gyaṕ-pa.*

Friends, to make, *hon.*	གྲོགས་པོ་སྐྱོན་པ་	*t́roḱ-po kyöm-pa.*
Fright (fear)	ཞེད་སྐྲག་	*sḱe-tra.*
Frighten	ཞེད་སྐྲག་སླང་བ་	*sḱe-tra lang-wa.*
Do. *hon.*	ཞེད་སྐྲག་སློང་ང་ (བ་) གནང་བ་	*sḱe-tra long-nga nang-wa.*
Frightened, to be	ཞེད་པ་	*sḱe-pa.*
Do. *hon.*	ཞེད་པ་གནང་བ་	*sḱe-pa nang-wa.*
Frightful	ཞེད་སྐྲག་ཚ་པོ་	*sḱe-tra tsha-po.*
Frigid	གྲང་མོ། བསིལ་པོ་	*t́rang-mo ; si-po.*
Do. *hon.*	སྐུ་བསིལ་པོ་	*ku-si-po.*
Fringe (of thread, etc.)	ཁ་ཚར། སྣེ་ཚར་	*kha-tshar ; ne-tshar.*
Frivolous	དོན་གནད་ཆུང་ཆུང་	*t́ön-ne chhung-chhung.*
Do. *hon.*	ཐུགས་དོན་ཆུང་ཆུང་	*thuḱ-t́ön chhung-chhung.*
Frog	སྦལ་པ་	*be-pa.*
From	ནས་	*ne.*
From within	ནང་ནས་	*nang-ne.*
Front of, in (ahead)	སྔན་ལ་ (སྔོན་ལ་)	*ngen-la.*
Do. (in presence of)	མདུན་ལ་	*dün-la.*
Do. *hon.*	སྐུ་མདུན་ལ་	*kun-dün-la.*
Front tooth	མདུན་སོ་	*dün-so.*
Do. *hon.*	མདུན་གྱི་ཚེམས་	*dün-ḱyi-tshem.*

Frontier	ས་མཚམས་	*san-tsham.*
Frost	ཁྱགས་པ་	*khyaḱ-pa.*
Frost-bitten, to be	གངས་ཀྱིས་འཚིག་པ་	*ḱang-ḱi tshiḱ-pa.*
Froth	ལྦུ་བ་	*bu-wa.*
Frown, to	ངོ་ནག་སྡུ་བ་	*ngo-na du-wa.*
Frozen, to be	ཁྱགས་པ་ཆགས་པ་	*khyaḱ-pa chhaḱ-pa.*
Fruit (of crops)	འབྲས་བུ་	*dre-ṕu.*
Fruit of tree (as orange, etc.)	ཤིང་འབྲས་	*shing-dre.*
Fruitful (fertile)	ལུད་ཆུ་འཛོམ་པོ་	*lü--chhu dzom-po.*
Fruitless, to be (useless)	ཕན་མི་ཐོགས་པ་	*phen mi thoḱ-pa.*
Do. *hon.*	ཐུགས་ཕན་མི་གསོ་བ་	*thu-phen mi so-wa.*
Fry, to	རྔོད་པ་	*ngö-pa.*
Do. *hon.*	རྔོད་པ་གནང་བ་	*ngö-pa nang-wa.*
Frying-pan	ཚལ་སླང་	*tshe-lang*
Fuel	མེ་ཤིང་	*me-shing.*
Fulfil, to	སྒྲུབ་པ་	*druṕ-pa.*
Do. *hon.*	སྒྲུབ་པ་གནང་བ་	*druṕ-ṕa nang-wa.*
Fulfilled, to be	ཚར་བ་	*tshar-wa.*
Do. *hon.*	གྲུབ་པ་	*t́ruṕ-pa.*
Full	གང་	*ḱang.*

Fun	བལྟས་མོ་	*te-mo.*
Function (work)	ལས་ཀ་	*le-ka.*
Do. *hon.*	ཕྱག་ལས་	*chha-le.*
Functionary	དཔོན་པོ་	*pöm-po.*
Fundament	ཀུབ་	*kuṕ.*
Do. *hon.*	ཞབས་ཕོངས་	*sḱam-phong.*
Fungus	ཤ་མོ་	*sha-mo.*
Funny	བགད་མོ་བྲོ་པོ་	*ge-mo t́ro-po.*
Do. *hon.*	ཞལ་མོ་བྲོ་པོ་	*sḱe-mo t́ro-po.*
Fur-coat	པགས་ཚ་	*paḱ-tsha.*
Do. *hon.*	སྐུ་ཚ་	*ku-tsha.*
Furnace	ཐབ་	*thaṕ.*
Furnish, to (supply)	སྒྲུབ་པ་	*druṕ-pa.*
Do. *hon.*	སྒྲུབ་པ་གནང་བ་	*druṕ-pa nang-wa.*
Furniture	ཅ་ལག་ (ཆ་ལག་)	*cha-la.*
Do. *hon.*	སྐུ་ཅས་ (སྐུ་ཆས་)	*ku-che.*
Furrow	རོལ་	*rö.*
Further (in distance)	ཕ་ཙ་ (ཕར་ཙམ་)	*pha-tsa.*
Do. (again)	ད་རུང་ཡང་། ཡང་སྐྱར་	*t́a-rung-yang ; yang-kyar.*
Fuse (for gun)	སྦིད་དི་ (སྦིད་དེ)	*bi-di.*

Futile, to be (useless)	ཕན་མི་ཐོགས་པ་	*phen mi thok-pa.*
Do. *hon.*	ཐུགས་ཕན་མི་གསོ་བ་	*thu-phen mi so-wa.*
Future	གཞུག་ལ་	*sKu-la.*

G

Gaiety	དགའ་ཚོར་	*ga-tshor.*
Gain (profit)	ཁེ་བཟང་	*khep̄-śang.*
Do. *hon.*	སྐུ་ཁེ་	*ku-khe.*
Gain a profit, to	ཁེ་བཟང་ཟ་བ་	*khep̄-śang śa-wa.*
Do. *hon.*	སྐུ་ཁེ་བཞེས་པ་	*ku-khe sKe-pa.*
Gain victory, to	རྒྱལ་བ་	*gye-wa.*
Do. *hon.*	རྒྱལ་ར་ (བ་) གནང་བ་	*gye-ra nang-wa.*
Gain, to (obtain)	འབྱོར་བ། ཐོབ་པ་	*jor-wa ; thop̄-pa.*
Do. *hon.*	ཕྱག་འབྱོར་ཡོང་བ་	*chhan-jor yong-wa.*
Gainsay, to (deny)	རྒྱབ་འགལ་ལབ་པ་	*gyam-ge lap̄-pa.*
Do. *hon.*	རྒྱབ་འགལ་གསུང་བ་	*gyam-ge sung-wa.*
Gainsay, to (dispute)	རྩོད་པ་རྒྱབ་པ་	*tsö-pa gyap̄-pa.*
Do. *hon.*	རྩོད་པ་སྐྱོན་པ་	*tsö-pa kyöm-pa.*
Gait	འགྲོ་སྟངས་	*dro-tang.*
Do. *hon.*	ཕེབ་སྟངས་	*phep̄-tang.*
Gale	ལྷགས་པ་ཚ་པོ་	*hlak-pa tsha-po.*
Gall (malignant feeling)	གནོད་སེམས་	*nö-sem.*
Gall-bladder	མཁྲིས་པ་	*thri-pa.*
Gallant, *adj.*	སྙིང་ཆེན་པོ་	*nying-chhem-po.*

Gallant *hon.*	ཐུགས་སྙིང་ཆེན་པོ་	*thu-nying chhem-po.*
Gallop, to	ཞམ་རེས་བཏང་ (གཏོང་) བ་	*sḱam-ṕe tang-wa.*
Do. *hon.*	ཆིབས་ཞམ་གནང་བ་	*chhiṕ-sḱam nang-wa*
Gamble, to	ཤོ་རྒྱབ་པ་	*sho-gyaṕ-pa.*
Do. *hon.*	ཕྱག་ཤོ་སྐྱོན་པ་གནང་བ་	*chha-sho kyöm-pa nang-wa.*
Gambler	ཤོ་པ་	*sho-pa.*
Game (play)	རྩེད་མོ་	*tse-mo.*
Do. *hon.*	སྐུ་རྩེད་	*ku-tse.*
Game (wild animals)	རི་དྭགས་	*ri-ťa.*
Gander	འང་པ་ (ངང་པ་)	*ang-pa.*
Gang	ཚོགས་	*tsho.*
Gaol	བཙོན་ཁང་	*tsön-khang.*
Gaoler	བཙོན་སྲུང་ང་ (པ་)	*tsön-sung-nga.*
Gap	སེར་ཀ་	*se-ka.*
Gape, to (of wounds)	ཁ་བཞག་བསྡད་ (སྡོད་) པ་	*kha-sḱa de-pa.*
Do. (yawn)	ཨ་སྟོང་རྒྱབ་པ་	*a-tong gyaṕ-pa.*
Do. *hon.*	ཨ་སྟོང་སྐྱོན་པ་	*a-tong kyöm-pa.*
Garb	དུག་ལོག་	*ťu-lo.*
Do. *hon.*	ན་བཟའ་	*nam-śa.*
Garden	ལྡུམ་ར་	*dum-ra.*

Garden, flower	མེ་ཏོག་གི་ལྡུམ་ར་	*me-tok-ki dum-ra.*
Do. vegetable	ཚོས་གཡང་ཚེ་ *ch.*	*tshe-yang-tse.*
Do. public	གླིང་ཀ་	*ling-ka.*
Gardener	གླིང་སྲུང་ང་ (པ་)	*ling-sung-nga.*
Gargle, to	ཁ་བཤལ་བཤལ་བཏང་ (གཏོང་) བ་	*kha-she-she tang wa.*
Do. *hon.*	ཞལ་བཤལ་བཤལ་གནང་བ་	*sḱe she-she nang-wa.*
Garland	མེ་ཏོག་འཕྲང་ང་ (འཕྲེང་བ་)	*me-to thrang-nga.*
Garlic	སྒོག་པ་	*goḱ-pa.*
Do. *hon.*	བཞེས་སྒོག	*sḱe-go.*
Garment	དུག་ལོག	*ťu-lo.*
Do. *hon.*	ན་བཟའ་	*nam-śa.*
Garnish, to (adorn)	རྒྱན་ཆ་བཏགས་ (འདོགས་) པ་	*gyen-cha taḱ-pa.*
Garrison	དམག་སྒར་	*ma-ga.*
Garter (for Tibetan boots)	ལྷམ་སྒྲོག	*hlam-dro.*
Do. *hon.*	ཞབས་སྒྲོག་	*sḱaṕ-dro.*
Gas	དུ་བའི་རླངས་པ་	*ťu-we lang-pa.*
Gas, poisonous	དུག་རླངས་	*ťuḱ-lang*
Gate (small)	ཕྱི་སྒོ་	*chhi-go.*

Gate (small), *hon.*	གཟིམ་སྒོ་ཕྱི་སྒོ་	*śim-go chhi-go.*
Gate (large)	རྒྱལ་སྒོ་	*gye-go.*
Do. *hon.*	གཟིམ་སྒོ་རྒྱལ་སྒོ་	*śim-go gye-go.*
Gather, to (pick up)	སྒྲུག་པ་	*druḱ-pa.*
Do. *hon.*	སྒྲུག་ག་ (པ་) གནང་བ་	*druḱ-ḱa nang-wa.*
Gather, to (pluck off tree)	གཏོག་པ་	*toḱ-pa.*
Do. *hon.*	གཏོག་ག་ (པ་) གནང་བ་	*toḱ-ḱa nang-wa.*
Gather, to (collect) *v.t.*	སྡུད་པ་	*dü-pa.*
Do. *hon.*	སྡུད་པ་གནང་བ་	*dü-pa nang-wa.*
Gather, to (assemble) *v.i.*	འཚོགས་པ། འཛོམས་པ་	*tsoḱ-pa ; dzom-pa.*
Do. *hon.*	ལྷན་རྒྱས་གནང་བ་	*hlen-gye nang-wa.*
Gaunt	ཤ་སྐམ་པོ་	*sha kam-po.*
Do. *hon.*	སྐུ་ཤ་སྐམ་པོ་	*ku-sha kam-po.*
Gay, to be	དགའ་བ། སྐྱིད་པོ་བྱས་ནས་སྡོད་པ་	*ga-wa ; kyi-po cḱe-ne dö-pa.*
Do. *hon.*	མཉེས་པོ་གནང་བ། སྤྲོ་པོ་གནང་ནས་བཞུགས་པ་	*nye-po nang-wa ; tro-po nang-ne sḱuḱ-pa.*
Do. *h. hon.*	ཐུགས་དགྱེས་པོ་གནང་བ་	*thu-gye-po nang-wa.*
Gaze, to	ལྟ་བ་	*ta-wa.*
Do. *hon.*	གཟིགས་པ་	*śi-pa.*

Gelding	ཕོ་རྟ་	*pho-ta.*
Gem	ནོར་བུ་	*nor-ṗu.*
Gender	ཕོ་མོ་	*pho-mo.*
Genealogy (of laymen)	རིགས་བརྒྱུད། མི་བརྒྱུད་	*ri-gyü ; mi-gyü.*
Do. *hon.*	སྐུ་བརྒྱུད་	*ku-gyü.*
Do. *hon.* (of lamas)	གདུང་བརྒྱུད་	*dung-gyü.*
Generally	ཕལ་ཆེར་	*phe-chher.*
Generate, to	སྐྱེད་པ་	*kye-pa.*
Generation	མི་བརྒྱུད་	*mi-gyü.*
Generosity	དྲིན་	*ťrin.*
Do. *hon*	བཀའ་དྲིན་	*ka-ťrin.*
Generous	ལག་པ་ཤོག་པོ་	*lak-pa shok-po.*
Do. *hon.*	ཕྱག་ཤོག་པོ་	*chha-shok-po.*
Genius	རིག་པ་	*rik-pa.*
Do. *hon.*	ཐུགས་རིག་	*thu-ri.*
Gentian	ཏིག་ཏ་	*tik-ta.*
Gentile	ཕྱི་པ་	*chhi-pa.*
Gentle	འཇམ་པོ་	*jam-po.*
Do. in speech	ཁ་འཇམ་པོ་	*kha jam-po.*
Do. *hon.*	ཞལ་འཇམ་པོ་	*ske jam-po.*

Gentle (tame, of animals)	མཉེན་པོ་	*nyem-po.*
Gentleman	སྐུ་དྲག་	*ku-t́ra.*
Gently (slowly)	ག་ལེ་	*ḱa-le.*
Do. (not roughly)	འཇམ་པོ་བྱས་ནས་	*jam-po cḱe-ne.*
Do. *hon.*	འཇམ་པོ་གནང་ནས་	*jam po nang-ne.*
Genuine	ངོ་ཐོག། དངོས་ནས་	*ngo-tho ; ngö-ne.*
Geography	འཛམ་གླིང་རྒྱས་བཤད་	*dzam-ling gye-she.*
Germinate, to	སྐྱེ་བ་	*kye-wa.*
Do. to cause to	སྐྱེད་པ་	*ḱye-pa.*
Gesture	བརྡབ་ (བརྡ་)	*daṕ.*
Gesture of hand	ལག་བརྡབ་ (ལག་བརྡ་)	*laḱ-daṕ.*
Do. *hon.*	ཕྱག་བརྡབ་ (ཕྱག་བརྡ་)	*chha-daṕ.*
Gesture of foot	རྐང་བརྡབ་ (རྐང་བརྡ་)	*kang daṕ.*
Do. *hon.*	ཞབས་བརྡབ་ (ཞབས་བརྡ་)	*sḱaṕ-daṕ.*
Get, to	འབྱོར་བ། ཐོབ་པ་	*jor-wa ; thoṕ-pa.*
Do. *hon.*	ཕྱག་འབྱོར་ཡོང་བ་	*chhan-jor yong-wa.*
Get by heart, to	བློ་ལ་ཟིན་པ་	*lo-la śim-pa.*
Do. *hon.*	ཐུགས་བློ་ལ་ཟིན་པ་གནང་བ་	*thu-lo-la śim-pa nang-wa.*
Get well, to	དྲག་པ་	*t́raḱ-pa.*
Do. *hon.*	སྐུ་དང་བ་	*ku-t́ang-wa.*

Get through, to	ཐར་བ་	*thar-wa.*
Get up, to, *v.i.*	ལང་བ་	*lang-wa.*
Do. *hon.*	བཞེང་བ་ (བཞེངས་པ་)	*sK̆ang-wa.*
Do. *h. hon.*	སྐུ་བཞེང་ (བཞེངས་) གནང་བ་	*k̆u-sK̆ang nang-wa.*
Ghastly (horrible)	ཞེད་སྣག་ཚ་པོ་	*sK̆e-tra tsha-po.*
Ghost	གདོང་འདྲེ། འདྲེ་	*dong-dre ; dre.*
Giant	མི་ཆེན་པོ་	*mi-chhem-po.*
Do. (mythological)	མི་རྒོད་	*mi-gö.*
Gibberish	དོན་དག་མེད་པའི་སྐད་ཆ་	*ťon-ťa me-pe ke-chha.*
Gibe, to	ཀྱག་ཀྱག་བྱས་ནས་ལབ་པ་	*kya-kya cK̆e-ne lap̆-pa.*
Do. *hon.*	ཀྱག་ཀྱག་གནང་ནས་གསུང་བ་	*kya-kya nang-ne sung-wa.*
Giddy, to be	མགོ་ཡུ་འཁོར་བ། བཟི་ཡོམ་ཡོམ་བྱེད་པ་	*go-yu khor-wa ; ṡi-yom-yom cK̆e-pa.*
Do. *hon.*	དབུ་ཡུ་འཁོར་བ་	*u-yu k̆hor-wa.*
Gift (alms to poor)	སྦྱིན་པ་	*jim-pa.*
Do. (to Lama)	འབུལ་བ་	*bül-wa.*
Do. (tip)	ཆང་རིན་	*chhang-rin.*
Do. *hon.*	གསོལ་རས། ཕྲུང་རིན་	*sö-re ; thrung-rin.*
Gigantic	ཆེ་ཐག་ཆོད་	*chhe-thak̆-chhö.*
Giggle, to	ཁ་ཚེ་ཚེ་བྱེད་པ་	*kha tshe-tshe cK̆e-pa.*

Giggle, to, *hon.*	ཞལ་ཚེ་ཚེ་གནང་བ་	*sḱe tshe-tshe nang wa.*
Gild, to (images, etc.)	མཚར་གསེར་བཏང་ (གཏོང་) བ་	*tsha-ser tang-wa.*
Do. *hon.*	མཚར་གསེར་གཏོང་ང་ (བ་) གནང་བ་	*tsha-ser tong-nga nang wa.*
Gilding	མཚར་གསེར་	*tsha-ser.*
Gilt, *s.*	མཚར་གསེར་	*tsha-ser.*
Gilt, to	མཚར་གསེར་བཏང་ (གཏོང་) བ་	*tsha-ser tang-wa.*
Gimlet	སོར་	*sor.*
Ginger	སྒ་སྨུག་	*ga-mu.*
Girdle	སྐེ་རགས་	*ke-ra.*
Do. *hon.*	སྐུ་སྐེ། སྐུ་རགས་	*ku-ke ; ku-ra.*
Girl	བུ་མོ་	*ṕu-mo.*
Do. *hon.*	སྲས་མོ་	*se-mo* or *tre-mo.*
Girth (of saddle)	གློ་	*lo.*
Do. *hon.*	ཆིབས་གློ་	*chhiṕ-lo.*
Gist (of letter, etc.)	དོན་སྙིང་	*tön-nying.*
Give, to	སྟེར་བ་	*ter-wa.*
Do. *hon.*	གནང་བ་	*nang-wa.*
Give, to (to superior)	ཕུལ་བ་ (འབུལ་བ་)	*phü-wa.*
Do. *hon.*	འབུལ་ར་ (བ་) གནང་བ་	*bü-ra nang-wa.*

Give over, to (deliver)	སྤྲད་པ་	*tre-pa.*
Do. *hon.*	གནང་བ་	*nang-wa.*
Give up, to (sins, certain kinds of foods, etc.)	སྤང་བ་	*pang-wa.*
Do. *hon.*	སྤོང་ང་ (བ་) གནང་བ་	*pong-nga nang-wa.*
Glacier	འཁྱགས་རུམ་	*khya-rum.*
Glad, to be	དགའ་བ་	*ga-wa.*
Do. *hon.*	མཉེས་པོ་གནང་བ་	*nye-po nang-wa.*
Do. *h. hon.*	ཐུགས་དགྱེས་པོ་གནང་བ་	*thu-gye-po nang-wa.*
Gladness	དགའ་ཚོར་	*ga-tshor.*
Do. *hon.*	མཉེས་ཚོར་	*nye-tshor.*
Glaring	འོད་ཆེམ་ཆེམ་	*ö-chhem-chhem.*
Glass	ཤེལ་	*she.*
Do. (looking glass)	ཤེལ་སྒོ་	*she-go.*
Do. *hon.*	སྤྱན་ཤེལ་	*chen-she.*
Gleam, to	འོད་རྒྱབ་པ་	*ö gyaṕ-pa.*
Do. (of the sun)	ཤར་བ་	*shar-wa.*
Do. (of the moon)	ཟླ་དཀར་ཤར་བ་	*da-ka shar-wa.*
Glee	དགའ་ཚོར་	*ga-tshor.*
Gleeful, to be	དགའ་བ་	*ga-wa.*

Gleeful, to be *hon.*	མཉེས་པོ་གནང་བ་	*nye-po nang-wa.*
Do. *h. hon.*	ཐུགས་དགྱེས་པོ་གནང་བ་	*thu-gye-po nang-wa.*
Glimmer, to	འོད་རྒྱབ་པ་	*ö gyap-pa.*
Do. (of the moon)	ཟླ་དཀར་ཤར་བ་	*da-ka shar-wa.*
Glisten, to	འོད་རྒྱབ་པ་	*ö gyap-pa.*
Glistening, *adj.*	འོད་ཆེན་པོ་	*ö chhem-po.*
Glitter, to	འོད་རྒྱབ་པ་	*ö gyap-pa.*
Globe	རིལ་རིལ་	*ri-ri.*
Globular	རིལ་རིལ་	*ri-ri.*
Gloom	མུན་ནག་	*mi-na.*
Glomy, to be (low-spirited)	སེམས་སྐྱོ་སྣང་བྱེད་པ་	*sem kyo-nang che-pa*
Do. *hon.*	ཐུགས་སེམས་སྐྱོ་སྣང་གནང་བ་	*thu-sem kyo-nang nang-wa.*
Glorious (in appearance)	གཟི་བརྗིད་ཆེན་པོ་	*śi-ji chhem-po.*
Do. (celebrated)	སྐད་གྲགས་ཆེན་པོ་	*ke-ṫra chhem-po.*
Do. *hon.*	སྙན་གྲགས་ཆེན་པོ་	*nyen-ṫra chhem-po.*
Glory (splendour)	གཟི་བརྗིད་	*śi-ji.*
Glossary	མིང་མཛོད་	*ming-dzö.*
Glossy (of silk)	ཀོན་ཡག་པོ་	*kön-yak-po.*
Do. (of wool or cotton)	ཙིག་ག་ (པ་) ཡག་པོ་	*tsik-ka yak-po.*
Glove	ལག་ཤུབས་	*lak-shup.*

Glove, *hon.*	ཕྱག་ཤུབས་	*chha-shuṕ.*
Glue	སྦྱིང་ (སྦྱིན་)	*ping.*
Gluttonous	གྲོད་ཆེན་པོ་	*t́rö-chhem-po.*
Gnash teeth, to	སོ་བདར་བ་	*so-dar-wa.*
Do. *hon.*	ཚེམས་བདར་ར་(བ་)གནང་བ་	*tshem dar-ra nang-wa.*
Gnat	སྦྲིན་སྦྲང་	*sin-drang.*
Gnaw, to	མུར་བ་	*mur-wa.*
Do. *hon.*	མུར་ར་ (བ་) གནང་བ་	*mur-ra nang-wa.*
Go, to	འགྲོ་བ་	*dro-wa.*
Do. *hon.*	ཕེབ་པ། ཐེས་པ་	*phe-pa ; the-pa.*
Do. *h. hon.*	འཆིབ་རྒྱུ་གནང་བ་	*chhiṕ-gyu nang-wa*
Go after, to	གཞུག་ལ་ཕྱིན་པ་	*sḱu-la chhim-pa.*
Do. *hon.*	གཞུག་ལ་ཕེབ་པ་	*sḱu-la phe-pa.*
Do. *h. hon.*	གཞུག་ལ་འཆིབ་རྒྱུ་གནང་བ་	*sḱu-la chhiṕ-gyu nang-wa.*
Go-between	བར་མི་	*ṕar-mi.*
Godown	དོས་ཁང་	*t́ö-khang.*
Go down, to (hill, etc.)	ཐུར་ལ་བབ་ (འབབ་) པ་	*thur-la ṕaṕ-pa.*
Do. *hon.*	ཐུར་ལ་ཕེབ་པ་	*thur-la phe-pa.*
Go down, to (diminish, of flood, etc.)	འཆག་པ་	*chhaḱ-pa.*
Go out, to	འཐོན་པ་	*thöm-pa.*

Go out, to, *hon.*	འཐོན་པ་གནང་བ་	*thöm-pa nang-wa.*
Go round, to	འཁོར་བ་	*khor-wa.*
Do. *hon.*	འཁོར་ར་ (བ་) གནང་བ་	*khor-ra nang-wa.*
Go up, to	འཛག་པ་ (འཛེག་པ་)	*dzak-pa.*
Do. *hon.*	འཛག་ག་ (འཛེག་པ་) གནང་བ་	*dzak-ka nang-wa.*
Gaol	བཙོན་ཁང་	*tsön-khang.*
Gaoler	བཙོན་སྲུང་ང་ (པ་)	*tsön-sung-nga.*
Goat	ར་	*ra.*
Goat, he-	ར་ཕོ་	*ra-pho.*
Goat, she-	ར་མོ་	*ra-mo.*
Goblin	གདོང་འདྲེ། འདྲེ་	*dong-dre ; dre.*
God	ཀུན་མཆོག་ (དཀོན་མཆོག་)	*kün-chho.*
God, a	ལྷ་	*hla.*
Goddess, a	ལྷ་མོ་	*hla-mo.*
Godless	ཆོས་སེམས་མེད་པ་	*chho sem me-pa.*
Goggles	མིག་ཤེལ་	*mik-she.*
Do. *hon.*	སྤྱན་ཤེལ་	*chen-she.*
Goitre	ལྦ་བ་	*ba-a.*
Do. *hon.*	མགུལ་ལྦ་	*gü-ba.*
Gold	གསེར་	*se.*

Gold, *hon.*	ཕྱག་གསེར་	*chha-se.*
Golden (made of gold)	གསེར་གྱི་	*se ḱi.*
Do. (colour)	སེར་པོ་	*se-po.*
Goldsmith	གསེར་བཟོ་བ་	*ser-śo-wa.*
Gong	འཁར་རྔ་	*kha-nga.*
Gonorrhoea	གྲང་གཞི་	*ťrang-sḱi.*
Good, *adj.*	ཡག་པོ་	*yaḱ-po.*
Do. (virtuous)	བཟང་པོ་	*śang-po.*
Good, *s.* (advantage)	ཕན་	*phen.*
Good for, to be	ཕན་ཐོགས་པ་	*phen thoḱ-pa.*
Do. *hon.*	ཐུགས་ཕན་གསོ་བ་	*thu-phen so-wa.*
Good-bye! (to person going)	འོ་ན་རྒྱུག་ཨ་	*o-na gyu-a.*
Do. *hon.*	ག་ལེ་ཕེབས་	*ḱa-le-phe.*
Do. *h. hon.*	ག་ལེ་འཆིབ་རྒྱུ་གནང་	*ḱa-le chhiṕ-gyu-nang.*
Good-bye! (to person remaining)	འོ་ན་སྡོད་ཨ་	*o-na dö-a.*
Do. *hon.*	ག་ལེ་བཞུགས་	*ḱa-le sḱu*
Do. *h. hon.*	ག་ལེ་བཞུགས་གདན་འཇག་	*ḱa-le sḱu-den ja.*
Goods	ཅ་ལག་ (ཆ་ལག་)	*cha-la.*
Do. *hon.*	སྐུ་ཅས་ (སྐུ་ཆས་)	*ku-che.*
Good-tempered	རྒྱུ་མ་རིང་པོ་	*gyu-ma ring-po.*

Good-tempered *hon.*	ཐུགས་རྒྱུ་རིང་པོ་	*thuk-gyu ring-po.*
Goose	ངང་པ་	*ngang-pa.*
Gorge	རོང་	*rong.*
Gorgeous (of persons)	རྔམ་ཟིག (བརྗིད་) ཆེན་པོ་	*ngam-śi chhem-po.*
Gossamer	སྡོམ་ཐག	*dom-tha.*
Gossip, to	ལབ་ལབ་རྡུང་བ། ཁ་ལས་བཤད་པ་	*lap-lap dung-wa; khap-le she-pa.*
Do. *hon.*	ཞལ་ཞོག་གནང་བ། ཞལ་ལས་གསུང་བ་	*ske-sko nang-wa; skel-le sung-wa.*
Gout	འབམ་	*bam.*
Do. *hon.*	སྐུ་འབམ་	*kun bam.*
Govern, to	དབང་བྱེད་པ་	*wang-che-pa.*
Do. *hon.*	སྐུ་དབང་གནང་བ་	*ku-wang nang-wa.*
Govern a country, to (secular government)	རྒྱལ་སྲིད་གནང་བ་	*gye-si nang-wa.*
Do. (spiritual government)	ཆོས་སྲིད་གནང་བ་	*chhö-si, nang-wa.*
Government	གཞུང་། གཞུང་ཐོག་	*sKung; sKung tho.*
Do. Tibetan	སྡེ་པ་གཞུང་	*de-pa sKung.*
Government revenue	གཞུང་གི་འབབ་	*sKung gi bap.*
Governor	བཀའ་བློན་	*ka-lön.*
Gown	ཆུ་པ་	*chhu-pa.*

Gown, *hon.*	ན་བཟའ་	*nam-śa.*
Grace (favour)	བཀའ་དྲིན། ཐུགས་རྗེ་	*ka-t́rin ; thuḱ-je.*
Graceful	མཛེས་པོ་	*dze-po.*
Gracious	དྲིན་ཆེན་པོ་	*t́rin-chhem-po*
Do. *hon.*	བཀའ་དྲིན་ཆེན་པོ་	*ka-t́rin-chhem-po.*
Grade (rank)	གོ་ས། གོ་གནས། རིམ་པ་	*ḱo-sa ; ḱo-ne ; rim-pa.*
Gradually	ག་ལེ་ག་ལེ་	*ḱa-le ḱa-le.*
Grain (for human beings)	འབྲུ་	*dru.*
Do. *hon.*	ཕྱག་འབྲུ་	*chhan-dru.*
Grain (for animals)	ཆག་	*chha.*
Grain, parched	ཡོས་	*yö.*
Do. *hon.*	བཞེས་ཡོས་	*sḱe-yö.*
Grammar (orthography)	དག་ཡིག་	*t́aḱ-yi.*
Granary	འབྲུ་བཀང་འཇུག་ འབྲུ་ཁང་	*dru-kang-juḱ ; dru-khang.*
Grand	ཆེན་པོ་	*chhem-po.*
Grand-daughter	བུའི་བུ་མོ། བུ་མོའི་བུ་མོ་	*ṕu-i ṕu-mo ; ṕu-mö ṕu-mo.*
Grandfather	པོ་འོ་	*po-o.*
Do. *hon.*	པོ་འོ་ལགས་	*po-o-la.*
Grandmother	རྨོ་འོ་	*mo-o.*

Grandmother, *hon.*	རྨོ་འོ་ལགས་	*mo-o-la.*
Grandson (son's son)	བུའི་བུ་	*ṕu-ï-ṕu.*
Do. (daughter's sou)	བུ་མོའི་བུ་	*ṕu-mö-ṕu.*
Grant, to	སྟེར་བ་	*ter-wa.*
Do. *hon.*	གནང་བ་	*nang-wa.*
Grape (fruit)	རྒུན་འབྲུམ་	*gün-drum.*
Grasp, to	ཟིན་པ་ (འཛིན་པ་)	*śim-pa.*
Do. *hon.*	ཟིན་ (འཛིན་) པ་གནང་བ་	*śím-pa nang-wa.*
Grasp, to (understand)	ཧ་གོ་བ་	*ha-ḱo-wa.*
Do. *hon.*	མཁྱེན་པ་	*khyem-pa.*
Do. *h. hon.*	དགོངས་པ་རྟོགས་པ་	*gong pa toḱ-pa.*
Grasping (avaricious)	ཧམ་པ་ཆེན་པོ་	*ham-pa chhem-po.*
Grass	རྩ་	*tsa.*
Grateful	བཀའ་དྲིན་ཆེན་པོ་	*ka-ťrin chhem-po.*
Grateful, to be	དྲིན་དྲན་པ་	*ťrin ťrem-pa.*
Do. *hon.*	དྲིན་དྲན་པ་གནང་བ་	*ťrin ťrem-pa nang-wa.*
Do. *inf.* to *sup.*	བཀའ་དྲིན་དྲན་པ་	*ka-ťrin ťrem-pa.*
Gratification (pleasure)	དགའ་ཚོར་	*ga-tshor.*
Do. *hon.*	མཉེས་ཚོར་	*nye-tshor.*
Gratified, to be	དགའ་བ་	*ga-wa.*

Gratified, to be, *hon.*	ཐུགས་མཉེས་པ་	*thu-nye-pa.*
Do. *h. hon.*	ཐུགས་དགྱེས་པ་	*thu-gye-pa.*
Grating (for windows)	ཁྲ་མ་ (དྲ་མ་)	*thra-ma.*
Do. iron	ལྕགས་ཁྲ་ (ལྕགས་དྲ་)	*chhaḱ-thra.*
Gratitude	བཀའ་དྲིན་སྙིང་བཅང་	*ka-t́rin nying-chang.*
Gratuity (tip)	ཆང་རིན་	*chhang-rin.*
Do. *hon.*	གསོལ་རས། ཁྲུང་རིན་	*sö-re ; trung-rin.*
Grave, *s.*	དུར་ཁུང་	*t́ur-khung.*
Grave, *adj.* (important)	གནད་ཁག་ཆེན་པོ། གལ་ཆེན་པོ་	*nen-kha chhem-po ; ḱe chhem-po.*
Gravity (importance)	གནད་ཁག་	*nen-kha.*
Gravy	ཤ་ཁུ་	*sha-khu.*
Do. *hon.*	སྐྲུང་ཁུ་ (སྐྲུམ་ཁུ་)	*trung-khu.*
Gray	སྔོ་སྐྱ་	*ngoṕ-kya.*
Graze, to (eat grass)	རྩ་ཟ་བ་	*tsa śa-wa.*
Grease	ཚིལ་ལུ་ (ཚིལ་བུ་)	*tshi-lu.*
Do. liquid	སྣུམ་རྩི་	*num-tsi.*
Greasy	ཞག་རྩི་ཆེན་པོ་	*sḱaḱ-tsi chhem-po.*
Great	ཆེན་པོ་	*chhem-po.*
Greed	ཧམ་པ་	*ham-pa.*

Greedy (avaricious)	འདོད་པ་ཆེན་པོ་	*dö-pa chhem-po.*
Do. (gluttonous)	གྲོད་ཆེན་པོ་	*ťrö-chhem-po.*
Green	ལྗང་ཁུ་	*jang-khu.*
Green (of grass)	སྔོན་པོ་	*ngöm po.*
Greet, to (by raising the hands)	ཐལ་མཇལ་བྱེད་པ་	*dam-jel cKe pa.*
Do. *hon.*	ཐལ་མཇལ་གནང་བ་	*dam-jel nang-wa.*
Greet, to, *inf.* to *sup.* (by removing the hat)	ཕྱག་འབུལ་ཞུ་བ་	*chham-bü sKu-wa.*
Do. (by kneeling)	ཕྱག་འཚལ་བ་	*chha tshe-wa.*
Do. *hon.*	སྐུ་ཕྱག་འཚལ་ར་ (བ་) གནང་བ་	*ku-chha tshe-ra nang-wa.*
Greet, to (by (postration)	བརྐྱང་ཕྱག་འཚལ་བ་	*kyang-chha tshe-wa.*
Do. *hon.*	བརྐྱང་ཕྱག་འཚལ་ར་ (བ་) གནང་བ་	*kyang-chha tshe-ra nang-wa.*
Grey	སྔོ་སྐྱ་	*ngop-kya.*
Grief (in serious matters)	སྡུག་བསྔལ། སེམས་འཁྲལ་	*du-nge ; sem-thre.*
Do. *hon.*	ཐུགས་འཁྲལ་	*thuk-thre.*
Grieve, to, *v. i.* (in serious matters)	སྡུག་བསྔལ་བྱེད་པ། མྱ་ངན་བྱེད་པ་	*du-nge cKe-pa ; nya-ngen cKe-pa.*
Do. *hon.*	ཐུགས་ངན་གནང་བ་	*thu-ngen nang-wa.*

Grieve, to, *v.i.* (in lesser matters)	སེམས་སྐྱོ་བ། སེམས་སྡུག་པ་	*sem-kyo-wa ; sem-duḱ-pa.*
Do. *hon.*	ཐུགས་སེམས་སྡུག་ག་ (པ་) གནང་བ་	*thu-sem duḱ-ḱa nang-wa.*
Grim	ཞེད་སྐྲག་ཚ་པོ་	*sḱe-tra tsha-po.*
Grind, to (steel, the teeth)	བདར་བ་	*dar-wa.*
Do. *hon.*	བདར་ར་ (བ་) གནང་བ་	*dar-ra nang-wa.*
Grind, to (corn)	བཏགས་པ་ (འཐག་པ་)	*taḱ-pa.*
Grindstone (for knives, &c.)	རྡར་རྡོ་	*dar-do.*
Do. (for corn)	རང་འཐག་	*rang-tha.*
Grip, to	ཟིན་པ་ (འཛིན་པ་)	*śim-pa.*
Do. *hon.*	ཟིན་ (འཛིན་) པ་གནང་བ་	*śim-pa nang-wa.*
Groan, to	སྐད་ཤོར་བ་	*ke-shor-wa.*
Do. *hon.*	གསུང་སྐད་ཤོར་ར་ (བ་) གནང་བ་	*sung-ke shor-ra nang-wa.*
Grog-shop	ཆང་ཁང་	*chhang-khang.*
Grog-seller	ཆང་མ་	*chhang-ma.*
Groom	ཆིབས་དཔོན་	*chhiṕ-pön.*
Do. *hon.*	ཆིབས་དཔོན་ལགས་	*chhiṕ-pön-la.*
Grotto	བྲག་ཕུག་	*traḱ-phu.*
Ground	ས་	*sa.*

Ground-rent	ས་གླ་	*sap̌-la.*
Group	ཚོགས་	*tsho.*
Grouse, sand	གངས་ཀ་ལིང་	*ǩang-ka-ling.*
Grove, pleasure	གླིང་ཀ་	*ling-ka.*
Grow, to	ཆེ་རུ་ཆེ་རུ་འགྲོ་བ་	*chhe-ru chhe-ru dro-wa.*
Do. *hon.*	ཆེ་རུ་ཆེ་རུ་ཕེབ་པ་	*chhe-ru chhe-ru phe-pa.*
Grow dark, to	ས་རིབ་ (འཁྲིབས་) པ་	*sa-rip̌-pa.*
Grow old, to	རྒད་རུ་རྒད་རུ་འགྲོ་བ་	*ge-ru ge-ru dro-wa.*
Do. *hon.*	བགྲེས་རུ་བགྲེས་རུ་ཕེབ་པ་	*dre-ru dre-ru phe-pa.*
Gruel	བག་ཐུག་	*p̌a thu.*
Do. *hon.*	བཞེས་ཐུག་བག་ཐུག་	*shé-thu p̌a-thu.*
Gruff (surly)	གྱོང་པོ་	*ǩyong-po.*
Grunt, to	སྐད་རྒྱབ་པ་	*ke-gyap̌-pa.*
Guarantee	ཁས་ཁྱགས་	*khe-khya.*
Do. *hon.*	ཞལ་ཁྱགས་	*sǩe-khya.*
Guarantee, to	ཁས་ཁྱགས་བྱེད་པ་	*khe-khya cǩe-pa.*
Do. *hon.*	ཞལ་ཁྱགས་གནང་བ་	*sǩe-khya nang-wa.*
Guarantor	ཁས་ཁྱགས་བྱེད་མཁན་	*khe-khya cǩe-khen.*
Do. *hon.*	ཞལ་ཁྱགས་གནང་མཁན་	*sǩe-khya nang-khen.*
Guard, *s.*	སྲུང་མཁན་	*sung-khen.*

Guard, to (a place, &c.)	སྲུང་བ་	*sung-wa.*
Do. *hon.*	སྲུང་ང་ (བ་) གནང་བ་	*sung-nga nang-wa.*
Guard, to (take care of goods, &c.)	ཉར་བ་	*nyar-wa.*
Do. *hon.*	ཉར་ར་ (བ་) གནང་བ་	*nyar-ra nang-wa.*
Do. *h. hon.*	ཐུགས་ཅག་གནང་བ་	*thu-cha nang-wa.*
Guardian	མགོ་འདོན་བྱེད་མཁན་	*gon-dön cKe-khen.*
Guess, *s.*	ཚོད་	*tshö.*
Guest	མགྲོན་པོ་	*dröm-po.*
Do. *hon.*	སྐུ་མགྲོན་	*kun-drön.*
Guide, *s.*	ལམ་རྒྱུད་བྱེད་མཁན། ལམ་ཁག་བསྟན་ (སྟོན་) མཁན་	*lam-gyü cKe-khen; lam-kha ten-khen.*
Do. *hon.*	ལམ་རྒྱུད་གནང་མཁན་	*lam-gyü. nang-khen.*
Guide, to	ལམ་རྒྱུད་བྱེད་པ། ལམ་ཁག་བསྟན་ (སྟོན་) པ་	*lam-gyü cKe-pa; lam-kha tem-pa.*
Do. *hon.*	ཕེབས་ལམ་རྒྱུད་གནང་བ་	*phep-lam-gyü nang-wa.*
Guile	གཡོ་སྒྱུ་	*yo-gyu.*
Guileful	གཡོ་སྒྱུ་ཚ་པོ་	*yo-gyu tsha-po.*
Guilt	སྐྱོན། ཉེས་པ་	*kyön; nye-pa.*
Guiltless	ཉེས་པ་མེད་པ་	*nye-pa me-pa.*

Guilty	སྐྱོན་ཆེན་པོ། ཉེས་པ་ཆེན་པོ་	*kyön-chhem-po; nye-pa chhem po*
Guinea-pig	ཨབ་ར་	*ab-ra.*
Guitar	སྒྲ་སྙན	*dram-nyen.*
Do. *hon.*	ཕྱག་སྙན་	*chha-nyen.*
Gull, to	མགོ་སྐོར་བཏང་ (གཏོང་) བ་	*go-kor tang-wa.*
Do. *hon.*	མགོ་སྐོར་གཏོང་ང་ (བ་) གནང་བ་	*go-kor tong-nga nang-wa.*
Do. *inf.* to *sup.*	དབུ་སྐོར་ཞུ་བ་	*u-kor sku-wa.*
Gullet	མིག་པ་ (མིད་པ་)	*mik-pa.*
Do. *hon.*	མགུལ་མིག་	*gü-mi.*
Gully	སང་འགག་	*hrang-ga.*
Gum	སྤྱིང་ (སྤྱིན་)	*ping.*
Do. for closing envelopes, etc.	ཁ་སྤྱིང་ (ཁ་སྤྱིན་)	*kha-ping.*
Do. *hon.*	ཞལ་སྤྱིང་ (ཞལ་སྤྱིན་)	*ske-ping.*
Gum (of teeth)	སོ་ཉིང་	*so-nying.*
Do. *hon.*	ཚེམས་ཉིང་	*tshem-nying.*
Gun	མེ་མདའ་	*men-da.*
Do. *hon.*	ཕྱག་མདའ་	*chhan-da.*
Gun-barrel	ལྕགས་ཧྲང་	*cha-hrang.*

Gun-fuse	སྦིད་རྡི་ (སྦིད་རྡེ་)	*bi-di.*
Gun, hammer of	སྐམ་པ་	*kam-pa.*
Gun-powder	རྫས་	*dze.*
Gun, ramrod of	སིན་འབིད་	*sim-bi.*
Gun-rest (of Tibetan fashion)	མེ་མདའི་རུ་	*men-de ru.*
Do. *hon.*	ཕྱག་མདའི་རུ་	*chhan-de ru.*
Gun, stock of	སྒྲུམ་ཤིང་	*gum-shing.*
Do. trigger of	སྐམ་པ་	*kam-pa.*
Guts	རྒྱུ་མ་	*gyu-ma.*
Do. *hon.*	སྐུ་རྒྱུ་	*ku-gyu.*
Gutter (on ground)	ཡོ་པོ་ (ཡུར་བོ་)	*yo-po.*
Do. (on roof of house)	འོག་ཆུ་	*o-chhu.*

H

Habit (custom)	ལུགས་སྲོལ་	*luḱ-sö.*
Habitation	ཁང་པ། ནང་། སྡོད་ས་	*khang-pa ; nang ; dö-sa.*
Do. *hon.*	གཟིམ་ཁང་། བཞུགས་ས་	*śim-khang ; sḱu-sa.*
Do. *h. hon*	གཟིམ་ཤག། བཞུགས་གདན་འཛགས་ས་	*śim-sha ; sḱu-den ja-sa.*
Habitually	རྟག་པར། རྣམ་རྒྱུན་	*taḱ-pa ; nam-gyün.*
Haemorrhoids (piles)	གཞང་ཐོར་	*ṫrang-thor.*
Haft	ཡུ་བ་	*yu-wa.*
Hag	མ་རྒན་	*ma-gen.*
Hail, *s.*	སེར་ར་ (སེར་བ་)	*se-ra.*
Hail, to (hail-storm)	སེར་ར་ བཏང་ (གཏོང་) བ་	*se-ra tang-wa.*
Do. to (call)	སྐད་བཏང་ (གཏོང་) བ་	*ke-tang-wa.*
Do. *hon.*	གསུངས་སྐད་གནང་བ། སྐད་གཏོང་ང་ (བ་) གནང་བ་	*sung-ke nang-wa ; ke tong-nga nang-wa.*
Hair (on human head)	སྐྲ་	*tra.*
Do. *hon.*	དབུ་སྐྲ་	*u-tra.*
Hair, to wash the	སྐྲ་འཁྲུད་པ་	*tra thrü-pa.*
Do. *hon.*	དབུ་བསིལ་གནང་བ་	*u-si nang-wa.*
Hair, a single	སྐྲ་ཀང་གཅིག་	*tra-kang chi.*

Hairs, two	སྐྲ་ཀང་གཉིས་	*tra-kang-nyi.*
Hair (of animals, and human hair other than that on head)	སྤུ་	*pu.*
Do. a single	སྤུ་ཀང་གཅིག་	*pu-kang-chi.*
Do. two	སྤུ་ཀང་གཉིས་	*pu-kang nyi.*
Hair-brush	ཕག་ཟེ་	*phaǩ-śe.*
Half	ཕྱེད་ཀ་	*chhe-ka.*
Hall of assembly	ཚོམས་ཆེན་	*tshom-chhen.*
Do. for monks	འདུ་ཁང་	*du-khang.*
Halo	འོད་སྐོར་	*ö-kor.*
Halt, to	ཞག་ས་སྡོད་པ་	*sǨaǩ-sa dö-pa.*
Do. *hon.*	བཞུགས་ཞག་གནང་བ་	*sǨuǩ-sǨa nang-wa.*
Halter	ཐོ་མགོ་ (ཐུར་མགོ་	*thong-go.*
Halting-place (for the day)	ཞག་ས་	*sǨaǩ-sa.*
Do. *hon.*	བཞུགས་ཞག་	*sǨu-sǨa.*
Hammer	ཐོ་བ་	*tho-wa.*
Do. of gun	སྐམ་པ་	*kam-pa.*
Hamper, *s.*	སླེ་ཀོག་ (སླེ་པོ་)	*le ko.*
Do. *hon.*	ཕྱག་སླེ་	*chha-le.*
Hamper, to (hinder).	བཀག་པ་ (འགེགས་པ་)	*kaǩ-pa.*

Hamper, to (hinder) *hon.*	བཀག་ག་ (འགེགས་པ་) གནང་བ་	*kaḱ-ḱa nang-wa.*
Hand	ལག་པ་	*laḱ-pa.*
Do. *hon.*	ཕྱག་	*chha.*
Handcuff, to	ལག་ལྕགས་རྒྱབ་པ་	*laḱ-cha gyaṕ-pa.*
Handcuffs	ལག་ལྕགས་	*laḱ-cha.*
Handful, a	སྤར་ར་ (བ་) གང་	*bar-ra ḱang.*
Do. *hon.*	ཕྱག་གང་	*chha-ḱang.*
Handicraft	ལས་ཀ་	*le-ka.*
Do. *hon.*	ཕྱག་ལས་	*chha-le.*
Handkerchief	སྣ་འཕྱིད་	*naṕ-chhi.*
Do. *hon.*	ཞངས་འཕྱིད་	*shang-chhi.*
Handkerchief (compliment ary)	ཁ་བཏགས་	*kha-ta.*
Do. *hon.*	མཇལ་དར་	*je-t́ar.*
Handle, straight (of knife, &c.)	ཡུ་བ་	*yu-wa.*
Do. *hon.*	ཕྱག་ཡུ་	*chha-yu.*
Handle, curved (of kettle, &c.)	ལུང་	*lung.*
Do. *hon.*	ཕྱག་ལུང་	*chha-lung.*
Handle, to	འཆང་བ་	*chhang-wa.*
Do. *hon.*	འཆང་ང་ (བ་) གནང་བ་	*chhang-nga nang-wa.*

Handmaid	གཡོག་མོ་	*yo-mo.*
Do. *hon.*	ཞལ་ལྟ་མ་	*sḱe-ta-ma.*
Handsome	ཚར་པོ། མཛེས་པོ་	*tshar-po; dze-po.*
Do. *hon.*	ཐུགས་ཚར་པོ་	*thu tshar po.*
Handwriting	ཡི་གེ་	*yi-ge.*
Do. *hon.*	ཕྱག་བྲིས་	*chha-ri.*
Hang, to, *v. t.*	བཀལ་བ་ (འགེལ་བ་)	*kel-wa.*
Do. *hon.*	བཀལ་ར་ (འགེལ་བ་) གནང་བ་	*ke-ra nang-wa.*
Hang, to (a man)	སྐེ་ལ་ཐག་པ་བསྣམས་ནས་བསད་ (གསོད་) པ་	*ke-la thaḱ-pa dam-ne se-pa.*
Hanker after, to	དྲན་པ་	*t́rem-pa*
Do. *hon.*	ཐུགས་དྲན་པ་གནང་བ་	*thu-t́rem-pa nang wa.*
Happen, to	བྱུང་བ་ (འབྱུང་བ་)	*cḱung-wa.*
Happiness	དགའ་ཚོར་	*ga tshor.*
Do. *hon.*	མཉེས་ཚོར་	*nye-tshor.*
Happy (comfortable)	སྐྱིད་པོ་	*kyi-po.*
Do. *hon.*	སྤྲོ་པོ་	*tro-po.*
Happy, to be	དགའ་བ་	*ga-wa.*
Do. *hon.*	མཉེས་པོ་གནང་བ་	*nye-po nang-wa.*
Do. *h. hon.*	ཐུགས་དགྱེས་པོ་གནང་བ་	*thu-gye-po nang-wa.*

Harass, to	སྡུག་པོ་བཏང་ (གཏོང་) བ་	*duk̄-po tang-wa.*
Do. *hon.*	སྡུག་པོ་གཏོང་ང་ (བ་) གནང་བ་	*duk̄-po tong-nga nang-wa.*
Hard (arduous)	དཀའ་ལས་ཁག་པོ་	*ka-le khak-po.*
Do. *hon.*	སྐུ་མཉེལ་པོ། སྐུ་ལས་ཁག་པོ་	*ku-nye-po ; ku-le khak̄-po.*
Hard (of substance)	མཁྲགས་པོ་ (མཁྲེགས་པོ)	*thrak̄-po.*
Hard-hearted, to be	སྙིང་རྗེ་མེད་པ་	*nying-je me-pa.*
Do. *hon.*	ཐུགས་རྗེ་མེད་པ་	*thuk̄-je me-pa.*
Hardship	དཀའ་ལས་	*ka-le.*
Hardware (of iron things)	ལྕགས་ཅས་ (ལྕགས་ཆས་)	*cha-che.*
Do. (of copper things)	ཟངས་ཅས་ (ཟངས་ཆས་)	*śang-che.*
Hardy	གཟུགས་པོ་ཐང་པོ་	*śuk̄-po thang-po.*
Do. *hon.*	སྐུ་གཟུགས་ཐང་པོ་	*ku-śu thang-po.*
Hare	རི་གོང་ (རི་བོང་)	*re-k̄ong.*
Hare-lip	ཞོ་རལ་	*sho-re.*
Hare-year	ཡོས་ལོ་	*yö-lo.*
Harlot	ཆལ་མོ། གཞང་ཚོང་མ། སྨད་ཚོང་མ་	*chhe-mo ; sk̄ang-tshong-ma ; me-tshong-ma.*
Harm, *s.*	སྐྱོན་	*kyön.*
Harm, to	སྐྱོན་བྱེད་པ་	*kyön-ck̄e-pa.*
Do. *hon.*	སྐྱོན་གནང་བ་	*kyön-nang-wa.*

Harm, to (by witchcraft, &c.)	གནོད་པ་	*nö-pa.*
Do. *hon.*	གནོད་པ་གནང་བ་	*nö-pa nang-wa.*
Harmony, to be in	མཐུན་པ་	*thüm-pa.*
Harp	སྒྲ་སྙན་	*dram-nyen.*
Do. *hon.*	ཕྱག་སྙན་	*chha-nyen.*
Harsh	གྱོང་པོ་	*ḱyong-po.*
Hart	ཤ་བ་	*sha a.*
Harvest	སྟོན་ཐོག་	*tön-tho.*
Haste	བྲེལ་བ་	*t́re-wa.*
Do. *hon.*	ཐུགས་བྲེལ་	*thu-t́re.*
Hasten, to	མགྱོགས་པོ་བྱེད་པ་	*gyoḱ-po cḱe-pa.*
Do. *hon.*	རྩོལ་པོ་གནང་བ་	*tsö-po nang-wa.*
Do. *h. hon.*	ཐུགས་རྩོལ་པོ་གནང་བ་	*thu tsö-po nang-wa.*
Hastily	ལམ་སང་	*lam-sang.*
Hasty (quick)	མགྱོགས་པོ་	*gyoḱ-po*
Do. *hon.*	རྩོལ་པོ་	*tsö-po.*
Hasty (rash)	ཁ་མེད་མིག་མེད་	*kha-me miḱ-me.*
Hate, to	སྡང་པོ་བྱེད་པ་	*dang po cḱe-pa.*
Do. *hon.*	སྡང་པོ་གནང་བ་	*dang-po nang-wa.*
Hat	ཞྭ་མོ་	*sḱa-mo.*

Hat, *hon.*	དབུ་ཞྭ་	*u-sḱa.*
Hatchet	སྟ་རེ། སྟ་གྲི་	*ta-ri ; ta-ťri.*
Hateful	སྐྱུག་བྲོ་བོ་	*kyuḱ-ťro-po.*
Haughtiness	ཉམས། ཛ་ཁོག་	*nyam ; dza-kho.*
Haughty	ཉམས་ཆེན་པོ། ཛ་ཁོག་ཆེན་པོ་	*nyam-chhem-po; dza-kho chhem-po.*
Haul, to	འཐེན་པ་	*them-pa*
Do. *hon.*	འཐེན་པ་གནང་བ་	*them-pa nang-wa.*
Haunt, *s.*	ཚང་	*tshang.*
Have, to	ཡོད་པ་	*yö-pa.*
Have, I	ང་ལ་ཡོད་	*nga-la yö.*
Haversack	ལྟོ་ཕད་	*to-phe.*
Hawk	ཁྲ་	*thra.*
Hay	གཟན་པ། རྩྭ་སྐམ་པོ་	*śem-pa ; tsa-kam-po.*
Do. *hon.*	ཆིབས་རྩྭ་	*chhiṕ-tsa.*
Hay-fork	ཁ་རག་ (ཁ་རྒྱག་)	*kheṕ-ra.*
Hay-sickle	ཟོར་ར་ (ཟོར་བ་)	*śor-ra.*
Hazard	ཉེན་ཁ་	*nyen-kha.*
Hazardous	ཉེན་ཁ་ཆེན་པོ་	*nyen-kha chhem-po.*
Haze	རྨུགས་པ་	*muḱ-pa.*
He	ཁོ། ཁོ་རང་	*kho ; kho-rang.*

He, *hon.*	ཁོང་	*khong.*
Head	མགོ་	*go.*
Do. *hon.*	དབུ་	*u.*
Head (leader)	མགོ་པ་	*go-pa.*
Head, having a shaved (as a monk)	མགོ་རིལ་	*go-ri.*
Do. *hon.*	དབུ་རིལ་	*u-ri.*
Headache, to have	མགོ་ན་བ་	*go-na-wa.*
Do. *hon.*	དབུ་སྙུང་བ་	*u-nyung-wa.*
Headman	འགོ་བྱེད་	*go-cḱe.*
Headstrong	གྱོང་པོ་	*ḱyong-po.*
Heal, to	དྲག་ག་ (པ་) བཟོ་བ་	*ťrak-ḱa śo-wa.*
Do. *hon.*	དྲག་ག་ (པ་) བཟོ་བ་གནང་བ་	*ťrak-ḱa śo-wa nang-wa.*
Heal, to (patient of good position)	སྐུ་དངང་ (པ་) བཟོ་བ་གནང་བ་	*ku-ťang-nga śo-wa nang-wa.*
Healed, to be	དྲག་པ་	*ťrak-pa.*
Do. *hon.*	སྐུ་དང་བ་	*ku-ťang-wa.*
Health	གཟུགས་པོ། ཁམས་	*śuk-po ; kham.*
Do. *hon.*	སྐུ་གཟུགས། སྐུ་ཁམས་	*ku-śuk ; kung-kham.*
Healthy	གཟུགས་པོ་བདེ་པོ་	*śuk-po de-po.*
Do. *hon.*	སྐུ་གཟུགས་བཟང་པོ་	*ku-śuk śang-po.*

Heap, *s.*	སྤུང་	*pung.*
Heap, to	སྤུང་བ་	*pung-wa.*
Do. *hon.*	སྤུང་ང་ (བ་) གནང་བ་	*pung-nga nang-wa.*
Hear, to	གོ་བ། ཨམ་མཆོག་གོ་བ་	*ḱo-wa ; am-chho ḱo-wa.*
Do. *hon.*	གསན་པ། སྙན་ལ་གསན་པ་	*sem-pa ; nyen-la sem-pa.*
Hearken, to	ཉན་པ་	*nyem-pa.*
Do. *hon.*	གསན་པ་	*sem-pa.*
Hearsay (report)	སྐད་ཆ། གཏམ་	*ke-chha ; tam.*
Heart	སྙིང་	*nying.*
Do. *hon.*	ཐུགས་སྙིང་། སྐུ་སྙིང་	*thu-nying ; ku-nying.*
Heart, to learn by	བློ་ལ་ཟིན་པ་	*lo-la śim-pa.*
Do. *hon.*	ཐུགས་ལ་ཟིན་པ་གནང་བ་	*thu-la śim-pa nang-wa.*
Hearth	ཐབ་	*thaṕ.*
Do. *hon.*	གསོལ་ཐབ་	*sö-thaṕ.*
Heartily	སྙིང་རུས་བྱས་ནས་	*nying-rü ćhe-ne.*
Do. *hon.*	ཐུགས་རུས་གནང་ནས་	*thuḱ-rü nang-ne.*
Heat	ཚད་པ་	*tshe-pa.*
Do. *hon.*	སྐུ་ཚད་	*ku-tshe.*
Heathen	ཕྱི་པ་	*chhi pa.*
Heaven (sky)	གནམ། ནམ་མཁའ་	*nam ; nam-kha.*

Heavy	ལྗི་པོ་	*ji-po.*
Hedge	ར་བ་	*ra-a.*
Hedgehog	གཟིག་མོ་	*śiǩ-mo.*
Heed, to	ཉན་པ་	*nyem-pa.*
Do. *hon.*	གསན་པ་	*sem-pa.*
Heel	རྟིང་པ་	*ting-pa.*
Do. *hon.*	ཞབས་མཐིལ་ (ཞབས་རྟིང་)	*sǩaṕ-thil.*
Heifer	པེ་བེ་	*pe-ṕe.*
Height (of human being)	རིང་ཐུང་	*ring-thung.*
Do. (of inanimate objects)	མཐོ་དམན་	*tho-men.*
Heir	ནོར་གྱི་བདག་པོ་	*nor-ǩyi daǩ-po.*
Heiress	ནོར་གྱི་བདག་མོ་	*nor-ǩyi daǩ-po.*
Hell	དམྱལ་ལ་ (བ་)	*nyel-la.*
Helmet	རྨོག་	*mo.*
Do. *hon.*	དབུ་རྨོག་	*u-mo.*
Help	རོགས་	*ro.*
Do. *hon.*	མགོ་འདྲེན་	*gön-dren.*
Help, to	རོགས་བྱེད་པ་	*ro cǩe-pa.*
Do. *hon.*	མགོ་འདྲེན་གནང་བ་	*gön-dren nang-wa.*
Helper	རོགས་བྱེད་མཁན་	*ro-cǩe-khen.*

Helper, *hon.*	མགོན་འདྲེན་གནང་མཁན་	*gön-dren nang-khen.*
Helpful, to be (useful)	ཕན་ཐོགས་པ་	*phen-thoḱ-pa.*
Do. *hon.*	ཐུགས་ཕན་གསོ་བ་	*thu-phen so-wa.*
Helpless	རོགས་ ·· མེད་པ་	*ro .....me pa.*
Hem, *s.*	སྣེ། སྣེ་མོ་	*ne ; ne-mo.*
Hem, to	སྣེ་ནས་འཚེམ་པ་	*ne-ne tshem-pa.*
Do. *hon.*	སྣེ་ནས་འཚེམ་པ་གནང་བ་	*ne-ne tshem-pa nang-wa.*
Hemp	སོ་མ་ར་ཙ་	*so-ma ra-tsa.*
Hen	བྱ་མོ་	*cḱa-mo.*
Hence (from this place)	འདི་ནས་	*di-ne.*
Do. (therefore)	དེའི་རྐྱེན་བྱས་ནས། དེའི་རྐྱེན་གྱིས་	*t́e-i-kyen cḱe-ne ; t́e-i kyen-kyi.*
Henceforth	ད་ནས་ཕྱིན་ཆད་	*t́a-ne chhin-chhe.*
Her	མོའི་	*mö.*
Herd	ཁྱུ་	*khyu.*
Herdsman	རྫི་བོ་	*dzi-o.*
Do. of cattle	བ་རྫི་	*ṕa-dzi.*
Do. of goats	ར་རྫི་	*ra-dzi.*
Do. of horses	རྟ་རྫི་	*ta-dzi.*
Do. of hogs	ཕག་རྫི་	*phaḱ-dzi.*

Herdsman of sheep	ལུག་རྫི་	*luḱ-dzi.*
Do. of yaks	གཡག་རྫི་	*ya-dzi.*
Do. of donkeys	བོང་རྫི་	*ṕong-dzi.*
Do. of fowls	བྱ་རྫི་	*cḱa-dzi.*
Here	འདིར་	*de.*
Hereafter	ད་ནས་ཕྱིན་ཆད་	*t́a-ne chhin-chhe.*
Heresy	ཆོས་ལོག་	*chhö lo.*
Heresy, to commit.	ཆོས་ལོག་བྱེད་པ་	*chhö-lo cḱe-pa.*
Herewith	འདི་དང་མཉམ་དུ་	*di-t́ang nyam-t́u.*
Heritage	ནོར་སྐལ་	*nor-ke.*
Hermit	སྒོམ་ཆེན་	*gom-chhen.*
Hermitage	དབེན་གནས་	*en-ne.*
Hero	དཔའ་བོ་	*pa-o.*
Heroine	དཔའ་མོ་	*pa-mo.*
Hers	མོའི་	*mö.*
Herself	མོ་རང་	*mo-rang.*
Hesitate, to	ཐེ་ཚོམ་ཟ་བ་	*the-tshom śa-wa.*
Do. *hon.*	ཐེ་ཚོམ་གནང་བ་	*the-tshom nang-wa.*
Hesitation	ཐེ་ཚོམ་	*the-tshom.*
Hew, to (length ways)	གཤག་པ་	*shaḱ-pa.*

Hew, to (breadthways)	བཙབ་པ་	*tsaṕ-pa.*
Hiccough, to	ཨི་ཀ་རྒྱབ་པ་	*i-ka gyaṕ-pa.*
Hidden (concealed)	སྦས་པ་	*be-pa.*
Do. (secret)	གསང་བ་	*sang-wa.*
Hide, *s.* (*e.g.* of yak, bullock, &c.)	ཀོ་བ་	*ko-wa.*
Do. (*i.e.* skin of sheep, goat, &c.)	པགས་པ་	*paḱ-pa.*
Hide, to, *v.t.*	སྦེད་པ་	*be-pa.*
Do. *hon.*	སྦེད་པ་གནང་བ་	*be-pa nang-wa.*
Hide, to, *v.i.*	ཡིབ་པ་	*yiṕ-pa.*
Do. *hon.*	ཡིབ་པ་གནང་བ་	*yiṕ-pa nang-wa.*
Hideous	ཞེད་སྣག་ཚ་པོ་	*sḱe-tra tsha-po.*
Hierarchy	ཆོས་སྲིད་	*chhö-si.*
High (of things, rank of persons	མཐོ་པོ་	*tho-po.*
Highway	རྒྱ་ལམ་	*gya-lam.*
Hill	རི་	*ri.*
Do. up	གྱེན་	*ḱyen.*
Do. down	ཐུར་	*thur.*
Hilt	ཡུ་བ་	*yu-wa.*
Him	ཁོ་ལ་	*kho-la.*

Himself	ཁོ་རང་	*kho-rang.*
Hinder, to	བཀག་བ་ (འཕེགས་པ)	*kak-pa.*
Do. *hon.*	བཀག་ག་ (འགེགས་པ་) གནང་བ་	*kak-ka nang-wa.*
Hind-foot	རྐང་པ་	*kang-pa.*
Hindrance	བཀག་ཆ་	*kak-chha.*
Hinge (of Tibetan make)	ཏིང་པ་	*ting-pa.*
Hip (of body)	དཔྱི་མགོ་	*ching-go.*
Hire (wages)	གླ། ཕོགས་	*la ; pho.*
Hire, to	གླས་པ་	*le-pa.*
Hired workman	མི་གླ། གླ་པ་	*mi-la ; la-pa.*
His	ཁོའི་	*khö.*
History	ལོ་རྒྱུས། རྣམ་ཐར་	*lo-gyü ; nam-tha.*
Do. *hon.*	གསུང་ཐར་	*sung-tha.*
Hit, to	ཁེས་པ། འཕོག་པ་	*khe-pa ; phok-pa.*
Hit at to (with a stick, fists, &c.)	གཀྲུ་བ་	*sku-wa.*
Hit, a	ལྕག་	*cha.*
Hither	ཚུར། འདི་རུ་	*tshur ; di-ru.*
Hitherto	ད་ཐུག་བར་དུ་	*ta-thu par-tu.*
Hive (of bees)	སྦྲང་ཚང་	*lrang-tshang.*

Hoard	བཀང་འཇུག་	*kang-juḱ.*
Hoar-frost	བ་མོ་	*ṕa-mo.*
Hoarse, to be	སྐད་འཛེར་བ་	*ke dzer-wa.*
Hobbling (lame)	རྐང་ཀྱོག་	*kang-kyo.*
Do. *hon.*	ཞབས་ཀྱོག་	*sḱaṕ-kyo.*
Hobgoblin	གདོང་འདྲེ། འདྲེ་	*dong-dre ; dre.*
Hoe	འཇོར་ (དོག་ཙེ་)	*jo.*
Hoe, to	རྐོ་བ་	*ko-wa.*
Hog	ཕག་པ་	*phaḱ-pa.*
Hoist, to	ཡར་འཕྱར་བ་	*yar-chhar-wa.*
Hold, to (catch hold of)	ཟིན་པ་ (འཛིན་པ་)	*śim-pa.*
Do. *hon.*	ཟིན་ (འཛིན་) པ་གནང་བ་	*śim-pa nang-wa.*
Hold up, to	སྟེན་པ་	*tem-pa.*
Hole (made by human being or animal)	ཁུང་	*khung.*
Do. (formed by nature)	ཨི་ཁུང་	*i-khung.*
Hole, peep-	སོ་ཁུང་	*so-khung.*
Holiday	དགོངས་པ་	*gong-pa.*
Hollo! *interj.*	ཝེའ	*we.*
Hollow, *s.* (in the ground)	ཀོང་སྟོང་	*kong-tong.*

Hollow, *adj.* (of metals, manufactured articles, &c.)	ཁོག་སྟོང་	*khoḱ-tong.*
Hollyhock	ཧ་ལོ་མེ་ཏོག་	*ha-lo me-to.*
Holy	དམ་པ། ཆོས་ལྡན་	*ťam-pa chhön-den.*
Homage, to do	ཕྱག་འཚལ་བ་	*chha-tshe-wa.*
Home	ནང་། ཁང་པ་	*nang ; khang-pa.*
Do. *hon.*	གཟིམ་ཁང་	*śim-khang.*
Do. *h. hon.*	གཟིམ་ཤག་	*śim-sha.*
Home, at	ནང་ལ་	*nang-la.*
Home-sick, to be	ལུང་པ་དྲན་པ་	*lung-pa ťrem-pa.*
Honest	དྲང་པོ་	*ťrang-po.*
Do. *hon.*	ཐུགས་དྲང་པོ་	*thu-ťrang-po.*
Honey	སྦྲང་རྩི་	*drang-tsi.*
Honour (respect)	བསྙེན་བཀུར་	*nyen-kur.*
Honour, to	བསྙེན་བཀུར་བྱེད་པ་	*nyen-kur cḱe-pa.*
Do. *inf.* to *sup.*	བསྙེན་བཀུར་ཞུ་བ་	*nyen-kur sḱu-wa.*
Hood (as scarf wound round the face to protect from cold, &c.)	ཁ་དཀྲིས་	*kha-tri.*
Do. *hon.*	ཞལ་དཀྲིས་	*sḱe-tri.*
Hoof	སྨིག་པ་	*miḱ-pa.*

Hook	ཀུག་	*kuk.*
Hook, fish-	ཉ་ཀུག་	*nya-kuk.*
Hook, iron-	ལྕགས་ཀྱུ་	*cha-kyu.*
Hookah	ཧོར་ཁ་ *Hind.*	*hor-kha.*
Do. *hon.*	བཞེས་ཧོར་	*ske-hor.*
Hookah, bowl of	ཅི་ལིམ་ *Hind.*	*chi-lim.*
Hoop	ཤན་	*shen.*
Do. iron	ལྕགས་ཤན་	*cha-shen.*
Hoopoe	པུ་པུ་ཁྲུ་ཤུད་ (ཕུ་ཤུད་)	*pu-pu khu-shü.*
Hope	རེ་བ་	*re-wa.*
Do. *hon.*	ཐུགས་རེ་	*thu-re.*
Hope, to	རེ་བ་བྱེད་པ་	*re-wa cke-pa.*
Do. *hon.*	ཐུགས་རེ་གནང་བ་	*thu-re nang-wa.*
Hopeless, to be	རེ་བ་མེད་པ་	*re-wa me-pa.*
Do. *hon.*	ཐུགས་རེ་མེད་པ་	*thu re me pa.*
Horizon	མཐོང་བའི་འཁོར་	*thong-we khor.*
Horn	རྭ་ཅོ་	*ra-cho.*
Hornet	སྦྲང་མ་	*drang-ma.*
Hornless	ཨ་ཡུ་	*a-yu.*
Horoscope	སྐྱེ་སྐར་རྟགས་པ་	*kye-ka tak-pa.*

Horoscope, *hon.*	འཁྲུངས་སྐར་རྟགས་པ་	*thrung-ka tak-pa.*
Horrible	ཞེད་སྐྲག་ཚ་པོ་	*sḱe-tra tsha-po.*
Horrid	ཞེད་སྐྲག་ཚ་པོ་	*sḱe-tra tsha-po.*
Horrifying	ཞེད་སྐྲག་ཚ་པོ་	*sḱe-tra tsha-po.*
Horror	ཞེད་སྐྲག་	*sḱe-tra.*
Horse	རྟ་	*ta*
Do. *hon.*	ཆིག་པ་ (ཆིབས་པ་)	*chhiḱ-pa.*
Horse, Chinese	སིང་རྟ་	*sing-ta.*
Horse, Indian country-bred	རྟི་པི་ཅག་	*ti pi-cha.*
Horse, saddle	ཞོན་རྟ་	*sḱön-ta.*
Do. *hon.*	ཆིབས་པ་	*chhiḱ-pa.*
Horse, pack	ཁལ་རྟ་	*khe-ta.*
Horse, saddle (of very high official or lama)	ཆིབས་ཆེན་	*chhiṕ-chhen.*
Horse-dung	རྟའི་སྦངས་	*te-bang.*
Horse-hair (of the tail)	རྟ་རྔ་	*ta-nga.*
Horse-whip	རྟ་ལྕག་	*te-cha.*
Do. *hon.*	ཆིབས་ལྕག་	*chhiṕ-cha.*
Horseman	རྟ་པ་	*ta-pa.*
Horsemen, body of	རྟ་རག་	*taṕ-ra.*
Do. *hon.*	ཆིབས་རག་	*chhiṕ-ra.*

Horse-shoe	རྨིག་ལྕགས་	*mik-cha.*
Hospitable	ལག་པ་ཤོག་པོ་	*lak-pa shok-po.*
Do. *hon.*	ཕྱག་ཤོག་པོ་	*chha-shok-po.*
Hospital	སྨན་ཁང་	*men-khang.*
Host (army)	དམག་	*ma.*
Do. (crowd of persons)	མི་དཔུང་	*mi-pung.*
Do. (owner of house, inn, &c.)	གནས་པོ་	*ne-po.*
Hostess	གནས་མོ་	*ne-mo.*
Hot	ཚ་པོ་	*tsha-po.*
Hot-tempered	རླུང་ལང་པོ་	*lung lang-po.*
Do. *hon.*	སྐུ་རླུང་བཞེང་པོ་	*ku lung sKang-po.*
Hot (of weather)	ཚད་པ་ཚ་པོ་	*tshe-pa tsha-po.*
Hot, to be (of body)	ཚད་པ་འཚིག་པ་	*tshe-pa tshiK-pa.*
Do. *hon.*	སྐུ་ཚད་ཚ་པོ་བྱུང་བ་	*ku-tshe tsha-po cKung-wa.*
Hotel	གནས་ཚང་	*ne-tshang.*
Hotel charges	གནས་གླ་	*ne-la.*
Hotel-keeper	གནས་པོ་	*ne-po.*
Do. *f.*	གནས་མོ་	*ne-mo.*
Hound	ཁྱི་	*khyi.*
Do. *hon.*	གཟིམ་ཁྱི་	*śim-khyi.*

Hour	ཆུ་ཚོད་	*chhu-tshö.*
House	ནང་། ཁང་པ་	*nang ; khang-pa.*
Do. *hon.*	གཟིམ་ཁང་	*śim-khang.*
Do. *h. hon.*	གཟིམ་ཤག་	*śim-sha.*
House-owner	ཁང་བདག་	*khang-dak̄.*
House agent	ཁང་གཉེར་	*khang-nyer.*
House, caretaker of	ཁང་སྲུང་ང་ (བ་)	*khang-sung-nga.*
House-rent	ཁང་གླ་	*khang-la.*
Household	ནང་མི་	*nang-mi.*
Housewife	གནས་མོ་	*ne-mo.*
Do. *hon.*	སྙི་སྙིང་ལགས་	*nyi-nying-la.*
Hovel	ནང་ཆུང་། ཁང་ཆུང་	*nang-chhung ; khang-chhung.*
How	ག་འདྲས་	*k̄an-dre.*
How much	ག་ཚོད་	*k̄a-tshö.*
Howbeit	ག་རེ་ཡིན་ནས་	*ka-re yin-ne.*
However	ཡིན་ནས། ཡིན་ཀྱང་། ཡིན་ན་ཡང་	*yin-ne ; yin-kyang ; yin-na-yang.*
Howl, to (of dogs)	སྡུག་སྐད་རྒྱབ་པ་	*duk̄-k̄e gyap̄-pa.*
Do. (of children crying)	ངུ་བ་	*ngu-wa.*
Hug, to	འཁྱུད་པ་	*khyü-pa.*

Huge	ཆེ་ཐག་ཆོད་	*chhe-thaḱ-chhö.*
Hullo! (expression of surprise)	ཨ་ཙི་	*a-tsi.*
Human	མིའི་	*mi-i.*
Humble	སེམས་ཆུང་ཆུང་	*sem-chhung-chhung.*
Do. *hon.*	ཐུགས་སེམས་ཆུང་ཆུང་	*thuḱ sem chhung-chhung.*
Humid	རློན་པ་	*löm-pa.*
Humorous	བགད་མོ་བྲོ་པོ་	*ge-mo ťro-po.*
Do. *hon.*	ཞལ་མོ་བྲོ་པོ་	*sḱe-mo ťro-po.*
Hunch-back	སྟོད་དགུར་	*tö-gur.*
Hundred	བརྒྱ་ཐམ་པ་	*gya-tham-pa.*
Hundredth	བརྒྱ་ཐམ་པ་	*gya-tham-pa.*
Hunger	ལྟོགས་པ་	*toḱ-pa.*
Do. *hon.*	བཀྲེས་པ་	*tre pa.*
Hungry, to be	གྲོ་ (གྲོད་) ཁོག་ལྟོགས་པ་	*ťro kho toḱ-pa.*
Do. *hon.*	གསོལ་གྲོད་བཀྲེས་པ་	*sö-ťrö tre-pa.*
Hunt, to	ཁྱི་ར་རྒྱབ་པ་	*khyi-ra gyaṕ-pa.*
Hunter	ཁྱི་ར་བ་	*khyi-ra-wa.*
Hurricane	ལྷགས་པ་ཚ་པོ་	*hlaḱ-pa tsha-po.*
Do. (with rain)	ཆར་རླུང་	*chhar-lung.*
Hurry, to	མགྱོགས་པོ་བྱེད་པ་	*gyoḱ-po cḱe-pa.*

Hurry, to, *hon.*	རྩོལ་པོ་གནང་བ་	*tsö-po nang-wa.*
Do. *h. hon.*	ཐུགས་རྩོལ་པོ་གནང་བ་	*thu tsö-po nang-wa.*
Hurry, in a great	བྲེལ་བ་ཚ་པོ་བྱས་ནས་	*t́re-wa tsha-po cḱe-ne.*
Do. *hon.*	མཛད་བྲེལ་ཆེན་པོ་གནང་ནས་	*dze-t́re chhem-po nang-ne.*
Hurt (physical)	རྨ་	*ma.*
Do. (by witchcraft, etc.)	གནོད་པ་	*nö-pa.*
Hurt, to (physically)	རྨ་བཟོ་བ་	*ma-śo-wa.*
Do. (by witchcraft, etc.)	གནོད་པ་བྱེད་པ་	*nö-pa cḱe-pa.*
Hurt, to (impair)	སྐྱོན་བྱེད་པ་	*kyön-cḱe-pa.*
Do. *hon.*	སྐྱོན་གནང་བ་	*kyön-nang-wa.*
Hurt, to be	སྐྱོན་བྱེད་པ་	*kyön-cḱe-pa.*
Husband	ཁྱོ་ག་	*khyo-ḱa.*
Husbandman	སོ་ནམས་བྱེད་མཁན་	*sö-nam cḱe-khen.*
Husband and wife	བཟའ་ཚང་	*śa-tshang.*
Husbandry (agriculture)	སོ་ནམས་	*sö-nam.*
Husk (of grain)	པགས་པ་	*paḱ-pa.*
Hut	ནང་ཆུང་། ཁང་ཆུང་	*nang-chhung; khang-chhung.*
Hydrophobia	ཁྱི་སྨྱོན་	*khyim-nyön.*
Hymn	མགུར་མ་	*gur-ma.*

I

I	ང་	*nga.*
Do. myself	ང་རང་	*nga-rang.*
Ice	ཁྱག་པ་	*khyak̓-pa.*
Icicle	ཁྱག་པ་	*khyak̓ pa.*
Icy, to be	ཁྱག་པ་ཡོད་པ་	*khyak̓-pa yö-pa.*
Idea (purport)	དོན་	*t̓ön.*
Do. *hon.*	སྐུ་དོན་	*ku-t̓ön.*
Idea (opinion)	བསམ་པ་	*sam pa.*
Do. *hon.*	ཐུགས་སེམས་	*thu-sem.*
Identical	གཅིག་པ་	*chik̓-pa.*
Identify, to	ངོ་འཕྲོད་སྤྲད་པ་	*ngo-thrö tre-pa.*
Do. *hon.*	ངོ་འཕྲོད་གནང་བ་	*ngo-thrö nang-wa.*
Idiom	སྐད་ལུགས་	*ke-lu.*
Idiot	ཀླུགས་པ། གླེན་པ་	*kuk̓-pa ; lem-pa.*
Idiotic (stupid)	ཀླུགས་པ། གླེན་པ་	*kuk̓-pa ; lem-pa.*
Idle	རྒྱུ་མ་རིང་པོ། ལེ་ལོ་ཆེན་པོ་	*gyu-ma ring po; le-lo chhem-po.*
Do. *hon.*	ཐུགས་རྒྱུ་རིང་པོ་	*thu-gyu ring-po.*
Idol	སྐུ་འདྲ་	*kun-dra.*
If	གལ་སྲིད་…ན་	*k̓e-si...na.*

Ignite, to	འབར་བ་	*bar-wa.*
Ignoble	སྐྱེ་ས་དམའ་པོ་	*kye-sa ma-po.*
Ignominious	ངོ་ཚ་པོ་	*ngo·tsha-po.*
Ignominy	ངོ་ཚ་	*ngo-tsha.*
Ignoramus	ལྐུགས་པ་	*kuk-pa.*
Ignorant	ཡོན་ཏན་མེད་པ་	*yön-ten me-pa.*
Do. *hon.*	སྐུ་ཡོན་མེད་པ་	*ku-yön me-pa.*
Ill, to be	ན་བ་	*na-wa.*
Do. *hon.*	སྙུང་བ་	*nyung-wa.*
Illegal	ཁྲིམས་མེད་	*thrim-me.*
Ill-fated	བསོད་བདེ་མེད་པ། བསོད་བདེ་ཆུང་ཆུང་།	*so-de me-pa ; so-de chhung-chhung.*
Do. *hon.*	སྐུ་བསོད་མེད་པ། སྐུ་བསོད་ཆུང་ཆུང་	*ku-sö me-pa ; ku-sö chhung-chhung.*
Ill-feeling, to cherish	སེམས་ལ་ངན་པ་བྱས་ནས་བཞག་ (འཇོག་) པ་	*sem-la ngem-pa che-ne shak-pa.*
Ill-luck	བསོད་བདེ་མེད་པ་	*so-de me-pa.*
Do. *hon.*	སྐུ་བསོད་མེད་པ་	*ku-sö me-pa.*
Ill-natured	སེམས་ངན་པ་	*sem-ngem-pa.*
Do. *hon.*	ཐུགས་སེམས་ངན་པ་	*thu-sem ngem-pa.*

Ill-will	སྙིང་ནད་	*nying-ne.*
Illegal	ཁྲིམས་མེད་	*thrim-me.*
Illegitimate	ཁྲིམས་མེད་	*thrim-me.*
Illicit	ཁྲིམས་མེད་	*thrim-me.*
Illimitable	ཚོད་མེད་པ་	*tshö-me-pa.*
Illiterate, to be	ཡོན་ཏན་མེད་པ་	*yön-ten me-pa.*
Do. *hon.*	སྐུ་ཡོན་མེད་པ་	*ku-yön me-pa.*
Illness	ན་ཚ་	*na-tsha.*
Do. *hon.*	སྙུང་གཞི་	*nyung-sk̃i.*
Illuminate, to	འོད་རྒྱབ་པ་	*ö-gyap̃-pa.*
Illusion (optical)	མིག་འཁྲུལ་	*mik̃-thrü.*
Illusive	མིག་འཁྲུལ་ཆེན་པོ་	*mik̃-thrü chhem-po.*
Illustrate, to	དཔེ་སྦྱར་ནས་བཤད་པ་	*pe-jar-ne she-pa.*
Do. *hon.*	དཔེ་སྦྱར་ནས་གསུང་བ་	*pe-jar ne sung-wa.*
Illustration	དཔེ་	*pe.*
Illustrious	སྐད་གྲགས་ཆེན་པོ་	*ke-t̃ra chhem-po.*
Do. *hon.*	མཚན་སྙན་གྲགས་ཆེན་པོ་	*tshen nyen-t̃ra chhem-po.*
Image (idol)	སྐུ་འདྲ་	*kun-dra.*
Imagination	དམིགས་པ་	*mik̃-pa.*
Imagine, to (think)	བསམ་པ་	*sam-pa.*

Imagine, to (think), *hon.*	ཐུགས་བསམ་བཞེས་པ་	*thu-sam sKe-pa.*
Imbecile	ཀླུགས་པ། གླེན་པ་	*kuk-pa ; lem-pa.*
Imbrue, to (soak)	སྦང་བ་	*bang-wa.*
Do. *hon.*	སྦང་ང་ (བ་) གནང་བ་	*bang-nga nang-wa.*
Imitate, to	མིག་འདྲེན་བྱེད་པ་	*mik-dren cKe-pa.*
Immaculate, to be	སྐྱོན་མེད་པ་	*kyön me pa.*
Immaterial (without substance)	གཟུགས་མེད་	*śu-me.*
Immeasurable (very great)	ཆེ་ཐག་ཆོད་	*chhe thaK chhö.*
Do. to be	ཚོད་མེད་པ་	*tshö me pa*
Immediately	ལམ་སང་། ལམ་ཀྱང་	*lam-sang ; lam-kyang.*
Immense	རྒྱ་ཆེན་པོ། ཆེ་ཐག་ཆོད་	*gya-chhem-po ; chhe thaK-chhö.*
Immoderate, to be	ཚོད་མེད་པ་	*tshö-me-pa.*
Do. *hon.*	ཐུགས་ཚོད་མེད་པ་	*thuk-tshö me-pa.*
Immodest, to be	ངོ་ཚ་མེད་པ་	*ngo-tsha me-pa.*
Immoral	བྱེད་སྟངས་ངན་པོ་	*cKe-tang ngem-po.*
Do. *hon.*	གནང་སྟངས་ངན་པོ་	*nang-tang ngem-po.*
Immortal, to be	ཤི་རྒྱུ་...མེད་པ་	*shi-gyu...me-pa.*
Do *hon.*	བཤག་ (གཤེགས་) རྒྱུ་... མེད་པ་	*sha-gyu...me-pa.*
Immovable	གཡོ་རྒྱུ་མེད་པ་	*yo-gyu me-pa.*

Impair, to	སྐྱོན་བྱེད་པ་	*kyön-cḱe-pa.*
Do. *hon.*	སྐྱོན་གནང་བ་	*kyön-nang-wa.*
Impale, to	ཤིང་ལ་བཀལ་ནས་བསད་ (གསོད་) པ་	*shing-la ke-ne se-pa.*
Impart, to	སྟེར་བ་	*ter-wa.*
Do. *hon.*	གནང་བ་	*nang-wa.*
Impartial	ཉེ་རིང་མེད་པ་	*nye-ring me-pa.*
Impartial (of judges)	ཁྲིམས་དྲང་པོ་	*thrim ťrang-po.*
Do. *hon.*	བཀའ་ཁྲིམས་དྲང་པོ་	*ka-thrim ťrang-po.*
Impassable, to be	མི་...ཐར་བ་	*mi ..thar-wa.*
Impassive	དྲན་པ་བརྒྱལ་བ་	*ťrem-pa gyel-wa.*
Impede, to	བཀག་པ་ (འགེགས་པ་)	*kaḱ-pa.*
Do. *hon.*	བཀག་ཀ་ (འགེགས་པ་) གནང་བ་	*kaḱ ḱa nang-wa.*
Impediment	བཀག་ཆ་	*kaḱ-chha.*
Imperceptible, to be	མཐོང་རྒྱུ་...མེད་པ་	*thong-gyu me-pa.*
Imperfect	མི་དག་པ་	*mi ťak-pa.*
Imperfection (defect)	སྐྱོན་	*kyön.*
Imperial	རྒྱལ་པོའི་	*gye-pö.*
Imperishable, to be	ཆག་རྒྱུ་མེད་པ་	*chha-gyu me-pa.*

Impertinent	འཛིང་པ་སྦོམ་པོ། གྱོང་པོ་	*jing-pa bom-po; kyong-po.*
Impetuous	རུ་ངར་པོ་	*ru-ngar-po.*
Do. *hon.*	ཐུགས་རུ་ངར་པོ་	*thuk-ru ngar-po.*
Impious	ཆོས་སེམས་མེད་པ་	*chhö-sem me-pa.*
Implements	ལག་ཆ་	*lak-chha.*
Implore, to	ཞུ་བ་	*sku-wa.*
Do. *hon.*	ཞུ་བ་གནང་བ་	*sku-wa nang-wa.*
Impolite	གྱོང་པོ་	*kyong-po.*
Import (meaning)	དོན་དག་	*tön-ta.*
Do. *hon.*	སྐུ་དོན་	*ku-tön.*
Importance	གནད་ཁག་	*nen kha.*
Important	གནད་ཁག་ཆེན་པོ། གལ་ཆེན་པོ་	*nen-kha chhem-po; ke-chhem-po.*
Impose, to (lay on)	སྐྱལ་བ་	*kü-wa.*
Impose on, to (deceive)	མགོ་སྐོར་བ་	*go-kor-wa.*
Do. *hon.*	དབུ་སྐོར་ར་ (བ་) གནང་བ་	*u-kor-ra nang-wa.*
Do. *inf.* to *sup.*	དབུ་སྐོར་ཞུ་བ་	*u-kor sku-wa.*
Imposition (deceit)	མགོ་སྐོར་	*go-kor.*
Do. *hon.*	དབུ་སྐོར་	*u-kor.*
Impossible	མི་ཐུབ་པ་	*mi-thup-pa.*

Impost (general)	ཁྲལ། འབབ་	thre ; baṕ.
Do. (customs-duty)	ཤོ་ཁྲལ་	sho-thre.
Do. (on land)	ས་ཁྲལ་	sa-thre.
Imposture	མགོ་སྐོར་	go-kor.
Do. *hon.*	དབུ་སྐོར་	u-kor.
Impotent, to be	སྟོབས་འཆག་པ་	toṕ-chhaḱ-pa.
Do. *hon.*	སྐུ་སྟོབས་འཆག་པ་	ku-toṕ chhaḱ-pa.
Impracticable, to be	བྱེད་…མི་ཐུབ་པ་	cḱe…mi thuṕ-pa.
Imprecate, to	དམོད་མོ་རྒྱབ་པ་	mö-mo gyaṕ-pa.
Do. *hon.*	དམོད་མོ་སྐྱོན་པ་	mö-mo kyöm-pa.
Impression, thumb	མཛུག་ཐེ་	dzuḱ-the.
Imprison, to	བཙོན་ལ་བཅུག་ (འཇུག་) པ་	tsön-la chuk-pa.
Improper	མི་ཆོག་པ་	mi-chhoḱ-pa.
Improve, to	བཟོ་སྐྱོར་བྱེད་པ་	śo-kyor cḱe-pa.
Do. *hon.*	བཟོ་སྐྱོར་གནང་བ་	śo-kyor nang-wa.
Impudent	འཇིང་པ་སྦོམ་པོ། ཁྱོང་པོ་	jing-pa bom-po ; ḱyong-po.
Impure	སྐྱུག་བྲོ་པོ་	kyuḱ-ťro-po.
Impurity	གྲིབ་	ťriṕ.
Impute wrongly, to	ཡ་ལ་བཞག་ (འཇོག་) པ་	ya-la sḱaḱ-pa.
Do. *hon.*	ཡ་ལ་གཞོག་ག་ (པ་) གནང་བ་	ya-la-sḱoḱ-ka nang-wa.

In (inside)	ནང་ལ་	*nang-la.*
Inaccessible	བཙན་པོ་	*tsem-po.*
Inaccurate, to be	མི་ . . དག་པ་	*mi...ťaǩ-pa.*
Inadequate, to be	མི་ . . འགྲིག་པ་	*mi...driǩ-pa.*
Inattentive, to be	སེམས་གཡང་ནས་བསྡད་ (སྡོད་) པ་	*sem-yang-ne de-pa.*
Do. *hon.*	ཐུགས་སེམས་གཡང་ནས་བཞུགས་པ་	*thuǩ-sem yang-ne sǨuǩ-pa.*
Inauspicious day	གཡང་གཟའ་	*yang-śa.*
Incalculable	གྲངས་མེད་	*ťrang-me.*
Incantation	སྔགས་	*nga.*
Incapable	མི་ . . ཐུབ་པ་	*mi...thup̓-pa.*
Incarcerate, to	བཙོན་ལ་བཅུག་ (འཇུག་) པ་	*tsön-la chuǩ-pa*
Incarnate, to be	སྤྲུལ་བ་	*trül-wa.*
Incarnation (of a deity)	སྤྲུལ་སྐུ་	*trül-ku.*
Incautious	སྣང་དག་མེད་པ་	*nang-ťa me-pa.*
Incense, *s.*	སྤོས་	*pö.*
Incense, to	ཁོང་ཁྲོ་སློང་བ་	*khong-thro lang-wa.*
Do. *hon.*	དགོངས་པ་དཀྲུག་པ་	*gong-pa truǩ-pa.*
Incessant	རྒྱུན་ཆད་རྒྱུ་མེད་པ་	*gyün-chhe-gyu me-pa.*

Incessantly	ནམ་རྒྱུན། དུས་རྒྱུན་	*nam-gyün ; tü-gyün.*
Inch (breadth of a finger)	སོར་	*sor.*
Inclination	འདོད་པ་	*dö-pa.*
Do. *hon.*	ཐུགས་འདོད་	*thung-dö.*
Incline, to (lean against)	སྦོ་སྙེ་རྒྱབ་པ་	*bo-nye gyaṕ-pa.*
Do. *hon.*	སྦོ་སྙེ་སྐྱོན་པ་	*bo-nye kyöm-pa.*
Inclined to be	འདོད་པ་ཡོད་པ་	*dö-pa yö-pa.*
Do. *hon.*	ཐུགས་འདོད་ཡོད་པ་	*thung-dö yö-pa.*
Inclosure	ར་བ་	*ra-wa.*
Include, to	སྡོམ་པ་	*dom-pa.*
Income	ཐོབ་ཐང་	*thoṕ-thang.*
Incompetent, to be	འོས་པོ་མེད་པ་	*ö-po me-pa.*
Do. *hon.*	ཐུགས་འོས་པོ་མེད་པ་	*thuḱ-ö-po me-pa.*
Incomplete, to be	མི་ཚང་བ་	*mi tshang-wa.*
Inconstant, to be	བརྟན་པོ་མེད་པ་	*tem-po me-pa.*
Incorporeal	གཟུགས་པོ་མེད་པ་	*ṡuk-po me-pa.*
Incorrect	མ་དག་པ་	*ma-ták-pa.*
Increase, to (in numbers)	འཕེལ་བ་	*phe-wa.*
Do. (in price)	འཕར་བ་	*phar-wa.*
Do. (in size)	ཆེ་རུ་ཆེ་རུ་འགྲོ་བ་	*chhe-ru chhe-ru dro-wa.*

Increase, to (in size), *hon.*	ཆེ་རུ་ཆེ་རུ་ཕེབ་པ་	*chhe-ru chhe-ru phe-pa.*
Indeed	ཏེན་ཏེན། ངོ་ཐོག་	*ten-ten ; ngo-tho.*
Indefatigable	སྙིང་རུས་ཆེན་པོ་	*nying-rü chhem-po.*
Do. *hon.*	ཐུགས་རུས་ཆེན་པོ་	*thu-rü chhem-po.*
Indefinite	ཏན་པོ་མེད་པ་	*tem-po me-pa.*
Indented	ཀྱོང་ཀྱོང་	*kyong-kyong.*
Independent	རང་མགོ་འཐོན་པ་	*rang-go thöm-pa.*
Indestructible	ཆག་རྒྱུ་མེད་པ་	*chha-gyu me-pa.*
Index	ཐོ་	*tho.*
India (plains of)	རྒྱ་ཐང་	*gya-thang.*
India	རྒྱ་གར་	*gya-k̓ar.*
Indian	རྒྱ་གར་གྱི་	*gya-k̓ar-k̓yi.*
Indicate, to	མིག་སྟོན་པ་	*mi-töm-pa.*
Do. *hon.*	མིག་སྟོན་པ་གནང་བ་	*mi-töm-pa nang-wa.*
Do. *inf.* to *sup.*	སྤྱན་ཕེབ་ཞུ་བ་	*chem-phe sk̓u-wa.*
Indifferent, to be	སྣང་དག་མི་བྱེད་པ་	*nang-t̓a mi-ck̓e-pa.*
Indigent	སྐྱོ་པོ་	*kyo-po.*
Indigestion	ལྟོ་མ་འཛུ་བའི་ནད་	*to ma ju-we ne.*
Indignant, to be	ཁོང་ཁྲོ་ཟ་བ། ཚིག་པ་ཟ་བ་	*khong-thro śa-wa ; tshik̓-pa śa-wa.*

Indignant, to be, *hon.*	དགོངས་པ་ཚུང་པ། རྣམ་མཁྱེན་འགལ་བ་	*gong-pa tshung-pa ; nam-khyen gel-wa.*
Indignation	ཚིག་པ། ཁོང་ཁྲོ་	*tshiḱ-pa ; khong-thro.*
Do. *hon.*	དགོངས་ཚུང་། རྣམ་མཁྱེན་	*gong-tshung ; nam-khyen.*
Indigo	རམས་	*ram.*
Indisposed, to be (unwell)	བདེ་པོ་མེད་པ། གཟུགས་པོ་ཐང་པོ་མེད་པ་	*de-po me-pa ; śuḱ-po thang-po me-pa.*
Do. *hon.*	སྐུ་གཟུགས་ཐང་པོ་མེད་པ་	*ku-śuḱ thang-po me-pa.*
Indisposition (illness)	ན་ཚ་	*na-tsha.*
Do. *hon.*	སྙུང་གཞི་	*nyung-sḱi.*
Indistinct	གསལ་པོ་མེད་པ་	*se-po me-pa.*
Indolent	རྒྱུ་མ་རིང་པོ། ལེ་ལོ་ཆེན་པོ་	*gyu-ma ring-po ; le-lo chhem-po.*
Do. *hon.*	ཐུགས་རྒྱུ་རིང་པོ་	*thu-gyu ring-po.*
Indra	ལྷའི་དབང་པོ་བརྒྱ་བྱིན་	*hlaï-wang-po gya-jin.*
Induce, to	ཨུ་ཚུགས་བྱེད་པ་	*u-tshu cḱe-pa.*
Do. *hon.*	ཨུ་ཚུགས་གནང་བ་	*u-tshu nang-wa.*
Industrious	སྙིང་རུས་ཆེན་པོ་	*nying-rü chhem-po.*
Do. *hon.*	ཐུགས་རུས་ཆེན་པོ་	*thu-rü chhem-po.*
Industry	སྙིང་རུས་	*nying-rü.*
Do. *hon.*	ཐུགས་རུས་	*thuḱ-rü.*

Ineffaceable, to be	སྲུབ་…མི་ཐུབ་པ་	*sup̌...mi thup̌-pa.*
Inefficient, to be	འོས་པོ་…མེད་པ་	*ö-po...me-pa.*
Inequitable, to be (unjust)	དྲང་པོ་…མེད་པ་	*ťrang-po...me-pa*
Inert, to be	ཧུར་པོ་…མེད་པ་	*hur-po . me-pa.*
Inexhaustible	ཛོགས་རྒྱུ་མེད་པ་	*dzo-gyu me-pa.*
Inexorable	སྨྲ་བ་ལེན་གཅིག་	*ma-wa len-chi.*
Inexpensive	ཁེ་པོ། གོང་ཆུང་ཆུང་	*khe-po ; ǩong-chhung-chhung.*
Infallible, to be	མི་ནོར་བ་	*mi-nor-wa.*
Infamy	མིང་ངན་	*ming ngen.*
Infant	བུ་གུ་ཆུང་ཆུང་	*p̌u-gu chhung-chhung.*
Do. *hon.*	ཨ་ལྦྲ་ཆུང་ཆུང་	*a-wa chhung-chhung.*
Infant (of a few weeks only)	མ་འབྱར་	*man-ja.*
Infantry	དམག་དཔུང་	*maǩ-pung.*
Infelicitous (unfortunate)	བསོད་བདེ་མེད་པ། བསོད་བདེ་ཆུང་ཆུང་	*so-de me-pa ; so-de chhung-chhung.*
Do. *hon.*	སྐུ་བསོད་མེད་པ། སྐུ་བསོད་ཆུང་ཆུང་	*ku-sö me-pa; ku-sö chhung-chhung.*
Inferior (of things)	སྡུག་པོ་	*duǩ-po.*
Do. (in rank of persons)	དམའ་པོ་	*ma-po.*
Infertile	རྩ་ཆུ་འཛོམ་པོ་…མེད་པ་	*tsa-chhu dzom-po...me-pa.*

Infidel	ཕྱི་པ་	*chhi-pa.*
Infinite	ཚད་མེད་པ་	*tshö me-pa.*
Infirm	ཤེད་མེད་ང་	*she me-pa.*
Do. *hon.*	སྐུ་ཤེད་ཆུང་ཆུང་	*ku-she chhung-chhung.*
Inflame, to (with anger)	ཁོང་ཁྲོ་སློང་བ་	*khong-thro lang-wa.*
Do. *hon.*	དགོངས་པ་དཀྲུག་པ་	*gong-pa truk-pa.*
Inflammation	ཚ་བ་	*tsha-wa.*
Do. of bone	རུ་གཟུག་རྒྱབ་པ་	*ru-śuk gyap-pa.*
Do. of joint	ཚིགས་ཚ་བ་	*tshi tsha-wa.*
Do. of muscle	རྩ་གཞི་འབར་བ་	*tsap-ski bar-wa.*
Inflamed, to be (of hands, &c.)	འཚིག་པ་	*tshik-pa.*
Inflate, to	གམ་ཕུ་རྒྱང་བ་	*kam-phu gyang-wa.*
Inflexible (stubborn)	གྱོང་པོ་	*kyong-po.*
Influence	དབང་	*wang.*
Do. *hon.*	སྐུ་དབང་	*ku-wang.*
Influential	དབང་ཆེན་པོ་	*wang-chhem-po.*
Do. *hon.*	སྐུ་དབང་ཆེན་པོ་	*ku-wang chhem-po.*
Inform, to	ལན་སྤྲོད་པ་	*len-trö-pa.*
Do. *inf.* to *sup.*	ཞུགས་ལན་ཕུལ་ (འབུལ་) བ་	*ja-len phü-wa.*
Do. *sup.* to *inf.*	བཀའ་ལན་གནང་བ་	*ka-len nang-wa.*

Information (news)	གནས་ཚུལ། གསར་འགྱུར་	*ne-tshül ; sang gyu.*
Informer	ལན་སྤྲད་མཁན་	*len-tre-khen.*
Ingenious	ཇུས་མཁས་པོ་	*cKü-khe-po.*
Do. *hon.*	སྐུ་ཇུས་མཁས་པོ་	*ku-cKü khe-po.*
Inhabit, to	བསྡད་པ་ (སྡོད་པ་)	*de-pa.*
Do. *hon.*	བཞུགས་པ་	*sKu-pa.*
Inhale, to	དབུགས་འཐེན་པ་	*u-them-pa.*
Do. *hon.*	ལྗགས་དབུགས་འཐེན་པ་ གནང་བ་	*ja-u them-pa nang-wa.*
Inherit, to	སྐལ་ལ་ (བ་) ཐོབ་པ་	*ke-la thop-pa.*
Do. *hon.*	སྐུ་སྐལ་ཐོབ་པ་	*ku-ke thop-pa.*
Inheritance	ཐོབ་སྐལ་	*thop-ke.*
Do. *hon.*	སྐུ་སྐལ་	*ku-ke.*
Inhibit, to (forbid)	བཀག་པ་ (འགོགས་པ་)	*kak-pa.*
Do. *hon.*	བཀག་ག་ (འགོགས་པ་) གནང་བ་	*kak-ka nang-wa.*
Inhuman, to be	སྙིང་རྗེ་མེད་པ་	*nying-je me-pa.*
Do. *hon.*	ཐུགས་རྗེ་མེད་པ་	*thuk-je me-pa.*
Inimical, to be	དགྲ་བྱེད་པ་	*dra-cKe-pa.*
Do. *hon.*	དགྲ་གནང་བ་	*dra-nang-wa.*

Iniquitous	ངན་པོ་	*ngem-po.*
Do. *hon.*	ཐུགས་ངན་པོ་	*thu ngem-po.*
Iniquity	ཉེས་པ། སྡིག་པ་	*nye-pa ; dik̄-pa.*
Do. *hon.*	སྐུ་སྡིག་	*ku-di.*
Inject, to	བཙུག་པ་ (འཛུག་པ་)	*chuk̄-pa.*
Do. *hon.*	བཙུག་ག་ (འཛུག་པ་) གནང་བ་	*chuk̄-k̄a nang-wa.*
Injunction	བཀའ་	*ka.*
Injure, to (by witchcraft, etc.)	གནོད་པ་བྱེད་པ་	*nö-pa ck̄e-pa.*
Do. (physically)	རྨ་བཟོ་བ་	*ma-śo-wa.*
Do. (impair)	སྐྱོན་བྱེད་པ་	*kyön-ck̄e-pa.*
Do. *hon.*	སྐྱོན་གནང་བ་	*kyön-nang-wa.*
Injured, to be	སྐྱོན་བྱེད་པ་	*kyön-ck̄e-pa.*
Injury	གནོད་པ་	*nö-pa.*
Injustice, to do	ཁྲིམས་མེད་བྱེད་པ་	*thrim-me ck̄e-pa.*
Do. *hon.*	ཁྲིམས་མེད་གནང་བ་	*thrim-me nang-wa.*
Ink	སྣག་ཚ་	*nak̄-tsha.*
Do. *hon.*	ཕྱག་སྣག་	*chha-na.*
Ink-pot	སྣག་བུམ་	*nak̄-p̄um.*
Do. *hon.*	ཕྱག་བུམ་	*chha-p̄um.*
Ink, red	མཚལ་	*tshe.*

Inlet (bay)	ཆུ་ལྷག་	*chhu-hla.*
Inmate (fellow-lodger)	ཐོ་ཚང་། ཐབ་རོགས་	*to-tshang ; thaṕ-ro.*
Inn	གནས་ཚང་	*ne-tshang.*
Inn-keeper	གནས་པོ་	*ne-po.*
Do. *f.*	གནས་མོ་	*ne-mo.*
Inner	ནང་གི་	*nang-ḱi.*
Innocent	ཉེས་པ་མེད་པ་	*nye-pa me-pa.*
Innumerable	གྲངས་མེད་	*ťrang me.*
Inoculate, to (for smallpox)	ལྷ་འབྲུམ་བཙུགས་ (འཛུག་) པ་	*hlan-drum tsuḱ-pa.*
Do. *hon.*	ལྷ་འབྲུམ་བཙུགས་ཀ་ (འཛུགས་པ་) གནང་བ་	*hlan-drum tsuḱ-ḱa nang-wa.*
Inordinate, to be.	ཚོད་མེད་པ་	*tshö me-pa.*
Do. *hon.*	ཐུགས་ཚོད་མེད་པ་	*thuḱ-tshö me-pa.*
Inquire, to (ask)	དྲི་བ་ (འདྲི་བ་)	*ťri-wa.*
Do. *hon.*	བཀའ་འདྲི་གནང་བ་	*kan-dri nang-wa.*
Do. *inf.* to *sup.*	ཞུ་བ་	*shu-wa.*
Inquire, to (into a matter)	རྩད་གཅོད་པ་	*tse chö-pa.*
Do. *hon.*	རྩད་གཅོད་གནང་བ་	*tse-chö nang-wa.*
Inquire, to (investigate)	ཞིབ་དཔྱོད་བྱེད་པ་	*shiṕ-chö che-pa.*
Do. *hon.*	ཞིབ་དཔྱོད་གནང་བ་	*shiṕ-chö nang-wa.*

Inquire, to (investigate) *h. hon.*	བཀའ་ཞིབ་གནང་བ་	*ka-sḱiṕ nang-wa.*
Inquiry (investigation)	ཞིབ་དཔྱོད་	*sḱiṕ-chö.*
Do. *hon.*	བཀའ་ཞིབ་	*ka-sḱiṕ.*
Insane	སྨྱོན་པ་	*nyöm-pa.*
Insane, to be	སྨྱོ་བ་	*nyo-wa.*
Inscription	རྡོ་བཀོད་	*do-kö.*
Insect	འབུ་	*bu.*
Insensible, to become	དྲན་པ་འཐོར་བ་	*t́rem-pa thor-wa.*
Inseparable, to be	བྲལ་ (འབྲལ་) མི་ཐུབ་པ་	*t́re...mi-thuṕ-pa.*
Insert, to	བཙུགས་པ་ (འཛུགས་པ་)	*tsuḱ-pa.*
Do. *hon.*	བཙུགས་ག་ (འཛུགས་པ་) གནང་བ་	*tsuḱ-ḱa nang-wa.*
Inside, *prep.*	ནང་ལ་	*nang-la.*
Insignificant (of matters)	དོན་དག་ཆུང་ཆུང་	*t́ön-t́a chhung-chhung.*
Do. *hon.*	སྐུ་དོན་ཆུང་ཆུང་	*ku-t́ön chhung-chhung.*
Insincere, to be	དྲང་པོ་…མེད་པ། དངོས་ནས་…མི་བྱེད་པ་	*t́rang-po . me-pa ; ngön-ne ...mi cḱe-pa.*
Insist, to	ཨུ་ཚུགས་བྱེད་པ་	*u-tshu cḱe-pa.*
Do. *hon.*	ཨུ་ཚུགས་གནང་བ་	*u tshu nang-wa.*
Insolent	འཇིང་པ་སྦོམ་པོ། གྱོང་པོ་	*jing-pa bom-po ; kyong-po.*

Insoluble	སྐུ་...མི་ཐུབ་པ་	*sku...mi thup-pa.*
Inspect, to	ལྟ་བ་	*ta-wa.*
Do. *hon.*	གཟིགས་པ་	*śi pa.*
Installation (of a ruler)	ཁྲི་འདོན་	*thrin-dön.*
Instance	དཔེ་	*pe.*
Instance, for	དཔེ་ན་ (དཔེར་ན་)	*pe-na.*
Instant, in an (presently)	ཧྲིབ་ཙམ་ཅིག་ལ་	*hrip-tsa-chi-la.*
Instantaneously	ལམ་སང་། ལམ་ཀྱང་	*lam-sang ; lam-kyang.*
Instantly	ལམ་སང་། ལམ་ཀྱང་	*lam-sang ; lam-kyang.*
Instead of	ཚབ་ལ་	*tshap-la.*
Instigate, to	ངན་པ་བསླབས་ (སློབ་) པ་	*ngen-pa lap-pa.*
Institute, to	བཙུགས་པ་ (འཛུགས་པ་)	*tsuk-pa.*
Instruct, to	བསླབས་པ་ (སློབ་པ་)	*lap-pa.*
Do. *hon.*	བསླབས་ (སློབ་) པ་གནང་བ་	*lap-pa nang-wa.*
Instructor	དགེ་རྒན། སློབ་དཔོན་	*ge-gen ; lo-pön.*
Do. (of Lama)	ཡོངས་འཛིན་	*yong-dzin.*
Instrument	ལག་ཆ་	*lak-chha.*
Insufficient	མི་...ལྡང་བ་	*mi...dang wa.*
Insult, *s.*	སྨད་ར་	*me-ra.*
Insult, to	སྨད་ར་བཏང་ (གཏོང་) བ་	*me-ra tang-wa.*

Insult, to, *hon.*	སྨད་ར་གཏོང་ང་ (བ་) གནང་བ་	*me-ra tong-nga nang-wa.*
Insurrection	སྡེ་འཁྲུག་	*de-thruḱ.*
Intellect	བློ་གྲོས་	*lo-t́ro.*
Intellectual	བློ་གྲོས་ཆེན་པོ་	*lo-t́ro chhem-po*
Do. *hon.*	དགོངས་པ་ཆེན་པོ་	*gong-pa chhem-po.*
Intelligence (news)	གནས་ཚུལ། གསར་འགྱུར་	*ne-tshül; sang-gyu.*
Do. (understanding)	རིག་པ་	*riḱ-pa.*
Do. *hon.*	ཐུགས་རིག་	*thu-ri.*
Intelligent	རིག་པ་ཡག་པོ་	*riḱ-pa yaḱ-po.*
Do. *hon.*	ཐུགས་རིག་ཡག་པོ་	*thu-ri yaḱ-po.*
Intemperate, to be	ཚོད་མེད་པ་	*tshö-me-pa.*
Do. *hon.*	ཐུགས་ཚོད་མེད་པ་	*thuḱ-tshö me-pa.*
Intend, to (purpose)	སེམས་ལ་བསམས་པ་	*sem-la sam-pa.*
Do. *hon.*	ཐུགས་ལ་དགོངས་པ་	*thuḱ-la gong-pa.*
Intent, *s.*	དོན་དག་	*t́ön-t́a.*
Do. *hon.*	སྐུ་དོན་	*ku-t́ön.*
Intention	དོན་དག་	*t́ön-t́a.*
Do. *hon.*	སྐུ་དོན་	*ku-t́ön.*
Inter, to (bury)	ས་ལ་སྦས་པ་	*sa-la be-pa.*
Intercede, to	བར་མི་བྱེད་པ་	*ṕar-mi cḱe-pa.*

Intercede, to, *hon.*	བར་མི་གནང་བ་	*par-mi nang-wa.*
Intercourse, to have (conversation)	སྐད་ཆ་བྱེད་པ་	*ḱe-chha cḱe-pa.*
Do. *hon.*	གསུང་གྲོས་གནང་བ་	*sung-t́rö nang-wa.*
Do. *inf. w. sup.*	གསུང་གྲོས་ཞུ་བ་	*sung-t́rö sḱu-wa.*
Interdict, to (forbid)	བཀག་པ་ (འགེགས་པ)	*kaḱ-pa.*
Do. *hon.*	བཀག་ག་ (འགེགས་པ་) གནང་བ་	*kaḱ-ḱa nang-wa.*
Interest (on loan)	སྐྱེད་	*ḱye.*
Do. *hon.*	ཕྱགས་སྐྱེད་	*ja-ḱye.*
Interior, *s.* (of a building)	ནང་	*nang.*
Do. (of a country)	གྲོང་གསེབ་	*t́rong-se.*
Internal	ནང་གི་	*nang-ḱi.*
Interpose, to (intercede)	བར་མི་བྱེད་པ་	*ṕar-mi cḱe-pa.*
Do. *hon.*	བར་མི་གནང་བ་	*ṕar-mi nang-wa.*
Interpreter	ལོ་ཙ་བ་	*lo-tsa-wa.*
Interrogate, to	དྲི་བ་ (འདྲི་བ་)	*t́ri-wa.*
Do. *hon.*	བཀའ་འདྲི་གནང་བ་	*kan-dri nang-wa.*
Interrupt, to	བཀག་པ་ (འགེགས་པ་)	*kaḱ-pa.*
Do. *hon.*	བཀག་ག་ (འགེགས་པ་) གནང་བ་	*kaḱ-ḱa nang-wa.*

Interruption	བཀག་ཆ་	*kak̄-chha.*
Interstice	སེར་ཀ་	*ser-ka.*
Interview (with lama)	མཇལ་ཁ་	*je-kha.*
Do. (with official)	སྐུ་མཇལ་	*ku-ja*
Interview, to (lama)	མཇལ་ཁ་ཞུ་བ་	*je-kha sh̄u-wa.*
Do. (official)	སྐུ་བཅར་ཞུ་བ་	*ku-cha sh̄u-wa.*
Intestines	རྒྱུ་མ་	*gyu-ma.*
Intimate, *adj.*	དགའ་པོ་ཉེ་པོ་	*ga-po nye-po.*
Do. *hon.*	ཐུགས་ཉེ་ཆགས་པོ་	*thuk̄-nye chhak̄-po.*
Intimidate, to	ཞེད་སྐྲག་སླང་བ་	*sh̄e-tra lang-wa.*
Do. *hon.*	ཞེད་སྐྲག་སློང་ང་ (བ་) གནང་བ་	*sh̄e-tra long-nga nang-wa.*
Into	ནང་ལ་	*nang-la.*
Intolerable (pain)	སྒོང་ (སྒོམ་) མི་ཐུབ་པ་	*gong mi thup̄-pa.*
Do. *hon.*	སྒོང་ང་ (སྒོམ་པ་) གནང་མི་ཐུབ་པ་	*gong-nga nang mi thup̄-pa.*
Intonation	མདངས་	*dang.*
Intoxicated	ར་བཟི་	*ra-śi.*
Do. to be	ར་བཟི་བ་	*ra-śi-wa.*
Do. *hon.*	སྐུ་ར་བྱེད་པ་	*ku-ra be-pa.*

Intrepid.	སྙིང་ཆེན་པོ་	*nying-chhem-po.*
Do. *hon.*	ཐུགས་སྙིང་ཆེན་པོ་	*thu-nying chhem-po.*
Intricate	མགོ་ཉོག་ཚ་པོ་	*go-nyo tsha-po.*
Do. *hon.*	དབུ་ཉོག་ཚ་པོ་	*u-nyo tsha-po.*
Intrigue	གྲོས་ངན་	*t'ö-ngen.*
Intrinsic (real)	ངོ་ཐོག། ངོས་ནས་	*ngo tho ; ngö-ne.*
Inundate, to	ཆུ་ཡིས་གནན་ (གནོན་) པ་	*chhu-yi nem-pa.*
Inundation	ཆུ་རུད་	*chhu-rü.*
Invalid, *s.*	ནད་པ་	*ne-pa.*
Do. *hon.*	སྙུང་མཁན་	*nyung-khen.*
Invective	སྨད་ར་	*me-ra.*
Inveigle, to	སླུ་བ་	*lu-wa.*
Do. *hon.*	སླུ་བ་གནང་བ་	*lu-wa nang-wa.*
Inventory	བརྗེད་ཐོ་	*je-tho.*
Do. *hon.*	བསྙེལ་ཐོ་	*nye-tho.*
Invert, to (upside down)	མགོ་གཞུག་ལོག་པ། ཨ་ལོག་རྒྱབ་པ་	*go-sku lok pa ; a-lo gyap-pa.*
Do. *hon.*	མགོ་གཞུག་ལོག་ག་ (པ་) གནང་བ། ཨ་ལོག་རྒྱབ་པ་གནང་བ་	*go-sku-lok-ka nang-wa ; a-lo gyap-pa nang wa.*

Invert, to (back to front)	ཁ་ཕྱོགས་ལོག་པ་	*kha-chho lok-pa.*
Do. *hon.*	ཞལ་ཕྱོགས་ལོག་ག་ (པ་) གནང་བ་	*ske-chho lok-ka nang-wa.*
Investigate, to	ཞིབ་དཔྱོད་བྱེད་པ་	*skip-chö cke-pa.*
Do. *hon.*	ཞིབ་དཔྱོད་གནང་བ	*skip-chö nang-wa.*
Do. *h. hon.*	བཀའ་ཞིབ་གནང་བ་	*ka-skip nang-wa.*
Investigation	ཞིབ་དཔྱོད་	*skip-chö.*
Do. hon.	བཀའ་ཞིབ་	*ka-skip.*
Invincible	གླགས་.....མི་ཁ་བ་	*la...mi kha-wa.*
Invisible	མི་.....མཐོང་བ་	*mi ..thong-wa.*
Invite, to (request)	ཞུ་བ་	*sku-wa.*
Do. *hon.*	ཞུ་བ་གནང་བ་	*sku-wa nang-wa.*
Invite, to (guest)	སྐད་བཏང་ (གཏོང་) བ་	*ke-tang-wa.*
Do. *hon.*	གདན་འདྲེན་ཞུ་བ་	*den-dren sku-wa.*
Involved (intricate)	མགོ་རྙོག་ཚ་པོ་	*go-nyo tsha-po.*
Inward	ནང་གི་	*nang-ki.*
Irascible	རུ་ངར་པོ་	*ru-ngar-po.*
Do. *hon.*	ཐུགས་རུ་ངར་པོ་	*thu-ru ngar-po.*
Ire	ཚིག་པ། ཁོང་ཁྲོ་	*tshik-pa ; khong-thro.*
Do. *hon.*	དགོངས་ཚུང་། རྣམ་མཁྱེན	*gong-tshung ; nam-khyen.*

Iris	སི་ལིང་ལྗང་པ་	*si-ling jang-pa.*
Irksome	དཀའ་ལས་ཁག་པོ་	*ka-le khaḱ-po.*
Do. *hon.*	སྐུ་མཉེལ་པོ་	*ku-nye-po.*
Iron, *s.*	ལྕགས་	*cha.*
Iron, *s.* (for clothes)	དབུར་ཏེ་	*ur-te.*
Iron, *adj.*	ལྕགས་ཀྱི་	*cha-kyi.*
Irrational	དོན་མེད་	*ťön-me.*
Irreligious, to be	ཆོས་སེམས་མེད་པ་	*chhö-sem me-pa.*
Do. *hon.*	ཆོས་སེམས་མི་གནང་བ་	*chhö-sem mi-nang-wa.*
Irreparable, to be	ཐབས་མེད་པ་	*thaṕ-me-pa.*
Irresistible, to be	བཀག་……མི་ཐུབ་པ་	*kaḱ...mi thuṕ-pa.*
Irresolute, to be	བརྟན་བརྟན་……མེད་པ་	*ten-ten...me-po.*
Irritable	རུ་ངར་པོ་	*ru-ngar-po.*
Do. *hon.*	ཐུགས་རུ་ངར་པོ་	*thu-ru ngar-po.*
Irritate, to	ཁོང་ཁྲོ་སློང་བ་	*khong-thro lang-wa.*
Do. *hon.*	དགོངས་པ་དཀྲུག་པ་	*gong-pa truḱ-pa.*
Is	རེད། འདུག་	*re ; du.*
Island	གླིང་ཕྲན་	*ling-thren.*
Isolated place	དབེན་གནས་	*en-ne.*
Issue (result)	སྙིང་པོ་	*nying-po.*

Issue, to (come out)	འཐོན་པ་	*thöm-pa.*
Do. *hon.*	ཕེབ་འཐོན་གནང་བ་	*phep-thön nang-wa.*
Do. *h. hon.*	ཕྱོགས་ཕེབས་གནང་བ་	*chho-phe nang-wa.*
It	དེ། འདི་	*te; di.*
Itch, *s.*	རྔོ་	*ngo.*
Itch, to (of body)	ཟ་བ། གཡའ་བ་	*śa-wa; ya-wa.*
Itching disease, to have	རྔོ་ཤོར་བ། རྔོ་རྒྱབ་པ་	*ngo-shor-wa; ngo-gyap-pa.*
Itself	འདི་རང་། དེ་རང་	*di-rang; te-rang.*
Ivory	བ་སོ་	*pa-so.*
Ivy	ཐག་འཁྱུད་མེ་ཏོག་	*tha-khyü me-tok.*

J

Jackal	ཁྱི་སྤྱང་	*khyiṕ-chang.*
Jackass	བུང་གུ་ (བོང་བུ་)	*ṕung-gu.*
Jackdaw	སྐྱུང་ཀ་	*kyung-ka.*
Jacket (without sleeves)	སྦྱ་སྦྱར་	*ja-ja.*
Do. *hon.*	ན་བཟའ་སྦྱ་སྦྱར་	*nam-śa ja-ja.*
Jacket (with sleeves)	འགོག་རྩེ་	*go-tse.*
Do. *hon.*	ན་བཟའ་འགོག་རྩེ་	*nam-śa go-tse.*
Jade (stone)	གཡང་སྟྲི་	*yang-tri.*
Jail	བཙོན་ཁང་	*tsön-khang.*
Jailor	བཙོན་སྲུང་ང་ (བ་)	*tsön-sung-nga.*
Jangle, to (wrangle)	རྒྱབ་འདྲེ་རྒྱབ་པ་	*gyam-dre gyaṕ-pa.*
Do. *hon.*	གསུང་འཁྲུག་སྐྱོན་པ་	*sung-thru kyöm-pa.*
Jar	ཛ་བུམ་	*dza-ṕum.*
Jaundice	སེར་ནད་	*ser-ne.*
Jaunt, to (ramble)	ཆན་ཆམ་ (འཁྱམ་འཁྱམ་) བྱེད་པ་	*chham-chham cḱe-pa.*
Do. *hon.*	སྐུ་ཆམ་ (འཁྱམ་) གནང་བ་	*kün-chham nang-wa.*
Javelin	མདུང་	*dung.*

Javelin, *hon.*	ཕྱག་མདུང་	*chhan-dung.*
Jaw	འགྲམ་པ་	*dram-pa.*
Jealous	ཕྲག་དོག་ཚ་པོ་	*thra-ťo tsha-po.*
Jealousy	ཕྲག་དོག་	*thra-ťo.*
Jealousy (between husband and wife)	མིག་སེར་	*miǩ-ser.*
Jeer, to	ཀྱག་ཀྱག་བྱས་ནས་ལབ་པ་	*kya-kya cǩe-ne lap̌-pa.*
Do. *hon.*	ཀྱག་ཀྱག་གནང་ནས་གསུང་བ་	*kya-kya nang-ne sung-wa.*
Jelly (meat)	ཕིག་ཕིག་	*phiǩ-phi.*
Jest, to	ཁབ་ལས་བཤད་པ་	*khap̌-le she-pa.*
Do. *hon.*	ཞལ་ལས་གསུང་བ་	*sǨe-le sung-wa.*
Do. *h. hon.*	ཞལ་ལས་གསུང་ང་ (བ་) གནང་བ་	*sǨe-le sung-nga nang-wa.*
Jester	དབུ་འཁོར་ཞུ་མཁན་	*u-khor sǨu-khen.*
Jesus	ཡེ་ཤུ་	*ye-shu.*
Jew	ཡ་ཧུ་དཱ་པ་	*ya-hu-da-pa.*
Jewel	ནོར་བུ་	*nor-p̌u.*
Job (work)	ལས་ཀ་	*le-ka.*
Jockey (for making horses)	རྟ་སྦྱང་མཁན་	*ta-jang-khen.*
Do. (for racing)	རྟ་རྒྱུག་བཏང་མཁན་	*tap̌-gyu tang-khen.*

Join, to	སྦྲེལ་བ། འཐུད་པ་	*drel-wa ; thü-pa.*
Do. *hon.*	སྦྲེལ་ལ་ (བ་) གནང་བ། འཐུད་པ་གནང་བ་	*drel-la nang-wa ; thü-pa nang-wa.*
Join, to (by glueing together, &c.)	སྦྱར་བ་	*jar-wa.*
Do. *hon.*	སྦྱར་ར་ (བ་) གནང་བ་	*jar-ra nang-wa.*
Joint, *s.* (of body)	ཚིགས་	*tshik.*
Jointly	མཉམ་སྦྲེལ་	*nyam-drel.*
Do. *hon.*	ཕྱག་སྦྲེལ་	*chha-drel.*
Joke, to	ཁབ་ལས་བཤད་པ་	*khap-le she-pa.*
Do. *hon.*	ཞལ་ལས་གསུང་བ་	*ske-le sung-wa.*
Do. *h. hon.*	ཞལ་ལས་གསུང་ང་ (བ་) གནང་བ་	*ske-le sung-nga nang-wa.*
Jollity	དགའ་ཚོར་	*ga-tshor.*
Do. *hon.*	མཉེས་ཚོར་	*nye-tshor.*
Jolly	དགའ་པོ་	*ga-po.*
Joss-stick	སྤོས་	*pö.*
Do. *hon.*	གཟིམ་སྤོས་	*sim-pö.*
Journey	ལམ་ཀ་	*lang-ka.*
Do. *hon.*	ཕེབ་ལམ་	*phep-lam.*
Joviality	དགའ་ཚོར་	*ga-tshor.*

Joviality, *hon.*	མཉེས་ཚོར་	*nye-tshor.*
Joy	དགའ་ཚོར་	*ga-tshor.*
Do. *hon.*	མཉེས་ཚོར་	*nye-tshor.*
Joyful, to be	དགའ་བ་	*ga-wa.*
Do. *hon.*	མཉེས་པོ་གནང་བ་	*nye-po nang-wa.*
Do. *h. hon.*	ཐུགས་དགྱེས་པོ་གནང་བ་	*thu-gye-po nang-wa.*
Judge, *s.* (if a Chinaman)	ཁྲིམས་དཔོན་	*thrim-pön.*
Do. (if a Tibetan)	མི་དཔོན་	*mi-pön.*
Judge, to	ཁྲིམས་བཅད་ (གཅོད་) པ་	*thrim-che-pa.*
Do. *hon.*	ཁྲིམས་གཅོད་པ་གནང་བ་	*thrim-chö-pa nang-wa.*
Judgment (opinion)	བསམ་པ་	*sam-pa.*
Do. *hon.*	ཐུགས་སེམས་	*thu-sem.*
Judgment (legal)	བཅད་མཚམས། ཁྲ་མ་	*che-tsham ; thra-ma.*
Do. to apply for	ཁྲ་མ་ཞུ་བ་	*thra-ma sḱu-wa.*
Do. to pass	ཁྲ་མ་གནང་བ་	*thra-ma nang-wa.*
Judgment-hall	ལས་ཁང་ (ལས་ཁུངས་)	*le-khung.*
Jug	ཆུ་སྣོད་	*chhu-nö.*
Do. *hon.*	ཆབ་སྣོད་	*chhaṕ-nö.*
Juggle, to (conjure)	མིག་འཕྲུལ་རྩེད་པ་	*miḱ-thrü tse pa.*
Do. *hon.*	མིག་འཕྲུལ་རྩེད་པ་གནང་བ་	*miḱ-thrü tse-pa nang-wa.*

Juggler	མིག་འཕྲུལ་རྩེད་མཁན་	*miḱ-thrü tse-khen.*
Do. *hon.*	མིག་འཕྲུལ་རྩེད་པ་གནང་མཁན་	*miḱ-thrü tse-pa nang-khen.*
Jugglery	མིག་འཕྲུལ་	*miḱ-thrü.*
Juice	ཁུ་བ་	*khu-wa.*
Jump, to	མཆོངས་པ། མཆོངས་རྒྱག་རྒྱབ་པ་	*chhong pa ; chhong-gya gyaṕ-pa.*
Do. *hon.*	མཆོངས་རྒྱག་སྐྱོན་པ་	*chhong-gya kyöm-pa.*
Junction of roads	ལམ་འཛོམ་	*lam-dzom.*
Do. of rivers	ཆུ་འཛོམ་	*chhu-dzom.*
Jungle	ཤིང་ནགས་	*shing-na.*
Juniper	ཤུག་པ་	*shuḱ-pa.*
Do. (another kind)	སྤ་མ་	*pa-ma.*
Jurisdiction	ས་གནས་	*sa-ne.*
Just, *adj.*	ཁྲིམས་དྲང་པོ་	*thrim-t́rang-po.*
Do. *hon.*	བཀའ་ཁྲིམས་དྲང་པོ་	*ka-thrim t́rang-po*
Just, *adv.*	རང་	*rang.*
Just by	ཙ་ལ་ (ཙར་)	*tsa-la.*
Just now	ད་ལྟ་རང་	*t́an-da-rang.*
Just so! (like that)	ད་ག་རེད་	*t́a-ḱa re.*
Do. *hon.*	ལགས་ད་ག་རང་རེད་	*la-t́a-ḱa-rang re.*

Just so! (like that) *h. hon.*	ལགས་བཀའ་གནང་རང་རེད་	*la ka nang-rang re.*
Justice	ཁྲིམས་དྲང་པོ་	*thrim ťrang-po.*
Do. *hon.*	བཀའ་ཁྲིམས་དྲང་པོ་	*ka-thrim ťrang-po.*
Justly	ཁྲིམས་ནང་བཞིན་	*thrim nang-sǩin.*
Do. *hon.*	བཀའ་ཁྲིམས་ནང་བཞིན་	*ka-thrim nang-sǩin.*
Jute	སོ་མ་ར་ཙ་	*so-ma ra-tsa.*
Juvenile	གཞོན་པ། ལོ་གཞོན་གཞོན་	*sǩöm-pa ; lo sǩön-sǩön.*

K

Keen (not blunt)	རྣོ་པོ་	*no-po.*
Keen (eager)	སྙིང་འདོད་པོ། སྙིང་བྲོ་པོ་	*nying-dö-po ; nying tro-po.*
Keep, to (have the care of)	ཉར་བ། ཆག་ག་བྱེད་པ་	*nyar-wa ; cha-k̆a ch̆e-pa.*
Do. *hon.*	ཉར་ར་ (བ་) གནང་བ། ཐུགས་ཆག་གནང་བ་	*nyar-ra nang-wa ; thuk̆-cha nang-wa.*
Keep, to (retain)	བཞག་པ་ (འཛོག་པ་)	*sh̆ak̆-pa.*
Do. *hon.*	གཞོག་ག་ (འཛོག་པ་) གནང་བ་	*sh̆ok̆-k̆a nang-wa.*
Keeper (guard)	སྲུང་མཁན་	*sung-khen.*
Kennel	ཁྱི་ཚང་	*khyi-tshang.*
Kerosene oil	ས་སྣུམ་	*sa num.*
Kettle (for tea)	ཁོ་ཏི་	*kho-ti.*
Do. *hon.*	གསོལ་ཏི་	*sö-ti.*
Key	ལྡེ་མིག་	*di-mi.*
Do. *hon.*	ཕྱག་ལྡེ་	*chhan-di.*
Kham (province in Eastern Tibet)	ཁམས་	*kham.*
Kham, inhabitant of	ཁམས་པ་	*kham-pa.*
Kick	རྡོག་རྒྱག་	*dong-gya.*

Kick, to	རྡོག་རྒྱག་གཞུ་བ་	*dong-gya sḱu-wa.*
Do. *hon.*	ཞབས་རྡོག་གཞུ་བ་གནང་བ་	*shap-do sḱu-wa nang-wa.*
Kid, *s.*	རེ་ཀོག་ (ར་ཕྲུག་)	*re-ko.*
Kidney	ཨ་རི་མཁལ་རི་	*a-ri khe-ri.*
Kill, to	བསད་པ་ (གསོད་པ་)	*se-pa.*
Do. *hon.*	བཀྲོངས་པ་ (འགྲོང་བ་)	*trong-pa.*
Do. *h. hon.*	བཀྲོངས་ང་ (འགྲོང་བ་) གནང་བ་	*trong-nga nang wa.*
Kind, *s.* (sort)	རྒྱུ་	*gyu.*
Kind, *adj.*	དྲིན་ཆེན་པོ་	*t́rin chhem-po.*
Do. *hon.*	བཀའ་དྲིན་ཆེན་པོ་	*ka-t́rin chhem-po.*
Kindle, to (fire)	བཏང་བ་ (གཏོང་བ་)	*tang-wa.*
Do. *hon.*	གཏོང་ང་ (བ་) གནང་བ་	*tong-nga nang-wa.*
Kindly	དྲིན་ཆེན་པོ་	*t́rin-chhem-po.*
Do. *hon.*	བཀའ་དྲིན་ཆེན་པོ་	*ka-t́rin chhem-po.*
Kindness	དྲིན་	*t́rin.*
Do. *hon.*	བཀའ་དྲིན་	*ka-t́rin.*
Kindness, to do	དྲིན་བྱེད་པ་	*t́rin cḱe-pa.*
Do. *hon.*	བཀའ་དྲིན་གནང་བ་	*ka-t́rin nang-wa.*
Kindred (relatives)	ཉེ་བ་	*nye-wa.*

Kindred (relatives) *hon.*	སྐུ་གཉེན་	*ku-nyen.*
Kinds, different	སྣ་ཚོགས་	*na-tsho.*
King	རྒྱལ་པོ་	*gye-po.*
King's business (administration)	རྒྱལ་སྲིད་	*gye-si.*
Kingdom	རྒྱལ་ཁབ་	*gye-khaṕ.*
Kiss, to	ཁ་སྐྱེལ་བ་	*kha-kyel-wa.*
Do. *hon.*	ཞལ་སྐྱེལ་ལ་ (བ་) གནང་བ་	*sḱe-kyel-la nang-wa.*
Kitchen	ཐབ་ཚང་	*thaṕ-tshang.*
Do. *hon.*	གསོལ་ཐབ་	*sö-thaṕ.*
Kitchen-garden	ཚལ་ཡང་ཙེ་	*tshe-yang-tse.*
Kite (bird)	ཕིང་ཀྱུ་མ་	*ping-kyu-ma.*
Kitten	ཞིམ་ཕྲུག་	*sḱim-thru.*
Knapsack	ལྟོ་ཕད་	*to-phe.*
Knave	བསྟན་བཞིག། འཛབ་ཆེན་	*ten-sḱi; dzaṕ-chhen.*
Knee	པུས་མོ་	*pi mo.*
Do. *hon.*	ཞབས་པུས་	*sḱaṕ-pi.*
Knee-joint	པུས་མོའི་ཚིགས་	*pi-mö-tshiḱ.*
Do. *hon.*	ཞབས་པུའི་ཚིགས་	*sḱaṕ-pi-i tshiḱ.*
Kneel, to	པུས་མོ་བཙུག་ (འཛུགས་) པ་	*pi-mo tsuḱ-pa.*

Kneel, to *hon.*	ཞབས་པུས་བཙུག་ག་ (འཛུགས་པ་) གནང་བ་	*sǩap̌-pi tsuǩ-ka nang-wa.*
Knife	གྲི་	*ťri.*
Do. *hon.*	ཕྱག་ཤན་	*chha-shen.*
Knife, clasp	ལྟེབ་གྲི་	*tap̌-ťri.*
Do. *hon.*	ཕྱག་ཤན་ལྟེབ་གྲི་	*chha-shen tap̌-ťri.*
Knit, to	སླེ་བ་	*le-wa.*
Do. *hon.*	སླེ་བ་གནང་བ་	*le-wa nang wa.*
Knitting-needle	ལྕགས་མདའ་	*chan-da.*
Knock, to	དག་དག་བཏང་ (གཏོང་) བ་	*taǩ-ta tang-wa.*
Do. *hon*	དག་དག་གཏོང་ང་ (བ་) གནང་བ་	*taǩ-ta tong-nga nang-wa.*
Knocking, *s.* (on door, &c.)	དག་དག་	*taǩ-ta.*
Knot, *s.*	མདུད་པ་	*dü-pa.*
Do. *hon.*	ཕྱག་མདུད་	*chhan-dü.*
Knot, to	མདུད་པ་རྒྱབ་པ་	*dü-pa gyap̌-pa.*
Do. *hon.*	ཕྱག་མདུད་སྐྱོན་པ་	*chhan-dü kyöm-pa.*
Knot, to untie a	མདུད་པ་བཤིག་པ་	*dü-pa sǩiǩ-pa.*
Do. *hon.*	ཕྱག་མདུད་བཤིག་ག་ (པ་) གནང་བ་	*chhan-dü sǩiǩ-ka nang-wa.*

Know, to (things)	ཤེས་པ་	*she-pa.*
Do. *hon.*	མཁྱེན་པ་	*khyem-pa.*
Do. *h. hon.*	དགོངས་པ་རྟོགས་པ་	*gong-pa tok-pa.*
Know, to (persons)	ངོ་ཤེས་པ་	*ngo-shem-pa.*
Know, to (a person of good position)	ཞལ་ཚོ་ (ཚོར་) བ་	*ske-tsho-wa.*
Do. *hon.*	ཐུགས་ངོ་མཁྱེན་པ་	*thu-ngo khyem-pa.*
Knowledge (in general)	ཤེས་བྱ། ཡོན་ཏན་	*she-cka ; yön-ten.*
Do. *hon.*	སྐུ་ཡོན་	*ku-yön.*
Knowledge (as to a specific matter)	རྒྱུས་	*gyü.*
Knuckle	ལག་པའི་ཚིགས་	*lak-pe tshik.*
Do. *hon.*	ཕྱག་གི་ཚིགས་	*chha-ki tshik.*

L

Laborious (difficult)	དཀའ་ལས་ཁག་པོ་	*ka-le khaḱ- po.*
Do. *hon.*	སྐུ་མཉེལ་པོ་	*ku-nye-po.*
Labour (pangs of child-birth)	སྐྱེ་གཟུག་	*kye-śu.*
Do. (work)	ལས་ཀ་	*le-ka.*
Do. *hon.*	ཕྱག་ལས་	*chha-le.*
Labour, forced	ཨུ་ལག་	*u-la.*
Do. hired	མི་ལག་	*mi-la.*
Labour, to	ལས་ཀ་བྱེད་པ་	*le-ka cḱe-pa.*
Do. *hon.*	ཕྱག་ལས་གནང་བ་	*chha-le nang-wa.*
Labourer	མི་གླ་	*mi la.*
Labourer's hire, a	གླ་	*la.*
Lac (dye)	རྒྱ་ཚོས་	*gya-tshö.*
Lac (number)	འབུམ་	*bum.*
Lacerate, to	གཤག་པ་	*shaḱ-pa.*
Do. *hon.*	གཤག་ག་ (པ་) གནང་བ་	*shaḱ-ka nang-wa.*
Lack, to	མི་‥ཚང་བ་	*mi. .tshang-wa.*
Lad	བུ་གུ་	*pu-gu.*
Do. *hon.*	ཨ་ཝ་	*a-wa.*
Ladak (name of province)	ལ་དྭགས་	*la-daḱ.*

Ladder	ཀན་རྩ་ (སྐས་འཛེག་)	*ken-tsa.*
Do. *hon.*	ཕེབ་སྐས་	*phep-ke.*
Lade, to	ཁལ་བཀལ་ (འགེལ་) བ་	*khe kel-wa.*
Do. *hon.*	ཁལ་བཀལ་ལ་ (བ་) གནང་བ་	*khe kel-la nang-wa.*
Ladle, *s.*	སྐྱོགས་	*kyo.*
Do. *hon.*	གསོལ་སྐྱོགས། ཕྱག་སྐྱོགས་	*sö-kyo ; chha-kyo.*
Ladle, to	སྐྱོགས་ཀྱིས་བླུག་པ་	*kyo-kyi luk-pa.*
Do. *hon.*	གསོལ་སྐྱོགས་ཀྱིས་བླུག་ག་ (པ་) གནང་བ་	*sö-kyo-kyi luk-ka nang-wa.*
Ladle, to, *inf.* to *sup.*	གསོལ་སྐྱོགས་ཀྱིས་ཞུ་བ་	*sö-kyo-kyi sKu-wa.*
Lady (wife of well-to-do villager)	སྙི་སྙིང་ལགས་	*nyi- nying-la.*
Do. (wife of ordinary official)	ལྕམ་སྐུ་གཞོགས་	*cham-ku-sKo.*
Do. (third grade and upwards)	ལྷ་ལྕམ་སྐུ་གཞོགས་	*hla-cham ku-sKo.*
Lady, young	སྲས་མོ་	*se-mo.*
Lag, to	འགོར་བ་	*gor-wa.*
Do. *hon.*	ཕེབ་འགོར་གནང་བ་	*phe-gor nang-wa.*
Lahoul (name of province)	གར་ཞ་	*kar-sKa.*
Laity	ཨའུ། འཇིག་རྟེན་པ་	*a-u ; jik-tem-pa.*

Lair	ཚང་	*tshang.*
Lake	མཚོ་	*tsho.*
Lakh (number)	འབུམ་	*bum.*
Lama	བླ་མ་	*la-ma.*
Lama, Grand (of Lhasa)	སྐྱབས་མགོན་རིན་པོ་ཆེ་	*kyam-gön rim-po-chhe.*
Lama, Grand (of Tashi Hlümpo)	པན་ཆེན་རིན་པོ་ཆེ་	*pen-chhen rim-po-chhe.*
Lamb	ལུག་ཕྲུག། ལུ་གུ་	*luk-thru ; lu-ku.*
Lame	ཀང་ཀྱོག་	*kang-kyo.*
Do. *hon.*	ཞབས་ཀྱོག་	*sKap-kyo.*
Lament, to	སྡུག་བསྔལ་བྱེད་པ། མྱ་ངན་བྱེད་པ་	*du-nge cKe pa ; nya-ngen cKe-pa.*
Do. *hon.*	ཐུགས་ངན་གནང་བ་	*thu-ngen nang-wa.*
Lamentation	མྱ་ངན་	*nya-ngen.*
Lamp	ཞུ་མར་	*sKu-ma.*
Do. *hon.*	གཟིམ་ཞུ་	*śim sKu.*
Lamp (as offering to deity)	མཆོད་མེ་	*chhö-me*
Lance, *s.*	མདུང་	*dung.*
Do. *hon.*	ཕྱག་མདུང་	*chhan-dung.*
Lancet	ཙའུ་	*tsa-u.*

Land (earth)	ས་	*sa.*
Do. (landed property)	ས་ཆ་	*sa-chha.*
Do. (country)	ལུང་པ། ཡུལ་	*lung-pa ; yü.*
Landing-place	གྲུ་ཁ་	*ťru-kha.*
Landlady (of inn, etc.)	གནས་མོ་	*ne-mo.*
Do. *hon.*	གནས་མོ་ལགས་	*ne-mo-la.*
Landlord (of inn, etc.)	གནས་པོ་	*ne-po.*
Do. *hon.*	གནས་པོ་ལགས་	*ne-po-la.*
Landlord (of land)	སའི་བདག་པོ་	*sa-i daǩ-po.*
Landslip	ས་རུད་	*sa-rü.*
Land-tax	ས་ཁྲལ་	*sa-thre.*
Lane	སྲང་འགག་	*hrang-ga.*
Language	སྐད་	*ke.*
Do. (honorific)	ཞེ་ས་	*sǩe-sa.*
Language (common, *i.e.* non-honorific)	ཞེ་ས་མེད་པའི་སྐད་ཆ་	*sǩe-sa me-pe ke-chha.*
Do. (colloquial)	ཕལ་སྐད། ཕལ་ཚིག་	*phe-ke ; phe-tshi.*
Do. (literary)	ཆོས་སྐད། ཆོས་ཚིག་	*chhö-ke ; chhö-tshi.*
Languid	ཉོབ་པོ་	*nyop̌-po.*
Lank (of persons and animals)	ཤ་སྐམ་པོ་	*sha kam-po.*
Do. *hon.* (of persons)	སྐུ་ཤ་སྐམ་པོ་	*ku-sha kam-po.*

Lank (of animals) *hon.*	བཞེས་ཤ་སྐམ་པོ་	*sKe sha kam-po.*
Lantern	སྒང་ཞུ་ (སྒོང་ཞུ་)	*gang-sKu.*
Do. *hon.*	ཕེབ་ཞུ་	*phep-sKu.*
Lap, *s.* (of women)	པང་པ་	*pang-pa.*
Do. *hon.*	སྐུ་པང་	*ku-pang.*
Lap up, to (water, &c.)	ལྡག་པ་	*daK-pa.*
Lapsus linguae, to make a	ཁ་ཤོར་བ་	*kha-shor-wa.*
Do. *hon.*	ཞལ་བཞེས་གནང་བ་	*sKe-sKe nang-wa.*
Larch	སྲ་ཤིང་	*śa-shing.*
Lard	ཕག་ཚིལ་	*phaK tshi.*
Large	ཆེན་པོ་	*chhem-po.*
Large (of country, etc.)	རྒྱ་ཆེན་པོ་	*gya-chhem-po.*
Larynx	སྐེ་	*ke.*
Do. *hon.*	མགུལ་	*gü.*
Lascivious	འདོད་ཆགས་ཆེན་པོ་	*dö-chha chhem-po.*
Lasciviousness	འདོད་ཆགས་	*dö-chha.*
Lash (of a whip)	རྟ་ལྕག་	*ta-cha.*
Do. *hon.*	ཆིབས་ལྕག་	*chhip-cha.*
Lash, to	རྟ་ལྕག་གཞུ་བ་	*ta-cha sKu-wa.*
Do. *hon.*	ཆིབས་ལྕག་སྐྱོན་པ་	*chhip-cha kyöm-pa.*

Lass	བུ་མོ་	*ṕu-mo.*
Do. *hon.*	སྲས་མོ་	*se-mo.*
Lassitude	ངལ་	*ngel.*
Do. *hon.*	སྐུ་ངལ་	*ku-ngel.*
Last, *adj.*	གཞུག་ཤོས་	*sḱuḱ-shö.*
Do. *adv.* (at last)	གཞུག་ལ་	*sḱuḱ-la.*
Last night	མདངས་དགོངས་	*dang-gong.*
Last year	ན་ཉིང་ (ན་ནིང་)	*da-nying.*
Last, to	ཐུབ་པ་	*thuṕ-pa.*
Lasting (durable)	གྲོག་ཆེན་པོ་	*tro chhem-po.*
Latch	ཨ་ཤིང་	*a-shing.*
Latchet	ལྷམ་སྒྲོགས་	*hlam-dro.*
Do. *hon*	ཞབས་སྒྲོགས་	*sḱaṕ-dro.*
Late	ཕྱི་པོ་	*chhi-po.*
Late, to be	ཕྱི་པོ་བྱེད་པ་	*chhi-po cḱe-pa.*
Late, the (the deceased)	ཤི་མཁན་	*shi-khen.*
Do. *hon.*	གྲོང་མཁན་	*ťrong-khen.*
Do. *h. hon.*	དམ་པ་	*ťam-pa.*
Lately	ཁ་སང་	*kha-sang.*
Latent	སྦེད་པ་	*be-pa.*

Later on (afterwards)	གཞུག་ལ་	*sḰu-la.*
Latest	གཞུག་ཤོས་	*sḰuḱ-shö.*
Latter	གཞུག་མ་	*sḰuḱ ma.*
Laud, to	སྟོད་ར་བཏང་ (གཏོང་) བ་	*tö-ra tang-wa.*
Do. *hon.*	སྟོད་ར་གཏོང་ང་ (བ་) གནང་བ་	*tö-ra tong-nga nang-wa.*
Do. *inf.* to *sup.*	སྟོད་ར་ཞུ་བ་	*tö-ra sḰu-wa.*
Laugh, *s.*	བགད་མོ་	*ge-mo.*
Laugh, to	བགད་མོ་བགད་པ། བགད་མོ་ཤོར་བ་	*ge-mo ge-pa ; ge mo shor-wa.*
Do. *hon.*	ཞལ་མོ་བཞེས་པ། ཞལ་མོ་ཤོར་བ་	*sḰe-mo sḰe-pa ; sḰe-mo shor-wa.*
Laughable	བགད་མོ་བྲོ་པོ་	*ge-mo t́ro-po.*
Do. *hon.*	ཞལ་མོ་བྲོ་པོ་	*sḰe-mo t́ro-po.*
Laughter	བགད་མོ་	*ge-mo.*
Do. *hon.*	ཞལ་མོ་	*sḰe-mo.*
Lavish (profuse)	འབེལ་པོ། ཛག་ཏོ་	*be po ; dzak-t́o.*
Law	ཁྲིམས་	*thrim.*
Do. *hon.*	བཀའ་ཁྲིམས་	*ka-thrim.*
Law (religious)	ཆོས་ཁྲིམས་	*chhö-thrim.*
Law, to go to	རྒྱུ་རྐྱེན་ཞུ་བ། ཁྲིམས་ལ་ཞུ་བ་	*gyu-kyen sḰu-wa ; thrim-la sḰu-wa.*

Laws, to obey	ཁྲིམས་འཁྱེར་བ། ཁྲིམས་འཁུར་བ་	*thrim khyer-wa; thrim khur-wa.*
Law-court	ཁྲིམས་ས་	*thrim-sa.*
Do. *hon.*	བཀའ་ཁྲིམས་ཀྱི་ས་ཆ་	*ka-thrim-kyi sa-chha.*
Lawful	ཁྲིམས་མཐུན་	*thrim-thün.*
Lawfully	ཁྲིམས་ནང་བཞིན་	*thrim-nang-sKin.*
Do. *hon.*	བཀའ་ཁྲིམས་ནང་བཞིན་	*ka-thrim nang-sKin.*
Lawless	ཁྲིམས་མེད་	*thrim-me.*
Lawn	ཐང་	*thang.*
Law-suit	ཁ་མཆུ་	*kham-chhu.*
Lay, to (place)	བཞག་པ་ (འཇོག་པ་)	*sKak-pa.*
Do. *hon.*	གཞོག་ག་ (འཇོག་པ་) གནང་བ་	*sKok-ka nang-wa.*
Lay, to (spread)	བཏིང་པ་ (འདིང་བ་)	*ting-pa.*
Do. *hon.*	བཏིང་ང་ (འདིང་བ་) གནང་བ་	*ting-nga nang-wa.*
Lay, to	བཞག་པ་ (འཇོག་པ་)	*sKak-pa.*
Do. *hon.*	གཞོག་ག་ (འཇོག་པ་) གནང་བ་	*sKok-ka nang-wa.*
Lay, to (down)	བསྙལ་བ་ (སྙོལ་བ་)	*nye-wa.*
Do. *hon.*	བསྙལ་ལ་ (སྙོལ་བ་) གནང་བ་	*nye-la nang-wa.*
Lay, to (eggs)	བཏང་བ་ (གཏོང་བ་)	*tang-wa.*
Lay the foundation of, to	རྩིག་རྟེན་བཏིང་ (འདིང་) བ་	*tsik-ten ting-wa.*

Lay the foundation of, to, *hon.*	ཙིག་སྟན་བཏིང་ང་ (བ་) གནང་བ་	*tsik-ten tingnga nang-wa.*
Layman	ཨུ། འཇིག་རྟེན་པ་	*a-u ; jik-tem-pa.*
Lazy	རྒྱུ་མ་རིང་པོ། ལེ་ལོ་ཆེན་པོ་	*gyu-ma ring-po ; le-lo chhem-po*
Do. *hon.*	ཐུགས་རྒྱུ་རིང་པོ་	*thu-gyu ring-po.*
Lead, *s.* (metal)	ཞ་ནི་	*sKa-ni.*
Lead (red-lead)	སི་ནྡྷུ་ར་	*sin-dhu-ra.*
Lead, to (towards)	འཁྲིད་ཡོང་བ་	*thri-yong-wa.*
Do. *hon.*	འཁྲིད་ཕེབ་པ་	*thri-phe-pa.*
Lead, to (away)	འཁྲིད་འགྲོ་བ་	*thri-dro-wa.*
Do *hon.*	འཁྲིད་ཕེབ་པ་	*thri-phe-pa.*
Leader	མགོ་པ་	*go-pa.*
Leaf (of a tree)	ལོ་མ། འདབ་མ་	*lo-ma ; da-ma.*
Do. (of a book)	ཤོག་ལེབ་	*shok-le.*
Leak, to (of water)	འཛག་པ་	*dzak-pa.*
Lean, *adj.* (of animals and persons)	ཤ་སྐམ་པོ་	*sha-kam-po.*
Do. *hon.* (of persons)	སྐུ་ཤ་སྐམ་པོ་	*ku-sha kam-po.*
Do. *hon.* (of meat)	བཞེས་ཤ་སྐམ་པོ་	*sKe-sha kam-po.*
Lean, to (against)	སྙེ་བསྡད་ (སྡོད་) པ་	*nye-de-pa.*

Lean, to (against) *hon.*	སྐུ་སྙེ་གནང་ནས་བཞུགས་པ་	*ku-nye nang-ne sḱu-pa.*
Do. *h. hon.*	སྐུ་སྙེ་གནང་ནས་བཞུགས་གདན་འཇག་པ་	*ku-nye nang-ne sḱu-den ja-pa.*
Lean, to (back)	རྒྱབ་བསྙེས་བྱས་ནས་བསྡད་ (སྡོད་) པ་	*gyaṕ-nye cḱe-ne de-pa.*
Do. *hon.*	སྐུ་བསྙེས་གནང་ནས་བཞུགས་པ་	*ku-nye nang-ne sḱu-pa.*
Leap, to	མཆོངས་པ། མཆོངས་རྒྱག་རྒྱབ་པ་	*chhong-pa ; chhong-gya gyaṕ-pa.*
Do. *hon.*	མཆོངས་རྒྱག་སྐྱོན་པ་	*chhong-gya kyöm-pa.*
Learn, to	བསླབས་པ་ (སློབ་པ་)	*laṕ-pa.*
Do. *hon.*	བསླབས་ (སློབ་) པ་གནང་བ་	*laṕ-pa nang-wa.*
Learn, to (by heart)	བློ་ལ་ཟིམ་པ་ (བཟུང་བ་)	*lo-la śim-pa.*
Do. *hon.*	ཐུགས་བློ་ལ་ཟིམ་པ་ (བཟུང་བ་) གནང་བ་	*thuḱ-lo la śim-pa nang-wa.*
Learned	ཤེས་བྱ་ཆེན་པོ། ཡོན་ཏན་ཆེན་པོ་	*she-cḱa chhem-po ; yön-ten chhem po.*
Do. *hon.*	སྐུ་ཡོན་ཆེན་པོ་	*ku-yön chhem-po.*
Learner (novice)	ཨེན་ཆུང་	*en-chhung.*
Learning	ཤེས་བྱ། ཡོན་ཏན	*she-cḱa ; yön-ten.*

Learning, *hon.*	སྐུ་ཡོན་	*ku-yön.*
Lease, *s.*	བཀའ་བརྟན་	*ka-ten.*
Do. to (let out on)	བོགས་མ་ལ་བཏང་ (གཏོང་) བ་	*ṕo-ma-la tang-wa.*
Do. *hon.*	བོགས་མ་ལ་གཏོང་ང་ (བ་) གནང་བ་	*ṕo-ma-la tong-nga nang-wa.*
Least	ཆུང་ཤོས་	*chhung-shö.*
Leather	ཀོ་བ་	*ko-wa.*
Leave of absence	དགོངས་པ་	*gong-pa.*
Leave, to (depart)	འཐོན་པ། ཕྱིན་པ་	*thöm-pa ; chhim-pa.*
Do. *hon.*	ཕེབ་པ་	*pheṕ-pa.*
Do. *h. hon.*	འཆིབ་རྒྱུ་གནང་བ་	*chhiṕ-gyu nang-wa.*
Leave off, to (renounce)	སྤང་བ་	*pang-wa.*
Do. *hon.*	སྤོང་ང་ (བ་) གནང་བ་	*pong-nga nang-wa.*
Leave, to (a country, etc.)	བཞག་ནས་ཡོང་བ་	*sḱa-ne yong-wa.*
Do. *hon.*	བཞག་ནས་ཕེབ་པ་	*sḱa-ne phe-pa.*
Do. *h hon.*	བཞག་ནས་འཆིབས་རྒྱུ་གནང་བ་	*sḱa-ne chhiṕ gyu nang-wa.*
Leave, to ask for	དགོངས་པ་ཞུ་བ་	*gong-pa sḱu-wa.*
Do. *hon.*	དགོངས་ཞུ་གནང་བ་	*gong-sḱu nang-wa.*
Leave, to grant	དགོངས་པ་སྟེར་བ་	*gong-pa ter-wa.*
Do. *hon.*	དགོངས་པ་གནང་བ་	*gong-pa nang-wa.*

Leaven (for fermenting liquor)	ཆང་རྩི་	*chhang-tsi.*
Do. (for fermenting dough for bread)	ཕྱེ་སྨན་	*chhi-men.*
Leaves (in a book), number of	ཤོག་གྲངས་	*shoḱ-ťrang.*
Leavings (things left)	ལྷག་མ་	*hla-ma.*
Lecherous	འདོད་ཆགས་ཆེན་པོ་	*dö-chha chhem-po.*
Lechery	འདོད་ཆགས་	*dö-chha.*
Leech	པད་པ་	*pe-pa.*
Left, *adj.* (opp. to right)	གཡོན་	*yön.*
Left, to be (not expended)	ལྷག་མ་ལུས་པ་	*hla-ma lü-pa.*
Left, to be (behind)	ལས་ (ལུས་) ནས་མེད་པ་	*le-ne me-pa.*
Do. *hon.*	ལས་ (ལུས་) པ་གནང་བ་	*le-pa nang-wa.*
Left-handed	གཡོན་ལག་	*yön-la.*
Do. *hon.*	ཕྱག་གཡོན་ལག་	*chha-yön-la.*
Leg	རྐང་པ་	*kang-pa.*
Do. *hon.*	ཞབས་	*sḱaṕ.*
Leg (of mutton, etc.)	རྐང་ཤ་	*kang-sha.*
Legal	ཁྲིམས་མཐུན་	*thrim-thün.*
Legally	ཁྲིམས་ནང་བཞིན་	*thrim-nang-sḱin.*

Legally, *hon.*	བཀའ་ཁྲིམས་ནང་བཞིན་	*ka-thrim nang-sKin.*
Legend	རྣམ་ཐར་	*nam-thu.*
Legged, bandy	རྐང་ཀྱོག་	*kang-kyo.*
Do. *hon.*	ཞབས་ཀྱོག་	*sKap-kyo.*
Legible, to be	ཀློག་ཤེས་པ་	*lok-she-pa.*
Do. *hon.*	ལྗགས་ཀློག་གནང་མཁྱེན་པ་	*ja-lo nang khyem-pa.*
Legitimate (lawful)	ཁྲིམས་མཐུན་	*thrim-thün.*
Legitimately	ཁྲིམས་ནང་བཞིན་	*thrim nang-sKin.*
Do. *hon.*	བཀའ་ཁྲིམས་ནང་བཞིན་	*ka-thrim nang-sKin.*
Leisure	ལོང་	*long.*
Leisure, to sit at	ལྷོད་ལྷོད་བསྡད་ (སྡོད་) པ་	*hlö-hlö de-pa.*
Do. *hon.*	ཐུགས་ལྷོད་ལྷོད་བཞུགས་པ་	*thu-hlö-hlö sKu-pa.*
Lend, to	གཡར་བ་	*yar-wa.*
Do. *hon.*	གཡར་པོ་གནང་བ་	*yar-po nang wa.*
Length	རིང་ཐུང་	*ring-thung.*
Length, at (afterwards)	གཞུག་ལ། རྗེས་ལ་	*sKu-la ; je-la.*
Lengthen, to	རིང་དུ་བཏང་ (གཏོང་) བ་	*ring-ṫu tang-wa.*
Do. *hon.*	རིང་དུ་གཏོང་ང་ (བ་) གནང་བ་	*ring-ṫu tong nga nang-wa.*
Lengthy	རིང་པོ་	*ring-po.*
Lenient, to be	འཆ་ཡང་གནང་བ་	*chha-yang nang-wa.*

Leopard	གཟིག་	*śik̄.*
Leper (male)	མཛེ་པོ་	*dze-po.*
Do. (female)	མཛེ་མོ་	*dze-mo.*
Leprosy	མཛེ་	*dze.*
Leprous, to be	མཛེ་རྒྱབ་པ་	*dze-gyap̄-pa.*
Do. *hon.*	མཛེ་སྐྱོན་པ་	*dze kyöm-pa.*
Less	ཉུང་བ་	*nyung-wa.*
Lessen, to, *v.i.*	ཉུང་རུ་ཕྱིན་པ་	*nyung-ru chhim pa.*
Do. to, *v.t.*	ཉུང་རུ་བཏང་ (གཏོང་) བ་	*nyung-ru tang-wa.*
Do. *hon.*	ཉུང་རུ་གཏོང་ང་ (བ་) གནང་བ་	*nyung ru tong-nga nang-wa.*
Lessen, to (price)	བཅག་པ་ (གཅོག་པ་)	*chak̄-pa.*
Do. *hon.*	གཅོག་ག་ (པ་) གནང་བ་	*chok̄-k̄a nang-wa.*
Lesson	ཡིག་རྒྱུགས་	*yi-gyuk̄.*
Let, to (allow)	བཅུག་པ་ (འཇུག་པ་)	*chuk̄-pa.*
Do. *hon.*	བཅུག་ག་ (པ་) གནང་བ་	*chuk̄-k̄a nang-wa.*
Let, to (down)	ཕབ་པ་ (འབེབས་པ་)	*phap̄-pa.*
Let, to (let in, let loose, etc.)	བཏང་བ་ (གཏོང་བ་)	*tang-wa.*
Do. *hon.*	གཏོང་ང་ (བ་) གནང་བ་	*tong-nga nang-wa.*
Let off, to	བཏང་བ་ (གཏོང་བ་)	*tang-wa.*
Do. *hon.*	གཏོང་ང་ (བ་) གནང་བ་	*tong-nga nang-wa.*

Letter (epistle)	ཡི་གེ་	*yi-ge.*
Do. *hon.*	ཕྱག་བྲིས་	*chha ri.*
Level, *adj.*	སྙོམས་པོ་	*nyom-po.*
Lewd	འདོད་ཆགས་ཆེན་པོ་	*dö-chha chhem-po.*
Lewdness	འདོད་ཆགས་	*dö-chha.*
Lhasa	ལྷ་ས་	*hla-sa.*
Lhasa man, a	ལྷ་སཱ་	*hla-sā.*
Liar	ཧམ་པ་ཤོད་མཁན་	*ham-pa shö-khen.*
Libation	གསེར་སྐྱེམས་	*ser-kyem.*
Libel, *s.*	སྨད་ར་	*me-ra.*
Libel, to	སྨད་ར་བཏང་ (གཏོང་) བ་	*me-ra tang-wa.*
Do. *hon.*	སྨད་ར་གཏོང་ང་ (བ་) གནང་བ་	*me-ra tong-nga nang-wa.*
Do *inf.* to *sup.*	སྨད་ར་ཞུ་བ་	*me-ra sk̄u wa.*
Liberal	ལག་པ་ཤོག་པོ་	*lak̄-pa shok̄-po.*
Do. *hon.*	ཕྱག་ཤོག་པོ་	*chha-shok̄-po.*
Liberate, to	བཏང་བ་ (གཏོང་བ་)	*tang-wa.*
Liberated, to be	ཐར་བ་	*thar-wa.*
Liberty	ཚེ་ཐར་	*tshe-thar.*
Do. to be at (to be allowed)	ཆོག་པ་	*chhok̄-pa.*

Liberty, to be set at	ཚེ་ཐར་བཏང་ (གཏོང་) བ་	*tshe-thar tang-wa.*
Do. *hon.*	ཚེ་ཐར་གཏོང་ང་ (བ་) གནང་བ་	*tshe-thar tong-nga nang-wa.*
Libidinous	འདོད་ཆགས་ཆེན་པོ་	*dö-chha chhem-po.*
Library	དཔེ་ཆ་ཁང་	*pe-chha-khang.*
Do. *hon.*	ཕྱག་དཔེ་ཁང་	*chha-pe-khang.*
License	བཀའ་ཤོག་	*ka-sho.*
Licentious	འདོད་ཆགས་ཆེན་པོ་	*dö-chha chhem-po.*
Licentiousness	འདོད་ཆགས་	*dö-chha.*
Lick, to (of animals)	ལྡག་པ་	*daḱ-pa.*
Do. (of persons)	ལྕེ་ལ་ (ལྡག་) རྒྱབ་པ་	*che-la gyaṕ-pa.*
Do. *hon.*	ལྕེ་ལ་ (ལྡག་) སྐྱོན་པ་	*che-la ḱyöm-pa.*
Lid	ཁ་གཅོད། ཁ་	*khaṕ-chö ; kha.*
Lid (of the eye)	མིག་པགས་	*miḱ-pa.*
Lie, *s.*	ཧམ་པ། ཀྱག་རྫུན་	*ham-pa ; kyaḱ-dzün.*
Do. *hon.*	ཞལ་རྫུན་	*sḱe-dzün.*
Lie, to (tell untruth)	ཧམ་པ་བཤད་ (ཤོད་) པ། ཀྱག་རྫུན་བཤད་ (ཤོད) པ་	*ham-pa she-pa ; kyaḱ-dzün she-pa.*
Do. *hon.*	ཞལ་རྫུན་གནང་བ་	*sḱe-dzün nang-wa.*
Lie, to (down)	ཉལ་བསྡད་ (སྡོད་) པ་	*nye-de-pa.*
Do. *hon.*	གཟིམ་བཞུགས་པ་	*śim-sḱu-pa.*

Lieu of, in (instead of)	ཚབ་	*tshap.*
Do. *hon.*	སྐུ་ཚབ་	*ku-tshap.*
Life	སྲོག། ཚེ་	*so* or *hro* ; *tshe.*
Do. *hon.*	སྐུ་སྲོག། སྐུ་ཚེ་	*ku-so* ; *ku-tshe.*
Life-time	ཚེ་གང་	*tshe-k̄ang.*
Do. *hon.*	སྐུ་ཚེ་གང་	*ku-tshe-k̄ang.*
Lift, to	ཡར་ཀྱག་ (འཁྱོག་) པ། ཡར་ལེན་པ་	*yar-kyak̄-pa* ; *yar-lem-pa.*
Do. *hon.*	ཡར་ཀྱག་ག་ (འཁྱོག་པ་) གནང་བ་	*yar-kyak̄-k̄a nang-wa.*
Light, *s.* (lamp)	ཞུ་མར་	*sk̄u-ma.*
Do. *hon.*	གཟིམ་ཞུ་	*śim-sk̄u.*
Light, *s.* (brightness)	འོད་	*ö.*
Light, *adj.* (bright)	འོད་ཆེན་པོ་	*ö chhem-po.*
Light, *adj.* (not heavy)	ཡང་པོ་	*yang-po.*
Light, to (fire)	བཏང་བ་ (གཏོང་བ་)	*tang-wa.*
Do. *hon.*	གཏོང་ང་ (བ་) གནང་བ་	*tong-nga nang-wa.*
Light, to (lamp)	སྤར་བ་	*par-wa.*
Do. *hon.*	སྤར་ར་ (བ་) གནང་བ་	*par-ra nang-wa.*
Lightning, *s.*	གློག་	*lo.*

Lightning (forked)	འཁྱུག་	*khyu.*
Lightning (sheet), to flash	གློག་རྒྱབ་པ་	*lo gyap̄-pa.*
Do. (forked), to flash	འཁྱུག་རྒྱབ་པ་	*khyu gyap̄-pa.*
Like (similar)	ནང་བཞིན། འདྲ་པོ་	*nang-sKin ; dra-po.*
Like, to	དགའ་བ་	*ga-wa.*
Do. *hon.*	ཐུགས་མཉེས་པོ་གནང་བ་	*thu-nye-po nang-wa.*
Do. *h. hon.*	ཐུགས་དགྱེས་པོ་གནང་བ་	*thu-gye-po nang-wa.*
Like this	འདི་འདྲ་	*din-dra.*
Like that	དེ་འདྲ་	*t́en-dra.*
Likely, it is	ཡིན་འགྲོ། ཡིན་པ་འདྲ་	*yin-dro ; yim-pa-dra.*
Likeness (form)	བཟོ་བལྟ་	*śop̄-ta.*
Do. *hon.*	སྐུ་བཟོ་	*ku-śo.*
Likewise	ཡང་	*yang.*
Limb (of human beings)	འཟུགས་ཀྱི་ཡན་ལག་	*śuk̄-kyi yen-la.*
Do. *hon.*	སྐུ་གཟུགས་ཀྱི་ཡན་ལག་	*ku-śuk-kyi yen-la.*
Limb (of animals)	སྲུག་ལག་	*suk̄-la.*
Lime	ས་དཀར། དཀར་རྩི་	*sa-kar ; kar-tsi.*
Limit	མཐའ་	*tha.*
Limitation	ཚོད་	*tshö.*
Do. *hon.*	ཐུགས་ཚོད་	*thu-tshö.*

Limp, to	རྐང་པ་འཁྱོག་འཁྱོག་བྱེད་པ་	*kang-pa khyo-khyo che-pa.*
Do. *hon.*	ཞབས་འཁྱོག་འཁྱོག་གནང་བ་	*skap khyo-khyo nang-wa.*
Limpid (clear)	དྭངས་པོ་	*tang-po.*
Line	ཐིག་	*thi.*
Line (in a book)	ཡིག་ཕྲེང་	*yik-threng.*
Lineage (of laymen)	རིགས་བརྒྱུད། མི་བརྒྱུད་	*ri-gyü ; mi-gyü.*
Do. *hon.*	སྐུ་བརྒྱུད་	*ku-gyü.*
Do. *hon.* (of lamas)	གདུང་བརྒྱུད་	*dung-gyü.*
Linen	རས་	*re.*
Do. *hon.*	སྐུ་རས་	*ku-re.*
Linger, to	འགོར་བ་	*gor-wa.*
Do. *hon.*	ཕེབ་འགོར་གནང་བ་	*phe-gor nang-wa.*
Lining	ནང་ཤ་	*nang-sha.*
Link, to	འཐུད་རྒྱབ་པ་	*thü-gyap-pa.*
Do. *hon.*	འཐུད་སྐྱོན་པ་	*thü-kyöm-pa.*
Lion	སེང་གེ་	*seng-ge.*
Lioness	སེང་གེ་མོ་	*seng-ge-mo.*
Lip	མཆུ་ཏོ་	*chho-to.*
Do. *hon.*	ཞལ་མཆུ་	*ske-chhu.*
Lip, upper	ཡ་མཆུ་	*yen-chhu.*

Lip, lower	མ་མཆུ་	*men-chhu.*
Liquefy, to	ཞུ་བ་	*sḱu-wa.*
Liquid	ཁུ་བ་	*khu-wa.*
Liquid medicine	འཐུང་སྨན་	*thung-men.*
Liquor, distilled	ཨ་རག་	*a-ra.*
Do. *hon.*	བཞེས་རག་	*sḱe-ra.*
List	ཐོ་	*tho*
Do. *hon.*	ཕྱག་ཐོ་	*chha-tho.*
Listen, to	ཉན་པ། ཨམ་ཆོག་ཉན་པ་	*nyem-pa ; am-chho nyem-pa.*
Do. *hon.*	གསན་པ། སྙན་ལ་གསན་པ་	*sem-pa ; nyen-la sem-pa.*
Literary language	ཆོས་སྐད་	*chhö-ke.*
Literature	ཆོས་	*chhö.*
Little	ཆུང་ཆུང་	*chhung-chhung.*
Little, a (few)	ཏོག་ཙ། ཉུང་ཉུང་	*toḱ-tsa ; nyung-nyung.*
Little time, a	ཧྲིབ་ཙ་ (ཙམ་) ཅིག	*hriṕ-tsa-chi.*
Live, *adj.*	གསོན་པོ་	*söm-po.*
Live, to (dwell)	བསྡད་པ་ (སྡོད་པ་)	*de-pa.*
Do. *hon.*	བཞུགས་པ་	*sḱu-pa.*
Do. *h. hon.*	བཞུགས་གདན་འཇག་པ་	*sḱu-den jaḱ-pa.*
Lively	ཧུར་པོ། གཅང་པོ་	*hur-po ; chang-po*

Liver	མཆིན་པ་	*chhim-pa.*
Do. *hon.*	སྐུ་མཆིན་	*ku-chhin.*
Living, *adj.*	གསོན་པོ་	*söm-po.*
Lizard, sand (small)	བྱེ་མ་ཉུ་གུ་	*cḱe-ma nyu-gu.*
Lizard, rock (large)	ཙམ་པ་ཁ་རལ་	*tsam-pa kha-re.*
Lo !	ལྟོས་ཤིག་	*tö-shi*
Load (of an animal)	ཁལ། དོ་པོ་	*khe ; ťo-po.*
Do. (of human being)	རྡོག་ཁྲེད། རྒྱབ་འཁུར་	*dok-thre ; gyaṕ-khur.*
Load, to (animal)	ཁལ་བཀལ་ (འགེལ་) བ་	*khe-ke-wa.*
Do. to (of human being)	རྡོག་ཁྲེད་སྐུར་བ་	*dok-thre kur-wa.*
Load, to (a gun)	རྫས་རྫོང་རྒྱབ་པ་	*dze-dzong gyaṕ-pa.*
Do. *hon.*	རྫས་རྫོང་སྐྱོན་པ་	*dze-dzong kyöm-pa.*
Loadstone	རྡོ་ཁབ་ལེན་	*do-khaṕ-len.*
Loaf	བག་ལེབ་	*ṕa-le.*
Loafer (tramp)	རྒྱལ་ཁམས་སྐོར་མཁན་	*gyeng-kham kor-khen.*
Loan	བུ་ལོན་	*ṕu-lön.*
Loathe, to	སྡང་པོ་བྱེད་པ་	*dang-po cḱe-pa.*
Do. *hon.*	སྡང་པོ་གནང་བ་	*dang-po nang-wa.*
Locality	ས་ཆ་	*sa-chha.*
Lock, *s.*	སྒོ་ལྕགས་	*gön-cha.*

Lock, *hon.*	གཟིམ་ལྕགས། ཕྱག་ལྕགས་	*śim-cha ; chha-cha.*
Lock, to	སྒོ་ལྕགས་རྒྱབ་པ་	*gön-cha gyaṕ-pa.*
Do. *hon.*	གཟིམ་ལྕགས་སྐྱོན་པ་	*śim-cha kyöm-pa.*
Locust	ཨ་ཚ་ཚག་པ་	*a-tsha tshaḱ-pa.*
Lodging-house	གནས་ཚང་	*ne-tshang.*
Lodging-house, landlady of	གནས་མོ་	*ne-mo.*
Do. *hon.*	གནས་མོ་ལགས་	*ne-mo-la.*
Lodging-house, landlord of	གནས་པོ་	*ne-po.*
Do. *hon.*	གནས་པོ་ལགས་	*ne-po-la.*
Lofty	མཐོ་པོ་	*tho-po.*
Log (piece of wood)	ཤིང་དུམ་	*shing-ťum.*
Loins	རྐེད་པ་	*ke-pa.*
Do. *hon.*	སྐུ་རྐེད་	*ku-ke.*
Loiter, to	འགོར་བ་	*gor-wa.*
Do. *hon.*	ཕེབ་འགོར་གནང་བ་	*phe-gor nang-wa.*
Lonely	གཅིག་པོ་	*chiḱ-po.*
Do. *hon.*	སྐུ་རྐྱང་	*ku-kyang.*
Lonely place	དབེན་གནས་	*en-ne.*
Long	རིང་པོ་	*ring-po.*
Long for, to	དྲན་པ་	*ťrem-pa.*

Long for, to, *hon.*	ཐུགས་དྲན་པ་གནང་བ་	*thu-t̃rem-pa nang-wa.*
Long life, to have	ཚེ་རིང་བ་	*tshe-ring-wa.*
Do. *hon.*	སྐུ་ཚེ་རིང་བ་	*ku-tshe ring-wa.*
Long-lived	ཚེ་རིང་པོ་	*tshe-ring-po.*
Do. *hon.*	སྐུ་ཚེ་རིང་པོ་	*ku-tshe ring-po.*
Look, to	ལྟ་བ་	*ta-wa.*
Do. *hon.*	གཟིགས་པ་	*śi-pa.*
Look for, to (search)	འཚོལ་བ་	*t́shö-wa.*
Do. *hon.*	འཚོལ་ལ་ (བ་) གནང་བ་	*tshö-lu nang-wa.*
Looking-glass	ཤེལ་སྒོ་	*she-go.*
Loom	འཐག་ཁྲི་	*thak̃-thri*
Loop	ལུང་	*lung.*
Loop-button	ཐུབ་ལུང་	*thup̃-lung.*
Do. *hon.*	མགུལ་ལུང་	*gü-lung.*
Loose (not tight)	ལྷུག་ལྷུག་	*lhu-lhu.*
Do. (lascivious)	འདོད་ཆགས་ཆེན་པོ་	*dö-chha chhem-po.*
Loose, to (liberate)	བཏང་བ་ (གཏོང་བ་)	*tang-wa.*
Do. *hon.*	གཏོང་ང་ (བ་) གནང་བ་	*tong-nga nang-wa.*
Loose, to (slacken)	ལྷོད་ལྷོད་བཏང་ (གཏོང་) བ་	*hlö-hlö tang-wa.*

Loose, to (slacken), *hon.*	ལྷོད་ལྷོད་གཏོང་ང་ (བ་) གནང་བ་	*hlö-hlö tong-nga nang-wa.*
Loosen, to	ལྷུག་ལྷུག་བྱེད་པ་	*lhu-lhu cḱe-pa.*
Do. *hon.*	ལྷུག་ལྷུག་གནང་བ་	*lhu-lhu nang-wa.*
Lord	དཔོན་པོ་	*pöm-po.*
Lose, to	བརླགས་པ་	*la-pa.*
Lose, to (in business transaction)	གྱོང་འཕོག་པ་	*ḱyong phoḱ-pa.*
Do. *hon.*	སྐུ་གྱོང་འཕོག་ག་ (པ་) གནང་བ་	*ku-ḱyong phoḱ-ḱa nang-wa.*
Lose, to (battle, law-suit, etc.)	ཤོར་བ	*shor-wa.*
Do. *hon.*	ཤོར་ར་ (བ་) གནང་བ་	*shor-ra nang-wa.*
Loss	གྱོང་	*ḱyong.*
Loss of appetite	དང་ཁ་མེད་པ་	*ṫang-kha me-pa.*
Do. *hon.*	གསོལ་དང་མེད་པ་	*sö-ṫang-me-pa.*
Lost, it is	བརླགས་ནས་མི་འདུག	*la-ne min-du.*
Do. *hon.*	བརླགས་ག་ (པ་) གནང་ནས་མི་འདུག	*laḱ-ḱa nang-ne min-du.*
Lot (many)	མང་པོ་	*mang-po.*
Do. (very many)	གཡོ་མ་སུ་	*yo-ma-su.*
Do. (chance)	མོ་	*mo.*
Do. *hon.*	ཕྱག་མོ་	*chha-mo*

Lot (fortune)	བསོ་བདེ་ (བསོད་བདེ་)	*so-de.*
Do. *hon.*	སྐུ་བསོད་	*ku-sö.*
Lot (share)	སྐལ་ལ་ (སྐལ་བ་)	*ke-la*
Do. *hon.*	སྐུ་སྐལ་	*ku-ke.*
Lots, to draw	མོ་རྒྱབ་པ་	*mo-gyap-pa.*
Do. *hon.*	ཕྱག་མོ་སྐྱོན་པ་	*chha-mo kyöm-pa.*
Lotus	པད་མ་	*pe-ma.*
Loud (noisy)	སྐད་ཆེན་པོ་	*ke chhem-po.*
Do. *hon.*	གསུང་སྐད་ཆེན་པོ་	*sung-ke chhem-po.*
Louse	ཤིག་	*shi.*
Do. *hon.*	སྐུ་ཤིག་	*ku-shi.*
Love	བྱམས་པོ་	*cKam-po.*
Love, to	བྱམས་པོ་བྱེད་པ་	*cKam-po cKe-pa.*
Do. *hon.*	བྱམས་པོ་གནང་བ་	*cKam-po nang-wa.*
Lovely	ཚར་པོ། མཛེས་པོ་	*tshar-po ; dze-po.*
Do. *hon.*	ཐུགས་ཚར་པོ་	*thu-tshar-po.*
Lover	སྙིང་སྡུག	*nying-du.*
Low	དམའ་པོ་	*ma-po.*
Low (cheap)	ཁེ་པོ་	*khe-po.*
Low, to be (shallow)	གཏིང་རིང་པོ་མེད་པ་	*ting-ring-po me-pa.*

Lower part of a thing	སྨད་	*me.*
Lower tooth	སྨད་སོ་	*me-so.*
Do. *hon.*	སྨད་ཀྱི་ཚེམས་	*me-kyi tshem.*
Lowland	སྨད་	*me.*
Lowly	སེམས་ཆུང་ཆུང་	*sem-chhung-chhung.*
Do. *hon.*	ཐུགས་སེམས་ཆུང་ཆུང་	*thuḱ-sem chhung-chhung.*
Low-spirited, to be	སེམས་སྐྱོ་སྣང་བྱེད་པ་	*sem-kyo-nang cḱe-pa*
Do. *hon.*	ཐུགས་སེམས་སྐྱོ་སྣང་གནང་བ་	*thu-sem kyo-nang nang-wa.*
Loyal, to be	བཀའ་མཐུན་ཞུ་བ་	*ka-thün sḱu-wa.*
Lucid	སྒྲ་དག་པོ་	*dra-ťaḱ-po.*
Luck (good)	བསོད་བདེ། བསོད་ནམས་	*so-de ; sö-nam.*
Do. *hon.*	སྐུ་བསོད་	*ku-sö.*
Luck (bad)	བསོད་བདེ་སྐམ་པོ། བསོད་ནམས་ཆུང་ཆུང་	*so-de kam-po ; sö-nam chhung-chhung.*
Do. *hon.*	སྐུ་བསོད་ཆུང་ཆུང་	*ku-sö chhung-chhung.*
Lucky	བསོད་བདེ་ཆེན་པོ། བསོད་ནམས་ཆེན་པོ་	*so-de chhem-po ; sö-nam chhem-po.*
Do. *hon.*	སྐུ་བསོད་ཆེན་པོ་	*ku-sö chhem-po.*
Ludicrous	དགོད་མོ་བྲོ་པོ་	*ge-mo ťro-po.*

Ludicrous, *hon.*	ཞལ་མོ་བྲོ་བོ་	*sḱe-mo t́ro-po.*
Luggage	ཅ་ལག་ (ཆ་ལག་)	*cha-la.*
Do. *hon.*	སྐུ་ཅས་ (སྐུ་ཆས་)	*ku-che.*
Lugubrious, to be	སེམས་སྐྱོ་བ། སེམས་སྡུག་པ་	*sem-kyo-wa : sem-duḱ-pa.*
Do. *hon.*	ཐུགས་སེམས་སྐྱོ་བ་གནང་བ། ཐུགས་སེམས་སྡུག་ག་ (པ་) གནང་བ་	*thu-sem kyo-wa nang-wa. thu-sem duḱ-ka nang-wa.*
Lukewarm	དྲོན་འཇམ་	*t́rön-jam.*
Lumbago, to have	སྐེད་པ་ན་བ་	*ke-pa na-wa.*
Do. *hon.*	སྐུ་སྐེད་སྙུང་བ་	*ku-ke nyung-wa.*
Luminous	འོད་ཆེན་པོ་	*ö chhem-po.*
Lump	རྡོག་རྡོག་	*doḱ-do.*
Lunatic	སྨྱོན་པ་	*nyöm-pa.*
Lunch	ཉིན་གུང་ཁ་ལག་	*nyin-ḱung kha-la.*
Do. *hon.*	ཉིན་གུང་ཞལ་ལག་	*nyin-ḱung sḱe-la.*
Lungs	གློ་ (གློ་བ་)	*lo.*
Do. *hon.*	སྐུ་གློ་	*ku-lo.*
Lurk, to	ཡིབ་ནས་བསྡད་ (སྡོད་) པ་	*yiṕ-ne de-pa.*
Do. *hon.*	ཡིབ་ནས་བཞུགས་པ་	*yiṕ-ne sḱu-pa.*
Lust	འདོད་ཆགས་	*dö-chha.*

Lustful	འདོད་ཆགས་ཆེན་པོ་	*dö-chha chhem-po.*
Lustre	གཟི་བརྗིད། འོད་	*śi-ji ;* ö.
Lustrous	གཟི་བརྗིད་ཆེན་པོ། འོད་ཆེན་པོ་	*śi-ji chhem-po ; ö chhem-po.*
Lusty	ཤེད་ཆེན་པོ་	*she chhem-po.*
Do. *hon.*	སྐུ་ཤེད་ཆེན་པོ་	*ku-she chhem-po.*
Luxuriant	འབེལ་པོ་	*be-po.*
Lynx	དབྱི་	*i.*

M

Machine, sewing	ཚེམ་བུའི་འཁོར་ལོ་	*tshem-bü khor-lo.*
Mad	སྨྱོན་པ་	*nyöm-pa.*
Mad, to be	སྨྱོ་བ་	*nyo-wa.*
Madam	ལྕམ་སྐུ་གཞོགས་	*cham-ku-sḱo.*
Magazine	མཛོད་	*dzö.*
Magic	མིག་འཕྲུལ་	*miḱ-thrü.*
Magician	མིག་འཕྲུལ་སྟོན་མཁན་	*miḱ-thrü tön-khen.*
Magistrate, city (Chinaman)	ཁྲིམས་དཔོན་	*thrim-pön.*
Do. (Tibetan)	མི་དཔོན་	*mi-pön.*
Do. in charge of district	རྫོང་དཔོན་	*dzong-pön.*
Magnanimity	དྲིན་	*t́rin.*
Do. *hon.*	བཀའ་དྲིན་	*ka-t́rin.*
Magnanimous	དྲིན་ཆེན་པོ་	*t́rin chhem-po.*
Do. *hon.*	བཀའ་དྲིན་ཆེན་པོ་	*ka-t́rin chhem-po.*
Magnet	རྡོ་ཁབ་ལེན་	*do-khaṕ-len.*
Magnificent	གཡང་མཛེས་	*yang-dze.*
Magnitude	ཆེ་ཆུང་	*chhe-chhung.*
Magnolia	ཙམ་པ་ཀ་ *Hin.*	*tsam-pa-ka.*
Magpie	ཀྲ་ཀ་ (སྐྲ་ཀ་)	*tra-ka.*

Mahommedan	ཁ་ཆེ་	*kha-chhe.*
Maid, maiden	བུ་མོ་	*ṕu-mo.*
Do. *hon.*	སྲས་མོ་	*se-mo* or *tre-mo.*
Maid-servant	གཡོག་མོ་	*yo-mo.*
Do. of person of high rank	ཞལ་ཏ་མ་	*sḱe-ta-ma.*
Main point	དོན་སྙིང་	*ťön-nying.*
Mainly	ཕལ་ཆེར་	*phe-chher.*
Maintain, to (affirm)	ལབ་པ་	*laṕ-pa.*
Do. *hon.*	གསུང་བ་	*sung-wa.*
Maintain, to (nourish)	གསོ་བ་	*so-wa.*
Do. *hon.*	གསོ་བ་གནང་བ་	*so-wa nang-wa.*
Maize	ཀན་ཛོམ་	*ken-dzom.*
Majestic	གཟི་བརྗིད་ཆེན་པོ་	*śi-ji chhem-po.*
Majesty, His	རིན་པོ་ཆེ་	*rim-po-chhe.*
Major (officer in command of 250 to 500 men)	རུ་དཔོན་	*ru-pön.*
Majority, the	མང་ང་ (མང་བ་)	*mang-nga.*
Make, to	བྱེད་པ་	*cḱe-pa.*
Do. *hon.*	གནང་བ་	*nang-wa.*
Make, to (construct)	བཟོ་བ་	*śo-wa.*

Make, to (construct), *hon.*	བཟོ་བ་གནང་བ་	*śo-wa nang-wa.*
Maker	བཟོ་མཁན་	*śo-khen.*
Do. *hon.*	བཟོ་བ་གནང་མཁན་	*śo-wa nang-khen.*
Malady	ན་ཚ་	*na-tsha.*
Do. *hon.*	སྙུང་གཞི་	*nyung-sKi.*
Male	ཕོ་	*pho.*
Malediction, to pronounce	དམོད་མོ་རྒྱབ་པ་	*mö-mo gyap-pa.*
Do. *hon.*	དམོད་མོ་སྐྱོན་པ་	*mö-mo kyöm-pa.*
Malefactor	འཛབ་ཆེན་	*dzap-chhen.*
Malice	གནོད་སེམས་	*nö-sem.*
Malicious	སེམས་ངན་པོ་	*sem ngem-po.*
Do. *hon.*	ཐུགས་སེམས་ངན་པོ་	*thu-sem ngem-po.*
Malign, to	སྨད་ར་བཏང་ (གཏོང་) བ་	*me-ra tang-wa.*
Do. *hon.*	སྨད་ར་གཏོང་ང་ (བ་) གནང་བ་	*me-ra tong-nga nang-wa.*
Do. *inf.* to *sup.*	སྨད་ར་ཞུ་བ་	*me-ra sKu-wa.*
Malignant	སེམས་ངན་པོ་	*sem ngem-po.*
Do. *hon.*	ཐུགས་སེམས་ངན་པོ་	*thu-sem ngem-po.*
Malignity	གནོད་སེམས་	*nö-sem.*
Mallet	ཤིང་གི་ཐོ་བ་	*shing-ki tho-a.*
Maltreat, to	སྡུག་པོ་བཏང་ (གཏོང་) བ་	*duk-po tang-wa.*

Maltreat, to, *hon.*	སྡུག་པོ་གཏོང་ང་ (བ་) གནང་བ་	*duk̔-po tong-nga nang-wa.*
Mamma	ཨ་མ་	*a-ma.*
Do. *hon.*	ཡུམ་	*yum.*
Mammon	ནོར་ལྷ་	*nor-hla.*
Man	མི་	*mi.*
Do. a short	ཏེ་པོ་	*te-po.*
Man-servant	གཡོག་པོ་	*yok̔-po.*
Do. of person in good position	ཞབས་ཕྱི་	*sk̔ap̔-chhi.*
Manacles	ལག་ལྕགས་	*lak̔-cha.*
Manage, to (supervise)	དོ་དམ་བྱེད་པ་	*t̔o-t̔am ck̔e-pa.*
Do. *hon.*	དོ་དམ་གནང་བ་	*t̔o-t̔am nang-wa*
Manager	དོ་དམ་པ་	*t̔o-t̔am-pa.*
Do. *hon.*	དོ་དམ་གནང་མཁན་	*t̔o-t̔am nang-khen.*
Mandate	བཀའ་	*ka.*
Do. written (of Government)	བཀའ་རྒྱ་	*ka-gya.*
Mane (of horse, etc.)	ཟེ་	*śe.*
Do. (of lion)	རལ་པ་	*re-pa.*
Mange	རྔོ་	*ngo.*
Do. to have	རྔོ་ཤོར་བ་	*ngo-shor-wa.*

Manger	བྲེས་ར་ (བྲེས་)	*t́re-ra.*
Mangle, to (tear)	བཀོག་པ་ (འགོག་པ་)	*koḱ-pa.*
Do. *hon.*	བཀོག་ག་ (འགོག་པ་) གནང་བ་	*koḱ-ḱa nang-wa.*
Maniac	སྨྱོན་པ་	*nyöm-pa.*
Manifest, *adj.*	མངོན་ནས། ངོ་ཐོག་	*ngön-ne ; ngo-tho.*
Manifold	སྣ་ཚོགས་	*na-tsho.*
Mankind	མི་རིགས་	*mi-ri.*
Manly (brave)	སྙིང་ཆེན་པོ། བློ་ཁོག་ཆེན་པོ་	*nying-chhem-po ; lo-kho chhem-po.*
Do. *hon.*	ཐུགས་སྙིང་ཆེན་པོ། ཐུགས་ཁོག་ཆེན་པོ་	*thu-nying chhem-po ; thu-kho chhem po.*
Manner (custom)	ལུགས་སྲོལ་	*luḱ-sö.*
Do. (behaviour)	བྱེད་སྟངས་	*cḱe-tang.*
Do. *hon.*	གནང་སྟངས་	*nang-tang.*
Manœuvre, to (troops)	དམག་སྦྱོང་བྱེད་པ་	*ma-jong cḱe-pa.*
Do. *hon.*	དམག་སྦྱོང་གནང་བ་	*ma-jong nang-wa.*
Mansion	གཟིམས་ཤག། ཕོ་བྲང་	*śim-sha ; pho-t́rang.*
Mantle	ཆུ་པ་	*chhu-pa.*
Do. *hon.*	ན་བཟའ་	*nam-śa.*

Manufacture, to	བཟོ་བ་	*ṡo-wa.*
Do. *hon.*	བཟོ་པ་གནང་བ་	*ṡo-wa nang-wa.*
Manure	ལུད་	*lü.*
Manuscript	བྲིས་མ་	*t́ri-ma.*
Many	མང་པོ་	*mang-po.*
Many, very	ཧ་ཅང་མང་པོ། གཡོ་མ་སུ་	*ha chang mang-po ; yo-ma-su.*
Many, too	ལྷག་པོ་	*hlaḱ-po.*
Many, how	ག་ཚོད་	*ḱa-tshö.*
Map	ས་ཁྲ་	*saṕ-thra.*
Mar, to	སྐྱོན་བྱེད་པ་	*kyön-cḱe-pa.*
Do. *hon.*	སྐྱོན་གནང་བ་	*kyön-nang-wa.*
March, to	འགྲོ་བ་	*dro wa.*
Do. *hon.*	ཕེབ་པ་	*phe-pa.*
Do. *h. hon.*	འཆིབ་སྒྱུ་གནང་བ་	*chhiṕ-gyu nang-wa.*
Mare	རྒོད་མ་	*gö-ma.*
Margin	མཐའ་	*tha.*
Marigold	གུར་གུམ་མེ་ཏོག་	*ḱur-ḱum me-to.*
Mark	རྟགས་	*ta.*
Mark, to (observe)	མིག་ལྟ་བ་	*miḱ-ta-wa.*
Do. *hon.*	གཟིགས་པ་	*ṡi-pa.*

Marked (famous)	སྐད་གྲགས་ཆེན་པོ་	*ke-ťra chhem-po.*
Do. *hon.*	སྙན་གྲགས་ཆེན་པོ་	*nyen-ťra chhem-po.*
Market-place	ཁྲོམ་	*throm.*
Marriage.	ཆང་ས་	*chhang-sa.*
Do. *hon.*	འཁྲུང་ས་	*thrung-sa.*
Marry, to (take a wife)	མནའ་མ་ལེན་པ་	*na-ma lem-pa.*
Do. *hon.*	མནའ་མ་བཞེས་པ་	*na-ma sḱe-pa.*
Marry, to (take a husband)	མག་པ་བསླང་ (སློང་) བ་	*maḱ-pa lang-wa.*
Do. *hon.*	སྐུ་བག་བཞེས་པ་	*ku ṕa sḱe-pa.*
Marvel, *s.*	ཡ་མཚན་	*yam tshen.*
Marvel, to	ཁྱད་མཚར་པོ་བྱེད་པ་	*khye-tsha-po cḱe-pa.*
Marvellous	ཡ་མཚན་པོ། ཁྱད་མཚར་པོ་	*yam-tshem-po ; khye-tsha-po.*
Mask	འབག་	*ba.*
Do. *hon.*	ཞལ་འབག་	*sḱem-ba.*
Mason	རྡོ་བཟོ་བ་	*doṕ-ṡo-wa.*
Masquerade	འཆམ་	*chham.*
Do. *hon.*	སྐུ་འཆམ་	*kun-chham.*
Massage, to	འཕུར་འཕུར་བྱེད་པ་	*phu-phu cḱe-pa.*
Massive (bulky)	སྦོམ་པོ་	*bom-po.*
Do. (heavy)	ལྗི་པོ་	*ji-po.*

Mast (flag-staff)	དར་པོ་ཆེ་	*ṫar-po-chhe.*
Master	སྦྱིན་བདག། བདག་པོ་	*jin-da ; dak̇-po.*
Do. *hon.*	དཔོན་པོ་	*pöm-po.*
Mastery (power)	དབང་	*wang.*
Do. *hon.*	སྐུ་དབང་	*ku-wang.*
Mastiff	འབྲོག་ཁྱི་	*drok̇-khyi.*
Mart	ཁྲོམ་	*throm.*
Mat	གདན་	*den.*
Match (lucifer)	མུ་ཟི་	*mu-śi.*
Match-box	མུ་ཟིའི་སྒམ་ཆུང་	*mu-śi gam-chhung.*
Mate	རོགས་	*ro.*
Material, *s.*	རྒྱུ་	*gyu.*
Material, *adj.* (important)	གནད་ཁག་ཆེན་པོ། གལ་ཆེན་པོ་	*nen-kha chhem-po ; k̇e chhem-po.*
Maternal aunt	སྲུ་མོ་	*su-mo.*
Matter (substance)	རྒྱུ་	*gyu.*
Do. (pus)	རྣག་	*na.*
Mattress	འབོལ་གདན་	*bö-den.*
Do. *hon.*	བཞུགས་འབོལ་	*sk̇um-böl.*
Mature, to be	ཚོས་པ་	*tshö-pa.*

Maxim	གདམ་དཔེ་	*tam-pe.*
Me	ང་ལ་	*nga-la.*
Meadow	སྤང་	*pang.*
Meagre (lean)	ཤ་སྐམ་པོ་	*sha-kam-po.*
Do. *hon.*	སྐུ་ཤ་སྐམ་པོ་	*ku-sha kam-po.*
Meagre (scanty)	ཉུང་ཉུང་	*nyung-nyung.*
Meal (food taken at one time)	ཁ་ལག། ལྟོ། ལྟོ་ཆས་	*kha-la ; to ; top-chhe.*
Do. *hon.*	ཞལ་ལག་	*sḱe-la.*
Mean (vulgar)	དཀྱུས་མ་	*kyü-ma.*
Mean (stingy)	ལག་པ་དམ་པོ་	*laḱ-pa t́am-po.*
Do. *hon.*	ཕྱག་དམ་པོ་	*chha t́am-po.*
Mean, to (purpose)	སེམས་ལ་བསམ་པ་	*sem-la sam-pa.*
Do. *hon.*	ཐུགས་ལ་དགོངས་པ་	*thuḱ-la gong-pa.*
Meaning	དོན་དག་	*t́ön-t́a.*
Do. *hon.*	སྐུ་དོན་	*ku-t́ön.*
Means, *s.*	ཐབས་	*thaṕ.*
Means, by all	ངེས་པར་	*nge-par.*
Means, by what	ག་འདྲས་	*ḱan-dre.*
Meantime, in the	ཁབ་སུ	*khaṕ-su.*

Meanwhile, in the	ཁབ་སུ་	*khaṕ-su.*
Measles	གསིལ་པ་	*si-pa.*
Measure, *s.*	ཚད་	*tshe.*
Measure, to	འཇལ་བ་	*je-wa.*
Do. *hon.*	འཇལ་ར་ (བ་) གནང་བ་	*je ra nang-wa.*
Meat	ཤ་	*sha.*
Do. *hon.*	བཞེས་ཤ་	*sḱe-sha.*
Mechanic	བཟོ་མཁན་	*śo-khen.*
Mediate, to	བར་མི་བྱེད་པ་	*ṕar-mi cḱe-pa.*
Do. *hon.*	བར་མི་གནང་བ་	*ṕar-mi nang-wa.*
Mediator	བར་མི་བྱེད་མཁན་	*ṕar-mi cḱe-khen.*
Medicine	སྨན་	*men.*
Medicine for internal use	ཁོང་སྨན་	*khong-men.*
Medicine, mineral	ས་སྨན་	*sa-men.*
Meditate, to	བསམ་པ་	*sam-pa.*
Do. *hon.*	དགོངས་པ་	*gong-pa.*
Meditate, to (on religious affairs)	སྒོམ་རྒྱབ་པ་	*gom-gyaṕ-pa.*
Do. *hon.*	སྒོམ་སྐྱོན་པ་	*gom-kyöm-pa.*
Meditation, religious	ཏིང་ངེ་འཛིན་	*ting-nge dzin.*

Medium (of quality)	འབྲིང་ཅིག། ཁྲིག་ཁྲིག་ཅིག་	*dring-chi ; thriḱ-thri-chi.*
Meek	སེམས་ཆུང་ཆུང་	*sem-chhung-chhung.*
Do. *hon.*	ཐུགས་སེམས་ཆུང་ཆུང་	*thuḱ-sem-chhung-chhung.*
Meek in speech	ཁ་འཇམ་པོ་	*kha jam-po.*
Do. *hon.*	ཞལ་འཇམ་པོ་	*sḱe jam-po.*
Meet, to	ཐུག་པ་	*thuḱ-pa.*
Do. (a superior)	མཇལ་བ་	*je-wa.*
Do. (between two of high position)	མཇལ་ར་ (བ་) གནང་བ་	*je-ra nang-wa.*
Meeting	ཐུག་ཕྲད་	*thuḱ-thre.*
Do. *hon.*	མཇལ་ཕྲད་	*je-thre.*
Melancholy, to be	སེམས་སྐྱོ་སྣང་བྱེད་པ་	*sem-kyo-nang cḱe-pa.*
Do. *hon.*	ཐུགས་སེམས་སྐྱོ་སྣང་གནང་བ་	*thu-sem kyo-nang nang-wa.*
Melt, to	ཞུ་བ་	*sḱu-wa.*
Memoir (story)	རྣམ་ཐར་	*nam-tha.*
Memory	དྲན་པ་	*t́rem-pa.*
Do. *hon.*	ཐུགས་དྲན་	*thu-t́ren.*
Menace, to	འཛོག་འཛོག་ (འཛིག་འཛིག་) བཏང་ (གཏོང་) བ་	*dziḱ-dziḱ tang-wa.*
Mend, to	སྒྲོག་པ་	*droḱ-pa.*

Mend, to, *hon.*	སྒྲོག་ག་ (པ་) གནང་བ་	*droḱ-ḱa nang-wa.*
Mend, to (by patching)	ལྷན་པ་རྒྱབ་པ་	*hlem-pa gyaṕ-pa.*
Do. *hon.*	ལྷན་པ་སྐྱོན་པ་	*hlem-pa kyöm-pa.*
Mendacious, to be	ཧམ་པ་ཤོད་པ། ཀྱག་རྫུན་ཤོད་པ་	*ham-pa shö-pa ; kyaḱ-dzün shö-pa.*
Do. *hon.*	ཞལ་རྫུན་གསུང་བ་	*sḱe-dzün sung-wa.*
Mendicant	སྤང་ཀོ་ (སྤྲང་པོ་)	*pang-ko.*
Menses	ཟླ་མཚན་	*da-tshen.*
Menstruate, to	ཟླ་ཁྲག་རྒྱབ་པ་	*da-thra, gyaṕ-pa.*
Mention, to	ལབ་པ་	*laṕ-pa.*
Do. *hon.*	གསུང་བ་	*sung-wa.*
Merchandise	ཚོང་ཟོག་	*tshong-śo.*
Merchant	ཚོང་པ་	*tshong-pa.*
Do. *hon.*	ཚོང་དཔོན་	*tshong-pön.*
Merciful	སྙིང་རྗེ་ཆེན་པོ་	*nying-je chhem-po.*
Do. *hon.*	ཐུགས་རྗེ་ཆེན་པོ་	*thuḱ-je chhem-po.*
Merciless, to be	སྙིང་རྗེ་མེད་པ་	*nying-je me-pa.*
Do. *hon.*	ཐུགས་རྗེ་མེད་པ་	*thuḱ-je me-pa.*
Mercury	དངུལ་ཆུ་	*ngü-chhu.*
Mercy	སྙིང་རྗེ་	*nying-je.*

Mercy, *hon.*	ཐུགས་རྗེ་	*thuk-je.*
Merely	ཤ་སྟག་	*sha-ta.*
Merit	དགེ་བ། ཚོགས་	*ge-wa ; tsho.*
Do. to accumulate	ཚོགས་བསག་ (གསོག་) པ་	*tsho saḱ-pa.*
Do. *hon.*	ཚོགས་གསོག་ག་ (པ་) གནང་བ་	*tsho soḱ-ḱa nang-wa.*
Merit, to	འོས་པ་	*ö-pa.*
Merriment	དགའ་ཚོར་	*ga-tshor.*
Do. *hon.*	མཉེས་ཚོར་	*nye-tshor.*
Merry, to be	དགའ་བ། སྐྱིད་པོ་བྱས་ནས་སྡོད་པ་	*ga-wa ; kyi-po cḱe-ne dö-pa.*
Do. *hon.*	མཉེས་པོ་གནང་བ། སྤྲོ་པོ་གནང་ནས་བཞུགས་པ་	*nye-po nang-wa ; tro-po nang-ne sḱuḱ-pa.*
Do. *h. hon.*	ཐུགས་དགྱེས་པོ་གནང་བ་	*thu-gye-po nang-wa.*
Message	ལན་	*len.*
Do. *hon.*	བཀའ་ལན་	*ḱa-len.*
Messenger	བང་ཆེན་	*ṕang-chhen.*
Method (means)	ཐབས་	*thaṕ.*
Do. (custom)	ལུགས་སྲོལ་	*luḱ-sö.*
Mewing, *s.* (of cat)	སྨྱོའོ་	*me-o.*

Mid-day	ཉིན་གུང་	*nyiṅ-k̄ung.*
Middle, *s.*	དཀྱིལ་	*kyi.*
Do. (waist)	ཀེད་པ་	*ke-pa.*
Do. *hon.*	སྐུ་ཀེད་	*ku-ke.*
Middle, *adj.*	འབྲིང་ཅིག། ཁྲིག་ཁྲིག་ཅིག་	*dring-chi ; thrik̄-thri-chi.*
Middle of, in the	དཀྱིལ་ལ་	*kyi-la.*
Midnight	ནམ་ཕྱེད་	*nam-chhe.*
Midst, in the	དཀྱིལ་ལ་	*kyi-la.*
Mien	བཟོ་ལྟ་	*śoṕ-ta.*
Do. *hon.*	སྐུ་བཟོ་	*ku-śo.*
Might (official authority)	དབང་	*wang.*
Do. *hon.*	སྐུ་དབང་	*ku-wang.*
Might (physical)	ཤེད་	*she.*
Do. *hon.*	སྐུ་ཤེད་	*ku-she.*
Mighty (officially)	དབང་ཆེན་པོ་	*wang chhem-po.*
Do. *hon.*	སྐུ་དབང་ཆེན་པོ་	*ku-wang chhem-po.*
Mighty (physically)	ཤེད་ཆེན་པོ་	*she chhem-po.*
Do. *hon.*	སྐུ་ཤེད་ཆེན་པོ་	*ku-she chhem-po.*
Milch cow	བཞོན་མ་	*sk̄ö-ma.*
Mild in speech	ཁ་འཇམ་པོ་	*kha jam-po.*

Mild in speech, *hon.*	ཞལ་འཇམ་པོ་	*sḱe jam-po.*
Mild (of climate)	བསིལ་དྲོས་སྙོམ་པོ་	*si-ťrö nyom-po.*
Militia (first) see "army"	འདོན་དམག་	*döm-ma.*
Do. (second)	སེར་དམག་	*ser-ma.*
Do. (final)	བཅོ་བརྒྱད་དྲུག་ཅུ་	*choṕ-gye truḱ-chu.*
Milk	འོ་མ་	*o-ma.*
Do. *hon.*	བཞེས་འོ་	*sḱe-o.*
Milk, to	བཞོ་བ་	*sḱo-wa.*
Do. *hon.*	བཞོ་བ་གནང་བ་	*sḱo-wa nang-wa.*
Milk-jug	འོ་སྣོད་	*o-nö.*
Million	ས་ཡ་	*sa-ya.*
Mimic, to	ལན་ལྟོས་བྱེད་པ་	*len-tö cḱe-pa*
Do. *hon.*	ལན་ལྟོས་གནང་བ་	*len-tö nang-wa.*
Mimicry	ལན་ལྟོས་	*len-tö*
Mina (bird)	མེ་ན་ *Hin.*	*me-na.*
Mince, to	བཙབ་པ་	*tsaṕ-pa.*
Do. *hon.*	བཙབ་པ་གནང་བ་	*tsaṕ-pa nang-wa.*
Mind	བློ། སེམས་	*lo ; sem.*
Do. *hon.*	ཐུགས་	*thu.*
Mind, to (take care of)	ཉར་བ་	*nyar-wa.*

Mind, to (take care of), *hon.*	ཉར་ར་ (བ་) གནང་བ་	*nyar-ra nang-wa.*
Mind! never	ཨའུ་ཙེ་	*a-u-tse.*
Mine, *pron.*	ངའི་	*nge.*
Mingle, to, *v.i.*	འདྲེ་བ་	*dre-wa.*
Mingle, to, *v.t.*	བསྲེ་བ་	*tre-wa.*
Do. *hon.*	བསྲེ་བ་གནང་བ་	*tre-a nang-wa.*
Minister of the Grand Council at Lhasa	ས་དབང་ཆེན་པོ། ཞབས་པད། བཀའ་བློན་	*sa-wang chhem-po ; sḱaṕ-pe ; ka-lön.*
Minister, Chief	བློན་ཆེན་	*lön-chhen.*
Mint	དངུལ་པར་ཁང་	*ngü-par-khang.*
Minute, *adj.*	ཞིབ་ཞིབ་	*sḱiṕ-sḱiṕ.*
Miracle	ཡ་མཚན་	*yam-tshen.*
Miraculous	ཡ་མཚན་པོ། ཁྱད་མཚར་པོ་	*yam-tshem po ; khye-tsha-po.*
Mire	འདམ། རྫབ་	*dam ; dzaṕ.*
Mirror	ཤེལ་སྒོ་	*she-go.*
Mirth	དགའ་ཚོར་	*ga-tshor.*
Do. *hon.*	མཉེས་ཚོར་	*nye-tshor.*
Mirthful, to be	དགའ་བ་	*ga-wa.*
Do. *hon.*	མཉེས་པོ་གནང་བ་	*nye-po nang-wa.*
Do. *h. hon.*	ཐུགས་དགྱེས་པོ་གནང་བ་	*thu-gye-po nang-wa.*

Mischief	སྐྱོན་	*kyön.*
Miscreant	འཛབ་ཆེན་	*dzaṕ-chhen.*
Miserable (unhappy)	སྡུག་བསྔལ་ཆེན་པོ་	*dung-nge chhem-po.*
Do. *hon.*	ཐུགས་བསྔལ་ཆེན་པོ་	*thuḱ-nge chhem-po.*
Miserliness	སེར་སྣ་	*ser-na.*
Miserly	སེར་སྣ་ཆེན་པོ་	*ser-na chhem-po*
Misery	སྡུག་བསྔལ་	*dung-nge.*
Do. *hon.*	ཐུགས་བསྔལ་	*thuḱ-nge.*
Misfortune	བསོད་བདེ་སྐམ་པོ་	*so-de ḱam-po.*
Do. *hon.*	སྐུ་བསོད་ཆུང་ཆུང་	*ku-sö chhung-chhung.*
Mist	སྨུགས་པ་	*muḱ-pa.*
Mistake, to	ནོར་བ་	*nor-wa.*
Do. *hon.*	ནོར་ར་ (བ་) གནང་བ་	*nor-ra nang-wa.*
Mistake in speech, to make a	ཁ་ནོར་བ་	*kha-nor-wa.*
Do. *hon.*	ཞལ་ནོར་བ་	*sḱe nor-wa.*
Mistress (wife of well-to-do villager)	སྙི་སྙིང་ལགས་	*nyi-nying-la.*
Mistress (wife of ordinary official)	ལྕམ་སྐུ་ཞོགས་	*cham-ku-sḱo.*
Do. (third grade and upwards)	ལྷ་ལྕམ་སྐུ་ཞོགས་	*hla-cham ku-sḱo*

Misunderstood, to be	གོ་ལོག་བྱུང་བ་	*ḱo-loḱ cḱung-wa.*
Do. *hon.*	གསན་འཛོལ་བྱུང་བ་	*sen-dzöl cḱung-wa.*
Mix, to, *v.t.*	བསྲེ་བ་	*tre-wa.*
Do. *hon.*	བསྲེ་བ་གནང་བ་	*tre-a nang-wa.*
Mix, to, *v.i.*	འདྲེ་བ་	*dre-wa.*
Mock, to	ཀྱག་ཀྱག་བྱས་ནས་ལབ་པ་	*kya-kya cḱe-ne laṕ-pa.*
Do. *hon.*	ཀྱག་ཀྱག་གནང་ནས་གསུང་བ་	*kya ḱya nang-ne sung-wa.*
Mode (custom)	ལུགས་སྲོལ་	*luḱ-sö.*
Do. (method)	ཐབས་	*thaṕ.*
Model	དཔེ་	*pe.*
Modelled well- (of metal-work, wood-work, etc.)	བཀོད་པ་དོད་པོ་	*ḱö-pa t́ö-po.*
Moderate, to be	ཚོད་ཟིན་པ་	*tshö-śim-pa.*
Modern	ད་རིང་སང་གི་	*t́e-ring sang-ḱi.*
Modest, to be	དམའ་ས་ཟིན་པ་	*ma-sa śim-pa.*
Do. *hon.*	དམའ་ས་ཟིན་པ་གནང་བ་	*ma-sa śim-pa nang-wa.*
Mohammadan	ཁ་ཆེ་	*kha-chhe*
Moist	རློན་པ་	*löm-pa.*
Moisten, to	སྦང་བ་	*bang-wa.*
Do. *hon.*	སྦང་ང་ (བ་) གནང་བ་	*bang-nga nang-wa.*

Moisture (of ground)	བཞའ་ཚན་	*sḱa-tshen.*
Molar tooth	འགྲམ་སོ་	*dram-so.*
Do. *hon.*	ཞལ་འགྲམ་གྱི་ཚེམས་	*sḱe-dram-ḱyi tshem.*
Mole	སྨན་ (སྨི་བ་)	*men.*
Molest, to	སྡུག་པོ་བཏང་ (གཏོང་) བ་	*duḱ-po tang-wa.*
Do. *hon.*	སྡུག་པོ་གཏོང་ང་(བ་)གནང་བ་	*duḱ-po tong-nga nang-wa.*
Moment (importance)	གནད་ཁག་	*nen-kha.*
Moment, in a	ཧྲིབ་ཙ་ (ཙམ་) ཅིག་	*hriṕ-tsa-chi.*
Momentous	གནད་ཁག་ཆེན་པོ། གལ་ཆེན་པོ་	*nen-kha chhem-po ; ḱe chhem-po.*
Monarch	རྒྱལ་པོ་	*gye-po.*
Monarch's administration	རྒྱལ་སྲིད་	*gye-si.*
Monastery	དགོན་པ་	*göm-pa.*
Monday	གཟའ་ཟླ་བ་	*śa-da-wa.*
Money	དངུལ་	*ngü.*
Mongol, Mongolian	སོག་པོ་	*soḱ-po.*
Monk	གྲྭ་པ་	*t́ra-pa.*
Do. *hon.*	དགེ་འདུན་	*gen-dün.*
Monkey	སྤྲེའུ་ (སྤྲེའུ་)	*pe-u.*
Monstrous (huge)	ཆེ་ཐག་ཆོད་	*chhe-thaḱ-chhö.*

Monstrous (horrible)	ཞེད་སྐྲག་ཚ་པོ་	*sKe-tra tsha-po.*
Month	ཟླ་བ་	*da-wa.*
Month, 1st half of	ཟླ་སྟོད། ཚེས་ཤར་	*da-tö ; tshe-shar.*
Do. middle of	ཟླ་དཀྱིལ། ཚེས་དཀྱིལ་	*da-kyi ; tshe-kyi.*
Do. last half of	ཟླ་སྨད། ཟླ་མཇུག། ཚེས་གཞུག་	*da-me ; dan-juK ; tshe-sKu.*
Do. last day of	ནམ་གང་	*nam-Kang.*
Moon	ཟླ་བ་	*da-wa.*
Moonlight	ཟླ་དཀར་	*da-ka.*
Moonlight, to be	ཟླ་དཀར་ཤར་བ་	*da-ka shar-wa.*
Moral, *adj.* (of persons)	ཚུལ་ལྡན་	*tshün-den.*
Morality	ཚུལ་ཁྲིམས་	*tshü-thrim.*
More	མང་ང་ (མང་བ།) ལྷག་ག་ (ལྷག་པ་)	*mang-nga ; hlaK-Ka.*
Moreover	ད་འདོ་ (ད་གདོས་)	*ťan-do.*
Morning	ཞོགས་གས། སྔ་དྲོ་	*sKoK-Ke ; nga-ťro.*
Do. (before dawn)	ཐོ་རངས་	*tho-rang.*
Do. forenoon (eight to ten o'clock)	ཚ་དིང་	*tsha-ting.*
Morrow	སང་ཉིན་	*sang-nyi.*

Morsel, a	དག་ག་ཅིག་	*ťaǩ-ǩa-chi.*
Mortal, *s.*	མི་	*mi.*
Mortar (for pounding)	སྒོག་དིང་	*goǩ-ting.*
Do. (cannon)	མེ་སྒྱོགས་	*me-gyoǩ.*
Mortification (shame)	ངོ་ཚ་	*ngo-tsha.*
Mortified, to feel	ངོ་ཚ་བ་	*ngo-tsha-wa*
Do. *hon.*	ཐུགས་ངོ་ཚ་བ་	*thu-ngo tsha-wa.*
Mosquito	དུག་སྦྲང་	*ťuǩ-drang.*
Most	མང་ཤོས་	*mang-shö.*
Most part, for the	ཕལ་ཆེར་	*phe-chher.*
Moth	ཕྱེ་འདྲེན་མ་	*chhem-drem-ma.*
Mother	ཨ་མ་	*a-ma.*
Do. *hon.*	ཡུམ་སྐུ་གཞོགས་	*yum-ku-sǩo.*
Do. *h. hon.*	ལྷ་ཡུམ་སྐུ་གཞོགས་	*hla-yum ku-sǩo*
Do. (of Dalai and Tashi Lamas)	རྒྱལ་ཡུམ་སྐུ་གཞོགས་	*gye-yum ku-sǩo*
Mother of pearl	ཉ་ཕྱིས་	*nyaṕ-chhi.*
Motive	དོན་དག་	*ťön-ťa.*
Do. *hon.*	སྐུ་དོན་	*ku-ťön.*
Mould (for shaping)	པར་	*par.*

Mouldy, to be	ཧམ་པ་རྒྱབ་པ་	*ham-pa gyaṗ-pa.*
Mound	ས་ཕུང་	*sa-phung.*
Mount for photograph	པར་གྱི་རྒྱབ་ཤ་ཤོག་བུ་	*par-k̇yi gyaṗ-sha shok̇-k̇u.*
Mount, to (a horse, &c.)	ཞོན་པ་	*sk̇öm-pa.*
Do. *hon.*	འཆིབ་པ་	*chhiṗ-pa.*
Mount, to (rise)	ལང་བ་	*lang-wa.*
Do. *hon.*	བཞང་བ་ (བཞེང་བ་)	*sk̇ang-wa.*
Do. *h. hon.*	སྐུ་བཞང་ (བཞེང་) གནང་བ་	*ku-sk̇ang nang-wa.*
Mount, to (climb)	འཛག་པ་ (འཛེག་པ་)	*dzak̇-pa.*
Do. *hon.*	འཛག་ག་ (འཛེག་པ་) གནང་བ་	*dzak̇-ka nang-wa.*
Mountain	རི་	*ri.*
Do. snowy	གངས་རི་	*k̇ang-ri.*
Mountain-pass	ལ་	*la.*
Mourn, to	སྡུག་བསྔལ་བྱེད་པ། མྱ་ངན་བྱེད་པ་	*du-nge ck̇e-pa; nya-ngen. ck̇e-pa.*
Do. *hon.*	ཐུགས་ངན་གནང་བ་	*thu-ngen nang-wa.*
Mouse	ཙི་ཙི་	*tsi-tsi.*
Moustache	ཨ་ར་	*a-ra.*
Do. *hon.*	ཞལ་ར་	*sk̇e-ra.*

Mouth	ཁ་	*kha.*
Do. *hon.*	ཞལ་	*sḱe.*
Mouthful	ཁམ་རྡོག་ཅིག་	*kham-do-chi.*
Move, to (go)	འགྲོ་བ་	*dro-wa.*
Do. *hon.*	ཕེབ་པ། ཐྲས་པ་	*phe-pa; the-pa.*
Do. *h. hon.*	འཆིབ་རྒྱུ་གནང་བ་	*chhiṕ-gyu nang-wa*
Move, to (persuade)	བསླབ་བྲ་བྱེད་པ་	*laṕ-cḱa cḱe-pa.*
Do. *hon.*	བཀའ་སློབ་གནང་བ་	*ka-loṕ nang-wa.*
Mow, to	རྔ་བ་	*nga-wa.*
Do. *hon.*	རྔ་བ་གནང་བ་	*nga-wa nang-wa.*
Much (many)	མང་པོ་	*mang-po.*
Do. (very many)	གཡོ་མ་སུ་	*yo-ma-su.*
Much, too	ལྷག་པ། ལྷག་མ་	*hlaḱ-pa; hla-ma.*
Much, very	ཧ་ཅང་མང་པོ་	*ha-chang mang-po.*
Mud	འདམ། རྫབ་	*dam; dzaṕ.*
Muddy (of water)	རྙོག་པོ་	*nyoḱ-po.*
Muhammadan	ཁ་ཆེ་	*kha-chhe.*
Mule	དྲེ་	*t́re.*
Mule, baggage	ཁལ་དྲེ་	*khe-t́re.*
Mule, riding	ཞོན་དྲེ་	*sḱön-t́re.*

Mule, riding, *hon.*	ཆིབས་དྲེ་	*chhiṕ-t́re.*
Muleteer	དྲེལ་པ་	*t́re-pa.*
Multitude (of men)	མི་ཚོགས་	*mi-tsho.*
Mumps	འགྲམ་པ་སྐྲང་བ་	*dram-pa trang-wa.*
Murder, to	བསད་པ་ (གསོད་པ་)	*se-pa.*
Do. *hon.* (*inf.* to *sup.*)	བཀྲོངས་པ་	*trong-pa.*
Do. *hon.* (between two of high position)	བཀྲོངས་ང་ (པ་) གནང་བ་	*trong-nga nang-wa.*
Murderer	མི་བསད་མཁན་	*mi-se-khen.*
Murky, to become (from clouds)	འཐིབས་པ་	*thiṕ-pa.*
Muscle	རྩ་	*tsa.*
Muse, to (meditate)	བསམ་པ་	*sam-pa.*
Do. *hon.*	དགོངས་པ་	*gong-pa.*
Mushroom (two kinds)	དཀར་ཤ། སེར་ཤ་	*ka-sha ; se-sha.*
Musk	གླ་རྩི་	*la-tsi.*
Musk-deer	གླ་བ་	*la-wa.*
Do. the young one of a	གླ་ཕྲུག་	*la-thru.*
Musket	མེ་མདའ་	*men-da.*
Musket ball	རྡེའུ་	*di-u.*

Mussalman	ཁ་ཆེ་	*kha-chhe.*
Must, *v.i.*	དགོ་བ་ (དགོས་པ་)	*go-wa.*
Mustard	པེ་གང་	*pe-k̄ang.*
Muster, to, *v.i.*	འཚོགས་པ། འཛོམས་པ་	*tshok̄-pa ; dzom-pa.*
Do. *hon.*	ལྷན་རྒྱས་གནང་བ་	*hlen-gye nang-wa.*
Musty, to be	ཧམ་པ་རྒྱབ་པ་	*ham-pa gyap̄-pa.*
Mute, *s.* (dumb person)	ལྐུགས་པ་	*kuk̄-pa.*
Mute, to be (silent)	ཁ་ཁ་བསྡད་ (སྡོད་) པ་	*kha-kha de-pa.*
Do. *hon.*	ཞལ་རགས་བཞུགས་པ་	*sk̄e-ra sk̄u-pa.*
Mutton	ལུག་ཤ་	*luk̄-sha.*
My	ངའི་	*nge.*
Myrabolam	ཨ་རུ་	*a-ru.*
Myrrh	ཨ་ཀ་རུ་	*a-ka-ru.*
Myself	ང་རང་	*nga-rang.*
Mystified, to be	མགོ་འཐོམས་པ་	*go-thom-pa.*
Do. *hon.*	དབུ་འཐོམས་པ་གནང་བ་	*u-thom-pa nang-wa.*
Myth	སྒྲུང་	*drum.*

N

Nail	གཟེར་	*śer.*
Do. finger	ལག་པའི་སེན་མོ་	*lak̄-pe se-mo.*
Do. *hon.*	ཕྱག་སེན་	*chhak̄-se.*
Nail, toe	རྐང་པའི་སེན་མོ་	*kang-pe se-mo.*
Do. *hon.*	ཞབས་སེན་	*sk̄ap̄-se.*
Nail, iron	ལྕགས་གཟེར་	*chak̄-śer.*
Do. wooden	ཕུར་པ་	*phur-pa.*
Nail, to	ལྕགས་གཟེར་རྒྱབ་པ་	*chak̄-śer gyap̄-pa.*
Do. *hon.*	ལྕགས་གཟེར་སྐྱོན་པ་	*chak̄-śer kyöm-pa.*
Naked	དམར་ཧྲང་ང་	*mar-hrang-nga.*
Name	མིང་	*ming.*
Do. *hon.*	མཚན་	*tshen.*
Name, to	མིང་འདོགས་པ་	*ming dok̄-pa.*
Do. *hon.*	མཚན་འདོགས་པ་	*tshen dok̄-pa.*
Nap (sleep)	གཉིད་	*nyi.*
Do. *hon.*	མཉལ་ (མནལ་)	*nye.*
Napkin	པང་ཁེབས་	*pang-khep̄.*
Do. *hon.*	སྐུ་ཁེབས་	*ku-khep̄.*
Narrate, to	བཤད་པ་	*she-pa.*

Narrate, to, *hon.*	གསུང་བ་	*sung-wa.*
Narrative	རྒྱུ་རྐྱེན། ལོ་རྒྱུས་	*gyu-kyen ; lo-gyü.*
Narrow	དོག་པོ། སྦུགས་སྦུབ་དོག་པོ་	*ťoǩ-po ; bu-su ťoǩ-po.*
Nasty	སྐྱུག་བྲོ་པོ་	*kyuǩ-ťro-po.*
Nation	མི་བརྒྱུད། རིགས་བརྒྱུད་	*mi-gyü ; ri-gyü.*
Native land	སྐྱེ་ས་	*kye-sa.*
Do. *hon.*	འཁྲུངས་ས་	*thrung-sa.*
Nature (species)	བརྒྱུད་	*gyü.*
Do. of different	སྣ་ཚོགས་	*na-tsho.*
Naught (cipher)	ཀླད་སྐོར་	*le-kor.*
Naughty	ངན་པ་	*ngem-pa.*
Nauseating	སྐྱུག་བྲོ་པོ་	*kyuǩ-ťro-po.*
Navel	ལྟེ་ (ལྟེ་བ་)	*te.*
Near, *adj.*	ཉེ་པོ། ཐག་ཉེ་པོ། ཙར། འགྲམ་ལ་	*nye-po ; tha-nye-po ; tsa ; dram-la.*
Nearly (almost)	ཧ་ལམ། ག་ཆེན་	*ha-lam ; ǩa-chhen.*
Neat	འདྲ་ཆགས་པོ་	*dra-chhaǩ-po.*
Necessary	དགོས་པ་	*gö-pa.*
Necessity	དགོས་པ། མཁོ་ཆེ་	*gö-pa ; kho-chhe*
Neck	སྐེ་	*ke.*

Neck, *hon.*	མགུལ་	*gü.*
Neck, back of	མཇིང་པ་	*jing-pa.*
Do. *hon.*	མགུལ་མཇིང་	*gü-jing.*
Necklace	སྐེ་རྒྱན་	*ke-gyen.*
Do. *hon.*	མགུལ་རྒྱན་	*gü-gyen.*
Nectar	བདུད་རྩི་	*dü-tsi.*
Need, to (require)	དགོས་པ་	*gö-pa.*
Do. *hon.*	ཐུགས་དགོས་པ་	*thu-gö-pa.*
Need, *s.* (necessity)	དགོས་པ། མཁོ་ཆེ་	*gö-pa; kho-chhe.*
Needful	དགོས་པ་	*gö-pa.*
Needfulness	དགོས་པ། མཁོ་ཆེ་	*gö-pa; kho-chhe.*
Needle	ཁབ་	*khaṕ.*
Do. *hon.*	མགུལ་ཁབ་	*gü-khaṕ.*
Needle, eye of	ཁབ་མིག་	*khaṕ-mi.*
Do. *hon.*	མགུལ་ཁབ་མིག་	*gü-khaṕ-mi.*
Needle, point of	ཁབ་རྩེ་	*khaṕ-tse.*
Do. *hon.*	མགུལ་ཁབ་རྩེ་	*gü-khaṕ-tse.*
Needy (poor)	སྐྱོ་པོ། སྙེམས་ཆུང་ (ཉམས་ཆུང་)	*kyo-po; nyem-chhung.*
Nefarious	ངན་པོ་	*ngem-po*

Nefarious, *hon.*	ཐུགས་ངན་པོ་	*thu ngem-po.*
Negotiate, to	འགྲིག་ཆགས་བྱེད་པ་	*drik-chha che-pa.*
Do. *hon.*	འགྲིག་ཆགས་གནང་བ་	*drik-chha nang-wa.*
Negotiation	བཀའ་མོལ། འགྲིག་ཆགས་	*ka-mön ; drik-chha.*
Neigh, to	རྟ་སྐད་རྒྱབ་པ་	*ta-ke gyap-pa.*
Neighbour	ཁྱིམ་མཚེས་	*khyim-tshe.*
Neighbourhood	ཉེ་འཁོར་	*nye-khor.*
Nepal	བལ་ཡུལ་	*pe-yü.*
Nepalese	བལ་པོ་	*pe-po.*
Nephew	ཚ་བོ་	*tsha-wo.*
Nerve	ཆུ་རྒྱུས་	*chhu-gyü.*
Nest	ཚང་	*tshang.*
Net	རྒྱ། དྲ་བ་	*gya ; tra-a.*
Do. fish	ཉ་དོལ། ཉ་རྒྱ་	*nya-tö ; nya-gya.*
Nettle, *s.*	ཟྭ་པོ་	*sa-po.*
Nettle, to (irritate)	ཁོང་ཁྲོ་སློང་བ་	*khong-thro lang-wa.*
Do. *hon.*	དགོངས་པ་དཀྲུག་པ་	*gong-pa truk-pa.*
Neuralgia	ཡ་མ་	*ya-ma.*
Never	ཙ་ནས་...མ། མ་ནས་...མ་	*tsa-ne...ma ; ma-ne...ma.*
Never mind !	ཨའུ་ཙེ་	*a-u-tse.*

Nevertheless	ཡིན་ནས། ཡིན་ཀྱང་། ཡིན་ན་ཡང་	*yin-ne ; yin-kyang ; yin-na-yang.*
New	གསར་པ་	*sa-pa.*
New year	ལོ་གསར་	*lo-sa.*
News	གནས་ཚུལ། གསར་འགྱུར་	*ne-tshü ; sang-gyu.*
Newspaper	གསར་འགྱུར་ཤོག་གུ་	*sang-gyu shok-ku.*
Next (at the side of)	རྩར། འགྲམ་ལ་	*tsa ; dram-la.*
Next (afterwards)	གཤུག་ལ། རྗེས་ལ་	*sku-la ; je-la.*
Nice (accurate)	ཁྲིག་ཁྲིག། ཏེན་ཏེན་	*thrik-thrik ; ten-ten.*
Nice (in flavour)	ཞིམ་པོ་	*skim-po.*
Do. *hon.*	སྤྲོ་པོ་	*tro-po.*
Nice (pleasant)	དར་པོ། ཡག་པོ་	*tar-po ; yak-po.*
Nickname	མིང་འདོགས། མིང་ངན་	*ming-do ; ming-ngen.*
Niece	ཚ་མོ་	*tsha-mo.*
Niggardly	ལག་པ་དམ་པོ་	*lak-pa tam-po.*
Do. *hon.*	ཕྱག་དམ་པོ་	*chha tam-po.*
Nigh	ཉེ་པོ། ཐག་ཉེ་པོ། རྩར། འགྲམ་ལ་	*nye-po ; tha-nye-po ; tsa ; dram-la.*
Night	མཚན། དགོངས་མོ་	*tshen ; gong-mo.*
Night, last	མདང་དགོངས་	*dang-gong.*

Night, in the middle of the	ནམ་ནག་གུང་། མཚན་ནག་གུང་	*nam-na kung; tshen-na-kung.*
Night-attack, to make	མཚན་ཐིག་ (མཚན་ཧྲིབ་) རྒྱབ་པ་	*tshen-thi gyap-pa.*
Nimble	ཧུར་པོ། མགྱོགས་པོ་	*hur-po; gyok-po.*
Do. *hon.*	རྩོལ་པོ་	*tsö po.*
Nine	དགུ་	*gu.*
Nineteen	བཅུ་དགུ་	*chu-gu.*
Nineteenth	བཅུ་དགུ་པ་	*chu-gu-pa.*
Ninetieth	དགུ་བཅུ་པ་	*gup-chu-pa.*
Ninety	དགུ་བཅུ་ཐམ་པ་	*gup-chu tham-pa.*
Ninny	ལྐུགས་པ། གླེན་པ།	*kuk-pa; lem-pa.*
Ninth	དགུ་པ་	*gu-pa.*
Nipple (of breast)	འོ་མའི་རྩེ། ནུ་སོར་	*o-me-tse; nu-sor.*
Do. *hon.*	ཆབ་ཞོའི་རྩེ་	*chhap-shö-tse.*
Noble, *s.*	སྐུ་དྲག་	*ku-tra.*
Do. *adj.* (illustrious)	སྐད་གྲགས་ཆེན་པོ་	*ke-tra chhem-po.*
Do. *hon.*	མཚན་སྙན་གྲགས་ཆེན་པོ་	*tshen-nyen-tro chhem-po.*
Nobleman	སྐུ་དྲག་	*ku-tra.*
Nobody	སུ་ཡང་ w. neg.	*su-yang* (w. neg.)
Nod, to	མགོ་འཇོག་འཇོག་བྱེད་པ་	*go jok-jok che-pa.*

Nod, to, *hon.*	དབུ་འཇོག་འཇོག་གནང་བ་	*u jok̄-jok̄ nang-wa.*
Noise	ཨུར་སྒྲ་	*u-dra.*
Noise, to make a	ཨུར་སྒྲ་རྒྱབ་པ་	*u-dra gyap̄-pa.*
Do. *hon.*	ཨུར་སྒྲ་སྐྱོན་པ་	*u-dra kyöm-pa.*
Noisome	སྐྱུག་བྲོ་པོ་	*kyuk̄-t̄ro-po.*
Nomad	འབྲོག་པ་	*drok̄-pa.*
Nominate, to	སྐོ་བ་	*ko-wa.*
Do. *hon.*	སྐོ་བ་གནང་བ་	*ko-wa nang-wa.*
None (nobody)	སུ་ཡང་ w. neg.	*su-yang* (w. neg.)
Do. (nothing)	ག་གས་ (གང་ཡང་) w. neg.	*k̄a-k̄e* (w. neg.)
Nonsensical	དོན་མེད་	*tön-me.*
Nook	ཟུར་	*ṡur.*
Noon	ཉིན་གུང་	*nyin-k̄ung.*
Noose	ཞགས་པ་	*shk̄ak̄-pa.*
North	བྱང་	*ck̄ang.*
Northward	བྱང་ངོས། བྱང་ཕྱོགས་	*ck̄ang-ngö ; ck̄ang-chho.*
Nose	སྣ་ཁུག་ (སྣ་)	*na-khu.*
Do. *hon.*	ཤངས་	*shang.*
Nostril	སྣ་ཁུག་གི་ཨི་ཁང་ (སྣ་ཁུང་)	*na-khu-ki i-khang.*

Nostril, *hon.*	ཤངས་ཀྱི་ཨི་ཁང་ (ཤངས་ཁུང་)	*shang-kyi i-khang.*
Not	མ། མི་	*ma ; mi.*
Not at all	ཙ་ནས་ w. neg.	*tsa-ne* (w. neg.)
Notable (celebrated)	སྙན་གྲགས་ཆེན་པོ་	*nyen-ťra chhem-po.*
Do. *hon.*	མཚན་སྙན་གྲགས་ཆེན་པོ་	*tshen nyen-ťra chhem-po.*
Note, *s.* (letter)	ཡི་གེ་	*yi-ge.*
Do. *hon.*	ཕྱག་བྲིས་	*chha-ri.*
Note, *s.* (reputation)	སྐད་གྲགས་	*ke-ťra.*
Do. *hon.*	སྙན་གྲགས་	*nyen-ťra.*
Note, to (observe)	མིག་ལྟ་བ་	*miǩ-ta-wa*
Do. *hon.*	གཟིགས་པ་	*śi-pa.*
Noted	སྐད་གྲགས་ཆེན་པོ་	*ke-ťra chhem-po.*
Do. *hon.*	མཚན་སྙན་གྲགས་ཆེན་པོ་	*tshen-nyen-ťra chhem-po.*
Nothing	ག་གས་ (གང་ཡང་) w. neg.	*ǩa-ǩe* (w. neg.)
Notice	ལན་ (ལོན་)	*len.*
Notice, to (mention)	ལབ་པ་	*lap̌-pa.*
Do. *hon.*	གསུང་བ་	*sung-wa.*
Notice, to (see)	མིག་ལྟ་བ་	*miǩ-ta-wa.*
Do. *hon.*	གཟིགས་པ་	*śi-pa.*

Notification (of Government)	བཀའ་རྒྱ་	*ka-gya.*
Do. (of official)	བསྐུལ་གཏམ་	*kü-tam.*
Notion (opinion)	བསམ་པ་	*sam-pa.*
Do. *hon.*	ཐུགས་སེམས་	*thu-sem.*
Notorious	སྐད་གྲགས་ཆེན་པོ་	*ke-t́ra chhem-po.*
Notwithstanding	ཡིན་ནས། ཡིན་ཀྱང་། ཡིན་ན་ཡང་	*yin-ne ; yin-kyang ; yin-na-yang.*
Noun	མིང་སྒྲ་	*ming-dra.*
Nourish, to	གསོ་བ་	*so-wa.*
Do. *hon.*	གསོ་བ་གནང་བ་	*so-wa nang-wa.*
Novel (new)	གསར་པ་	*sa-pa.*
Novice, religious	དགེ་ཚུལ་	*ge-tshü.*
Now (at this time)	ད་ལྟ་	*t́an-da.*
Now (well, yes)	འོ་ན་	*o-na.*
Now-a-days	དེ་རིང་སང་། དེང་སང་	*t́e-ring-sang ; t́eng-sang.*
Now and then	མཚམས་མཚམས་	*tsham-tsham.*
Nowhere	ག་པ་...མ། ག་རེ་...མ་	*ḱa-pa...ma ; ḱa-re...ma.*
Noxious	སྐྱུག་བྲོ་པོ་	*kyuḱ-t́ro-po.*
Nude	དམར་ཧྲང་ང་	*mar-hrang-nga.*
Nullify, to	མེད་པར་བཟོ་བ་	*me-pa ś o-wa.*

Nullify, to, *hon.*	མེད་པར་བཟོ་བ་གནང་བ་	*me-pa śo-wa nang-wa.*
Number (numeral)	གྲངས་ཀ། ཨང་གི་	*t́rang-ka; ang-ki.*
Do. amount	མང་ཉུང་	*mang-nyung.*
Number, to	གྲངས་ཀ་རྒྱབ་པ་	*t́rang-ka gyap̈-pa.*
Do. *hon.*	ཕྱགས་གྲངས་སྐྱོན་པ་	*ja-t́rang kyöm-pa.*
Numberless	གྲངས་མེད་	*t́rang-me.*
Numerous	མང་པོ་	*mang-po.*
Numerous, very	གཡོ་མ་སུ་	*yo-ma-su.*
Nun	ཨ་ནི	*a-ni.*
Do. *hon.*	རྗེ་བཙུན་	*je-tsün.*
Nuptials	ཆང་ས་	*chhang-sa.*
Do. *hon.*	འཁྲུང་ས་	*thrung-sa.*
Nurse (of children)	དབུ་རྫི། བུ་རྫི་	*u-dzi; p̈u-dzi.*
Do. *hon.*	ཞལ་ལྟ་མ་	*sḱe-ta-ma.*
Nurture, to	གསོ་བ་	*so-wa.*
Do. *hon.*	གསོ་བ་གནང་བ་	*so-wa nang-wa.*
Nutmeg	ཛ་ཏི་	*dza-ti.*
Nutrition	ཁ་ལག། ལྟོ་	*kha-la; to.*
Do. *hon.*	ཞལ་ལག་	*sḱe-la.*

O

Oar	གྲུ་སྐྱ་	*ťru-kya.*
Oath	མནའ་	*na.*
Do. *hon.*	དབུ་མནའ་	*u-na.*
Oath, to take an	མནའ་སྐྱེལ་བ་	*na kyel-wa.*
Do. *hon.*	དབུ་མནའ་བཞེས་པ་	*u-na sǩe-pa.*
Obdurate, to be (hard-hearted)	སྙིང་རྗེ་མེད་པ་	*nying-je me-pa.*
Do. *hon.*	ཐུགས་རྗེ་མེད་པ་	*thuǩ-je me-pa.*
Obdurate, to be (obstinate)	གྱོང་པོ་	*ǩyong-po.*
Obedient	ཁ་ལ་ཉན་པོ་	*kha-la nyem-po.*
Do. *hon.*	ཞལ་ལ་གསན་པོ་	*sǩe-la sem-po.*
Obeisance, to make (by kneeling)	ཕྱག་འཚལ་བ་	*chha-tshe-wa.*
Do. *hon.*	སྐུ་ཕྱག་འཚལ་ལ་(བ་)གནང་བ་	*ku-chha tshe-la nang-wa.*
Obeisance, to make (by removing hat)	རྡབ་མཇལ་བྱེད་པ་	*ďam-jel cǩe-pa.*
Do. *hon.*	རྡབ་མཇལ་གནང་བ་	*dam-jel nang-wa.*
Obeisance, to make (by raising hand)	ཕྱག་འབུལ་ཞུ་བ་	*chham-bü sǩu-wa.*
Do. *hon.*	ཕྱག་འབུལ་ཞུ་བ་གནང་བ་	*chham-bü sǩu-a nang-wa.*
Obeisance, to make (by prostration)	ཕྱག་འཚལ་བ་	*chha-tshe-wa.*

Obeisance, to make (by prostration), *hon.*	སྐུ་ཕྱག་འཚལ་བ་	*ku-chha tshe-wa.*
Obese	ཤ་རྒྱགས་པ་	*sha-gyaḱ-pa.*
Do. *hon.*	སྐུ་ཤ་འབྱོར་པོ་	*ku-sha jor-po.*
Obey, to	ཁ་ལ་ཉན་པ་	*kha-la nyem-pa.*
Do. *hon.*	ཞལ་ལ་གསན་པ་	*sḱe-la sem-pa.*
Obey laws, to	ཁྲིམས་འཁྱེར་བ། ཁྲིམས་འཁུར་བ་	*thrim khyer-wa; thrim khur-wa.*
Object (intention)	དོན་དག་	*t́ön-t́a.*
Do. *hon.*	སྐུ་དོན་	*ku-t́ön.*
Object, to	བཀག་པ་ (འགེགས་པ་)	*kaḱ-pa.*
Do. *hon.*	བཀག་ག་ (འགེགས་པ་) གནང་བ་	*kaḱ-ḱa nang-wa.*
Obliged, to be (thankful)	དྲིན་དྲན་པ་	*t́rin t́rem-pa.*
Do. *hon.*	དྲིན་དྲན་པ་གནང་བ་	*t́rin t́rem-pa nang-wa.*
Do. *inf.* to *sup.*	བཀའ་དྲིན་དྲན་པ་	*ka-t́rin t́rem-pa.*
Obliging	དྲིན་ཆེན་པོ་	*t́rin chhem-po.*
Do. *hon.*	བཀའ་དྲིན་ཆེན་པོ་	*ka-t́rin chhem-po.*
Oblique	ཀྱོག་ཀྱོག་	*kyoḱ-kyo.*
Obliterate, to	སུབ་པ་	*suṕ-pa.*

Obliterate, to, ***hon.***	སྦུབ་པ་གནང་བ་	*suṕ-pa nang-wa.*
Obscure (dark)	ནག་པོ་	*naḱ-po.*
Do. (undefined)	ཧན་པོ་མེད་པ་	*tem-po me-pa.*
Obscurity (darkness)	མུན་ནག་	*min-na.*
Observe, to	མིག་ལྟ་བ་	*miḱ-ta-wa.*
Do. ***hon.***	གཟིགས་པ་	*śi-pa.*
Obstacle	བཀག་ཆ་	*kaḱ-chha.*
Obstinate	གྱོང་པོ་	*ḱyong-po.*
Obstruct, to	བཀག་པ་ (འགོགས་པ་)	*kaḱ pa.*
Do. ***hon.***	བཀག་ག་ (འགོགས་པ་) གནང་བ་	*kaḱ-ḱa nang-wa.*
Obtain, to	འབྱོར་བ། ཐོབ་པ་	*jor wa ; thoṕ-pa.*
Do. ***hon.***	ཕྱག་འབྱོར་ཡོང་བ་	*chhan-jor yong-wa.*
Obtuse (dull)	རྐུགས་པ། གླེན་པ་	*kuḱ-pa ; lem-pa.*
Occasion (cause)	རྐྱེན། རྒྱུ་རྐྱེན་	*kyen ; gyu-kyen.*
Do. (opportunity)	ཐབས་	*thaṕ.*
Do. (time)	དུས། དུས་ཚོད་	*ṫü ; ṫü-tshö.*
Occasionally	མཚམས་མཚམས་	*tsham-tsham.*
Do. ***hon.***	ཐུགས་སངས་ཐུགས་སངས་ལ་	*thuḱ-sang thuḱ-sang la.*
Occupation	ལས་ཀ་	*le-ka.*

Occupation, *hon.*	ཕྱག་ལས་	*chha-le.*
Occupied with work, to be	བྲེལ་བ་ཡོད་པ་	*ťre-wa yö-pa.*
Do. *hon.*	ཐུགས་བྲེལ་ཡོད་པ་	*thu-ťre yö-pa.*
Occur, to	ཡོང་བ་	*yong-wa.*
Ocean	རྒྱ་མཚོ་	*gyam-tsho.*
O'clock	ཆུ་ཚོད་	*chhu-tshö.*
Odd (not a pair)	ཡ་གཅིག་	*ya-chi.*
Odious	སྐྱུག་བྲོ་པོ་	*kyuǩ-ťro-po.*
Odour	དྲི་མ་	*ťri-ma.*
Odour, to have	དྲི་མ་ཁ་བ་	*ťri-ma kha-wa.*
Of, *post.*	གི། ཀྱི། གྱི་	*ǩi ; kyi ; ǩyi.*
Off, *adv.*	ནས་	*ne.*
Offal	བཙོག་པ་	*tsoǩ-pa.*
Offence (anger)	ཚིག་པ། ཁོང་ཁྲོ་	*tshiǩ-pa ; khong-thro.*
Do. (insult)	སྨོད་ར་	*me-ra.*
Do. (moral fault)	ཉེས་པ་	*nye-pa.*
Offence, to commit	ཉེས་པ་བསག་ (གསོག་) པ་	*nye-pa saǩ-pa.*
Do. *hon.*	སྐུ་སྡིག་བསག་ག་ (གསོག་པ་) གནང་བ་	*ku-di saǩ-ǩa-nang-wa.*
Offence, to give	ཁོང་ཁྲོ་སློང་བ་	*khong-thro lang-wa.*

Offence, to give, *hon.*	དགོངས་པ་དཀྲུག་པ་	*gong-pa truḱ-pa.*
Offence, to take	འཚེར་བ་	*tsher-wa.*
Do. *hon.*	ཐུགས་འཚེར་གནང་བ་	*thu-tsher nang-wa.*
Offend, to	དམའ་འབེབས་བྱེད་པ་	*mam-be cḱe-pa.*
Do. *hon.*	དམའ་འབེབས་གནང་བ་	*m̃am-be nang-wa.*
Offensive (disgusting)	སྐྱུག་བྲོ་པོ་	*kyuḱ-t́ro-po.*
Do. (insolent)	འཛིང་པ་སྦོམ་པོ། གྱོང་པོ་	*jing-pa bom-po; ḱyong-po.*
Offer, to	སྟེར་བ་	*ter-wa.*
Do. *hon.*	གནང་བ་	*nang-wa.*
Do. *inf.* to *sup.*	ཕུལ་བ་ (འབུལ་བ་)	*phü-wa.*
Offering (presents)	འབུལ་བ་	*bül-wa.*
Do. (sacrifice)	མཆོད་པ་	*chhö-pa.*
Office (employment)	ལས་ཀ་	*le-ka.*
Do. *hon.*	ཕྱག་ལས་	*chha-le.*
Office-room	ཡིག་ཚང་	*yiḱ-tshang.*
Officer	དཔོན་པོ་	*pöm-po.*
Official	དཔོན་པོ་	*pöm-po.*
Officiate, to	ལས་ཚབ་བྱེད་པ་	*le-tshaṕ cḱe-pa.*
Do. *hon.*	སྐུ་ཚབ་གནང་བ་	*ku-tshaṕ nang-wa.*
Offspring	ཕྲུ་གུ་	*pu-gu.*

Often	ཚར་མང་པོ་	*tshar mang-po.*
Oh !	ཨ་ཁ་ཁ་	*a-kha-kha.*
Oil	སྣུམ་	*num.*
Do. (kerosene)	ས་སྣུམ་	*sa-num.*
Ointment	བྱུགས་པ་	*chuk-pa.*
Old (of persons and animals)	རྒ་པུ་ (རྒན་པོ་)	*ga-pu.*
Old man	རྒ་པུ་ (རྒན་པོ་)	*ga-pu.*
Do. *hon.*	བགྲེས་པོ་	*dre-po.*
Old woman	རྒ་མུ་ (རྒན་མོ་)	*ga-mu.*
Do. *hon.*	བགྲེས་མོ་	*dre-mo.*
Old (of things)	རྙིང་པ་	*nying-pa.*
Old, to grow	རྒས་པ་	*ge-pa.*
Do. *hon.*	བགྲེས་པ་	*dre-pa.*
Omen	རྟེན་འབྲེལ་	*tem-dre.*
Omit, to	སྐུབ་པ་	*sup-pa.*
Do. *hon.*	སྐུབ་པ་གནང་བ་	*sup-pa nang-wa.*
On	སྒང་ལ། སྟེང་ལ་	*gang-la ; teng-la.*
Once	ཚར་གཅིག། ཐེངས་གཅིག་	*tshar-chi ; theng-chi.*
Once, at (immediately)	ལམ་སང་	*lam-sang.*

Once more	ད་འདོ་ (ད་འདོས་) ཚར་གཅིག། ད་རུང་ཚར་གཅིག་	*t́an-t́o tshar-chi ; t́a-rung tshar-chi.*
One	གཅིག་	*chi.*
One (in the sense of one full or complete)	གང་	*ḱang.*
One-eyed	ཞར་ར་ (ཞར་བ།) མིག་ཞར་	*sḱar-ra ; mik-sḱar.*
Onion	བཙོང་	*tsong.*
Only, *adj.* (alone)	གཅིག་པོ་	*chiḱ-po.*
Do. *adv.* (entirely)	ཤ་སྟག་	*sha-ta.*
Onward (forward)	སྔན་ལ་ (སྔོན་ལ་)	*ngen-la.*
Open, to	ཁ་ཕྱེས་ (འབྱེད་) པ་	*kha-chhe-pa.*
Do. *hon.*	ཁ་ཕྱེས་ (འབྱེད་) པ་གནང་བ་	*kha-chhe-pa nang wa.*
Open (frank)	དྲང་པོ་	*t́rang-po.*
Do. *hon.*	ཐུགས་རྒྱུ་དྲང་པོ་	*thu-gyu t́rang-po.*
Opening	ཨི་ཁུང་	*i-khung.*
Openly (frankly)	མ······གསང་བ་	*ma...sang-ẉa.*
Operation	ཁྲིས་བཤག་པ་	*t́ri-shaḱ-pa.*
Opinion	བསམ་པ་	*sam-pa.*
Do. *hon.*	ཐུགས་སེམས་	*thu-sem.*
Opium	གཡའ་ཕིན། *Ch.* ཉལ་ཐ་ཁ་	*ya-phin ; nye-tha-ḱha.*

Opponent	དགྲ་	*dra.*
Opportunity	ཐབས་	*thap.*
Oppose, to (dispute)	རྩོད་པ་རྒྱབ་པ་	*tsö-pa gyap-pa.*
Do. *hon.*	རྩོད་པ་སྐྱོན་པ་	*tsö-pa kyöm-pa.*
Oppose, to (thwart)	བཀག་པ་ (འགོགས་པ་)	*kak-pa.*
Do. *hon.*	བཀག་ཀ་ (འགོགས་པ་) གནང་བ་	*kak-ka nang-wa.*
Opposite (different)	མི་...གཅིག་པ་	*mi . chik-pa.*
Do. (facing)	ཁ་ཐུག་ལ་	*kha-thu-la.*
Opposite side	ཕར་ཕྱོགས་	*pha-chho.*
Oppress, to (press against)	གནན་པ་ (ནོན་པ་)	*nem-pa.*
Do. *hon.*	གནན་ (ནོན་) པ་གནང་བ་	*nem-pa nang-wa.*
Oppress, to (use severely)	སྡུག་པོ་བཏང་ (གཏོང་) བ། བཟོ་བལྟ་བཟོ་བ་	*duk-po tang-wa ; śop-ta śo-wa.*
Do. *hon.*	སྡུག་པོ་བཏོང་ང་ (བ་) གནང་བ་	*duk-po tong-nga nang wa.*
Opthalmia	མིག་ནད་	*mik-ne.*
Do. *hon.*	སྤྱན་སྙུང་བ་	*chen nyung-wa.*
Optical deception	མིག་འཁྲུལ་	*mik-thrü.*
Option	ཐང་	*thang.*
Opulent	ཕྱུག་པོ། ཅ་ (ཆ་) ལག་ཆེན་པོ་	*chhuk-po; cha-la chhem-po.*

Opulent, *hon.*	སྐུ་ཅས་ (ཆས་) ཆེན་པོ་	*ku-che chhem-po.*
Or	ཡང་མེན་ན། ཡང་ན་	*yang-men-na; yang-na.*
Oracle (prophecy)	ལུང་བསྟན་	*lung-ten.*
Do. *hon.*	བཀའ་ལུང་	*ka-lung.*
Oracle, to deliver (by beads or dice)	མོ་རྒྱབ་པ་	*mo gyap̄-pa.*
Do. *hon.*	ཕྱག་མོ་སྐྱོན་པ་	*chha-mo kyöm-pa.*
Oral	ཁའི་	*khe.*
Orally	ཁ་ནས་	*kha-ne.*
Orange	ཚ་ལུམ་མ་ (པ་)	*tsha-lum-ma.*
Orchard	ལྡུམ་ར་	*dum-ra.*
Order, *s.* (command)	བཀའ་	*ka.*
Order (rank)	གོ་ས། གོ་གནས། རིམ་པ་	*k̄o-sa ; k̄o-ne ; rim-pa.*
Order, written (of Government)	བཀའ་རྒྱ་	*ka-gya.*
Do. (of official)	བསྐུལ་གཏམ་	*kü-tam.*
Do. verbal (of official)	བཀའ་ཁྱབ། བཀའ་བཀོད་	*ka-khyap̄ ; ka-kö.*
Do. (written judgment in a judicial case).	བཅད་མཚམས། ཁྲ་མ་	*che-tsham ; thra-ma.*
Do. (series)	རིམ་པ་	*rim-pa.*
Do. (rank)	གྲལ་	*t̄re.*

Order, to	བཀའ་གནང་བ་	*ka-nang-wa.*
Order, to (things from shop, etc.)	མངག་པ་	*ngaḱ-pa.*
Do. *hon.*	བཀའ་མངག་གནང་བ་	*ka-nga nang-wa.*
Order to, in	དོན་ལ་	*t́ön-la.*
Ordinarily	ཕལ་ཆེར་	*phe-chher.*
Ordinary language, *opp.* to *hon.*	ཞེ་ས་མེད་པ་	*sḱe-sa me-pa.*
Ordinary (in quality)	དཀྱུས་མ་	*kyü-ma.*
Orifice	ཨི་ཁུང་	*i-khung.*
Origin	བྱུང་སྟངས་ (འབྱུང་ཁུང་)	*cḱung-tang.*
Ornament	རྒྱན་ཆ་	*gyen-chha.*
Do. *hon.*	སྐུ་རྒྱན་	*ku-gyen.*
Orphan	དྭ་ཕྲུག་	*t́a-thru.*
Orthography	དག་ཡིག་	*t́aḱ-yi.*
Ostentatious	ཉམས་དོད་པོ་	*nyam-t́ö-po.*
Do. *hon.*	སྐུ་ཉམས་དོད་པོ་	*ku-nyam t́ö-po.*
Other	གཞན་པ། ཡན་པ་	*sḱem-pa ; yem-pa.*
Otter	སྲམ་	*hram.*
Ought	དགོས་པ་	*gö-pa.*
Our	ང་ཚོའི་	*nga-tshö.*

Out (outside)	ཕྱི་ལོགས་ལ་	*chhi-lo-la.*
Out of	ནས་	*ne.*
Outcry	འུར་སྒྲ་	*u-dra.*
Outlet	སྒོ་	*go.*
Outside, *adv.*	ཕྱི་ལོགས་ལ་	*chhi-lo-la.*
Outward	ཕྱིའི་	*chhi-i.*
Oven	ཐབ་	*thap̍.*
Do. *hon.*	གསོལ་ཐབ་	*sö-thap̍.*
Over (above)	ཡ་གེའི་	*ya-k̇e.*
Do. (more)	ལྷག་	*hla.*
Overbear, to	རྒྱལ་བ། ཀླག་འཁས་པ་	*gye-wa ; la khe-pa.*
Do. *hon.*	རྒྱལ་ར་ (བ་) གནང་བ། ཀླག་འཁས་ར་ (པ་) གནང་བ་	*gye-ra nang-wa ; la khe-ra nang-wa.*
Overbearing	ཉམས་ཆེན་པོ། ཛ་ཁོག་ཆེན་པོ་	*nyam-chhem-po ; dza-kho chhem-po.*
Overcome, to	རྒྱལ་བ། ཀླག་འཁས་པ་	*gye-wa ; la khe-pa.*
Do. *hon.*	རྒྱལ་ར་ (བ་) གནང་བ། ཀླག་འཁས་ར་ (པ་) གནང་བ་	*gye-ra nang-wa ; la khe-ra nang-wa*

Overflow, to	ལྷུད་པ་	*lü-pa.*
Overpower, to	རྒྱལ་བ། ལྷག་འཁས་པ་	*gye-wa ; la khe-pa.*
Do *hon.*	རྒྱལ་ར་ (བ་) གནང་བ། ལྷག་འཁས་ར་ (པ་) གནང་བ་	*gye-ra nang-wa ; la khe-ra nang-wa.*
Overtake, to	རྗེས་ཟིན་པ་	*je-śim-pa.*
Do. *hon.*	རྗེས་ཟིན་པ་གནང་བ་	*je-śim-pa nang-wa.*
Do. *inf.* to *sup.*	ཕེབ་རྗེས་ཟིན་པ་	*phep-je śim-pa.*
Overthrow, to	རྒྱལ་བ་	*gye-wa.*
Do. *hon.*	རྒྱལ་ར་ (བ་) གནང་བ་	*gye-ra nang-wa.*
Overturn, to	མགོ་གཞུག་ལོག་པ། ཨ་ལོག་རྒྱབ་པ་	*go-sku lok-pa ; a-lo gyap-pa.*
Do. *hon.*	མགོ་གཞུག་ལོག་ག་ (པ་) གནང་བ། ཨ་ལོག་སྐྱོན་པ་	*go-sku lok-ka nang-wa ; a-lo kyöm-pa.*
Owe, to	བུ་ལོན་གཟུག་པ་	*pu-lön śuk-pa.*
Do. *hon.*	ཕྱག་བུན་གཟུག་པ་	*chha pün śuk-pa.*
Owl	འུག་པ་	*uk-pa.*
Own, *adj.*	རང་གི་	*rang-ki.*
Owner	བདག་པོ་	*dak-po.*
Ox	གླང་། གླང་གོག་	*lang ; lang-ko.*

P

Pace (stride)	གོམ་པ་	*ḱom-pa.*
Do. *hon.*	ཞབས་གོམ་	*sḱaṕ-ḱom.*
Paces (of a horse)	འགྲོས་	*drö.*
Do. *hon.*	ཆིབས་འགྲོས་	*chhiṕ-drö.*
Pack (load)	ཁལ་	*khe.*
Pack on, to (load)	བཀལ་བ་ (འགེལ་བ་)	*kel-wa.*
Do. *hon.*	བཀལ་ར་ (འགེལ་བ་) གནང་བ་	*ke ra nang-wa*
Pack-horse	ཁལ་རྟ་	*khe-ta.*
Pack-mule	ཁལ་དྲེ་	*khe-ťre.*
Pack-pony	ཁལ་རྟ་	*khe-ta.*
Pack-saddle	སྒ་	*ga.*
Packet of paper, large	ཤོག་སྒྲིལ་	*shoḱ-dri.*
Do. small	ཤོག་གུའི་ (ཤོག་བུའི་) ཆག་པ་	*shoḱ-kü chhuḱ-pa.*
Padlock	སྒོ་ལྕགས་	*gö-cha*
Do. *hon.*	གཟིམ་ལྕགས། ཕྱག་ལྕགས་	*sim-cha: chha-cha*
Pagan	ཕྱི་པ་	*chhi-pa.*
Page of book	ཤོག་ལེབ་	*shoḱ-le.*
Do. number of, in a book	ཤོག་གྲངས་	*shoḱ-ťrang.*
Do. (attendant)	གཡོག་པོ་	*yoḱ-po.*

Page (attendant), *hon.*	ཞབས་ཕྱི་	*sḱap-chhi.*
Pail (of wood)	ཟོ་ལག་	*śo-la.*
Do. (of iron)	ལྕགས་ཀྱི་ཟོ་ལག་	*cha-kyi śo-la.*
Pain, bodily	གཟུག་	*śu.*
Do. *hon.*	སྙུང་གཟུག་	*nyung-śu.*
Pain, mental	སྡུག་བསྔལ་	*dung-nge.*
Do. *hon.*	ཐུགས་འཁྲལ་	*thuḱ-thre.*
Pain (punishment by beating)	ཁྲིམས་	*thrim.*
Do. *hon.*	བཀའ་ཁྲིམས་	*ka-thrim.*
Pain (punishment by fine)	ཉེས་པ། ཆད་པ་	*nye-pa ; chhe-pa.*
Do. *hon.*	བཀའ་ཉེས། བཀའ་ཆད	*ka-nye ; ka-chhe.*
Painful	གཟུག་ཆེན་པོ་	*śuḱ-chhem-po.*
Painstaking	སྙིང་རུས་ཆེན་པོ་	*nying-rü chhem-po.*
Paint, *s.*	ཚོན་	*tshön.*
Paint, to (cover with colour)	ཚོན་བཏང་ (གཏོང་) བ་	*tshön tang-wa.*
Do. *hon.*	ཚོན་གཏོང་ང་ (བ་) གནང་བ་	*tshön tong-nga nang-wa.*
Paint, to (picture)	བྲིས་པ་ (འབྲི་བ་)	*t́ri-pa.*
Do. *hon.*	བྲིས་པ་ (འབྲི་བ་) གནང་བ་	*t́ri-pa nang-wa.*
Painter	ལྷ་བྲི་ (འབྲི་) པ་	*hlap-ri-pa.*

Painting	རི་མོ་	*ri-mo.*
Pair	ཆ་	*chha.*
Palace	ཕོ་བྲང་	*pho-t́rang.*
Palanquin	མགྱོགས་དཔྱང་ (འཁྱོགས་དཔྱང་)	*gyo-chang.*
Do. *hon.*	ཕེབ་དཔྱང་	*pheṕ-chang.*
Palate	དཀན་	*ken.*
Pale	དཀར་པོ་དཀར་ཀྱང་	*kar-po kar-kyang.*
Pallid	དཀར་པོ་དཀར་ཀྱང་	*kar-po kar-kyang.*
Palm (of hand)	ལག་མཐིལ་	*laḱ-thi.*
Do. *hon.*	ཕྱག་མཐིལ་	*chha-thi.*
Palsy	གྲུམ་བུ་ཆུ་སེལ་	*t́rum-ṕu chhu-se.*
Paltry	དོན་དག་ཆུང་ཆུང་	*t́ön-t́a chhung-chhung.*
Do. *hon.*	སྐུ་དོན་ཆུང་ཆུང་	*ku t́ön chhung-chhung.*
Pan	སླ་ང་	*la-nga.*
Pang, mental	སྡུག་བསྔལ་	*du-nge.*
Do. *hon.*	ཐུགས་འཁྲལ་	*thu-thre.*
Pang, physical	གཟུག་	*śu.*
Do. *hon.*	སྙུང་གཟུག་	*nyung-śu.*
Pankah	རླུང་ཡབ་	*lung-yaṕ.*

Pang (of grief)	སྡུག་བསྔལ་	*dung-nge.*
Pant, to (for breath)	དབུགས་བསགས་ (གསོག་) པ་	*u saḱ-pa.*
Do. *hon.*	ལྷུགས་དབུགས་བསགས་ག་ (གསོག་པ་) གནང་བ་	*ja-u saḱ-ḱa nang-wa.*
Pant, to (when the breath is taken away by cold water)	ངམ་པ་	*ngam-pa.*
Do. *hon.*	ངམ་པ་གནང་བ་	*ngam-pa nang-wa.*
Pantaloons	གོས་ཐུང་། དོར་མ་	*ḱo-thung ; t́or-ma.*
Do. *hon.*	ཞབས་དོར་	*sḱaṕ-t́o.*
Panther	གཟིག་	*śiḱ.*
Pantry	གཉེར་ཚང་	*nyer-tshang.*
Paper	ཤུ་གུ་ (ཤོག་བུ་)	*shu-gu.*
Do. *hon.*	ཕྱག་ཤོག་	*chha-sho.*
Parable	དཔེ། འདྲ་དཔེ་	*pe ; dra-pe.*
Paradise	བདེ་བ་ཅན་གྱི་ཞིང་ཁམས་	*de-wa-chen-kyi sḱing-kham.*
Parasol	ཉི་གདུགས་	*nyi-du.*
Do. *hon.*	དབུ་གདུགས་	*u-du.*
Parcel (round)	ཐུམ་དི་	*thum-ti.*
Parcel out, to	བགོད་པ། བགོ་བཤའ་རྒྱབ་པ་	*gö-pa ; goṕ-sha gyaṕ-pa.*

Parcel out, to, *hon.*	བགོད་པ་གནང་བ། བགོ་བ་ཤབ་སྐྱོན་པ་	*gö-pa nang-wa ; gop-sha kyöm-pa.*
Parched (dry)	སྐམ་པོ་	*kam-po.*
Pardon	དགོངས་པ་	*gong-pa.*
Pardon, to	དགོངས་པ་བཏང་ (གཏོང་) བ་	*gong-pa tang-wa.*
Do. *hon.*	དགོངས་པ་གཏོང་ང་ (བ་) གནང་བ་	*gong-pa tong nga nang-wa.*
Pardon, to ask	ཐུགས་དགོངས་དག་ཞུ་བ་	*thu-gong-t́a sḱu-wa.*
Pare, to	པགས་པ་ཤུ་བ་	*pak-pa shu-wa.*
Do. *hon.*	པགས་པ་ཤུ་བ་གནང་བ་	*pak-pa shu-wa nang-wa.*
Parents	ཕ་མ་	*pha-ma.*
Do. *hon.*	ཡབ་ཡུམ་	*yap-yum.*
Park	གླིང་ཀ་	*ling-ka.*
Parrot	ཨཙུ་ནེ་ཙོ། ནེ་ཙོ་	*a-u-nen tso ; nen-tso.*
Parsimonious	ལག་པ་དམ་པོ་	*lak-pa t́am-po.*
Do. *hon.*	ཕྱག་དམ་པོ་	*chha-t́am-po.*
Part	དུམ་བུ་	*t́um-ṕu.*
Do. (share)	སྐལ་ལ་ (སྐལ་བ་	*ke-la.*
Do. *hon.*	སྐུ་སྐལ་	*ku-ke.*
Part, to	ཁ་བྱེས་པ་ (འབྱེ་བ་)	*kha-kye-pa.*

Part, to, *hon.*	ཞལ་གྲེས་ར་ (འགྲེབ་) གནང་བ་	*sK̃e-K̃ye-ra nang-wa.*
Partial, to be (biassed)	ཉེ་རིང་བྱེད་པ་	*nye-ring-cK̃e-pa.*
Do. *hon.*	ཉེ་རིང་གནང་བ་	*nye-ring nang-wa.*
Particular (exact)	ཁྲིག་ཁྲིག། ཏེན་ཏེན་	*thrik̃-thrik̃ ; ten-ten.*
Particularly	ཁྱད་པར་དུ་	*khye-par-t̃u.*
Partly	དོག་ཙ་	*tok̃-tsa.*
Partner (in business)	ཚོང་རོགས་	*tshong-ro.*
Party (faction)	ཕྱོགས་	*chho.*
Do. (in lawsuit)	གྱོད་ཡ་	*k̃yo-ya.*
Pass, *s.* (over mountains)	ལ་	*la.*
Pass, to (go), *v.i.*	འགྲོ་བ་	*dro-wa.*
Do. *hon.*	ཕེབ་པ་	*phe-pa.*
Pass, to, *h. hon.*	འཆིབ་རྒྱུ་གནང་བ་	*chhip̃-gyu nang-wa.*
Pass the time, to	མགོ་འཁོར་བ་	*go-khor-wa.*
Do. *hon.*	དབུ་འཁོད་བ་	*u-khor-wa.*
Passenger (traveller)	འགྲུལ་པ་	*drü-pa.*
Passion (rage)	ཚིག་པ། ཁོང་ཁྲོ་	*tshik̃-pa ; khong-thro.*
Do. *hon.*	དགོངས་པ། རྣམ་མཁྱེན་	*gong-pa ; nam-khyen.*
Passion (lust)	འདོད་ཆགས་	*dö-chha.*

Passionate	རུ་ངར་པོ་	*ru-ngar-po.*
Passport	ལམ་ཡིག་	*lam-yi.*
Pastime (game)	རྩེད་མོ་	*tse-mo.*
Do. *hon.*	སྐུ་རྩེད་	*ku-tse.*
Pastry-puff	མོག་མོག་	*mo mo.*
Do. *hon.*	བཞེས་མོག་	*sḱe-mo.*
Patch, *s.*	ལྷན་པ་	*hlem-pa*
Patch, to	ལྷན་པ་རྒྱབ་པ་	*hlem-pa gyap̸ pa.*
Do. *hon.*	ལྷན་པ་སྐྱོན་པ་	*hlem-pa kyöm-pa.*
Path	ལམ་ཀ་	*lang-ka.*
Do. *hon.*	ཕེབ་ལམ་	*phep̸-lam.*
Path (by cliff)	ཕྲང་	*thrang.*
Patience (forbearance)	བཟོད་པ་	*śö-pa.*
Patient, to be (to endure)	བཟོད་པ་སྒོམ་པ་	*śö-pa gom pa.*
Do. *hon.*	བཟོད་པ་སྒོམ་པ་གནང་བ་	*śö-pa gom-pa nang-wa.*
Patiently, to wait	བསྒུགས་བསྡད་ (སྡོད་) པ་	*gu de-pa.*
Do. *hon.*	བསྒུགས་བཞུགས་པ་	*gu sḱuḱ-pa.*
Patron	མགོ་འདྲེན་གནང་མཁན་	*gön-dren nang-khen.*
Patronage	མགོ་འདྲེན་	*gön-dren.*
Patronize, to	མགོ་འདྲེན་གནང་བ་	*gön-dren nang-wa.*

Pattern	དཔེ་	*pe.*
Do. (sample)	སྤུས་ཚད་	*pü-tshe.*
Pauper	སྙེམས་ཆུང་། སྐྱོ་པོ་	*nyem chhung; kyo-po.*
Paw	སྡེར་མོ་	*der-mo.*
Pawn, to	གཏའ་མ་བཞག་ (འཛོག) པ་	*ta-ma sKak-pa.*
Do. *hon.*	གཏའ་མ་གཞོག་ག་ (འཛོག་པ་) གནང་བ་	*ta-ma sKok-Ka nang-wa.*
Pay	གླ། ཕོགས་	*la; pho.*
Do. *hon.*	གསོལ་ཕོགས་	*sö-pho.*
Pay, to	གླ་སྤྲད་པ། ཕོགས་སྤྲད་པ་	*la-tre-pa; pho-tre-pa.*
Do. *hon.*	གླ་གནང་བ། ཕོགས་གནང་བ་	*la nang-wa; pho nang-wa.*
Pay back, to	སྐྱིར་ཚབ་སྤྲད་པ་	*kyin tshap tre-pa.*
Do. *hon.*	སྐྱིར་ཚབ་གནང་བ་	*kyin-tshap nang-wa.*
Do. *inf.* to *sup.*	སྐྱིན་ཚབ་ཕུལ་ (འབུལ་) བ་	*kyin-tshap phü-wa.*
Pay taxes, to	ཁྲལ་འཇལ་བ་	*thre je-wa.*
Paymaster	ཕོགས་དཔོན་	*pho-pön.*
Pea	སྲན་མ་	*trem-ma.*
Peace	སྐྱིད་པོ། དུས་བདེ་པོ་	*kyi-po; tü de-po.*
Peaceable (condition of country)	ལྷིངས་ཆག་པོ། འཇམ་ཐིང་ཐིང་	*hling-chhak-po; jam-thing-thing.*

Peaceful (condition of country)	ཧླིངས་ཆག་པོ། འཇམ་ཐིང་ཐིང་	*hling-chhak-po; jam-thing-thing.*
Peach	ཁམ་བུ་	*kham-pu.*
Peacock	རྨ་བྱ་	*map-che.*
Peak (of mountain)	རྩེ་	*tse.*
Pear	སླི་	*li.*
Do. *hon.*	བཞེས་སླི་	*ske-li*
Pearl	མུ་ཏིག་	*mu-ti.*
Do. *hon.*	དབུ་ཏིག་	*u-ti.*
Peasant	སོ་ནམས་བྱེད་མཁན་	*so-nam che-khen.*
Pebble	རྡོ་ཧྲུག་	*do-hru.*
Peculiar	ཁྱད་མཚར་པོ། ཡ་མཚན་པོ་	*khye-tsha po; yam-tshem-po.*
Pedestrian	རྐང་ཐང་ང་ (པ་)	*kang-thang-nga.*
Peel, *s.*	པགས་པ་	*pak-pa.*
Peel, to	པགས་པ་ཤུ་བ་	*pak pa shu-wa.*
Do. *hon.*	པགས་པ་ཤུ་བ་གནང་བ་	*pak-pa shu wa nang-wa.*
Peg, iron	ལྕགས་ཕུར་	*cha-phu.*
Do. wooden	ཕུར་པ་	*phu pa.*
Pelt, to (stone)	གཀྲུ་བ་	*sku wa.*
Do. *hon.*	གཀྲུ་བ་གནང་བ་	*sku-wa nang-wa.*

Pen	སྨྱུ་གུ་	*nyu-ḱu.*
Do. *hon.*	ཕྱག་སྨྱུ་	*chha-nyu.*
Penalty	ཆད་པ། ཉེས་པ་	*chhe-pa ; nye-pa.*
Do. *hon.*	བཀའ་ཆད། བཀའ་ཉེས་	*ka chhe ; ka-nye.*
Pencil	སྨྱུ་གུ་	*nyu-ḱu.*
Do. *hon.*	ཕྱག་སྨྱུ་	*chha-nyu.*
Pending	མ་ཚར་བ་	*ma-tshar-wa.*
Penetrate, to (enter)	འཛུལ་བ་	*dzü-wa.*
Do. (pierce)	ཕིགས་པ་ (འབིགས་པ་)	*phi-pa.*
Do. *hon.*	འབིགས་ཀ་ (པ་) གནང་བ་	*bi-ḱa nang-wa.*
Penis	མཇེ། ཕོ་རྟགས་	*je ; pho-ta.*
Do. *hon.*	སོ་མཇེ་	*so je.*
Penurious	སྐྱོ་པོ། སྙེམས་ཆུང་ (ཉམས་ཆུང་)	*kyo-po ; nyem-chhung.*
People	མི་	*mi.*
Do. (nation)	མི་བརྒྱུད། རིགས་བརྒྱུད་	*mi-gyü ; ri-gyü*
Pepper	ཕོ་བ་རིལ་བུ་	*pho-wa ri-pu.*
Peradventure	གཅིག་བྱེད་ན་	*chiḱ-cḱe-na.*
Perceive, to (with the eye)	མཐོང་བ་	*thong-wa.*
Do. *hon.*	གཟིགས་པ་	*śi-pa.*

Perceive, to (understand)	ཤེས་པ། ཧ་གོ་བ་	*she-pa ; ha-ḱo-wa.*
Do. *hon.*	མཁྱེན་པ་	*khyem-pa.*
Do. *h. hon.*	དགོངས་པ་རྟོགས་པ་	*gong-pa toḱ-pa.*
Perfect (possessed of grace, glory, and wealth)	ཕུན་སུམ་ཚོགས་པ་	*phün-sum tshoḱ-pa.*
Perform, to	བྱེད་པ་	*cḱe-pa.*
Do. *hon.*	གནང་བ་	*nang-wa.*
Perfume	དྲི་མ་	*ťri-ma.*
Perhaps	གཅིག་བྱེད་ན་	*chiḱ-cḱe-na.*
Peril	ཉེན་ཁ་	*nyen-kha.*
Perilous	ཉེན་ཁ་ཆེན་པོ་	*nyen-kha chhem-po.*
Period	དུས། བསྐལ་པ་	*ťü, kel-pa.*
Perish, to	ཞི་བ་	*shi-wa.*
Do. *hon.*	གྲོངས་པ་ (འགྲོང་བ་)	*ťrong-pa.*
Do. *h. hon.*	བཞགས་པ་	*shaḱ-pa.*
Permission	དགོངས་པ་	*gong-pa.*
Permit, to	བཅུག་པ་ (འཇུག་པ་)	*chuḱ-pa.*
Do. *hon.*	བཅུག་ག་ (འཇུག་པ་) གནང་བ་	*chuḱ-ḱa nang-wa.*
Permitted, to be	ཆོག་པ་	*chhoḱ-pa.*
Perpetual	རྒྱུན་ཆད་རྒྱུ་མེད་པ་	*gyün-chhe-gyu me-pa.*

Perpetually	རྣམ་རྒྱུན། དུས་རྒྱུན	*nam-gyün ; tü-gyün.*
Perplexed, to be	མགོ་འཐོམས་པ་	*go-thom-pa.*
Do. *hon.*	དབུ་འཐོམས་པ་གནང་བ་	*u thom-pa nang-wa.*
Perplexing	མགོ་ཉོག་ཚ་པོ་	*go-nyo tsha-po.*
Perplexity	མགོ་ཉོག་	*go-nyo.*
Persecute, to	གནོད་པ་བྱེད་པ་	*nö-pa cḱe-pa.*
Do. *hou.*	གནོད་པ་གནང་བ་	*nö-pa nang wa.*
Persecution	གནོད་པ་	*nö-pa.*
Perseverance	སྙིང་རུས་	*nying-rü.*
Do. *hon.*	ཐུགས་རུས་	*thu-rü.*
Persevere, to	སྙིང་རུས་བྱེད་པ་	*nying-rü cḱe-pa.*
Do. *hon.*	ཐུགས་རུས་གནང་བ་	*thuḱ-rü nang-wa.*
Persia	ད་ཟིག་	*ta-śi.*
Persian	ད་ཟིག་པ་	*ta śiḱ-pa.*
Persist, to	ཨུ་ཚུགས་བྱེད་པ་	*u tshu cḱe-pa.*
Do. *hon.*	ཨུ་ཚུགས་གནང་བ་	*u-tshu nang-wa.*
Persistence	ཨུ་ཚུགས་	*u tshu.*
Person	མི་	*mi.*
Personally	རང་	*rang.*
Perspiration	རྔུལ་ནག་	*ngü-na.*

Perspire, to	རྔུལ་ནག་འཐོན་པ་	*ngü-na thöm-pa.*
Do. *hon.*	རྔུལ་ནག་འཐོན་པ་གནང་བ་	*ngü-na thöm-pa nang-wa.*
Persuade, to	བསླབ་བྱ་བྱེད་པ་	*laṕ-cḱa cḱe-pa.*
Do. *hon.*	བཀའ་སློབ་གནང་བ་	*ka-loṕ nang-wa.*
Peruse, to	ཀློག་པ་	*loḱ-pa.*
Do. *hon.*	ལྗགས་ཀློག་གནང་བ་	*ja-lo nang-wa.*
Perverse	གྱོང་པོ་	*ḱyong-po.*
Pessimistic, to be (hopeless)	རེ་བ་མེད་པ་	*re-wa me-pa.*
Do. *hon.*	ཐུགས་རེ་མེད་པ་	*thu-re me-pa.*
Pestle	ཡ་རྒྱག། གཏུན་རིལ་	*ya-gya; ting-ri.*
Pet, to	གཅེས་པོ་བྱེད་པ་	*che-po cḱe-pa.*
Do. *hon.*	གཅེས་པོ་གནང་བ་	*che-po nang-wa.*
Petition	སྙན་ཞུ་	*nye-sḱu.*
Petition, to	སྙན་ཞུ་ཞུ་བ་	*nye-sḱu sḱu-wa.*
Petroleum	ས་སྣུམ་	*sa-num.*
Petticoat	སྨད་གཡོགས་	*me-yo.*
Do. *hon.*	ཞབས་ཁྲིན་	*sḱaṕ-khyen.*
Petty (matter)	དོན་གནད་ཆུང་ཆུང་	*tön-ne chhung-chhung.*
Do. *hon.*	ཐུགས་དོན་ཆུང་ཆུང་	*thuḱ-tön chhung-chhung.*

Pewter	དིག་ཚ་	*tik-tsha.*
Phantom	གདོང་འདྲེ། འདྲེ་	*dong-dre ; dre.*
Pheasant, Blood	ཟྲེ་མོ་	*se-mo.*
Do. Monal	བྱ་མདངས་	*cKam-dang.*
Phlegm	ལུད་པ་	*lü-pa.*
Do. *hon.*	ལྗགས་ལུད་	*ja-lü.*
Photographic mount	པར་གྱི་རྒྱབ་ཤ་ཤོག་གུ་ (བུ་)	*par-kyi gyap-sha shok-ku.*
Phthisis	གཅོང་ནད་	*chong-ne.*
Physic	སྨན་	*men.*
Do. *hon.*	གསོལ་སྨན་	*sö-men.*
Physician	ཨེམ་ཆི་	*am-chhi.*
Do. *hon.*	ཨེམ་ཆི་ལགས་	*am-chhi-la.*
Pick, to (flowers, etc.)	གཏོག་པ་	*tok-pa.*
Do. *hon.*	གཏོག་ག་ (པ་) གནང་བ་	*tok-ka nang-wa.*
Pick, to (a quarrel)	སྙད་སྐོ་བ་	*nye-ko-wa.*
Do. (choose)	འདམ་པ་	*dam-pa.*
Do. *hon.*	འདམ་པ་གནང་བ་	*dam-pa nang-wa.*
Pick up, to	ཡར་སྒྲུག་པ། ཡར་ཁྱག་ (འཁྱགས་) པ་	*ya-druk-pa ; ya-khyak-pa.*

Pick up, to, *hon.*	ཡར་སྒྲུག་ག་ (པ་) གནང་བ། ཡར་ཁྱག་ག་ (འཁྱོགས་པ་) གནང་བ་	*ya-druk-ka nang-wa ; ya-khyak-ka nang·wa.*
Pictorial representation	རི་མོ་	*ri-mo.*
Picture	ཐང་ཀ་	*thang-ka.*
Do. *hon.*	ཞལ་ཐང་	*ske-thang.*
Piebald (horse)	རྟ་ཁྲ་	*tap-thra.*
Piece	རྡུམ་བུ་	*tum-pu.*
Do. (round in shape)	རྡོག་རྡོག་	*dok-do.*
Do. (roll of cotton cloth)	ཐ་ན་ *Hind.*	*tha-na.*
Do. (roll of silk)	ཡུག་	*yuk.*
Do. (roll of woollen cloth)	ཏྲུབས་	*pup.*
Pierce, to	ཕིགས་པ (འབིགས་པ་)	*phi-pa.*
Do. *hon.*	འབིགས་ག་ (པ་) གནང་བ་	*bi-ka nang-wa.*
Piety	ཆོས་སེམས། དགེ་སེམས་	*chhö-sem ; ge-sem.*
Pig	ཕག་པ་	*phak-pa.*
Pig-sty	ཕག་ཚང་	*phak-tshang.*
Pig-tail	ལྕང་ལོ་	*chang-lo.*
Do. *hon.*	དབུ་ལྕང་	*u-chang.*
Pigeon	ཨང་གུ། (ཕུག་རོན་)	*ang-ku.*

Pike (spear)	མདུང་	*dung.*
Do. *hon.*	ཕྱག་མདུང་	*chhan-dung.*
Pile, *s.*	སྤུང་	*pung.*
Pile, to	སྤུང་ནས་བཞག་ (འཇོག་) པ་	*pung-ne sḱak-pa.*
Do. *hon.*	སྤུང་ནས་གཞོག་ག་ (པ་) གནང་བ་	*pung-ne sḱok-ḱa nang-wa.*
Piles	གྲང་ཐོར་	*t́rang-thor.*
Pilgrim	གནས་སྐོར་ར་ (པ་)	*ne-kor-ra.*
Pilgrimage	གནས་སྐོར་	*ne-kor.*
Do. to go on	གནས་སྐོར་ལ་འགྲོ་བ་	*ne-kor-la dro-wa.*
Do. *hon.*	གནས་སྐོར་ལ་ཕེབ་པ་	*ne-kor-la phe-pa.*
Do. *h. hon.*	གནས་སྐོར་ལ་འཆིབ་རྒྱུ་ གནང་བ་	*ne-kor-la chhiṕ-gyu nang-wa.*
Pill	རིལ་བུ་	*ri-ṕu.*
Pillage, to (rob)	ཇག་པ་རྒྱབ་པ་	*cḱak-pa gyaṕ-pa.*
Pillar	ཀ་བ་	*ka-a.*
Pillow	སྔས། སྔས་འབོལ་	*nge ; ngem böl.*
Do. *hon.*	དབུ་སྔས་	*u-nge.*
Pimple	ཐོར་པ་	*thor-pa.*
Do. *hon.*	མགུལ་ཐོར་	*gü-thor.*

Pin	གཟེར་	*śer.*
Pincers	སྐམ་པ་	*kam-pa.*
Pinch, to	སེན་འཐོག་རྒྱབ་པ་	*sem-tho gyaṕ-pa.*
Do. *hon.*	སེན་འཐོག་སྐྱོན་པ་	*sem-tho kyöm-pa.*
Pinch, to (twisting the skin)	ཤ་བཙུས་ (འཛུས་) རྒྱབ་པ་	*shaṕ-chü gyaṕ-pa.*
Do. *hon.*	ཤ་བཙུས་ (འཛུས་) སྐྱོན་པ་	*shaṕ-chü kyöm-pa.*
Pine-tree (Pinus Excelsa)	ཐང་ཤིང་	*thang-shing.*
Pinnacle	ལྷ་བཙུགས། ཅོག་	*hla-tsuḱ ; cho.*
Pions	ཆོས་སེམས་ཆེན་པོ་	*chhö-sem chhem-po.*
Pipe (musical) instrument)	གླིང་བུ་	*ling-ṕu.*
Do. *hon.*	ཞལ་གླིང་	*she-ling.*
Pipe (tobacco)	གང་ཟག་	*ḱang-śa.*
Do. *hon.*	བཞེས་ཟག་	*sḱe-śa.*
Pistol	ཏྲོ་མདའ་	*trom-da.*
Pit	ས་དོང་། དོང་	*sa-ťong ; ťong.*
Pitch (of the voice)	གདངས་	*dang.*
Pitcher	ཆུ་སྣོད། ཆུ་བན་	*chhu-nö ; chhu-ṕen.*
Pitiless, to be	སྙིང་རྗེ་...མེད་པ་	*nying-je...me-pa.*
	བྱམས་སྙིང་རྗེ་...མེད་པ་	*cḱam-nying-je ...me pa.*
Do. *hon.*	ཐུགས་རྗེ་...མེད་པ་	*thuḱ-je...me-pa.*

Pity	སྙིང་རྗེ། བྱམས་སྙིང་རྗེ	*nying-je ; cKam-nying-je.*
Do. *hon.*	ཐུགས་རྗེ	*thuk-je.*
Place, *s.*	ས་ཆ	*sa-chha.*
Place, to	བཞག་པ (འཇོག་པ)	*sKak-pa.*
Do. *hon.*	གཞོག་ག (འཇོག་པ) གནང་བ	*sKok-Ka nang-wa.*
Place in, to	བཅུག་པ (འཇུག་པ)	*chuk-pa.*
Do. *hon.*	བཅུག་ག (འཇུག་པ) གནང་བ	*chuk-Ka nang-wa.*
Placenta	ཤ་མ	*sha-ma*
Plague	གཉན་ནད	*nyen-ne.*
Plain	ཐང	*thang.*
Plain, *adj.* (clear)	གསལ་པོ	*se-po.*
Do. (level)	སྙོམས་པོ	*nyom-po.*
Plaintiff	ཀྲུ་གཏུག་བྱེད་པོ	*sKu-tuK cKe-po.*
Do. *hon.*	ཀྲུ་གཏུག་གནང་མཁན	*sKu-tuK nang-khen.*
Plait (of hair)	ལྕང་ལོ	*chang-lo.*
Do. *hon.*	དབུ་ལྕང	*u-chang.*
Plan (pattern)	རི་མོ	*ri-mo.*
Do. (map)	ས་ཁྲ	*sap-thra.*
Do. (contrivance)	ཐབས	*thap.*
Plane	བྱུ་ལྷན	*bu-hlen.*

Plane, to	སྦུ་ལྷན་རྒྱབ་པ་	*bu-hlen gyap-pa.*
Do. *hon.*	སྦུ་ལྷན་སྐྱོན་པ་	*bu hlen kyöm-pa.*
Planet	གཟའ་	*śa.*
Plank	སྤང་ལེབ་	*pang-le.*
Plant, to	བཙུགས་པ་ (འཛུགས་པ་)	*tsuk-pa.*
Do. *hon.*	བཙུགས་ག་ (འཛུགས་པ་) གནང་བ་	*tsuk-ka nang-wa.*
Plantain	སྐྱེ་སྡོང་ *Sik.*	*kye-dong.*
Plat, to (weave)	འཐག་འཐག་པ་	*tha thak-pa.*
Do. *hon.*	འཐག་ཐག་ག་གནང་བ་	*tha thak-ka nang-wa.*
Plate	སྡེར་མ། ཐར་དཔག་	*der-ma ; tha-pa.*
Do. *hon.*	གསོལ་སྡེར་	*sö-der.*
Play	རྩེད་མོ་	*tse-mo.*
Do. *hon.*	སྐུ་རྩེད་	*ku-tse.*
Play, to	རྩེད་མོ་རྩེ་བ་	*tse mo tse-wa.*
Do. *hon.*	སྐུ་རྩེད་གནང་བ་	*ku-tse nang-wa.*
Play-fellow	རྩེད་རོགས་	*tse-ro.*
Do. *hon.*	སྐུ་རྩེད་གནང་རོགས་	*ku-tse nang-ro.*
Plea (controversy)	ལབ་གཞི། རྩོད་པ་	*lap-ski ; tsö-pa.*
Plead, to	ཞུ་བ་	*sku-wa.*

Plead, to, *hon.*	ཞུ་བ་གནང་བ་	*sḰu-wa nang-wa.*
Pleader	བར་མི་བྱེད་མཁན་	*ṕar-mi cḰe-khen.*
Do. *hon.*	བར་མི་གནང་མཁན་	*ṕar-mi nang-khen.*
Pleasant	སྐྱིད་པོ་	*kyi-po.*
Do. *hon.*	སྤྲོ་པོ་	*tro-po.*
Please, if you	རོགས་གནང་། རོགས་བྱེད་	*ro nang; ro-cḰe.*
Pleased, to be	དགའ་བ་	*ga-wa.*
Do. *hon.*	ཐུགས་མཉེས་པ་	*thu nye-pa.*
Do. *h. hon.*	ཐུགས་དགྱེས་པ་	*thu-gye-pa.*
Pleasure	དགའ་ཚོར་	*ga-tshor.*
Do. *hon.*	མཉེས་ཚོར་	*nye-tshor.*
Pledge	གཏའ་མ་	*ta-ma.*
Plenteous	འབེལ་པོ། ཛག་ཏོ་	*be-po; dzaḱ-ťo.*
Plentiful	འབེལ་པོ། ཛག་ཏོ་	*be-po; dzaḱ-ťo.*
Pliable	མཉེན་པོ་	*nyem-po.*
Pliant (flexible)	མཉེན་པོ་	*nyem-po.*
Plough, *s.*	གཤོལ་	*shö.*
Plough, to	རྨོན་པ་རྒྱབ་པ་	*möm-pa gyaṕ-pa.*
Ploughman	རྨོན་པ་རྒྱབ་མཁན། ཐོན་མཁན་ (ཐོང་པ་)	*möm-pa gyang-khen; thön-khen.*

Pluck, to (*e.g.* from tree)	གཏོག་པ་	*tok̓-pa.*
Do. *hon.*	གཏོག་ག་ (པ་) གནང་བ་	*tok̓-k̓a nang-wa.*
Plump	ཤ་རྒྱགས་པ་	*sha-gyak̓-pa.*
Do. *hon*	སྐུ་ཤ་འབྱོར་པོ་	*ku-sha jor-po.*
Plunder, to (by stealth)	རྐུ་བ་	*ku-wa.*
Do. (by highway robbery)	ཇག་པ་རྒྱབ་པ་	*ck̓ak̓-pa gyap̓ pa.*
Pneumonia	བད་ཁྲག་	*p̓e-thra.*
Pocket	ཨམ་ཕྲག་	*am-p̓a.*
Do. *hon.*	སྐུ་ཕྲག་	*kum-p̓a.*
Pock-mark	འབར་ཙག་	*bar-tsa.*
Pod	གང་བུ་	*k̓am-p̓u.*
Do. *hon.*	བཞེས་གང་	*sk̓e-k̓am.*
Poem	སྙན་ངག་	*nye-nga.*
Poet	སྙན་ངག་བྲིས་མཁན་	*nye-nga t̓ri-khen.*
Point (*e.g.*, of nail)	རྩེ་	*tse.*
Do. (of argument)	དོན་དག་	*t̓ön-t̓a.*
Do. *hon.*	སྐུ་དོན་	*ku-t̓ön.*
Point out, to (indicate)	མིག་སྟོན་པ་	*mi-töm-pa.*
Do. *hon.*	མིག་སྟོན་པ་གནང་བ་	*mi-töm-pa nang-wa.*

Point out, to (indicate) *inf.* to *sup.*	སྤྱན་ཕེབ་ཞུ་བ། སྤྱན་དར་ཞུ་བ་	*chem-phe sKu-wa ; chen-ťar sKu-wa.*
Poised evenly, to be	ཡང་ལྗི་མེད་པ་	*yang-ji me-pa.*
Poison	དུག་	*ťu.*
Do. *hon.*	གསོལ་དུག་	*sö-ťu.*
Policeman	སྐོར་ལྕག་པ་	*ko-chak-pa.*
Policy	ལུགས་སྲོལ་	*luk-sö.*
Polite language	ཞེ་ས་	*sKe-sa.*
Pollute, to	བཙོག་པ་བཟོ་བ་	*tsok-pa so-wa.*
Do. *hon.*	བཙོག་པ་བཟོ་བ་གནང་བ་	*tsok-pa so-wa nang-wa.*
Pollution	གྲིབ་	*ťrip.*
Do. *hon.*	སྐུ་གྲིབ་	*ku-ťrip.*
Pond	ཆུ་འཁྱིལ་	*chhu-khyil.*
Ponder, to	བསམ་བློ་བཏང་ (གཏོང་) བ་	*sam-lo tang-wa.*
Do *hon.*	ཐུགས་བསམ་བཞེས་པ་	*thu-sam sKe-pa.*
Ponderous (heavy)	ལྗི་པོ་	*ji-po.*
Pony	རྟ་	*ta.*
Do. *hon.*	ཆིབས་པ་	*chhik-pa.*
Pony, riding	ཞོན་རྟ་	*sKön-ta.*
Do. *hon.*	ཆིབས་པ་	*chhik-pa.*

Pony, riding (of very high official or lama)	ཆིབས་ཆེན་	*chhiṕ-chhen.*
Pony, pack	ཁལ་རྟ་	*khe-ta.*
Pool (small)	ཆུ་འཁྱིལ་	*chhu-khyil.*
Poor	སྐྱོ་པོ། སྙེམས་ཆུང་ (ཉམས་ཆུང་)	*kyo-po ; nyem-chhung.*
Poplar	སྦྱར་པ་	*ja-pa.*
Poppy	སྟོབས་ལྡན་མེ་ཏོག་	*tom-den me to.*
Population	མི་གྲངས་	*mi-ťrang.*
Porch	ཕྱི་སྒོ་	*chhi-go.*
Porcupine	གཟིག་མོ་	*śiḱ-mo.*
Pork	ཕག་ཤ་	*phaḱ-sha.*
Porridge	བག་ཐུག་	*ṕa-thu.*
Do. *hon.*	བཞེས་བག་བག་ཐུག་	*sḱe-ṕa ṕa-thu.*
Portent	རྟེན་འབྲེལ་	*tem-dre.*
Portion	སྐལ་ལ་ (སྐལ་བ་)	*ke-la.*
Do. *hon.*	སྐུ་སྐལ་	*ku-ke.*
Position (in society)	རྒྱུད་	*gyü.*
Positive	རྟེན་རྟེན་	*ten-ten.*
Possessor	བདག་པོ་	*daḱ-po.*

Possible, to be	ཐུབ་པ་	*thup-pa.*
Post (pillar)	ཀ་བ་	*ka-a.*
Post-office	ཡིག་ཁང་	*yik-khang.*
Posterior (anus)	ཀུབ་	*kup.*
Do. *hon.*	ཞབས་ཕོང་	*sKam-phong.*
Postpone, to (adjourn)	བཞག་པ་ (འཇོག་པ་)	*sKak-pa.*
Do. *hon.*	གཞོག་ག་ (འཇོག་པ་) གནང་བ་	*sKok-ka nang-wa.*
Posture	བཙབ་ (བཙ་)	*dap.*
Pot	ཁོག་མ་	*kho-ma.*
Do. earthen	རྫ་ཁོག་	*dza-kho.*
Do. flower	མེ་ཏོག་ཁོག་མ་	*me-to kho-ma.*
Potato	ཞོ་ཀོག་	*sKo-Ko.*
Do. (a sweet variety)	གྲོ་མ་	*tro-ma.*
Do. *hon.*	བཞེས་གྲོ་	*she-tro.*
Potency	དབང་	*wang.*
Do. *hon.*	སྐུ་དབང་	*ku-wang.*
Potter	རྫ་མཁན་	*dza-khen.*
Pouch (for tobacco)	ཐ་ཁུག་	*tha-khu.*
Do. *hon.*	བཞེས་ཁུག་	*sKe-khu.*

Pound, to (crush)	རྫོག་པ་	*dzok-pa.*
Do. *hon.*	རྫོག་ག་ (པ་) གནང་བ་	*dzok-ka nang-wa.*
Pour, to	བླུག་པ་	*luk-pa.*
Do. *hon.*	བླུག་ག་ (པ་) གནང་བ་	*luk-ka nang-wa.*
Powder	ཕྱེ་མ་	*chhe-ma.*
Do. gun	རྫས་	*dze.*
Power (official)	དབང་	*wang.*
Do. *hon.*	སྐུ་དབང་	*ku-wang.*
Power (physical)	ཤེད་	*she.*
Do. *hon.*	སྐུ་ཤེད་	*ku-she.*
Powerful (officially)	དབང་ཆེན་པོ་	*wang chhem-po.*
Do. *hon.*	སྐུ་དབང་ཆེན་པོ་	*ku-wang chhem-po.*
Powerful (physically)	ཤེད་ཆེན་པོ་	*she chhem-po.*
Do. *hon.*	སྐུ་ཤེད་ཆེན་པོ་	*ku-she chhem-po.*
Practicable, to be	ཐུབ་པ་	*thup-pa.*
Practice (custom)	ལུགས་སྲོལ་	*luk-sö.*
Practise, to	སྦྱང་བ་	*jang-wa.*
Do. *hon.*	སྦྱང་ང་ (བ་) གནང་བ་	*jang-nga nang-wa.*
Praise, *s.*	སྟོད་ར་	*tö-ra.*
Praise, to	སྟོད་ར་བཏང་ (གཏོང་) བ་	*tö-ra tang-wa.*

Praise, to, *hon.*	སྟོད་ར་གཏོང་ང་ (བ་) གནང་བ་	*tö-ra tong-nga nang-wa.*
Do. *inf.* to *sup.*	སྟོད་ར་ཞུ་བ་	*tö-ra sKu-wa.*
Pray, to (request)	ཞུ་བ་	*sKu-wa.*
Do. *hon.*	ཞུ་བ་གནང་བ་	*sKu-wa nang-wa.*
Pray to deity, to (extempore prayer)	སྨོན་ལམ་བཏབ་ (འདེབས་) པ་	*mö-lam tap-pa.*
Do. *hon.*	ཐུགས་སྨོན་གནང་བ་	*thu-mön nang wa.*
Do. (written prayers)	ཁ་འདོན་བྱེད་པ་	*khan-dön cKe-pa.*
Do. *hon.*	ཞལ་འདོན་གནང་བ་	*sKen-dön nana-wa.*
Prayer (extempore)	སྨོན་ལམ་	*mö-lam.*
Do. *hon.*	ཐུགས་སྨོན་	*thu-mön.*
Prayer (written)	ཁ་འདོན་	*khan-dön.*
Do. *hon.*	ཞལ་འདོན་	*sKen-dön.*
Prayer-wheel	མ་ཎི། ལག་སྐོར་	*ma-ni ; la-kor.*
Do. *hon.*	ཕྱག་སྐོར་	*chha-kor.*
Preach, to	ཆོས་བཤད་པ་	*chhö she-pa.*
Do. *hon.*	བཀའ་ཆོས་གསུང་བ་	*ka-chhö sung-wa.*
Precede, to	སྔན་ (སྔོན་) ལ་འགྲོ་བ་	*ngen-la dro-wa.*
Do. *hon.*	སྔན་ (སྔོན་) ལ་ཕེབ་པ་	*ngen-la phe-pa.*

Precede, to, *h. hon.*	སྔན་ (སྔོན་) ལ་འཆིབ་རྒྱུ་ གནང་བ་	*ngen-la chhip-gyu nang-wa.*
Preceding	སྔོན་གྱི། དང་པོ་	*ngön-ḱyi ; t́ang-po.*
Precept (maxim)	གདམ་དཔེ་	*tam-pe.*
Precious	ཙ་ཆེན་པོ་	*tsa-chhem-po.*
Precipice	གཡང་	*yang.*
Precipitate (rash)	ཁ་མེད་མིག་མེད་	*kha-me mik-me.*
Precise	ཁྲིག་ཁྲིག། ཏེན་ཏེན་	*thrik-thrik ; ten-ten.*
Precisely	རང་	*rang.*
Preclude, to	བཀག་པ་ (འགོགས་པ་)	*kaḱ-pa.*
Do. *hon.*	བཀག་ག་ (འགོགས་པ་) གནང་བ་	*kaḱ-ḱa nang-wa.*
Predict, to	མངོན་ཤེས་བཤད་པ་	*ngön-she she-pa.*
Do. *hon.*	མངོན་མཁྱེན་གསུང་བ་	*ngön-khyen sung-wa.*
Prediction	ལུང་བསྟན་	*lung-ten.*
Do. *hon.*	བཀའ་ལུང་	*ka-lung.*
Prefix, *s.*	སྔོན་འཇུག་	*ngön-ju.*
Pregnant, to be	བུ་གུ་སྐྱེད་རྒྱུ་ཡོད་པ་	*pu-gu kye-gyu yö-pa.*
Do. *hon.*	ཨ་ལྭ་འཁྲུང་རྒྱུ་ཡོད་པ་	*a-wa thrung-gyu yö-pa.*
Prejudice	རྣམ་རྟོག་	*nam-to.*

Prepare, to	གྲལ་སྒྲིག་བྱེད་པ་	*t́ra-dri cḱe-pa.*
Do. *hon.*	གྲལ་སྒྲིག་གནང་བ་	*t́ra-dri nang-wa.*
Prerogative	ཐོབ་ཐང་	*thoṕ-thang.*
Presage, *s.*	རྟེན་འབྲེལ་	*tem dre.*
Presence of, in the	མདུན་ལ་	*dün-la.*
Do. *hon.*	སྐུ་མདུན་ལ་	*kun-dün-la.*
Present, *s.* (alms to poor)	སྦྱིན་པ་	*jim-pa.*
Do. (to lama)	འབུལ་བ་	*bül-wa.*
Do. (tip)	ཆང་རིན་	*chhang-rin.*
Do. *hon.*	གསོལ་རས། ཁྲུང་རིན་	*sö-re ; thrung-rin.*
Present, to	སྟེར་བ་	*ter-wa.*
Do. *hon.*	གནང་བ་	*nang-wa.*
Do. *inf.* to *sup.*	ཕུལ་བ་	*phü-wa.*
Do. *hon.*	འབུལ་ར་ (བ་) གནང་བ་	*bü-ra nang wa.*
Present, to be	བསྡད་ (སྡོད་) ཡོད་པ་	*de yö-pa.*
Do. *hon.*	བཞུགས་ཡོད་པ་	*sḱu yö-pa.*
Do. *h. hon.*	བཞུགས་གདན་འཛག་ཡོད་པ་	*sḱu-den-ja yö-pa.*
Present, at	ད་ལྟ་	*t́an-da.*
Presently (in a few minutes)	ཕྲིབ་ཙ་ (ཙམ་) གཅིག། མགྱོགས་པོ་	*hrip-tsa-chi ; gyok-po.*

Preserve, to (keep care of)	ཉར་བ་	*nyar-wa.*
Do. *hon.*	ཉར་ར་ (བ་) གནང་བ་	*nyar-ra nang-wa.*
Do. *h. hon.*	ཐུགས་ཅག་གནང་བ་	*thuk-cha nang-wa.*
Press, to (physically)	གནན་པ་ (གནོན་པ་)	*nem-pa.*
Do. *hon.*	གནན་ (གནོན་) པ་གནང་བ་	*nem-pa nang-wa.*
Press, to (insist)	ཨུ་ཚུགས་བྱེད་པ་	*u-tshu cke-pa.*
Do. *hon.*	ཨུ་ཚུགས་གནང་བ་	*u-tshu nang-wa.*
Pressing (work)	ཕྲལ་ཕྲལ་བྱེད་དགོས་ཡ་	*thre-thre cke gö-ya.*
Pretend, to	གྱོད་བཤད་པ་	*kyö she-pa.*
Do. *hon.*	གྱོད་གསུང་བ་	*kyö sung-wa.*
Pretty (of woman)	ཚར་པོ། མཛེས་པོ་	*tshar-po ; dze-po.*
Do. *hon.*	ཐུགས་ཚར་པོ་	*thu tshar-po.*
Pretty (of things)	སྙིང་རྗེ་པོ་	*nying-je-po.*
Prevail over, to (overcome)	རྒྱལ་བ། ལྷག་འཁས་པ་	*gye-wa ; la khe-pa.*
Do. *hon.*	རྒྱལ་ར་ (བ་) གནང་བ། ལྷག་འཁས་ར་ (པ་) གནང་བ་	*gye-ra nang-wa ; la khe-ra nang-wa.*
Prevent, to	བཀག་པ་ (འགེགས་པ་)	*kak-pa.*
Do. *hon.*	བཀག་ག་ (འགེགས་པ་) གནང་བ་	*kak-ka nang-wa.*

Previous	སྔོན་གྱི། དང་པོ་	*ngön-k̔yi ; t̔ang-po.*
Previously	སྔན་མ། སྔོན་ལ་	*ngen-ma ; ngen-la.*
Price	གོང་། རིན་	*k̔ong ; ring.*
Do. *hon.*	ཕྱག་གོང་	*ja-k̔ong.*
Prick, to	བཙུགས་པ་ (འཛུགས་པ་)	*tsuk̔-pa.*
Do. *hon.*	བཙུགས་ག་ (འཛུགས་པ་) གནང་བ་	*tsuk̔-k̔a nang-wa.*
Pride	ཉམས། ཛག་ཁོག་	*nyam ; dza-kho.*
Priest	བླ་མ་	*la-ma.*
Prince	རྒྱལ་སྲས་	*gye-se.*
Princess	རྒྱལ་པོའི་སྲས་མོ་	*gye-pö sé-mo.*
Principal	ཆེ་ཤོས་	*chhe-shö.*
Do. (of a loan)	མ་རྩ་	*ma-tsa.*
Principally	ཕལ་ཆེར་	*phe-chher.*
Principle (origin)	བྱུང་སྟངས་ (འབྱུང་ཁུང་)	*c̔hung-tang.*
Do. (cause)	རྐྱེན། རྒྱུ་རྐྱེན་	*kyen ; gyu-kyen.*
Do. (motive)	དོན་དག་	*t̔ön-t̔a.*
Do. *hon.*	སྐུ་དོན་	*ku-t̔ön.*
Print, to	པར་རྒྱབ་པ་	*par-gyap̔-pa.*
Do. *hon.*	སྐུ་པར་སྐྱོན་པ་	*ku-par kyöm-pa.*

Printed matter	པར་མ་	*par-ma.*
Printer	པར་པ་	*par-pa.*
Printer (cutter of types)	པར་རྐོད་ (རྐོ་) པ་	*par-kö-pa.*
Do. *hon.*	པར་དཔོན་	*par-pön.*
Printing-office	པར་ཁང་	*par-khang.*
Prior, *adj.*	སྔོན་གྱི། དང་པོ་	*ngön-kyi ; tang-po.*
Prison	བཙོན་ཁང་	*tsön-khang.*
Prisoner	བཙོན་པ་	*tsöm-pa.*
Private	གསང་བ་	*sang-wa.*
Private property, *hon.*	སྐུ་སྒེར་གྱི་སྐུ་ཆས་	*ku-ger-kyi ku-chhe.*
Privately	གསང་བ་བྱས་ནས་	*sang-wa che-ne.*
Do. *hon.*	གསང་བ་གནང་ནས་	*sang-wa nang-ne.*
Privilege (right)	ཐོབ་ཐང་	*thop-thang.*
Prize	གསོལ་རས་	*sö-re.*
Probably	གཅིག་བྱེད་ན་	*chik-che-na.*
Probationer (in monastery)	ཨེན་ཆུང་	*en-chhung.*
Proceed, to	འགྲོ་བ། ཕྱིན་པ་	*dro-wa ; chhim-pa.*
Do. *hon.*	ཕེབ་པ། ཐས་པ་	*phe-pa ; the-pa.*
Do. *h. hon.*	འཆིབ་རྒྱུ་གནང་བ་	*chhip-gyu nang-wa.*
Proclaim, to	སྒྲོག་པ་	*drok-pa.*

Proclaim, to, *hon.*	སྒྲོག་ཀ་ (པ་) གནང་བ་	*drok̄-k̄a nang wa.*
Proclamation (of Government)	བཀའ་རྒྱ་	*ka-gya.*
Do. (of official)	བསྐུལ་གཏམ་	*kü-tam.*
Procrastinating	ཉ་སི་དགུ་སི་	*nya-si-gu-si.*
Procreate, to	སྐྱེད་པ་	*kye-pa.*
Procure, to	འབྱོར་བ། ཐོབ་པ་	*jor-wa ; thop̄-pa.*
Do. *hon.*	ཕྱག་འབྱོར་ཡོང་བ་	*chhan-jor yong-wa.*
Prodigal (profuse)	འབེལ་པོ། ཛག་ཏོ་	*be-po ; dzak̄-t̄o.*
Prodigious	ཆེ་ཐག་ཆོད་	*chhe-thak̄-chhö.*
Prodigy	ཡ་མཚན་	*yam-tshen.*
Produce, to (bring)	འཁྱེར་ཡོང་བ་	*khyer-yong-wa.*
Do. *hon.*	བསྣམས་ (སྣོམས་) ཕེབ་པ་	*nam-phe-pa.*
Productive (of soil)	ལུད་ཆུ་འཛོམ་པོ་	*lü-chhu dzom-po.*
Profane	ཆོས་སེམས་མེད་པ་	*chhö-sem me-pa.*
Profession	ལས་ཀ་	*le-ka.*
Do. *hon.*	ཕྱག་ལས་	*chha-le.*
Professor	མཁན་པོ་	*khem-po.*
Profit	ཁེ་བཟང་	*khep-śang.*
Do. *hon.*	སྐུ་ཁེ་	*ku-khe.*
Profit, to make a	ཁེ་བཟང་ཟ་བ་	*khep̄-śang śa wa.*

Profit, to make a, *hon.*	སྐུ་ཁེ་བཞེས་པ་	*ku-khe sḱe-pa.*
Profitable, to be	ཕན་ཐོགས་པ་	*phen-thoḱ-pa.*
Do. *hon.*	ཐུགས་ཕན་གསོལ་བ་	*thu-phen söl-wa.*
Profound (deep)	གཏིང་རིང་པོ་	*ting-ring-po.*
Profuse	འབེལ་པོ། ཛག་ཏོ་	*be-po ; dzaḱ-t́o.*
Progeny	ཕྲུ་གུ་	*pu-gu.*
Prognostication	ལུང་བསྟན་	*lung-ten.*
Do. *hon.*	བཀའ་ལུང་	*ka-lung.*
Prohibit, to	བཀག་པ་ (འགེགས་པ་)	*kaḱ-pa.*
Do. *hon.*	བཀག་ག་ (འགེགས་པ་) གནང་བ་	*kaḱ-ka nang-ẇa.*
Prolific (of soil)	ལུད་ཆུ་འཛོམ་པོ་	*lü-chhu dzom-po.*
Prominent (eminent)	སྐད་གྲགས་ཆེན་པོ་	*ke-t́ra chhem-po.*
Do. *hon.*	སྙན་གྲགས་ཆེན་པོ་	*nyen-t́ra chhem-po.*
Promise, to	ཁས་བླང་བ་	*khe-lang-wa.*
Do. *hon.*	ཞལ་བཞེས་པ་	*sḱe-sḱe-pa.*
Promoted, to be	གོ་གནས་འཕར་བ་	*ḱo-ne phar-wa.*
Do. *hon.*	གོ་གནས་འཕར་ར་ (བ་) གནང་བ་	*ḱo-ne phar-ra nang-wa.*
Promptly	མགྱོགས་པོར་	*gyoḱ-po.*

Promptly, *hon.*	རྩོལ་པོར་	*tsö-po.*
Promulgate, to	སྒྲོག་པ་	*drok-pa.*
Do. *hon.*	སྒྲོག་ག་ (པ་) གནང་བ་	*drok-ka nang-wa.*
Pronunciation	ལབ་སྟངས། ཤོད་སྟངས་	*lap-tang ; shö-tang.*
Do. *hon.*	གསུང་སྟངས་	*sung-tang.*
Proof	རྟགས་	*ta.*
Prop, *s.*	ཀ་སྐྱོར་	*ka-kyor.*
Prop, to	སྐྱོར་བ་	*kyor-wa.*
Do. *hon.*	སྐྱོར་ར་ (བ་) གནང་བ་	*kyor-ra nang-wa.*
Proper (befitting)	འོས་པོ་	*ö po.*
Property (in land)	ས་ཆ་	*sa-chha.*
Do. (in goods)	ཆ་ལག་	*cha-la.*
Do. *hon.*	སྐུ་ཆས་	*ku-che.*
Prophecy	ལུང་བསྟན་	*lung-ten.*
Do. *hon.*	བཀའ་ལུང་	*ka-lung.*
Prophesy, to	མངོན་ཤེས་ཤེས་པ་	*ngön-she she-pa.*
Do. *hon.*	མངོན་མཁྱེན་མཁྱེན་པ་	*ngön-khyen khyem-pa.*
Propitious	རྟེན་འབྲེལ་ཡག་པོ་	*tem-dre yak-po.*
Proportion	ཚོད་	*tshö.*
Proprietor	བདག་པོ་	*dak-po.*

Prose	ལྷུག་མ་	*lhuk-ma.*
Prosperity (good fortune)	བསོ་བདེ་ (བསོད་བདེ།) བསོད་ནམས་	*so-de ; sö-nam.*
Do. *hon.*	སྐུ་བསོད་	*ku-sö.*
Prosperous	གཡང་ཆེན་པོ་	*yang-chhem-po.*
Prostrate oneself, to	ཕྱག་འཚལ་བ་	*chha-tshe-wa.*
Do. *hon.*	སྐུ་ཕྱག་འཚལ་ར་ (བ་) གནང་བ་	*ku-chha tshe-ra nang-wa.*
Prostitute	ཆལ་མོ། ཞང་ཚོང་མ་	*chhe-mo ; skang-tshong-ma.*
Protect, to	སྲུང་བ་	*sung-wa.*
Do *hon.*	སྲུང་ང་ (བ་) གནང་བ་	*sung-nga nang-wa.*
Protector	སྐྱབས་མགོན་	*kyam-gön.*
Protectorate (over a country)	སྐྱབས་ཁོངས་	*kyap-khong.*
Proud	ཉམས་ཆེན་པོ། ཛག་ཁོག་ཆེན་པོ་	*nyam-chhem-po ; dza-kho chhem-po.*
Prove, to (a case)	ར་འཕྲོད་པ་	*ra-thrö-pa.*
Do. *hon.*	ར་འཕྲོད་པ་གནང་བ་	*ra-thrö-pa nang-wa.*
Prove, to (test)	ཚོད་ལྟ་བ་	*tshö ta-wa.*
Do. *hon.*	ཚོད་གཟིགས་པ་	*tshö śi-pa.*

Proverb	གཏམ་དཔེ་	*tam-pe.*
Provide, to	སྒྲུབ་པ་	*drup-pa.*
Do. *hon.*	སྒྲུབ་པ་གནང་བ་	*drup-pa nang-wa.*
Province	ཞིང་ཆེན། ཁུལ་	*sKing-chhen ; khü.*
Provisions	ཁ་ལག། ལྟོ་	*kha-la ; to.*
Do. *hon.*	ཞལ་ལག་	*sKe-la.*
Provisions for journey	ལམ་ཆས་	*lam-chhe.*
Provoke, to (annoy)	ཁོང་ཁྲོ་སློང་བ་	*khong-thro lang-wa.*
Do. *hon.*	དགོངས་པ་དཀྲུག་པ་	*gong-pa truk-pa.*
Proximity	ཉེ་འཁོར་	*nye-khor.*
Proxy	ཚབ་	*tshap.*
Do. *hon.*	སྐུ་ཚབ་	*ku-tshap.*
Prudence (wisdom)	བློ་གྲོས་	*lo-trö.*
Prudent	མཁས་པོ་	*khe-po.*
Puddle (small pool)	ཆུ་འཁྱིལ་	*chhu-khyil.*
Puff (pastry)	མོག་མོག་	*mo-mo.*
Do. *hon.*	བཞེས་མོག་	*sKe-mo.*
Pull, to	འཐེན་པ་	*them-pa.*
Do. *hon.*	འཐེན་པ་གནང་བ་	*them-pa nang-wa.*
Pull, to (of horses)	ངར་པོ་བྱེད་པ་	*ngar-po cKe-pa.*

Pulling, *adj.* (of horses)	ངར་པོ་	*ngar-po.*
Pulse (of the body)	རྩ་	*tsa.*
Do. *hon.*	ཕྱག་རྩ་	*chha-tsa*
Punctually	ཏེན་ཏེན་བྱས་ནས། མ་འཁྱུག་པ་བྱས་ནས་	*ten-ten cḱe-ne; ma-chhuḱ-pa cḱe-ne.*
Do. *hon.*	ཏེན་ཏེན་གནང་ནས། མ་འཁྱུག་པ་གནང་ནས་	*ten-ten nang-ne; ma-chhuḱ-pa nang-ne.*
Pungent	ཁ་ཚ་པོ་	*kha-tsha-po.*
Do. *hon.*	ཞལ་ཚ་པོ་	*sḱe-tsha-po.*
Punish, to (by fine)	ཉེས་པ་བཏང་ (གཏོང་) བ་	*nye-pa tang-wa.*
Do. *hon.*	བཀའ་ཉེས་གནང་བ་	*ka-nye nang-wa.*
Punish, to (by beating)	ཁྲིམས་བཏང་ (གཏོང་) བ་	*thrim tang-wa.*
Do. *hon.*	བཀའ་ཁྲིམས་གནང་བ་	*ka-thrim nang-wa.*
Punishment (by fine)	ཉེས་པ། ཆད་པ	*nye-pa; chhe-pa.*
Do. *hon.*	བཀའ་ཉེས། བཀའ་ཆད་	*ka-nye; ka-chhe.*
Punishment (by beating)	ཁྲིམས་	*thrim.*
Do. *hon.*	བཀའ་ཁྲིམས་	*ka-thrim.*
Pupil	བསླབ་ཕྲུག	*laṕ-thru.*
Do. (monk)	དགེ་ཕྲུག་	*ge-thru.*
Puppy	ཨ་ཡོ་ (ཁྱི་ཕྲུག་)	*a-yo.*

Purchase, to	ཉོ་བ་	*nyo-wa.*
Do. *hon.*	གཟིགས་པ་	*śi-pa.*
Pure	གཙང་མ་	*tsang-ma.*
Purgative	འགྲིད་སྨན། བཤལ་སྨན་	*dri-men ; she-men.*
Purge, to	འགྲིན་པ། བཤལ་བ་	*drim-pa ; she-wa*
Do. *hon.*	འགྲིན་པ་གནང་བ། བཤལ་ར་ (བ་) གནང་བ་	*drim-pa nang-wa ; she-ra nang-wa.*
Purified	དག་པོ་	*ťaḱ-po.*
Purple	རྒུན་འབྲུམ་མདོག་	*gün-drum-do.*
Purport	དོན་དག་	*ťön-ťa.*
Do. *hon.*	སྐུ་དོན་	*ku-ťön.*
Purpose, *s.*	དོན་དག་	*ťön-ťa.*
Do. *hon.*	སྐུ་དོན་	*ku-ťön.*
Purpose, to	སེམས་ལ་བསམ་པ་	*sem-la sam-pa.*
Do. *hon.*	ཐུགས་ལ་དགོངས་པ་	*thuḱ-la gong-pa.*
Purr, to	ངུག་པ་རྒྱབ་པ་	*nguḱ-pa gyaṕ-pa.*
Purse	སྦ་ཁུག་ (སྦྲིད་ཁུག་)	*ba-khu.*
Do. *hon.*	ཕྱག་ཁུག་	*chha-khu.*
Pursue, to	གཞུག་དེད་ཕྱིན་པ་	*sḱuḱ-de chhim pa.*
Do. *hon.*	གཞུག་དེད་ཕེབ་པ་	*sḱuḱ-de phe-pa.*

Pus	རྣག་	*na.*
Do. *hon.*	སྐུ་རྣག་	*ku-na.*
Push, to	འབིད་ཀྱག་བཏང་ (གཏོང་) བ་	*be-kya tang-wa.*
Do. *hon.*	འབིད་ཀྱག་གཏོང་ང་ (བ་) གནང་བ་	*be-kya tong-nga nang-wa.*
Pustule	ཐོར་པ་	*thor-pa.*
Do. *hon.*	མགུལ་ཐོར་	*gü-thor.*
Put, to (place)	བཞག་པ་ (འཇོག་པ་)	*skak-pa.*
Do. *hon.*	བཞོག་ག་ (འཇོག་པ་) གནང་བ་	*skok-ka nang-wa.*
Put in, to	བཅུག་པ་ (འཇུག་པ་)	*chuk-pa.*
Do. *hon.*	འཇུག་ག་ (པ་) གནང་བ་	*juk-ka nang-wa.*
Put in order, to	སྒྲིག་པ་	*drik-pa.*
Do. *hon.*	སྒྲིག་ག་ (པ་) གནང་བ་	*drik-ka nang-wa.*
Put on, to (clothes)	གོན་པ་	*köm-pa.*
Do. *hon.*	བཞེས་པ་	*ske-pa.*
Put off, to (defer)	པ་རུ་བཞག་ (འཇོག་) པ་	*pa-ru skak-pa.*
Do. *hon.*	པ་རུ་གཞོག་ག་ (འཇོག་པ་) གནང་བ་	*pa-ru skok-ka nang-wa.*
Put off, to (divest)	ཕིས་པ་ (འབུད་པ་)	*pi-pa.*
Do. *hon.*	ཕིས་ (འབུད་) པ་གནང་བ་	*pi-pa nang-wa.*

Putrefy, to	རུལ་འགྲོ་བ་	*rü-dro-wa.*
Putrid, to be	རུལ་བ་	*rü-wa.*
Puzzled, to be	མགོ་འཐོམས་པ་	*go-thom-pa.*
Do. *hon.*	དབུ་འཐོམས་པ་གནང་བ་	*u-thom-pa nang-wa.*

Q

Quaint	ཡ་མཚན་པོ། ཁྱད་མཚར་པོ་	*yam-tshen-po; khye-tsha-po.*
Quake, to (shudder)	འདར་བ་	*dar-wa.*
Do. *hon.*	སྐུ་འདར་སྐྱོན་པ་	*kün-dar kyöm-pa.*
Qualified	འོས་པོ་	*ö-po.*
Quality	ཡག་ཉེས། སྤུས་ཁ་	*ya-nye; pü-kha.*
Quarrel	རྒྱབ་འདྲེ་	*gyam-dre.*
Do. *hon.*	གསུང་འཁྲུག་	*sung-thru.*
Quarrel, to	རྒྱབ་འདྲེ་རྒྱབ་པ་	*gyam-dre gyap-pa.*
Do. *hon.*	གསུང་འཁྲུག་སྐྱོན་པ་	*sung-thru kyöm-pa.*
Quarrel, to pick a	སྙད་སྐོ་བ་	*nye-ko-wa.*
Quarrelsome	རུ་ངར་པོ་	*ru-ngar-po.*
Queen	རྒྱལ་མོ་	*gye-mo.*
Queen-consort	རྒྱལ་པོའི་བཙུན་མོ་	*gye-pö tsö-mo.*
Queer	ཁྱད་མཚར་པོ་	*khye-tsha-po.*
Query, to (question)	དྲི་བ་ (འདྲི་བ་)	*ťri-wa.*
Do. *hon.*	བཀའ་འདྲི་གནང་བ་	*kan-dri nang-wa.*
Do. *inf.* to *sup.*	ཞུ་བ་	*sku-wa.*
Question, to	དྲི་བ་ (འདྲི་བ་)	*ťri-wa.*
Do. *hon.*	བཀའ་འདྲི་གནང་བ་	*kan-dri nang-wa.*

Queue (pig-tail)	ལྕང་ལོ་	*chang-lo.*
Do. *hon.*	དབུ་ལྕང་	*u-chang.*
Quick (rapid)	མགྱོགས་པོ་	*gyok-po.*
Do. *hon.*	རྩོལ་པོ་	*tsö-po.*
Quick (active)	ཧུར་པོ་	*hur-po.*
Do. (clever)	རིག་པ་ཆེན་པོ་	*rik-pa chhem-po.*
Do. *hon.*	ཐུགས་རིག་ཆེན་པོ་	*thu-rik chhem-po.*
Quick (irritable)	རུ་ངར་པོ་	*ru-ngar-po.*
Do. *hon.*	ཐུགས་རུ་ངར་པོ་	*thu-ru ngar-po.*
Quick (living)	གསོན་པོ་	*söm-po.*
Quickly (rapidly)	མགྱོགས་པོར་	*gyok-po.*
Do. *hon.*	རྩོལ་པོར་	*tsö-po.*
Quick-silver	དངུལ་ཆུ་	*ngü-chhu.*
Quiet (of persons)	ཁ་ཉུང་ཉུང་	*kha nyung-nyung.*
Do. *hon.*	ཞལ་ཉུང་ཉུང་	*ske nyung-nyung.*
Quiet (of places)	ཁ་གུ་སིམ་པོ་	*kha-ku sim-po.*
Do. (calm condition of country)	ལྷིང་ཆགས་པོ། འཇམ་ཐིང་ཐིང་	*hling-chhak-po ; jam-thing-thing.*
Do. (of horses)	ལྷིང་བུ་	*hling-pu.*
Quilt	ཉལ་གཟན་	*nye-sen.*

Quilt, *hon.*	གཟིམ་གཟན་	*śim-śen.*
Quill-pen	སྒྲོ་སྨྱུག་	*dro-nyu.*
Quit, to (depart)	འཐོན་པ། ཕྱིན་པ་	*thöm-pa ; chhim-pa.*
Do. *hon.*	ཕེབ་པ་	*phe-pa.*
Do. *h. hon.*	འཆིབ་རྒྱུ་གནང་བ་	*chhiṕ-gyu nang-wa.*
Quit, to (a country, etc.)	བཞག་ནས་ཡོང་བ་	*sḱa-ne yong-wa.*
Do. *hon.*	བཞག་ནས་ཕེབ་པ་	*sḱa-ne phe-pa.*
Do. *h. hon.*	བཞག་ནས་འཆིབ་རྒྱུ་གནང་བ་	*sḱa-ne chhiṕ-gyu nang-wa.*
Quite (used negatively)	བད་དེ། ཁྱོན་ནས་	*be-ťe ; khyön-ne.*
Quite so !	ད་ག་རང་རེད་	*ťa-ḱa-rang-re.*
Do. *hon.*	ལགས་ད་ག་རང་རེད་	*la ťa-ḱa-rang-re.*
Do. *h. hon.*	བཀའ་གནང་རང་རེད་	*ka-na-rang-re.*
Quiver, *s.*	མདའ་དོང་	*da-ťong.*
Quiver, to (of animate things)	འདར་བ་	*dar-wa.*
Do. *hon.*	སྐུ་འདར་སྐྱོན་པ་	*kün-dar kyöm-pa.*
Quiver, to (of inanimate things)	འཁྲུག་པ་	*thruḱ-pa.*
Quota	སྐལ་ལ་ (སྐལ་བ་)	*ke-la.*
Do. *hon.*	སྐུ་སྐལ་	*ku-ke.*

R

Rabbit	རི་གོང་ (རི་བོང་)	*ri-kong.*
Rabid	སྨྱོན་པ་	*nyöm-pa.*
Rabid, to be	སྨྱོ་བ་	*nyo-wa.*
Race, foot	མི་རྒྱུག་	*mi-gyu.*
Do. horse	རྟ་རྒྱུག་	*ta-gyu.*
Race (tribe)	མི་བརྒྱུད། རིགས་བརྒྱུད་	*mi-gyü ; ri-gyü.*
Radiance	གཟི་བརྗིད། འོད་	*śi-ji ; ö.*
Radiant	གཟི་བརྗིད་ཆེན་པོ། འོད་ཆེན་པོ་	*śi-ji chhem-po ; ö chhem-po.*
Radish	ལ་ཕུག་	*la-phu.*
Do. *hon.*	བཞེས་ལབ་	*ske-lap.*
Rafter	ལྕམ་	*cham.*
Rag	ཨ་ཚོར་	*a-chho.*
Do. *hon.*	ཞལ་ཚོར་	*ske-chho.*
Rage	ཚིག་པ། ཁོང་ཁྲོ་	*tshik-pa ; khong-thro.*
Do. *hon.*	དགོངས་ཚུང་། རྣམ་མཁྱེན་	*gong-tshung ; nam-khyen.*
Ragged	བཙབ་རལ་ (རྡུལ་པོ་)	*tsap-re.*
Railing (fence)	ར་བ་	*ra-wa.*
Do. iron	ལྕགས་ཀྱི་ར་བ་	*cha-kyi ra-wa.*
Raiment	དུག་ལོ་	*tu-lo.*

Raiment, ***hon.***	ན་བཟའ་	*nam-śa.*
Rain	ཆར་པ་	*chhar-pa.*
Do. ***hon.***	སྐུ་ཆར་	*sk̄u-chhar.*
Rain, light shower of	སྦྲིན་ཆར་	*tring-chhar.*
Do. mixed with hail	དྲག་ཆར་	*t́rak̄-chhar.*
Rain, to	ཆར་པ་བཏང་ (གཏོང་) བ་	*chhar-pa tang-wa.*
Do. ***hon.***	སྐུ་ཆར་བཏང་ (གཏོང་) བ་	*sk̄u-chhar tang-wa.*
Rain heavily, to	ཆར་པ་ཞེ་སྐྲག་རྒྱབ་པ་	*chhar-pa sk̄e-tra gyap̄-pa.*
Rainbow	འཇའ་	*ja.*
Raise up, to	ཡར་ཀྱག་ (འཁྱོག་) པ། ཡར་ལེན་པ་	*yar-kyak̄-pa; yar-lem-pa.*
Do. ***hon.***	ཡར་ཀྱག་ག་ (འཁྱོག་པ་) གནང་བ་	*yar-kyak̄-ka nang-wa.*
Raisin	རྒྱུན་འབྲུམ་དཀར་པོ་	*gün-drum ka-po*
Rake	རྒྱ་གཟེབ་	*gya-śep̄.*
Ram	ལུག་ཕོ་	*luk̄-pho.*
Ramble, to	ཆམ་ཆམ་ (འཁྲམས་ འཁྲམས་) བྱེད་པ་	*chham-chham ck̄e-pa.*
Do. ***hon.***	སྐུ་ཆམ་ (འཁྲམས་) གནང་བ་	*kün-chham nang-wa.*
Ramrod of gun	སིན་འབིད་	*sim-bi.*

Rancid	ཁ་རྩུབ་པོ་	*kha-tsup-po.*
Rancour	གནོད་སེམས་	*nö-sem.*
Range, to (rove over)	ཆམ་ཆམ་ (འཁྲམས་འཁྲམས་) ལ་འགྲོ་བ་	*chham-chham la dro-wa.*
Do. *hon.*	སྐུ་ཆམ་ (འཁྲམས་) ལ་ཕེབ་པ་	*kün-chham la phe-pa.*
Do. *h. hon.*	སྐུ་ཆམ་ (འཁྲམས་) ལ་འཆིབ་རྒྱུ་གནང་བ་	*kün-chham la chhip-gyu nang-wa.*
Rank (degree)	གོ་ས། གོ་གནས། རིམ་པ་	*ko-sa ; ko-ne ; rim-pa.*
Do. (row)	གྲལ་	*tre.*
Ransack, to	ཇག་པ་རྒྱབ་པ་	*chak-pa gyap-pa*
Ransom (for killing a man)	སྟོང་	*tong.*
Ransom, to	བླུ་བ་	*lu-wa.*
Do. *hon.*	བླུ་བ་གནང་བ་	*lu-wa nang-wa.*
Rap, *s.* (on door, etc.)	དག་དག་	*tak-tak.*
Rap, to	དག་དག་བཏང་ (གཏོང་) བ་	*tak-tak tang-wa.*
Do. *hon.*	དག་དག་གཏོང་ང་(བ་) གནང་བ་	*tak-tak tong-nga nang-wa.*
Rapacious	འདོད་པ་ཆེན་པོ། ཧམ་པ་ཚ་པོ་	*dö-pa chhem-po ; ham-pa tsha-po.*
Rapacity	ཧམ་པ་	*ham-pa.*
Rapid	མགྱོགས་པོ་	*gyok-po.*

Rapid, *hon.*	རྩོལ་པོ་	*tsö-po.*
Rare	དཀོན་པོ་	*köm-po.*
Rascal	བསྟན་བཞིག། འཛབ་ཆེན་	*ten-ski ; dzap-chhen.*
Rase, to	བཤིག་པ་ (འཇིག་པ་)	*shik-pa*
Do. *hon.*	བཤིག་ག་ (འཇིག་པ་) གནང་བ་	*shik-ka nang-wa*
Rash, *adj.*	ཁ་སྨེད་མིག་མེད་	*kha-me mik-me.*
Rat	ཙི་ཙི་ (ཙིག་གེ་)	*tsi-tsi.*
Rate (price)	གོང་	*kong.*
Do. *hon.*	ཕྱགས་གོང་	*ja-kong.*
Rate (tax)	ཁྲལ། འབབ་	*thre ; bap.*
Do. on land	ས་ཁྲལ་	*sa-thre.*
Ratify, to (confirm)	གཏན་ལྡན་བྱེད་པ་	*ten-den cke-pa.*
Do. *hon.*	གཏན་ལྡན་གནང་བ་	*ten-den nang-wa.*
Rattle, to, *v.t.*	དཀྲོག་དཀྲོག་བཏང་ (གཏོང་) བ་	*trok-tro tang-wa.*
Do. *hon.*	དཀྲོག་དཀྲོག་གཏོང་ང་ (བ་) གནང་བ་	*trok-tro tong-nga nang-wa.*
Ravage, to (rob)	ཇག་པ་རྒྱབ་པ་	*ckak-pa gyap-pa.*
Raven	ཕོ་རོག་	*pho-ro.*

Ravine	རོང་	*rong.*
Raw (uncooked)	རྗེན་པ་	*jem-pa.*
Do. (of weather)	གྲང་མོ། བསིལ་པོ་	*ťrang-mo ; si-po.*
Do. *hon.*	སྐུ་བསིལ་པོ་	*ku-si-po.*
Ray	འོད་གཟེར་	*ö-śer.*
Raze, to	བཤིག་པ་ (འཇིག་པ་)	*shiǩ-pa.*
Do. *hon.*	བཤིག་ག་ (འཇིག་པ་) གནང་བ་	*shiǩ-ǩa nang-wa.*
Razor	སྤྲ་གྲི་	*tra-ťri.*
Reach, to (by stretching hand, etc.)	སྙོབ་པ་	*nyop̌-pa.*
Do. *hon.*	སྙོབ་པ་གནང་བ་	*nyop̌-pa nang-wa.*
Reach, to (arrive at)	སླེབ་པ་	*lep̌-pa*
Do. *hon.*	ཕེབ་པ་	*p̌he-pa.*
Do. *h. hon.*	འཆིབ་སྒྱུ་གནང་བ་	*chhip̌-gyu nang-wa.*
Read, to	ཀློག་པ་	*loǩ-pa.*
Do. *hon.*	ཀློག་ག་ (པ་) གནང་བ་	*loǩ-ǩa nang-wa.*
Do. *h. hon.*	ལྗགས་ཀློག་གནང་བ་	*ja-lo nang-wa.*
Ready	གྲལ་སྒྲིག་	*ťra-dri.*
Ready, to make	གྲལ་སྒྲིག་བྱེད་པ་	*ťra-dri cǩe-pa.*

Ready, to make, *hon.*	གྲལ་སྒྲིག་གནང་བ་	*ťra-dri nang-wa.*
Real	ངོ་ཐོག། དངོས་ནས་	*ngo-tho ; ngö-ne.*
Do. (of price, etc.)	ཡང་ཏིག་	*yang-tiǩ.*
Realise, to (obtain)	འབྱོར་བ། ཐོབ་པ་	*jor-wa ; thop̌-pa.*
Do. *hon.*	ཕྱག་འབྱོར་ཡོང་བ་	*chhan-jor yong-wa.*
Realise, to (understand)	ཤེས་པ། ཧ་གོ་བ་	*she-pa ; ha-ǩo-wa.*
Do. *hon.*	མཁྱེན་པ་	*khyem-pa.*
Do. *h. hon.*	དགོངས་པ་རྟོགས་པ་	*gong-pa toǩ-pa.*
Really	ངེས་པར་། དངོས་ནས་དྲང་ནས་	*nge-par ; ngö-ne ťrang-ne.*
Realm (kingdom)	རྒྱལ་སྲིད་	*gye-si.*
Reap, to	རྔ་བ་	*nga-wa.*
Do. *hon.*	རྔས་པ་གནང་བ་	*nge-pa nang-wa.*
Reaper	རྔ་མཁན་	*nga-khen.*
Do. *hon.*	རྔ་བ་གནང་མཁན་	*nga-a nang-khen.*
Rear, in the	རྒྱབ་ལ་	*gyap̌-la.*
Reason (mind)	བློ། སེམས་	*lo ; sem.*
Do. *hon.*	ཐུགས་	*thu.*
Reason (purpose)	དོན་དག་	*ťon-ťa.*
Do. *hon.*	སྐུ་དོན་	*ku-ťön.*
Reason, to (argue)	རྩེ་རྒྱབ་པ་	*tse gyap̌-pa.*

Reason, to (argue), *hon.*	ཞལ་རྩེ་སྐྱོན་པ་	*sḱe-tse kyöm-pa.*
Reasoning	རྩོད་པ་	*tsö-pa.*
Rebel, to	སྡེ་འཁྲུག་པ་	*de-thruḱ-pa.*
Rebellion	སྡེ་འཁྲུག་	*de-thru.*
Rebuke, *s.*	གཤེ་གཤེ་	*she-she.*
Do. *hon.*	བཀའ་བཀྱོན་	*kaṕ-kyön.*
Rebuke, to	གཤེ་གཤེ་བཏང་ (གཏོང་) བ་	*she-she tang-wa.*
Do. *hon.*	བཀའ་བཀྱོན་གནང་བ་	*kaṕ-kyön nang-wa.*
Recede, to (retreat)	ཕྱིར་ལོག་རྒྱབ་པ་	*chhi-lo gyaṕ-pa.*
Do. *hon.*	ཕྱིར་ལོག་སྐྱོན་པ་	*chhi-lo kyöm-pa.*
Receipt	འཛིན་	*dzin.*
Do. *hon.*	ཕྱག་འཛིན་	*chhan-dzin.*
Receive, to	འབྱོར་བ། ཐོབ་པ་	*jor-wa; thoṕ-pa.*
Do. *hon.*	ཕྱག་འབྱོར་ཡོང་བ་	*chhan-jor yong-wa.*
Recent	གསར་པ་	*sa-pa.*
Recently	ཁ་སང་ནས་	*kha-sang-ne.*
Recite, to	ཆོས་ཀློག་པ་	*chhö loḱ-pa.*
Do. *hon.*	ཆོས་ཀློག་ག་ (པ་) གནང་བ་	*chhö loḱ-ka nang-wa.*
Reckless	ཁ་མེད་མིག་མེད་	*kha-me miḱ-me.*
Reckon, to	རྩིས་རྒྱབ་པ་	*tsi-gyaṕ-pa.*

Reckon, to, *hon.*	ཕྱག་རྩིས་སྐྱོན་པ་	*ja-tsi kyöm-pa.*
Reckoning	རྩིས་	*tsi.*
Do. *hon.*	ཕྱག་རྩིས་	*ja-tsi.*
Recline, to	ཉལ་ནས་བསྡད་ (སྡོད་) པ་	*nye-ne de-pa.*
Do. *hon.*	གཟིམ་ནས་བཞུགས་པ་	*śim-ne sḱu-pa.*
Recluse	སྒོམ་ཆེན་	*gom-chhen.*
Recognise, to (a person)	ངོ་ཤེས་པ་	*ngo-shem-pa.*
Do. *hon.*	ཐུགས་ངོ་མཁྱེན་པ།ཞལ་ཚོར་བ་	*thu-ngo khyem-pa; she-tsho-wa.*
Recollect, to	དྲན་གསོ་བ་	*ťren-so-wa.*
Do. *hon.*	ཐུགས་དྲན་གསོ་བ་གནང་བ་	*thu-tren so-wa nang-wa.*
Recollection	དྲན་པ་	*ťrem-pa.*
Do. *hon.*	ཐུགས་དྲན་	*thu-tren.*
Reconcile, to	ནང་སྒྲིག་བྱེད་པ་	*nang-dri cḱe-pa.*
Do. *hon.*	ནང་སྒྲིག་གནང་བ་	*nang-dri nang-wa.*
Reconciliation	ནང་སྒྲིག་	*nang-dri.*
Record	ཐོ་	*tho.*
Do. *hon.*	ཕྱག་ཐོ་	*chha-tho.*
Recover, to (health)	དྲག་པ་	*ťrak-pa.*
Do. *hon.*	སྐུ་དྲངས་པ་	*ku-ťang-pa.*

Recover, to (find)	རྙེད་པ་	*nye-pa.*
Do. *hon.*	རྙེད་པ་གནང་བ་	*nye-pa nang-wa.*
Recreation (game)	རྩེད་མོ་	*tse-mo.*
Do. *hon.*	སྐུ་རྩེད་	*ku-tse.*
Recreation, to have	ཐུགས་སྤྲོ་བཏང་ (གཏོང་) བ་	*thu-tro tang-wa.*
Do. *hon.*	ཐུགས་སྤྲོ་གཏོང་ང་ (བ་) གནང་བ་	*thu-tro tong-nga nang-wa.*
Rectify, to (correct)	ཞུ་དག་བྱེད་པ་	*sḱu-ťa cḱe-pa.*
Do. *hon.*	ཞུ་དག་གནང་བ་	*sḱu-ťa nang-wa.*
Red	དམར་པོ་	*ma-po.*
Redeem, to	བླུ་བ་	*lu-wa.*
Do. *hon.*	བླུ་བ་གནང་བ་	*lu-wa nang-wa.*
Redeemer	སྐྱབས་མགོན་	*kyam-gön.*
Redemption	ཐར་པ་	*thar-pa.*
Reduce in number, to	ཉུང་རུ་ (དུ་) བཟོ་བ་	*nyung-ru śo-wa.*
Do. *hon.*	ཉུང་རུ་ (དུ་) བཟོ་བ་གནང་བ་	*nyung-ru śo-wa nang-wa.*
Reduce in price, to	གོང་བཅག་ (གཅོག་) པ་	*ḱong chaḱ-pa.*
Do. *hon.*	ཕྱགས་གོང་གཅོག་ག་ (པ་) གནང་བ་	*ja-ḱong choḱ-ḱa nang-wa.*
Reduce, to (conquer)	རྒྱལ་བ། ཀླག་འཁས་པ་	*gye-wa ; la khe-pa.*

Reduce, to (conquer), *hon.*	རྒྱལ་ར་ (བ་) གནང་བ། ཀླག་འཁམས་ར་ (པ་) གནང་བ་	*gye-ra nang-wa ; la khe-ra nang-wa.*
Reduce, to (degrade)	གོ་གནས་བབ་པ་	*ḱo-ne ṕaṕ-pa.*
Reed	སྨྱུག་མ་	*nyung-ma.*
Reel, to (stagger)	འཁྱོར་ནས་འགྲོ་བ་	*khyor-ne dro-wa.*
Do. *hon.*	སྐུ་འཁྱོར་ནས་ཕེབ་པ་	*ku-khyor-ne phe-pa.*
Do. *h. hon.*	སྐུ་འཁྱོར་ནས་འཆིབ་རྒྱུ་གནང་བ་	*ku-khyor-ne chhiṕ-gyu nang-wa.*
Reflect, to	བསམ་བློ་བཏང་ (གཏོང་) བ་	*sam-lo tang-wa.*
Do. *hon.*	ཐུགས་བསམ་བཞེས་པ་	*thu-sam sḱe-pa.*
Reform, to (amend)	བཟོ་སྐྱོར་བྱེད་པ་	*śo-kyor cḱe-pa.*
Do. *hon.*	བཟོ་སྐྱོར་གནང་བ་	*śo-kyor nang-wa.*
Refrain, to (forbear)	ཁོག་པ་བྱེད་པ་	*khoḱ-pa cḱe-pa.*
Do. *hon.*	ཐུགས་ཁོག་གནང་བ་	*thu-kho nang-wa*
Refuge (shelter)	སྐྱབས་གནས་	*kyam-ne.*
Refuse, to (withhold)	མི་...སྟེར་བ་	*mi...ter-wa.*
Do. *hon.*	མི་...གནང་བ་	*mi...nang-wa.*
Refuse, to (a request)	མི་...ཉན་པ་	*mi...nyem-pa.*
Do. *hon.*	མི་...གསན་པ་	*mi...śem-pa.*
Regard, to (look at)	ལྟ་བ་	*ta-wa.*

Regard, to (look at), *hon.*	གཟིགས་པ་	*si-pa.*
Regarding (concerning)	དོན་ལ། སྐོར་ལ་	*tön-la ; kor-la.*
Regent	རྒྱལ་ཚབ་	*gye-tshap̀.*
Regent of Tibet	བོད་རྒྱལ་པོ་	*ṕö-gye-po.*
Regiment	དམག་དཔུང་	*ma-pung.*
Region	ལུང་པ་	*lung-pa.*
Register, *s.*	ཐོ་	*tho.*
Do. *hon.*	ཕྱག་ཐོ་	*chha-tho.*
Register, to	ཐོ་འབྲིས་པ་ (འབྲི་པ་)	*tho-t́ri-pa.*
Do. *hon.*	ཕྱག་ཐོ་སྐྱོན་པ་	*chha-tho ḱyöm-pa.*
Regret, *s.* (heavy sorrow)	སྡུག་བསྔལ། སེམས་འཁྲལ་	*du-nge ; sem-thre.*
Do. *hon.*	ཐུགས་འཁྲལ་	*thuḱ-thre.*
Regret, *s.* (repentance)	འགྱོད་པ་	*gyö-pa.*
Do. *hon.*	ཐུགས་འགྱོད་	*thung-gyö.*
Regret, to, *v.i.* (heavy sorrow)	སྡུག་བསྔལ་བྱེད་པ། མྱ་ངན་བྱེད་པ་	*du-nge cḱe-pa ; nya-ngen cḱe-pa.*
Do. *hon.*	ཐུགས་ངན་གནང་བ་	*thu-ngen nang-wa.*
Regret, to, *v.i.* (in lesser matters)	སེམས་སྐྱོ་བ། སེམས་སྡུག་པ་	*sem-kyo-wa ; sem-duḱ-pa.*
Do. *hon.*	ཐུགས་སེམས་སྐྱོ་བ་གནང་བ་	*thu-sem kyo-wa nang-wa.*
Regulate, to (arrange)	སྒྲིག་པ་	*driḱ-pa.*

Regulate, to (arrange), *hon.*	གྲིག་ག་ (བ་) གནང་བ་	*drik-ka nang-wa.*
Regulation (law)	ཁྲིམས་	*thrim.*
Do. *hon.*	བཀའ་ཁྲིམས་	*ka-thrim.*
Regulation (religious)	ཆོས་ཁྲིམས་	*chhö-thrim.*
Reign, *s.*	རྒྱལ་སྲིད་	*gye-si.*
Reign, to	རྒྱལ་སྲིད་གནང་བ་	*gye-si nang-wa.*
Reinforcement	རྒྱབ་སྣོན་	*gyam-nön.*
Reins	སྲབ་ཐག་	*trap-tha.*
Reject, to	སྤང་བ་	*pang-wa.*
Do. *hon.*	སྤོང་ང་ (བ་) གནང་བ་	*pong-nga nang-wa.*
Rejoice, to	དགའ་བ་	*ga-wa.*
Do. *hon.*	མཉེས་པོ་གནང་བ་	*nye-po nang-wa.*
Do. *h. hon.*	ཐུགས་དགྱེས་པོ་གནང་བ་	*thu-gye-po nang-wa.*
Rejoicing, *s.*	དགའ་ཚོར་	*ga-tshor.*
Relate, to	བཤད་པ་	*she-pa.*
Do. *hon.*	གསུང་བ་	*sung-wa.*
Relation	ཉེ་བ་	*nye-wa.*
Do. *hon.*	སྐུ་གཉེན་	*ku-nyen.*
Relative, *s.*	ཉེ་བ་	*nye-wa.*
Do. *hon.*	སྐུ་གཉེན་	*ku-nyen.*

Relative to (concerning)	དོན་ལ། སྐོར་ལ་	*tön-la; kor-la.*
Release, to	ཐར་ར་ (བར་) བྱེད་པ། བཏང་བ་ (གཏོང་བ་)	*thar-ra cḱe-pa; tang-wa.*
Do. *hon.*	ཐར་ར་ (བར་) གནང་བ། གཏོང་ང་ (བ་) གནང་བ་	*thar-ra nang-wa; tong-nga nang-wa.*
Release, to (by ransom)	བླུ་བ་	*lu-wa.*
Do. *hon.*	བླུ་བ་གནང་བ་	*lu-wa nang-wa.*
Released, to be	ཐར་བ་	*thar-wa.*
Relentless, to be	སྙིང་རྗེ་མེད་པ་	*nying-je me-pa.*
Do. *hon.*	ཐུགས་རྗེ་མེད་པ་	*thuḱ-je me-pa.*
Reliable	བློས་ (བློ་) ཁེལ་བ་	*lö khe-wa.*
Do. *hon.*	ཐུགས་བློས་ཁེལ་བ་	*thu-lö khe-wa.*
Reliance	བློ་གཏད་	*lo-te.*
Relief (help)	རོགས་	*ro.*
Do. *hon.*	མགོ་འདྲེན་	*gön-dren.*
Relief (in coming troops)	རྗེས་ཚབ་	*je-tshaṕ.*
Relieve, to (help)	རོགས་བྱེད་པ་	*ro cḱe-pa.*
Do. *hon.*	མགོ་འདྲེན་གནང་བ་	*gön-dren nang-wa.*
Religion	ཆོས་	*chhö.*
Religion, to practise	ཆོས་བྱེད་པ་	*chhö cḱe-pa.*

Religion, to practise, *hon.*	སྐུ་ཆོས་གནང་བ་	*ku-chhö nang-wa.*
Religious	ཆོས་སེམས་ཆེན་པོ་	*chhö-sem chhem-po.*
Relinquish, to (abandon)	སྤང་བ་	*pang-wa.*
Do. *hon.*	སྤོང་ང་ (བ་) གནང་བ་	*pong-nga nang-wa.*
Relish, *s.* (taste)	བྲོ་བ་	*ťro-a.*
Do. *hon.*	ལྗགས་བྲོ་	*ja-ťro.*
Rely on, to	བློས་ (བློ་) བཀལ་བ་	*lö kel-wa.*
Do. *hon.*	ཐུགས་བློ་བཀལ་ར་ (བ་) གནང་བ་	*thu-lo ke-ra nang-wa.*
Remain, to	བསྡད་པ་ (སྡོད་པ་)	*de-pa.*
Do. *hon.*	བཞུགས་པ་	*sḱu-pa.*
Do. *h. hon.*	བཞུགས་གདན་འཛག་པ་	*sḱu-den jaḱ-pa.*
Remainder	ལྷག་མ་	*hla-ma.*
Remains (corpse)	རོ་	*ro.*
Do *hon.*	སྐུ་སྤུར། སྐུ་ཕུང་	*ku-pur ; ku-phung.*
Do. *hon.* (of lamas)	སྐུ་གདུང་	*ku-dung.*
Remarkable	ཁྱད་མཚར་པོ་	*khye-tsha-po.*
Remedy, to	བཅོས་ཐབས་བྱེད་པ་	*chö-thaṕ cḱe-pa.*
Do. *hon.*	བཅོས་ཐབས་གནང་བ་	*chö-thaṕ nang-wa.*
Remember, to	དྲན་གསོ་བ་	*ťren-so-wa.*

Remember, to, *hon.*	ཐུགས་དྲན་གསོ་བ་གནང་བ་	*thu-ťren so-wa nang-wa.*
Remembrance	དྲན་པ་	*ťrem-pa.*
Do. *hon.*	ཐུགས་དྲན་	*thu-ťren.*
Remind, to	དྲན་གསོས་བཏང་ (གཏོང་) བ་	*ťren-sö tang-wa.*
Do. *hon.*	དྲན་གསོས་གནང་བ་	*ťren-sö nang-wa.*
Do. *inf.* to *sup.*	བསྙིལ་གསོལ་ཞུ་བ་	*nye-sö sǩu-wa.*
Reminder	དྲན་གསོ་	*ťren-so.*
Do. *hon.*	བསྙིལ་གསོ་	*nye-so.*
Remorse (regret)	འགྱོད་པ་	*gyö-pa.*
Do. *hon.*	ཐུགས་འགྱོད་	*thung-gyö.*
Remorseless, to be (merciless)	སྙིང་རྗེ་མེད་པ་	*nying-je me-pa.*
Do. *hon.*	ཐུགས་རྗེ་མེད་པ་	*thuǩ-je me-pa.*
Remote	ཐག་རིང་པོ་	*tha-ring-po.*
Do. *hon.*	ཕེབ་ཐག་རིང་པོ་	*phep-tha-ring-po.*
Remove, to	ཕར་ཞིད་པ་	*pha shi-pa.*
Do. *hon.*	ཕར་ཞིད་པ་གནང་བ་	*pha shi-pa nang-wa.*
Remove, to (take off)	ཕྱིས་པ་ (འབུད་པ་)	*pi-pa.*
Do. *hon.*	བསིལ་ར་ (བ་) གནང་བ་	*si-ra nang-wa.*
Remuneration	རྔན་པ་	*ngem-pa.*
Rend, to	གཤག་པ་	*shaǩ-pa.*

Rend, to, *hon.*	གཤག་ག་ (པ་) གནང་བ་	*shak-ka nang-wa.*
Renounce, to (sins, certain kinds of foods, etc.)	སྤང་བ་	*pang-wa.*
Do. *hon.*	སྤོང་ང་ (བ་) གནང་བ་	*pong-nga nang-wa.*
Renown	སྐད་གྲགས་	*ke-tra.*
Do. *hon.*	སྙན་གྲགས་	*nyen-tra.*
Renowned	མིང་ཆེན་པོ་	*ming chhem-po.*
Do. *hon.*	མཚན་ཆེན་པོ་	*tshen chhem-po.*
Rent	སེར་ཀ་	*se-ka.*
Rent of a house	ཁང་གླ་	*khang-la.*
Do. *hon.*	གཟིམ་ཁང་གི་གླ་	*sim-khang ki-la.*
Rent, to (house)	ཁང་གླ་བྱས་ནས་བསྡད་ (སྡོད་) པ་	*khang-la che-ne de-pa.*
Do. *hon.*	ཁང་གླ་གནང་ནས་བཞུགས་པ་	*khang-la nang-ne sku-pa.*
Repair, to	གསོས་སྐྱོར་བྱེད་པ་	*sö-kyor che-pa.*
Do. *hon.*	གསོས་སྐྱོར་གནང་བ་	*sö-kyor nang-wa.*
Repair, to (a house)	ཞིག་གསོས་བྱེད་པ་	*shik-sö che-pa.*
Do. *hon.*	ཞིག་གསོས་གནང་བ་	*shik-sö nang-wa.*
Repast	ཁ་ལག། ཏོ་	*kha-la; to.*
Do. *hon.*	ཞལ་ལག་	*she-la.*

Repay, to	སྐྱིན་ཚབ་སྤྲོད་པ་	*khin-tshap̄ tre-pa.*
Do. *hon.*	སྐྱིན་ཚབ་གནང་བ་	*kyin-tshap̄ ṅang-wa.*
Do. *inf.* to *sup.*	སྐྱིན་ཚབ་ཕུལ་བ་	*kyin-tshap̄ phü-wa.*
Repeat, to (recite)	ཆོས་ཀློག་པ་	*chhö-lok̄-pa.*
Do. *hon.*	ཆོས་ཀློག་ཀ་ (པ་) གནང་བ་	*chhö-lok̄-k̄a nang-wa.*
Repent, to	འགྱོད་པ་སྐྱེད་པ་	*gyö-pa kye-pa.*
Do. *hon.*	ཐུགས་འགྱོད་གནང་བ་	*thung-gyö nang-wa.*
Repentance	འགྱོད་པ་	*gyö-pa.*
Do. *hon.*	ཐུགས་འགྱོད་	*thung-gyö.*
Reply, *s.*	ལན་	*len.*
Do. *hon.*	བཀའ་ལན་	*ka-len.*
Reply to a letter, *s.*	ཡིག་ལན་	*yik̄-len.*
Do. *hon.*	ཕྱག་བྲིས་བཀའ་ལན་	*chha-ri ka-len.*
Reply, to	ལན་རྒྱབ་པ་	*len gyap̄-pa.*
Do. *hon.*	ལྗགས་ལན་སྐྱོན་པ་	*ja-len kyöm-pa.*
Reply, to (letter)	ཡིག་ལན་བཏང་ (གཏོང་) བ་	*yik̄-len tang-wa.*
Do. *hon.*	ཕྱག་བྲིས་བཀའ་ལན་གནང་བ་	*chha-ri ka-len nang-wa.*
Report (rumour)	སྐད་ཆ། གཏམ་	*ke-chha ; tam.*
Report, to	སྙན་ཞུ་བཏང་ (གཏོང་) བ་	*nyen-šk̄u tang-wa.*
Do. *inf.* to *sup.*	སྙན་ཞུ་ཕུལ་ (འབུལ་) བ་	*nyen-šk̄u phü-wa.*

Report, to (after investigation), *inf.* to *sup.*	ཁྲ་མ་ཕུལ་ (འབུལ་) བ་	*thra-ma phü-wa.*
Do. *hon.*	ཁྲ་མ་འབུལ་ར་ (བ་) གནང་བ་	*thra-ma bü-ra nang-wa.*
Repository	བང་མཛོད་	*ṕang-dzö.*
Representative, *s.*	ཚབ། འཐུས་མི་	*tsh́aṕ ; thü-mi.*
Do. *hon.*	སྐུ་ཚབ་	*ku tshaṕ.*
Reprimand, *s.*	གཤེ་གཤེ་	*she-she.*
Do. *hon.*	བཀའ་བཀྱོན་	*kaṕ-kyön.*
Reprimand, to	གཤེ་གཤེ་བཏང་ (གཏོང་) བ་	*she-she tang-wa.*
Do. *hon.*	བཀའ་བཀྱོན་གནང་བ་	*kaṕ-kyön nang-wa.*
Reproduce, to (copy)	དཔེ་ཞུ་བ་	*pe-shu-wa.*
Do. *hon.*	དཔེ་ཞུ་བ་གནང་བ་	*pe-shu-wa nang-wa.*
Reproduce, to (imitate)	མིག་འདྲེན་བྱེད་པ་	*mik-dren ćhe-pa.*
Repulsive	སྐྱུག་བྲོ་པོ་	*kyuḱ-t́ro-po.*
Reprove, to	གཤེ་གཤེ་བཏང་ (གཏོང་) བ་	*she-she tang-wa.*
Do. *hon.*	བཀའ་བཀྱོན་གནང་བ་	*kaṕ-kyön nang-wa.*
Reputable	ཡ་རབས་	*ya-raṕ.*
Reputation (fame)	སྐད་གྲགས་	*ke-t́ra.*
Do. *hon.*	སྙན་གྲགས་	*nyen-t́ra.*
Repute, *s.*	སྐད་གྲགས་	*ke-t́ra.*

Repute, *s. hon.*	སྙན་གྲགས་	*nyen-ťra.*
Request, *s.*	ཞུ་བ་	*sǩu-wa.*
Request, to	ཞུ་བ་	*sǩu-wa.*
Do. *hon.*	ཞུ་བ་གནང་བ་	*sǩu-wa nang-wa.*
Require, to	དགོས་པ་	*gö-pa.*
Do. *hon.*	ཐུགས་དགོས་པ་	*thu-gö-pa.*
Requisite	དགོས་པ་	*gö-pa.*
Do. *hon.*	ཐུགས་ཁོ་	*thung-kho.*
Requite, to (revenge)	དགྲ་ལན་ལོག་པ་	*dra-len loǩ-pa.*
Do. *hon.*	དགྲ་ལན་ལོག་ག་ (པ་) གནང་བ་	*dra-len loǩ-ǩa nang-wa.*
Rescue, to	བསྐྱབས་པ་ (སྐྱོབ་པ།) སྐྱོང་བ་	*kyaṗ-pa; kyong-wa.*
Do. *hon.*	སྐྱབས་འཇུག་གནང་བ་	*kyam-juǩ nang-wa.*
Resent, to	འཚེར་བ་	*tsher-wa.*
Do. *hon.*	ཐུགས་འཚེར་གནང་བ་	*thu-tsher nang-wa.*
Resentment	ཚིག་པ།, ཁོང་ཁྲོ་	*tshiǩ-pa; khong-thro.*
Do. *hon.*	དགོངས་ཚུང་། རྣམ་མཁྱེན་	*gong-tshung; nam-khyen.*
Resentment, to cause	ཁོང་ཁྲོ་སློང་བ་	*khong-thro lang-wa.*
Do. *hon.*	དགོངས་པ་དཀྲུག་པ་	*gong-pa truǩ pa.*

Reside, to	བསྡད་པ་ (སྡོད་པ་)	*de-pa.*
Do. *hon.*	བཞུགས་པ་	*sḱu-pa.*
Do. *h. hon.*	བཞུགས་གདན་འཛག་པ་	*sḱu-den jaḱ-pa.*
Residence (house)	ཁང་པ། ནང་། སྡོད་ས་	*khang-pa; nang; dö-sa.*
Do. *hon.*	གཟིམ་ཁང་། བཞུགས་ས་	*śim-khang; sḱuḱ-sa.*
Do. *h. hon.*	གཟིམ་ཤག། བཞུགས་གདན་འཛག་ས་	*śim-sha; sḱu-den ja-sa.*
Resident	སྡོད་མཁན་	*dö-khen.*
Do. *hon.*	བཞུགས་མཁན་	*sḱu-khen.*
Do. *h. hon.*	བཞུགས་གདན་འཛག་མཁན་	*sḱu-den ja-khen.*
Residue	ལྷག་མ་	*hla-ma.*
Resistless, to be	བཀག་...མི་ཐུབ་པ་	*kaḱ...mi-thup-pa.*
Resolute	བརྟན་པོ་	*tem-po.*
Resolve, to (decide)	ཐག་བཅད་ (གཅོད་) པ་	*tha-che-pa.*
Do. *hon.*	ཐག་གཅོད་པ་གནང་བ་	*tha-chö-pa nang-wa.*
Do. *h. hon.*	ཐུགས་ཐག་གཅོད་པ་གནང་བ་	*thu-tha chö-pa nang-wa.*
Respect to, with	དོན་ལ། སྐོར་ལ་	*ṫön-la; kor-la.*
Respect (reverence)	བསྙེན་བཀུར་	*nyen-kur.*
Respect, to	བསྙེན་བཀུར་བྱེད་པ་	*nyen-kur cḱe-pa.*
Do. *inf.* to *sup.*	བསྙེན་བཀུར་ཞུ་བ་	*nyen-kur sḱu-wa.*

Respectable (socially)	ཡ་རབས་	*ya-rap.*
Respectful language	ཞེ་ས་	*sKe-sa.*
Respecting (concerning)	དོན་ལ། སྐོར་ལ་	*t́ön-la; kor-la.*
Respiration	དབུགས་	*u.*
Do. *hon.*	ལྗགས་དབུགས་	*ja-u.*
Resplendence	གཟི་བརྗིད་	*śi-ji.*
Resplendent	གཟི་བརྗིད་ཆེན་པོ། འོད་ཆེན་པོ་	*śi-ji chhem-po; ö chhem-po.*
Respond, to	ལན་རྒྱབ་པ་	*len gyap-pa.*
Do. *hon.*	ལྗགས་ལན་སྐྱོན་པ་	*ja-len kyöm-pa.*
Responsibility	ཁག། འགན་	*kha; gen.*
Do. *hon.*	ཐུགས་ཁག་	*thu-kha.*
Responsible, to become	ཁས་ཁྱག་ (ཁག་ཐེག་) པ་	*khe-khyaK-pa.*
Do. *hon.*	ཞལ་ཁྱག་ (ཐེག་) གནང་བ་	*sKe-khya nang-wa.*
Rest (for Tibetan gun)	མེ་མདའི་རུ་	*men-de ru.*
Do. *hon.*	ཕྱག་མདའི་རུ་	*chhan-de ru.*
Rest, to	ངལ་གསོ་བ་	*nge-so-wa.*
Do. *hon.*	སྐུ་ངལ་གསོ་བ་གནང་བ་	*ku-nge so-wa nang-wa.*
Rest, to (elbows on table, etc.)	སྦོ་སྙེ་རྒྱབ་པ་	*bo-nye gyap-pa.*
Do. *hon.*	སྐུ་སྙེ་སྐྱོན་པ་	*ku-nye kyöm-pa.*
Rest, to (lean back)	རྒྱབ་སྙེ་རྒྱབ་པ་	*gyam-nye gyap-pa.*

Rest, to (lean back), *hon.*	སྐུ་སྙེ་སྐྱོན་པ་	*ku-nye kyöm-pa.*
Rest, to (lie down)	ཉལ་བསྡད་ (སྡོད་) པ་	*nye-de-pa.*
Do. *hon.*	གཟིམ་བཞུགས་པ་	*śim-sḱu-pa.*
Restaurant	ཟ་ཁང་	*śa-khang.*
Restrain, to	བཀག་པ་ (འགེགས་པ་)	*kaḱ-pa.*
Do. *hon.*	བཀག་ག་ (འགེགས་པ་) གནང་བ་	*kaḱ-ḱa nang-wa.*
Result	སྙིང་པོ་	*nying-po.*
Retain, to	བཞག་པ་ (འཇོག་པ་)	*sḱaḱ-pa.*
Do. *hon.*	གཞོག་ག་ (འཇོག་པ་) གནང་བ་	*sḱoḱ-ḱa nang-wa.*
Retaliate, to	དགྲ་ལན་ལོག་པ་	*dra-len loḱ-pa.*
Do. *hon.*	དགྲ་ལན་ལོག་ག་ (པ་) གནང་བ་	*dra-len loḱ-ḱa nang-wa.*
Retaliation	དགྲ་ལན་	*dra-len.*
Retard to (obstruct)	བཀག་པ་ (འགེགས་པ་)	*kaḱ-pa.*
Do. *hon.*	བཀག་ག་ (འགེགས་པ་) གནང་བ་	*kaḱ-ḱa nang-wa.*
Retinue	འཁོར་གཡོག་	*khor-yo.*
Do. *hon.*	ཞབས་ཕྱི་	*sḱaṕ-chhi.*

Retire, to (retreat)	ཕྱིར་ལོག་རྒྱབ་པ་	*chhi-lo gyaṕ-pa.*
Do. *hon.*	ཕྱིར་ལོག་སྐྱོན་པ་	*chhi-lo kyöm-pa.*
Retreat, *s.* (shelter)	སྐྱབས་གནས་	*kyam-ne.*
Retreat, to	ཕྱིར་ལོག་རྒྱབ་པ་	*chhi-lo gyaṕ-pa.*
Do. *hon.*	ཕྱིར་ལོག་སྐྱོན་པ་	*chhi-lo kyöm-pa.*
Return, to	ལོག་པ་	*loḱ-pa.*
Do. *hon.*	ཚུར་ཕེབ་པ་	*tshur-phe-pa.*
Do. *h. hon.*	ཚུར་འཆིབ་རྒྱུ་གནང་བ་	*tshur-chhiṕ-gyu nang-wa.*
Return, to, *v.t.* (property committed to one's charge)	རྩིས་སྤྲོད་པ་	*tsi tre-pa.*
Do. *hon.*	ཕྱག་རྩིས་གནང་བ་	*ja-tsi nang-wa.*
Revenge, *s.*	དགྲ་ལན་	*dra-len.*
Revenge, to	དགྲ་ལན་ལོག་པ་	*dra-len loḱ-pa.*
Do. *hon.*	དགྲ་ལན་ལོག་ག་ (པ་) གནང་བ་	*dra-len loḱ-ka nang-wa.*
Revenue	ཁྲལ་དངུལ་	*thre-ngü.*
Revenue, government	གཞུང་གི་འབབ་	*sḱung-gi baṕ.*
Revere, to	བསྙེན་བཀུར་བྱེད་པ་	*nyen-kur cḱe-pa.*
Do. *inf.* to *sup.*	བསྙེན་བཀུར་ཞུ་བ་	*nyen-kur sḱu-wa.*
Reverence, *s.*	བསྙེན་བཀུར་	*nyen-kur.*

Reverence, to	བསྙེན་བཀུར་བྱེད་པ་	*nyen-kur ch̔e-pa.*
Do. *inf.* to *sup.*	བསྙེན་བཀུར་ཞུ་བ་	*nyen-kur sh̔u-wa.*
Reverend (title)	རྗེ་བཙུན་	*je-tsün.*
Reverse, to (turn up-side down)	མགོ་གཞུག་ལོག་པ། ཨ་ལོག་རྒྱབ་པ་	*go-sh̔u lok̔-pa ; a-lo gyap̔-pa.*
Do. *hon.*	མགོ་གཞུག་ལོག་ག་ (པ་) གནང་བ། ཨ་ལོག་སྐྱོན་པ་	*go-sh̔u lok̔-k̔a nang-wa; a-lo kyöm-pa.*
Reverse, to (turn back to front)	ཁ་ཕྱོགས་ལོག་པ་	*kha-chho lok̔-pa.*
Do. *hon.*	ཞལ་ཕྱོགས་ལོག་ག་ (པ་) གནང་བ་	*sh̔e-chho lok̔-k̔a nang-wa.*
Revile, to	སྨད་ར་བཏང་ (གཏོང་) བ་	*me-ra tang-wa.*
Do. *hon.*	སྨད་ར་གཏོང་ང་ (བ་) གནང་བ་	*me-ra tong-nga nang-wa.*
Do. *inf.* to *sup*	སྨད་ར་ཞུ་བ་	*me-ra sh̔u-wa.*
Revise, to	ཞུ་དག་བཏང་ (གཏོང་) བ་	*sh̔u-t̔a tang-wa.*
Do. *hon.*	ཞུ་དག་གཏོང་ང་ (བ་) གནང་བ་	*sh̔u-t̔a tong-nga nang-wa.*
Revision	ཞུ་དག་	*sh̔u-t̔a.*
Revolt, *s.*	སྡེ་འཁྲུགས་	*de-thru.*
Revolt, to	སྡེ་འཁྲུག་པ་	*de-thruk̔-pa.*
Revolting (disgusting)	སྐྱུག་བྲོ་པོ་	*kyuk̔-t̔ro-po.*
Revolve, to	འཁོར་བ་	*khor-wa.*

Reward	རྔན་པ་	*ngem-pa.*
Do. *hon.*	གསོལ་རས་	*sö-re.*
Reward, to	རྔན་པ་སྟེར་བ་	*ngem-pa ter-wa.*
Do. *hon.*	གསོལ་རས་གནང་བ་	*sö-re nang-wa.*
Rheumatism	འབམ་	*bam.*
Do. *hon.*	ཞབས་འབམ་	*sKam-bam.*
Rhinoceros	བསེ་རུ་	*se-ru.*
Rhododendron	སྟག་མ་ཤིང་	*ta-ma-shing.*
Rhubarb	ཆུ་ཆུ་	*chhu-chhu.*
Rib	རྩིབ་མ་	*tsi-ma.*
Ribbon	ལྷས་མ་	*hle-ma.*
Rice	འབྲས་	*dre.*
Do. *hon.*	བཞེས་འབྲས་	*sKen-dre.*
Rich (wealthy)	ཕྱུག་པོ། ཅ་ (ཆ་) ལག་ཆེན་པོ་	*chhuk-po; cha-la chhem-po.*
Do. *hon.*	སྐུ་ཅས་ (ཆས་) ཆེན་པོ་	*ku-che chhem-po.*
Rich (fertile)	ལུད་ཆུ་འཛོམ་པོ་	*lü-chhu dzom-po*
Ride, to	ཞོན་པ་	*sKöm-pa.*
Do. *hon.*	འཆིབ་པ་	*chhip-pa.*
Ridge	སྒང་	*gang.*

Ridiculous	དོན་མེད་	*t́ön-me.*
Riding horse	ཞོན་རྟ་	*sḱön-ta.*
Do. *hon.*	ཆིབས་པ་	*chhiḱ-pa.*
Riding horse (of very high official or lama)	ཆིབས་ཆེན་	*chhiṕ-chhen.*
Riding mule	ཞོན་དྲེ་	*sḱön-t́re.*
Do. *hon.*	ཆིབས་དྲེ་	*chhiṕ-t́re.*
Riding pony	ཞོན་རྟ་	*sḱön-ta.*
Do. *hon.*	ཆིབས་པ་	*chhiḱ-pa.*
Riding pony (of very high official or lama)	ཆིབས་ཆེན་	*chhiṕ-chhen.*
Rifle	མེ་མདའ་	*men-da.*
Do. *hon.*	ཕྱག་མདའ་	*chhan-da.*
Rift	སེར་ཀ་	*se-ka.*
Right (privilege)	ཐོབ་ཐང་	*thoṕ-thang.*
Right (not left)	གཡས་	*ye.*
Right (not wrong)	དག་པོ་	*t́aḱ-po.*
Right, to be	འགྲིག་པ་	*driḱ-pa.*
Right! (very well)	ལགས་སི། ལགས་ལགས་སི་	*la-si; la-la-si.*
Righteous	དྲང་པོ་	*t́rang-po.*
Rigid	མཁྲགས་པོ་ (མཁྲེགས་པ་)	*thraḱ-po.*

Rind	པགས་པ་	*pak-pa.*
Rinderpest	ཡོར་	*yor.*
Ring (for finger)	ཚིགས་ཁོག་	*tshi-kho.*
Do. *hon.*	ཕྱག་རྒྱུས་	*chha-gyü.*
Ring (for thumb)	སྲས་ཁོག་	*tre-kho.*
Do. *hon.*	ཕྱག་སྲས་	*chha-tre.*
Ring (circle)	ཨ་ལོང་	*a-long.*
Ring, to (bell)	དཀྲོལ་བ་ (འཁྲོལ་བ་)	*tröl-wa.*
Ringleader	གདེ་པོ། མི་བྱེད་མགོ་བྱེད་བྱེད་མཁན་	*te-po; mi-che go-che che-khen.*
Rinse, to	བཤལ་བཤལ་བཏང་ (གཏོང་) བ་	*she-she tang-wa.*
Do. *hon.*	བཤལ་བཤལ་གནང་བ་	*she-she nang-wa.*
Ripen, to	སྨིན་པ་	*mim-pa.*
Rise, to (get up)	ལང་བ་	*lang-wa.*
Do. *hon.*	བཞང་བ་ (བཞེང་བ་)	*shang-wa.*
Do. *h. hon.*	སྐུ་བཞང་ (བཞེང་) གནང་བ་	*ku-shang nang-wa.*
Rise, to (of sun)	ཤར་བ་	*shar-wa.*
Do. (of water)	རྒྱས་པ་	*gye-pa.*
Risk	ཉེན་ཁ་	*nyen-kha.*
Risky	ཉེན་ཁ་ཆེན་པོ་	*nyen-kha chhem-po.*

Rite, religious	ཆོས་ལུགས་	*chhö-lu.*
Rival	ཁ་ཐེག་	*khap-the.*
River, large	གཙང་པོ་	*tsang-po.*
Do. small	ཆུ་	*chhu.*
Road	ལམ་ཀ་	*lang-ka.*
Do. *hon.*	ཕེབ་ལམ་	*phep-lam.*
Road, main	རྒྱ་ལམ་	*gya-lam.*
Roam, to	ཆམ་ཆམ་ (འཁྱམ་འཁྱམ་) བྱེད་པ་	*chham-chham che-pa.*
Do. *hon.*	སྐུ་ཆམ་ (འཁྱམ་) གནང་བ་	*kün-chham nang-wa.*
Roar, to (wild beasts)	ངར་སྐད་རྒྱབ་པ་	*ngar-ke gyap-pa.*
Roast, to	རྔོད་པ་	*ngö-pa.*
Do. *hon.*	རྔོད་པ་གནང་བ་	*ngö-pa nang-wa.*
Rob, to (by stealth)	རྐུ་ (རྐུན་) མ་རྐུ་བ་	*ku-ma ku-wa.*
Do. (openly)	ཇག་པ་རྒྱབ་པ་	*chak-pa gyap-pa.*
Robber (by stealth)	རྐུ་མ་ (རྐུན་མ་)	*ku-ma.*
Do. (openly)	ཇག་པ་	*chak-pa.*
Robe	དུག་ལོག་	*tu-lo.*
Do *hon.*	ན་བཟའ་	*nam-sa.*
Robust	ཤེད་ཆེན་པོ་	*she chhem-po.*

Robust, *hon.*	སྐུ་ཤེད་ཆེན་པོ་	*ku-she chhen-po.*
Rock	བྲག་	*ťra.*
Rod	འཁར་རྒྱུག་	*khar-gyu.*
Roe (of fish)	ཉའི་སྒོ་ང་	*nye-go-nga.*
Do. *hon.*	བཞེས་ཉའི་བཞེས་སྒོང་	*sǩe-nye sǩe-gong.*
Rogue	བསྟན་བཞིག། འཛབ་ཆེན་	*ten-sǩi; dzap̌-chhen.*
Roll (of woollen cloth)	ཏུབས་	*p̌up̌.*
Do. (of cotton cloth)	ཐ་ན། *Hin.* ཡུག་	*tha-na; yuǩ.*
Do. (of silk)	དབ་རིལ་	*tap̌-ri.*
Roll, to	སྒྲིལ་བ་	*dril-wa.*
Do. *hon.*	སྒྲིལ་ར་ (བ་) གནང་བ་	*dri-ra nang-wa.*
Roof	ཐོག་ཁ་	*tho-kha.*
Rook	ཁྭ་ཏ་	*kha-ta.*
Room (in house)	ཁང་མིག་	*khang-mi.*
Do. *hon.*	གཟིམས་ཆུང་	*śim-chhung.*
Room (space)	ས་ཆ་	*sa-chha.*
Root	རྩ་བ་	*tsa-wa.*
Rope	ཐག་པ་	*thaǩ-pa*
Rosary	འཕྲང་ང་ (འཕྲེང་བ་)	*thrang-nga.*
Do. *hon.*	ཕྱག་འཕྲང་ (ཕྱག་འཕྲེང་)	*chhan-thrang.*

Rose	སེ་བའི་མེ་ཏོག་	*se-we me-to.*
Rosin	ཐང་ཆུ་	*thang-chhu.*
Rot, to	རུལ་བ་	*rül-wa.*
Rotten	རུལ་པ་	*rü-pa.*
Rough	རྩུབ་པོ། རྩིང་པོ་	*tsup-po*; *tsing-po.*
Round (like a disc)	སྒོར་སྒོར་	*go-gor.*
Do. (like a sphere)	རྡོག་རྡོག་	*dok-do.*
Rouse, to (from sleep)	གཉིད་བསད་ (གསོད་) པ་	*nyi se-pa.*
Do. *hon.*	གཉིད་གསོད་པ་གནང་བ་	*nyi sö-pa nang-wa.*
Do. *inf.* to *sup.*	མཉེན་ (མཉལ་) སད་པ་	*nyen se-pa.*
Route	ལམ་ཀ་	*lang-ka.*
Do. *hon.*	ཕེབ་ལམ་	*phep-lam.*
Route (highway)	རྒྱ་ལམ་	*gya-lam.*
Rove, to	ཆམ་ཆམ་ (འཁྱམ་འཁྱམ་) བྱེད་པ་	*chham-chham che-pa.*
Do. *hon.*	སྐུ་ཆམ་ (འཁྱམ་) གནང་བ་	*kün-chham nang wa.*
Row (noise)	ཨུར་སྒྲ་	*u-dra.*
Do. (quarrel)	རྒྱབ་འདྲེ་	*gyam-dre.*
Do. *hon.*	གསུང་འཁྲུག་	*sung-thru.*
Row (line)	གྲལ་	*tre.*

Row, to (boat)	སྐྱ་རྒྱབ་པ་	*kya-gyap-pa.*
Royal	རྒྱལ་པོའི་	*gye-pö.*
Rub, to	འཕུར་འཕུར་བྱེད་པ་	*phu-phu che-pa.*
Do. *hon.*	འཕུར་འཕུར་གནང་བ་	*phu-phu nang-wa.*
Rub out, to (erase)	སུབ་པ་	*sup-pa.*
Do. *hon.*	སུབ་པ་གནང་བ་	*sup-pa nang-wa*
Rubber	སྒྱིགས་	*gyi.*
Rubbish (refuse)	གད་སྙིགས། ཕྱག་སྙིགས་	*ke-nyi ; chha-nyi.*
Ruby	པདྨ་རཱ་ག་	*pe-ma ra-ga.*
Rudder	སྐྱ་མཇུག་	*kyam-ju.*
Rude (impolite)	འཇིང་པ་སྦོམ་པོ། ཀྱོང་པོ་	*jing-pa bom-po ; kyong-po.*
Do. (ignorant)	ཡོན་དན་མེད་པ་	*yön-ten me-pa.*
Do. (rough)	རྩུབ་པོ་	*tsup-po.*
Do. (robust)	ཤེད་ཆེན་པོ་	*she chhem-po.*
Do. *hon.*	སྐུ་ཤེད་ཆེན་པོ་	*ku-she chhem-po.*
Ruffian	འཛབ་ཆེན་	*dzap-chhen.*
Rug (bedding)	ཉལ་གཟན་	*nye-śen.*
Do. *hon.*	གཟིམ་གཟན་	*śim-śen.*
Rugged	རྩུབ་པོ་	*tsup-po.*
Ruin, to	མེད་པར་བཟོ་བ་	*me-pa śo-wa.*

Ruin, to, *hon.*	མེད་པར་བཟོ་བ་གནང་བ་	*me-pa śo-wa nang-wa.*
Rule (government)	གཞུང་། གཞུང་ཐོག་	*sKung ; sKung-tho.*
Rule (law)	ཁྲིམས་	*thrim.*
Do. *hon.*	བཀའ་ཁྲིམས་	*ka-thrim.*
Do. (religious)	ཆོས་ཁྲིམས་	*chhö-thrim.*
Rule (maxim)	གཏམ་དཔེ་	*tam-pe.*
Rule (power)	དབང་	*wang.*
Do. *hon.*	སྐུ་དབང་	*ku-wang.*
Rule, as a (usually)	ནམ་རྒྱུན་	*nam-gyün.*
Rule, to (govern)	དབང་བྱེད་པ་	*wang cKe-pa.*
Do. *hon.*	སྐུ་དབང་གནང་བ་	*ku-wang nang-wa.*
Rule, to (decide)	ཐག་བཅད་ (གཅོད་) པ་	*tha-che-pa.*
Do. *hon.*	ཐག་གཅོད་པ་གནང་བ་	*tha-chö-pa nang-wa.*
Do. *h. hon.*	ཐུགས་ཐག་གཅོད་པ་གནང་བ་	*thu-tha chö-pa nang-wa.*
Rule a country, to (secular rule)	རྒྱལ་སྲིད་གནང་བ་	*gye-si nang-wa.*
Do. (spiritual rule)	ཆོས་སྲིད་གནང་བ་	*chhö-si nang-wa.*
Ruler (king)	རྒྱལ་པོ་	*gye-po.*
Do. (for drawing lines)	ཐིག་ཤིང་	*thik-shing.*
Rumour	སྐད་ཆ། གཏམ་	*ke-chha ; tam.*

Rump (anus)	ཀུབ་	*kuṕ.*
Do. *hon.*	ཞབས་ཕོངས་	*sḱam-phong.*
Run, to	རྒྱུག་པ་	*gyuḱ-pa.*
Do. *hon.*	རྒྱུག་ཕེབ་པ་	*gyuḱ phe-pa.*
Do. *h. hon.*	རྒྱུག་འཆིབ་རྒྱུ་གནང་བ་	*gyuḱ chhiṕ-gyu nang-wa.*
Run away, to (flee)	བྲོས་ཕྱིན་པ་	*ṕö-chhim-pa.*
Do. *hon.*	བྲོས་ཕེབ་པ་	*ṕö-pheṕ-pa.*
Do. *h. hon.*	བྲོས་འཆིབ་རྒྱུ་གནང་བ་	*ṕö-chhiṕ-gyu nang-wa.*
Rupee	སྒོར་མོ་	*gor-mo.*
Rush, to (run)	རྒྱུག་པ་	*gyuḱ-pa.*
Do. *hon.*	རྒྱུག་ཕེབ་པ་	*gyuḱ phe-pa.*
Do. *h. hon.*	རྒྱུག་འཆིབ་རྒྱུ་གནང་བ་	*gyuḱ chhiṕ-gyu nang-wa.*
Russia	ཨུ་རུ་སུ་	*u-ru-su.*
Russian	ཨུ་རུ་སུ་ཀི་	*u-ru-su-ḱi.*
Rust	བཙའ་	*tsa.*
Rut (furrow)	རོལ་	*röl.*
Ruthless, to be	སྙིང་རྗེ་མེད་པ་	*nying-je me-pa.*
Do. *hon.*	ཐུགས་རྗེ་མེད་པ་	*thuḱ-je me-pa.*

S

Sabbath	ངལ་གསོ་བའི་ཉི་མ་	*nge-so-we nyi-ma.*
Sabre	ཞོག་ལང་	*sho-lang.*
Sack (small)	ཕད་གོག་	*phe-k̄o.*
Do. (large)	སྒྱེ་མོ་	*gye-mo.*
Do. (small, of cotton)	རས་ཁུག་	*re-khu.*
Do. (large, of cotton)	རས་ཕད་	*re-phe.*
Do. leather	རྐྱལ་པ་	*kye-pa.*
Sacred	དམ་པ། ཆོས་ལྡན་	*t́am-pa; chhön-den.*
Sacrifice (religious offering)	མཆོད་པ་	*chhö-pa.*
Sacrifice, to	མཆོད་པ་ཕུལ་ (འབུལ་) བ་	*chhö-pa phü-wa.*
Do. *hon.*	མཆོད་པ་འབུལ་ར་ (བ་) གནང་བ་	*chhö-pa bü-ra nang-wa.*
Sad, to be	སེམས་སྐྱོ་བ། སེམས་སྡུག་པ་	*sem-kyo-wa; sem-duk̄-pa.*
Do. *hon.*	ཐུགས་སེམས་སྐྱོ་བ་གནང་བ། ཐུགས་སེམས་སྡུག་ག་ (པ་) གནང་བ་	*thu-sem kyo-wa nang-wa; thu-sem duk̄-k̄a nang-wa.*
Saddle	སྒ། རྟའི་སྒ་	*ga; te-ga.*
Do. *hon.*	ཆིབས་སྒ་	*chhip̄-ga.*
Saddle, pack	ཁལ་སྒ་	*khe-ga.*

Saddle, to	རྟའི་སྒ་རྒྱབ་པ་	*te-ga gyap̄-pa.*
Do. *hon.*	ཆིབས་སྒ་སྐྱོན་པ་	*chhip̄-ga kyöm-pa.*
Saddle-bag	རྟ་སྒྲོག་	*ta-dro.*
Do. *hon.*	ཆིབས་སྒྲོག་	*chhip̄-dro.*
Saddle-cloth	སྨ་སྤྲན་ *Ch.*	*ma-tren.*
Do. *hon.*	ཆིབས་སྨ་སྨ་སྤྲན་	*chhip̄-ma ma-tren.*
Saddle-girth	གློ་	*lo.*
Do. *hon.*	ཆིབས་གློ་	*chhip̄-lo.*
Safe (steadfast)	བརྟན་པོ་	*tem-po.*
Safflower (Saffron)	གུར་གུམ་	*k̄ur-k̄um.*
Saffron	ཁ་ཆེ་ཤ་ཀ་མ་	*kha-chhe sha-ka-ma.*
Sagacious	རིག་པ་ཆེན་པོ་	*rik̄-pa chhem-po.*
Do. *hon.*	ཐུགས་རིག་ཆེན་པོ་	*thu-ri chhem-po.*
Sagacity	རིག་པ་	*rik̄-pa.*
Do. *hon.*	ཐུགས་རིག་	*thu-ri.*
Sailor	མཉན་པ་	*nyem-pa.*
Do. *hon.*	མཉན་དཔོན་ལགས་	*nyem-pön-la.*
Saint, Buddhist	བྱང་ཆུབ་སེམས་དཔའ་	*cħang-chhup̄ sem-pa.*
Saintly	དམ་པ། ཆོས་ལྡན་	*t̄am-pa; chhön-den.*
Sake of, for the	དོན་ལ་	*t̄ön-la.*

Sake of, for the *hon.*	སྐུ་དོན་ལ་	*ku-ťön-la.*
Sal ammoniac	རྒྱ་ཚྭ་	*gya-tsha.*
Salary	ཕོགས་	*pho.*
Do. *hon.*	གསོལ་ཕོགས་	*sö-pho.*
Salesman	ཚོང་པ་	*tshong-pa.*
Do. *hon.*	ཚོང་དཔོན་	*tshong-pön.*
Saliva	ཁ་ཆུ་	*kha-chhu.*
Do. *hon.*	ཞལ་ཆུ་	*sḱe-chhu.*
Salt	ཚྭ་	*tsha.*
Do. *hon.*	ལྗགས་ཚྭ་	*ja-tsha.*
Saltpetre	ཟེ་ཚྭ་	*śe-tsha.*
Salute, to	ཕྱག་འབུལ་ཞུ་བ་	*chham-bü sḱu-wa.*
Do. *hon.*	ཕྱག་འབུལ་ཞུ་བ་གནང་བ་	*chham-bü sḱu-wa nang-wa.*
Salvation	ཐར་པ་	*thar-pa.*
Same	གཅིག་པ་	*chik-pa.*
Sample	དཔེ། སྤུས་ཚད་	*pe; pü-tshe.*
Sanctify, to (consecrate)	རབ་གནས་བྱེད་པ་	*raṕ-ne cḱe-pa.*
Do. *hon.*	རབ་གནས་གནང་བ་	*raṕ-ne nang-wa.*
Sanction	དོན་སྨིན་	*ťön-min.*
Sand	ཕྱེ་མ་	*chhe-ma.*

Sand-grouse	གང་ག་ལིང་	*k̄ang-k̄a-ling.*
Sandal	ཀྲད་པ་	*tre-pa.*
Sandal-wood	ཙན་དན་	*tsen-t̄en.*
Sanskrit	སྔགས་སྐད་	*nga-ke.*
Sap	ཆུ་	*chhu.*
Sapient	ཡོན་ཏན་ཆེན་པོ་	*yön-ten chhem-po.*
Do. *hon.*	སྐུ་ཡོན་ཆེན་པོ་	*ku-yön chhem-po.*
Sapphire	ཨིནྡྲ་ནཱི་ལ་	*in-t̄ra-ni-la.*
Sash	སྐེ་རགས་	*ke-ra.*
Do. *hon.*	སྐུ་རགས་	*ku-ra.*
Satan	བདུད་	*dü.*
Satin (cloth)	ཟུབ་	*śup.*
Satisfied, to be	འདོད་པ་གང་བ་	*dö-pa k̄ang-wa.*
Do. *hon.*	ཐུགས་འདོད་གང་བ་	*thung-dö k̄ang-wa.*
Satisfied, to be (with food)	འགྲང་བ་	*drang-wa.*
Do. (with water)	ཁ་ངོམས་པ་	*kha ngom-pa.*
Do. *hon.*	ཞལ་ངོམས་པ་གནང་བ་	*sk̄e ngom-pa nang-wa.*
Saturday	གཟའ་སྤེན་པ་	*śa-pem-pa.*
Sauce	ཤ་ཁུ་	*sha-khu.*
Do. *hon.*	སྐྲུམ་ཁུ་	*trung-khu.*

Saucepan	ཚལ་སླང་	*tshe-lang.*
Saucer	ཏྲ་ཀྱ་	*ťra-kya.*
Do. *hon.*	ཞལ་ཀྱ་	*sǩe-kya.*
Saucy (rude)	འཛིང་པ་སྦོམ་པོ། གྱོང་པོ་	*jing-pa bom-po; ǩyong-po.*
Saunter, to (linger)	འགོར་བ་	*gor-wa.*
Do. *hon.*	ཕེབ་འགོར་གནང་བ་	*phe-gor nang-wa.*
Sausage	རྒྱུ་མ་	*gyu-ma.*
Do. *hon.*	བཞེས་རྒྱོང་ (བཞེས་རྒྱུ་)	*sǩe-gyong.*
Savage, *s.* (barbarian)	ཀླ་ཀློ་	*la-lo.*
Do. *adj.* (ferocious)	ངན་པ་	*ngem-pa.*
Save, to (rescue)	བསྐྱབས་པ་ (སྐྱོབ་པ་)	*kyap̌-pa.*
Do. *hon.*	སྐྱབས་འཇུག་གནང་བ་	*kyam-juǩ nang-wa.*
Save, to (money)	བསགས་པ་ (གསོག་པ་)	*saǩ-pa.*
Do. *hon.*	གསོག་ག་ (པ་) གནང་བ་	*soǩ-ǩa nang-wa.*
Saviour	སྐྱབས་མགོན་	*kyam-gön.*
Savour	བྲོ་	*ťro.*
Do. *hon.*	ལྗགས་བྲོ་	*ja-ťro.*
Savoury	ཞིམ་པོ་	*sǩim-po.*
Do. *hon.*	སྤྲོ་པོ་	*tro-po.*
Saw (cutting instrument)	སོག་ལེ་	*so-le.*

Saw (proverb)	གཏམ་དཔེ་	*tam-pe.*
Saw, to	སོག་ལེ་རྒྱབ་པ་	*so-le gyaṕ-pa.*
Say, to	ལབ་པ། ཟེར་བ་	*laṕ-pa ; śe-wa.*
Do. *hon.*	གསུང་བ་	*sung-wa.*
Saying	སྐད་ཆ་	*ke-chha.*
Scab	རྨ་ཁོག་	*ma-kho.*
Scabbard	ཤུབས་	*shuṕ.*
Scalded, to be	ཆུ་འཁོལ་མས་འཚིག་པ་	*chhu-khö-me tshiḱ-pa.*
Do. *hon.*	ཆབ་ཆུ་འཁོལ་མས་འཚིག་པ་	*chhaṕ-chhu khö-me tshiḱ-pa.*
Scales, a pair of	ཉ་ག་	*nya-ga.*
Scamp	བསྟན་བཤིག། འཛབ་ཆེན་	*ten-sḱi ; dzaṕ-chhen.*
Scan, to (look at)	ལྟ་བ་	*ta-wa.*
Do. *hon.*	གཟིགས་པ་	*śi-pa.*
Scanty	ཉུང་ཉུང་	*nyung-nyung.*
Scar	རྨ་རྗེས་	*ma-je.*
Do. *hon.*	སྐུ་རྨའི་རྗེས་	*ku-me-je.*
Scarce	དཀོན་པོ་	*köm-po.*
Scare, to	ཞེད་སྐྲག་སླང་བ་	*sḱe-tra lang-wa.*
Do. *hon.*	ཞེད་སྐྲག་སློང་ང་ (བ་) གནང་བ་	*sḱe-tra long-nga nang-wa.*
Scared, to be	ཞེད་པ་	*sḱe-pa.*

Scared, to be, *hon.*	ཞེད་པ་གནང་བ་	*sḱe-pa nang-wa.*
Scarf, complimentary	ཁ་བཏགས་	*kha-ta.*
Do. *hon.*	མཇལ་དར་	*je-ťar.*
Scarf, complimentary, best	ནང་མཛོད་	*nang-dzö.*
Do. second best	ཨ་ཤེ་	*a-she.*
Do. third best	ཕྱི་སྤྲག་	*chhi-pa.*
Do. fourth best	ཟུར་ཨ་ཤེ་	*su a-she.*
Do. fifth best	ཕྱི་མཛོད་	*chhi-dzö.*
Do. sixth best	ཁ་སྔོན་	*kha-ngön.*
Do. seventh best	གསོལ་བཏགས་	*sö-ta.*
Do. cheapest	རྒྱུས་སྤྲག་	*gye-pa.*
Scarlet	དམར་པོ་	*ma-po.*
Scatter, to (strew)	གཏོར་བ་	*tor-wa.*
Do *hon.*	གཏོར་ར་ (བ་) གནང་བ་	*tor-ra nang-wa.*
Schedule	ཟུར་ཐོ་	*ṡur-tho.*
Scent, *s.*	དྲི་མ་	*ťri-ma.*
Sceptre (thunder bolt)	རྡོ་རྗེ་	*dor-je.*
Scholar (pupil)	བསླབ་ཕྲུག་	*laṗ-thru.*
Scholarly (learned)	ཡོན་ཏན་ཆེན་པོ་	*yön-ten chhem-po.*
Do. *hon.*	སྐུ་ཡོན་ཆེན་པོ་	*ku-yön chhem-po.*

School	བསླབ་གྲྭ་	*laṕ-t́ra.*
School-master	དགེ་རྒན་	*ge-gen.*
Science (skill)	རིག་པ	*riḱ-pa.*
Do. *hon.*	ཐུགས་རིག་	*thu-ri.*
Science (knowledge)	ཤེས་བྱ་	*she-cḰa.*
Scissors	ཛེམ་ཙེ་ (ཅེམ་ཙེ་)	*cḰem-tse.*
Do. *hon.*	ཕྱག་ཛེམ་ (ཕྱག་ཅེམ་)	*chha-cḰem.*
Scoff, to	ཀྱག་ཀྱག་བྱས་ནས་ལབ་པ་	*kya-kya cḰe-ne laṕ-pa.*
Do. *hon.*	ཀྱག་ཀྱག་གནང་ནས་གསུང་བ་	*kya-kya nang-ne sung-wa.*
Scold, to	གཤེ་གཤེ་བཏང་ (གཏོང་) བ་	*she-she tang-wa.*
Do. *hon.*	བཀའ་བཀྱོན་གནང་བ་	*kaṕ-kyön nang-wa.*
Scoop, *s.*	སྐྱོགས་	*kyo.*
Scoop, to	སྐྱོགས་ཀྱིས་བཏོན་ (འདོན་) པ་	*kyo-kyi töm-pa.*
Do. *hon.*	སྐྱོགས་ཀྱིས་འདོན་པ་གནང་བ་	*kyo-kyi dom-pa nang-wa.*
Scope (intention)	དོན་དག་	*t́ön-t́a.*
Do. *hon.*	སྐུ་དོན་	*ku-t́ön.*
Scorch, to	འཚིག་པ་	*tshiḱ-pa.*
Score (twenty)	ཉི་ཤུ་	*nyi-shu.*
Scorn, to	ཀྱག་ཀྱག་བྱས་ནས་ལབ་པ་	*kya-kya cḰe-ne laṕ-pa.*
Do. *hon.*	ཀྱག་ཀྱག་གནང་ནས་གསུང་བ་	*kya-kya nang-ne sung-wa.*

Scorpion	སྡིག་པ་ར་ཛ་	*diḱ-pa ra-dza.*
Scoundrel	བསྟན་བཞིག ། འཛབ་ཆེན་	*ten-sḱi; dzaṕ-chhen.*
Scourge, to	རྟའི་ལྕུག་གཞུ་བ་	*te-cha sḱu-wa.*
Scraggy (of persons and animals)	ཤ་སྐམ་པོ་	*sha kam-po.*
Do. *hon.* (of persons)	སྐུ་ཤ་སྐམ་པོ་	*ku-sha kam-po.*
Do. *hon.* (of animals)	བཞེས་ཤ་སྐམ་པོ་	*she-sha kam-po.*
Scrap	དུམ་བུ་	*t́um-ṕu.*
Scrape, to	བྲད་བྲད་ (འབྲད་འབྲད་) བཏང་ (གཏོང་) བ་	*t́re-t́re tang-wa.*
Do. *hon.*	བྲད་བྲད་ (འབྲད་འབྲད་) གཏོང་ང་ (བ་) གནང་བ་	*t́re-t́re tong-nga nang-wa*
Scrape off, to	ཞུད་ཞུད་བྱེད་པ་	*shü-shü cḱe-pa.*
Do. *hon.*	ཞུད་ཞུད་གནང་བ་	*shü-shü nang-wa.*
Scratch, to	སྦར་ཤད་རྒྱབ་པ་	*bar-she gỵaṕ-pa.*
Do. *hon.*	ཕྱག་ཤད་སྐྱོན་པ་	*chha-she kyöm-pa.*
Scream, to	སྐད་རྒྱབ་པ་	*ke-gyaṕ-pa.*
Do. *hon.*	གསུང་སྐད་སྐྱོན་པ་	*sung-ke kyöm-pa.*
Screen	ཡོལ་ལ་ (ཡོལ་བ་)	*yö-la.*
Scriptures	གསུང་རབ་	*sung-raṕ.*

Scroll	ཤུག་གུའི་ཆག་པ་	*shuḱ-ḱü chhaḱ-pa.*
Scruple	ཐེ་ཚོམ་	*the-tshom.*
Sea	རྒྱ་མཚོ་	*gyam-tsho.*
Seal	དམ་ཕྲུག། ཐེ་ཙེ་	*t́am-thru ; the-tse.*
Do. *hon.*	ཕྱག་དམ་	*chha-t́am.*
Seal, to	དམ་ཕྲུག་རྒྱབ་པ། ཐེ་ཙེ་རྒྱབ་པ་	*t́am-thru gyaṕ-pa ; the-tse gyaṕ-pa.*
Do. *hon.*	ཕྱག་དམ་སྐྱོན་པ་	*chha-t́am-kyöm-pa.*
Sealing-wax	ལ་ཆ་	*la-chha.*
Seam	ཚེམ་བུ་	*tshem-ṕu.*
Do. *hon.*	ཕྱག་ཚེམ་	*chha-tshem.*
Search, to	འཚལ་བ་ (འཚོལ་བ་)	*tshel-wa.*
Do. *hon.*	འཚལ་ར་ (འཚོལ་བ་) གནང་བ་	*tshe-ra nang-wa.*
Season	ནམ་དུས་	*nam-t́ü.*
Seat	ཀུབ་ཀྱག། ཁྲིའུ་ཤིང་	*kuṕ-kya ; thri-u-shing.*
Do. *hon.*	ཞབས་ཀྱག་	*sḱaṕ-kya.*
Secluded place	དབེན་གནས་	*en-ne.*
Second	གཉིས་པ་	*nyi-pa.*
Secondly	གཉིས་པར་	*nyi-pa.*
Secret	གསང་བ་	*sang-wa.*

Secretary	དྲུང་ཡིག་བགྲེས་པ་	*ťrung-yi dre-pa.*
Secretary, Chief	དྲུང་ཡིག་ཆེན་མོ་བ་	*ťrung-yi chhem-mo-wa.*
Secrete, to	སྦེད་པ་	*be-pa.*
Do. *hon.*	སྦེད་པ་གནང་བ་	*be-va nang-wa.*
Sect (religious)	ཆོས་ལུགས་	*chhö-lu.*
Secular	འཇིག་རྟེན་པ་	*jiǩ-tem-pa.*
Secure (steadfast)	བརྟན་པོ་	*tem-po.*
Security (bail)	ཁས་ཁྱགས་	*khe-khya.*
Do. *hon.*	ཞལ་ཁྱགས་	*sǩe-khya.*
Security, to give	ཁས་ཁྱགས་བྱེད་པ་	*khe-khya cǩe-pa.*
Do. *hon.*	ཞལ་ཁྱགས་གནང་བ་	*sǩe-khya nang-wa.*
Sedan-chair	མགྱོགས་དབྱང་ (འགྱོགས་དབྱང་)	*gyo-chang.*
Do. *hon.*	ཕེབ་དབྱང་	*phep̌-chang.*
Sediment	སྙིགས་	*nyi.*
Seduce, to	སླུ་བ་	*lu-wa.*
Do. *hon.*	སླུ་བ་གནང་བ་	*lu-wa nang-wa.*
See, to	མཐོང་བ་	*thong-wa.*
Do. *hon.*	གཟིགས་པ་	*ši-pa.*
Seed	སོན། ས་བོན་	*sön ; sa-p̌ön.*

Seek, to	འཚལ་བ་ (འཚོལ་བ་)	*tshel-wa.*
Do. *hon.*	འཚལ་ར་ (འཚོལ་བ་) གནང་བ་	*tshe-ra nang-wa.*
Seemingly (probably)	ཡིན་པ་འདྲ་	*yim-pa-dra.*
Seemly (becoming)	འོས་པོ་	*ö-po.*
Seize, to	ཟིན་པ་ (འཛིན་པ་)	*śim-pa.*
Do *hon.*	ཟིན་ (འཛིན་) པ་གནང་བ་	*śim-pa nang-wa.*
Select, to	འདམ་པ་	*dam-pa.*
Do. *hon.*	འདམ་པ་གནང་བ་	*dam-pa nang-wa.*
Self	རང་	*rang.*
Selfish	རང་འདོད་ཆ་པོ་	*rang-dö tsha-po.*
Selfishness	རང་འདོད་	*rang-dö.*
Sell, to	འཚོང་བ་	*tshong-wa.*
Do. *hon.*	འཚོང་ང་ (བ་) གནང་བ་	*tshong-nga nang-wa.*
Send, to	བཏང་བ་ (གཏོང་བ་)	*tang-wa.*
Do. *hon.*	གཏོང་ང་ (བ་) གནང་བ་	*tong-nga nang-wa.*
Senior	རྒན་པ་	*gem-pa.*
Sense (opinion)	བསམ་པ་	*sam-pa.*
Do. *hon.*	ཐུགས་སེམས་	*thu-sem.*
Sense (purport)	དོན་དག་	*tön-ta.*
Do. *hon.*	སྐུ་དོན་	*ku-tön.*

Sense (understanding)	བློ་གྲོས་	*lo-trö.*
Senseless (nonsensical)	དོན་མེད་	*tön-me.*
Do. (unconscious)	དྲན་མེད་	*trem-me.*
Sensible (intelligent)	རིག་པ་ཡག་པོ་	*rik-pa yak-po.*
Do. *hon.*	ཐུགས་རིག་ཡག་པོ་	*thu-ri yak-po.*
Sentence *s.* (in a book)	ཤོག་ལོ་	*shok-lo.*
Do. a single	ཤོག་ལོ་ཁ་གཅིག་	*shok-lo kha-chi.*
Sentence, to (punish)	ཁྲིམས་བཏང་ (གཏོང་) བ་	*thrim tang-wa.*
Do. *hon.*	ཁྲིམས་གཏོང་ང་ (བ་) གནང་བ་	*thrim tong-nga nang-wa.*
Do. *h. hon.*	བཀའ་ཁྲིམས་གནང་བ་	*ka-thrim nang-wa.*
Sentence, to (fine)	ཉེས་པ་བཏང་ (གཏོང་) བ་	*nye-pa tang-wa.*
Do. *hon.*	ཉེས་པ་གནང་བ་	*nye-pa nang-wa.*
Do. *h. hon.*	བཀའ་ཉེས་གནང་བ་	*ka-nye nang-wa.*
Sentiment (opinion)	བསམ་པ་	*sam-pa.*
Do. *hon.*	ཐུགས་སེམས་	*thu-sem.*
Sentinel	སོ་པ་	*so-pa.*
Separate, to	དབྱེན་ (དབྱེ་བ་) ཕྱེ་བ་	*yen chhe-wa.*
Do. *hon.*	དབྱེན་ (དབྱེ་བ་) ཕྱེ་བ་གནང་བ་	*yen chhe-wa nang-wa.*
Separately	ཁ་ཁ་བྱས་ནས་	*kha-kha che-ne.*
Sepoy	དམག་མི་	*ma-mi.*

Sepulchre	རོ་སྦེད་ས་	*ro be-sa.*
Series	རིམ་པ་	*rim-pa.*
Serpent	སྦྲུལ་	*drü.*
Serpent-demon	ཀླུ་	*lu.*
Servant	གཡོག་པོ་	*yoḱ-po.*
Do. *hon.*	ཞབས་ཕྱི་	*sḱaṕ-chhi.*
Servant, female	ཞལ་ལྟ་མ་	*sḱe-ta-ma.*
Serve, to	གཡོག་བྱེད་པ་	*yo cḱe-pa.*
Do. *hon.*	ཞབས་ཕྱི་ཞུ་བ་	*sḱaṕ-chhi sḱu-wa.*
Service, religious	ཆོ་ག། སྐུ་རིམ་	*chho-ga ; ku-rim.*
Serviceable, to be	ཕན་ཐོགས་པ་	*phen-thoḱ-pa.*
Do. *hon.*	ཐུགས་ཕན་གསོ་བ་	*thu-phen so-wa.*
Sesamum	ཏིལ་ *Hind.*	*til.*
Set, to (place)	བཞག་པ་ (འཛོག་པ་)	*sḱaḱ-pa.*
Do. *hon.*	གཞོག་ག་ (འཛོག་པ་) གནང་བ་	*sḱoḱ-ḱa nang-wa.*
Set, to (of the sun)	རྒས་པ་	*ge-pa.*
Set out, to (depart)	འཐོན་པ་	*thöm-pa.*
Do. *hon.*	ཕེབ་བ་	*phe-pa.*
Set right, to (adjust)	སྒྲིག་པ་	*driḱ-pa.*

Set right, to (adjust), *hon.*	སྒྲིག་ག་ (པ་) གནང་བ་	*driǩ-ǩa nang-wa.*
Settle, to (decide)	ཐག་བཅད་ (གཅོད་) པ་	*tha che-pa.*
Do. *hon.*	ཐག་གཅོད་པ་གནང་བ་	*tha chö-pa nang-wa.*
Do. *h. hon.*	ཐུགས་ཐག་གཅོད་པ་གནང་བ་	*thu-tha chö-pa nang-wa.*
Settle, to (a law-suit out of court)	འདུམ་བཏང་ (གཏོང་) བ་	*dum tang-wa.*
Do. *hon.*	བཀའ་འདུམ་གནང་བ་	*kan-dum nang-wa.*
Settle, to (arrange)	སྒྲིག་པ་	*driǩ-pa.*
Do. *hon.*	སྒྲིག་ག་ (པ་) གནང་བ་	*driǩ-ǩa nang-wa.*
Seven	བདུན་	*dün.*
Seventh	བདུན་པ་	*dün-pa.*
Seventeen	བཅུ་བདུན་	*chup̌-dün.*
Seventeenth	བཅུ་བདུན་པ་	*chup̌-dün-pa.*
Seventieth	བདུན་ཅུ་པ་	*dün-chu-pa.*
Seventy	བདུན་ཅུ་	*dün-chu.*
Sever, to (cut)	བཅད་པ་ (གཅོད་པ་)	*che-pa.*
Do. *hon.*	བཅད་ (གཅོད་) པ་གནང་བ་	*che-pa nang-wa.*
Several	འགའ་ཆེན་	*ga-chhen.*
Severally	སོ་སོ་བྱས་ནས་	*so-so cǩe-ne.*
Severe (harsh, of human beings)	གྱོང་པོ་	*ǩyong-po.*

Severe (of gods)	དྲག་པོ་	*t́raḱ-po.*
Severe (strict)	དམ་པོ། བཙན་པོ་	*t́am-po ; tsem-po.*
Sew, to	འཚེམ་པ། འཚེམ་བུ་རྒྱབ་པ་	*tshem-pa; tshem-ṕu gyaṕ-pa.*
Do. *hon.*	ཕྱག་འཚེམ་གནང་བ། ཕྱག་འཚེམ་སྐྱོན་པ་	*chha-tshem nang-wa; chha-tshem kyöm-pa.*
Sew, to (together)	སྦྲེལ་བ་	*drel-wa.*
Do. *hon.*	སྦྲེལ་ར་ (བ་) གནང་བ་	*dre-ra nang-wa.*
Shackles (for hands)	ལག་ལྕགས་	*laḱ-cha.*
Do. (for feet)	རྐང་ལྕགས་	*kang-cha.*
Shade	བསིལ་གྲིབ་	*sil-t́riṕ.*
Shadow	གྲིབ་མ་	*t́ri-ma.*
Shaggy	རྩུབ་པོ་	*tsuṕ-po.*
Shake, to *v.t.*	འགུལ་འགུལ་བཏང་ (གཏོང་)བ། དཀྲུག་དཀྲུག་བྱེད་པ་	*gü-gü tang-wa; truḱ-truḱ ćhe-pa.*
Do. *hon.*	འགུལ་འགུལ་གཏོང་ང་ (བ་) གནང་བ། དཀྲུག་དཀྲུག་གནང་བ་	*gü-gü tong-nga nang-wa; truḱ-truḱ nang-wa.*
Shake, to *v.i.*	འཁྲུག་པ་	*thruḱ-pa.*
Do. (of human being)	འདར་བ་	*dar-wa.*

Shake, to (of human being), *hon.*	སྐུ་འདར་སྐྱོར་པ་	*kün-dar kyöm-pa.*
Shake, to (of bridge, etc.)	ལྡེམ་ལྡེམ་བྱེད་པ་	*dem-dem cḱe-pa.*
Shallow, to be	གཏིང་རིང་པོ་མེད་པ་	*ting-ring-po me-pa.*
Sham (false)	རྫུས་མ་	*dzü-ma.*
Sham, to	གྱོད་བཤད་པ་	*ḱyö she-pa.*
Do. *hon.*	གྱོད་གསུང་བ་	*ḱyö sung-wa.*
Sham illness, to	ན་རྫུ་བཏབ་ (འདེབས་) པ་	*na-dzu taṕ-pa.*
Do. *hon.*	སྙུང་རྫུ་བཏབ་ (འདེབས་) པ་	*nyung-dzu taṕ-pa.*
Shame	ངོ་ཚ་	*ngo-tsha.*
Shame, to feel	ངོ་ཚ་བ་	*ngo-tsha-wa.*
Do. *hon.*	ཐུགས་ངོ་ཚ་བ་	*thu-ngo-tsha-wa.*
Shamefaced	ངོ་ཚ་པོ་	*ngo-tsha-po.*
Shameful	ངོ་ཚ་པོ་	*ngo-tsha-po.*
Shameless, to be	ངོ་ཚ་མེད་པ་	*ngo-tsha me-pa.*
Shape, *n.*	བཟོ་བལྟ་	*śoṕ-ta.*
Do. *hon.*	སྐུ་བཟོ་	*ku-śo.*
Share	སྐལ་ལ་ (སྐལ་བ་)	*ke-la.*
Do. *hon.*	སྐུ་སྐལ་	*ku-ke.*
Share, to	བགོད་པ། བགོ་བཤའ་རྒྱབ་པ་	*gö-pa ; goṕ-sha gyaṕ-pa.*

Share, to, *hon.*	བགོད་པ་གནང་བ། བགོ་བཤའ་སྐྱོན་པ་	*gö-pa nang-wa; gop-sha kyöm-pa.*
Sharp (not blunt)	རྣོ་པོ་	*no-po.*
Do. (shrewd)	གཅང་པོ་	*chang-po.*
Do. *hon.*	ཐུགས་གཅང་པོ་	*thu-chang-po.*
Sharpen, to	བདར་བ་	*dar-wa.*
Do. *hon.*	བདར་ར་ (བ་) གནང་བ་	*dar-ra nang-wa.*
Sharpen, to (by blacksmith)	ཁ་འདོན་བྱེད་པ་	*khan-dön cKe-pa.*
Shatter, to	ཧྲུག་ཧྲུག་བཏང་ (གཏོང་) བ་	*hru-hru tang-wa.*
Shave, to	སྐྲ་བཞར་བ་	*tra sKar-wa.*
Do. *hon.*	དབུ་སྐྲ་བཞར་བ་	*u-tra sKar-wa.*
Shaved head, having a (as a monk)	མགོ་རིལ་རིལ་	*go-ri-ri.*
Do. *hon.*	དབུ་རིལ་རིལ་	*u-ri-ri.*
Shawl (of lamas)	གཟན་	*śen.*
Do. *hon.*	སྐུ་གཟན་	*ku-śen.*
She	མོ་	*mo.*
Sheaf	ཚག་པ་	*chhaK-pa.*
Shear, to	བལ་བག་ (འབྲེག་) པ་	*ṕe ṕaK-pa.*

Shear, to, *hon.*	བལ་བག་(འབྲེག་) ག་(པ་) གནང་བ་	*ṕe ṕak-ḱa na ng-wa.*
Sheath	ཤུབས་	*shuṕ.*
Sheep	ལུག་	*lu.*
Sheep, flock of	ལུག་ཁྱུ་	*luḱ-khyu.*
Sheep-skin	ལུག་པགས་	*luḱ-pa.*
Sheet of paper	ཤོག་གུ་ (ཤོག་བུ་)	*shu-ḱu.*
Do. *hon.*	ཕྱག་ཤོག་	*chha-sho.*
Shelf	བང་ཁྲི། བང་ག་	*ṕang-thri; ṕang-ḱa.*
Shell	འགྲོན་བུ་	*dröm-ṕu.*
Shell, conch	དུང་	*ṫung.*
Shelter (refuge)	སྐྱབས་གནས་	*kyam-ne.*
Shepherd	ལུག་རྫི་	*luḱ-dzi.*
Shield	ཕུབ་	*phuṕ.*
Shift, to (move)	སྤོ་བ་	*po-wa.*
Do. *hon.*	སྤོ་བ་གནང་བ་	*po-wa nang-wa.*
Shin, shin-bone	ངར་དུང་	*ngar-ṫung.*
Do. *hon.*	ཞབས་པིས་ངར་དུང་	*sḱaṕ-pi ngar-ṫung.*
Shine (brightness)	འོད་	*ö.*
Shine, to	འོད་རྒྱབ་པ་	*ö gyaṕ-pa.*

Shine, to (of the sun)	ཤར་བ་	*shar-wa.*
Do. (of the moon)	ཟླ་དཀར་ཤར་བ་	*da-ka shar-wa.*
Ship	གྲུ་	*tru.*
Shirt	འོག་འཇུག་	*ön-ju.*
Do. *hon.*	སྐུ་འཇུག་	*kün-ju.*
Shiver, to (with fear, cold, etc.)	འདར་བ་	*dar-wa.*
Do. *hon.*	སྐུ་འདར་སྐྱོན་པ་	*kun-dar kyöm-pa.*
Shock	ཧམས་སྐྲག་	*ngam-tra.*
Shoe	ལྷམ། ལྷམ་ཁོག་	*hlam ; hlam-kho.*
Do. *hon.*	ཞབས་ཆགས་	*shap-chha.*
Shoe (European style)	འཇུ་ཏ་ *Hin.*	*ju-ta.*
Shoe-maker	ལྷམ་བཟོ་	*hlam-śo.*
Shoot, to (with gun, etc.)	རྒྱབ་པ་	*gyap-pa.*
Do. *hon.*	སྐྱོན་པ་	*kyöm-pa.*
Shop	ཚོང་ཁང་	*tshong-khang.*
Shore	འགྲམ་	*dram.*
Short	ཐུང་ཐུང་	*thung-thung.*
Short man	ཏེ་པོ་	*te-po.*
Do. *hon.*	སྐུ་གཟུགས་ཆུང་ཆུང་	*ku-śu chhung chhung.*

Short-cut (road)	མགྱོགས་ལམ་	*gyo-lam.*
Shorten, to (abbreviate)	སྡུད་པ། དུམ་དུམ་བྱེད་པ་	*dü-pa ; dum-dum cḱe-pa.*
Shortly (soon)	ཧྲིབ་ཙ་ (ཙམ་) གཅིག་ལ་	*hrip-tsa-chi-la.*
Shoulder	དཔུང་པ་	*pung-pa.*
Do. *hon.*	ཕྱག་དཔུང་	*chha-pung.*
Shout, to	སྐད་རྒྱབ་པ་	*ke-gyaṕ-pa.*
Do. *hon.*	གསུང་སྐད་སྐྱོན་པ་	*sung-ke kyöm-pa.*
Shovel	འཇག་མ་	*ja-ma.*
Show	བལྟས་མོ་	*te-mo.*
Do. *hon.*	གཟིགས་མོ་	*śi-mo.*
Show, to	བསྟན་པ་ (སྟོན་པ་)	*tem-pa.*
Do. *hon.*	བསྟན་ (སྟོན་) པ་གནང་བ་	*tem-pa nang-wa.*
Do. *inf.* to *sup.*	སྤྱན་ཕེབ་ཞུ་བ། སྤྱན་དར་ཞུ་བ་	*chen-phe sḱu-wa; chen-ťar sḱu-wa.*
Show off, to (in dress)	དང་འདོད་བྱེད་པ་	*ťang-dö cḱe-pa.*
Do. *hon.*	ཐུགས་དང་འདོད་གནང་བ་	*thu ťang-dö nang-wa.*
Shower of rain, light	སྦྲིན་ཆར་	*tring-chhar.*
Do. mixed with hail	དྲག་ཆར་	*ťrak-chhar.*
Shrewd	གཅང་པོ་	*chang-po.*
Do. *hon.*	ཐུགས་གཅང་པོ་	*thu-chang-po.*
Shrine	ལྷ་ཁང་	*hla-khang.*

Shrink, to (of cloth, etc.)	འཁུམ་པ་	*khum-pa.*
Shrivel, to	འཁུམ་པ་	*khum-pa.*
Shrub	ཤིང་སྡོང་ཆུང་ཆུང་	*shing-dong-chung-chung.*
Shudder, to	འདར་བ་	*dar-wa.*
Do. *hon.*	སྐུ་འདར་སྐྱོན་པ་	*kün-dar kyöm-pa.*
Shun, to (persons)	དབྱོལ་བ། ཟུར་ནས་འགྲོ་བ་	*yö-wa ; śur-ne dro-wa.*
Do. *hon.*	ཟུར་ནས་ཕེབ་པ་	*śur-ne phe-pa.*
Shun, to (things)	དབྱུག་བཞག་ (འཛོག་) པ། སྤང་བ་	*yuḱ-sḱaḱ-pa ; pang-wa.*
Do. *hon.*	དབྱུག་གཞོག་ག་ (འཛོག་པ་) གནང་བ། སྤོང་ང་ (ཀ་) གནང་བ་	*yuḱ-sḱo-ḱa nang-wa ; pong-nga nang-wa.*
Shut, to (door)	རྒྱབ་པ་	*gyaṕ-pa.*
Do. *hon.*	སྐྱོན་པ་	*kyöm-pa.*
Shut the mouth, to	ཁ་བཙུམ་ (འཛུམ་) པ་	*kha tsum-pa.*
Shut up! (keep quiet)	ཁ་ཁ་སྡོད། ཁ་བཙུམ་ (ཁ་ཚུམ་)	*kha-kha-dö ; kha-tsum.*
Do. *hon.*	ཞལ་བཙུམ་ (ཞལ་ཚུམ་)	*sḱe-tsum.*
Shutter	སྒོ་སྤང་	*go-pang.*
Shuttle-cock	ཐེ་བེ་	*the-be.*
Shy, to (of horses)	འདྲོག་པ་	*droḱ-pa.*

Shy, to be (bashful)	ངོ་ཚ་བ་	*ngo-tsha-wa.*
Do. *hon.*	ཞལ་རས་ཚ་བ་གནང་བ་	*ske-re tsha-wa nang-wa.*
Sick, to be	ན་བ་	*na-wa.*
Do. *hon.*	སྙུང་བ་	*nyung-wa.*
Sickle	ཟོར་ར་ (ཟོར་བ་)	*śor-ra.*
Sickness	ན་ཚ་	*na-tsha.*
Do. *hon.*	སྙུང་གཞི་	*nyung-ski.*
Side (of the body)	ཟུར་	*śur.*
Do. (direction)	ཕྱོགས། ངོས་	*chho; ngö.*
Side of, at the	རྩ་ལ་ (རྩར་ལ་)	*tsa-la.*
Side of, the far	ཕར་ཕྱོགས་	*phar-chho.*
Side of, the near	ཚུར་ཕྱོགས་	*tshur-chho.*
Sides, on all	ཕན་ཚུན་	*phen-tshün.*
Sift, to	བཙག་པ་ (འཚག་པ་)	*tsak-pa.*
Do. *hon.*	བཙག་ག་ (འཚག་པ་) གནང་བ་	*tsak-ka nang-wa.*
Sigh	དབུགས་རིང་	*u-ring.*
Sigh, to	དབུགས་རིང་བཏང་ (གཏོང་) བ་	*u-ring tang-wa.*
Do. *hon.*	དབུགས་རིང་གཏོང་ང་ (བ་) གནང་བ་	*u-ring tong-nga nang-wa.*
Sight (of a gun)	སོ་ཁུང་	*so-khung.*

Sightless	ལོང་ང་ (ལོང་བ་)	*long-nga.*
Do. *hon.*	སྤྱན་ལོང་ང་ (བ་)	*chen-long-nga.*
Sign (mark)	རྟགས་	*ta.*
Signal	ལག་བརྡ་	*lak̔-da.*
Signature	ལག་རྟགས་	*lak̔-ta.*
Do *hon.*	ཕྱག་རྟགས་	*chha-ta.*
Significant (important)	གནད་ཁག་ཆེན་པོ། གལ་ཆེན་པོ་	*nen-kha chhem-po ; k̔e chhem-po.*
Signification	དོན་དག་	*t̔ön-t̔a.*
Do. *hon.*	སྐུ་དོན་	*ku-t̔ön.*
Sikkim	འབྲས་ལྗོངས་	*dren-jong.*
Silent, to be	ཁ་ཁ་བསྡད་ (སྡོད་) པ་	*kha-kha de-pa.*
Do. *hon.*	ཞལ་རགས་བཞུགས་པ་	*sk̔e-ra sk̔u-pa.*
Silk	གོས་ཆེན་	*k̔ö-chhen.*
Do. (tussore silk)	འབུ་རས་	*bu-re.*
Silly (weak in intellect)	ཀླུགས་པ། གླེན་པ་	*kuk̔-pa ; lem-pa.*
Do. (nonsensical)	དོན་མེད་	*t̔ön-me.*
Silver, *s.*	དངུལ་	*ngü.*
Do. *adj.*	དངུལ་གྱི་	*ngü-k̔yi.*
Silversmith	དངུལ་བཟོ་བ་	*ngü śo-wa.*

Similar	ནང་བཞིན། འདྲ་པོ། གཅིག་པ། འདྲ་འདྲ་	*nang-shin; dra-po; chik-pa; dran-dra.*
Simple (easy)	ལས་སླ་པོ་	*le-la-po.*
Do. (foolish)	ཀླུགས་པ། གླེན་པ་	*kuk-pa; lem-pa.*
Simpleton	ཀླུགས་པ། གླེན་པ་	*kuk-pa; lem-pa.*
Simply (merely)	གཅིག་གོ་ (གཅིག་པོ་)	*chik-ko.*
Simulate, to	གྱོད་བཤད་པ་	*kyö she-pa.*
Do. *hon.*	གྱོད་གསུང་བ་	*kyö sung-wa.*
Sin	སྡིག་པ་	*dik-pa.*
Do. *hon.*	སྐུ་སྡིག་	*ku-di.*
Sin, to	སྡིག་པ་བསགས་ (སོག་) པ་	*dik-pa sak-pa.*
Do. *hon.*	སྐུ་སྡིག་བསགས་ག་ (སོག་པ་) གནང་བ་	*ku-di sak-ka nang-wa.*
Since (afterwards)	གཞུག་ལ། རྗེས་ལ་	*shu-la; je-la.*
Sincere	དྲང་པོ་	*trang-po.*
Do. *hon.*	ཐུགས་དྲང་པོ་	*thuk-trang-po.*
Sincerely	དངོས་ནས་དྲང་ནས་	*ngö-ne trang-ne.*
Sinew	རྒྱུས་པ་	*gyü-pa.*
Sinful	ངན་པོ་	*ngem-po.*
Do. *hon.*	ཐུགས་ངན་པོ་	*thu ngem-po.*

Sing, to	གཞེས་བཏང་ (གཏོང་) བ་	*sKe tang-wa.*
Do. *hon.*	མགུལ་གླུ་བཞེས་པ་	*gü-lu sKe-pa.*
Sing, to (hymns)	མགུར་མ་ལེན་པ་	*gur-ma lem-pa.*
Do. *hon.*	གསུང་མགུར་བཞེས་པ་	*sung-gur sKe-pa.*
Single (separate)	གཅིག་པོ་	*chiK-po.*
Do. *hon.*	སྐུ་རྐྱང་	*ku-kyang.*
Single (individual)	རེ་རེ་	*re-re.*
Singly	རེ་རེ་བྱས་ནས་	*re-re cKe-ne.*
Sink, to (of persons)	ཐིམ་པ་	*thim-pa.*
Do. *hon.*	ཐིམ་པ་གནང་བ་	*thim-pa nang-wa.*
Sink, to (of things)	གཟགས་པ་ (འཛོག་པ་)	*śaK-pa.*
Do. *hon.*	གཟགས་ག་ (འཛོག་པ་) གནང་བ་	*śaK-Ka nang-wa*
Sinner	སྡིག་ཅན་	*diK-chen.*
Sinuous	ཀྱོག་ཀྱོག་	*kyo-kyo.*
Sip, to	ཏོག་ཙོ་ཏོག་ཙོ་འཐུང་བ་	*toK-tso toK-tso thung-wa.*
Do. *hon.*	ཏོག་ཙོ་ཏོག་ཙོ་བཞེས་པ་	*toK-tso toK-tso sKe-pa.*
Sir	སྐུ་གཞོགས་ (སྐུ་ཞབས་)	*ku-sKo.*
Sister (general term)	སྤུན་ཀྱག་	*pün-kya.*
Do. *hon.*	སྐུ་མཆེད་	*kum-chhe.*

Sister, elder	ཨ་ཆེ་	*a-chhe.*
Sister, young	སྤུན་ཀྱག་ཆུང་ང་ (བ་)	*pün-kya chhung-nga.*
Do. *hon.*	སྐུ་མཆེད་ཆུང་ང་ (བ་)	*kum-chhe chung-nga.*
Sister-in-law (husband's sister)	ཁྱོ་གའི་སྤུན་ཀྱག་	*khyo-ge pün-kya.*
Do. *hon.*	སྐུ་ཟླའི་སྐུ་མཆེད་	*kum-de kum-chhe.*
Sister-in-law (wife's sister)	སྐྱེ་དམན་གྱི་སྤུན་ཀྱག་	*kyi-men-ḱyi pün-kya.*
Do. *hon.*	སྐུ་ཟླའི་སྐུ་མཆེད་	*kum-de kum-chhe.*
Sister-in-law (brother's wife)	སྤུན་ཀྱག་གི་སྐྱེ་དམན་	*pün-kya ḱi kyi-men.*
Do. *hon.*	སྐུ་མཆེད་ཀྱི་སྐུ་ཟླ་	*kum-chhe kyi kum-da.*
Sit, to	བསྡད་པ་ (སྡོད་པ་)	*de-pa.*
Do. *hon.*	བཞུགས་པ་	*sḱu-pa.*
Do. *h. hon.*	བཞུགས་གདན་འཛག་པ་	*sḱu-den jaḱ-pa.*
Sit cross-legged, to	སྐྱིལ་ཀྲུང་བྱས་ནས་བསྡད་ (སྡོད་) པ་	*kyi-trung cḱe-ne de-pa.*
Site	ས་ཆ་	*sa-chha.*
Situation (locality)	ས་ཆ་	*sa-chha.*
Do. (state of affairs, etc.)	གནས་ཚུལ་	*ne-tshü*
Six	དྲུག་	*ťruḱ.*
Sixteen	བཅུ་དྲུག་	*chu-ťruḱ.*

Sixteenth	བཅུ་དྲུག་པ་	*chu-t́ruḱ-pa.*
Sixth	དྲུག་པ་	*t́ruḱ-pa.*
Sixtieth	དྲུག་ཅུ་པ་	*t́ruḱ-chu-pa.*
Sixty	དྲུག་ཅུ་	*t́ruḱ-chu.*
Size	ཆེ་ཆུང་	*chhe-chhung.*
Skeleton	རུས་ཀྲང་	*rü-trang.*
Sketch	རི་མོ་	*ri-mo.*
Sketch, to	རིས་མོ་བྲིས་པ་ (འབྲི་བ་)	*ri-mo t́ri-pa.*
Do. *hon.*	རིས་མོ་བྲིས་པ་ (འབྲི་བ་) གནང་བ་	*ri-mo t́ri-pa nang-wa.*
Skilful	མཁས་པོ་	*khe-po.*
Skill	རིག་པ་	*riḱ-pa.*
Do. *hon.*	ཐུགས་རིག་	*thu-ri.*
Skin	པགས་པ་	*paḱ-pa.*
Skin, to	པགས་པ་ཤུ་བ་	*paḱ-pa shu-wa.*
Do. *hon*	པགས་པ་ཤུ་བ་གནང་བ་	*paḱ-pa shu-wa nang-wa.*
Skinny (of persons and animals)	ཤ་སྐམ་པོ་	*sha kam-po.*
Do. *hon.* (of persons)	སྐུ་ཤ་སྐམ་པོ་	*ku-sha kam-po.*
Do. *hon.* (of animals)	བཞེས་ཤ་སྐམ་པོ་	*sḱe-sha kam-po.*

Skull	ཐོད་པ། ཀ་པཱ་ལི་ *Hind.*	*thö-pa ; kap̆-li.*
Skull-drum	ཐོད་ཏམ་	*thön-tam.*
Sky	གནམ། ནམ་མཁའ་	*nam ; nam-kha.*
Slack (languid)	ཉ་རེ་ (ར་) ཉོ་རེ་	*nya-re nyo-re.*
Do. (slow)	འགོར་པོ་	*gor-po.*
Slacken, to	ལྷོད་ལྷོད་བཏང་ (གཏོང་) བ་	*hlö-hlö tang-wa.*
Do. *hon.*	ལྷོད་ལྷོད་གཏོང་ང་ (བ་) གནང་བ་	*hlö-hlö tong-nga nang-wa.*
Slander, *s.*	སྨད་ར་	*me-ra.*
Slander, to	སྨད་ར་བཏང་ (གཏོང་) བ་	*me-ra tang-wa.*
Do. *hon.*	སྨད་ར་གཏོང་ང་ (བ་) གནང་བ་	*me-ra tong-nga nang-wa.*
Do. *inf.* to *sup.*	སྨད་ར་གཞུ་བ་	*me-ra sǩu-wa.*
Slap, to	གཞུ་བ་	*sǩu-wa.*
Do. *hon.*	གཞུ་བ་གནང་བ་	*sǩu-wa nang-wa.*
Slate (for writing)	ཡང་བག་	*yam-p̆a.*
Do. wooden	སྦྱང་ཤིང་	*jang-shing.*
Slaughter, to	བསད་པ་ (གསོད་པ་)	*se-pa.*
Do. *hon.*	བསད་ (གསོད་) པ་གནང་བ་	*se-pa nang-wa.*
Slave	ཚེ་གཡོག་	*tshe-yo.*
Slay, to	བསད་པ་ (གསོད་པ་)	*se-pa.*

Slay, to *hon.*	བསད་ (གསོད་) པ་གནང་བ་	*se-pa nang-wa.*
Slay, to (a person of good position)	བཀྲོངས་པ་ (འགྲོང་བ་)	*trong-pa.*
Sleep, *s.*	གཉིད་	*nyi.*
Do. *hon.*	མཉལ་ (མནལ་)	*nye.*
Sleep, to	ཉལ་བསྡད་ (སྡོད་) པ་	*nye de-pa.*
Do. *hon.*	གཟིམ་བཞུགས་པ་	*śim sḱu-pa.*
Sleep, to go to	གཉིད་ཁུག་པ་	*nyi khuḱ-pa.*
Do. *hon.*	མཉལ་ (མནལ་) གཟིམ་པ་	*nye śim-pa.*
Sleeping draught	ཞི་སྨན་	*sḱi-men.*
Sleepy, to be	གཉིད་ཚོག་རྒྱབ་པ་	*nyi-tso gyaṕ-pa.*
Do. *hon.*	མཉལ་ (མནལ་) ཚོག་སྐྱོན་པ་	*nye-tso kyöm-pa.*
Sleeve	ཕུ་དུང་	*phu-ťung.*
Do. *hon.*	ཕྱག་ཕུང་	*chha-phung.*
Slender	ཕྲ་པོ་	*thra-po.*
Slice, to	གཏུབ་པ་	*tuṕ-pa.*
Do. *hon.*	གཏུབ་པ་གནང་བ་	*tuṕ-pa nang-wa.*
Slice	བྲ་པོ་	*tra-po.*
Slight, *adj.* (thin)	ཤ་སྐམ་པོ་	*sha kam-po.*
Do. *hon.*	སྐུ་ཤ་སྐམ་པོ་	*ku-sha kam-po.*

Sling (for stone)	སྒུ་རྡོ་	*gu-do.*
Slip, to, *v.i.*	འདྲེད་དག་ཤོར་བ་	*dre-ťa shor-wa.*
Do. *hon.*	ཞབས་འདྲེད་ཤོར་བ་	*sKam-dre shor-wa.*
Slit (fissure)	སེར་ཀ་	*ser-ka.*
Slit, to be (cloth)	རལ་བ་	*re-wa.*
Slope (upward)	གྱེན་	*kyen.*
Do. (downward)	ཐུར་	*thur.*
Slothful	སྙོབས་པོ། ལེ་ལོ་ཆེན་པོ་	*nyop-po ; le-lo chhem-po.*
Slow	འགོར་པོ་	*gor-po.*
Slowly	ག་ལེ་ག་ལེ་	*ka-le ka-le.*
Sluggard	སྙོབས་པོ་	*nyop-po.*
Sluggish (languid)	ཉ་རེ་ (ར་) ཉོ་རེ་	*nya-re nyo-re.*
Slumber, to	གཉིད་ཚོག་རྒྱབ་པ་	*nyi-tso gyap-pa.*
Do. *hon.*	མཉལ་ (མནལ་) ཚོག་སྐྱོན་པ་	*nye-tso kyöm-pa.*
Sly (artful)	གཅང་པོ་	*chang-po.*
Do. *hon.*	ཐུགས་གཅང་པོ་	*thu-chang-po.*
Small	ཆུང་ཆུང་	*chhung-chhung.*
Small-pox	ལྷན་འབྲུམ་	*hlan-drum.*
Smash, to	བཅག་པ་ (གཅོག་པ་)	*chak-pa.*
Do. *hon.*	བཅག་ག་ (པ་) གནང་བ་	*chak-ka nang-wa.*

Smear, to	བྱུག་པ་ (འབྱུག་པ།) སྐུ་བ་	*chuḱ-pa ; ḱu-wa.*
Do. *hon.*	བྱུགས་ག་ (འབྱུག་པ་) གནང་བ། སྐུ་བ་གནང་བ་	*chuḱ-ḱa nang-wa ; ḱu-wa nang-wa.*
Smell	དྲི་མ་	*t́ri-ma.*
Smell, to (use the sense of smell)	སྣོམ་པ་	*nom-pa.*
Do. *hon.*	སྣོམ་པ་གནང་བ་	*nom-pa nang-wa.*
Smell, to (have odour)	དྲི་མ་ཁ་བ་	*t́ri-ma kha-wa.*
Smile, to	ཁ་ཚེ་ཚེ་བྱེད་པ་	*kha tshe-tshe cḱe-pa.*
Do. *hon.*	ཞལ་ཚེ་ཚེ་གནང་བ་	*sḱe tshe-tshe nang-wa.*
Smite, to	གཞུ་བ། རྡུང་བ་	*sḱu-wa ; dung-wa.*
Do. *hon.*	གཞུ་བ་གནང་བ། ཕྱག་འཇུག་ (འཇུས་) གནང་བ་	*sḱu-wa nang-wa ; chhan-ju nang-wa.*
Smith	མགར་ར་ (མགར་བ་)	*gar-ra.*
Smoke, *s.*	དུ་བ་ (དུད་པ་)	*t́u-wa.*
Smoke, to (tobacco)	འཐུང་བ། འཐེན་པ་	*thung-wa ; them-pa.*
Do. *hon.*	བཞེས་པ་	*sḱe-pa.*
Smooth	སྙོམ་པོ་	*nyom-po.*
Smother, to	གློ་སུབ་རྒྱབ་པ་	*lo-suṕ gyaṕ-pa.*
Do. *hon.*	གློ་སུབ་སྐྱོན་པ་	*lo-suṕ kyöm-pa.*
Snake	སྦྲུལ་	*drü.*

Snap the finger, to	སིར་གོར་ (སེ་གོལ་) རྡབ་པ་	*sir-ḱor daṕ-pa.*
Do. *hon.*	སིར་གོར་ (སེ་གོལ་) རྡབ་པ་ གནང་བ་	*sir-ḱor daṕ-pa nang-wa.*
Snare	ཉི་	*nyi.*
Snatch, to	འཕྲོག་པ་	*throḱ-pa.*
Do. *hon.*	འཕྲོག་ག་ (པ་) གནང་བ་	*throḱ-ḱa nang-wa.*
Sneeze, to	ཧབ་བྲིད་ (སྦྲིད་) རྒྱབ་པ་	*haṕ-t́ri gyaṕ-pa.*
Do. *hon.*	ཧབ་བྲིད་ (སྦྲིད་) སྐྱོན་པ་	*haṕ-t́ri kyöm-pa.*
Sneer, to	ཀྱག་ཀྱག་བྱས་ནས་ལབ་པ་	*kya-kya cḱe-ne laṕ-pa.*
Do. *hon.*	ཀྱག་ཀྱག་གནང་ནས་གསུང་བ་	*kya-kya nang-ne sung-wa.*
Snore, to	སྔུར་པོ་རྒྱབ་པ་	*ngur-po gyaṕ-pa.*
Do. *hon.*	སྔུར་པོ་སྐྱོན་པ་	*ngur-po kyöm-pa.*
Snow	གངས་	*ḱang.*
Snow, to	གངས་རྒྱབ་པ་	*ḱang gyaṕ-pa.*
Snow, eye-shade for	མིག་ར་	*miḱ-ra.*
Do. *hon.*	སྤྱན་ར་	*chen-ra.*
Snow-avalanche	གངས་རུད་	*ḱang-rü.*
Snow-blindness	གངས་ཁྲིད་	*ḱang-chhi.*
Snow-cock,	ལྷ་བྱ་གོང་མོ་	*lhaṕ-cḱa ḱong-mo.*
Snow-leopard	གསའ་	*sa.*

Snow-storm	གངས་ཚུབ་	*ḱang-tshuṕ.*
Snuff	སྣ་ཐག་	*na-tha.*
Do. *hon.*	ཞངས་ཐག་	*shang-tha.*
Snuff-box	སྣ་རུ་	*na-ru.*
Do. *hon.*	ཞངས་རུ་	*shang-ru.*
So and so	དེ་འདྲས་	*den-dre.*
Soak, to	སྦང་བ་	*bang-wa.*
Do. *hon.*	སྦང་ང་ (བ་) གནང་བ་	*bang-nga nang-wa.*
Soap	ཡི་རྩེ་ *Ch.*	*yi-tse.*
Do. globular (for washing clothes)	གླང་གླད་	*lang-le.*
Do. powdered (of Tibetan manufacture)	སྦུག་པ་	*suḱ-pa.*
Do. *hon.*	ཕྱག་སུག་	*chha-su.*
Soar, to	ལྡིང་བ་	*ding-wa.*
Sob, to	ངུ་བ་	*ngu-wa.*
Do. *hon.*	ཤུམ་པ་	*shum-pa.*
Sober (not drunk), to be	ར་མ་ཟི་པ་	*ra ma śi-pa.*
Do. *hon.*	སྐུ་ར་མ་བེད་པ་	*ku-ra ma be-pa.*
Sock	ཨོ་མོ་སུ་ *Mon.*	*o-mo-su.*
Do. *hon.*	ཞབས་སུ་	*shaṕ-su.*

Socket of the eye	མིག་ཁུང་	*mik-khung.*
Do. *hon.*	སྤྱན་ཁུང་	*chen-khung.*
Sod	སྤང་	*pang.*
Soda	བུལ་ཏོག་	*pü-to.*
Soft	འཇམ་པོ་	*jam-po.*
Softly	ག་ལེ་ག་ལེ་	*ka-le ka-le.*
Soil (earth)	ས་	*sa.*
Soil, to	བཙོག་པ་བཟོ་བ་	*tsok-pa śo-wa.*
Do. *hon.*	བཙོག་པ་བཟོ་བ་གནང་བ་	*tsok-pa śo-wa nang-wa.*
Sojourn, to	བསྡད་པ་ (སྡོད་པ་)	*de-pa.*
Do. *hon.*	བཞུགས་པ་	*sku-pa.*
Do. *h. hon.*	བཞུགས་གདན་འཇག་པ་	*sku-den jak-pa.*
Solace, to	སེམས་གསོ་བཏང་ (གཏོང་) བ་	*sem-so tang-wa.*
Do. *hon.*	སེམས་གསོ་གཏོང་ང་ (བ་) གནང་བ་	*sem-so tong-nga nang-wa.*
Do. *inf. to sup.*	ཐུགས་གསོ་ཕུལ་ (འབུལ་) བ་	*thu-so phü-wa.*
Solder, *s.*	དཀར་ཡ་	*ka-ya.*
Soldier	དམག་མི་	*ma-mi.*
Sole (of foot)	རྐང་མཐིལ་	*kang-thi.*
Do. *hon.*	ཞབས་མཐིལ་	*skap-thi.*

Sole, *adj.*	གཅིག་པོ་	*chik-pa.*
Do. *hon.*	སྐུ་རྐྱང་	*ku-kyang.*
Solely	ཤ་སྟག་	*sha-ta.*
Solicit, to	ཞུ་བ་	*sku-wa.*
Do. *hon.*	ཞུ་བ་གནང་བ་	*sku-wa nang-wa.*
Solitary	གཅིག་པོ་	*chik-po.*
Do. *hon.*	སྐུ་རྐྱང་	*ku-kyang*
Solitary place	དབེན་གནས་	*en-ne.*
Solid (firm)	བརྟན་པོ་	*tem-po.*
Sombre, to be, (melancholy)	སེམས་སྐྱོ་སྣང་བྱེད་པ་	*sem kyo-nang che-pa.*
Do. *hon.*	ཐུགས་སེམས་སྐྱོ་སྣང་གནང་བ་	*thu-sem kyo-nang nang-wa.*
Some (a little, *e.g.* salt)	ཏོག་ཙ་	*tok-tsa.*
Some (a few, *e.g.* men)	ཁ་ཤས་	*kha-she.*
Something	ག་རེ་ཡིན་ནས་གཅིག་	*ka-re yin-ne chi.*
Sometimes	མཚམས་མཚམས་	*tsham-tsham.*
Do. *hon.*	ཐུགས་སངས་ཐུགས་སངས་ལ་	*thuk-sang thuk-sang la.*
Somnolent, to be	གཉིད་ཚོག་རྒྱབ་པ་	*nyi-tso gyap-pa.*
Do. *hon.*	མཉལ་ (མནལ་) ཚོག་སྐྱོན་པ་	*nye-tso kyöm-pa.*
Son	བུ་	*pu.*
Do. *hon.*	སྲས་	*se.*

Son-in-law	མག་པ་	*mak-pa.*
Do. *hon.*	སྐུ་བག་	*ku-pá.*
Song	གཞས་	*she.*
Do. *hon.*	གསུང་གཞས་	*sung-she.*
Song, religious	མགུར་མ་	*gur-ma.*
Do. *hon.*	གསུང་མགུར་	*sung-gur.*
Soon	མགྱོགས་པོར་	*gyok-po.*
Soothsay, to	མངོན་ཤེས་ཤེས་པ་	*ngön-she she-pa.*
Do. *hon.*	མངོན་མཁྱེན་མཁྱེན་པ་	*ngön-khyen khyem-pa.*
Soothsay, to (in a trance)	ལུང་བསྟན་ (སྟོན་) པ་	*lung tem-pa.*
Do. *hon.*	བཀའ་ལུང་བསྟན་ (སྟོན་) པ་གནང་བ་	*ka-lung tem-pa nang-wa.*
Soothsayer	རྩིས་པ་	*tsi-pa.*
Soothsaying	མངོན་ཤེས་	*ngon-she.*
Do. *hon.*	མངོན་མཁྱེན་	*ngön-khyen.*
Soothsaying (in a trance)	ལུང་བསྟན་	*lung-ten.*
Do. *hon.*	བཀའ་ལུང་	*ka-lung.*
Sorcerer	མཐུ་རྒྱབ་མཁན་	*thu-gyap-khen.*
Do. *hon.*	མཐུ་སྐྱོན་མཁན་	*thu kyön-khen.*
Sorcery	མཐུ་	*thu.*

Sordid (niggardly)	ལག་པ་དམ་པོ་	*laḱ-pa ťam-po.*
Do. *hon.*	ཕྱག་དམ་པོ་	*chha ťam-po.*
Sore, *s.*	རྨ་	*ma.*
Sore throat, to have a	སྐེ་ན་བ་	*ke-na-wa.*
Sorrow	སྡུག་བསྔལ་	*du-nge.*
Do. *hon.*	ཐུགས་འཁྲལ། ཐུགས་བསྔལ་	*thu-thre ; thu-nge.*
Sorrowful, to be	སེམས་སྐྱོ་བ། སེམས་སྡུག་པ་	*sem-kyo-wa; sem-duḱ-pa.*
Do. *hon.*	ཐུགས་སེམས་སྐྱོ་བ་གནང་བ། ཐུགས་སེམས་སྡུག་ག་ (པ་) གནང་བ་	*thu-sem kyo-wa nang-wa ; thu-sem duḱ-ḱa nang-wa.*
Sorry, to be	སེམས་སྐྱོ་བ་	*sem-kyo-wa.*
Do. *hon.*	ཐུགས་སེམས་སྐྱོ་བ་གནང་བ་	*thu-sem kyo-wa nang-wa.*
Sort, *s.* (class of man)	རྒྱུ། རིགས་	*gyu ; ri.*
Do. *hon.*	སྐུ་རྒྱུ། སྐུ་རིགས་	*ku-gyu ; ku-ri.*
Sort, *s.* (of things)	རྒྱུ་དག་	*gyu-ťa.*
Sorts, different	སྣ་ཚོགས་	*na-tsho.*
Soul	སེམས་	*sem.*
Do. *hon.*	ཐུགས་སེམས་	*thu-sem.*
Sound (noise)	སྐད་	*ke.*
Sound (healthy)	གཟུགས་པོ་བདེ་པོ་	*śuḱ-po de-po.*

Sound (healthy), *hon.*	སྐུ་གཟུགས་བཟང་པོ་	*ku-śuk śang-po.*
Soup	ཁུ་བ་	*khu-a.*
Do. *hon.*	སྒྲུམ་ཁུ་	*trung-khu.*
Soup (made from meat)	ཤ་ཁུ་	*sha-khu.*
Do. *hon.*	སྒྲུམ་ཁུ་	*trung-khu.*
Sour (acid)	སྐྱུར་པོ་	*kyur-po.*
Source (of river, etc.)	ཆུ་ཐང་ (འབྱུང་ཁུངས་)	*cḱung-tang.*
Do. (cause)	རྐྱེན་	*kyen.*
South	ལྷོ་	*hlo.*
Sovereign (king)	རྒྱལ་པོ་	*gye-po.*
Sow, *s.*	ཕག་མོ་	*pha-mo.*
Sow, to (seed)	བཏབ་པ་ (འདེབས་པ་)	*tap̍-pa.*
Do. (broadcast)	སོན་རྒྱབ་པ་	*sön gyap̍-pa.*
Sower	སོན་རྒྱབ་མཁན་	*sön gyam-khen.*
Space for, sufficient	ཤོང་ས་	*shong-sa.*
Spacious	ཁུ་ཡངས་པོ་	*ḱu-yang-po.*
Spade	འཇག་མ་	*ja-ma.*
Span	མཐོ་	*tho.*
Spare (thin)	ཤ་སྐམ་པོ་	*sha kam-po.*
Do. *hon.*	སྐུ་ཤ་སྐམ་པོ་	*ku-sha kam-po.*

Spare time (leisure)	ལོངས་	*long.*
Spark	མེ་ཚག་	*me-tsha.*
Sparkle, to, *v.i.*	འོད་རྒྱབ་པ་	*ö gyaṕ-pa.*
Speak, to	ལབ་པ་	*laṕ-pa.*
Do. *hon.*	གསུང་བ་	*sung-wa.*
Spear	མདུང་	*dung.*
Do. *hon*	ཕྱག་མདུང་	*chhan-dung.*
Specially	ཁྱད་པར་དུ་	*khye-par-ťu.*
Species (of human beings)	རྒྱུ། རིགས་	*gyu ; ri.*
Do. *hon.*	སྐུ་རྒྱུ། སྐུ་རིགས་	*ku-gyu ; ku-ri.*
Species (of things)	རྒྱུ་དག་	*gyu-ťa.*
Do. (different)	སྣ་ཚོགས་	*na-tsho.*
Specimen	དཔེ་	*pe.*
Spectacle	བལྟད་མོ་	*te-mo.*
Do. *hon.*	གཟིགས་མོ་	*śi-mo.*
Spectacles	མིག་ཤེར་ (མིག་ཤེལ་)	*miḱ-sher.*
Do. *hon.*	སྤྱན་ཤེར་ (སྤྱན་ཤེལ་)	*chen-sher.*
Spectre (ghost)	གདོང་འདྲེ། འདྲེ་	*dong-dre ; dre.*
Speech	སྐད་	*ke.*
Do. *hon.*	གསུང་སྐད་	*sung-ke.*

Speechless, to be	ཁ་ཁ་བསྡད་ (སྡོད་) པ་	*kha-kha de-pa.*
Do. *hon.*	ཞལ་རགས་བཞུགས་པ་	*sḱe-ra sḱu-pa.*
Speed	ཚ་དྲག་	*tsha-t́ra.*
Speed, to	མགྱོགས་པོ་བྱེད་པ་	*gyoḱ-po cḱe-pa.*
Do. *hon.*	རྩོལ་པོ་གནང་བ་	*tsö-po nang-wa.*
Do. *h. hon.*	ཐུགས་རྩོལ་པོ་གནང་བ་	*thu-tsö-po nang-wa.*
Speedy	མགྱོགས་པོ་	*gyoḱ-po.*
Do. *hon.*	རྩོལ་པོ་	*tsö-po.*
Spell, to	སྦྱོང་ཀློག་རྒྱབ་པ་	*jong-lo gyaṕ-pa.*
Spelling	སྦྱོང་ཀློག་	*jong-lo.*
Spend wastefully, to (money)	གཏོར་བ་	*tor-wa.*
Do. *hon.*	གཏོར་ར་ (བ་) གནང་བ་	*tor-ra nang-wa.*
Spice	ཤ་སྨན་	*sha-men.*
Spider	འདོམ་	*dom.*
Spider's web	འདོམ་ཐག་	*dom-tha.*
Spike, iron	ལྕགས་ཕུར་	*chaḱ-phur.*
Do. wooden	ཕུར་པ་	*phu-pa.*
Spill, to	ཕོ་བ་ (འཕོ་བ་)	*pho-wa.*
Do. *hon.*	ཕོ་ (འཕོ་) བ་གནང་བ་	*pho-wa nang-wa.*

Spin, to	འཁལ་བ་	*khe-wa.*
Do. *hon.*	འཁལ་ར་ (བ་) བནང་བ་	*khe-ra nang-wa.*
Spindle	ཡོ་ག་	*yo-ga.*
Do. (another kind)	འཕང་	*phang.*
Spine	སྒལ་ཚིགས་	*ge-tshi.*
Spirit (soul)	སེམས་	*sem.*
Do. (wine)	ཨ་རག་	*a-ra.*
Do. *hon.*	བཞེས་རག་	*ske-ra.*
Spirit, evil	གདོང་འདྲེ། བདུད་	*dong-dre; dü.*
Spirited	ཧུར་པོ་	*hur-po.*
Spiritual	དགེ་སེམས་ཆེན་པོ་	*ge-sem chhem-po*
Spit, to	མཆིལ་མ་གཏོར་བ་	*chhi-ma tor-wa.*
Do. *hon.*	ལྗགས་ཆུ་གཏོར་ར་ (བ་) གནང་བ་	*ja-chhu tor-ra nang-wa.*
Spite	གནོད་སེམས་	*nö-sem.*
Spittle	མཆིལ་མ་	*chhi-ma.*
Do. *hon.*	ལྗགས་ཆུ་	*ja-chhu.*
Splendid	གཟི་བརྗིད་ཆེན་པོ། གཡང་མཛེས་	*śi-ji chhem-po; yang-dze.*
Splendour	གཟི་བརྗིད་	*śi-ji.*

Splice, to	འཐུད་རྒྱབ་པ་	*thü gyaṕ-pa.*
Do. *hon.*	འཐུད་སྐྱོན་པ་	*thü kyöm-pa.*
Split, to	གཤགས་པ་	*shaḱ-pa.*
Do. *hon.*	གཤག་ག་ (པ་) གནང་བ་	*shaḱ-ḱa nang-wa.*
Spoil, to	མེད་པར་བཟོ་བ་	*me-pa śo-wa.*
Do. *hon.*	མེད་པར་བཟོ་བ་གནང་བ་	*me-pa śo-wa nang-wa.*
Spoon	ཐུར་མ་	*thur-ma.*
Do. *hon.*	བཞེས་ཐུར་	*sḱiṕ-thu.*
Sport, *s.*	རྩེད་མོ་	*tse-mo.*
Do. *hon.*	སྐུ་རྩེད་	*ku-tse.*
Sport, to	རྩེད་མོ་རྩེ་བ་	*tse-mo tse-wa.*
Do. *hon.*	སྐུ་རྩེད་གནང་བ་	*ku-tse nang-wa*
Spot (stain)	ཐིག་པ་	*thiḱ-pa.*
Do. (place)	ས་ཆ་	*sa-chha.*
Spouse (wife)	སྐྱེས་དམན་	*kyi-men.*
Do. *hon.* (of well-to-do villager)	ཉི་སྙིང་ལགས་	*nyi-nying-la.*
Do. (of ordinary official)	ལྕམ་སྐུ་གཞོགས་	*cham ku-sḱo.*
Do. (of third grade and upwards)	ལྷ་ལྕམ་སྐུ་གཞོགས་	*hla-cham ku-sḱo*
Sprain, to	ཚིགས་འཁྲོག་ (འཁྲུད་) པ་	*tshi throḱ-pa.*

Sprain, to, *hon.*	ཞབས་ཚིགས་འཁྲོག་ག་ (འབུད་པ་) གནང་བ་	*sKap-tshi throk-ka nang-wa.*
Spread, to (mat, etc.)	བཏིང་བ་ (འདིང་བ་)	*ting-wa.*
Do. *hon.*	བཏིང་ང་ (འདིང་བ་) གནང་བ་	*ting-nga nang-wa.*
Spring (season)	དཔྱིད་ཀ་	*chi-ka.*
Spring (of water)	ཆུ་མིག་	*chhu-mi.*
Spring, to (jump)	མཆོངས་པ། མཆོངས་རྒྱག་ རྒྱབ་པ་	*chhọng-pa ; chhong-gya gyap-pa.*
Do. *hon.*	མཆོངས་རྒྱག་སྐྱོན་པ་	*chhong-gya kyöm-pa.*
Sprinkle, to (*e.g.* water on ground)	གཏོར་བ་	*tor-wa.*
Do. *hon.*	གཏོར་ར་ (བ་) གནང་བ་	*tor-ra nang-wa.*
Sprite	གདོང་འདྲེ། འདྲེ་	*dong-dre ; dre.*
Sprout, to	སྐྱེ་བ་	*kye-wa.*
Spruce (tree)	སད་ཤིང་	*se-shing.*
Spur (of mountain)	སྒང་	*gang.*
Spy, *s.*	སོ་པ་	*so-pa.*
Spy, to	སོ་ལྟ་བ་	*so ta-wa.*
Squabble (row)	རྒྱབ་འདྲེ་	*gyam-dre.*
Do. *hon.*	གསུང་འཁྲུག་	*sung-thru.*

Squabble, to	རྒྱབ་འདྲེ་རྒྱབ་པ་	*gyam-dre gyaṕ-pa.*
Do. *hon.*	གསུང་འཁྲུག་སྐྱོན་པ་	*sung-thru kyöm-pa.*
Squander, to	གཏོར་བ་	*tor-wa.*
Do. *hon.*	གཏོར་ར་ (བ་) གནང་བ་	*tor-ra nang-wa.*
Square	གྲུ་བཞི་	*t́ruṕ-sḱi.*
Squeeze, to	བཙིར་བ་ (འཚིར་བ)	*tsir-wa.*
Do. *hon.*	བཙིར་ར་ (བ་) གནང་བ་	*tsir-ra nang-wa.*
Squirrel	སྲེ་མོང་	*tre-mong.*
Stab, to	བཙུགས་པ་ (འཛུགས་པ་)	*tsuḱ-pa.*
Do. *hon.*	བཙུགས་ག་ (འཛུགས་པ་) གནང་བ་	*tsuḱ-ḱa nang-wa.*
Stable, *adj.* (firm)	བརྟན་པོ་	*tem-po.*
Stable, *s.*	རྟ་ར་	*ta-ra.*
Do. *hon.*	ཆིབས་ར་	*chhiṕ-ra.*
Stable gear	རྟ་ཆས་	*taṕ-chhe.*
Stack, to	རྩིག་བཞག་ (འཛོག་) པ་	*tsiḱ sḱaḱ-pa.*
Do. *hon.*	རྩིག་གཞོག་ག་ (འཛོག་པ་) གནང་བ་	*tsiḱ sḱoḱ-ḱa nang-wa.*
Staff	འཁར་རྒྱུག། རྒྱུག་པ་ (དབྱུག་པ་)	*khar-gyu ; gyuḱ-pa.*

Stag	ཤ་ཕོ་	*sha-pho.*
Do. young	ཤ་ཕྲུག་	*sha-thru.*
Stage of a journey	ཞག་ས། རྒྱ་ཚུག་	*sǩak-sa ; gya-tshu.*
Do. *hon.*	བཞུགས་ཞག་	*sǩu-sǩa.*
Stagger, to, *v.i.*	འཁྱོར་ནས་འགྲོ་བ་	*khyor-ne dro-wa.*
Do. *hon.*	སྐུ་འཁྱོར་ནས་ཕེབ་པ་	*ku-kyyor-ne phe-pa.*
Do. *h. hon.*	སྐུ་འཁྱོར་ནས་འཆིབ་རྒྱུ་གནང་བ་	*ku-khyor-ne chhiṕ-gyu nang-wa.*
Stagger, to (astonish)	ཡ་མཚན་བྱེད་པ་	*yam-tshen cǩe-pa.*
Do. *hon.*	ཡ་མཚན་གནང་བ་	*yam-tshen nang-wa.*
Stain, *s.*	ཐིག་པ་	*thiǩ-pa.*
Stain, to	བཙོག་པ་བཟོ་བ་	*tsoǩ-pa śo-wa.*
Do. *hon.*	བཙོག་པ་བཟོ་བ་གནང་བ་	*tsoǩ-pa śo-wa nang-wa.*
Stair-case	ཀན་ཙ་ (སྐས་འཛེག་)	*ken-tsa.*
Do. *hon.*	ཕེབ་སྐས་	*pheṕ-ke.*
Staircase (of stone)	རྡོ་ཀྱག་	*doṕ-kya.*
Stake (wager)	རྒྱན་	*gyen.*
Do. *hon.*	སྐུ་རྒྱན་	*ku-gyen.*
Stake, to	རྒྱན་བཞག་ (འཛོག་) པ་	*gyen sǩak-pa.*

Stake, to, *hon.*	སྐུ་རྒྱན་གཞོག་ག་ (འཛོག་པ་) གནང་བ་	*ku-gyen sḱok-ḱa nang-wa.*
Stake	སྙིང་པ་	*nying-pa.*
Stalk	ཀང་	*ḱang.*
Stallion	གསེབ་	*seṕ.*
Do. *hon.*	ཆིབས་གསེབ་	*chhiṕ-seṕ.*
Stalwart	ཤེད་ཆེན་པོ་	*she chhem-po.*
Do. *hon.*	སྐུ་ཤེད་ཆེན་པོ་	*ḱu-she chhem-po.*
Stammering	ཁ་ལྡིག་	*kha-di.*
Stamp, *s.* (seal)	ཐེ་ཙེ། དམ་ཕྲུག་	*the-tse ; ťam-thru.*
Do. *hon.*	ཕྱག་དམ་	*chha-ťam.*
Stampede, to	འདྲོག་ནས་བོས་ (འབྲོས་) པ་	*droḱ-ne ṕö-pa.*
Stand, to	ལངས་ནས་བསྡད་ (སྡོད་) པ་	*lang-ne de-pa.*
Do. *hon.*	བཞེང་ (བཞེངས་) ནས་བཞུགས་པ་	*sḱang-ne sḱu-pa*
Standard (flag)	དར་ལྕོག་	*ťar-cho.*
Star	སྐར་མ་	*ḱar-ma.*
Stare, to	མིག་འདིར་ (བསྒྲིམས་) ནས་ལྟ་བ་	*miḱ-dir-ne ta-wa.*

Stare, to, *hon.*	སྤྱན་འདིར་ (བསྒྲིམས་) ནས་ གཟིགས་པ་	*chen-dir-ne śi-pa.*
Start, to (on a journey)	འགྲོ་བ། ཕྱིན་པ་	*dro-wa ; chhim-pa.*
Do. *hon.*	ཕེབ་པ་	*phe-pa.*
State (condition)	གནས་ཚུལ་	*ne-tshü.*
Do. (kingdom)	རྒྱལ་སྲིད་	*gye-si.*
Station (rank)	གོ་ས་	*ḱo-sa.*
Statue	སྐུ་འདྲ་	*kun-dra.*
Status quo	ཆབ་སྲིད་སྔོན་ཡོད་	*chhaṕ-si ngön-yö*
Status quo, maintenance of	ཆབ་སྲིད་སྔོན་ཡོད་རང་འཇགས་བཞག་རྒྱུ་	*chhaṕ-si ngön-yö rang-ja sḱaḱ-gyu.*
Stay, to	བསྡད་པ་ (སྡོད་པ་)	*de-pa.*
Do. *hon.*	བཞུགས་པ་	*sḱu-pa.*
Do. *h. hon.*	བཞུགས་གདན་འཇག་པ་	*sḱu-den jaḱ-pa.*
Stay, to (wait)	སྒུག་བསྡད་ (སྡོད་) པ་	*gu de-pa.*
Do. *hon.*	སྒུག་བཞུགས་པ་	*gu sḱu-pa.*
Steadfast	བརྟན་པོ་	*tem-po.*
Steadily	ཏེན་ཏེན་བྱས་ནས་	*ten-ten ćhe-ne.*
Steady (resolute)	བརྟན་པོ་	*tem-po.*
Steal, to	རྐུན་མ་རྐུ་བ། རྐུ་བ་	*kü-ma ku-wa ; ku-wa.*

Steam	རླངས་པ་	*lang-pa.*
Steed	རྟ་	*ta*
Do. *hon.*	ཆིབས་པ་	*chhi-pa.*
Steel	ཁ་ལྕགས་	*ḱha-cha.*
Steep	གཟར་པོ་	*śar-po.*
Steep, to	སྦང་བ་	*bang-wa.*
Do. *hon.*	སྦང་ང་ (བ་) གནང་བ་	*bang-nga nang-wa.*
Stem	སྡོང་པོ་	*dong-po.*
Stench, to	དྲི་མ་ཁ་བ་	*t́ri-ma ḱha-wa.*
Step (pace)	གོམ་པ་	*ḱom-pa.*
Do. *hon.*	ཞབས་གོམ་	*sḱaṕ-ḱom.*
Step, to (move by paces)	གོམ་པ་རྒྱབ་པ་	*ḱom-pa gyaṕ-pa.*
Do. *hon.*	ཞབས་གོམ་སྐྱོན་པ་	*sḱaṕ-ḱom kyöm-pa.*
Step-father	ཕ་གཡར་	*p̱ha-ya.*
Step-mother	མ་གཡར་	*ma-ya.*
Steps, flight of wooden	ཀན་ཙ་ (སྐས་འཛེག་)	*ken-tsa.*
Do. *hon.*	ཕེབ་སྐས་	*pheṕ-ke.*
Steps, stone	རྡོ་ཀྱག་	*doṕ-kya.*
Sterile (of women)	རབས་ཆད་	*raṕ-chhe.*
Do. (of land)	ཙ་ཆུ་འཛོམ་པོ་...མེད་པ་	*tsa-chhu dzom-po...me-pa.*

Stern, *adj.*	གྱོང་པོ་	*ḱyong-po.*
Steward	ཕྱག་མཛོད་	*chhang-dzö.*
Stick, *s.*	འཁར་རྒྱུག། རྒྱུག་པ་ (དབྱུག་པ་)	*khar-gyu ; gyuḱ-pa.*
Stick, to (paste) *v.t.*	སྦྱར་བ་	*jar-wa.*
Do. *hon.*	སྦྱར་ར་ (བ་) གནང་བ་	*jar-ra nang-wa.*
Stiff	གྱོང་པོ་	*ḱyong-po.*
Stifle to	གློ་སུབ་རྒྱབ་པ་	*lo-suṕ gyaṕ-pa.*
Do. *hon.*	གློ་སུབ་སྐྱོན་པ་	*lo-suṕ ḱyöm-pa.*
Still, *adv.*	ད་རུང་། ད་འདོ་	*t́a-rung ; t́an-do.*
Still, to sit	ཁ་ཁ་བསྡད་ (སྡོད་) པ་	*kha-kha de-pa.*
Do. *hon.*	ཁ་ཁ་བཞུགས་པ་	*kha-kha sḱu-pa.*
Still-birth	ཤི་རོ་སྐྱེས་པ་	*shi-ro kye-pa.*
Sting, to	སོ་རྒྱབ་པ་	*so gyaṕ-pa.*
Stingy	ལག་པ་དམ་པོ་	*laḱ-pa t́am-po.*
Do. *hon.*	ཕྱག་དམ་པོ་	*chha-t́am-po.*
Stink, to	དྲི་མ་ཁ་བ་	*t́ri-ma kha-wa.*
Stipend	གླ། ཕོགས་	*la ; pho.*
Do. *hon.*	གསོལ་ཕོགས་	*sö-pho.*
Stir, to (move), *v.t.*	དཀྲུག་པ་	*truḱ-pa.*

Stir, to (move), *v.t., hon.*	དཀྲུག་ག་ (པ་) གནང་བ་	*truḱ-ḱa nang-wa.*
Stir, to, *v.i.*	འཁྲུག་པ་	*thruḱ-pa.*
Do. *hon.*	འཁྲུག་ག་ (པ་) གནང་བ་	*thruḱ-ḱa-nang-wa.*
Stirrup	ཡོབ་	*yoṕ.*
Do. *hon.*	ཆིབས་ཡོབ་	*chhiṕ-yoṕ.*
Stirrup-leather	ཡོབ་ཐག་	*yoṕ-tha.*
Do. *hon.*	ཆིབས་ཡོབ་ཀྱི་ཐག་པ་	*chhiṕ-yoṕ kyi thaḱ-pa.*
Stitch, to (clothes)	འཚེམ་པ་	*tshem-pa.*
Do. *hon.*	ཕྱག་འཚེམ་སྐྱོན་པ་	*chha-tshem kyöm-pa.*
Stitch, to (together)	སྦྲེལ་བ་	*drel-wa.*
Do. *hon.*	སྦྲེའ་ར་ (བ་) གནང་བ་	*dre-ra nang-wa.*
Stock (of gun)	སྒུམ་ཤིང་	*gum-shing.*
Stocking	ཨོ་མོ་སུ་ *Mon.*	*o-mo-su.*
Stocks (for criminals)	ཨན་གདས་	*an-de.*
Stomach	གྲོ་ཁོག་ (གྲོད་ཁོག་)	*ťro-kho.*
Do. *hon.*	གསོལ་གྲོད་	*sö-ťrö.*
Stone	རྡོ་	*do.*
Do. *hon.*	ཕྱག་རྡོ་	*chha-do.*
Stool (foot-stool)	རྐང་སྟེགས་	*kang-teḱ.*
Do. *hon.*	ཞབས་སྟེགས་	*sḱaṕ-teḱ.*

Stoop, to	ཁྱུག་ཁྱུག་ (ཁྲུར་ཁྲུར་) བྱེད་པ་	*ḱuk-ḱu cḱe-pa.*
Do. *hon.*	ཁྱུག་ཁྱུག་ (ཁྲུར་ཁྲུར་) གནང་བ་	*ḱuk-ḱu nang-wa.*
Stop, to, *v.t.*	བཀག་པ་ (འགེགས་པ་)	*kak-pa.*
Do. *hon.*	བཀག་ག་ (འགེགས་པ་) གནང་བ་	*kak-ḱa nang-wa.*
Stop, to, *v.i.*	བསྡད་པ་ (སྡོད་པ་)	*de-pa.*
Do. *hon.*	བཞུགས་པ་	*sḱu-pa.*
Do. *h. hon.*	བཞུགས་གདན་འཇག་པ་	*sḱu-den jak-pa.*
Stop raining, to	ཆར་པ་འཆད་པ་	*chhar-pa chhe-pa.*
Store-house	མཛོད། མཛོད་ཁང་	*dzö ; dzö-khang.*
Stork	ཀྲུང་ཀྲུང་དཀར་མོ་	*trung-trung ka-mo.*
Storm	རླུང་ཚུབ་	*lung-tshuṕ.*
Do. snow	གངས་ཚུབ་	*ḱang-tshuṕ.*
Story (of house)	ཐོག་	*tho.*
Do. second	བར་ཐོག་	*ṕar-tho.*
Do. third	གསུམ་ཐོག་	*sum-tho.*
Do. top	རྩེ་ཐོག་	*tse-tho.*
Story (legend)	སྒྲུང་། རྣམ་ཐར་	*drum ; nam-thar.*
Do. *hon.*	ཞལ་སྒྲུང་	*sḱe-drum.*

Stout (of men and animals)	ཤ་རྒྱགས་པ་	*sha gyaḱ-pa.*
Do. *hon.*	སྐུ་ཤ་འབྱོར་པོ་	*ku-sha jor-po.*
Stout (of things)	སྦོམ་པོ་	*bom-po.*
Stove, iron	ལྕག་ཐབ་	*chaḱ-thaṕ.*
Straight	འདྲོང་པོ་ (དྲང་པོ་)	*drong-po.*
Do. (of road)	ཁ་ཐུག་	*kha-thu.*
Do. (honourable)	དྲང་པོ་	*t́rang-po.*
Straighten, to	འདྲོང་ (དྲང་) པོ་བཟོ་བ་	*drong-po śo-wa.*
Do. *hon.*	འདྲོང་ (དྲང་) པོ་བཟོ་བ་ གནང་བ་	*drong-po śo-wa nang-wa.*
Straightforward (just)	ཁྲིམས་དྲང་པོ་	*thrim-t́rang-po.*
Do. *hon.*	བཀའ་ཁྲིམས་དྲང་པོ་	*ka-thrim t́rang-po.*
Straightway	ལམ་སང་	*lam-sang.*
Strain, to	བཙག་པ་ (འཚག་པ་)	*tsaḱ-pa.*
Do. *hon.*	བཙག་ག་ (འཚག་པ་) གནང་བ་	*tsaḱ-ḱa nang-wa.*
Strainer, tea	ཇ་འཚག་	*cḱa-tsha.*
Strait (narrow)	དོག་པོ། སྦུགས་སྦུབ་དོག་པོ་	*toḱ-po ; bu-su toḱ-po.*
Strange	ཁྱད་མཚར་པོ་	*khye-tsha-po.*
Stranger	ཕྱི་མི་	*chhi-mi.*

Strangle, to	སྐེ་བཀག་བཏང་ནས་བསད་ (གསོད་) པ་	*ke-kaḱ tang-ne se-pa.*
Strategy	དམག་ཇུས་	*maḱ-cḱü.*
Do. *hon.*	སྐུ་ཇུས་	*ku-cḱü.*
Straw	ཟན་པ་	*śem-pa.*
Strawberry (Chumbi Valley dialect)	དམར་ལུམ་	*ma-lum.*
Stray, to	ལམ་ཀ་ནོར་བ་	*lang-ka nor-wa.*
Do. *hon.*	ཕེབ་ལམ་ནོར་ར་ (བ་) གནང་བ་	*pheṕ-lam nor-ra nang-wa.*
Stream	རྒྱུག་ཆུ་	*gyuḱ-chhu.*
Street	ལམ་ཀ་	*lang-ka.*
Do. narrow	སྲང་འགག་	*hrang-ga.*
Strength	ཤེད་	*she.*
Do. *hon.*	སྐུ་ཤེད་	*ku-she.*
Stretch, to	བརྐྱང་བ་ (རྐྱོང་བ་)	*kyang-wa.*
Do. *hon.*	རྐྱོང་ང་ (བ་) གནང་བ་	*kyong-nga nang-wa.*
Strew, to (grass, etc.)	གཏོར་བ་	*tor-wa.*
Do. *hon.*	གཏོར་ར་ (བ་) གནང་བ་	*tor-ra nang-wa.*
Strewing oblation	གཏོར་མ་	*tor-ma.*

Strict	དམ་པོ། བཙན་པོ་	*ťam-po; ťsem-po.*
Strife	རྒྱབ་འདྲེ་	*gyam-dre.*
Do. *hon.*	གསུང་འཁྲུག་	*sung-thru.*
Strike, to (hit)	འཕོག་པ་	*phoḱ-pa.*
Strike, to (a blow)	རྡུང་བ་	*dung-wa.*
Do. *hon.*	ཕྱག་འཇུག་ (འཇུས་) གནང་བ་	*chhan-ju nang-wa.*
String	སྐུད་པ་	*kü-pa.*
Do. *hon.*	ཕྱག་སྐུད་	*chha-kü.*
Strive, to	སྙིང་རུས་བྱེད་པ་	*nying-rü cḱe-pa.*
Do. *hon.*	ཐུགས་རུས་གནང་བ་	*thuḱ-rü nang-wa.*
Strip, to	ཤུ་བ་	*shu-wa.*
Stroke	ལྕག་	*cha.*
Stroll, to	ཆམ་ཆམ་ (འཁྱམ་འཁྱམ་) ལ་འགྲོ་བ་	*chham-chham-la dro-wa.*
Do. *hon.*	ཆམ་ཆམ་ (འཁྱམ་འཁྱམ་) ལ་ཕེབ་པ་	*chham-chham la phe-pa.*
Do. *h. hon.*	ཆམ་ཆམ་ (འཁྱམ་འཁྱམ་) ལ་འཆིབ་རྒྱུ་གནང་བ་	*chham-chham la chhiṕ-gyu nang-wa.*

Strong (of human beings, animals, etc.)	ཤེད་ཆེན་པོ་	*she chhem-po.*
Do. *hon.*	སྐུ་ཤེད་ཆེན་པོ་	*ku-she chhem-po.*
Strong (of forts, houses, etc.)	བཙན་པོ་	*tsem-po.*
Struggle, to (wrestle)	འཛིང་བ། འཛིང་རེ་བཏང་ (གཏོང་) བ་	*dzing-wa ; dzing-re tang-wa.*
Do. *hon.*	འཛིང་ང་ (བ་) གནང་བ་	*dzing-nga nang-wa.*
Stubble	སོག་མ་	*so-ma.*
Stubborn	གྱོང་པོ་	*k̓yong-po.*
Student	བསླབ་གྲྭ་	*lap̓-tra.*
Do. religious	གྲྭ་པ་	*t̓ra-pa.*
Stumble, to (of persons)	ཁ་རྡབ་པ་	*kha dap̓-pa.*
Do. *hon.*	ཞལ་རྡབ་པ་གནང་བ་	*sk̓e dap̓-pa nang-wa.*
Stumble, to (of animals)	ཚིགས་བུར་རྒྱབ་པ་	*tshik̓-p̓u gyap̓-pa.*
Stupid (weak in intellect)	ལྐུགས་པ། གླེན་པ་	*kuk̓-pa ; lem-pa.*
Do. (senseless, of things)	དོན་མེད་	*t̓ön-me.*
Sturdy	ཤེད་ཆེན་པོ་	*she chhem-po.*
Do. *hon.*	སྐུ་ཤེད་ཆེན་པོ་	*ku-she chhem-po.*
Stuttering	ཁ་ལྡིག་	*kha-di.*
Sty	ཕག་ཚང་	*phak̓-tshang.*

Style (of persons)	རྒྱུ། རིགས་	*gyu; ri.*
Do. *hon.*	སྐུ་རྒྱུ། སྐུ་རིགས་	*ku-gyu; ku-ri.*
Style (of things)	རྒྱུ་དག་	*gyu-ťa.*
Styles, different	སྣ་ཚོགས་	*na-tsho.*
Subdue, to	རྒྱལ་བ། ལྷག་འཁས་པ་	*gye-wa; la khe-pa.*
Do. *hon.*	རྒྱལ་ར་ (བ་) གནང་བ། ལྷག་འཁས་ར་ (པ་) གནང་བ་	*gye-ra nang-wa; la khe-ra nang-wa.*
Subject (of a government), *s.*	མངའ་འབངས་	*nga-bang.*
Do. *hon.*	མངའ་ཞབས་	*nga-sǩap̌.*
Subjoin, to	འཐུད་རྒྱབ་པ་	*thü gyap̌-pa.*
Do. *hon.*	འཐུད་སྐྱོན་པ་	*thü kyöm-pa.*
Subjugate, to	རྒྱལ་བ། ལྷག་འཁས་པ་	*gye-wa; la khe-pa.*
Do. *hon.*	རྒྱལ་ར་ (བ་) གནང་བ། ལྷག་འཁས་ར་ (པ་) གནང་བ་	*gye-ra nang-wa; la khe-ra nang-wa.*
Sublime	གཡང་མཛེས་	*yang-dze.*
Submissive (humble)	སེམས་ཆུང་ཆུང་	*sem-chhung-chhung.*
Do. *hon.*	ཐུགས་སེམས་ཆུང་ཆུང་	*thuǩ-sem chhung-chhung.*
Submit, to	མགོ་དགུར་བ་	*go gur-wa.*
Do. *hon.*	དབུ་དགུར་ར་ (བ་) གནང་བ་	*u gur-ra nang-wa.*

Submit, to (a petition or report)	འབུལ་བ། འབུལ་ལམ་ཞུས་པ་ (ཞུ་བ་)	*bül-wa ; bü-lam sḱü-pa.*
Do. *hon.*	འབུལ་ར་ (བ་) གནང་བ། འབུལ་ལམ་ཞུ་བ་གནང་བ་	*bü-ra nang-wa ; bü-lam sḱu-wa nang-wa.*
Subside, to (of water, flood, etc.)	ཆག་པ་	*chhaḱ-pa.*
Substance	དངོས་པོ། རྒྱུ་	*ngö-po ; gyu.*
Do. (of document, etc.)	དོན་སྙིང་	*ťön-nying.*
Substantiate, to (statement)	གཏན་ལྡན་བྱེད་པ་	*ten-den cḱe-pa.*
Do. *hon.*	གཏན་ལྡན་གནང་བ་	*ten-den nang-wa.*
Substitute	ཚབ་	*tshaṕ.*
Do. *hon.*	སྐུ་ཚབ་	*ku-tshaṕ.*
Subtility	གཡོ་སྒྱུ་	*yo-gyu.*
Subtle	གཡོ་ཆེན་པོ་	*yo chhem-po.*
Subtract, to	འཐེན་པ་	*them-pa.*
Do. *hon.*	འཐེན་པ་གནང་བ་	*them-pa nang-wa.*
Succeed, to (be successful)	ཐུབ་པ་	*thuṕ-pa.*
Do. (follow)	གཞུག་ལ་ཕྱིན་པ་	*sḱu-la chhim-pa.*
Do. *hon.*	གཞུག་ལ་ཕེབ་པ་	*sḱu-la phe-pa.*
Do. *h. hon.*	གཞུག་ལ་འཆིབ་རྒྱུ་གནང་བ་	*sḱu-la chhiṕ-gyu nang-wa*

Successful, to be	མགོ་འཐོན་པ་	*go thöm-pa.*
Succession, (descendants)	རིགས་བརྒྱུད། མི་བརྒྱུད་	*ri-gyü ; mi-gyü.*
Do. *hon.* (of laity)	སྐུ་བརྒྱུད་	*ku-gyü.*
Do. *hon.* (of lamas)	གདུང་བརྒྱུད་	*dung-gyü.*
Succour, *s.*	རོགས་	*ro.*
Do. *hon.*	མགོན་འདྲེན་	*gön-dren.*
Succour, to	རོགས་བྱེད་པ་	*ro cḱe-pa.*
Do. *hon.*	དབུ་འདྲེན་གནང་བ་	*u-dren nang-wa.*
Such	འདི་འདྲ་	*din-dra.*
Suck, to	འཇིབ་པ་	*jiṕ-pa.*
Do. *hon.*	འཇིབ་པ་གནང་བ་	*jiṕ-pa nang-wa.*
Suckle, to	འོ་མ་སྟེར་བ་	*o-ma ter-wa.*
Do. *hon.*	འོ་མ་གནང་བ་	*o-ma nang-wa.*
Suddenly	ལམ་སང་	*lam-sang.*
Suffer, to (endure)	བཟོད་པ་སྒོམ་པ་	*śö-pa gom-pa.*
Do. *hon.*	བཟོད་པ་བཞེས་པ་	*śö-pa sḱe-pa.*
Suffer, to (pain)	གཟུག་རྒྱབ་པ་	*śu-gyaṕ-pa.*
Do. *hon.*	སྙུང་གཟུག་སྐྱོན་པ་	*nyung-śu kyöm-pa.*
Suffer, to (permit)	བཅུག་པ་ (འཇུག་པ་)	*chuḱ-pa.*
Do. *hon.*	བཅུག་ག་ (འཇུག་པ་) གནང་བ་	*chuḱ-ḱa nang-wa.*

Suffering (mental)	སྡུག་བསྔལ་	*du-nge.*
Do. *hon.*	ཐུགས་འཁྲལ་	*thu-thre.*
Suffering (physical)	གཟུག་	*śu.*
Do. *hon.*	སྙུང་གཟུག་	*nyung-śu.*
Sufficient, to be	ལྡང་བ། འགྲིག་པ་	*dang-wa; drik-pa.*
Suffocate, to	གློ་སུབ་རྒྱབ་པ་	*lo-suṕ gyaṕ-pa.*
Do. *hon.*	གློ་སུབ་སྐྱོན་པ་	*lo-suṕ kyöm-pa.*
Suffocated, to be	དབུགས་འགག་པ་	*u gaḱ-pa.*
Sugar	བྱེ་མ་ཀ་ར་	*cḱe-ma ka-ra.*
Sugar-candy	ཤེལ་ཀ་ར་	*she ka-ra.*
Suicide, to commit	རང་སྲོག་བཅད་ (གཅོད་) པ་	*rang-sa che-pa.*
Do. *hon.*	རང་སྲོག་གཅོད་པ་གནང་བ་	*rang-so chö-pa nang-wa.*
Suit, to (befit)	འོས་པ་	*ö-pa.*
Do. (agree)	འགྲིག་པ། འཆམ་པ་	*driḱ-pa; chham-pa.*
Suitable	འོས་པོ། འོས་བབས་	*ö-po; ö-ṕaṕ.*
Suite	འཁོར་གཡོག་	*khor-yo.*
Sulk, to	གདོང་ནག་པོ་བསྟན་ (སྟོན་) པ་	*dong naḱ-po tem-pa.*
Do. *hon.*	ཞལ་རས་ནག་པོ་སྟོན་པ་གནང་བ་	*sḱe-re naḱ-po töm-pa nang-wa.*
Sullen	གྱོང་པོ་	*ḱyong-po.*

Sully, to	བཙོག་པ་བཟོ་བ་	soḱ-pa śo-wa.
Do. *hon.*	བཙོག་པ་བཟོ་བ་གནང་བ་	tsoḱ-pa śo-wa nang-wa.
Sulphur	མུ་ཟི་	mu-śi.
Sum up, to	སྡོམ་པ་	dom-pa.
Do. *hon.*	སྡོམ་པ་གནང་བ་	dom-pa nang-wa.
Summer	དབྱར་ཀ་	yar-ka.
Summit	རྩེ་	tse.
Summon, to	སྐད་བཏང་ (གཏོང་) བ་	ke tang-wa.
Do. *hon.*	ཤོག་བཀའ་གནང་བ་	sho ka-nang-wa.
Sun	ཉི་མ་	nyi-ma.
Do. *hon.*	ཞོ་ཉི་ (ཞུ་ཉི་)	sḱo-nyi.
Sunbeam	ཉི་མའི་གཟེར་	nyi-me śer.
Sunrise	ཉི་མ་ཤར་ར་ (བ་)	nyi-ma shar-ra.
Sunset	ཉི་མ་རྒས་པ་	nyi-ma ge-pa.
Sunstroke, to get	ཉི་གཟེར་འཕོག་པ་	nyi-śer phoḱ-pa.
Sunday	གཟའ་ཉི་མ་	śa-nyi-ma.
Sundry (various)	མི་གཅིག་པ་	mi-chiḱ-pa.
Superabundant	ཧ་ཅང་མང་པོ། གཡོ་མ་སུ་	ha-chang mang-po; yo-ma-su.
Superb	གཡང་མཛེས་	yang-dze.
Supercilious (haughty)	ཉམས་ཆེན་པོ། ཛ་ཁོག་ཆེན་པོ་	nyam-chhem-po; dza-kho chhem-po.

Superfluous	ལྷག་པོ་	*hlaḱ-po.*
Superintend	དོ་དམ་བྱེད་པ་	*ťo-ťam cḱe-pa.*
Do. *hon.*	དོ་དམ་གནང་བ་	*ťo-ťam nang-wa.*
Superintendent	དོ་དམ་པ་	*ťo-ťam-pa.*
Superstition	རྣམ་རྟོག་	*nam-to.*
Superior (rank of persons)	མཐོ་པོ་	*tho-po.*
Do. (of things)	ཡག་པོ་	*yaḱ-po.*
Supervise, to	དོ་དམ་བྱེད་པ་	*ťo-ťam cḱe-pa.*
Do. *hon.*	དོ་དམ་གནང་བ་	*ťo-ťam nang-wa.*
Supper	དགོངས་མོའི་ཁ་ལག་	*gong-mö kha-la.*
Do. *hon.*	དགོངས་མོའི་ཞལ་ལག་	*gong-mö sḱe-la.*
Supple	མཉེན་པོ་	*nyem-po.*
Supplicate, to	ཞུ་བ་	*sḱu-wa.*
Do. *hon.*	ཞུ་བ་གནང་བ་	*sḱu-wa nang-wa.*
Supplication	ཞུ་བ་	*sḱu-wa.*
Supply, to	སྒྲུབ་པ་	*drup̓-pa.*
Do. *hon.*	སྒྲུབ་པ་གནང་བ་	*drup̓-pa nang-wa.*
Support, to (prop up)	སྐྱོར་བ་	*kyor-wa.*
Do. *hon.*	སྐྱོར་ར་ (བ་) གནང་བ་	*kyor-ra nang-wa.*
Support to. (endure)	བཟོད་པ་སྒོམ་པ་	*śö-pa gom-pa.*

Support, to (endure), *hon.*	བཟོད་པ་སྒོམ་པ་གནང་བ་	*sö-pa gom-pa nang-wa.*
Support, to (nourish)	གསོ་བ་	*so-wa.*
Do. *hon.*	གསོ་བ་གནང་བ་	*so-wa nang-wa.*
Suppose, to	བསམ་པ་	*sam-pa.*
Do. *hon.*	དགོངས་པ་	*gong-pa.*
Supposition (opinion)	བསམ་པ་	*sam-pa.*
Do. *hon.*	ཐུགས་སེམས་	*thu-sem.*
Suppress, to (restrain)	བཀག་པ་ (འགེགས་པ་)	*kak-pa.*
Do. *hon.*	བཀག་ག་ (འགེགས་པ་) གནང་བ་	*kak-ka nang-wa.*
Suppression of urine, to suffer from	གཅིན་པ་འགག་པ་	*chim-pa gak-pa.*
Suppurate, to	རྣག་བསག་ (གསོག་) པ་	*na sak-pa.*
Do. *hon.*	རྣག་བསག་ག་ (གསོག་པ་) གནང་བ་	*na sak-ka nang-wa.*
Sure	ཏེན་ཏེན། ཁྲིག་ཁྲིག	*ten-ten ; thrik-thri.*
Surely	ངེས་པར་	*nge-par.*
Surety	ཁས་ཁྲུགས་	*khe-khya.*
Do. *hon.*	ཞལ་ཁྲུགས་	*sKe-khya.*
Surety, to stand	ཁས་ཁྲུགས་བྱེད་པ་	*khe-kya cKe-pa.*

Surety, to stand, *hon.*	ཞལ་ཁྱགས་གནང་བ་	*sḱe-khya nang-wa.*
Surgeon	ཨེམ་ཆི་	*am-chhi.*
Surly	གྱོང་པོ་	*ḱyong-po.*
Surmise, to (suspect)	དོགས་པ་ཟ་བ་	*t́ok-pa śa-wa.*
Do. *hon.*	ཐུགས་དོགས་གནང་བ་	*thu-t́o nang-wa.*
Surmise, to (conjecture)	བསམ་པ་	*sam-pa.*
Do. *hon.*	དགོངས་པ་	*gong-pa.*
Surplus	ལྷག་མ་	*hla-ma.*
Surprise, *s.*	ཡ་མཚན་	*yam-tshen.*
Surprise, to	ཡ་མཚན་བྱེད་པ་	*yam-tshen cḱe-pa.*
Do. *hon.*	ཡ་མཚན་གནང་བ་	*yam-tshen nang-wa.*
Surprising	ཡ་མཚན་པོ། ཁྱད་མཚར་པོ་	*yam-tshem-po; khye-tsha-po.*
Surrender, to (abandon)	སྤང་བ་	*pang-wa.*
Do. *hon.*	སྤོང་ང་ (བ་) གནང་བ་	*pong-nga nang-wa.*
Surrender, to (submit)	མགོ་བཏགས་ཞུ་བ་	*goṕ-te sḱu-wa.*
Surround, to	སྐོར་ར་རྒྱབ་པ་	*kor-ra gyaṕ-pa.*
Do. *hon.*	ཞབས་སྐོར་སྐྱོན་པ་	*sḱaṕ-kor kyöm-pa.*
Survey, to (look at)	ལྟ་བ་	*ta-wa.*
Do. *hon.*	གཟིགས་པ་	*śi-pa.*
Suspect, to	དོགས་པ་ཟ་བ་	*t́ok-pa śa-wa.*

Suspect, to, *hon.*	ཐུགས་དོགས་གནང་བ་	*thu-ťo nang-wa.*
Suspense (doubt)	ཐེ་ཚོམ་	*the-tshom.*
Suspense, to be in (doubt)	ཐེ་ཚོམ་ཟ་བ་	*the-tshom śa-wa.*
Do. *hon.*	ཐེ་ཚོམ་གནང་བ་	*the-tshom nang-wa.*
Suspend, to	བཀལ་བ་ (འགེལ་བ་)	*kel-wa.*
Do. *hon.*	བཀལ་ར་ (འགེལ་བ་) གནང་བ་	*ke-ra nang-wa.*
Suspend, to (from office)	བཏོན་པ་ (འདོན་པ་)	*töm-pa.*
Do. *hon.*	བཏོན་ (འདོན་) པ་གནང་བ་	*töm-pa nang-wa.*
Suspicion	དོགས་པ་	*ťoǩ-pa.*
Do. *hon.*	ཐུགས་དོགས་	*thu-ťo.*
Suspicious and angry, to be	བལྟ་ཕྱོགས་བྱེད་པ་	*ta-chhoǩ cȟe-pa.*
Do. *hon.*	གཟིགས་ཕྱོགས་གནང་བ་	*śi-chhoǩ nang-wa.*
Sustain, to (endure)	བཟོད་པ་སྒོམ་པ་	*śö-pa gom-pa.*
Do. *hon.*	བཟོད་པ་སྒོམ་པ་གནང་བ་	*śö-pa gom-pa nang-wa.*
Sustain, to (nourish)	གསོ་བ་	*so-wa.*
Do. *hon.*	གསོ་བ་གནང་བ་	*so-wa nang-wa.*
Sustain, to (prop)	སྐྱོར་བ་	*kyor-wa.*
Do. *hon.*	སྐྱོར་ར་ (བ་) གནང་བ་	*kyor-ra nang-wa.*
Swallow, to	མིད་པ་	*mi-pa.*

Swarm (crowd)	ཚོགས་	*tsho.*
Sway	དབང་	*wang.*
Do. *hon.*	སྐུ་དབང་	*ku-wang.*
Sway, to (govern)	དབང་བྱེད་པ་	*wang-cḱe-pa.*
Do. *hon.*	སྐུ་དབང་གནང་བ་	*ku-wang nang-wa.*
Swear, to	མནའ་སྐྱེལ་བ་	*na kyel-wa.*
Do. *hon.*	དབུ་མནའ་བཞེས་པ་	*u-na sḱe-pa.*
Sweat, *s.*	རྔུལ་ནག་	*ngü-na.*
Sweat, to	རྔུལ་ནག་འཐོན་པ་	*ngü-na thöm-pa.*
Do. *hon.*	རྔུལ་ནག་འཐོན་པ་གནང་བ་	*ngü-na thöm-pa nang-wa.*
Sweep, to	གེ་རྒྱབ་པ་	*ḱe gyaṕ-pa.*
Do. *hon.*	གེ་སྐྱོན་པ་	*ḱe-kyöm-pa.*
Sweeper	གེ་པ། ར་རྒྱ་པ་	*ḱe-pa; ra-gya-pa.*
Do. chief	ར་རྒྱ་དཔོན་པོ་	*ra-gya pöm-po.*
Sweet, *adj.*	མངར་མོ། ཞིམ་པོ་	*ngar-mo; sḱim-po.*
Sweetheart	སྙིང་སྡུག་	*nying-du.*
Sweetmeat	བྱི་རིལ་	*cḱi-ri.*
Sweet-scented	དྲི་མ་ཞིམ་པོ་	*t́ri-ma sḱim-po.*
Swell, to	སྐྲང་བ་	*trang-wa.*
Do. *hon.*	སྐྲང་ང་ (བ་) གནང་བ་	*trang-nga nang-wa.*

Swift	མགྱོགས་པོ་	*gyoḱ-po.*
Do. *hon.*	རྩོལ་པོ་	*tsö-po.*
Swim, to	རྐྱལ་རྒྱབ་པ་	*kye gyaṕ-pa.*
Do. *hon.*	རྐྱལ་སྐྱོན་པ་	*kye kyöm-pa.*
Swine	ཕག་པ་	*phaḱ-pa.*
Swineherd	ཕག་རྫི་	*phaḱ-dzi.*
Swing, (*e.g.* branch in wind)	ལིང་ལིང་བྱེད་པ་	*ling-ling cḱe-pa.*
Do. (brandish)	དབྱུག་དབྱུག་བྱེད་པ་	*yuḱ-yuḱ cḱe-pa.*
Do. *hon.*	དབྱུག་དབྱུག་གནང་བ་	*yuḱ-yuḱ nang-wa.*
Switch	རྟའི་ལྕག། ལྕང་སྨྱུག་	*te-cha ; chang-nyu.*
Do. *hon.*	ཆིབས་ལྕག་	*chhiṕ-cha.*
Swoon, to	དྲན་མེད་བརྒྱལ་བ་	*t́ren-me gyel-wa.*
Do. *hon.*	ཐུགས་དྲན་མེད་བརྒྱལ་ར་ (བ་) གནང་བ་	*thu-t́ren-me gye-ra nang-wa.*
Sword	དཔའ་དམ། ཤོག་ལང་	*pa-dam ; sho-lang.*
Do. (two-edged)	རལ་གྲི་	*re-t́ri.*
Do. short	རྩེབ་སག་	*tseṕ-sa.*
Symbol	རྟགས་	*ta.*
Symmetry (proportion)	ཚོད་	*tshö.*

Sympathy	སྙིང་རྗེ། ཁྱམས་སྙིང་རྗེ་	*nying-je; cḱam-nying-je.*
Do. *hon.*	ཐུགས་རྗེ་	*thuḱ-je.*
Symptom (of disease)	ན་སྟངས་	*na-tang.*
Do. *hon.*	སྙུང་སྟངས་	*nyung-tang.*
Syphilis	སྲི་མོག་	*se-mo.*
System (method)	ཐབས་	*thaṕ.*

T

Table, small	ལྕོག་ཙེ་	*choḱ-tse.*
Do. *hon.*	གསོལ་ལྕོག་	*sö-cho.*
Table, European	རྒྱ་ལྕོག་	*gya-cho.*
Table-cloth	ལྕོག་ཁེབས་	*cho-kheṕ.*
Taciturn, to be	ཁ་ཁ་བསྡད་ (སྡོད་) པ་	*kha-kha de-pa.*
Do. *hon.*	ཞལ་ཁ་བཞུགས་པ་	*sḱe-kha sḱu-pa.*
Tact	ཐབས་མཁས་	*thaṕ-khe.*
Tail	གཞུག་གུ་	*sḱu-gu.*
Tailor	ཚེམ་བུ་	*tshem-ṕu.*
Do. *hon.*	དབུ་མཛད་	*um-dze.*
Taint (contamination)	གྲིབ་	*t́riṕ.*
Do. *hon.*	སྐུ་གྲིབ་	*ku-t́riṕ.*
Take, to	ལེན་པ་	*lem-pa.*
Do. *hon.*	བཞེས་པ་	*sḱe-pa*
Take, to (carry)	འཁྱེར་འགྲོ་བ་	*khe dro-wa.*
Do. *hon.*	སྣོམ་ཕེབ་པ་	*nom phe-pa.*
Do. *h. hon.*	སྣོམ་འཆིབ་རྒྱུ་གནང་བ་	*nom chhiṕ-gyu nang-wa.*
Take, to (conduct)	འཁྲིད་འགྲོ་བ་	*thri dro-wa.*
Do. *hon.*	འཁྲིད་ཕེབ་པ་	*thri phe-pa.*

Take, to (conduct), *h. hon.*	འཁྲིད་འཆིབ་རྒྱུ་གནང་བ་	*thri chhiṕ-gyu nang-wa.*
Take, to (forcibly	འཕྲོག་པ་	*phoḱ-pa.*
Do. *hon.*	འཕྲོག་ག་ (པ་) གནང་བ་	*phoḱ-ḱa nang-wa.*
Take hold of, to	ཟིན་པ་	*śim-pa.*
Do. *hon.*	ཟིན་པ་གནང་བ་	*śim-pa nang-wa.*
Take off, to (clothes, etc.)	ཕིས་པ་ (འབུད་པ་)	*pi-pa.*
Do. *hon.*	བསིལ་ར་ (བ་) གནང་བ་	*si-ra nang-wa.*
Take out, to	བཏོན་པ་ (འདོན་པ་)	*t́öm-pa.*
Do. *hon.*	འདོན་པ་གནང་བ་	*döm-pa nang-wa.*
Tale	སྒྲུང་། རྣམ་ཐར་	*drum; nam-thar.*
Do. *hon.*	ཞལ་སྒྲུང་	*sḱe-drum.*
Talent (natural gift)	ཡོན་ཏན་	*yön-ten.*
Talented (person)	རིག་པ་ཆེན་པོ་	*riḱ-pa chhem-po.*
Do. *hon.*	ཐུགས་རིག་ཆེན་པོ་	*thu-ri chhem-po.*
Talisman	སྲུང་བ་	*hrung-nga.*
Do. (used by high lamas)	སྲིད་པ་ཧོ་	*si-pa-ho.*
Talk, *s.* (conversation)	སྐད་ཆ་	*ke-chha.*
Do. *hon.*	གསུང་གྲོས་	*sung-t́rö.*
Talk (rumour)	སྐད་ཆ། གཏམ་	*ke-chha; tam.*
Talk, to	ལབ་པ་	*laṕ-pa.*

Talk, to, *hon.*	གསུང་བ་	*sung-wa.*
Do. *h. hon.*	བཀའ་གནང་བ་	*ka nang-wa.*
Tall	གཟུགས་པོ་རིང་པོ་	*śuk-po ring-po.*
Do. *hon.*	སྐུ་གཟུགས་རིང་པོ་	*ku-śu ring-po.*
Tallow	ཚིལ་ལུ་ (ཚིལ་བུ་)	*tshi-lu.*
Talon	སྡེར་མོ་	*der-mo.*
Tame, to	ཀླིང་པོ་བཟོ་བ་	*hling-po śo-wa.*
Do. *hon.*	ཀླིང་པོ་བཟོ་བ་གནང་བ་	*hling-po śo-wa nang-wa.*
Tan, to	མཉེད་པ་	*nye-pa.*
Tanner	ཀོ་བ་མཉེད་མཁན་	*ko-wa nye-khen.*
Tap, to	དག་དག་བཏང་ (གཏོང་) བ་	*taǩ-ta tang-wa.*
Do. *hon.*	དག་དག་གཏོང་ང་ (བ་) གནང་བ་	*taǩ-ta tong-nga nang-wa.*
Tape, measuring	ཐག་ཚད་	*thaǩ-tshe.*
Tape-worm	ཀུབ་འབུ་	*kup̌-bu.*
Tardy	ཕྱི་པོ་	*chhi-po.*
Target	རྒྱབ་འབེན་	*gyam-be.*
Tarnish, to	བཙོག་པ་བཟོ་བ་	*tsoǩ-pa śo-wa.*
Do. *hon.*	བཙོག་པ་བཟོ་བ་གནང་བ་	*tsoǩ-pa śo-wa nang-wa.*
Tarry, to	འགོར་པོ་བྱེད་པ་	*gor-po cǩe-pa.*

Tarry, to, *hon.*	འགོར་པོ་གནང་བ་	*gor-po nang-wa.*
Tartar (on the teeth)	སོ་དྲེག་	*so-t́re.*
Do. *hon.*	ཚེམས་དྲེག་	*tshem-t́re.*
Task	ལས་ཀ་	*le-ka.*
Do. *hon.*	ཕྱག་ལས་	*chha-le.*
Task, school	ཡིག་ཚད་	*yiḱ-tshe.*
Tassel (for hat)	དོང་སྐུད་	*tong-kü.*
Taste, *s.*	བྲོ་བ་	*t́ro-a.*
Do. *hon.*	ལྗགས་བྲོ་	*ja-t́ro.*
Taste, to	བྲོ་བ་ལྟ་བ་	*t́ro-a ta-wa.*
Do. *hon.*	ལྗགས་བྲོ་གཟིགས་པ་	*ja-t́ro śi-pa.*
Taunt, to	ཀྱག་ཀྱག་བྱས་ནས་ལབ་པ་	*kya-kya cḱe-ne laṕ-pa.*
Do. *hon.*	ཀྱག་ཀྱག་གནང་ནས་གསུང་བ་	*kya-kya nang-ne sung-wa.*
Tavern	ཆང་ཁང་	*chhang-khang.*
Tax (general)	ཁྲལ། འབབ་	*thre; baṕ.*
Do. (customs-duty)	ཤོ་ཁྲལ་	*sho-thre.*
Do. on land	ས་ཁྲལ་	*sa-thre.*
Tax, to pay	ཁྲལ་འཇལ་བ་	*thre-je-wa.*
Tea	ཇ་	*cḱa.*
Do. *hon.*	གསོལ་ཇ་	*sö-cḱa.*

Tea, best quality	འབྲུ་ཐང་	*dru-thang.*
Do. 2nd quality	འབྲུ་གཉིས་	*dru-nyi.*
Do. 3rd quality	བཅུ་པ་	*chu-pa.*
Do. 4th quality	བརྒྱད་པ་	*gye-pa.*
Tea, brick of	ཇ་པག་	*cḱa-ṕa-ka.*
Do. *hon.*	གསོལ་ཇ་པག་	*sö-cḱa ṕa-ka.*
Tea-pot	ཁོག་ཏི་	*k̇ho-ti.*
Do. *hon.*	གསོལ་ཏི་	*sö-ti.*
Tea-strainer	ཇ་ཚགས་	*cḱa-tsha.*
Teach, to	བསླབ་པ་ (སློབ་པ་)	*laṕ-pa.*
Do. *hon.*	བསླབས་ (སློབ་) པ་གནང་བ་	*laṕ-pa nang-wa.*
Teacher	དགེ་རྒན། སློབ་དཔོན་	*ge-gen; lo-pön.*
Tear, *s.*	མིག་ཆུ་	*miḱ-chhu.*
Do. *hon.*	སྤྱན་ཆབ་	*chen-chhaṕ.*
Tear, to (cloth, etc.)	རལ་བ་	*re-wa.*
Do. *hon.*	རལ་ར་ (བ་) གནང་བ་	*re-ra nang-wa.*
Tear, to (flesh)	བཀོག་པ་ (འགོག་པ་)	*koḱ-pa.*
Do. *hon.*	བཀོག་ག་ (འགོག་པ་) གནང་བ་	*koḱ-ḱa nang-pa.*
Tears, to shed	མིག་ཆུ་ཤོར་བ་	*miḱ-chhu shor-wa.*

Tears, to shed, *hon.*	སྤྱན་ཆབ་ཤོར་བ་	*chen-chhaṕ shor-wa.*
Tedious	དཀའ་ལས་ཁག་པོ་	*ka-le khak̄-po.*
Do. *hon.*	སྐུ་མཉེལ་པོ་	*ku-nye-po.*
Telegram	གློག་སྐུད་ཡི་གེ་	*lo-kü yi-ge.*
Telegraph	ལྕགས་སྐུད། གློག་སྐུད་	*cha-kü; lo-kü.*
Telephone	ཁ་པར་	*kha-ṕar.*
Do. *hon.*	ཞལ་པར་	*sk̄e-ṕar.*
Telescope	རྒྱང་ཤེལ་	*gyang-she.*
Tell, to	ལབ་པ་	*laṕ-pa.*
Do. *hon.*	གསུང་བ་	*sung-wa.*
Do. *h. hon.*	བཀའ་གནང་བ་	*ka nang-wa.*
Temper (passion)	ཚིག་པ། ཁོང་ཁྲོ་	*tshik̄-pa ; khong-thro.*
Tempered, good	བློ་རྒྱུ་རིང་པོ་	*lo-gyu ring-po.*
Do. *hon.*	ཐུགས་རྒྱུ་རིང་པོ་	*thu-gyu ring-po.*
Tempered, bad	རུ་ངར་པོ་	*ru ngar-po.*
Do. *hon.*	ཐུགས་རུ་ངར་པོ་	*thu-ru ngar-po.*
Temperate (climate)	བསིལ་དྲོས་སྙོམས་པོ་	*si-t́rö nyom-po.*
Temperate, to be (moderate)	ཚོད་ཟིན་པ་	*tshö-śim-pa.*
Temperature	གྲང་ལོས་	*t́rang-lö.*
Tempest	རླུང་ཚུབ་	*lung-tshuṕ.*

Temple	མཆོད་ཁང་	*chhö-khang.*
Tempt, to (cheat)	མགོ་སྐོར་བཏང་ (གཏོང་) བ་	*go-kor tang-wa.*
Do. *hon.*	མགོ་སྐོར་གཏོང་ང་ (བ་) གནང་བ་	*go-lor tong-nga nang-wa.*
Tempt, to (entice)	སེམས་བསླུས་པ་	*sem lü-pa.*
Do. *hon.*	སེམས་བསླུས་པ་གནང་བ་	*sem lü-pa nang-wa.*
Do. *inf.* to *sup.*	ཐུགས་སེམས་བསླུས་པ་	*thuk-sem lü-pa.*
Tenacious (obstinate)	གྱོང་པོ་	*kyong-po.*
Tenant	མི་སེར། འབངས་	*mi-ser; bang.*
Do. poorer class of	མོ་ཡན་	*mo-yen.*
Tender	འཇམ་པོ་	*jam-po.*
Tendon	རྒྱུས་པ་	*gyü-pa.*
Tenet	ཆོས་ལུགས་	*chhö-lu.*
Ten	བཅུ་	*chu.*
Tenth	བཅུ་པ་	*chu-pa.*
Ten thousand	ཁྲི་	*thri.*
Tent	གུར་	*kur.*
Do. *hon.*	དབུ་གུར་	*u-kur.*
Tent-pole	གུར་རྒྱུག་	*kur-gyu.*
Tepid	དྲོན་འཇམ་	*trön-jam.*

Term (limit)	མཐའ་	*tha.*
Do. (period)	དུས། བསྐལ་པ་	*tü ; kel-pa.*
Do. (word)	ཚིག་	*tshi.*
Terminate, to	འཚར་བ་	*tshar-wa.*
Do. *hon.*	གྲུབ་པ་	*ťruṕ-pa.*
Terrible	ཞེད་སྐྲག་ཚ་པོ་	*sḱe-tra tsha-po.*
Terribly	ཞེད་སྐྲག་	*sḱe-tra.*
Terrified, to be	ཞེད་པ་	*sḱe-pa.*
Do. *hon.*	ཞེད་པ་གནང་བ་	*sḱe-pa nang-wa.*
Terrify, to	ཞེད་སྐྲག་སླང་བ་	*sḱe-tra lang-wa.*
Do. *hon.*	ཞེད་སྐྲག་སློང་ང་ (བ་) གནང་བ་	*sḱe-tra long-nga nang-wa.*
Terrifying	ཞེད་སྐྲག་ཚ་པོ་	*sḱe-tra tsha-po.*
Territory	ས་ཆ་	*sa-chha.*
Terror	ཞེད་སྐྲག་	*sḱe-tra.*
Test, to	ཚོད་ལྟ་བ་	*tshö ta-wa.*
Do. *hon.*	ཚོད་གཟིགས་པ་	*tshö śi-pa.*
Testament (will)	ཁ་ཆེམས་	*kha-chhem.*
Do. *hon.*	ཞལ་ཆེམས་	*sḱe-chhem.*
Testicle	རླིག་པ་	*liḱ-pa.*

Testify, to	དཔང་པོ་བྱེད་པ་	*pang-po cḱe-pa.*
Do. *hon.*	དཔང་པོ་གནང་བ་	*pang-po nang-wa.*
Than	ལས་	*le.*
Thankful, to be	དྲིན་དྲན་པ་	*ťrin ťrem-pa.*
Do. *hon.*	དྲིན་དྲན་པ་གནང་བ་	*ťrin ťrem-pa rang-wa.*
Do. *inf.* to *sup.*	བཀའ་དྲིན་དྲན་པ་	*ka-ťrin ťrem-pa.*
Thank you!	འོ་ཡག་བྱུང་	*o ya-cḱung.*
Do. *hon.*	ཐུགས་ཆེ་	*thu-chhe.*
Do. *h. hon.*	ཐུགས་རྗེ་ཆེ་གནང་	*thu-je chhe-nang.*
That	དེ་	*ťe.*
That down there	མ་གི་	*ma-ḱi.*
That, just like	ད་ག་རང་། དེ་འདྲ་	*ťa-ḱa-rang; ťen-dra.*
That over there	ཕ་གི་	*pha-ḱi.*
That up there	ཡ་གི་	*ya-ḱi.*
That very	ཕ་གེ་རང་	*pha-ḱe-rang.*
Thaw, to	ཞུ་བ་	*sḱu-wa.*
The, *def. art.*	འདི། དེ་	*di; ťe.*
Theft	རྐུན་མ་	*ku-ma.*
Their	ཁོང་ཚོའི་	*khon-tshö.*
Them	ཁོང་ཚོ་	*khon-tsho.*

Then (after that)	དེ་ནས་	*ťe-ne.*
Do. (at that time)	དེའི་སྐང་ལ་	*ťe-i gang-la.*
There	དད་ (དེ་རུ།) ཕ་གི་	*ťe ; pha-gi.*
Therefore	བྱས་ཚང་། དེའི་རྐྱེན་བྱས་ནས། དེའི་རྐྱེན་གྱིས་	*cKe-tsang ; ťe-i kyen cKe-ne ; ťe-i kyen-Kyi*
Thermometer	ཚ་གྲང་ལྟ་ཡ་	*tsha-ťrang ta-ya.*
These	འདི་ཚོ་	*di-tsho.*
They	ཁོ་ཚོ་	*khon-tsho.*
Thibet	བོད་	*ṕo.*
Thibetan	བོད་པ་	*ṕö-pa.*
Do. language	བོད་སྐད་	*ṕö-ke.*
Do. manuscript characters	དབུ་མེད་	*u-me.*
Do. printed characters	དབུ་ཅན་	*u-chen.*
Thick(of flat objects)	འཐུག་པོ་	*thuK-po.*
Do. (of round objects)	སྦོམ་པོ་	*bom-po.*
Do. (turbid)	རྙོག་པོ་	*nyoK-po.*
Thief	རྐུན་མ་	*ku-ma.*
Thieve, to	རྐུན་མ་རྐུ་བ་	*ku-ma ku-wa.*
Thigh	བརླ་ཤ་	*le-sha.*

Thigh-bone trumpet	རྐང་གླིང་	*kang-ling.*
Thimble	ཅོ་མོ་	*cho-mo.*
Thin (of flat objects)	སྲབ་པོ་	*traṗ-po.*
Do. (of round objects)	ཕྲ་པོ་	*thra-po.*
Do. (of persons and animals)	ཤ་སྐམ་པོ་	*sha kam-po.*
Do. *hon.* (of persons)	སྐུ་ཤ་སྐམ་པོ་	*ku-sha kam-po.*
Do. *hon.* (of animals)	བཞེས་ཤ་སྐམ་པོ་	*sk̄e-sha kam-po.*
Thine	ཁྱོད་རེའི་ (ཁྱོད་ཀྱི་)	*khyö-re.*
Do. *hon.*	ཁྱེད་ཀྱི་	*khye-kyi.*
Do. *h. hon.*	སྐུ་གཞོགས་ཀྱི་	*ku-sk̄o kyi.*
Thing	ཅ་ལག་ (ཆ་ལག་)	*cha-la.*
Do. *hon.*	སྐུ་ཅས་ (སྐུ་ཆས་)	*ku-che.*
Think, to (suppose)	བསམ་པ་	*sam-pa.*
Do. *hon.*	དགོངས་པ་	*gong-pa.*
Think, to (reflect)	བསམ་བློ་བཏང་ (གཏོང་) བ་	*sam-lo tang-wa.*
Do. *hon.*	ཐུགས་བསམ་བཞེས་པ་	*thu-sam sk̄e-pa.*
Third	གསུམ་པ་	*sum-pa.*
Thirdly	གསུམ་པར་	*sum-pa.*
Thirsty, to be	ཁ་སྐོམ་པ་	*kha kom-pa.*
Do. *hon.*	ཞལ་སྐྱེམས་པ་	*sk̄e kyem-pa.*

Thirteen	བཅུ་གསུམ་	*chuǩ-sum.*
Thirteenth	བཅུ་གསུམ་པ་	*chuǩ-sum-pa.*
Thirty	སུམ་ཅུ་	*sum-chu.*
Thirtieth	སུམ་ཅུ་པ་	*sum-chu-pa.*
This	འདི་	*di.*
This very	ད་ག་རང་	*ťa-ǩa-rang*
Thither	དེར་ (དེ་རུ་)	*ťe.*
Thorn	ཚེར་མ་	*tsher-ma.*
Thorough, to be (complete)	ཕུགས་འཁྱོལ་བ་	*phu khyö-wa.*
Thoroughly	ཐད་དེ་	*be-ťe.*
Those	དེ་ཚོ་	*ťe-tsho.*
Thou	ཁྱོད། ཁྱོད་རང་	*khyö; khyö-rang.*
Do. *hon.*	ཁྱེད་	*khye.*
Do. *h. hon.*	སྐུ་གཞོགས་	*ku-sǩo.*
Though	ནས། ཀྱང་། རུང་། ན་ཡང་	*ne; kyang; rung na-yang.*
Thought (intention)	དོན་དག་	*ťön-ťa.*
Do. *hon.*	སྐུ་དོན་	*ku-ťön.*
Thought (opinion)	བསམ་པ་	*sam-pa.*
Do. *hon*	ཐུགས་སེམས་	*thu-sem.*

Thousand	སྟོང་ཕྲག་	*tong-thra.*
Thousand, hundred	འབུམ་	*bum.*
Thousand, ten	ཁྲི་	*thri.*
Thrash, to	གཡོ་མ་སྲུ་རྡུང་བ་	*yo-ma-su dung-wa.*
Thread	སྐུད་པ་	*kü-pa.*
Threaten, to	འཛེག་འཛེག་ (འཛིག་འཛིག་) བཏང་ (གཏོང་) བ་	*dzik-dzik tang-wa.*
Three	གསུམ་	*sum.*
Thresh, to (corn)	རྡུང་བ་	*dung-wa.*
Threshhold	ཐེམ་པ་	*them-pa.*
Thrice	ཚར་གསུམ་	*tshar-sum.*
Thriving	གཡང་ཆེན་པོ་	*yang-chhem-po.*
Throat	མིག་པ་	*mik-pa.*
Do. *hon.*	མགུལ་མིག་	*gü-mi.*
Throne	བཞུགས་ཁྲི་	*skuk-thri.*
Throng (of men)	མི་ཚོགས་	*mi-tsho.*
Through (by the agency of)	བརྒྱུད་ནས	*gyü-ne.*
Throw, to	རྒྱབ་པ། དབྱུག་པ་	*gyap-pa; yuk-pa.*
Do. *hon.*	དབྱུག་ག་ (པ་) གནང་བ	*yuk-ka nang-wa.*
Throw at, to	གཞུ་བ་	*sku-wa.*

Throw at, to, *hon.*	སྐྱོན་པ་གནང་བ་	*kyöm-pa nang-wa.*
Thumb	མཐེ་བོ་	*the-po.*
Do. *hon.*	ཕྱག་མཐེ་	*chha-the.*
Thunder	འབྲུག་སྐད།	*druk-ke.*
Thunder, to	འབྲུག་སྐད་སྐྱོན་པ་	*druk-ke kyöm-pa.*
Thunderbolt	ཐོག་	*tho.*
Do. sacred	རྡོ་རྗེ་	*dor-je.*
Thursday	གཟའ་ཕུར་བུ་	*śa-phur-ṕu.*
Thus	འདི་འདྲས། དག་ག་ཟེ་	*din-dre ; t́a-ḱa-śe.*
Thwart, to	བཀག་པ་ (འགེགས་པ་)	*kaḱ-pa.*
Do. *hon.*	བཀག་ག་ (འགེགས་པ་) གནང་བ་	*kaḱ-ḱa nang-wa.*
Tibet	བོད་	*ṕö.*
Tibetan	བོད་པ་	*ṕö-pa.*
Do. language	བོད་སྐད་	*ṕö-ke.*
Do. printed characters	དབུ་ཅན་	*u-chen.*
Do. manuscript characters	དབུ་མེད་	*u-me.*
Tickle, to	ཨི་ཀུ་ལུ་ཀུ་སག་པ་	*i-ḱu lu-ḱu sak-pa.*
Tidings	གནས་ཚུལ། གསར་འགྱུར་	*ne-tshü ; sang-gyu.*

Tiffin	ཉིན་གུང་ཁ་ལག་	*nyin-kung kha-la.*
Do. *hon.*	ཉིན་གུང་ཞལ་ལག་	*nyin-ḱung sḱe-la.*
Tie, to	བསྡམས་པ་ (སྡོམ་པ་)	*dam-pa.*
Do. *hon.*	བསྡམས་ (སྡོམ་) པ་གནང་བ་	*dam-pa nang-wa.*
Tiger	སྟག་	*ta.*
Tight	དམ་པོ་	*t́am-po.*
Till	ཐུག་ལ། བར་དུ་	*thuḱ-la; ṕar-t́u.*
Till, to	རྨོན་པ་རྒྱབ་པ་	*möm-pa gyaṕ-pa.*
Tillage	སོ་ནམས་	*so-nam.*
Tiller, *s.* (one who tills)	རྨོན་པ་རྒྱབ་མཁན། ཐོན་ཁས་ (ཐོང་པ་)	*möm-pa gyang-ḱhen; thön-ḱhe.*
Timber	ཤིང་ཆ་	*shing-chha.*
Time	དུས། དུས་ཚོད་	*t́ü; t́ü-tshö.*
Do. (o'clock)	ཆུ་ཚོད་	*chhu-tshö.*
Do. (proper time for doing something)	རན་	*ren.*
Do. (three times, etc.)	ཚར། ཐེངས་	*tshar; theng.*
Do. (life)	ཚེ་	*tshe.*
Time, at the present (now-a-days)	དེ་རིང་སང་། དེང་སང་	*t́e-ring sang; t́eng-sang.*
Time, to pass the	དགོ་འཁོར་བ་	*go-khor-wa.*

Time, to pass the, *hon.*	དབུ་འཁོར་བ་	*u-khor-wa.*
Tin	ཤ་དཀར་	*sha-ka.*
Tinder	སྤྲ་བ་	*pa-a.*
Tip (point)	རྩེ་	*tse.*
Tip (gratuity)	ཆང་རིན་	*chhang-ring.*
Do. *hon.*	གསོལ་རས་	*sö-re.*
Tipsy	ར་བཟི་	*raṕ-śi.*
Do. to be	ར་བཟི་བ་	*ra-śi-wa.*
Do. *hon.*	སྐུ་ར་བྱེད་པ་	*ku-ra be-pa.*
Tired	བཀའ་ལས་ཁག་པོ་	*ka-le khaḱ-po*
Do. *hon.*	སྐུ་མཉེལ་པོ་	*ku-nye-po.*
Tired, to be	ཐང་ཆད་པ་	*thang-chhe-pa.*
Do. *hon.*	སྐུ་ཐང་ཆད་པ་གནང་བ་	*ku-thang chhe-pa nang-wa.*
Tiresome (tedious)	དཀའ་ལས་ཁག་པོ་	*ka-le khaḱ-po.*
Do. *hon.*	སྐུ་མཉེལ་པོ་	*ku-nye-po.*
Titan (demi-god)	ལྷ་མ་ཡིན་	*hla-ma-yin.*
Title	གོ་ས། གོ་གནས་	*ḱo-sa; ḱo-ne.*
To (in presence of a person)	རྩ་ལ་	*tsa-la.*
Do. *inf.* to *sup.*	སྐུ་མདུན་ལ་	*kun-dün-la.*
To (as far as)	བར་ལ་	*ṕar-la.*

Tobacco	ཐ་མག་	*tha-ma.*
Do. *hon.*	བཞེས་ཐ་	*sḱe-tha.*
Tobacco pipe	གང་ཟག་	*ḱang-śa.*
Do. *hon.*	བཞེས་ཟག་	*sḱe-śa.*
Tobacco pouch	ཐ་ཁུག་	*tha-khu.*
Do. *hon.*	བཞེས་ཁུག་	*sḱe-khu.*
To-day	དེ་རིང་	*ťe-ring.*
Toe	རྐང་པའི་མཛུག་གུ་	*ḱang-pe dzuḱ-ḱu.*
Do. *hon.*	ཞབས་ཀྱི་ཕྱག་མཛུག་	*sḱaṕ-kyi chhan-dzu.*
Toe, the big	རྐང་པའི་མཐེ་བོ་	*kang-pe the-ṕo.*
Do. *hon.*	ཞབས་ཀྱི་མཐེ་བོ་	*sḱaṕ-kyi the-ṕo.*
Together with, *prep.*	དང་མཉམ་དུ་	*ťang-nyam-ťu.*
Together, *adv.* (jointly)	མཉམ་སྦྲེལ་	*nyam-drel.*
Do. *hon.*	ཕྱག་སྦྲེལ་	*chha-drel.*
Toilsome	དཀའ་ལས་ཁག་པོ་	*ka-le khaḱ-po.*
Do. *hon.*	སྐུ་མཉེལ་པོ་	*ku-nye-po.*
Token	རྟགས་	*ta.*
Tolerate, to (endure)	བཟོད་པ་སྒོམ་པ་	*śö-pa gom-pa.*
Do. *hon.*	བཟོད་པ་སྒོམ་པ་གནང་བ་	*śö-pa gom-pa nang-wa.*
Tolerate to (permit)	བཅུག་པ་ (འཇུག་པ་)	*chuḱ-pa.*

Tolerate, to (permit), *hon.*	བཅུག་ག་ (འཇུག་པ་) གནང་བ་	*chuḱ-ḱa nang-wa.*
Tomb	དུར་ཁུང་	*t́ur-khung.*
Tom-cat	ཕོ་ཞིམ་	*pho-sḱim.*
To-morrow	སང་ཉིན་	*sang-nyi.*
To-morrow morning	སང་ཞོགས་སྔ་པོ་	*sang-sḱo nga-po.*
Tone	གདངས་	*dang.*
Tongue	ལྕེ་	*che.*
Do. *hon.*	ལྗགས་	*ja.*
Tongue (dialect)	སྐད་ལུགས་	*ke-lu.*
To-night	དོ་དགོངས་དགོངས་མོ་	*t́o-gong gong-mo.*
Too, *conj.*	ཡང་	*yang.*
Too (very)	ཧ་ཅང་	*ha-chang.*
Too few, to be	ཉུང་དྲག་པ་	*nyung t́raḱ-pa.*
Too little, to be	ཆུང་དྲག་པ་	*chhung t́raḱ-pa.*
Too many, to be	མང་དྲག་པ་	*mang t́raḱ-pa.*
Too much, to be	ལྷག་པ་	*hlaḱ-pa.*
Tool	ལག་ཆ་	*laḱ-chha.*
Tooth	སོ་	*so.*
Do. *hon.*	ཚེམས་	*tshem.*

Toothless	སོ་མེད་	*so-me.*
Do. *hon.*	ཚེམས་མེད་	*tshem-me.*
Tooth, front	མདུན་སོ་	*dün-so.*
Do. *hon.*	མདུན་གྱི་ཚེམས་	*dün-k̄yi tshem.*
Tooth, lower	སྨད་སོ་	*me-so.*
Do. *hon.*	སྨད་ཀྱི་ཚེམས་	*me-kyi tshem.*
Tooth, molar	འགྲམ་སོ་	*dram-so.*
Do. *hon.*	ཞལ་འགྲམ་གྱི་ཚེམས་	*sk̄e-dram k̄yi-tshem*
Tooth, upper	ཡ་སོ་	*ya-so.*
Do. *hon.*	ཡས་ཀྱི་ཚེམས་	*ye-kyi tshem.*
Top (summit)	རྩེ	*tse.*
Do. (lid)	ཁ་གཅོད་	*khaṕ-chö.*
Do. *hon.*	ཞལ་གཅོད་	*sk̄e-chö.*
Torch	སྤོད་འབར་ (སྤ་འབར་)	*pem-bar.*
Torment, to (annoy)	ཁོང་ཁྲོ་སློང་བ་	*khong-thro lang-wa.*
Do. *hon.*	དགོངས་པ་དཀྲུག་པ་	*gong-pa truk̄-pa.*
Torn, to be	རལ་བ་	*re-wa.*
Tortoise	རུས་སྦལ་	*rü-be.*
Tortuous (crooked)	ཀྱོག་ཀྱོག་	*kyo-kyo.*
Do. (deceitful)	གཡོ་ཅན། བློ་སྐྱོགས་སྐྱོགས་	*yo-chen ; lo kyok̄-kyok̄.*

Tortuous (deceitful), *hon.*	ཐུགས་གཡོ་ཅན། ཐུགས་སྐྱོགས་སྐྱོགས་	*thu yo-chen; thu kyok-kyok.*
Torture (agony of mind)	སྡུག་བསྔལ་	*du-nge.*
Do. *hon.*	ཐུགས་འཁྲལ་	*thu-thre.*
Total, in the	བསྡོམས་ནས་	*dom-ne*
Totter, to	འཁྱོར་ནས་འགྲོ་བ་	*khyor-ne dro-wa.*
Do. *hon.*	སྐུ་འཁྱོར་ནས་ཕེབ་པ་	*ku-khyor-ne phe-pa.*
Do. *h. hon.*	སྐུ་འཁྱོར་ནས་འཆིབ་རྒྱུ་གནང་བ་	*ku-khyor-ne chhip-gyu nang-wa.*
Touch, to	ཐུག་པ། འཆང་བ་	*thuk-pa; chhang-wa.*
Do. *hon.*	ཐུག་ག་ (པ་) གནང་བ་	*thuk-ka nang-wa.*
Touch, to (by stretching out hand, etc.)	སྙོབ་པ་	*nyop-pa.*
Do. *hon.*	སྙོབ་པ་གནང་བ་	*nyop-pa nang-wa.*
Towards	ཕྱོགས་ལ། ངོས་ལ་	*chhok-la; ngö-la.*
Towel	ཨ་ཅོར་	*a-chor.*
Do. *hon.*	ཞལ་ཅོར་	*ske-chor.*
Town	གྲོང་ཁྱེར་	*trong-khyer.*
Toy	རྩེད་མོ་རྩེ་ཡ་	*tse-mo tse-ya.*
Do. *hon.*	སྐུ་རྩེ་གནང་ཡ་	*ku-tse nang-ya.*

Track (path)	ལམ་ཀ་	*lang-ka.*
Do. *hon.*	ཕེབ་ལམ་	*pheṕ-lam.*
Track (on face of cliff)	ཕྲང་	*thrang.*
Track (foot-print)	རྐང་རྗེས་	*kang-je.*
Do. *hon.*	ཞབས་རྗེས་	*sh́aṕ-je.*
Tract (of country)	ལུང་པ་	*lung-pa.*
Trade, *s.*	ཚོང་	*tshong.*
Do. *hon.*	རྒྱ་ཚོང་	*gya-tshong.*
Trade, to	ཚོང་རྒྱབ་པ་	*tshong-gyaṕ-pa.*
Do. *hon.*	རྒྱ་ཚོང་སྐྱོན་པ་	*gya-tshong kyöm-pa.*
Trader, tradesman	ཚོང་པ་	*tshong-pa.*
Do. *hon.*	ཚོང་དཔོན་	*tshong-pön.*
Traduce, to	སྨད་ར་བཏང་ (གཏོང་) བ་	*me-ra tang-wa.*
Do. *hon.*	སྨད་ར་གཏོང་ང་ (བ་) གནང་བ་	*me-ra tong-nga nang-wa.*
Do. *inf.* to *sup.*	སྨད་ར་ཞུ་བ་	*me-ra sh́u-wa.*
Traffic	ཚོང་	*tshong.*
Do. *hon.*	རྒྱ་ཚོང་	*gya-tshong.*
Train, to (teach)	བསླབས་པ་ (སློབ་པ་)	*laṕ-pa.*
Do. *hon.*	བསླབས་ (སློབ་) པ་གནང་བ་	*laṕ-pa nang-wa.*
Trammel *s.* (hindrance)	བཀག་ཆ་	*kaḱ-chha.*

Trammel, to	བཀག་པ་ (འགེགས་པ་)	*kaḱ-pa.*
Do. *hon.*	བཀག་ག་ (འགེགས་པ་) གནང་བ་	*kaḱ-ḱa nang-wa.*
Tramp, *s* (loafer)	རྒྱལ་ཁམས་སྐོར་མཁན་	*gyeng-kham kor-khen.*
Trample, to	རྐང་པས་རྫི་བ་	*kang-pe dzi-wa.*
Do. *hon.*	ཞབས་ཀྱིས་རྫི་བ་གནང་བ་	*sḱaṕ-kyi dzi-wa nang-wa.*
Tranquil (of places)	ཁ་གུ་སིམ་བུ་	*kha-ḱu sim-ṕu.*
Do. *hon.*	ཞལ་གུ་སིམ་བུ་	*sḱe-ḱu sim-ṕu.*
Transfer, to	རྗེ་བ་	*je-wa.*
Do. (soldiers, etc.)	རྗེ་པོ་རྒྱབ་པ་	*je-po gyaṕ-pa.*
Do. *hon.*	རྗེ་པོ་སྐྱོན་པ་	*je-po kyöm-pa.*
Transgress, to	སྡིག་པ་བསགས་ (སོག་) པ་	*diḱ-pa saḱ-pa.*
Do. *hon.*	སྐུ་སྡིག་བསགས་ག་ (སོག་པ་) གནང་བ་	*ku-di saḱ-ḱa nang-wa.*
Transgression	སྡིག་པ་	*diḱ-pa.*
Do. *hon.*	སྐུ་སྡིག་	*ku-di.*
Translate, to	སྒྱུར་བ་	*gyur-wa.*
Do. *hon.*	སྒྱུར་ར་ (བ་) གནང་བ་	*gyur-ra nang-wa.*
Transmigrate, to	སྐྱེ་བ་འཕོས་པ་	*kye-wa phö-pa.*
Do. *hon.*	སྐུ་སྐྱེ་འཕོས་པ་	*ku-kye phö-pa.*

Transmigration, cycle of	སྲིད་པ་འཁོར་ལོ་	*si-pa khor-lo.*
Transport	ཁལ་མ་	*khe-ma.*
Do. *hon.*	ཆིབས་ཁལ་	*chhiṕ-khe.*
Transport (compulsory service)	ཏའུ་	*ta-u.*
Do. *hon.*	ཆིབས་ཏའུ་	*chhiṕ-ta-u.*
Transport, to	ཏའུ་སྐྱེལ་བ་	*ta-u kyel-wa.*
Do. *hon.*	ཆིའུ་སྐྱེལ་ར་ (བ་) གནང་བ་	*chhi-u kye-ra nang-wa.*
Trap	རྙི་	*nyi.*
Travail (child-birth)	སྐྱེ་གཟུག་	*kye-śu.*
Traveller	འགྲུལ་པ་	*drü-pa.*
Tray	ཤིང་ཁྲོལ་	*shing-thrö.*
Do. *hon.*	གསོལ་ཁྲོལ་	*sö-thrö.*
Tread, to	རྐང་ལེབ་འཐེབ་པ་	*kang-le theṕ-pa.*
Do. *hon.*	ཞབས་ལེབ་འཐེབ་པ་	*sȟaṕ-le theṕ-pa.*
Treasure, *s.*	བཀང་འཛུག་	*kang-juḱ.*
Treasurer	ཕྱག་མཛོད་	*chhan-dzö.*
Treasury	དངུལ་ཁང་	*ngü-khang.*
Treat, *s.* (feast)	མགྲོན་པོ་	*dröm-po.*
Do. *hon.*	ཐུགས་སྤྲོ་	*thu-tro.*

Treat, to (entertain)	མགྲོན་པོ་བཏང་ (གཏོང་) བ་	*dröm-po tang-wa.*
Do. *hon.*	ཐུགས་སྤྲོ་གཏོང་ང་ (བ་) གནང་བ་	*thu-tro tong-nga nang-wa.*
Treaty	འཆིང་ཡིག་	*chhing-yi.*
Tree	ཤིང་སྡོང་	*shing-dong.*
Tremble, to (of animate beings)	འདར་བ་	*dar-wa.*
Do. *hon*	སྐུ་འདར་སྐྱོན་པ་	*kun-dar kyöm-pa.*
Tremble, to (of inanimate things)	འཁྲུག་པ་	*thruk-pa.*
Trench	རྡོང་	*ťong.*
Trial (experiment)	ཞིབ་ཆ་	*sḱiṕ-chha.*
Do. (by judge)	ཞིབ་དཔྱོད་	*sḱiṕ-chö.*
Do. *hon.*	བཀའ་ཞིབ་	*ka-sḱiṕ.*
Trial, to make a	ཞིབ་ཆ་ལྟ་བ་	*sḱiṕ-chha ta-wa.*
Do. *hon.*	ཞིབ་ཆ་གཟིགས་པ་	*sḱiṕ-chha śi-pa*
Triangle	ཟུར་གསུམ་	*śur-sum.*
Tribe	མི་བརྒྱུད། རིགས་བརྒྱུད་	*mi-gyü ; ri-gyü.*
Tribunal	ཁྲིམས་ཁང་	*thrim-khang.*
Tribute	ཁྲལ། འབབ་	*thre ; bap.*
Trick (deceit)	མགོ་སྐོར་	*go-kor.*

Trick (deceit), *hon.*	དབུ་སྐོར་	*u-kor.*
Trickle, to	ཐིགས་པ་རྒྱབ་པ་	*thiḱ-pa gyaṕ-pa.*
Tricky (artful)	གཅང་པོ་	*chang-po.*
Do. *hon.*	ཐུགས་གཅང་པོ་	*thu-chang-po.*
Trident	ཁ་ཊཾ་	*kha-tam.*
Trifling, (matter), *adj.*	དོན་གནད་ཆུང་ཆུང་	*ťön-ne chhung-chhung.*
Do. *hon.*	ཐུགས་དོན་ཆུང་ཆུང་	*thuḱ-ťön chhung-chhung.*
Trigger	སྐམ་པ་	*kam-pa.*
Tripod	རྐང་གསུམ་	*kang-sum.*
Do. iron (for fire)	ལྕགས་སྒྱིད་	*cha-gyi.*
Trivial	དོན་གནད་ཆུང་ཆུང་	*ťön-ne chhung-chhung.*
Do. *hon.*	ཐུགས་དོན་ཆུང་ཆུང་	*thuḱ-ťön chhung-chhung.*
Tromowa (inhabitant of Chumbi Valley)	གྲོ་མོ་བ་	*ťro-mo-wa.*
Troop	དམག་དཔུང་	*maḱ-pung.*
Trot, to	གོམ་ས་རྒྱབ་པ་	*ḱom-sa gyaṕ-pa.*
Do. *hon.*	གོམ་ས་སྐྱོན་པ་	*ḱom-sa kyöm-pa.*
Trouble	དཀའ་ལས་	*ka-le.*
Do. to be in	དཀའ་ལས་ཁྱུང་བ་	*ka-le cḱung-wa.*

Troublesome (of persons)	ཚ་སྲུན་པོ་	*cha-sing-po.*
Do. *hon.*	ཐུགས་ཚ་སྲུན་པོ་	*thuk̄-cha sing-po.*
Troublesome (of things)	དཀའ་ལས་ཁག་པོ་	*ka-le khak̄-po.*
Do. *hon.*	སྐུ་མཉེལ་པོ་	*ku-nye-po.*
Trousers	གོ་ཐུང་ (གོས་ཐུང་།) དོར་མ་	*k̄o-thung ; t̄or-ma.*
Do. *hon.*	ཞབས་དོར་	*sk̄ap-t̄o.*
True	ངོ་ཐོག། དངོས་ནས་	*ngo-tho : ngö-ne.*
Truly	དངོས་ནས་	*ngö-ne.*
Trumpet	དུང་	*t̄ung.*
Trumpet, thigh bone	རྐང་གླིང་	*kang-ling.*
Trunk (box)	སྒམ་	*gam.*
Do. *hon.*	ཕྱག་སྒམ་	*chha-gam.*
Trunk (of elephant)	མཆུ་རྡོ་	*chhu-do.*
Trunk, iron (box)	ལྕགས་སྒམ་	*cha-gam.*
Do. leather (box)	ཀོ་སྒམ་	*ko-gam.*
Trunk (of tree)	སྡོང་པོ་	*dong-po.*
Trust (confidence)	བློ་གཏད་	*lo-te.*
Trust, to	བློས་བཀལ་བ་	*lö ke-wa.*
Do. *hon*	ཐུགས་བློ་བཀལ་ར་ (བ་) གནང་བ་	*thu-lo ke-ra nang-wa.*

Trustworthy	བློས་ (བློ་) ཁེལ་ར་ (བ་)	*lö khe-ra.*
Do. *hon.*	ཐུགས་བློ་ཁེལ་ར་ (བ་)	*thu-lo khe-ra.*
Truth	ངོ་ཐོག། ངོས་ནས་	*ngo-tho; ngö-ne.*
Try, to (make effort)	སྙིང་རུས་བྱེད་པ་	*nying-rü che-pa.*
Do. *hon.*	ཐུགས་རུས་གནང་བ་	*thuk-rü nang-wa.*
Try, to (test)	ཚོད་ལྟ་བ། ཁོག་པ་ལེན་པ་	*tshö ta-wa; khok-pa lem-pa.*
Do. *hon.*	ཚོད་གཟིགས་པ་	*tshö śi-pa.*
Tuesday	གཟའ་མིག་དམར་	*śa mik-mar.*
Tumble, to (on ground which one is already touching)	འགྱེལ་བ་	*gye-wa.*
Do. *hon.*	འགྱེལ་ར་ (བ་) གནང་བ་	*gye-ra nang-wa.*
Tumble, to (from a height)	གཟགས་པ་ (འཛོག་པ་)	*śak-pa.*
Do. *hon.*	གཟགས་ཀ་ (འཛོག་པ་) གནང་བ་	*śak-ka nang-wa.*
Tumour	གཉེན་འབུར་	*nyem-bur.*
Tumult	རྒྱབ་འདྲེ། འཁྲུག་པ་	*gyam-dre; thruk-pa.*
Tune	གདངས་	*dang.*
Turban	ལེ་ཏོས་	*le-tö.*
Turbid	རྙོག་པོ་	*nyok-po.*

Turf	སྤང་	*pang.*
Turkistan	ཧོར་ལུང་པ། ཧོར་ཡུལ་	*hor lung-pa ; hor-yü.*
Do. man of	ཧོར་པ་	*hor-pa.*
Turn round, to, *v.i.*	འཁོར་བ་	*khor-wa.*
Do. *hon.*	ཞབས་འཁོར་གནང་བ་	*sKap-khor nang-wa.*
Turn round, to, *v.t.*	སྐོར་ར་ (བ་) རྒྱབ་པ་	*kor-ra gyap-pa.*
Do. *hon.*	སྐོར་ར་ (བ་) སྐྱོན་པ་	*kor-ra kyöm-pa.*
Turn back to front, to	ཁ་ཕྱོགས་ལོག་པ་	*kha-chho lok-pa.*
Do. *hon.*	ཁ་ཕྱོགས་ལོག་ག་ (པ་) གནང་བ་	*kha-chho lok-ka nang-wa.*
Turn upside down, to	མགོ་གཞུག་ལོག་པ། ཨ་ལོག་རྒྱབ་པ་	*go-sKu lok-pa ; a-lo gyap-pa.*
Do. *hon.*	མགོ་གཞུག་ལོག་ག་ (པ་) གནང་བ། ཨ་ལོག་སྐྱོན་པ་	*go-sKu lok-ka nang-wa; a-lo kyöm-pa.*
Turnip	ཉུང་མ་	*nyung-ma.*
Do. *hon.*	བཞེས་ཉུང་	*sKe-nyung.*
Turquoise	གཡུ་	*yu.*
Do. *hon.*	ཕྱག་གཡུ་	*chha-yu.*
Turquoise ear-ring	ཟི་གཡུ་	*ṡi-yu.*
Turquoise (worn in head-dress)	གཡུ་	*yu.*

Turquoise (worn in head-dress) *hon.*	དབུ་གཡུ་	*u-yu.*
Tusk	མཆེ་བ་	*chhe-wa.*
Tutelary deity	ཡི་དམ་	*yi-dam.*
Tutor	དགེ་རྒན་	*ge-gen.*
Do. *hon.*	དགེ་རྒན་ལགས་	*ge-gen-la.*
Twelfth	བཅུ་གཉིས་པ་	*chu-nyi-pa.*
Twelve	བཅུ་གཉིས་	*chu-nyi.*
Twentieth	ཉི་ཤུ་པ་	*nyi-shu-pa.*
Twenty	ཉི་ཤུ་	*nyi-shu.*
Twice	ཚར་གཉིས་	*tshar-nyi.*
Twilight, at	ས་རིབ་ (སྲིབ་) ནས་	*sa rip-ne.*
Twin	མཚེ་མ་	*tshe-ma.*
Do. *hon.*	ཨ་ཝ་མཚེ་མ་	*a-wa tshe-ma.*
Twine	སྐུད་པ་	*kü-pa.*
Do. *hon.*	ཕྱག་སྐུད་	*chha-kü.*
Twist, to	སྒྲིམ་པ་	*drim-pa.*
Do. *hon.*	སྒྲིམ་པ་གནང་བ་	*drim-pa nang-wa.*
Two	གཉིས་	*nyi.*
Do. (in weighing, measuring, etc.)	དོ་	*t́o.*

U

Udder	གཞོས་	*sKö.*
Ugly	ཁ་མདོག་ཉེས་པོ་	*kha-do nye-po.*
Do. *hon.*	ཞལ་མདོག་ཉེས་པོ་	*sKe-do nye-po.*
Ulcer	ཤུ་བ་	*shu-wa.*
Do. *hon.*	སྐུ་ཤུ་	*ku-shu.*
Ultimate	གཞུག་ཤོས་	*sKuk-shö.*
Umbrage, to take	འཚེར་བ་	*tsher-wa.*
Do. *hon.*	ཐུགས་འཚེར་གནང་བ་	*thu-tsher nang-wa.*
Umbrella	ཉི་གདུགས་	*nyi-du.*
Do *hon.*	དབུ་གདུགས་	*u-du.*
Unable, to be	མི་ཐུབ་པ་	*mi thup-pa.*
Unavailing, to be (useless)	ཕན་མི་ཐོགས་པ་	*phen mi thok-pa.*
Do. *hon.*	ཐུགས་ཕན་མི་གསོ་བ	*thu-phen mi so-wa.*
Unbearable (pain)	སྒྲོང་མི་ཐུབ་པ་	*gong mi thup-pa.*
Do. *hon.*	སྒྲོང་ང་ (སྒྲོམ་པ་) གནང་མི་ ཐུབ་པ་	*gong-nga nang mi thup-pa.*
Unbiassed	ཁྲིམས་དྲང་པོ་	*thrim trang-po.*
Do. *hon.*	བཀའ་ཁྲིམས་དྲང་པོ་	*ka-thrim trang-po.*
Unbreakable, to be	ཆག་རྒྱུ་མེད་པ་	*chhak-gyu me-pa.*

Unbridled (licentious)	འདོད་ཆགས་ཆེན་པོ་	*dö-chha chhem-po.*
Unceasing	རྒྱུན་ཆད་རྒྱུ་མེད་པ་	*gyün-chhe-gyu me-pa.*
Unceasingly	རྣམ་རྒྱུན། དུས་རྒྱུན་	*nam-gyün; ťü-gyün.*
Uncertain, to be	ཐེ་ཚོམ་ཟ་བ་	*the-tshom śa-wa.*
Do. *hon.*	ཐེ་ཚོམ་གནང་བ་	*the-tshom nang-wa.*
Uncertainty	ཐེ་ཚོམ་	*the-tshom.*
Unchaste	འདོད་ཆགས་ཆེན་པོ་	*dö-chha chhem-po.*
Uncivil	སྒྲིག་མེད་	*driǩ-me.*
Uncle, maternal	ཞང་ཞང་ (ཨ་ཞང་)	*sǩang sǩang.*
Do. paternal	ཨ་ཁུ་	*a-ǩu.*
Unclean	བཙོག་པ་	*tsoǩ-pa.*
Unclothed	དམར་ཧྲང་ང་	*mar-hrang-nga.*
Uncommon (rare)	དཀོན་པོ་	*köm-po.*
Unconquerable	གླགས་····མི་ཁ་བ་	*la...mi kha-wa.*
Undaunted	བློ་ཁོག་ཆེན་པོ་	*lo-kho chhem-po.*
Do. *hon.*	ཐུགས་ཁོག་ཆེན་པོ་	*thu-kho chhem-po.*
Undefined	བརྟན་པོ་མེད་པ་	*tem-po me-pa.*
Under	འོག་ལ་	*o-la.*
Understand, to	ཤེས་པ། ཧ་གོ་བ་	*she-pa; ha-ǩo-wa.*
Do. *hon.*	མཁྱེན་པ་	*khyem-pa.*

Understand, to, *h. hon.*	དགོངས་པ་རྟོགས་པ་	*gong-pa tok-pa.*
Understanding	རིག་པ་	*rik-pa.*
Do. *hon.*	ཐུགས་རིག་	*thu-ri.*
Undo, to (nullify)	མེད་པར་བཟོ་བ་	*me-pa so-wa.*
Do. *hon.*	མེད་པར་བཟོ་བ་གནང་བ་	*me-pa so-wa nang-wa.*
Undo, to (untie)	བཀྲོལ་བ་ (འགྲོལ་བ།) བཤིག་པ་	*tröl-wa ; sKik-pa.*
Do. *hon.*	བཀྲོལ་ར་ (འགྲོལ་བ་) གནང་བ། བཤིག་ག་ (པ་) གནང་བ་	*trö-ra nang-wa ; sKik-ka nang-wa.*
Undress, to	ཕྱིས་པ་ (འབུད་པ་)	*pi-pa.*
Do. *hon.*	ཕིས་ (འབུད་) པ་གནང་བ་	*pi-pa nang-wa.*
Unendurable (pain)	སྒྲོང་ (སྒྲོམ་) མི་ཐུབ་པ་	*gong mi thup-pa.*
Do. *hon.*	སྒྲོང་ང་ (སྒྲོམ་པ་) གནང་མི་ཐུབ་པ་	*gong-nga nang mi thup-pa.*
Uneven, to be	སྙོམས་པོ་མེད་པ་	*nyom-po me-pa.*
Unfasten, to (button, etc.)	སྤྱིད་པ་	*pi-pa.*
Do. *hon.*	སྤྱིད་པ་གནང་བ་	*pi-pa nang-wa.*
Untasten, to (knot, etc.)	བཤིག་པ་	*sKik-pa.*
Do. *hon.*	བཤིག་ག་ (པ་) གནང་བ་	*sKik-ka nang-wa.*

Unfit	འོས་པོ་མེད་པ་	*ö-po me-pa.*
Do. *hon.*	ཐུགས་འོས་པོ་མེད་པ་	*thu-ö-po me-pa.*
Unfortunate	བསོད་བདེ་མེད་པ། བསོད་བདེ་ཆུང་ཆུང་	*so-de me-pa; so-de chhung-chhung.*
Do. *hon.*	སྐུ་བསོད་མེད་པ། སྐུ་བསོད་ཆུང་ཆུང་	*ku-sö me-pa; ku-sö chhung-chhung.*
Unfortunate, to be	བསོད་བདེ་མེད་པ་	*so-de me-pa.*
Do. *hon.*	སྐུ་བསོད་མེད་པ་	*ku-sö me-pa.*
Unintelligible	མི་གོ་བ་	*mi k̓o-wa.*
Do. *hon.*	མི་གསན་པ་	*mi sem-pa.*
Unhappy, to be	སྐྱིད་པོ་མེད་པ་	*kyi-po me-pa.*
Do. *hon.*	ཐུགས་སྤྲོ་པོ་མེད་པ་	*thu-tro-po me-pa.*
Uniform (dress)	དམག་ཆས་	*mak̓-chhe.*
Uniform (alike)	གཅིག་པ། འདྲ་འདྲ་	*chik̓-pa; dran-dra.*
Unimportant	དོན་དག་ཆུང་ཆུང་	*t̓ön-t̓a chhung-chhung.*
Do. *hon.*	ཐུགས་དོན་ཆུང་ཆུང་	*thuk̓-t̓ön chhung-chhung.*
Uninterrupted	རྒྱུན་ཆད་རྒྱུ་མེད་པ་	*gyün-chhe-gyu me-pa.*
Uninterruptedly	རྣམ་རྒྱུན། དུས་རྒྱུན་	*nam-gyün; t̓ü-gyün.*
Unite, to	འཐུད་རྒྱབ་པ་	*thü-gyap̓-pa.*
Do. *hon.*	འཐུད་སྐྱོན་པ་	*thü-kyöm-pa.*

Unitedly (jointly)	མཉམ་སྦྲེལ་	*nyam-drel.*
Do. *hon.*	ཕྱག་སྦྲེལ་	*chha-drel.*
Universal (all)	ཚང་མ། ཐམས་ཅད། སྒང་ཁ། རུ་	*tshang-ma; thum-che; gang-kha; ru.*
Unlawful	ཁྲིམས་མེད་	*thrim-me.*
Unlearned	ཡོན་ཏན་མེད་པ་	*yön-ten me-pa.*
Do. *hon.*	སྐུ་ཡོན་མེད་པ་	*ku-yön me-pa.*
Unless, with *verb* "to do"	མ་བྱེད་ན་	*ma cḱe-na.*
Unlimited	ཚོད་མེད་པ་	*tshö me-pa.*
Unloose, to (dress, etc.)	སྤྱིད་པ་	*pi-pa.*
Do. *hon.*	སྤྱིད་པ་གནང་བ་	*pi-pa nang-wa.*
Unlucky	བསོད་བདེ་མེད་པ། བསོ་ (བསོད་) བདེ་ཆུང་ཆུང་	*so-de me-pa; so-de chhung-chhung*
Do. *hon.*	སྐུ་བསོད་མེད་པ། སྐུ་བསོད་ཆུང་ཆུང་	*ku-sö me-pa; ku-sö chhung-chhung.*
Unlucky, to be	བསོད་བདེ་མེད་པ་	*so-de me-pa.*
Do. *hon.*	སྐུ་བསོད་མེད་པ་	*ku-sö me-pa.*
Unmarried man	ཕོ་ཧྲང་ང་	*pho-hrang-nga.*
Do. woman	མོ་ཧྲང་ང་	*mo-hrang-nga.*
Unmerciful, to be	སྙིང་རྗེ་མེད་པ་	*nying-je me-pa.*

Unmerciful, to be, *hon.*	ཐུགས་རྗེ་མེད་པ་	*thuǩ-je me-pa.*
Unprejudiced (of judge)	ཁྲིམས་དྲང་པོ་	*thrim ťrang-po.*
Do. *hon.*	བཀའ་ཁྲིམས་དྲང་པོ་	*ka-thrim ťrang-po.*
Unprofitable, to be	ཕན་མི་ཐོགས་པ་	*phen mi thoǩ-pa.*
Do. *hon.*	ཐུགས་ཕན་མི་གསོ་བ་	*thu-phen mi so-wa.*
Unreasonable	དོན་མེད་	*ťon-me.*
Unrelenting, to be	སྙིང་རྗེ་མེད་པ་	*nying-je me-pa.*
Do. *hon.*	ཐུགས་རྗེ་མེད་པ་	*thuǩ-je me-pa.*
Unserviceable, to be	ཕན་མི་ཐོགས་པ་	*phen mi thoǩ-pa.*
Do. *hon.*	ཐུགས་ཕན་མི་གསོ་བ་	*thu-phen mi so-wa.*
Unsettled (indefinite)	བརྟན་པོ་མེད་པ་	*tem-po me-pa.*
Untie, to	བཀྲོལ་བ་ (འགྲོལ་བ།) བཤིག་པ་	*tröl-wa ; sǩik-pa.*
Do. *hon.*	བཀྲོལ་ར་ (འགྲོལ་བ་) གནང་བ། བཤིག་ག་ (པ་) གནང་བ་	*trö-ra nang-wa ; sǩik-ǩa nang-wa.*
Until	ཐུག་ལ་	*thuǩ-la.*
Untruth	ཧམ་པ། ཀྱག་རྫུན་	*ham-pa ; kyaǩ-dzün.*
Do. *hon.*	ཞལ་རྫུན་	*sǩe-dzün.*
Unusual (rare)	དཀོན་པོ་	*köm-po.*

Unusual (extraordinary)	ཡ་མཚན་པོ། ཁྱད་མཚར་པོ་	*yam-tshem-po ; khye-tsha-po.*
Unwell, to be	བདེ་པོ་མེད་པ། གཟུགས་པོ་ཐང་པོ་མེད་པ་	*de-po me-pa ; śuk̄-po thang-po me-pa.*
Do. *hon.*	སྐུ་གཟུགས་བདེ་པོ་མེད་པ། སྐུ་གཟུགས་ཐང་པོ་མེད་པ་	*ku-śu de-po me-pa ; ku-śu thang-po me-pa.*
Up	ཡར་	*ya.*
Up to	ཐུག་ལ་	*thuk̄-la.*
Up-hill	གྱེན་	*k̄yen.*
Do. steep	གྱེན་དམ་པོ་	*k̄yen-ťam-p̄o.*
Upon	སྟེང་ལ། སྒང་ལ་	*teng-la ; gang-la.*
Upper	ཡ་གི་	*ya-k̄i.*
Upper arm	ལག་ཉ་	*lak̄-nya.*
Do. *hon.*	ཕྱག་ཉ་	*chha-nya.*
Upper tooth	ཡ་སོ་	*ya-so.*
Do. *hon.*	ཡས་ཀྱི་ཚེམས་	*ye-kyi tshem.*
Upraid, to	གཞི་གཞི་བཏང་ (གཏོང་) བ་	*she-she tang-wa.*
Do. *hon.*	བཀའ་བཀྱོན་གནང་བ་	*kap̄-kyön nang-wa.*
Upright (erect)	ཀྱེ་རེ་	*kye-re.*
Do. (just)	ཁྲིམས་དྲང་པོ་	*thrim ťrang-po.*
Do. *hon.*	བཀའ་ཁྲིམས་དྲང་པོ་	*ka-thrim ťrang-po.*

Upright (moral, virtuous)	ཚུལ་ལྡན་	*tshün-den.*
Upshot	སྙིང་པོ་	*nying-po.*
Upstairs	ཡ་ཐོག་	*yaṕ-tho.*
Urge, to (insist)	ཨུ་ཚུགས་བྱེད་པ་	*u-tshu cḱe-pa.*
Do. *hon.*	ཨུ་ཚུགས་གནང་བ་	*u-tshu nang-wa.*
Urgent (work)	འཕྲལ་འཕྲལ་བྱེད་དགོས་ཡ་	*thre-thre cḱe gö-ya.*
Urine	གཅིན་པ་	*chim-pa.*
Do. *hon.*	ཆབ་གསང་	*chhaṕ-sang.*
Do. *h. hon.*	སྐུ་གསང་	*ku-sang.*
Urine, to discharge	གཅིན་པ་བཏང་ (གཏོང་) བ་	*chim-pa tang-wa.*
Do. *hon.*	ཆབ་གསང་བཏང་ (གཏོང་) བ་	*chhaṕ-sang tang-wa.*
Do. *h. hon.*	སྐུ་གསང་གནང་བ་	*ku-sang nang-wa.*
Urn (containing ashes of dead lama)	སྐུ་གདུང་	*ku-dung.*
Us	ང་ཚོ་	*nga-tsho.*
Usage	ལུགས་སྲོལ་	*luḱ-sö.*
Use (custom)	ལུགས་སྲོལ་	*luḱ-sö.*
Use, to (employ)	སྐོ་བ་	*ko-wa.*
Do. *hon.*	སྐོ་བ་གནང་བ་	*ko-wa nang-wa.*
Use, to be of	ཕན་ཐོགས་པ་	*phen thoḱ-pa.*

Use, to be of *hon.*	ཐུགས་ཕན་གསོ་བ་	*thu-phen so-wa.*
Used to, to be	གོམས་པ་	*k̄om-pa.*
Used to, to become	གོམས་སོང་བ་	*k̄om-song-wa.*
Used up, to be	རྫོགས་པ་	*dzok̄-pa.*
Do. *hon.*	རྫོགས་ཀ་ (པ་) གནང་བ་	*dzok̄-k̄a nang-wa.*
Useful, to be	ཕན་ཐོགས་པ་	*phen thok̄-pa.*
Do. *hon.*	ཐུགས་ཕན་གསོ་བ་	*thu-phen so-wa.*
Useless, to be	ཕན་མི་ཐོགས་པ་	*phen mi thok̄-pa*
Do. *hon.*	ཐུགས་ཕན་མི་གསོ་བ་	*thu-phen mi so-wa.*
Usually	ཕལ་ཆེར་	*phe-chhe.*
Usurp, to	འཕྲོག་པ་	*throk̄-pa.*
Do. *hon.*	འཕྲོག་ཀ་ (པ་) གནང་བ་	*throk̄-k̄a nang-wa.*
Utensils	ལག་ཆ་	*lak̄-chha.*
Do. cooking	ཐབ་ཆས་	*thap̄-chhe.*
Utter (entire)	ཚང་མ། ཐམས་ཅད། སྒང་ཁ་.	*tshang-ma; tham-che; gang-kha.*
Utter, to (speak)	ལབ་པ་	*lap̄-pa.*
Do. *hon.*	གསུང་བ་	*sung-wa.*
Utterance	སྐད་	*ke.*
Do. *hon.*	གསུང་སྐད་	*sung-ke.*
Utterly (used negatively)	ཐད་དེ། ཁྱོན་ནས་	*be-t̄e; khyön-ne.*

V

Vacant	སྟོང་པ་	*tong-pa.*
Vagrant	རྒྱལ་ཁམས་སྐོར་མཁན་	*gyeng-kham kor-khen.*
Vaccine lymph	ཐོར་པའི་སྨན་	*thor-pe-men.*
Vacillate, to	ཐེ་ཚོམ་ཟ་བ་	*the-tshom ża-wa.*
Do. *hon.*	ཐེ་ཚོམ་གནང་བ་	*the-tshom ṅang-wa.*
Vacillation	ཐེ་ཚོམ་	*the-tshom.*
Vague	ཏན་པོ་མེད་པ་	*tem-po me-pa.*
Vain	རང་སྟོད་ཚ་པོ་	*rang-tö tsha-po.*
Do. in personal appearance	དང་འདོད་ཚ་པོ་	*ťang-dö tsha-po.*
Valiant	སྙིང་ཆེན་པོ་	*nying-chhem-po.*
Do. *hon.*	ཐུགས་སྙིང་ཆེན་པོ་	*thu-nying chhem-po.*
Valley	རོང་། ལུང་པ་	*rong ; lung-pa.*
Do. upper part of	ལུང་པའི་ཕུ་	*lung-pe phu.*
Do. lower part of	ལུང་པའི་མདོ་	*lung-pe do.*
Valorous	སྙིང་ཆེན་པོ་	*nying-chhem-po.*
Do. *hon.*	ཐུགས་སྙིང་ཆེན་པོ་	*thu-nying chhem-po.*
Valuable	རྩ་ཆེན་པོ་	*tsa chhem-po.*
Value. *s.*	གོང་	*kong.*

Value, *hon.*	ལྗགས་གོང་	*ja-ḱong.*
Valueless	གོང་མེད་	*ḱong-me.*
Vanish, to	ཡལ་བ་	*ye-wa.*
Vanity	རང་སྟོད་	*rang-tö.*
Do. in personal appearance	དང་འདོད་	*ťang-dö.*
Vanquish, to	རྒྱལ་བ། ཀླག་འཁས་པ་	*gye-wa ; la khe-pa.*
Do. *hon.*	རྒྱལ་ར་ (བ་) གནང་བ། ཀླག་འཁས་ར་ (པ་) གནང་བ་	*gye-ra nang-wa ; la khe-ra nang-wa.*
Vanquished, to be	འཕམ་པ་	*pham-pa.*
Do. *hon.*	འཕམ་པ་གནང་བ་	*pham-pa nang-wa.*
Vapour	རླངས་པ་	*lang-pa.*
Variable, to be	བརྟན་པོ་……མེད་པ་	*tem-po...me-pa.*
Variation (difference)	ཁྱད། ཧེ་བག་	*khye ; he-ṕa.*
Do. *hon.*	ཐུགས་ཁྱད་	*thu-khye.*
Variety	ཁྱད། ཧེ་བག་	*khye; he-ṕa.*
Do. *hon.*	ཐུགས་ཁྱད་	*thu-khye.*
Various	མི་གཅིག་པ། མི་འདྲ་བ་	*mi chik-pa ; min dra-wa.*
Various kinds of	སྣ་ཚོགས་	*na-tsho.*
Vase	བུམ་པ་	*ṕum-pa.*

Vase, *hon.*	ཕྱག་བུམ་	*chha-pum.*
Vast	རྒྱ་ཆེན་པོ་	*gya-chhem-po.*
Vaunt, to	རང་སྟོད་བྱེད་པ་	*rang-tö cḱe-pa.*
Veal	པེ་པེའི་ཤ་	*ṕe-ṕe sha.*
Vegetable	ཚལ་ *Ch.*	*tshe.*
Vegetable drug	སྔོ་སྨན་	*ngo-men.*
Vegetable garden	ཚལ་གཡང་ཙེ་ *Ch.*	*tshe yang-tse.*
Vein	རྩ་	*tsa.*
Do. *hon.*	སྐུ་རྩ་	*ku-tsa.*
Velveteen	སྤུ་མ་	*pu-ma.*
Venerable (title)	རྗེ་བཙུན་	*je-tsün.*
Venerate, to	བསྙེན་བཀུར་བྱེད་པ་	*nyen-kur cḱe-pa.*
Do. *inf.* to *sup.*	བསྙེན་བཀུར་ཞུ་བ་	*nyen-kur sḱu-wa.*
Veneration	བསྙེན་བཀུར་	*nyen-kur.*
Vengeance	དགྲ་ལན་	*dra-len.*
Vengeance, to take	དགྲ་ལན་ལེན་པ་	*dra-len lem-pa.*
Do. *hon.*	དགྲ་ལན་བཞེས་པ་	*dra-len sḱe-pa.*
Venial (trivial)	དོན་གནད་ཆུང་ཆུང་	*ťön-ne chhung-chhung.*
Do. *hon.*	ཐུགས་དོན་ཆུང་ཆུང་	*thuḱ-ťon chhung-chhung.*
Venison	ཤ་གི་ཤ་ (ཤ་བའི་ཤ་)	*sha-ḱi sha.*

Venom (poison)	དུག་	*ťu.*
Do. *hon.*	གསོལ་དུག་	*sö-ťu.*
Venom (spite)	གནོད་སེམས་	*nö-sem.*
Venture, to	ནུས་པ་	*nü-pa.*
Do. *hon.*	ནུས་པ་གནང་བ་	*nü-pa nang-wa.*
Venturesome	ཁ་མེད་མིག་མེད་	*kha-me miḱ-me.*
Verandah (roofed in)	ཐོག་གཡང་	*tho-yang.*
Do. (in upper story)	གཡབ་སྟེང་	*yaṕ-teng.*
Do. (upper, running round a house)	གཡབ་འཁོར་	*yaṕ-khor.*
Verbal	ཁའི་	*khe.*
Verbally	ཁ་ནས་	*kha-ne.*
Verdict (judgment)	བཅད་མཚམས་། ཁྲ་མ་	*che-tsham ; thra-ma.*
Vermilion	མཚལ། རྒྱ་མཚལ་	*tshe; gyam-tshe.*
Vermin	འབུ་	*bu.*
Verse	ཚིགས་བཅད་	*tshiḱ-che.*
Vertebræ	སྒལ་ཚིགས་	*ge-tshi.*
Do. *hon.*	སྐུ་སྟོད་ཚིགས་	*ku-tö tshi.*
Vertigo	བད་རླུང་མགོ་འཁོར་	*ṕe-lung go-khor.*
Very	ཧ་ཅང་	*ha-chang.*

Vessel (for water)	ཆུ་སྣོད་	*chhu-nö.*
Do. *hon.*	ཆབ་སྣོད་	*chhaṕ-nö.*
Vessel (ship)	གྲུ་	*t́ru.*
Do. *hon.*	ཕེབ་གྲུ་	*pheṕ-t́ru.*
Vex, to	ཁོང་ཁྲོ་སློང་བ་	*khong-thro lang-wa.*
Do. *hon.*	དགོངས་པ་དཀྲུག་པ་	*gong-pa truḱ-pa.*
Vexed, to be	ཚིག་པ་ཟ་བ་	*tshiḱ-pa śa-wa.*
Do. *hon.*	དགོངས་པ་ཚུང་བ་	*gong-pa tshung-pa.*
Viands	ཁ་ལག། ལྟོ་	*kha-la ; to.*
Do. *hon.*	ཞལ་ལག་	*sḱe-la.*
Vibrate, to	འཁྲུག་པ་	*thruḱ-pa.*
Vice	སྡིག་པ་	*diḱ-pa.*
Do. *hon.*	སྐུ་སྡིག་	*ku-di.*
Vicinity	ཉེ་འཁོར་	*nye-khor.*
Vicious	ངན་པོ་	*ngem-po.*
Do. *hon.*	ཐུགས་ངན་པོ་	*thu ngem-po.*
Victorious, to be	རྒྱལ་བ་	*gye-wa.*
Do. *hon.*	རྒྱལ་ར་ (བ་) གནང་བ་	*gye-ra nang-wa.*
Victuals	ཁ་ལག། ལྟོ་	*kha-la ; to.*
Do. *hon.*	ཞལ་ལག་	*sḱe-la.*

View (opinion)	བསམ་པ་	*sam-pa.*
Do. *hon.*	ཐུགས་སེམས་	*thu-sem.*
View (purpose)	དོན་དག་	*ťön-ťa.*
Do. *hon.*	སྐུ་དོན་	*ku-ťön.*
View, to	མཐོང་བ། ལྟ་བ་	*thong-wa ; ta-wa.*
Do. *hon.*	གཟིགས་པ་	*śi-pa.*
Vigorous	ཤེད་ཆེན་པོ་	*she chhem-po.*
Do. *hon.*	སྐུ་ཤེད་ཆེན་པོ་	*ku-she chhem-po.*
Vigour	ཤེད་	*she.*
Do. *hon.*	སྐུ་ཤེད་	*ku-she.*
Vile (dirty)	བཙོག་པ་	*tsoǩ-pa.*
Do. (odious)	སྐྱུག་བྲོ་པོ་	*kyuǩ-ťro-po.*
Vilification	སྨད་ར་	*me-ra.*
Vilify, to	སྨད་ར་བཏང་ (གཏོང་) བ་	*me-ra tang-wa.*
Do. *hon.*	སྨད་ར་གཏོང་ང་ (བ་) གནང་བ་	*me-ra tong-nya nang-wa.*
Do. *inf.* to *sup.*	སྨད་ར་ཞུ་བ་	*me-ra sǩu-wa.*
Village	གྲོང་པ་	*ťrong-pa.*
Villager	གྲོང་པ་	*ťrong-pa.*
Villain	འཛབ་ཆེན་	*dzap̌-chhen.*
Vine	རྒུན་འབྲུམ་ཤིང་	*gün-drum-shing.*

Vinegar	ཚུའུ་ *Ch.*	*tshu-u.*
Violence (force)	དབང་ཡོད་	*wang-yö.*
Violence, to show	དབང་ཡོད་བྱེད་པ་	*wang-yö cḱe-pa.*
Violet (colour)	ཀུན་འབྲུམ་མདོག	*gün-drum do.*
Virgin	བུ་མོ་	*ṕu-mo.*
Virtue	དགེ་བ་	*ge-wa.*
Virtuous	ཚུལ་ལྡན་	*tshün-den.*
Virus (poison)	དུག་	*ṫu.*
Do. *hon.*	གསོལ་དུག་	*sö-tu.*
Visible, to be	མཐོང་བ་	*thong-wa.*
Do. *hon.*	གཟིགས་པ་	*śi-pa.*
Vision (spectre)	གདོང་འདྲེ། འདྲེ་	*dong-dre ; dre.*
Visit, to (a person)	བཅར་བ་	*char-wa.*
Do. *inf.* to *sup.*	སྐུ་མདུན་ལ་བཅར་བ་	*kun-dün-la char-wa.*
Vituperate, to	སྨད་ར་བཏང་ (གཏོང་) བ་	*me-ra tang-wa.*
Do. *hon.*	སྨད་ར་གཏོང་ང་ (བ་) གནང་བ་	*me-ra tong-nga nang-wa.*
Do. *inf.* to *sup.*	སྨད་ར་ཞུ་བ་	*me-ra sḱu-wa.*
Vituperation	སྨད་ར་	*me-ra.*
Vocabulary	མིང་མཛོད་	*ming-dzö.*
Vocation	ལས་ཀ་	*le-ka.*

Vocation, *hon.*	ཕྱག་ལས་	*chha-le.*
Voice	སྐད། སྒྲ་	*ke ; dra.*
Do. *hon.*	གསུང་	*sung.*
Void (empty)	སྟོང་པ་	*tong-pa.*
Volume (of book)	པོ་ཏི་	*po-ti.*
Vomit, to	སྐྱུག་པ་	*kyuk-pa.*
Do. *hon.*	ཞལ་སྐྱུག་གནང་བ་	*sKo-kyu nang-wa.*
Voracious (gluttonous)	གྲོད་ཆེན་པོ་	*ťrö-chhem-po.*
Vouch, to	ཁས་ཁྱགས་བྱེད་པ་	*khe-khya cKe-pa.*
Do. *hon.*	ཞལ་ཁྱགས་གནང་བ་	*sKe-khya nang-wa.*
Voucher (guarantor)	ཁས་ཁྱགས་བྱེད་མཁན་	*khe-khya cKe-khen.*
Do. *hon.*	ཞལ་ཁྱགས་གནང་མཁན་	*sKe-khya nang-khen.*
Vow (religious)	དམ་བཅའ་	*ťam-cha.*
Do. to make)	དམ་བཅའ་ཕུལ་ (འབུལ་) བ་	*ťam-cha phü-wa.*
Do. *hon.*	དམ་བཅའ་འབུལ་ར་ (བ་) གནང་བ་	*ťam-cha bü-ra nang-wa.*
Vowels	དབྱངས་	*yang.*
Vulgar (of language, *opp.* to *hon.*)	ཞེ་ས་མེད་པ་	*sKe-sa me-pa.*
Do. (of persons, *opp.* to high-born)	དཀྱུས་མ་	*kyü-ma.*

W

Wag (jester)	དབུ་འཁོར་ཞུ་མཁན་	*u-khor sKu-khen.*
Wag, to (shake)	དབྱུག་དབྱུག་བྱེད་པ་	*yuk-yu cKe-pa.*
Do. *hon.*	དབྱུག་དབྱུག་གནང་བ་	*yuk-yu nang-wa.*
Wag, to (dog's tail)	རིལ་རིལ་བྱེད་པ་	*ri-ri cKe-pa.*
Wager	རྒྱན་	*gyen.*
Do. *hon.*	སྐུ་རྒྱན་	*ku-gyen.*
Wager, to	རྒྱན་བཞག་ (འཛོག་) པ་	*gyen sKak-pa.*
Do. *hon.*	སྐུ་རྒྱན་གཞོག་ག་ (འཛོག་པ་) གནང་བ་	*ku-gyen sKok-ka nang-wa.*
Wages	གླ། ཕོགས་	*la; pho.*
Waggish	བགད་མོ་བྲོ་པོ་	*ge-mo tro-po.*
Do. *hon.*	ཞལ་མོ་བྲོ་པོ་	*sKe-mo tro-po.*
Waggon	ཤིང་རྟ་འཁོར་ལོ་	*shing-ta khor-lo.*
Wail, to	ངུ་བ་	*ngu-wa.*
Do. *hon.*	ཤུམ་པ་	*shum-pa.*
Waist	ཀེད་པ་	*ke-pa.*
Do. *hon.*	སྐུ་ཀེད་	*ku-ke.*
Waist band	སྐེད་རགས་	*ke-ra.*
Do. *hon.*	སྐུ་རགས་	*ku-ra.*

Waistcoat	ཁན་སྦྱར་	*khen-jar.*
Wait, to, *v.t.*	སྒུག་བསྡད་ (སྡོད་) པ་	*gu de-pa.*
Do. *hon.*	སྒུག་བཞུགས་པ་	*gu-sḱu-pa.*
Wait on, to	སྐུ་མདུན་ལ་བཅར་བ་	*kun-dün-la char-wa.*
Wake, to	གཉིད་སད་པ་	*nyi se-pa.*
Do. *hon.*	མཉན་ (མནལ་) སད་པ་	*nyen se-pa.*
Walk, to	ཀང་ཐང་ལ་འགྲོ་བ་	*kang-thang la dro-wa.*
Do. *hon.*	ཞབས་ཐང་ལ་ཕེབ་པ་	*sḱap-thang la phe-pa.*
Do. *h. hon.*	ཞབས་ཐང་ལ་འཆིབ་རྒྱུ་གནང་བ་	*sḱap-thang la chhiṕ-gyu nang-wa.*
Walk, to (of horses)	གོམ་པ་འགྲོ་བ་	*ḱom-pa dro-wa.*
Walk, to take a	ཆམ་ཆམ་ (འཁྲུམ་འཁྲུམ་) ལ་འགྲོ་བ་	*chham-chham la dro-wa.*
Do. *hon.*	སྐུ་ཆམ་ (འཁྲུམ་) ལ་ཕེབ་པ་	*kün-chham la phe-pa.*
Do. *h. hon.*	སྐུ་ཆམ་ (འཁྲུམ་) ལ་འཆིབ་རྒྱུ་གནང་བ་	*kün-chham la chhiṕ-gyu nang-wa.*
Wall	རྩིག་པ་	*tsiḱ-pa.*
Do. city	ལྕགས་རི་	*cha-ri.*
Do. fortified	འཛིང་ར་	*dzing-ra.*
Walnut	སྟར་ཀ་	*tar-ka.*

Wan	དཀར་པོ་དཀར་ཀྱང་	*kar-po kar-kyang.*
Wander, to (stroll)	ཆམ་ཆམ་ (འཁྲམ་འཁྲམ་) ལ་འགྲོ་བ་	*chham-chham la dro-wa.*
Do. *hon.*	སྐུ་ཆམ་ (འཁྲམ་, ལ་ཕེབ་པ་	*kün-chham la phe-pa.*
Do. *h. hon.*	སྐུ་ཆམ་ (འཁྲམ) ལ་འཆིབ་རྒྱུ་གནང་བ་	*kün-chham la chhip-gyu nang-wa.*
Wander, to (go astray)	ལམ་ཀ་ནོར་བ་	*lam-ka nor-wa.*
Do. *hon.*	ཕེབ་ལམ་ནོར་ར་ (བ་) གནང་བ་	*phep-lam nor-ra nang-wa.*
Want, to (need)	དགོ་བ་ (དགོས་པ་)	*go-wa.*
Do. *hon.*	དགོ་བ་གནང་བ་	*go-wa nang-wa.*
Want, to (wish)	འདོད་པ་བྱེད་པ་	*dö-pa cke-pa.*
Do. *hon.*	ཐུགས་འདོད་གནང་བ་	*thung-dö nang-wa.*
Wanton	འདོད་ཆགས་ཆེན་པོ་	*dö-chha chhem-po.*
War	དམག་	*ma.*
Wardrobe	དུག་ལོག་ལྒྱུག་སའི་སྒམ་	*ṭu-lo luk-se gam.*
Do. *hon.*	ན་བཟའ་ལྒྱུག་སའི་ཕྱག་སྒམ་	*nam-śa luk-se chha-gam.*
Wares	ཚོང་ཡ་	*tshong-ya.*
Do. *hon.*	རྒྱ་ཚོང་གནང་ཡ་	*gya-tshong nang-ya.*
Warm	དྲོ་པོ་	*ṭro-po.*
Warn, to	བསླབ་བྱ་བྱེད་པ་	*lap-cka cke-pa.*

Warn, to, *hon.*	བསླབ་བྱ་གནང་བ་	*laṕ-cḱa nang-wa.*
Warp, *s.* (of loom)	རྒྱུ་	*gyu.*
Do. *hon.*	ཕྱག་རྒྱུ་	*chha-gyu.*
Warrant, to (authorize)	དབང་སྤྲད་པ་	*wang tre-pa.*
Do. *hon.*	དབང་གནང་བ་	*wang nang-wa.*
Warrant, to (guarantee)	ཁས་ཁྱགས་བྱེད་པ་	*khe-khya cḱe-pa.*
Do. *hon.*	ཞལ་ཁྱགས་གནང་བ་	*sḱe-khya nang-wa.*
Warranty	ཁས་ཁྱགས་	*khe-khya.*
Do. *hon.*	ཞལ་ཁྱགས་	*sḱe-khya.*
Warrior	དམག་མི་	*ma-mi.*
Wart, *s.*	སྨན་ (སྨེ་བ་)	*men.*
Do *hon.*	སྐུ་སྨན་ (སྐུ་སྨེ་)	*ku-men.*
Wash, to	འཁྲུད་པ་	*thrü-pa.*
Do. *hon.*	བསིལ་ར་ (བ་) གནང་བ་	*si-ra nang-wa.*
Wasp	དུག་སྦྲང་	*t́uk-drang.*
Waste, to	གཏོར་བ་	*tor-wa.*
Do. *hon.*	གཏོར་ར་ (བ་) གནང་བ་	*tor-ra nang-wa.*
Watch, *s.*	ཆུ་ཚོད་འཁོར་ལོ་	*chhu-tshö khor-lo.*
Watch, to	མིག་ལྟ་བ་	*mik ta-wa.*
Do. *hon.*	སྤྱན་གཟིགས་པ་	*chen śi-pa.*

Watch, to (guard)	སྲུང་བ་	*sung-wa.*
Do. *hon.*	སྲུང་ང་ (བ་) གནང་བ་	*sung-nga nang-wa.*
Watchman	མིག་ལྟ་མཁན། སྲུང་མཁན་	*mik-ta-khen; sung-khen.*
Water	ཆུ་	*chhu.*
Do. *hon.*	ཆབ་	*chhap.*
Water (for drinking)	འཐུང་ཡ་གི་ཆུ་	*thung-ya-ki chhu.*
Do. *hon.*	བཞེས་ཡ་གི་ཆབ་	*ske-ya-ki chhap.*
Waterfall	བབ་ཆུ་ (འབབ་ཆུ་)	*pap-chhu.*
Do. over rocks	བྲག་ཆུ་	*trak-chhu.*
Water-mill	ཆུ་འཁོར་	*chhu-kho.*
Water-vessel	ཆུ་སྣོད་	*chhu-nö.*
Do. *hon.*	ཆབ་སྣོད་	*chhap-nö.*
Wave, *s.*	དབའ་རླབས་	*ba-lap.*
Wave, to	དབྱུག་དབྱུག་བྱེད་པ་	*yuk-yu cke-pa.*
Waver, to	ཐེ་ཚོམ་ཟ་བ་	*the-tshom sa-wa.*
Do. *hon.*	ཐེ་ཚོམ་གནང་བ་	*the-tshom nang-wa.*
Wavering	ཐེ་ཚོམ་	*the-tshom.*
Wax, sealing	ལ་ཆ་	*la-chha.*
Way (road)	ལམ་ཀ་	*lang-ka.*
Do. *hon.*	ཕེབ་ལམ་	*phep-lam.*

Way (highway)	རྒྱ་ལམ་	*gya-lam.*
Way (manner)	ཐབས་	*thaṕ.*
We	ང་ཚོ། ང་རང་ཚོ་	*nga-tsho ; nga-rang-tsho.*
Weak (in muscle)	ཤེད་ཆུང་ཆུང་	*she chhung-chhung.*
Do. *hon.*	སྐུ་ཤེད་ཆུང་ཆུང་	*ku-she chhung-chhung.*
Weak (prone to illness)	གཟུགས་པོ་གཅོང་པོ་	*śuḱ-po chong-po.*
Do. *hon.*	སྐུ་གཟུགས་གཅོང་པོ་	*ku-śuḱ chong-po.*
Weakminded	ལྐུགས་པ། གླེན་པ་	*kuḱ-pa ; lem-pa.*
Wealthy	ཕྱུག་པོ། ཅ་ (ཆ་) ལག་ཆེན་པོ་	*chhuḱ-po ; cha-la chhem-po.*
Do. *hon.*	སྐུ་ཅས་ (ཆས་) ཆེན་པོ་	*ku-che chhem-po.*
Weapon	མཚོན་ཆ་	*tshön-chha.*
Wear, to	གྱོན་པ་	*ḱöm-pa.*
Do. *hon.*	བཞེས་པ་	*sḱe-pa.*
Wearisome	དཀའ་ལས་ཁག་པོ་	*ka-le khaḱ-po.*
Do. *hon.*	སྐུ་མཉེལ་པོ་	*ku-nye-po.*
Weariness	ངལ་	*ngel.*
Do. *hon.*	སྐུ་ངལ་	*ku-ngel.*
Weary, to be	ཐང་ཆད་པ་	*thang chhe-pa.*
Do. *hon.*	སྐུ་ཐང་ཆད་པ་གནང་བ་	*ku-thang chhe-pa nang-wa.*

Weasel	སྲེ་མོང་	*tre-mong.*
Weather	གནམ་	*nam.*
Do. clear	གནམ་དྭངས་པོ་	*nam ťang-po.*
Weave, to	འཐག་འཐག་པ་	*tha thaḱ-pa.*
Do. *hon:*	འཐག་འཐག་ག་ (པ་) གནང་བ་	*ťha thaḱ-ḱa nang-wa.*
Weaver	འཐག་མཁན་	*thang-khen.*
Web	ཐགས་	*tha.*
Do. *hon.*	ཕྱག་ཐགས་	*chha-tha.*
Wed, to (take husband)	མག་པ་བསླང་ (སློང་) བ་	*maḱ-pa lang-wa*
Do. *hon.*	སྐུ་བག་བཞེས་པ་	*ku-ṕa sḱe-pa.*
Wed, to (take wife)	མནའ་མ་ལེན་པ་	*na-ma lem-pa.*
Do. *hon.*	མནའ་མ་བཞེས་པ་	*na-ma sḱe-pa.*
Wedding	ཆང་ས་	*chhang-sa.*
Do. *hon.*	འཁྲུང་ས་	*thrung-sa.*
Wedge	ཀེའུ་	*ke-u.*
Wednesday	གཟའ་ལྷག་པ	*śa-hlaḱ-pa.*
Weed	རྩྭ་ངན་	*tsa-ngen.*
Weed, to	ཡུར་མ་རྒྱབ་པ་	*yur-ma gyaṕ-pa.*
Do. *hon.*	ཡུར་མ་སྐྱོན་པ་	*yur-ma kyöm-pa*
Week	བདུན་ཕྲག་	*dün-thra.*

Weep, to	ངུ་བ་	*ngu-wa.*
Do. *hon.*	ཤུམ་པ་	*shum-pa.*
Weft	སྤུན་	*pün.*
Do. *hon.*	ཕྱག་སྤུན་	*chha-pün.*
Weigh, to	ཀྱག་ (འགྱོགས་) པ་	*kyak-pa.*
Do. *hon.*	ཀྱག་ག་ (འགྱོགས་པ་) གནང་བ་	*kyak-ka nang-wa.*
Weigh, to (consider)	བསམ་བློ་བཏང་ (གཏོང་) བ་	*sam-lo tang-wa.*
Do. *hon.*	ཐུགས་བསམ་བཞེས་པ་	*thu-sam ske-pa.*
Weight	ཡང་ལྗི་	*yang-chi.*
Weighty (heavy)	ལྗི་པོ་	*ji-po.*
Do. (important)	གནད་ཁག་ཆེན་པོ། གལ་ཆེན་པོ་	*nen-kha chhem-po ; ke chhem-po.*
Welcome!	ཕྱག་ཕེབ་གནང་བྱུང་	*chha-phe nang-chung.*
Well, *s.*	ཁྲོམ་པ་ (ཁྲོན་པ་)	*throm-pa.*
Do. *adj.*	ཡག་པོ་	*yak-po.*
Well, to be (in health)	གཟུགས་པོ་བདེ་པོ་ཡོད་པ་	*śuk-po de-po yö-pa.*
Do. *hon.*	སྐུ་གཟུགས་བཟང་པོ་ཡོད་པ་	*ku-śuk śang-po yö-pa.*
Well! *interj.*	འོ་ན་	*o-na.*
Well-behaved	ཡ་རབས་	*ya-rap.*
Well-known (celebrated)	སྐད་གྲགས་ཆེན་པོ་	*ke-tra chhem-po.*

Well-known (celebrated), *hon.*	མཚན་སྙན་གྲགས་ཆེན་པོ་	*tshen-nyen-t́ra chhem-po.*
Well-modelled (of metal-work, wood-work, etc.)	བཀོད་པ་རྡོད་པོ་	*kö-pa t́ö-po.*
West	ནུབ་	*nuṕ.*
Westward	ནུབ་ངོས། ནུབ་ཕྱོགས་	*nuṕ-ngö ; nuṕ-chho.*
Wet	རློན་པ་	*löm-pa.*
Wet, to	སྦང་བ་	*bang-wa.*
Do. *hon.*	སྦང་ང་ (བ་) གནང་བ་	*bang-nga nang-wa.*
Wether	ལུག་ཕོ་	*luḱ-pho.*
What, *interr.* and *rel.*	ག་རེ་	*ḱa-re.*
Whatever it is	ག་རེ་ཡིན་ནས་	*ḱa-re yin-ne.*
Wheat	གྲོ་	*t́ro.*
Wheat-flour	གྲོ་ཞིབ་	*t́ro-sḱiṕ.*
Wheedle, to (for good object)	བསླབ་བྱ་རྒྱབ་པ་	*laṕ-cḱa gyaṕ-pa.*
Do. *hon.*	བཀའ་སློབ་གནང་བ་	*ka-loṕ nang-wa.*
Wheedle, to (for bad object)	སླུ་བ་	*lu-wa.*
Do. *hon.*	སླུ་བ་གནང་བ་	*lu-wa nang-wa.*
Wheel	འཁོར་ལོ་	*khor-lo.*
When, *rel.*	དུས་ (w. root of verb)	*tü.*

When, *interr.*	ག་དུས་	*ḱa-tü.*
Whenever	ག་དུས་……ཡང་	*ḱa-tü…yang.*
Whence	ག་ནས་	*ḱa-ne.*
Where, *interr.* and *rel.*	ག་པ་	*ḱa-pa.*
Wherever	ག་པ་……ཡང་	*ḱa-pa…yang*
Whet, to	རྡར་བ་	*dar-wa.*
Do. *hon.*	རྡར་ར་ (བ་) གནང་བ་	*dar-ra nang-wa.*
Whether	ནས་ (ན་)	*ne.*
Whetstone	བདར་རྡོ་	*dar-do.*
Which, *interr.* and *rel.*	ག་རེ་	*ḱa-re.*
Which of them	ག་གི་	*ḱa-ki.*
While, *adv.*	དུས་ (w. root of verb)	*tü.*
Whip	རྟའི་ལྕག་	*te-cha.*
Do. *hon.*	ཆིབས་ལྕག་	*chhiṕ-cha.*
Whirlwind	རླུང་ཚུབ་	*lung-tshuṕ.*
Whiskers	རྒྱའུ་	*gya-u.*
Whisper, *s.*	ཞབ་ཞོབ་ (ཞབ་ཞུབ་)	*shaṕ-shoṕ.*
Whisper, to	ཞབ་ཞོབ་ (ཞབ་ཞུབ་) ལབ་པ་	*shaṕ-shoṕ laṕ-pa.*
Do. *hon.*	ཞབ་ཞོབ་ (ཞབ་ཞུབ་) གསུང་བ་	*shaṕ-shoṕ sung-wa.*

Whistle, to	སི་རྒྱབ་པ་	*si gyap̄-pa.*
Do. *hon.*	སི་སྐྱོན་པ་	*si kyöm-pa.*
Whistle a tune, to	སི་གླུ་བཏང་ (གཏོང་) བ་	*si-lu tang-wa.*
Do. *hon.*	སི་གླུ་བཞེས་པ་	*si-lu sk̄e-pa.*
White	དཀར་པོ་	*kar-po.*
Whitewash	ས་དཀར། དཀར་རྩི་	*sa-kar; kar-tsi.*
Whisher	ག་པ་	*k̄a-pa.*
Who	སུ་	*su.*
Whoever (you, he, tc.) be	སུ་ཡིན་ནས་	*su yin-ne.*
Whole	ཚང་མ། ཐམས་ཅད། སྒང་ཁ་	*tshang-ma, tham-che; gang-kha.*
Do. (healthy)	གཟུགས་པོ་བདེ་པོ་	*śuk̄-po de-po.*
Do. *hon.*	སྐུ་གཟུགས་བཟང་པོ་	*ku-śuk̄ śang-po.*
Wholly (used negatively)	བད་དེ། ཁྱོན་ནས་	*be-t́e; khyön-ne*
Whore	གཞང་ཚོང་མ་	*sk̄ang-tshong-ma.*
Why, *interr.*	ག་རེ་དོན་ལ་	*k̄a-re t́ön-la.*
Do. *interj.*	འོ་ན་	*o-na.*
Wick	སྡོང་རས་	*dong-re.*
Wicked	ངན་པོ་	*ngem-po.*
Do. *hon.*	ཐུགས་ངན་པོ་	*thu ngem-po.*

Wickedness	སྡིག་པ་	*dik-pa.*
Do. *hon.*	སྐུ་སྡིག་	*ku-di.*
Wide	ཞང་ (ཞེང་) ཆེན་པོ་	*sKang-chhem-po.*
Do. (of valley, etc.)	རྒྱ་ཆེན་པོ་	*gya chhem-po.*
Widow (term of reproach)	ཡུགས་ཟ་མ་	*yuk-śa-ma.*
Width	ཞང་ (ཞེང་)	*sKang.*
Wife	སྐྱེ་དམན་	*kyi-men.*
Do. (of well-to-do villager)	སྙི་སྙིང་ལགས་	*nyi-nying-la.*
Do. (of ordinary official)	ལྕམ་སྐུ་གཞོགས་	*cham ku-sKo.*
Do. (of third grade and upwards)	ལྷ་ལྕམ་སྐུ་གཞོགས་	*hla-cham ku-sKo.*
Wild (fierce, of human beings)	ངན་པ་	*ngem-pa.*
Do. (of animals)	ཚུབ་པོ་	*tshuṕ-po.*
Wild animal	རི་དྭགས་	*ri-t́a.*
Wilderness	ཁྲེ་ཐང་	*cKe-thang.*
Wile, *s.*	མགོ་སྐོར་	*go-kor.*
Do. *hon.*	དབུ་སྐོར་	*u-kor.*
Will, *s.* (wish)	འདོད་པ་	*dö-pa.*
Do. *hon.*	ཐུགས་འདོད་	*thung-dö.*
Will, *s.* (testament)	ཁ་ཆེམས་	*kha-chhem.*

Will, *s.* (testament), *hon.*	ཞལ་ཆེམས་	*sḱe-chhem.*
Willing, to be	འདོད་པ་ཡོད་པ་	*dö-pa yö-pa.*
Do. *hon.*	ཐུགས་འདོད་ཡོད་པ་	*thung-dö yö-pa*
Willow	ལྕང་མ་	*chang-ma.*
Wily	གཅང་པོ་	*chang-po.*
Do. *hon.*	ཐུགས་གཅང་པོ་	*thu chang-po.*
Win, to (conquer)	རྒྱལ་བ་	*gyel-wa.*
Do. *hon.*	རྒྱལ་ར་ (བ་) གནང་བ་	*gye-ra nang-wa.*
Win, to (obtain)	འབྱོར་བ། ཐོབ་པ་	*jor-wa ; thoṕ-pa.*
Do. *hon.*	ཕྱག་འབྱོར་ཡོང་བ་	*chhan-jor yong-wa.*
Wind	ལྷགས་པ། རླུང་	*hlaḱ-pa ; lung.*
Wind, to	སྒྲིལ་བ་	*dril-wa.*
Do. *hon.*	སྒྲིལ་ར་ (བ་) གནང་བ་	*dri-ra nang-wa.*
Winding	ཀྱོག་ཀྱོག་	*kyo-kyo.*
Window	སྒེ་ཁུང་ (རྒྱལ་ཁུང་)	*gi-khung.*
Window-grating	ཁྲ་མ་ (དྲ་མ་)	*thra-ma.*
Do. *hon.*	ཞལ་ཁྲ་	*sḱe-thra.*
Wine (beer)	ཆང་	*chhang.*
Do. *hon.*	མཆོད་ཆང་	*chhö-chhang.*
Wing	གཤོག་པ་	*shoḱ-pa.*

Wink, to	མིག་ཁྲབ་ཁྲབ་བྱེད་པ་	*miḱ thraṕ-thraṕ cḱe-pa.*
Do. *hon.*	སྤྱན་ཁྲབ་ཁྲབ་གནང་བ་	*chen thraṕ-thraṕ nang-wa.*
Winter	དགུན་ཁ་	*gün-ka.*
Wintry (cold)	གྲང་མོ། བསིལ་པོ་	*ťrang-mo ; si-po.*
Do. *hon.*	སྐུ་བསིལ་པོ་	*ku-si-po.*
Wipe, to	འཕྱིད་པ་	*chhi-pa.*
Do. *hon.*	འཕྱིད་པ་གནང་བ་	*chhi-pa nang-wa.*
Wipe out, to (efface)	སུབ་པ་	*suṕ-pa.*
Do. *hon.*	སུབ་པ་གནང་བ་	*suṕ-pa nang-wa.*
Wire	ལྕགས་སྐུད་	*cha-kü.*
Wireless telegraphy	ལྕགས་སྐུད་མེད་པའི་ཏར་	*cha-kü me-pe tar.*
Wisdom	བློ་གྲོས་	*lo-ťrö.*
Wise (skilful)	མཁས་པོ་	*khe-po.*
Do. (learned)	ཡོན་ཏན་ཆེན་པོ་	*yön-ten chhem-po.*
Do. *hon.*	སྐུ་ཡོན་ཆེན་པོ་	*ku-yön chhem-po.*
Wish	འདོད་པ་	*dö-pa.*
Do. *hon.*	ཐུགས་འདོད་	*thung-dö.*
Wish, to	འདོད་པ་བྱེད་པ་	*dö-pa cḱe-pa.*
Do. *hon.*	ཐུགས་འདོད་གནང་བ་	*thung-dö nang-wa.*
Wit (intellect)	བློ་གྲོས་	*lo-ťrö.*

Witchcraft	མཐུ་	*thu.*
With (together with)	དང་མཉམ་དུ་	*t́ang-nyam-t́u.*
Do. *hon.*	ལྷན་རྒྱས་	*hlen-gye.*
With regard to	དོན་ལ། སྐོར་ལ་	*t́ön-la ; kor-la.*
Withdraw, to, *v.i.* (retreat)	ཕྱིར་ལོག་རྒྱབ་པ་	*chhi-lo gyaṕ-pa.*
Do. *hon.*	ཕྱིར་ལོག་སྐྱོན་པ་	*chhi-lo kyöm-pa.*
Wither, to	རྙིད་པ་	*nyi-pa.*
Within	ནང་ལ་	*nang-la.*
Withhold, to (restrain)	བཀག་པ་ (འགོགས་པ)	*kaḱ-pa.*
Do. *hon.*	བཀག་ག་ (འགོགས་པ་) གནང་བ་	*kaḱ-ḱa nang-wa.*
Without (*opp.* to "with")	མེད་པར་	*me-pa.*
Without (*opp.* to "within")	ཕྱི་ལོགས་ལ་	*chhi-lo-la.*
Withstand, to (restrain)	བཀག་པ་ (འགོགས་པ་)	*kaḱ-pa.*
Do. *hon.*	བཀག་ག་ (འགོགས་པ་) གནང་བ་	*kaḱ-ḱa nang-wa.*
Witless	ལྐུགས་པ། གླེན་པ་	*kuḱ-pa ; lem-pa.*
Witness	དཔང་པོ་	*pang-po.*
Witness, to	དཔང་པོ་བྱེད་པ་	*pang-po cḱe-pa.*
Do *hon.*	དཔང་པོ་གནང་བ་	*pang-po nang-wa.*

Woe	སྡུག་བསྔལ། སེམས་འཁྲལ་	*du-nge ; sem-thre.*
Do. *hon.*	ཐུགས་འཁྲལ་	*thuk-thre.*
Wolf	སྤྱང་ཀུ་	*chang-ku.*
Woman	སྐྱེས་དམན་	*kyi-men.*
Do. (wife of well-to-do villager)	སྙི་སྙིང་ལགས་	*nyi-nying-la.*
Do. (wife of ordinary official)	ལྕམ་སྐུ་གཞོགས་	*cham ku-sko.*
Do. (third grade and upwards)	ལྷ་ལྕམ་སྐུ་གཞོགས་	*hla-cham ku-sko.*
Womb	ཕུ་སྣོད་	*ṗu-nö.*
Wonder	ཡ་མཚན་	*yam-tshen.*
Wonder, to	ཁྱད་མཚར་བ་	*khye tshar-wa.*
Do. *hon.*	ཐུགས་ཁྱད་མཚར་ར་ (བ་) གནང་བ་	*thu-khye tshar-ra nang-wa.*
Wonderful	ཡ་མཚན་པོ། ཁྱད་མཚར་པོ་	*yam-tshem-po ; khye-tsha-po.*
Wondrous	ཡ་མཚན་པོ། ཁྱད་མཚར་པོ་	*yam-tshem-po ; khye-tsha-po.*
Wood	ཤིང་	*shing.*
Do. (forest)	ཤིང་ནགས། ནགས་གསེབ་	*shing-na ; nak-seṗ.*
Wooden	ཤིང་གི་	*shing-ki.*
Woof, *s.* (of loom)	སྤུན་	*pün.*

Woof, *s.* (of loom), *hon.*	ཕྱག་སྤུན་	*chha-pün.*
Wool	བལ་	*ṕe.*
Woollen	བལ་གྱི་	*ṕe-ḱyi.*
Woollen cloth	སྣམ་བུ་	*nam-ṕu.*
Do. *hon.*	ཕྱག་སྣམ་	*chha-nam.*
Word	ཚིག་	*tshi.*
Do. (tidings)	གནས་ཚུལ། གསར་འགྱུར་	*ne-tshü ; sang-gyu.*
Do. (command)	བཀའ་	*ka.*
Word, to give one's (promise)	ཁས་བླང་བ་	*khe-lang-wa.*
Do. *hon.*	ཞལ་བཞེས་པ་	*sḱe-sḱe-pa.*
Work	ལས་ཀ་	*le-ka.*
Do. *hon.*	ཕྱག་ལས་	*chha-le.*
Work, to	ལས་ཀ་བྱེད་པ	*le-ka cḱe-pa.*
Do. *hon.*	ཕྱག་ལས་གནང་བ་	*chha-le nang-wa.*
Work, to be, occupied with	བྲེལ་བ་ཡོད་པ་	*t́re-wa yö-pa.*
Do. *hon.*	ཐུགས་བྲེལ་ཡོད་པ་	*thu-t́re yö-pa.*
World	འཛམ་བུ་གླིང་། འཇིག་རྟེན་	*dzam-ṕu-ling ; jiḱ-ten.*
Worm	འབུ་	*bu.*
Worry, to, *v.t.* (vex)	ཁོང་ཁྲོ་སློང་བ་	*khong-thro lang-wa.*
Do. *hon.*	དགོངས་པ་དཀྲུག་པ་	*gong-pa truk-pa*

Worry, to, *v.i.*	སེམས་འཁྲལ་བྱེད་པ་	*sem-thre cḱe-pa.*
Do. *hon.*	ཐུགས་འཁྲལ་གནང་བ་	*thuḱ-thre nang-wa.*
Worship, to (extempore prayers)	སྨོན་ལམ་བཏབ་ (འདེབས་) པ་	*mö-lam tap̄-pa.*
Do. *hon.*	ཐུགས་སྨོན་གནང་བ་	*thu-mön nang-wa.*
Worship, to (written prayers)	ཁ་འདོན་བྱེད་པ་	*khan-dön cḱe-pa.*
Do. *hon.*	ཞལ་འདོན་གནང་བ་	*sḱen-dön nang-wa.*
Worst	སྡུག་ཤོས་	*duḱ-shö.*
Worst of, to get the	འཕམ་པ་	*pham-pa.*
Do. *hon.*	འཕམ་པ་གནང་བ་	*pham-pa nang-wa.*
Worth	གོང་	*ḱong.*
Do. *hon.*	ལྗགས་གོང་	*ja-ḱong.*
Worth, to be	གོང་བྱེད་པ་	*ḱong-cḱe-pa.*
Worthless (valueless)	གོང་མེད་	*ḱong-me.*
Do. (useless)	དོན་མེད་	*t́ön-me.*
Do. (wicked)	ངན་པོ་	*ngem-po.*
Do. *hon.*	ཐུགས་ངན་པོ་	*thu ngem-po.*
Worthy	འོས་པོ་	*ö-po.*
Wound, *s.*	རྨ་	*ma.*
Wound, to	རྨ་བཟོ་བ་	*ma ṡo-wa.*

Wound, to, *hon.*	རྨ་བཟོ་བ་གནང་བ་	*ma śo-wa nang-wa.*
Wrangle, to	རྒྱབ་འདྲེ་རྒྱབ་པ་	*gyam-dre gyap̄-pa.*
Do. *hon.*	གསུང་འཁྲུག་སྐྱོན་པ་	*sung-thru kyöm-pa.*
Wrap, to	སྒྲིལ་བ་	*dril-wa.*
Do. *hon.*	སྒྲིལ་ར་ (བ་) གནང་བ་	*dri-ra nang-wa.*
Wrath	ཚིག་པ། ཁོང་ཁྲོ་	*tshik̄-pa ; khong-thro.*
Do. *hon.*	དགོངས་ཚུང་། རྣམ་མཁྱེན་	*gong-tshung ; nam-khyen.*
Wrathful, to be	ཚིག་པ་ཟ་བ། ཁོང་ཁྲོ་ཟ་བ་	*tshik̄-pa śa-wa ; khong-thro śa-wa.*
Do. *hon.*	དགོངས་པ་ཚུང་པ། རྣམ་མཁྱེན་འགལ་བ་	*gong-pa tshung-pa ; nam-khyen gel-wa.*
Wrest, to	འཕྲོག་པ་	*throk̄-pa.*
Do *hon.*	འཕྲོག་ག་ (པ་) གནང་བ་	*throk̄-ka nang-wa.*
Wrestle, to	འཛིང་རེ་བཏང་ (གཏོང་) བ་	*dzing-re tang-wa.*
Wretched (bad)	སྡུག་རྡུལ་	*duk̄-rü.*
Do. (unhappy)	སྡུག་བསྔལ་ཆེན་པོ་	*dung-nge chhem-po.*
Do. *hon.*	ཐུགས་བསྔལ་ཆེན་པོ་	*thuk̄-nge chhem-po.*
Wretchedness	སྡུག་བསྔལ། སེམས་འཁྲལ་	*dung-nge ; sem-thre.*
Do. *hon.*	ཐུགས་འཁྲལ་	*thuk̄-thre.*
Wring, to (twist)	སྒྲིམ་པ་	*drim-pa.*

Wring, to. (twist), *hon.*	སྒྲིམ་པ་གནང་བ་	*drim-pa nang-wa*
Wrinkle (on face)	གཉེར་མ་	*nye-ma.*
Wrist	ལག་ཚིགས་	*laḱ-tshi.*
Do. *hon.*	ཕྱག་ཚིགས་	*chhaḱ-tshi.*
Write, to	བྲིས་པ་ (འབྲི་བ་)	*t́ri-pa.*
Do. *hon.*	ཕྱག་བྲིས་གནང་བ་	*chha-t́ri nang-wa.*
Writer (author)	རྩོམ་མཁན་	*tsom-khen.*
Do. *hon.*	རྩོམ་པ་གནང་མཁན་	*tsom-pa nang-khen.*
Writer (clerk)	དྲུང་ཡིག་	*t́rung-yi.*
Do. *hon.*	དྲུང་ཡིག་ལགས་	*t́rung-yi-la.*
Wrong, *adj.* (incorrect)	མ་དག་པ་	*ma…t́ak-pa.*
Do. (unjust)	ཁྲིམས་མེད་	*thrim-me.*
Do. (wicked)	ངན་པ་	*ngem-pa.*
Wrong, *s.* (error)	ནོར་	*nor.*
Do. (guilt)	སྐྱོན། ཉེས་པ་	*kyön; nye-pa.*
Do. (sin)	སྡིག་པ་	*diḱ-pa.*
Do. *hon.*	སྐུ་སྡིག་	*ku-di.*
Wrong (crime), to commit	ཁྲིམས་འགལ་བ་	*thrim gel-wa.*
Do. *hon.*	བཀའ་ཁྲིམས་འགལ་ར་ (བ་) གནང་བ་	*ka-thrim ge-ra nang-wa.*

X

Xylograph, to make a	ཤིང་བསྐོས་རྒྱབ་པ་	*shing-kö gyap-pa.*
Do. *hon.*	ཤིང་བསྐོས་སྐྱོན་པ་	*shing-kö kyöm-pa.*

Y

Yak, *m.*	གཡག་	*ya.*
Do. *f.*	འབྲི་	*dri.*
Yak, wild	འབྲོང་	*drong.*
Yak, half-breed with ordinary cattle	མཛོ་	*dzo.*
Yak-dung	ལྕོ་ (ལྕི་བ་)	*cho.*
Yak's meat	ཚག་ཤ་	*tshak-sha.*
Yama	གཤིན་རྗེ་ཆོས་རྒྱལ་	*shin-je chhö-gye.*
Yap, to	འཆང་བ་	*chhang-wa.*
Yard, court	སྒོ་ར་	*go-ra.*
Yarn	སྲིང་སྐུད་	*hring-kü.*
Do. black	སྲིང་ནག་	*hring-na.*
Do. blue	སྲིང་སྔོན་	*hring-ngön.*
Do. green	སྲིང་ལྗང་	*hring-jang.*
Do. red	སྲིང་དམར་	*hring-mar.*
Do. white	སྲིང་དཀར་	*hring-kar.*
Do. yellow	སྲིང་སེར་	*hring-ser.*
Yawn, to	ཨ་སྟོང་རྒྱབ་པ་	*a-tong gyap-pa.*
Do. *hon.*	ཨ་སྟོང་སྐྱོན་པ་	*a-tong kyöm-pa.*

Year	ལོ་	*lo.*
Year, this	ད་ལོ་	*t́a-lo.*
Year, last	ཟླ་སྙིང་ (ན་ནིང་)	*da-nyi.*
Year before last	ཞི་སྙིང་ (ཞི་ནིང་)	*sḱi-nyi.*
Year, next	ཕྱི་ལོ། སང་སྤོད་	*chhi-lo; sang-pö.*
Year, first four months of a	ཟླ་སྟོད་	*da-tö.*
Year, middle four months of a	ཟླ་དཀྱིལ་	*da-kyi.*
Year, last four months of a	ཟླ་སྨད་	*da-me.*
Yearn for, to	དྲན་པ་	*t́rem-pa.*
Do. *hon.*	ཐུགས་དྲན་པ་གནང་བ་	*thu-t́rem-pa nang-wa.*
Yeast (for bread)	ཕྱི་སྨན་	*chhi-men.*
Do. (for fermenting liquor)	ཕབ་	*phaṕ.*
Yell, to (of children crying)	ངུ་བ་	*ngu-wa.*
Do. *hon.*	ཤུམ་པ་	*shum-pa.*
Yell, to (of dogs)	ཁྱུག་སྐད་རྒྱབ་པ་	*duḱ-ḱe gyaṕ-pa.*
Yellow	སེར་པོ་	*se-po.*
Yellow, dark	སྨུག་སེ་	*nyuḱ-se.*
Yelp, to (of dogs)	འཆང་བ་	*chhang-wa.*
Yes	ལགས་སི། ལགས་ w. auxiliary verb	*la-si; la.*

Yes, *hon.*	ལགས་ལགས་སི། ལ་འོང་	*la-la-si; la-ong.*
Do. *h. hon.*	ལགས་བཀའ་གནང་རང་	*la ka-nang-rang.*
Yesterday	ཁས་ས་ (ཁ་སང་)	*khe-sa.*
Yesterday evening	མདང་དགོང་	*dang-gong.*
Yet, *adv.* (in addition)	ད་འདོ། ད་རུང་	*ťan-do; ťa-rung.*
Yet, *conj.* (nevertheless)	ཡིན་ནས། ཡིན་ཀྱང་། ཡིན་ན་ཡང་	*yin-ne; yin-kyang; yin-na-yang.*
Yield, to (admit)	ཁས་ལེན་པ་	*khe-lem-pa.*
Do. *hon.*	ཞལ་བཞེས་གནང་བ། ཞལ་གྱིས་བཞེས་པ་	*sǩe-sǩe nang-wa; sǩe-ǩyi sǩe-pa.*
Yield, to (forego)	སྤང་བ་	*pang-wa.*
Do. *hon.*	སྤོང་ང་ (བ་) གནང་བ་	*pong-nga nang-wa.*
Yield, to (give)	སྟེར་བ་	*ter-wa.*
Do. *hon.*	གནང་བ་	*nang-wa.*
Yield, to (surrender)	མགོ་དགུར་བ་	*go gur-wa.*
Do. *hon.*	དབུ་དགུར་ར་ (བ་) གནང་བ་	*u gur-ra nang-wa.*
Yielding (flexible)	མཉེན་པོ་	*nyem-po.*
Yoke (for oxen)	གཉའ་ཤིང་	*nya-shing.*
Yolk	སེར་སྒོང་། སེར་སྤྲིན་	*ser-gong; ser-trin.*
Yonder	ཕ་གི་	*pha-gi.*

You	ཁྱོད། ཁྱོད་རང་	*khyö ; khyö-rang.*
Do. *hon.*	ཁྱེན་ (ཁྱེད་)	*khyen.*
Do. *h. hon.*	སྐུ་གཞོགས་	*ku-sK̄o.*
Young	གཞོན་པ། ལོ་གཞོན་གཞོན་	*sK̄öm-pa ; lo sK̄ön-sK̄ön.*
Your	ཁྱོད་རེའི་ (ཁྱོད་ཀྱི་)	*khyö-re.*
Do. *hon.*	ཁྱེན་གྱི་ (ཁྱེད་ཀྱི་)	*khyen-k̄yi.*
Do. *h. hon.*	སྐུ་གཞོགས་ཀྱི་	*ku-sK̄o kyi.*
Youthful	གཞོན་པ། ལོ་གཞོན་གཞོན་	*sK̄öm-pa ; lo sK̄ön-sK̄ön.*

Z

Zeal	སྙིང་རུས་	*nying-rü.*
Do. *hon.*	ཐུགས་རུས་	*thu-rü.*
Zealous	སྙིང་རུས་ཆེན་པོ་	*nying-rü chhem-po.*
Do. *hon.*	ཐུགས་རུས་ཆེན་པོ་	*thu-rü. chhem-po.*
Zealous, to be	སྙིང་རུས་བྱེད་པ་	*nying-rü cKe-pa.*
Do. *hon.*	ཐུགས་རུས་གནང་བ་	*thu-rü nang-wa.*
Zealously	སྙིང་རུས་བྱས་ནས་	*nying-rü cKe-ne.*
Do. *hon.*	ཐུགས་རུས་གནང་ནས་	*thu-rü nang-ne.*
Zero	ལྷད་སྐོར་	*le-kor.*
Zigzag	ལམ་སྐྱོགས་	*lam-kyo.*

THE END.